MEMBERS OF PARLIAMENT
1734–1832

MEMBERS OF
PARLIAMENT
1734-1832

BY GERRIT P. JUDD, IV

ARCHON BOOKS
1972

Library of Congress Cataloging in Publication Data

Judd, Gerrit Parmele, 1915–
    Members of Parliament, 1734-1832.

    Reprint of the 1955 ed. which was issued as no. 61
of the Yale historical publications, Miscellany series.
    Includes bibliographical references.
    1. Gt. Brit. Parliament. House of Commons--Registers.
    2. Gt. Brit.--Biography. I. Title.
II. Series: Yale historical publications. Miscellany
61.
[JN672.J8 1972]   328.42'0922 [B]   73-179572
ISBN 0-208-01230-3

Preface

THIS BOOK, which has occupied most of my leisure for the past eight years, is an attempt to show the relationship between the British ruling class and the House of Commons 1734–1832. The method is experimental. In establishing terms of reference I drew freely on concepts about social classes as used in sociology. Having assembled biographical material about the men elected to the House of Commons in this period, I used a machine to make the statistical part of the analysis. Admittedly both the sociological terms of reference and the machine technique are departures from usual historical practice, but such departures seem well worth making. By venturing into fields of research other than his own the historian sometimes finds a new approach to old problems.

I am especially indebted to the Social Science Research Council, which granted me a fellowship to undertake this work, to the International Business Machines Corporation for advice and financial aid, and to Hofstra College for a grant which facilitated publication. Sir Lewis Namier and his colleagues, J. Brooke, I. R. Christie, J. B. Owen, E. A. Smith, and L. V. Sumner, of the Institute of Historical Research, Senate House, London, made a number of extremely valuable suggestions and corrections. The staff of the Sterling Memorial Library, Yale University, gave their usual unfailing assistance.

May I also express gratitude to the following, who gave so unstintedly of their talents and their time: President John C. Adams of Hofstra College; Charles H. Bennett of Yale University; the Reverend Cyril Britton of London; Maj. J. R. Bush; the Reverend George Craggs of Heston; the Reverend E. H. L. Crosby of Dublin; Lewis P. Curtis of Yale University; J. K. Glynn of London; the Reverend F. H. E. Harfitt of London; Charles Hemingfield of Bognor Regis; Cmdr. E. H. Stuart Jones, R.N., of Wells; John Bean King of Lincoln; George L. Lam of Yale University; the Reverend H. J. Matthew of London; C. H. Philips of London; Canon J. G. Richardson of Abberley; E. C. Schroedel of New York; Elbridge Sibley of Washington, D.C.; Warren H. Smith of Yale University; John Sutherland of Yale University; C. Twynam of Soberton; J. A. Venn of Queen's College, Cambridge; Lewis M. Wiggin of Yale University; J. F. Wolfenden of

Shrewsbury; the Hon. H. A. Wyndham of London; and the Reverend D. A. Yerbury of Steeple Ashton. Above all I am grateful to my wife for her tireless cooperation and encouragement.

G. P. J.

Contents

"The history of Western democracy is, for centuries, the history of the growth of the English House of Commons, as it separated itself from the upper chamber of the peers, as it vindicated its right to levy taxes and to make accountable to it the spending policies of the executive, as it fought against the tyranny of kings and gradually bereft them of power, as it attacked the prerogatives of class and weakened to final extinction the control exercised over it by the House of Lords, as it broadened its own basis by successive stages that extended the franchise until it denied all political distinction between rich and poor, and at length between men and women."

Robert M. MacIver, *The Web of Government* (New York, Macmillan, 1947), p. 185.

1. Introduction

OVER FIVE THOUSAND MEN sat in the House of Commons in the years 1734–1832, that is, in the ninety-nine years between the election of Sir Robert Walpole's next to last Parliament and the passage of the Reform Act. These five thousand men came from all walks of life, and they left their mark not only upon Britain but upon the distant parts of the civilized and uncivilized world. It would be difficult to name a country unvisited by at least one of them, or a way of life—from grand larceny to the cloth—in which one of them did not excel. In the government service, both military and civil, they traversed Asia Minor, Africa, China, and the Americas. Merchant adventurers among them made vast profits in such faraway places as Calcutta, Trinidad, and the Hudson Bay region. Some traveled on their own, not seeking a fortune, but for the sheer love of travel, and those who stayed at home proved no less venturesome. The sons of bakers, hairdressers, clockmakers, and market gardeners acquired wealth and took their places at Westminster beside scions of ancient families. Barristers and physicians sat next to bankers and merchants. Scholars learned in botany and archaeology exchanged repartee with artists, writers, and young men of fashion, while on the back benches sat the ruddy-faced country gentlemen, foxhunting, inarticulate, and deeply conservative.

Many members of Parliament were also army officers. Robert Barker and John Johnstone had served at Plassy. John Leland and Isaac Barré accompanied Wolfe to Quebec. Robert Douglas and Charles Ross fell at Fontenoy. John Rutherford and George Augustus Howe were killed at Ticonderoga. Sir Peter Halkett was among those slaughtered in Braddock's defeat. Henry Clinton commanded at Bunker Hill. A number of M.P.'s saw service at Waterloo, and not a few at one time or other served with foreign forces. John Milley Doyle was a lieutenant colonel in the Portuguese army. James Duff (later fourth Earl of Fife) fought for Spain. Christopher Hely-Hutchinson once served in the Russian army, and John Mackenzie joined a Swedish regiment. At least one M.P. had taken up arms against England during the American Revolution. Unlike John Jaffray, a loyalist, and Paul Wentworth, who was a British secret agent, John Barker Church fought

1

on the American side. Following a family rumpus, the details of which remain obscure, Church left England as a young man and settled in New York, where he married the daughter of Gen. Philip Schuyler. During the Revolution he supported the American side, acting as aide to the French general Rochambeau. After the Peace of Paris he returned to England, and in 1790—a scant seven years later—he sat for Wendover, one of the rotten boroughs. Toward the end of his life he became a close friend of Charles James Fox and the Prince of Wales.

Members of Parliament in the naval service included George Anson, known for his cruise around the world; Edward Vernon of Porto Bello fame; as well as Hugh Pigot, who entered the navy as an enlisted man and rose to be an admiral; and, of course, the unfortunate John Byng, who was executed because of his failure to relieve Minorca. The naval M.P.'s certainly equaled the army members in the breadth of their travels. Home Riggs Popham, having joined the navy in 1778, took a leave of absence to enter the China trade 1787–94, and returned to the navy to serve off Jamaica, Copenhagen, Buenos Aires, and the Cape of Good Hope; George Harris saw service off Java; Samuel Cornish fought his ship in Philippine waters; and Adm. Thomas Cochrane found time in his turbulent career to serve with the navies of Chile, Brazil, and Greece.

Not a few M.P.'s at one time or another served abroad as members of the British diplomatic corps. Robert Stephen Fitzgerald and Benjamin Keene represented England in Portugal. Thomas Grenville, the book collector, was ambassador to Berlin and Vienna, while Edward Finch-Hatton, Robert Murray Keith, and Hans Stanley served in Russia. Robert Sutton, John Edward Fitzroy, Charles Fane, and Henry Grenville were ambassadors at Constantinople. The last, incidentally, prefaced his service in Turkey with a seven-year tour of duty as governor of Barbados, while Richard Master began as consul at Algiers and ended as governor of Tobago.

India and China attracted a number of adventurers who ultimately found seats in the House. Early in life Matthew Martin entered the naval service of the East India Company, and obtained both prominence and a handsome reward for successfully defending his ship against three French men-of-war. William Fitzhugh had lived in China as a factor of the East India Company, and James Andrew John Lawrence Charles Drummond

(later Viscount Strathallan) was head of the British settlement at Canton. Sir Edward Hyde East, born in Jamaica, was chief justice of Calcutta for nine years. Conversely, William Fullarton saw service as an army officer in India and later in life was commissioner of Trinidad. Probably Josias Dupré Porcher had the most cosmopolitan background of all. His great grandfather was a Huguenot refugee and his father a native of South Carolina who later settled in England. Porcher himself lived twenty-two years in India before his election to the House.

Several M.P.'s had extensive American connections. Anthony Bacon ran a store in Maryland, before branching out as a government contractor, tobacco merchant, shipowner, and gun manufacturer. Brice Fisher owned estates in South Carolina, and Barlow Trecothick, a supporter of John Wilkes, had lived in America as a merchant before becoming agent in London for New Hampshire. Edward Ellice, a Canadian-born Scot, as a young man entered the Canadian fur trade, and George Richard Robinson, the son of a surgeon at Wareham, made a fortune in commerce in Newfoundland before returning to England, where he became a shipowner, East India proprietor, director of the Bank of England, and chairman of Lloyd's.

Others traded in Europe. Sir William Duff-Gordon was brought up in his uncle's countinghouse in Cadiz. Robert Herries was a merchant in Spain, and William Mayne (later Lord Newhaven) was a merchant in Portugal. Christopher Potter owned a large porcelain factory in France, and Sir Robert Smyth was a banker in Paris.

Those who did not travel in the government service, or in trade, toured the world on their own. During the eighteenth century, and after the Napoleonic Wars, thousands of young Englishmen invaded the Continent on the grand tour to France and Italy, as a supplement to their formal education. A few, who later entered the House of Commons, strayed farther afield. Robert Curzon (later fourteenth Baron Zouche) became an authority on monasticism in the Levant. Henry Gally-Knight toured Palestine, and Maurice Bagenal St. Leger Keating wrote a book describing his adventures in Morocco. John Bacon Sawrey Morritt and James Dawkins, the archaeologist, traveled extensively in Greece and Asia Minor.

Several M.P.'s received high honors from foreign governments. For his services in reforming the Portuguese army, William Carr

Beresford was made a peer of Portugal. Dr. Nathaniel Dimsdale, who inoculated Catherine the Great, accepted a Russian title. John Mackenzie was made a count in the nobility of Sweden. Thomas Francis Fremantle was a baron of Austria. John Hookham Frere was a peer of Spain. Richard Le Poer Trench (Earl of Clancarty in the peerage of Ireland) was also a Dutch peer; and Thomas Villiers (Earl of Clarendon in the English peerage) was at the same time a Prussian count.

Those Englishmen in the House of Commons who stayed at home represented in their origins all gradations of the social hierarchy, and in their ambition to rise in the world they equaled the vigor of the M.P.'s who ventured abroad. Thomas Vere was the son of a baker. Edward Burtenshaw Sugden (later Baron St. Leonards) was the son of a hairdresser. The father of William Roscoe was a market gardener. The father of Henry Isherwood was a servant in an inn. Richard Ironmonger had been a coachmaster at Charing Cross. Benjamin Hammett began life as a porter in a bookseller's shop. Luke White, a former itinerant bookseller, became one of the wealthiest men in Ireland. James Sanderson, the son of a grocer, was a hop merchant, banker, and finally lord mayor of London. Robert Gifford (later Baron Gifford), also the son of a grocer, became chief justice of the Common Pleas. Frederick Hodgson, a brewer, became nationally famous for the quality of his India pale ale. Joseph Cripps, a banker, also owned two cloth mills. Most spectacular of all was Frederick Gye, who won £30,000 in a lottery, with the money established wine and tea companies, and operated Vauxhall Gardens.

The road to success lay in the professions as well as in trade. The army and navy were amply represented, and a large number of jurists, many eminent, also entered the House. Blackstone, famous for his *Commentaries*, sat for almost nine years. Samuel Romilly, the great legal reformer, George Spence, the reformer of chancery, Lord Mansfield, and Thomas Erskine all served in the Commons for varying periods, as did the lesser known judges William Grant and Codrington Edmund Carrington, the latter of whom wrote the legal code of Ceylon. A few taught law. Thomas Francis Wenman and Joseph Phillimore were professors of civil law at Oxford; William Kirkpatrick taught public law at Edinburgh; and James Mackintosh was professor of law in the East India Company's college at Heytesbury.

Other members had a direct connection with phases of education not related to law. Sir George Downing, founder of Downing College, Cambridge, was in the House, as was Francis Annesley, a master of Downing College. George Newland taught geometry at Gresham College. John Baillie was a professor of Arabic at Fort William College in Bengal. John Bruce taught logic at Edinburgh. Thomas Reade endowed a lecture at Cambridge. Samuel Holden left money to Harvard. Paul Wentworth was a benefactor of Dartmouth. John Sargent, a correspondent of Benjamin Franklin, offered a gold medal as a prize to the University of Pennsylvania. Sir Watkin Williams-Wynn is remembered as a patron of charity schools.

Literary scholars and scientists there were as well. Thomas Johnes translated Froissart. George John Warren, who lived the greater part of his life in Florence, was an editor of Dante. Edward King edited Mexican antiquities, and Richard Griffin edited Pepys' diary. Stephen Rumbold Lushington and John Malcolm were Persian scholars, and Nathaniel Brassey Halhed was an authority on Sanskrit. In the field of history—aside from such figures as Gibbon, Macaulay, and Stanhope—Henry Bankes wrote a history of Rome; Malcolm Laing published a work on the history of Scotland; and George Ellis wrote a study of the Dutch Revolution. David Ricardo and Sir John Sinclair are well known in the field of economics. Sir James Hall, geologist and chemist, wrote also on Gothic architecture. James Nasmith and Robert More studied botany under Linnaeus. Sir Philip de Malpas Grey-Egerton was a student of paleontology. William Parsons (later Earl of Rosse), an amateur astronomer of some note, was a president of the Royal Society. Philip Rashleigh was a mineralogist; Robert Wood an archaeologist; and Henry Penruddocke Wyndham a topographer.

A few M.P.'s found varying degrees of fame in the literary and graphic arts. William Beckford, author of *Vathek;* the critic John Wilson Croker; James Macpherson, author of *Ossian;* and Matthew Gregory ("Monk") Lewis were of the House, as well as lesser figures like Francis Jeffrey, editor of the *Edinburgh Review;* Horace Twiss, the biographer of Eldon; Henry James Pye, a forgotten poet laureate; William Pitt Lennox, a novelist of dubious merit; and William Herbert, who wrote learned verse about flowers. Among the artists in the House, Nathaniel Holland was an original member of the Royal Academy, and William Elford, a banker and amateur painter, exhibited at the Academy for sixty-three years. George Howland Beaumont was a landscape artist, and Robert Adam was architect to George III.

As for rogues in the House, there were several of more than passing interest. Andrew Robinson Bowes, John Mytton, Robert Paris Taylor, and Frederick William De Moleyns all died in prison —the first three for debt and the fourth for having forged a power-of-attorney. Andrew James Cochrane-Johnstone was expelled from the House in 1814 for a fraud on the stock exchange; and Peter Moore, a nabob, reportedly the last wearer of a peruke in London society, became involved in a number of companies of questionable repute. Both men fled the country to escape arrest. In even more colorful fashion, Thomas Benson, one-time proprietor of Lundy Island, Devonshire, hit upon the scheme of secretly unloading one of his ships, scuttling her, claiming full value from the insurance company, and pocketing not only the proceeds of the cargo but the insurance money as well. He also fled, and died in Portugal. But such were comparatively few, and in number they are more than balanced by young men, such as Richard Bagwell and Charles Henry Barham, who forsook political life for a career in the church.

One large group remains, the country gentlemen, numerically stronger than any other in the House, but almost by definition less prominent as individuals. Taciturn, bluff, and tradition steeped, the country gentlemen generally preferred the silent distinction of being the backbone of a society which was still primarily agricultural. When they stepped forward in private life they excelled mainly in farming and in sports. The Whig agriculturist Thomas William Coke of Holkham epitomizes the best in this group. But there were others like Coke, such as Thomas Gisborne, interested in Manchester lime, who wrote essays on agriculture; John Bennett, another writer on farming; and John Christian-Curwen, who twice refused a peerage. Among sportsmen were Philip Dehany, an authority on cricket; George Osbaldeston, master of the Quorn hounds; Thomas Tyrwhitt-Drake, master of the Bicester hounds; Richard Grosvenor and George Cholmley, both breeders of racehorses; and Richard Vernon, the founder of the Jockey Club.

The foregoing examples can only hint at the variety of interests and the divergence of character of these five thousand M.P.'s. Here a soldier wounded in the North American wilderness; a sailor who remembered the breakers of a South Pacific reef; a diplomatist schooled in dealing with Middle Eastern nomads;

a nabob who recalled the acrid smells of Calcutta; London merchants, many of them beginning life in tiny courtyards and foul
alleys, climbing doggedly up the social pyramid; the bankers and
manufacturers, lawyers, scholars, scientists, and artists; a few
rogues; a few clerics; and a large body of country gentlemen interested in farming, foxhunting, and the status quo. Few legisla-
tive bodies in world history have had a more diverse and colorful
membership.

2. Method

AT FIRST GLANCE the diversity of the 5,034 men elected to the House of Commons in the years 1734–1832 appears overwhelming. What, for example, can the banker Joseph Cripps have in common with the Whig agriculturist Thomas William Coke, save that they were both Englishmen living in the same century? What are the grounds for a comparison of the buccaneering sea captain Matthew Martin with such a literary scholar as Thomas Johnes; the porcelain manufacturer William Taylor Copeland with a legalist of Blackstone's caliber; the venom-tongued orator Isaac Barré with the artist Nathaniel Holland; the former coachmaster Richard Ironmonger with Richard Plantagenet Temple-Nugent-Brydges-Chandos-Grenville, later Duke of Buckingham and Chandos? Facing such a formidable array of men, each unique in personality, background, and experience, the historian may well conclude that he cannot discover a pattern or even a common denominator in the mountain of disorderly information which these men represent.

Customarily the historian of Parliament, schooled as he has been in textual criticism and the literary techniques of presenting material, limits himself to a more or less haphazard sampling. Having described the various types of men in the House, such as the rakes, the nabobs, the landed proprietors, and the men of trade, he proceeds to draw conclusions based on an intuitive grasp of his subject. Often he uses as corroboration a few apparently judicious comments made by contemporary writers of letters and memoirs. Subsequent scholars admire and copy his work, until by sheer weight of repetition it passes for "history."

Such an approach is unsound both in theory and in technique. The historian's categories of description are inadequate because they proceed from a literary rather than a sociological view of his subject. Moreover, he has based his conclusions upon only a fraction of the available evidence, and the statements of contemporary writers, which he has used to bolster his argument, may prove to be unreliable.

The problem of method, then, has two main aspects: theoretical definition and practical procedure. Otherwise stated, what are the pertinent questions for the historian to ask about the Members of Parliament and how shall he go about answering them?

8

At the outset one may assume that the men elected to the House of Commons 1734–1832 belonged to Britain's ruling class. The historian may further assume that, because the House of Commons in this period was one of the main instruments through which the ruling class expressed its political will, a study of the House's membership becomes in effect an analysis in miniature of the ruling class itself. In other words, the House's membership may serve as a case study of the composition of the ruling class, and the social-economic forces underlying the representation may be presumed to be generally similar to the forces which were molding the upper classes in the nation at large.

The historian then may borrow from the sociologist a number of concepts about social classes in general and ruling classes in particular. By using these concepts he may derive a coherent pattern from the apparently chaotic materials before him.

Although not all sociologists agree about the conditions which determine social classes, there is general consensus that in modern societies family background, education, occupation, and wealth are among the most important.[1] The historian may now pose four broad questions about the Members of Parliament: What were their family backgrounds? How were they educated? What did they do for a living? And how much wealth did they have?

The historian then adapts his general questions to the historical environment of the years 1734–1832. That is, he frames his specific questions to fit the special circumstances of the old regime, eliminating some inquiries as irrelevant and adding others. The following are some of the questions in their final, modified form: How many M.P.'s had connections with the peerage? How many were baronets? What proportion had had ancestors in the House? How many belonged to politically important families? How many had gone to one of the traditionally great public schools or the universities? What schools? What universities? What colleges within the universities? Which of the professions predominated? How many members were in trade? What trades? How does the strength of the domestic merchants compare with the bloc that traded overseas? How long did members of these various categories sit in the House? And how did the representation change in character throughout the period?

Other related questions arise. Of what nationalities were the members? What were some of their non-British national origins?

1. See below, p. 36.

How old were the members? Did their age vary according to their social status, education, occupation, and wealth? How did their age at death compare to that of the nation at large? These and similar queries provide the historian with a coherent frame of reference in dealing with the theoretical aspect of his problem.

With respect to technique, the historian rejects the practice of sampling and decides to seek his answers in the entire body of the evidence. Here two apparently insurmountable obstacles appear. First, how can he possibly unearth enough biographical information about 5,034 Members of Parliament to make his study more than a ragged web of estimates? Second, even presuming the data to be reasonably complete, how can he make a selective analysis of this vast compendium of material without spending endless years shuffling and reshuffling the cards in his file?

The first obstacle, as to the availability of biographical data, is far less serious than it seems, because certain kinds of information abound for these Members of Parliament. Exact or approximate birthdates have been found for over 90 per cent of the 5,034 M.P.'s in this period, and presumably the material on their family background, education, and occupation is complete in about the same proportion.

Nor is the second obstacle insurmountable, for the historian may use a mechanical device to assist him in analyzing the large body of material which he has assembled. Once he has converted his information to a simple numerical code, he may have it completely sorted by machine in a matter of days. In this process he breaks down the data into a code of numbers, to be transferred to perforated punch cards, each containing up to eighty columns of twelve spaces each. Once in this form, any phase of the data (that is, any number in any column or any combination of numbers and columns) readily lends itself to mechanical tabulation.[2] The use of machines renders practicable the study of large masses of material hitherto passed over because of their bulk. Scholars in the physical sciences and in some of the social sciences, as well as industrialists and government bureaus, civil and military, have long used the punch-card method. Faced as he is with an increasing volume of documentary remains, the historian may benefit by following their example, for mechanical tabulation by means of punch

2. For a full discussion see George Walter Baehne, ed., *Practical Applications of the Punched Card Method in Colleges and Universities* (New York, Columbia University Press, 1935).

cards has unquestionably revolutionized the technique of quantitative analysis.

At this stage the historian has compiled many statistics in answer to his questions. He knows in general the class structure of the political representation in these years. His next problems are those of interpretation and comparison, in relating his findings to the historical environment of the old regime, and in comparing his findings to conditions in past and future periods. For example, having found out how many members were in trade and what their trades were, the historian investigates the economic structure of the old regime in order to illuminate his discovery. In one instance he compares the proportion of bankers and manufacturers in the House to the relative importance of banking and manufacturing in the nation's economy. He then compares the strength of the M.P.'s in banking and manufacturing 1734–1832 with their strength in preceding and succeeding periods. In these ways he tries to fit his discoveries into their proper historical context.

The present study contains a number of limitations, some inherent in the method itself and others imposed by the material under investigation. Since the analysis is primarily statistical, it deals with groups of men rather than with individuals, so that conclusions reached about any given group do not necessarily apply to every individual within the group. Also, being mainly quantitative in nature, this study omits many of the imponderables in history, much drama, emotional conflict, and intellectual predilection. Further, some parts of the data are at present lacking. The sources consulted failed to yield adequate information, for example, on the wealth of members, so that conclusions about this part of the problem perforce rest upon inference; and as new information becomes available all the statistics here presented are subject to modification. But the margin of error appears small, and such modification as may be necessary should not destroy the validity of the main conclusions.

The date 1734 has been selected as the *terminus a quo* because in that year occurred one of the three most important general elections in the eighteenth and early nineteenth centuries, and because biographical information on M.P.'s before 1734 becomes increasingly scanty. The date 1832, of course, marks the passage of the Reform Act, which rang down the curtain on the old regime and brought a new series of tensions into British life.

3. Nationality [1]

THE UNREFORMED House of Commons contained 513 English seats, in addition to 45 Scots, and after 1801, 100 Irish. In the years 1734–1832, 3,856 Englishmen were elected to the House, slightly over 75 per cent of the total number returned. Nonetheless the English fell somewhat short of obtaining their expected numerical share of members (92 per cent before 1801 and 78 per cent 1801–32) because of the disproportionately large number of Scots and Irish entering the House in these years.

The Scots with 647 M.P.'s 1734–1832, about 13 per cent of the total, comprise the largest non-English group in the representation. At every general election between 1734 and 1832 more than the expected number of 45 Scots entered the House, for the twenty general elections show an average of 65 Scots per election, from a low of 49 in 1741 to a high of 86 in 1830. A tendency appears for an increasing number of Scots to be elected: an average of 56 per election entered 1734–90 as contrasted to an average of 74 in the ten general elections 1796–1831. As the Scots obtained progressively more than their allotted 45 seats, they invaded every species of constituency. Seven Scots sat for English counties, 171 for English rotten boroughs, and 99 for English open boroughs. One Scot, John Campbell (ca 1695–1777), whose mother was Elizabeth Lort of Stackpole Court, Pembroke, represented the Welsh county of Pembroke 1727–47. Others of his family represented Welsh boroughs, as did four descendants of the Scottish Earl of Bute. After the Union with Ireland in 1801, two Scots represented Irish counties and ten Scots sat for Irish boroughs. But only one Englishman represented a Scottish county in the period 1734–1832, Francis Leveson-Gower (who changed his name to Egerton), M.P. Sutherland 1826–31; and only 12 Englishmen represented

---

1. See Appendixes 1 and 2. Three-quarters of the members were clearly English. Lacking evidence to the contrary, I have considered as Scottish all members who fell into one or more of the following groups: (1) M.P.'s for Scottish seats (for most of these seats were occupied by Scots); (2) M.P.'s with Scottish places of residence as given in the Official Return and other sources; (3) M.P.'s connected with the Scottish peerage; (4) M.P.'s with characteristic Scottish family names. The Irish have been identified mainly through their place of residence. I have considered as American only those M.P.'s born in continental North America.

Scottish burghs, the first being the London merchant Chauncy Townsend, M.P. for Wigtown burghs in 1768. The only other outsiders in the Scottish constituencies were the American-born Staats Long Morris, M.P. Kintore 1774–84, and five Irishmen— mainly because the Scottish seats, few in number and generally "managed" by the government, could not meet the home demand, while south of the Tweed many more seats were available to the Scottish aspirant.[2]

The appearance of Scots in increasing numbers aggravated the traditional resentment which the English bore them. Dr. Johnson's gibes at Scotland have become classic, and no small measure of John Wilkes' success as a political agitator came from his skill in playing upon the anti-Scottish prejudices of his audience. As Graham has observed, "the unpopularity of Lord Bute, the royal favorite, was more owing to his being a Scotsman than to being an incompetent statesman." [3] Likewise the government's virtual domination of the Scottish representation—with the result that the 45 Scottish members tended to support government measures as a solid phalanx—made the Scots natural targets for the highly vocal attacks of the opposition. In Henry Fox's blunt words, "Every man has at some time or other found a Scotchman in his way, and everybody has therefore damned the Scotch: and this hatred their excessive nationality has continually inflamed." [4] Also, particularly in the first half of the eighteenth century, the unmistakable burr of the Scottish accent made them unduly conspicuous in the House, to the point that Scottish members dreaded

2. Edward Porritt, *The Unreformed House of Commons* (Cambridge, Eng., the University Press, 1903), *2*, 138–40. Porritt names eight Englishmen as having represented Scottish burghs, including Charles James Fox, M.P. Kirkwall 1784. But Fox later chose to sit for Westminster, where in 1784 his election was under scrutiny. That Fox was a bona fide member for a Scottish constituency may be disputed. Five other Englishmen not named by Porritt held Scottish burgh seats: Chauncy Townsend, M.P. Wigtown 1768–70; Sir Henry Watkin Dashwood, M.P. Wigtown 1775–80; William Henry Fremantle, M.P. Wick 1808–12; Dudley Long-North, M.P. Haddington 1818–20; and Nicholas Conyngham Tindal, M.P. Wigtown 1824–26. The five Irishmen representing Scottish constituencies were: Sir Archibald Edmonstone, M.P. Dumbarton 1761–80 and 1790–96, also M.P. Ayr 1780–90; Sir Charles Edmonstone, M.P. Dumbarton 1806–7 and Stirling 1812–21; Lyndon Evelyn, M.P. Wigtown 1809–12; George Macartney, M.P. Ayr 1774–75; and James George Stopford, M.P. Linlithgow 1796–1802 and Ayr 1803–6.

3. Henry Grey Graham, *The Social Life of Scotland in the Eighteenth Century* (London, 1906), pp. 67, 178.

4. Fox's memoir in *The Life and Letters of Lady Sarah Lennox,* ed. the Countess of Ilchester and Lord Stavordale (London, 1901), *1*, 68.

the open ridicule which their participation in debate often provoked.[5] Smollett noted:

> I think the Scots would do well for their own sakes, to adopt
> the English idioms and pronunciation; those of them especially,
> who are resolved to push their fortunes in South-Britain. I
> know, by experience, how easily an Englishman is influenced
> by the ear, and how apt he is to laugh, when he hears his own
> language spoken with a foreign or provincial accent. I have
> known a member of the House of Commons speak with great
> energy and precision, without being able to engage attention,
> because his observations were made in the Scotch dialect.[6]

Nevertheless, although the Scots increasingly flocked to the House
and occupied almost half again as many seats as allotted to their
native land, they were by no means present in the vast numbers
which contemporary animosity alleged.

The Irish with 512 M.P.'s 1734–1832, or about 10 per cent
of the total, make up the third and only other numerically important non-English bloc of members. The House contained no Irish
constituencies before the Union of 1801, but an average of 17
Irishmen per election entered in the eleven general elections
1734–96, including such prominent debaters as Burke and Sheridan. After 1801 and until 1832, with Ireland allocated 100 seats
at Westminster, an average of 110 Irishmen entered the House at
the general elections. Irishmen sat for every type of consistuency
except that of a Welsh county. Four Irishmen represented English
counties, including Wilkes' intrepid opponent, Henry Lawes Luttrell, who emerged from the political dogfight of 1769 as M.P. for
Middlesex. One hundred twenty-three sat for English rotten boroughs—about 50 less than the Scots in this type of constituency—
and 97 Irishmen (almost as many as the Scots) represented English open boroughs. Two Irishmen sat for Scottish counties; three
others represented Scottish burghs; and two entered the House
as representatives of boroughs in Wales. The Irish, then, were
nearly as ubiquitous as their Scottish cousins. Even before 1801
they sent a not inconsequential number of men to the House, and
thereafter they returned slightly more than their quota.

A few colonials also received election. In the countermigration
from New England to the mother country in the years 1640–60,

5. Graham, *Social Life of Scotland,* pp. 76 n., 82, 118.
6. Tobias Smollett, *The Expedition of Humphrey Clinker* (Oxford, 1925), *2,* 59.

five residents of New England entered the House.[7] In 1699 Sir Robert Davers, born in the Barbados, became M.P. for Bury, and two years later Joseph Dudley, a New Englander, was M.P. for Newtown, Isle of Wight.[8] The West Indians in the House will receive separate consideration,[9] but in all 17 natives of continental North America were elected 1734–1832, five before 1783 and the remainder thereafter. In addition the House contained a number of men with more or less intimate North American connections or experience, such as merchants trading to North America, American colonial agents, army and navy officers who had served in America, speculators in American lands, and former governors of North American colonies.

Of the native North, Americans, John Huske of New Hampshire, M.P. for Maldon 1763–73, was the first to enter the House in the period beginning 1734. In 1774 two other North Americans were elected: Henry Cruger of New York and Bristol, a wealthy merchant who made speeches in Parliament against the American war and in 1790 left England to live out the rest of his life in the United States; [10] and Staats Long Morris of New York, who became governor of Quebec in 1800. In 1780 two other North Americans entered the House: Edward Rushworth of New York, who incidentally took deacon's orders before his election and was sometime mayor of Yarmouth, Isle of Wight; and Paul Wentworth, a connection of the New Hampshire Wentworths, notorious for his activities as a British secret agent in America during the Revolution. After 1783 the North Americans in the House were the Scots-American brothers Charles and David Barclay of Philadelphia; the American-born general, Napier Christie-Burton, later lieutenant governor of Upper Canada; the Boston-born admiral, Sir Isaac Coffin; John Singleton Copley, the younger, son of the eminent Bostonian portrait painter; the loyalist general, Oliver De Lancey of Huguenot stock, who fought against the Americans at Brooklyn, White Plains, and Charleston; the Scots-Canadian brothers Edward and William Ellice; Sir William Middleton-Fowle, who was born in Charleston, S. C.; another South Carolinian, the nabob Josias Dupré Porcher, of Huguenot descent; Richard ("Con-

7. William L. Sachse, "The Migration of New Englanders to England, 1640–1660," *American Historical Review, 53* (1948), 273.

8. *Notes and Queries,* 11th Ser., *2,* 387.

9. See Chapter 9.

10. *Parliamentary History of England,* ed. William Cobbett (London, 1806–20), *19,* 584 and *21,* 579.

versation") Sharp, who was born in Newfoundland; and Sir Grey
Skipwith, who left his birthplace in Virginia at an early age to
receive formal education at Eton and Cambridge.

Namier has treated exhaustively the members of the 1761 Parliament who had direct personal knowledge of North America,
either from residence in the colonies or from various colonial af-
filiations.[11] He has, for example, named seven M.P.'s who were
former governors of North American colonies, four sitting in the
1761 Parliament and three elected thereafter. But in all a total
of 13 former governors of North American colonies—eight naval
officers, three army officers, and two civilians—entered the House
in the generation or so preceding the outbreak of the American
Revolution.[12]

Among the naval officers all but George Johnstone were governors of Newfoundland: George Clinton in 1731; Charles Hardy
in 1744; Brydges Rodney in 1749; Francis William Drake in
1750; Thomas Graves in 1761; Hugh Palliser in 1764; and Molineux Shuldham in 1772. Only three held a North American post
elsewhere: George Johnstone in West Florida in 1763; and Clinton
and Hardy in New York following their Newfoundland appointments. Thus the majority of North American colonial governors
who were elected to the House before 1776 were naval officers with
a special and distracting professional interest. Moreover, a tour
of duty in barren Newfoundland doubtless provided little opportunity to acquire understanding of colonial problems.

Much the same may be said of the three army officers among
the ex-governors in the House before 1776. The Eton-trained son
of a peer, Edward Cornwallis, later a general, interrupted his

11. L. B. Namier, *England in the Age of the American Revolution* (London,
Macmillan, 1930), pp. 265–327; see also his article on Brice Fisher in *The English
Historical Review, 42* (1927), 514–32. Namier has considered Barlow Trecothick
as an American. In a letter to the author dated 4 September 1951, Professor Namier
states that Trecothick was born at sea, outbound from England to America.

12. This total does not include a colonial governor who entered the House after
1776: Richard Penn, M.P. 1784–91 and 1796–1806, who was deputy governor of
Pennsylvania 1771–73. Nor does it include five colonial governors who had been
M.P.'s but who did not re-enter the House after their American appointments
expired: Norborne Berkeley, M.P. 1741–63 and governor of Virginia 1768–70;
Thomas Bladen, M.P. 1727–41 and lieutenant governor of Maryland 1742–46; Lord
William Campbell, M.P. 1764–66 and governor of Newfoundland in 1766 and
South Carolina in 1773; Lord Charles Greville Montagu, M.P. 1762–65 and governor
of South Carolina in 1766; and Sir Danvers Osborn, M.P. 1747–53 and governor
of New York in 1753. A list of American colonial governors 1685–1783 appears
in *The Annual Report of the American Historical Association* (1911), *1*, 395–528.

parliamentary career of almost twenty years with a three-year tour as governor of Nova Scotia 1749–52. Robert Monckton, schooled at Westminster, also a general and a peer's son, was governor of New York for less than a month in 1761. Their appointments do little more than illustrate the tendency for upper-class Englishmen to receive a colonial governorship as a kind of political reward.[13] The third army officer, James Grant, also a general, had a long and distinguished record of service at Culloden, in the Seven Years' War, and in America during the Revolution. His duty as governor of East Florida beginning in 1763 may be considered as little more than an interlude.

In all, only five of the 13 former governors in the House of Commons before 1776 had held posts in colonies which in 1783 became part of the United States. These were the naval officers Clinton and Hardy in New York; the army officer Monckton, also in New York; William Henry Lyttelton, governor of South Carolina 1756–60, who later spoke in favor of drastic armed coercion of the colonies; [14] and the remarkable writer on colonial administration, Thomas Pownall, M.P. 1767–80, who had served as lieutenant governor of New Jersey 1755–57 and governor of Massachusetts 1757–60.

The members of Parliament before 1776 who were either native-born North Americans, who had lived long in America, or who had kept close connections with the new continent, do not constitute a large group. Nor were all of them well informed on matters colonial. In consequence they were not able to bring to their fellows in the House that depth of understanding which might have averted the breach. At least two large forces operated against them: the relative geographical isolation of North America in an era before science had begun to annihilate distances; and the colonial tendency to seek representation in their own provincial legislatures, which they looked upon "as local Parliaments, coordinate in status with the Parliament of Great Britain." [15]

The 65 M.P.'s of French Huguenot descent comprise a minor but distinguished group which cut across territorial lines, since 53 were from families settled in England, 10 from Ireland, and two

13. See Leonard W. Labaree, *Royal Government in America* (New Haven, Yale University Press, 1930), pp. 37–42.

14. *Parliamentary History, 18,* 733.

15. Labaree, *Royal Government,* p. 217; see also, *inter alia,* Charles M. Andrews, *The Colonial Background of the American Revolution* (New Haven, Yale University Press, 1931), p. 36.

from North America. During the persecution after the revocation of the Edict of Nantes in 1685 an estimated half million Huguenots fled from France, and of these thousands in all ranks of society came to Britain, bringing with them much professional, artistic, and industrial talent.[16] An average of between six and seven entered the House at each general election 1734–1831, from a low of two in 1820 and 1826 to a high of 12 in 1802.

The Huguenots in the House represent in microcosm the various activities in which they excelled nationwide. Among the Huguenot M.P.'s who achieved military prominence were the admirals Peter and John Spratt Rainier, uncle and nephew; also Sir Peter Denis, who served on the court martial of the unfortunate Byng; and Gen. John Carnac, who carved out for himself a brilliant career with the Indian army. In the legal profession one may mention the eminent reformer Samuel Romilly; Thomas Langlois Lefroy, later chief justice of the Queen's Bench in Ireland; and the Chancery expert John De Grenier-Fonblanque. Six members of the Dublin banking family of Latouche appear, along with three directors of the Bank of England: Martin Fonnereau, Henry Porcher, and Peter Isaac Thellusson. Among merchants were George and John Amyand, father and son, also William Wilberforce Bird, silk dealer of Coventry. Josias Dupré Porcher, formerly of South Carolina and father of Henry Porcher, the banker, tried his fortunes in India, and three other M.P.'s of Huguenot descent became East India Company directors: Paul Le Mesurier, a lord mayor of London; William Devaynes; and Zachary Philip Fonnereau. Others of Huguenot descent in the House include Dr. Johnson's friend, Anthony Chamier; the litterateur and man of fashion, Philip Champion De Crespigny; and Benjamin Langlois, Undersecretary of State 1779–82.

In this period five Jews received election. Sir Samuel Eardley, later Baron Eardley, was the only son of a Jewish stockbroker and sat for various constituencies, including the county of Cambridge, in the years 1770–1802. Manasseh Masseh Lopes, a merchant created a baronet in 1805, was born in Jamaica of a family of Spanish Jews, and having conformed to the Church of England, sat in the House for four English boroughs beginning in 1802. His nephew, Sir Ralph Lopes, became M.P. for Westbury·in 1814 and remained in the House for twenty years. Another Jew of

16. Samuel Smiles, *The Huguenots* (London, 1867), p. 339, also *passim* pp. 205–405.

Spanish descent with interests in the West Indies, Ralph Bernal, the art collector, was elected for the city of Lincoln in 1818 and continued as member for over thirty years. In 1819 the political economist David Ricardo, a Jew of Dutch descent, was elected for the Irish borough of Portarlington.[17]

Three further remarkable individuals deserve brief mention. François Joseph Marie Henry de Viry, later Baron de la Perière and Comte de Viry, the grandson of the Sardinian ambassador to England, represented the borough of Huntingdon 1790–96 under the name of Henry Speed. Field Marshal John Louis Ligonier, who was born at Castres in France, represented Bath from 1748 until 1763, when he received an English peerage. And the Russian-born John Julius Angerstein, naturalized by private Act of Parliament (10 George III, c. 19) distinguished himself as an underwriter in Lloyds and represented Camelford in the years 1796–1802. Although de Viry might claim British nationality because his birthplace was London and his mother was English, the elections of Ligonier and Angerstein appear to have been illegal under existing statutes, which excluded not only aliens but also naturalized Englishmen from the Privy Council and the House of Commons.[18]

17. Cf. Porritt, *1*, 142–43.

18. For a summary of this legislation, see Porritt, *1*, 235–36. For Ligonier's birthplace and the possible legality of de Viry's citizenship I am indebted to a suggestion from Professor L. B. Namier.

4. The Age of Members [1]

TAKEN ALONE, the age of a man, of a group of men, or of a Parliament of men, has little significance, for among other considerations the world has known too many old fools to accept longevity as an index of worth. A. L. Rowse has commented tartly on the youthful statesmen of the Long Parliament in contrast to "Parliaments of elderly men since 1918 who have such a record of disservice to their country." [2] The fact that the younger Pitt entered the House of Commons in 1781 before his twenty-second birthday and became head of the government before his twenty-fifth may divert the biographer, and possibly the psychologist may make something of it, but Pitt's extreme youth assumes historical perspective and social meaning only in relation to the society in which he lived—a society, incidentally, which saw nothing remarkable in George III's accession to the throne (and to real political responsibility) in 1760 at the age of 22. Further illustrations abound. In 1752 Henry Fielding could refer to himself as an old man when still in his forty-fifth year.[3] In 1789 William Wyndham Grenville became Speaker of the House of Commons aged only 29, and in 1816 Lord Glenbervie was distressed that his son, aged only 26, contemplated joining the opposition instead of seeking the greener pastures of advancement as a supporter of the administration.[4] By contrast the elder Forsytes in a later era considered Soames at 40 as barely entering into man's estate. In each case the age of a man acquires its significance only in relation to the general social pattern, and this statement applies also to the various groups of men in the House of Commons. Taken alone, their average ages evoke little more than passing interest, but taken together and in relation to the structure of society, the ages of members attain real importance, not only as yardsticks to measure social privilege but also as barometers to measure social change.

The average age of members at the twenty general elections

1. See Appendixes 1, 3, and 4.
2. Alfred Leslie Rowse, *The English Spirit* (New York, Macmillan, 1946), pp. 163–64.
3. Henry Fielding, *The Covent-Garden Journal,* ed. Gerard E. Jensen (New Haven, Yale University Press, 1915), *1,* 4.
4. *The Diaries of Sylvester Douglas (Lord Glenbervie),* ed. Francis Bickley (London, 1928), *2, 158.*

1734–1831 was 43.3 years.[5] About one-sixth were under 30, one-quarter were 30 to 39 inclusive, one-quarter 40 to 49 inclusive, and about one-third were 50 or older. By way of contrast, the average age of members returned in the seven general elections 1918–35 was considerably higher, 50.1 years, with only one M.P. in five being under 40 and almost half over 50.[6] At the general election of 1950 the average age of members was 49.[7] Obviously a marked change upward has taken place as one proceeds from the old regime to the twentieth century.

The rising age of M.P.'s mirrors the upsurge toward longer life of the nation at large, as scientific advances lowered the deathrate and raised the level of life expectancy.[8] Evidence exists that the span of life of Western man has increased phenomonally since prehistoric times, from about 18 years in the Bronze Age in Greece to about 66 in the United States in 1946.[9] At the close of the seventeenth century the Englishman of 21 could expect (on an average) to live until his late forties or early fifties, but at the time of the Reform Act of 1832 he could normally expect ten more years of life, that is, to die in his late fifties or early sixties.[10] Seen in this perspective, the youthfulness of M.P.'s 1734–1832 relative to their successors in the twentieth century reflects the ascending mean age of the population at large.

Further examination reveals still closer relationship to national trends, for the elected Parliaments increased slightly in age 1734–1831. The average age of members at the ten elections 1734–90 was 42.7 years, but the next ten elections show an increase of just over one year, to 43.8. Also, the average age at death for M.P.'s

5. This average, of course, does not include the members who entered the House at bye elections and who were never returned at a general election.

6. James Frederick Stanley Ross, *Parliamentary Representation* (New Haven, Yale University Press, 1944), pp. 27, 32.

7. *The Times House of Commons 1950* (London, Times Pub. Co., 1950), gives the ages of 540 of the 625 members. The average age comes to 49.04 years.

8. M. C. Buer, *Health, Wealth, and Population in the Early Days of the Industrial Revolution* (London, 1926), p. 35; G. T. Griffith, *Population Problems of the Age of Malthus* (Cambridge, Eng., 1926), pp. 39–40; Ephraim Lipson, *The Economic History of England* (London, Black, 1915–31), *3*, 166.

9. Louis I. Dublin, Alfred J. Lotka, and Mortimer Spiegelman, *Length of Life* (New York, Ronald Press, 1949), p. 42.

10. T. Birch, *A Collection of the Yearly Bills of Mortality from 1657 to 1758* (London, 1759), pp. 147–51; Francis Baily, *The Doctrine of Life Annuities and Assurances* (London, 1810), pp. 528, 598; Buer, *Health, Wealth, and Population*, pp. 13–14; T. R. Edmonds, *Life Tables* (London, 1832), Appendix, p. 15; Dublin et al., *Length of Life*, pp. 35–39; J. R. McCulloch, *A Statistical Account of the British Empire* (London, 1837), *1*, 418–19.

increased about two years in conformance to the lengthening life span nationwide. The 2,200 M.P.'s known to have been born before 1750 lived to an average age of 64.7 years, but the 2,285 members born in 1750 or later died at the average age of 66.6 years.[11]

The average life span for M.P.'s of 65.6 years appears to have been much greater than the presumed national average for adults. In explanation one may suggest that the M.P.'s were more highly privileged than the general public and enjoyed better living conditions, therefore longer life. Nevertheless, the tendency toward increasingly long life among the M.P.'s partakes of the larger national movement in the same direction—indication, if indeed formal indication be needed, that the House of Commons functioned as a highly sensitive barometer of social change.

At the same time an ostensibly contradictory tendency shows itself, for analysis of age data reveals an extraordinary stability, both in average ages and in age groupings. For example, the total spread in the average age of members returned in the ten general elections 1734–90 was only 2.2 years, the difference between the youngest Parliament (1768) averaging 42.0 years and the oldest (1761) averaging 44.2 years. The same general conditions prevailed at the next ten general elections, with a total spread of only 2.4 years, the difference between the youngest Parliament (1796) averaging 42.6 years and the oldest (1826) averaging 45.0 years. Four Parliaments 1796–1831 averaged between 43.9 and 44.1 years at the time of general elections. The age groupings share this stability in impressive degree, in that although the Parliaments were becoming somewhat older, the relative proportions of the young, the middle-aged, and the elderly men remained about the same.[12] Such stability in average ages and in age groupings suggests that the political machinery was functioning smoothly, for aside from a persistent upward movement no marked fluctuations appear.

The age on first election of the 4,540 M.P.'s 1734–1832 whose

11. Ordinarily age analysis rests upon 4,540 of the 5,034 M.P.'s, but in 55 instances only the birthdate is known, so that age-at-death averages rest upon a total of 4,485 cases.

12. In the twenty general elections the first quartile (the age of the 25th man in a series of 100) varied from 31 to 35 years, and the third quartile (the age of the 75th man in a series of 100) varied from 51 to 55, so that half of each elected Parliament (the M.P.'s between the two quartiles, i.e., the 26th to and including the 74th member in a series of 100) remained within an age span of no more than about 20 years.

birthdates are known averages 34.6 years. Of the 494 members with unknown ages, about half were of the landed interest (entering the House relatively early in life), and about half were professional men or of the commercial interest (entering the House relatively late in life). One may presume, therefore, that the members with ages unknown approximated the national average and would cause no serious variation from the known figure of 34.6 years. To be completely safe, one may place the average age on first election at somewhere between 34 and 35 years.

One-quarter of the M.P.'s 1734–1832 first entered the House at the age of 25 or younger. In such perspective Pitt's youthful political prominence loses much of its glamor. Another quarter entered between 26 and 33 inclusive, the third quarter between 34 and 42, and the rest at the age of 43 or over. Only 11 per cent of the members were 50 years old or older when they received first election, and only 49 men waited until they were 65 to enter the House.[13] By way of contrast—and the contrast is striking—the average age on first election for members 1918–35 was 44.4 years.[14] In other words the Parliaments 1918–35 were composed of men who had first entered the House almost ten years later in life than their more precocious predecessors 1734–1832. In 1918–35 only one member in forty received his first election at the age of 25 or younger; one member in four did so 1734–1832. Also, in 1918–35 one-quarter were over 50 at the time of their first election, as opposed to only one-tenth in the earlier period.

The lengthening life span explains only in part the increasing age of members, for in contrast to the leveling democracy of a later era the ruling class of the old regime was a highly privileged group, which maintained much of its political power through the rotten boroughs in the electoral system. As indication of the degree of privilege which this class enjoyed, not a few embryo statesmen—81 in all 1734–1832, including six first elected before 1734—did not wait until their twenty-first birthdays before seeking election

13. The detailed distribution of ages on first election follows:

Under 21	81	45 to 49	361
21 to 24	946	50 to 54	230
25 to 29	831	55 to 59	177
30 to 34	698	60 to 64	77
35 to 39	586	65 to 69	38
40 to 44	504	70 and over	11

N.B. "21 to 24" means from 21 years, 0 months to 24 years, 11 months, inclusive.

14. Ross, *Parliamentary Representation*, pp. 21, 26.

to the House. Such action violated the statute (7 and 8 William III, c. 25) passed in 1695, but in only one instance 1734–1832 did the House take effective action to enforce the law. The single exception occurred in 1797, when the House expelled Sir Thomas Mostyn, who had been elected the year before just a few weeks after his twentieth birthday. All of the remaining minors were allowed to retain their seats.

Two boys were elected aged only 18: Robert Lowther in 1759 and Robert Jocelyn (later Earl of Roden) in 1806. Ten were elected aged 19, of whom the most prominent was Charles James Fox, who not only took his seat but made a reputation as an orator before his twenty-first birthday. The remainder of the minors, 69 in number, were elected between the ages of 20 and 21, and of these 14 were within a month of coming of age, so that they had actually reached their majority before the House met.

At least one boy under age was elected to each of the twenty Parliaments 1734–1832 except that of 1830, and in addition to Fox at least one other, Charles William Wentworth-Fitzwilliam, styled Viscount Milton (later Earl Fitzwilliam), not only took his seat but engaged prominently in debate.[15] Two minors were elected as late as 1831: John Charles Savile, later fourth Earl of Mexborough, who died in August 1899 as the last surviving member of the unreformed House; and Algernon George Percy, later sixth Duke of Northumberland, the next to last surviving member, who died in January 1899. Enforcement of the 1695 statute did not come until 1832, after which date no minor has been elected to the House.[16]

The minors in the House came from the inner circle of the ruling class. Two-thirds of them were sons of peers, 32 being elder and 21 younger sons. In addition, nine minors were or became baronets; and of the 19 remaining, three were grandsons of peers, three were the sons of men who later received peerages, one was the great nephew of a viscount, and one was himself created a baron later in life. Twenty-five of the minors belonged to eleven aristo-

15. Cf. Porritt, *The Unreformed House of Commons, 1,* 230. Viscount Milton was born on 4 May 1786 and elected M.P. for Malton 3 November 1806; he spoke on the slave trade at some length on 23 February 1807.

16. William R. Anson, *The Law and Custom of the Constitution* (Oxford, 1909), *1,* 79. The American constitution makers had the English situation in mind, when in 1789, despite mention of Pitt's youthful services to the state, the convention agreed that no member of the House of Representatives should be under 25 and no senator under 30 (see Charles Warren, *The Making of the Constitution* [Cambridge, Mass., Harvard University Press, 1947], pp. 412–13).

cratic families. Three Lowthers (Lonsdale earldom), three Manners (dukedom of Rutland), and three Seymours (Hertford earldom) were elected under age, as were two members apiece from families with the following titles: Abercorn, Bedford, Cornwallis, Holland, Marlborough, Northumberland, Shelburne, and Uxbridge.

If the minors in the House represented a high degree of social prominence, the average ages of various other groups of members may serve as a measure of their relative privilege within the social hierarchy. For example, the M.P.'s with ancestors or close relatives in the House first entered at the average age of 31, while the "new" members without parliamentary forebears received their first election aged almost 40. The eldest sons of English peers averaged only 23.7 years on first election, and the younger sons averaged 27.3—both figures being well under the national average. The Irish peers in the House first entered at the average age of 33. For the members who were baronets when first elected the average entry age rose somewhat, to just over 35 years, but for the remaining members—who were neither sons of peers, Irish peers, or baronets on first election—the average age was 36.6 years. Clearly, members with superior social standing first entered the House considerably earlier in life than did those with less patrician backgrounds.

By the same token, the M.P.'s who had attended one of the seven traditionally great public schools first entered the House at the average age of 30, while the members without a public-school education first received election at the average age of 37. The M.P.'s who had attended one of the universities entered the House at the average age of 32.4 years, but the remaining members first entered almost five years later in life. On the basis of age analysis, therefore, M.P.'s with a public-school or a university background enjoyed greater social privilege than did the rest.

The average entry age for professional men was over 36 years, a little higher than the national average, but considerable variation existed among the professions. The M.P.'s with army service first entered on an average just under 33, but the naval officers and the lawyers averaged about 39 years on first election. Among the lawyers the 34 solicitors and attorneys first entered at the average age of 48, a situation in keeping with the relatively undignified position of nonbarristers in the legal profession. The age figures suggest that the army was the most fashionable profession and that the other professional members enjoyed a lesser degree of privilege than the generality of parliamentarians.

Most impressive of all are the entry-age figures for the M.P.'s in the commercial interest, whose average age on first election comes to just over 40 years, almost six years higher than the national average. The businessmen in the House were mostly self-made, lacking many of the privileges of the older segment of the ruling class.

By contrast, the M.P.'s who belonged neither to the professional nor the commercial interest, that is, the country gentlemen, first entered the House at the average age of 31.9 years, almost three years under the national average, over four years earlier than the professional men, and over eight years earlier than the members in the commercial interest. On the basis of age analysis alone, the landed proprietors of the old regime enjoyed far greater social and political privilege than did the other members.

With the entry age of members as a standard of measurement, the more privileged part of the ruling class in the House included M.P.'s closely connected with the peerage, those belonging to parliamentary families, those with a public-school or university education, the army officers, and the landed gentry. The remaining members were in process of acquiring what their more fortunate colleagues had inherited.

5. Length of Service [1]

In DISCUSSING the qualities making for leadership in the House of Commons Harold Laski has given prominence to the stability of its membership:

> Men who have to live together and work together for years on end can hardly, even amid the conditions of modern party warfare, help developing between one another the habits of good fellowship . . . Members who are not accustomed to one another for fairly long periods cannot take one another for granted; they cannot know one another's personality in a way that builds a tradition, an esprit de corps, a sense, despite differences, of a mutual adventure in search of great ends.[2]

The average length of service of the 5,034 M.P.'s 1734–1832 was 13.4 years. Of the total representation 257, or about 5 per cent, were members for a year or less, and a few were M.P.'s in a technical sense only, such as Henry Cornwallis, elected on 30 March 1761, who died in April before the House met, and Thomas Noel, elected on 20 October 1774, who succeeded as second Viscount Wentworth eleven days later, before the House began sitting on 29 November. About one-quarter of the representation sat for less than six years, and half served less than 11 years, but the third quarter served between 11 and 19 years, and the upper quarter served 19 years or more apiece. Seven hundred sixty-three members (roughly one in seven) were in the House 25 years or longer, and of these 451 sat for over 30 years. At the top of the list, 23 M.P.'s in this period served more than a half century each.[3] William Aislabie, with the longest service in this period, was M.P. 1721–81;

1. See Appendixes 1 and 5.
2. Harold J. Laski, *Parliamentary Government in England* (New York, Viking Press, 1938), pp. 129, 131.
3. 1,136 M.P.'s served under 5 years each; 1,261 from 5 to 10 (that is, from 5 years, 0 months to and including 9 years, 11 months); 799 from 10 to 15; 645 from 15 to 20; 430 from 20 to 25; 312 from 25 to 30; 234 from 30 to 35; 106 from 35 to 40; 58 from 40 to 45; 30 from 45 to 50; and 23 for 50 or more years. Service has been calculated to the nearest month, from the date of election to either the date the M.P. left the House (as nearly as can be determined), or the date the Parliament was dissolved. The intervals between the dissolution and the subsequent re-election have not been included in the totals, since technically the members became private citizens in the interval.

Christopher Rice Mansel-Talbot, the last sitting survivor of the unreformed House, came second, with service as M.P. 1830–90; and Sir John Aubrey, third on the list, was M.P. 1768–1826. The psychological effect on the House of such men is incalculable, as month by month, session by session, decade by decade they took their seats in the same familiar surroundings. In their persons they symbolized that sense of permanence which was so characteristic of the old regime.

As a group, the 23 members with over 50 years' service exhibit upper-class characteristics in high degree. With one exception, Philips Gybbon, they had attended a public school or a university, or had had a blood relative (in the male line) in the House before them. Five only had entered professional life, Henry Cecil Lowther, who retired from the army in 1831, and four barristers: Sir James Lowther, George Granville Harcourt, Clement Tudway, and Charles Watkin Williams-Wynn. Six of the 23 were baronets and four were sons of peers. Their average age on first election was just under 25 years, and of their number only William Edwardes, first elected aged 36, was older than the national average.

In general, M.P.'s with ancestors previously in the House, those with fashionable educational backgrounds, and those without stated occupations (i.e., the country gentlemen) tended not only to enter the House earlier in life but also to serve longer as members. Thus length of service as well as youthfulness on first election appears as a means of identifying the privileged groups in the Commons.

As further evidence of the stability of membership, 4,569 men without previous service entered the House in the 95.6 years in which a Parliament was legally in being 1734–1832, or an average of only 48 per year. An average of only 138 new members per election entered the House at the twenty general elections in this period, from a high of 166 in 1802 to a low of 89 in 1807, following the short Parliament of 1806.[4] Otherwise expressed, at

4. M.P.'s without previous service, by general elections:

1734	155	1768	164	1796	139	1818	157
1741	156	1774	148	1802	166	1820	90
1747	154	1780	143	1806	147	1826	144
1754	127	1784	138	1807	89	1830	143
1761	130	1790	134	1812	127	1831	118

In making this and other tabulations by general elections, I have disregarded hedgers, i.e., M.P.'s returned for two or more seats at the same election. In each case, when the hedger gave up his superfluous seat(s), I have considered his successor as the originally returned member. In this respect I have followed the

the ten general elections 1734–90 on an average three-quarters of the House had had previous parliamentary experience, and at the next ten elections four-fifths of the M.P.'s returned had served sometime before.

In Queen Elizabeth's time the proportion of experienced members was much lower, being about one-third of the House at the general elections of 1571 and 1584, and about one-half at the election of 1593.[5] At the general elections 1918–50 on an average just about 70 per cent of the House had served before.[6] Insofar as such measurements may be valid, it appears that the House enjoyed greater stability of membership in the years 1734–1832 than in either the earlier or later period.

---

practice of Namier (*England in the Age of the American Revolution,* pp. 248–49). M.P.'s without previous service returned at bye elections:

1734–41	98	1768–74	99	1796–1802	211	1818–20	36
1741–47	99	1774–80	103	1802–06	99	1820–26	105
1747–54	93	1780–84	72	1806–07	7	1826–30	60
1754–61	114	1784–90	102	1807–12	103	1830–31	20
1761–68	140	1790–96	108	1812–18	110	1831–32	21

The total for 1796–1802 includes 97 Irish M.P.'s without previous service in the British Parliament, who entered at the Union in 1801.

5. John E. Neale, *The Elizabethan House of Commons* (London, Cape, 1949), p. 309.

6. Ross, *Parliamentary Representation,* pp. 36–37; Ronald B. McCallum and Alison Readman, *The British General Election of 1945* (London, Oxford University Press, 1947), p. 274; in 1950, 129 new members were elected, see *The Times House of Commons 1950* (London), *passim.*

6. Social Status and Family Backgrounds [1]

IT HAS BECOME customary to speak of the British ruling class of the old regime as an oligarchy, and to emphasize the degree of control which a few families exercised over the organs of government, particularly in the era of Whig domination 1714–60. This view, which takes its root in the novels of Disraeli and the essays of Macaulay, states that the nobility in cooperation with important nontitled landed families controlled the powers of the crown, the royal patronage, local government, the cabinet, and both Houses of Parliament. One encounters such statements as the following: the "House of Commons [was] packed with the nominees of landowners and peers"; [2] "the House, by means of the rotten boroughs, falls under the control of the greater nobility"; [3] "Parliament and the ministerial offices were the preserve of a few great families"; [4] "the landed gentry became omnipotent in central and local government"; [5] "sixty families supply, and for generations have supplied, one-third of the House of Commons, one-third of the ultimate governing power for an empire which includes a fourth of the human race." [6] All such remarks lean toward overstatement, for recent research has shown that the nobility neither monopolized the cabinet, nor did they control a majority in the House of Commons by bribery and manipulation of the archaic electoral machinery. One historian, Barnes, in reviewing the evidence, has concluded, "We are justified in dismissing the conventional picture of the eighteenth-century Whig oligarchy as a myth." [7] Nonetheless, the aristocracy in cooperation with the great territorial families exercised an impressive

1. See Appendixes 1, 6, 7, 8, and 9.
2. J. R. M. Butler, *The Passing of the Great Reform Bill* (London, 1914), p. 18.
3. Philip A. Gibbons, *Ideas of Political Representation in Parliament, 1651–1832* (Oxford, 1914), p. 9.
4. John Donald Kingsley, *Representative Bureaucracy* (Yellow Springs, Ohio, Antioch Press, 1944), p. 39.
5. Paschal Larkin, *Property in the Eighteenth Century, with Special Reference to England and Locke* (Dublin, Cork University Press, 1930), p. 112.
6. J. L. Sanford and Meredith Townsend, *The Great Governing Families of England* (London, 1865), *1*, 15.
7. Donald Barnes, "The Myth of the Eighteenth Century Whig Oligarchy," *Proceedings of the Pacific Coast Branch of the American Historical Association, 25* (1929), 119–32; of the 306 cabinet members 1801–1924, 182 were sons of aristocrats (see Harold J. Laski, "The Personnel of the English Cabinet, 1801–1924," *American Political Science Review, 12* [1928], 16–20).

degree of control over the government, even if that control was incomplete. The traditional view of an oligarchy should be modified and qualified, rather than completely discarded.

Of the 5,034 M.P.'s 1734–1832, 883 were sons of peers (or of peeresses in their own right), 452 were baronets, and 64 were Irish peers at the time of their first election. Thus over one-quarter of the members began their service in a formally privileged social category. While in the House 330 members changed status: nine sons of peers and five baronets received Irish peerages, as did 41 other M.P.'s; 244 members became baronets; and 31 men became sons of peers as their fathers acquired titles. In all, 1,715 members, over one-third of the representatives in this period, ended their careers in the Commons with preferential social standing, in addition to an untold number of others who were related to peers or baronets by birth or marriage.

If one then follows the members beyond their years in the House of Commons the results are even more striking. At death 787 of the 5,034 members had become baronets and 876 had become peers (including 176 Irish peers and 24 in the peerage of Scotland). Otherwise stated, about one-third of the representatives died as baronets or peers, and since another one-fifth died as sons of peers, over half of the M.P.'s in this period ended their lives in an extremely elevated social sphere—to say nothing of the members with more remote aristocratic connections.

The sons of peers outnumbered the baronets at every general election except that of 1734, and increased steadily in number as time went on, from a low of 68 in 1734 to a high of 154 in 1826. The presence of such a formidable and growing bloc of peers' sons received the sanction of a venerable political tradition, for as early as Tudor times, when the House began to attract members "of a better class," [8] it was customary for the eldest sons or heirs apparent of peers to seek election to the Commons before passing on to the Upper House. As Mahon said in a speech in the House of Commons in 1832: "I do think it of the highest importance, if we are to have a House of Lords at all, that those who are to compose it should be trained in the habits of business . . . Of all the many eminent statesmen who are to be found in the House of Lords at present, I only remember one—Lord Holland—who has not received his po-

8. Wallace Notestein, *The Winning of the Initiative by the House of Commons* (London, 1924), pp. 48–49; see also Neale, *The Elizabethan House of Commons*, pp. 146–47, 301.

litical education here." [9] Similarly, Basil Williams has pointed out that Carteret, who inherited a title as a child of five, missed the important schooling in practical politics ordinarily obtained "in the hurly-burly of the House of Commons." [10] But a more obvious explanation of the increase of peers' sons in the Commons is simply that the peerage itself almost doubled in size between 1780 and 1832. Particularly as the sources of patronage in the form of sinecures began to dry up following the Whig program of economical reform, the crown began to bestow peerages instead of offices as political rewards, and as the newly created peers were recruited mainly from politically prominent families, whose sons would have entered the Commons whether their fathers had a title or not, the sons of peers in the House naturally grew in number.[11]

Other evidence shows that a relatively small group exercised a high degree of political control. Of the 5,034 M.P.'s 1734–1832, 2,813 or well over half, had had a blood relative in the male line in the House before them, and only 2,221 were "new" men.[12] If one had the patience to make a family tree for each member extending back three or four generations, and if one then searched for previous M.P.'s on both sides of the family, or if one took into account members connected to parliamentary families by marriage, the proportion of "new" men would decline still further.

The members with parliamentary ancestors belonged to the inner circle of the political elite. They first entered the House on an average about nine years earlier in life than did the "new" men, and they accounted for two-thirds of the knights of the shire, the English county seats being the most sought-after constituencies in the unreformed House. Further, of the 897 M.P.'s in the commercial interest, only 303, or about one-third, had had blood relatives (in the male line) previously in the House, but of noncommercial mem-

9. *Parliamentary Debates,* ed. T. C. Hansard, 3d Ser. (London, 1830–85), *11,* 421.

10. Basil Williams, *Carteret and Newcastle* (Cambridge, Eng., University Press, 1943), p. 122; see also Charles Grant Robertson, *Chatham and the British Empire* (New York, Macmillan, 1948), p. 38.

11. G. C. Richards, "The Creation of Peers recommended by the Younger Pitt," *American Historical Review, 34* (1928), 49–53; A. S. Turberville, *The House of Lords in the XVIIIth Century* (London, 1927), pp. 4–5, 420; A. S. Turberville, "The Younger Pitt and the House of Lords," *History,* N.S., *21* (1936–37), 351–54; Nathaniel William Wraxall, *Historical and Posthumous Memoirs,* ed. Henry B. Wheatley (New York, 1884), *2,* 286 and *3,* 107.

12. 1,014 were the sons of members; 789 were preceded by both fathers and (paternal) grandfathers; 339 had had (paternal) grandfathers but not fathers previously in the House; and 671 were preceded by other blood relatives in the male line.

bers almost two-thirds could claim at least one ancestor (in the male line) who had served in the House before them.

Of the 5,034 M.P.'s 1734–1832, 3,045 belonged to 922 families; and of these, 1,527 M.P.'s belonged to only 247 families.[13] Some family groups almost achieved the stature of dynasties. The Manners family sent 21 of its members to the House in this period; the Townshend family sent 17; the families of Buller, Finch, and Fitzroy sent 15 apiece; there were 14 Cavendishes, 14 Fanes, 14 Stuarts (Bute earldom), 13 Grenvilles, 13 Spencers, 12 Bouveries, 12 Ponsonbys, 12 Stewarts (Galoway earldom), and 12 Yorkes. The following families sent 11 members each: Cavendish-Bentinck, Clive, Dundas, Foley, Heathcote, Herbert, Hope, Leveson-Gower, Paget, Pitt, Seymour, Smith (Carrington barony), and Walpole; and the following sent 10 members each: Lowther, Onslow, Percy, and Williams-Wynn. These 31 families sent a total of 382 members to the House 1734–1832, or one M.P. in every 13 returned. One may only concur in Namier's judgment that "English history, and especially English Parliamentary history, is made by families rather than by individuals." [14]

Among statesmen family pride usually went hand in hand with personal ambition. Both Marlborough and Chatham sought to elevate their families to the first rank in the kingdom,[15] and there is profound truth in Becky Sharp's remarks to Sir Pitt Crawley: "I know what you want. You want to distinguish yourself in Parliament . . . You want to be member for the county, where, with your own vote and your borough at your back, you can command anything. And you want to be Baron Crawley of Queens Crawley." [16] Mosca in his monumental work has stated that all ruling classes tend to become hereditary.[17] The dynastic emphasis in the House of Commons of the old regime tends to corroborate his thesis.

13. A family group is here defined as any two or more M.P.'s 1734–1832 descended from a common great grandfather or bearing a closer relationship in the male line. The M.P.'s in family groups include the majority of members with parliamentary ancestors but not all, since an M.P. 1734–1832 might have been the first of his family in the House but at the same time the founder of a parliamentary family. Conversely, a given M.P. with parliamentary ancestors might have been the only member of his family in the House 1734–1832.

14. Namier, *England in the Age of the American Revolution,* p. 22.

15. Winston S. Churchill, *Marlborough* (New York, Scribner's, 1933–38), *4,* 171; Robertson, *Chatham,* pp. 131, 184–85.

16. W. M. Thackeray, *Vanity Fair* (1848), ch. 45.

17. Gaetano Mosca, *The Ruling Class,* ed. Arthur Livingston, trans. H. D. Kahn (New York and London, McGraw-Hill, 1939), p. 61.

Illegitimate birth was in itself no barrier to a political career, provided one's father belonged to the elite. There were 25 bastards in the House 1734–1832, 13 being natural sons of peers. All but six had had parliamentary ancestors, and all but three belonged to parliamentary family groups. Five became baronets, and one acquired an Irish title. Among the bastards was Chesterfield's Philip Stanhope. Two illegitimate sons of the first Marquis of Waterford entered the House: Adm. John Poo Beresford, who died a baronet; and his brother William Carr Beresford, the reformer of the Portuguese army, who received an Irish title. The other M.P.'s born out of wedlock remained for the most part undistinguished.

Since the majority of M.P.'s shared a common social background, tinged as it was with aristocracy and family pride, the House of Commons itself has often been compared to an exclusive club for the upper classes.[18] As such, membership in the House at times became a matter of social prestige rather than political stewardship, and occasionally members found themselves faced with political responsibilities which they were not equipped to meet. For example, James Boswell, himself an unsuccessful aspirant for membership in the House, noted in his London journal for 5 April 1773: "I called on Mr. David Kennedy, and found him the same joker as formerly and nothing more. It struck me a little to think that the gentlemen of Ayrshire should be represented in Parliament by a good, honest, merry fellow indeed, but one so totally incapable of the business of legislation, and so devoid of the talents which distinguish a man in public life." [19] Kennedy was by no means the only incapable member of the club, and a number of others like him neglected their parliamentary duties.[20]

How far such incapacity and laxness were peculiar to the unreformed House may be left for the philosophers and political scientists to decide. Lecky and Laski alike have argued eloquently in favor of a system which gave young men of rank easy and early entrance into public life.[21] But at least—and despite all its

18. See, *inter alia,* H. Taine, *Notes on England,* trans. W. F. Rae (New York, 1874), p. 223; William I. Jennings, *Parliament* (Cambridge, Eng., University Press; New York, Macmillan, 1940), p. 31.

19. James Boswell, *Private Papers,* ed. Geoffrey Scott and Frederick A. Pottle (Mount Vernon, New York, Rudge, privately printed, 1928–34), *6,* 82.

20. Porritt, *The Unreformed House of Commons, 1,* 250–51.

21. William E. H. Lecky, *A History of England in the Eighteenth Century* (New York, 1887), *1,* 194–95; Laski, *Parliamentary Government in England,* pp. 131–32.

failings—the unreformed House contained a central bloc of members, connected by birth and marriage in a relatively small web of family interrelationships. Of similar and privileged social standing, the majority of members shared a homogeneous social heritage and a common political tradition. Although this bloc of members did not monopolize the representation, they were the most dominant single group in the house, and their presence set the tone and character of British political life before 1832.

7. Education [1]

How FAR EDUCATION acts as a cohesive and binding force to mold a social class has received the thoughtful attention of a number of scholars. Morris Ginsberg, for example, has given education due prominence in his statement:

> Classes in modern societies may be described as groups of individuals who, through common descent, similarity of occupation, wealth and education have come to have a similar mode of life, a similar stock of ideas, feelings, attitudes and forms of behavior and who, on any or all these grounds, meet one another on equal terms and regard themselves, although with varying degrees of explicitness, as belonging to one group. [2]

In his discussion of the landed gentry Bagehot emphasized the sense of unity which they derived from a common educational tradition, and other scholars have observed that the British upper classes tended to monopolize the sources of education in order to maintain their privileged position within the state. [3] In a conversation with Boswell in 1775 Topham Beauclerk set aside the importance of family in favor of education and wealth as hallmarks of social acceptability: "He said that now in England being of an old family was of no consequence. People did not inquire far back. If a man was rich and well educated, he was equally well received as the most ancient gentleman, though if inquiry were made, his extraction might be found to be very mean." [4] Beauclerk's remarks may be disputed, but similarity of educational background, in the public schools, the universities, and the law, went a long way to bolster the esprit de corps of the upper classes, particularly as it fortified the social and intellectual standards by which they lived.

1. See Appendixes 1, 10, and 11.
2. Morris Ginsberg, "Class Consciousness," *Encyclopedia of the Social Sciences* (New York, Macmillan, 1935), *3*, 536.
3. Walter Bagehot, *The English Constitution* (new ed. Boston, 1873), pp. 225–26; see also J. R. M. Butler, *The Passing of the Great Reform Bill* (London, 1914), p. 233; Mosca, *The Ruling Class*, p. 417; Dorothy Ross, "Class Privilege in Seventeenth-Century England," *History*, N.S., *28* (1943), 149; Richard Henry Tawney, *Equality* (London, Allen & Unwin, 1931), pp. 69–70.
4. James Boswell, *Private Papers*, ed. Scott and Pottle, *10*, 156.

Of the 5,034 M.P.'s 1734–1832, 1,714, or about a third had gone to one or more of the seven English public schools of the old regime: Charterhouse, Eton, Harrow, Rugby, Shrewsbury, Westminster, and Winchester.[5] As time passed and the schools themselves grew in size and prestige, the proportion of M.P.'s with a public-school education increased accordingly, from about one in five at the general election of 1734 to almost half the House at the general election of 1830, and the high proportion of former public-school boys in the House has continued on into the twentieth century.[6]

Eton headed the roster of politically prominent public schools, for 785 M.P.'s 1734–1832, or about one member in six, were old Etonians, including Robert Walpole, Henry and Charles James Fox, Chatham, Grenville, North, Camden, Canning, Tierney, Wellington, Grey, and Melbourne. Throughout this period the number of Etonians in the House increased threefold, from a low of 43 in 1734 to 144 at the general election of 1830. The second oldest of the public schools after Winchester, Eton enjoyed a large endowment and controlled the appointments to scholarships and fellowships at King's College, Cambridge. Although smaller than Westminster in 1734, Eton outstripped Westminster in the next two decades, and thereafter, in part owing to the partiality shown by George III, Eton rose to first rank among the public schools.[7] About 5,000 boys born after 1750 entered Eton in time to seek parliamentary election before 1832, and of these one boy in ten actually reached the unreformed House of Commons. By contrast, only one Winchester boy in fifty became an M.P. in the same period. Eton's greatness was to extend far beyond the Reform Act, for former Etonians comprised over one-quarter of the cabinet members 1801–1924, one-seventh of the M.P.'s 1918–35, and about

5. A public school has been defined as "a non-local endowed boarding school for the upper classes" (see Edward C. Mack, *Public Schools and British Opinion, 1780 to 1860* [London, Methuen, 1938], p. xiii). Only seven schools came within the limits of this definition before 1832, and before 1780 Harrow, Rugby, and Shrewsbury were of doubtful status. Merchant Taylor and St. Paul's have been excluded because strictly speaking they were day and not boarding schools. Besides, they had only eleven M.P.'s apiece in this period.

6. In 1918–35, 43 per cent of the M.P.'s had attended a public school, and at the general elections in these years 56 per cent of the M.P.'s were former public-school boys (see Ross, *Parliamentary Representation*, pp. 43, 46); in 1945 the proportion fell to under 30 per cent (see McCallum and Readman, *The British General Election of 1945*, p. 273).

7. Mack, *Public Schools*, pp. 4, 11–13, 17–19.

one-tenth of the members elected in both 1945 and 1950.[8] Trevelyan has commented in his biography of Earl Grey: "At nine years
old he was sent to Eton . . . It was here that he first touched the
great world of politics and fashion, to which Eton was then an
antechamber . . . Eton was a recruiting ground for Parliament,
not only because of its peculiar education, but by reason of its
personal connections. An 'Eton reputation' was a long step towards a seat in the House." [9]

Westminster, with 544 M.P.'s 1734–1832, ranked second to
Eton, but Westminster's story is one of deterioration rather than
growth. Third oldest of the public schools after Winchester and
Eton, re-endowed by Henry VIII and Elizabeth, and maintaining
twenty scholars at Oxford and Cambridge, Westminster at the
time of the Restoration became, under headmaster Busby, England's foremost public school and enjoyed a second period of greatness under John Nicholl in the years 1733–53.[10] Westminster's high
point in political prestige 1734–1832 came at the general election
of 1761, when 111 "Old Westminsters" entered the House of Commons to 79 Etonians. But in the succeeding years, in part because
of reduced finances and restricted physical boundaries, Westminster entered a slow decline, until in 1831 Westminster sent only
65 former students to the House to 135 from Eton. Nevertheless,
"Old Westminsters" in the unreformed House included Henry Pelham, Lord Mansfield, Gibbon, and Lord John Russell.

Harrow had 270 M.P.'s 1734–1832, about half as many as
Westminster and a third as many as Eton. Harrow's story in these
years is one of rapid and phenomenal growth under a succession of
remarkably able headmasters, as from a meagerly financed grammar school in the 1720's Harrow became Eton's most serious rival
by the end of the eighteenth century.[11] Harrow sent only one member to the House of Commons at the general election of 1747; only
two in 1734, 1741, and 1754; and no more than nine at any elec-

8. Harold J. Laski, "The Personnel of the English Cabinet 1801–1924," *American Political Science Review, 12* (1928), 16; Ross, *Parliamentary Representation,*
p. 52; McCallum and Readman, *Election of 1945,* p. 273; *The Times House of
Commons 1950* (London), contains biographies of the 625 members returned and
of these 69 were old Etonians.

9. George M. Trevelyan, *Lord Grey of the Reform Bill* (London, 1929), pp. 4, 6.

10. Mack, *Public Schools,* pp. 4, 11, 18, 74; John W. Adamson, *English Education
1789–1902* (Cambridge, Eng., University Press, 1930), pp. 61–62.

11. Mack, *Public Schools,* pp. 4, 11, 74; Adamson, *English Education,* pp. 61–62;
Geddes MacGregor, "Public Schools in the 18th Century," *Quarterly Review, 285*
(1947), 582; William T. J. Gun, ed., *The Harrow School Register, 1571–1800*
(London and New York, Longmans, Green, 1934), p. xv.

tion before 1780. But at the three elections of 1826, 1830, and 1831 Harrow had more M.P.'s than Westminster and was second only to Eton in the House. In less than one hundred years Harrow had risen from obscurity to second place on the roster of politically prominent public schools, a position which was maintained in the years 1918–35.[12] In the unreformed House former Harrow students included Sheridan, Palmerston, and Peel.

Winchester, the oldest of the schools, sent only 70 of its students to the House 1734–1832, from a low of four at the general elections of 1734, 1741, and 1768 to a high of 19 at the elections of 1826 and 1830. Winchester suffered from tenacious medievalism, to the point that by 1750 it had only ten paying students. Except for a brief rejuvenation in the 1790's, Winchester had almost ceased to be an upper-class school.[13] Winchester's most prominent political figure in this period was Henry Addington.

Former Rugby students numbered 51 in the House 1734–1832, with as few as two at the general elections of 1784 and 1790, and a high of 12 at the election of 1826. Like Harrow, Rugby began as a local grammar school without a rich endowment, and enjoyed little prominence before Dr. James became headmaster in 1777. Rugby's greatness, as yet unachieved, was reserved for the future.[14]

Charterhouse sent only 32 members to the House in this period, with no more than three at any election before 1796, and a high of eight thereafter. Like Rugby, Charterhouse fared somewhat better in the later years, but Charterhouse's sudden rise in the 1820's came too late to be reflected in the unreformed House.[15] Aside from Blackstone, Charterhouse's most prominent M.P. in this period was the second Earl of Liverpool.

Shrewsbury had only 15 M.P.'s 1734–1832. From a position of strength at the close of the seventeenth century, Shrewsbury had declined to near extinction, having only 18 students in 1798, when Samuel Butler became headmaster. Under Butler's direction the school underwent a splendid revival, but like Rugby, Shrewsbury's real greatness was yet to come.[16]

The relative size of the public schools determined only in part

12. Ross, *Parliamentary Representation*, p. 51.

13. Mack, *Public Schools*, pp. 4, 17, 74; MacGregor, p. 582; A. F. Leach, *A History of Winchester College* (New York, 1899), pp. 378–80, 410.

14. Mack, *Public Schools*, pp. 11, 13, 19, 74.

15. *Ibid.*, pp. 18, 74.

16. *Ibid.*, pp. 19, 74; G. W. Fisher, *Annals of Shrewsbury School* (London, 1899), pp. 229, 308.

the number of their former students entering the House of Commons. On the basis of incomplete statistics, Eton, Harrow, and Westminster had together about two-thirds of the total public-school enrollment in this period, but they accounted for nine-tenths of the public-school boys in the House.[17] Clearly some force other than mere weight of numbers was at work. Throughout the eighteenth century the ruling class overran the public schools—particularly Eton, Harrow, and Westminster—until the poor scholars, for whose benefit the schools were originally established, found themselves wholly submerged.[18] The extent to which a school received upper-class support determined not only its prestige but also the degree to which its students entered public life. Relatively few M.P.'s came from Winchester and Charterhouse, not because they were small schools but because they were less fashionable than some of the others.

In corroboration, the M.P.'s with a public-school education enjoyed a high degree of social privilege. They first entered the House on an average seven years earlier in life and they served an average of two years longer than the other members. Of their number, 806, or almost half, were Irish peers, baronets, or sons of peers, in addition to a number of others more distantly connected with the aristocracy.

As a unifying force, the classical curriculum of the schools, albeit often dreary and uninspired,[19] at least provided an intellectual meeting ground for all public-school boys, along with the comforting realization that they all "spoke the same language." To

17. Enrollment figures for Eton, Westminster, and Winchester are almost complete for this period, but they exist only in fragmentary form for the other schools. The following have been used in gathering data on the relative size of the public schools: Fisher, *Annals of Shrewsbury,* pp. 229, 264, 270 n., 278, 308, 329; Gun, *Harrow School Register,* p. xv; Leach, *Winchester College,* pp. 378–80, 410; R. A. Austen-Leigh, *Eton College Lists 1678–1790* (Eton, 1907), pp. 364–68; G. F. Russell Barker and Alan M. Stenning, *The Record of Old Westminsters* (London, 1928), *2,* 1094–95; Gerald S. Davies, *Charterhouse in London* (London, 1921), pp. 254–55; *The Eton Calendar* (Eton, 1889), p. 196; Frederic H. Forshall, *Westminster School, Past and Present* (London, 1884), pp. 107, 113; Clifford W. Holgate, ed., *Winchester Long Rolls, 1653–1721* (Winchester, 1899), pp. lxxii, lxxvi; *Report of Her Majesty's Commissioners Appointed to Inquire into the Revenues and Management of Certain Colleges and Schools* (London, 1864), *1,* 179, 310 and *2,* 112, 218; W. H. D. Rouse, *A History of Rugby School* (London, 1899), p. 120; Percy Thornton, *Harrow School and Its Surroundings* (London, 1885), pp. 112, 132, 196 n., 230, 251, 257.

18. Mack, *Public Schools,* pp. 10, 16–17, 20, 35, 41; MacGregor, p. 582; Adamson, *English Education,* p. 65.

19. Mack, *Public Schools,* pp. 26–30.

speak in debate brilliantly and according to classical standards of oratory could go a long way toward establishing a political reputation. After the younger Pitt had spoken only three times in the House an observer predicted that his eloquence would soon lead to "a high situation." [20] Again, to use poor grammar or to mispronounce a word could endanger a political career.[21] The ungrammatical speech of the hop merchant Sir James Sanderson provoked ridicule when he moved the address in 1792,[22] and the Scots suffered equally because of their accent.[23] If a public-school education in the classics could not make a boy a brilliant speaker, it could teach him to speak correctly in the accepted manner of the day.

But the primary function of the schools was moral and social rather than intellectual, as ruling classes generally and upper-class Englishmen in particular tend to emphasize character and good form rather than intelligence and learning.[24] As the masters retired more and more into the background, the boys themselves assumed control of school life, and by devices such as the prefect-fagging system found means to enforce their own code of gentlemanly conduct.[25] Oliver Goldsmith commented in 1759: "A boy will learn more true wisdom in a public school in a year, than by a private education in five. It is not from masters but from their equals, youth learn a knowledge of the world: the little tricks they play each other, the punishment that frequently attends the commission, is a just picture of the great world; and all the ways of men are practised in a public school in miniature." [26] Somewhat later Greville expressed concern that a nobleman's son had received a private education "without receiving correction from any of those levelling circumstances which are incidental to public

20. Wraxall, *Historical and Posthumous Memoirs, 2,* 119.

21. Lord Chesterfield's *Letters to His Son,* 24 November 1749 and 19 November 1750.

22. *Notes and Queries,* 8th Ser., *12,* 73 (cited in Cokayne's *Baronetage*). Despite reports to the contrary, he spoke at least three times thereafter (*Parliamentary History,* ed. Cobbett, *30,* 543, *31,* 88 and 122).

23. See above, p. 13.

24. Mack, *Public Schools,* pp. 26–30; Adamson, *English Education,* p. 59; Mosca, *The Ruling Class,* p. 63; Kingsley, *Representative Bureaucracy,* p. 153; Lewis P. Curtis, "Gibbon's Paradise Lost," *The Age of Johnson, Essays Presented to Chauncey Brewster Tinker,* ed. F. W. Hilles (New Haven, Yale University Press, 1949), p. 86.

25. Mack, *Public Schools,* pp. 34–36, 40.

26. Oliver Goldsmith, *The Bee,* No. 6, 10 November 1759; see also Butler, *Great Reform Bill,* pp. 232–33; Elie Halévy, *A History of the English People in 1815* (London, 1924), p. 467.

schools." [27] Although the public schools neglected scholarship in favor of moral training, they etched deeply on the minds of impressionable youths the values, both social and intellectual, which prevailed in the aristocratic world. In so doing the public schools strengthened immeasurably the mental and moral foundations of the ruling class.

Of the 5,034 M.P.'s 1734–1832, 2,416, or just under half, had attended a university, either Oxford or Cambridge, one of the four universities in Scotland, Trinity College in Dublin, or one of eleven universities outside of Great Britain. Throughout the period the proportion of university-trained M.P.'s increased from about 45 per cent at the general elections 1734–61 and about half at the elections 1768–1812 to almost 60 per cent in 1818–31, with a low of 236 in 1741 and a high of 396 in 1830. The tendency for more and more university men to enter the House dates from Queen Elizabeth's reign, when the proportion rose from one in six in 1563 to one in three in 1584 and 1593.[28] A sampling of the representation 1604–29 indicates that just over half the members had gone to some university.[29] In the years 1734–1832 the number of university men in the House rose to a point higher than that attained in the past, or in the years 1918–50.[30]

Oxford with 1,286 M.P.'s and Cambridge with 873 accounted for seven-eighths of the university-trained members 1734–1832. In the eighteenth century Oxford outnumbered Cambridge in enrollment about three to two,[31] and Oxford exceeded Cambridge in M.P.'s in about the same proportion. On an average Oxford had 50 more M.P.'s than Cambridge per election, and as many as 87 more in 1741.

Of the Oxford colleges, Christ Church, with 550 M.P.'s 1734–1832, far overshadowed the others, accounting for more than two-fifths of the Oxford men who entered the House in these years.

27. *The Greville Memoirs*, ed. Henry Reeve (3d ed. London, 1875), *1*, 76.

28. Neale, *The Elizabethan House of Commons*, pp. 302–3.

29. Harold Hulme, *A Study of the Personnel of the House of Commons between 1604 and 1629*, abstract of Ph.D. thesis at Cornell University (Ithaca, New York [1925]).

30. In 1918–35, 743 (or 41 per cent) of the 1,823 M.P.'s were university men (Ross, *Parliamentary Representation*, p. 53); in 1945 there were 248 (or 39 per cent) of the 640 returned (McCallum and Readman, *Election of 1945*, p. 273); in 1950 there were 307 (or 49 per cent) of the 625 returned (*The Times House of Commons 1950, passim*).

31. John A. Venn, *Oxford and Cambridge Matriculations 1544–1906* (Cambridge, Eng., 1908), p. 11.

Christ Church had about one-tenth of Oxford's undergraduates 1730–70 and about one-seventh in the next forty years,[32] but Christ Church had one-quarter of Oxford's M.P.'s in the elections 1734–90 and over 60 per cent in the elections 1796–1831. From 1806 on, Christ Church sent more members to the House than all the rest of the Oxford colleges put together. Brasenose, Christ Church's nearest rival, had only 83 M.P.'s in this period.[33]

To a somewhat lesser degree the same general situation prevailed at Cambridge, where Trinity with 299 M.P.'s and St. John's with 201 M.P.'s accounted for about half of the student body and almost 60 per cent of the Cambridge men in the House.[34] Throughout most of the eighteenth century St. John's was the largest college in the university, but in the 1780's Trinity took the lead. Trinity had about one-quarter of the student body and one-third of the Cambridge men who entered the House 1734–1832, but as Trinity grew in size its share of the representation increased, from eight M.P.'s in 1741 to more than all the other Cambridge colleges in 1826, 1830, and 1831. No other college in the university approached the stature of Trinity and St. John. Their nearest rival, Trinity Hall, had only 51 M.P.'s in this period.[35]

Although as a whole the relative size of Oxford and Cambridge determined the number of men which each sent to the House of Commons, the colleges within the universities varied in M.P.'s as much as the public schools, with Christ Church, Oxford, and Trinity College, Cambridge, corresponding roughly to Eton and West-

32. *The Historical Register of the University of Oxford* (Oxford, 1900), p. 909; Joseph Foster, ed., *Alumni Oxonienses, 1715–1886* (London, 1887–88), 4 vols. (Christ Church matriculations counted in Foster average 31 per year in the years 1730–1810.)

33. The remaining Oxford colleges had M.P.'s 1734–1832 as follows: Oriel, 76; University, 70; Magdalen, 64; Queens, 60; Trinity, 58; New College, 49; Balliol, 42; Corpus, 37; St. John, 29; Exeter, 27; Wadham, 27; Hart, 22; Merton, 21; Pembroke, 18; St. Mary, 16; Jesus, 14; Worcester, 11; Lincoln, 5; Alban, 3; Edmund, 2; New Inn, 2.

34. John A. Venn, *A Statistical Chart to Illustrate the Entries at the Various Colleges in the University of Cambridge, 1544–1907* (Cambridge, Eng., 1908); *The Historical Register of the University of Cambridge* (Cambridge, Eng., 1917), pp. 989–90; R. F. Scott, ed., *Admissions to . . . St. John . . . Cambridge*, Vols. *3* and *4* (Cambridge, Eng., 1903 and 1931); (Matriculations counted in Scott average 40 per year in the years 1730–1802); W. W. R. Ball and J. A. Venn, *Admissions to Trinity College* (London, 1911), *3*, v and *4*, iv.

35. The remaining Cambridge colleges had M.P.'s 1734–1832 as follows: Clare, 48; Emmanuel, 39; Kings, 39; Christs, 31; St. Peters, 31; Corpus, 27; Pembroke, 27; Queens, 26; Jesus, 16; Magdalen, 11; Gonville and Caius, 11; Sidney, 9; Catherine, 7.

minster. As in the public schools, both universities began to show a marked cleavage along class lines, with the poor scholars receding into the background and the sons of the elite, who paid higher fees and enjoyed special privileges, gradually taking control.[36] In the process some colleges, such as Christ Church and Trinity, became more fashionable than others, and the degree to which a college sent its undergraduates on to the House of Commons may be taken as an index of its social prestige.

Only 125 M.P.'s 1734–1832 had studied at a Scottish university: 71 at Glasgow, 53 at Edinburgh, 10 at Aberdeen, and 6 at St. Andrews, including 15 who had attended more than one. The distribution of M.P.'s among the Scottish universities bore little relation to their respective enrollments.[37] Glasgow, for example, had half as many students as Edinburgh but 18 more M.P.'s. Aberdeen and St. Andrews together accounted for one-quarter of the Scottish undergraduates but only one-tenth of the M.P.'s educated in Scottish universities.

All in all the Scottish universities made a relatively slight contribution to the education of M.P.'s in this period. Only one-fifth of the Scots in the House had studied at one of them, and only about one Scottish undergraduate in 300 later found his way to the House. In one sense the Scottish universities were not centers of higher learning at all, since their students entered at about the age of 14, or even younger.[38] Sir James Lamb, for example, studied first at Edinburgh, then at Westminster, before seeking admittance to Oxford. But the Union of 1707 was bringing to Scotland increasing prosperity, which led to the gradual rehabilitation of her universities.[39] In this period the M.P.'s trained in Scottish uni-

36. A. D. Godley, *Oxford in the Eighteenth Century* (2d ed. London, 1909), pp. 121, 134–35; John R. Green, *Studies in Oxford History* (Oxford, 1901), pp. 46–47, 51; Halévy, p. 479; Venn, *Oxford and Cambridge Matriculations 1544–1906*, pp. 12–13; Denys A. Winstanley, *Unreformed Cambridge* (Cambridge, Eng., University Press, 1935), pp. 197–200; Christopher Wordsworth, *Social Life at the English Universities in the Eighteenth Century* (Cambridge, Eng., 1874), p. 97.

37. Material on the relative size of the Scottish universities was taken from the following: W. I. Addison, ed., *The Matriculation Albums of the University of Glasgow, from 1728 to 1858* (Glasgow, 1913), p. 538; James M. Anderson, ed., *The Matriculation Roll of the University of St. Andrews 1747–1897* (Edinburgh and London, 1905), p. lxxxvii; Peter John Anderson, ed., *Roll of Alumni in Arts of the University and King's College of Aberdeen 1596–1860* (Aberdeen, 1900), pp. 207–10; Alexander Grant, *The Story of the University of Edinburgh* (London, 1884), *2*, 492; Graham, *The Social Life of Scotland in the Eighteenth Century*, p. 471.

38. Halévy, p. 469.

39. *Ibid.*, pp. 471–73; Graham, *Social Life of Scotland*, p. 471; Grant, *Edinburgh*, *1*, 259 and *2*, 492.

versities almost doubled, from an average of ten per election
1734–90 to about 19 per election 1796–1831. Slight as it was,
Scotland's contribution to the higher education of M.P.'s was increasing.

Trinity College, Dublin, with 176 M.P.'s 1734–1832, provided higher education for one-third of all the Irish elected to the
House of Commons in these years. Trinity more than doubled in
size during the eighteenth century, and in contrast to the universities of England and Scotland, Trinity maintained an excep-
tionally high academic standard.[40] Trinity's most distinguished
alumnus in this period was Edmund Burke.

Thirty-seven M.P.'s 1734–1832 had attended continental universities, including John Wilkes at Leyden and Chatham at
Utrecht. Leyden headed the list with 24 M.P.'s and (in addition to
Utrecht) a lesser number had studied at Brunswick, Freiburg,
Göttingen, Neuchâtel, Paris, and Turin. Of the M.P.'s educated
on the Continent, 16 were Scots, including eleven lawyers, all but
one of whom had previously attended a Scottish university. Since
Scottish and Dutch law both developed from the Roman system,
many Scots sought their legal education in Holland, until toward
the end of the eighteenth century Edinburgh in particular began
to emphasize the teaching of law, and the need to journey to Holland disappeared.[41] In consequence, and because the Napoleonic
Wars restricted travel abroad, 28 of the 37 M.P.'s educated in
continental universities were men born before 1750, and only ten sat
in the House in 1796 or later.

To complete the panorama of university education, and to
underscore once again the cosmopolitan quality of the House,
Henry Cruger, the Bristol merchant, was educated at King's College (now Columbia) in New York, and the nabob Richard Jenkins
had studied at Fort William College in Bengal.

University education in the old regime followed generally the
pattern set by the public schools in that the emphasis appears to
have been social and moral rather than intellectual. Gibbon and
Malmesbury alike denounced the intellectual sloth at Oxford, and
at Cambridge peers and sons of peers could receive their degrees
without examinations—so that any inquiry into the number of

40. Constantia Maxwell, *A History of Trinity College, Dublin, 1591–1892* (Dublin, University Press, Trinity College, 1946), pp. 130, 166; Dixon Wecter, *Edmund
Burke and His Kinsmen,* University of Colorado Studies in the Humanities, *1,*
No. 1 (Boulder, Colo., 1939), pp. 5–6.
41. Graham, *Social Life of Scotland,* pp. 465–66, 471.

M.P.'s with university degrees becomes meaningless.[42] There was some good scholarship at both Oxford and Cambridge, which doubtless had due effect in shaping the minds of the elite along conventional classical lines, but the graces of social life predominated.[43] As centers of ethical training the universities were probably less effective than the public schools, since they received their students at a less impressionable age and kept them for a shorter period.

Over and above the 2,416 M.P.'s educated at one of the universities, an additional 248 M.P.'s who had not gone to college received their higher education at one of the English Inns of Court or by reading law elsewhere for the bar.[44] The Inns of Court, as Fortescue noted in the sixteenth century, were never exclusively centers of legal knowledge, and in Queen Elizabeth's reign they trained more M.P.'s than Oxford and Cambridge.[45] After the Restoration they specialized increasingly in legal studies,[46] but they still retained something of their character as institutions of general education. Many a young man placed there had no intention of becoming a lawyer.[47] Nevertheless, neither the law itself nor the Inns of Court seriously rivaled the universities in providing higher education for members of Parliament 1734–1832.

In all, 3,138 of the 5,034 M.P.'s in this period had received some form of upper-class education. The public-school enrollment included 1,714 M.P.'s; an additional 1,214 members without a public-school education had gone to a university at home or abroad; and 210 M.P.'s without previous study at a public school or a university had entered one of the Inns of Court or read law for the bar elsewhere. The total is impressive and does much to ex-

42. Edward Gibbon, *Autobiography* (Everyman Library, 1939), p. 40; Green, *Studies in Oxford History*, p. 53; Godley, *Oxford in the Eighteenth Century*, p. 67; Winstanley, *Unreformed Cambridge*, p. 79.

43. Christopher Wordsworth, *Scholae Academicae* (Cambridge, Eng., 1877), p. 269.

44. Of the 248, 38 had attended a public school.

45. Fortescue's *De Laudibus Legum Angliae*, ch. 49, cited in William R. Douthwaite, *Gray's Inn* (London, 1876), p. 28; Neale, *Elizabethan House of Commons*, pp. 302–3.

46. Reginald J. Fletcher, ed., *The Pension Book of Gray's Inn 1669–1800* (London, 1910), p. x.

47. Jonathan Swift, "A Project for the Advancement of Religion and the Reformation of Manners" (1709), in *Prose Works*, ed. Herbert Davis (Oxford, Shakespeare Head Press, 1939–), *2*, 52; *The Spectator*, No. 21, 24 March 1711. Of the 248 M.P.'s mentioned in the text, 40 had attended one of the Inns of Court but were not called to the bar.

plain the social and intellectual unity of the House in these years, but two out of every five M.P.'s lacked formal training in one of the upper-class centers of learning. Obviously other forces, such as family background and occupation, operated along with education to mold the rulers of Britain into a group with the cultural solidarity of a class.

8. *The Professions* [1]

IN ANALYZING the structure of a social class, the occupation of its members deserves as much consideration as their family background or their education, for as society becomes more complex, in the growing division of labor some occupations become more socially acceptable than others until the ruling class tends to monopolize the "honorable" occupations and to leave the more menial ones to the lower orders. A man's occupation, therefore, becomes a badge of his social status, and almost invariably anyone with a menial occupation drops out of the upper social ranks.[2]

In general, the professions which a gentleman of the old regime in Great Britain might follow without damage to his social position were the church, the law, and the military and naval services. Many people considered medicine a pursuit not quite fit for a gentleman, and within the law barristers had much more prestige than either attorneys or solicitors.[3]

Customarily the clergy were not eligible to sit in the House of Commons. On three occasions between 1553 and 1662 (the last recorded instance) the House by its own vote refused to seat a churchman named in the election writs. There the matter slumbered until 1801, when the volatile and radical John Horne-Tooke, a deacon, took his seat as M.P. for Old Sarum. An investigation committee recommended on a technicality that he be allowed to keep his seat, but the House passed a bill (which became law as 41 George III, c. 63) to exclude in future any clergyman who might be elected. The committee also found that in 1784 Edward Rushworth, a deacon, had retained his seat as M.P. for Newport, in spite of a

1. See Appendixes 1, 12, and 13.
2. See Geoffrey Gorer, "Society as Viewed by the Anthropologist," *The Cultural Approach to History,* ed. Caroline F. Ware (New York, Columbia University Press, 1940), p. 23; Gunnar Landtman, *The Origin of the Inequality of the Social* Classes (Chicago, University of Chicago Press, 1938), p. 37; Robert M. MacIver, *The Web of Government* (New York, Macmillan, 1947), p. 116; P. Sorokin, *Social Mobility* (New York, 1927), p. 12; Tawney, *Equality,* pp. 69–70.
3. A. M. Carr-Saunders and P. A. Wilson, *The Professions* (Oxford, Clarendon Press, 1933), pp. 7–9, 19, 294–95, 300; Octavius F. Christie, *The Transition from Aristocracy* (London, Seely, Service, 1927), p. 22; Graham, *The Social Life of Scotland in the Eighteenth Century,* p. 33; R. H. Gretton, *The English Middle Class* (London, 1917), p. 204.

petition to unseat him because of his connection with the Church.[4] Another instance appears to have escaped the committee's attention, that of Sir Robert Palk, who took deacon's orders and went to Madras as a chaplain in the East India Company; but Palk chose the company's civil service, became governor of Madras 1763–67, and on his return to England sat in the House of Commons 1767–87. Otherwise no clergyman was elected to the House in this period, although eleven other M.P.'s abandoned their parliamentary careers for the Church: Richard Bagwell, Charles Henry Barham, Richard Boyle Bernard (a lawyer), Henry Bowyer, James Somers Cocks (1790–1856), Henry Glynne, John Gordon (1794–1843), William Herbert (1778–1847), John William Drage Merest, Edward Stewart (another lawyer), and Sir Richard Wrottesley.

Of the 5,034 M.P.'s 1734–1832, 1,753, or just over one-third had followed one of the four other professions, the army, the navy, the law, and medicine. In Queen Elizabeth's time only about half a dozen M.P.'s had made a career of the military or naval services,[5] but in the years 1734–1832 the army officers formed the largest single professional group in the House, for 827 of the 5,034 M.P.'s, or about one in six, had at some time held an army commission. Of these, about three-fifths were career officers, since membership in the House was a recognized avenue to professional advancement.[6] Their number did not fluctuate greatly in the period. The remaining 317 army M.P.'s were men with temporary military service. Some regarded a short tour of army duty, like the grand tour of Europe, as an adjunct to their formal education,[7] but the majority had served in wartime only. Their numbers rose steadily as the Seven Years' War, the American War, and the protracted Napoleonic Wars drew an increasing number of civilians into uniform. At the general election of 1741, the regular officers outnumbered the temporary officers 49 to 16; but at the election of 1831 there were 74 temporary officers to 47 regulars. Much the same situation occurred in 1945, when two-thirds of the World War II veterans in the House were men who had been civilians when the war started.[8]

4. Porritt, *The Unreformed House of Commons, 1,* 125–27.
5. Neale, *The Elizabethan House of Commons,* p. 302.
6. L. B. Namier, *The Structure of Politics at the Accession of George III* (London, Macmillan, 1929), p. 36.
7. Halévy, *A History of the English People in 1815,* p. 83.
8. McCallum and Readman, *The British General Election of 1945,* p. 274.

Despite the traditional fear of a standing army, founded in Cromwell's military rule and bolstered by classical precepts,[9] Englishmen of the old regime recognized the need for a permanent military establishment, and upon occasion baldly justified the army as a means of preserving order in the state. Lord Hinton, for example, told the House of Lords in 1737, "There is such a spirit of licentiousness among the vulgar, as can neither be corrected or restrained by the civil power, without the assistance of regular troops." [10] During the same debate Bathurst argued, "Our liberties and properties, my Lords, depend upon the laws of our country, but it is by the military force of the country only that those laws can be made effectual." [11] In spite of much loose talk about standing armies leading to tyranny, the army remained an attractive and fashionable occupation, since it required little more than the money to buy a commission, to the point that many officers regarded their pay as interest on their original investment.[12]

The army M.P.'s mainly came from the inner circle of the ruling class, for the obvious reason that the elite appeared in strength in the army's commissioned ranks. The army officers first entered the House two years earlier in life than the national average; 391, or almost half, were baronets, sons of peers, or Irish peers; and 322, or almost two-fifths, had attended one of the public schools.

Only 234 naval officers entered the House 1734–1832, from a low of ten at the general election of 1734 to a high of 34 in 1806. The representation of the army and the navy did not reflect the relative size of the two services. The army was certainly the larger, particularly in time of war, but it did not outnumber the navy in the proportion of seven to two which obtained in the House of Commons.[13] The army had greater parliamentary strength, not because it was overwhelmingly larger than the navy but because it was a less arduous and more fashionable occupation. Halévy went straight to the heart of the matter when he wrote:

9. John S. Omond, *Parliament and the Army, 1642–1904* (Cambridge, Eng., University Press, 1933), pp. 5, 44–49.

10. *Parliamentary History of England,* ed. Cobbett, *10,* 530.

11. *Parliamentary History, 10,* 543.

12. J. W. Fortescue, *The British Army 1783–1802* (London, 1905), p. 7.

13. See C. M. Clode, *The Military Forces of the Crown* (London, 1869), *1,* 271, 398–400; W. L. Clowes, *The Royal Navy* (London, 1897–1903), *3, 5,* 327; *4,* 153; *5,* 9; and *6,* 190. The figures should be used with caution, since the army totals apparently do not include the ordnance and the foreign garrisons.

Though, generally speaking, to become a naval officer a man must belong to the governing classes of the country, the aristocracy or the gentry, the rule was not absolute. To become a midshipman gentle birth was not essential, nor even wealth, provided the consent of a commander were obtained . . . The [army] officers were, as a body, aristocratic, certainly more aristocratic than the officers of the navy . . . Perhaps this is the reason why there were more soldiers than sailors in the House of Commons.[14]

Although 111, or almost half of the navy M.P.'s, were baronets, sons of peers, or Irish peers, the navy as a whole was underrepresented, and among sons of peers in the House four had served in the army to one in the navy. Proportionately fewer navy members had attended one of the public schools, only 72, or 30 per cent, compared to 40 per cent of the army officers in the House. Their age on first election averaged over 39 years, higher than the entry age of either lawyers or army officers, and more than four years above the national average. Alone among the professional M.P.'s the naval officers served three years less in the House than the national average. Also, among the navy M.P.'s 207, or almost nine-tenths, were career officers, while four out of every ten army M.P.'s resigned their commissions. Relatively few young men took temporary service in the navy to broaden their education, and in time of war the navy, as the more stable service, required fewer additional officers.[15] In consequence, when the elite gravitated to the House of Commons more came with army than with navy commissions.

The 700 lawyers in the House 1734–1832 (including 34 attorneys and solicitors) formed the second largest group of professional M.P.'s and accounted for about one-seventh of the total representation. As early as the fourteenth century lawyers had achieved some prominence in the Commons, and by Queen Elizabeth's time they had obtained about the same proportion of the representation as in 1734–1832.[16] After 1832 the proportion of lawyers rose somewhat, being about one-quarter of the House in Queen Victoria's last Parliament and about one-fifth of the House 1918–50.[17] Even within the period 1734–1832 the proportion of

14. Halévy, pp. 51, 72.
15. Omond, p. 74.
16. Neale, pp. 304–5; Porritt, *1*, 512.
17. Porritt, *1*, 518; McCallum and Readman, *Election of 1945*, p. 273; Ross,

lawyers increased slightly, from about one M.P. in eight at the elections 1734–90 to one M.P. in six at the next ten elections.

For the most part the lawyers acted as the retainers or the professional servants of the elite, and the law, requiring brilliance and hard work, remained open to the underprivileged as a recognized means of getting on in the world.[18] In the old regime, as in the twentieth century,[19] the House of Commons was a convenient steppingstone to the bench, for 158 of the 700 lawyers in the House 1734–1832 ultimately became judges. Relatively few M.P.'s of privileged social status followed the law, probably for the reason inherent in Goldsmith's remark that "the nobility are fond of wisdom, but they are also fond of having it without study." [20] The sons of peers made up about one-sixth of the representation, but they accounted for only 50 of the 700 lawyers in the House. As further indication that the lawyers were a relatively unprivileged group, they first entered the House at the average age of almost 39 years, over four years later in life than the national average, and the solicitors and attorneys in their number did not receive first election until they had reached the average age of 48. Because of their origins and the somewhat pedantic nature of their calling, the lawyers received considerable abuse from the more fashionable (and more leisured) segment of the governing class.[21] As a group they had far less social prestige than either the army or the navy M.P.'s.

Only eleven men connected with the medical profession sat in the House of Commons 1734–1832. Of these the most celebrated were Thomas and Nathaniel Dimsdale, father and son, who made a trip to Russia to inoculate Catherine the Great against smallpox. Five others had practised medicine in the Orient, including Joseph Hume, the well-known opponent of the combination laws. Of the

Parliamentary Representation, p. 76; *The Times House of Commons 1950* (London), contains biographies of the 625 M.P.'s returned, and of these 110 were lawyers.

18. Halévy, p. 19; Namier, p. 53; Notestein, *The Winning of the Initiative by the House of Commons,* pp. 49–50; M. M. Knappen, *Constitutional and Legal History of England* (New York, Harcourt, Brace, 1942), p. 545.

19. Ross, *Parliamentary Representation*, p. 73.

20. Oliver Goldsmith, *The Citizen of the World* (1762), Letter No. 34; see also *Boswell's London Journal 1762–1763,* ed. Frederick A. Pottle (London, Heinemann, 1950), p. 141.

21. Porritt, *1, 518*; Bathurst to Swift 29 March 1733 in Jonathan Swift's *Correspondence,* ed. F. E. Ball (London, 1914), *4,* 411; *The Diaries of Sylvester Douglas (Lord Glenbervie),* ed. Bickley, *1,* 328.

four remaining, two had only a tenuous connection with the medical profession: Charles Cotes and James Mackintosh held M.D. degrees, but they both left medicine to practise law. The small number of physicians in the House in this period indicates that in the old regime medicine did not enjoy the prestige accorded to the other professions.

No dentist sat in the House in these years, although the father of George Spence, M.P., had long practised dentistry in London. A few M.P.'s were teachers, but in general teaching remained an underpaid and unfashionable occupation.[22] On the fringe of the professions three M.P.'s were or had been apothecaries; George Gipps, who made a fortune in hops; Sir Samuel Hannay, a merchant; and Sir Matthew Wood, a lord mayor of London, who began his career as an apprentice to a druggist. But all three belonged to the commercial rather than the professional interest.

The English, with three-quarters of the representation, accounted for only 1,193 or about two-thirds of the professional M.P.'s. The Irish had about the expected number. But the Scots, with only one-eighth of the representation, had 352, or one-fifth of the professional men in the House: 194 army officers, 131 lawyers, 38 naval officers, and one physician (including 12 in more than one profession). Over half of the Scots members elected in this period belonged to some profession. Here is evidence that the Scots, underprivileged as a nation, were flocking to the professions as a means of climbing up the social ladder, and that each profession remained open to those men of ability who would take advantage of the opportunities which lay before them.

The presence of 1,753 professional men in the House of Commons in these years went a long way to stimulate the esprit de corps of the representation. Similarity of occupation, added to similarity of social background and of education, acted as a dynamic force to bind together into one cohesive group those members of the ruling class who entered the House of Commons in the old regime.

22. See, *inter alia*, Oliver Goldsmith, *The Bee*, No. 6, 10 November 1759; also above, p. 5.

9. The Landed and Commercial Interests [1]

ALTHOUGH SOME HISTORIANS have described the British ruling class of the old regime as a landed aristocracy, a large segment of that class was far from aristocratic, and much of its economic strength came from sources other than the land. Laski and other recent scholars were much closer to the truth when they characterized the ruling class as a partnership between the landed and the moneyed interests; for in the old regime there was a constant interchange between the money lords and the land lords, as capital passed from land to trade and back again, as the aristocracy and the landed gentry entered the world of business, and as part of the trading community managed eventually to enter the charmed inner circle of the elite.[2]

Younger sons of the aristocracy and gentry frequently went into trade in order to make their way in the world.[3] Particularly in Scotland poverty often forced young men of good families to seek a livelihood in commercial pursuits.[4] But by entering trade these young men did not lose their social standing.[5] To the contrary, since wealth was usually necessary to enter the upper-class

1. See Appendixes 1, 14, 15, 16, 17, 18, 19, 20, and 21. In placing a member in the commercial interest I have followed the biographical notices literally. If an M.P. is stated to be a banker or a merchant, I have so considered him, even if he also possessed wealth in land. Since many members were interested in both trade and land, no absolute distinctions can be made, and probably no two historians will agree exactly in their definitions and conclusions about the economic structure of the House.

2. Harold J. Laski, *The Rise of European Liberalism* (London, Allen & Unwin, 1936), p. 103; T. S. Ashton and J. Sykes, *The Coal Industry of the Eighteenth Century* (Manchester, 1929), p. 2; Ernest Barker, "An Attempt at Perspective" in his edition of *The Character of England* (Oxford, Clarendon Press, 1947), p. 563; Roy Lewis and Angus Maude, *The English Middle Classes* (New York, Knopf, 1950), p. 25; Ralph J. Robson, *The Oxfordshire Election of 1754* (London, Oxford University Press, 1949), p. 65; William M. Sale, "From Pamela to Clarissa," *The Age of Johnson, Essays Presented to Chauncey Brewster Tinker*, ed. F. W. Hilles, p. 129; George M. Trevelyan, *England under Queen Anne, Blenheim* (London and New York, Longmans, Green, 1930), p. 33.

3. Lewis and Maude, *The English Middle Classes*, p. 25; Trevelyan, *Blenheim*, p. 33.

4. Graham, *The Social Life of Scotland in the Eighteenth Century*, p. 34.

5. See, *inter alia*, William Henry Irving, *John Gay's London* (Cambridge, Mass., Harvard University Press, 1928), p. 4; Namier, *England in the Age of the American Revolution*, p. 9.

world or to remain long within it,[6] the ruling class tended to give automatic approval to the activities by which its wealth was acquired.

The men and women of the old regime did not hesitate to associate riches with virtue and poverty with vice.[7] In 1717 Sir Thomas Hanmer told the House of Commons, "The only strength of this nation must always consist in the riches of it; riches must be the fruits of public liberty." [8] Ten years later in his immensely popular *Beggar's Opera* John Gay wrote, "But money, wife, is the true fuller's earth for reputations, there is not a spot or a stain but what it can take out." [9] And Lady Mary Wortley Montagu put into one of her letters a rhapsody on money which in sheer naïveté would be difficult to equal: "I need not enlarge upon the advantages of money; every thing we see, and every thing we hear, puts us in remembrance of it . . . As the world is, and will be, 'tis a sort of duty to be rich, that it may be in one's power to do good; riches being another word for power." [10] A few undertones of contempt for trade and the new wealth certainly appear,[11] but seldom if ever do they approach the intensity which Thackeray expressed in *Vanity Fair:* "The selling of goods by retail is a shameful and infamous practise, meriting the contempt and scorn of all real gentlemen . . . I've been accustomed to live with gentlemen, and men of the world and fashion, Emmy, not with a parcel of turtle-fed tradesmen." [12] In the opinion of one authority trade was not considered to be socially lowering until the nineteenth century.[13] It may be further suggested that a snobbish antagonism to trade reached its peak only in the Victorian period, when the landed interest, on the defensive with its economic pre-eminence lost and the cult of land worship dying, gave a last determined counterblast to

6. See Churchill, *Marlborough, 2,* 166; Mary Ellen Chase, *This England* (New York, Macmillan, 1936), p. 132.

7. Larkin, *Property in the Eighteenth Century, with Special Reference to England and Locke,* pp. 88–89.

8. *Parliamentary History of England,* ed. Cobbett, 7, 520.

9. Act I, scene 9.

10. To Edward Wortley 24 September 1714, *Letters of Lady Mary Wortley Montagu* (Everyman Library), pp. 51–52.

11. *The Spectator,* No. 108, 4 July 1711; Smollett, *The Expedition of Humphrey Clinker, 1,* 52; Carlisle to Selwyn 9 March 1768 in *George Selwyn and His Contemporaries,* ed. John Heneage Jesse (London, 1882), *2,* 273.

12. W. M. Thackeray, *Vanity Fair* (1848), chs. 5 and 20.

13. Richard Law, "The Individual and the Community" in Barker, ed., *The Character of England,* p. 48; Lewis and Maude, *The English Middle Classes,* pp. 44–45.

the rising industrial order. For, as MacIver has indicated, "the most complete exposition of a social myth often comes when the myth itself is waning." [14]

If it was habitual and respectable for the aristocracy and the landed gentry to enter trade, the converse remained true, in that trade formed a convenient avenue by which to enter the ranks of the governing class. Here the complete story remains to be told, but recent scholarship has indicated that a substantial proportion of the landed gentlemen of the old regime had as their immediate ancestors businessmen who had bought up land for purposes of profit and social prestige.[15] Pitt and Peel shared their commercial backgrounds with many lesser political figures.

In broader terms, during an era of expanding economic opportunity there existed in Great Britain a high degree of "vertical mobility," or movement up and down the social scale.[16] Although a few historians have spoken loosely of the "caste" system of the old regime,[17] Britain operated rather upon a more flexible "class" system, in which men of ability in the professions or in trade could rise from undistinguished origins, until ultimately they or their sons mingled on terms of perfect equality with the other members of the ruling class.[18] As Emerson happily expressed it, "English history is aristocracy with the doors open. Who has courage and faculty, let him come in." [19]

Of the 5,034 M.P.'s 1734–1832, 897, or more than one in six, had engaged in commercial activity or had associated themselves with some commercial interest. As time passed the proportion of members connected with trade increased, from about one member in nine at the elections 1734–61 to about one member in four

14. MacIver, *The Web of Government*, p. 72.

15. H. J. Habakkuk, "English Landownership, 1680–1740," *Economic History Review, 10* (1939–40), 12; E. Chesney, "The Transference of Lands in England 1640–1660," Royal Historical Society *Transactions*, 4th Ser., *15* (1932), 210; Gretton, *The English Middle Class*, p. 171; Trevelyan, *Blenheim*, p. 33. Disraeli's novels contain a number of suggestive passages bearing on this matter.

16. Sorokin, *Social Mobility*, pp. 141, 381, 444.

17. Andrews, *The Colonial Background of the American Revolution*, p. 189; J. B. Botsford, *English Society in the Eighteenth Century* (New York, 1924), p. 2; Christie, *The Transition from Aristocracy*, p. 29.

18. M. D. George, *London Life in the Eighteenth Century* (London, 1925), p. 318; Halévy, *A History of the English People in 1815*, pp. 94, 467; Albert F. Pollard, *Factors in Modern History* (3d ed. London, Constable, 1932), pp. 44–47; Mark A. Thomson, *A Constitutional History of England, 1642 to 1801* (London, Methuen, 1938), p. 467.

19. Ralph Waldo Emerson, *English Traits* (Boston, 1876), p. 134.

1818–31. Such an increase reflects a larger tendency in British life, for the proportion of M.P.'s in the mercantile interest 1734–61 was just about the same as in the last two Parliaments of Queen Elizabeth and in the Parliaments 1604–29.[20] But after 1832, with the industrial revolution in full blast, the proportion of commercial members rose sharply, until they vastly outnumbered the members in the older economic interests.[21] The period 1734–1832, as it shows the gradual rise of the moneyed men in the House, lies in between the predominantly agrarian economy of the later Middle Ages and the predominant industrialism of a later era.

The social-economic forces at work in the nation appear once again, in that the M.P.'s with commercial connections differed considerably in characteristics from the representation as a whole. Only 145 in their number, or about one in six, ended their parliamentary careers in a formally privileged social category (117 as baronets, six as Irish peers, and 22 as sons of peers), while of the noncommercial members well over one-third achieved such standing before leaving the House. The commercial members first entered the House at the average age of 40, almost six years later in life than the national average. Only 110, or about one in eight, had attended a public school, and 237, or about one-quarter, had attended a university, while of the noncommercial members two-fifths were former public-school boys and over half had attended a university. As a group the trading members came from a less fashionable stratum of society than did the others in the House.

But at the same time there is considerable evidence of interpenetration between the aristocracy and the men of business. It is no less than remarkable that so many businessmen in the House had gone to the public schools and the universities, and to find 22 sons of peers among the M.P.'s in the trading interest pointedly illustrates the nationwide tendency for the aristocracy to mingle in the commercial world. Among the merchants in the House were Thomas Harley and William Bouverie, sons respectively of the Earls of Oxford and Radnor; among the bankers were another Bouverie and two Walpoles, Richard and Thomas; and among the nabobs were Arthur Henry Cole (son of the Earl of Enniskil-

20. Neale, *The Elizabethan House of Commons*, p. 147; see also the unpubl. diss. (Cornell, 1925) by Harold Hulme, "A Study of the Personnel of the House of Commons between 1604 and 1629," p. 178.

21. John A. Thomas, *The House of Commons 1832–1901* (Cardiff, University of Wales Press, 1939), pp. 9, 18–19; Ross, *Parliamentary Representation*, p. 60.

len), Edward Monckton (son of Viscount Galway), and Frederick Stuart (son of George III's mentor, Lord Bute). While as a whole the commercial members tended to be self-made men, it is apparent that not a few in their number had socially eligible backgrounds.

In still another way the commercial men in the House of Commons reflected larger national tendencies, for as the sources of national wealth varied with the passing years the character of the commercial interest in the House varied accordingly. During the old regime trade and banking facilities in Britain grew hand in hand, but the greater part of the new wealth came from abroad, with fortunes to be made in European markets, in the Orient (particularly in India), and in the colonies (particularly in the West Indies).[22] As John Gay expressed it:

> Now Commerce, wealthy goddess, rears her head,
> And bids Britannia's fleets their canvas spread;
> Unnumbered ships the peopled ocean hide,
> And wealth returns with each revolving tide.[23]

Toward the end of the eighteenth century, manufacturing with power-driven machines began to provide a new source of wealth to rival its predecessors. In the House of Commons representatives of each of these sources of wealth appear: the bankers, the East India interest and the nabobs, the investors and merchants in the West Indies, and mainly in the latter part of the period, the manufacturers. In addition there remains a miscellaneous body of "merchants" not primarily associated with any of the above special groups, businessmen trading within England as well as with Europe and continental America.

But it is impossible to assign each of the 897 commercial members to only one specific activity, for the world of business is a web of economic interests so interwoven that no one commercial group ever completely disassociates itself from the rest. An economic crisis could drive interested members to act temporarily as a unit, which disintegrated after the crisis passed. A number of M.P.'s engaged in two or more spheres of business enterprise. Joseph Cripps, for example, was a banker, an East India proprietor, a brewer, and the owner of cloth mills. John Irving was an East and West Indian

---

22. Lipson, *The Economic History of England, 3,* 209–10; Botsford, *English Society,* p. 116.

23. "An Epistle to a Lady" (1714) in *Poetical Works,* ed. G. C. Faber (Oxford, 1926), p. 151.

proprietor, an army contractor, banker, and insurance underwriter.

Many "merchants"—a term often used to denote any form of commercial activity—also participated in banking, and have been grouped with the bankers; many "merchants" also traded in India or the West Indies (and a few traded in both), and have been classified as belonging to one (or both) of these special groups; some "merchants" also engaged in manufacturing, and so appear with the new industrialists. Nevertheless, even after assigning as many "merchants" as possible to special groups, the remainder, 257 in number, engaged in miscellaneous business pursuits, form the largest single part of the commercial representation. An average of 30 "merchants" was returned at each general election 1734–1831, with little significant rise or fall during the period.

At least 37 "merchants" engaged directly in the liquor trade, including 27 brewers, prominent among whom were four members of the Calvert family; three Whitbreads; Robert and William Hucks, father and son; Henry and Ralph Thrale of Johnson's circle; and Henry Isherwood, who sold the family business for £70,000. Four "hop merchants" appear, including the former apothecary George Gipps and Thomas Godfrey, a speculator in hops. At least four "merchants" were primarily interested in the wine trade; and two appear as distillers: Samuel Kent, distiller to the court during Walpole's administration, and Sir Joseph Mawbey, who made a fortune in vinegar. In addition, at least three other commercial members dealt in wine: the East India proprietor George Schonswar; the nabob Robert Jones; and the West India merchant Alexander Grant.

Fourteen or more "merchants" were active in the clothing trade. Robert Waithman, a lord mayor of London, was a linen draper; Michael Thomas Sadler engaged in the importation of linen from Ireland; Thomas Vere, mayor of Norwich, was a weaver; both Wynne Ellis and William Wilberforce Bird dealt in silk; and William Spicer was a glover. The wool trade found representation in such members as the army contractor Sir Lawrence Dundas; the barrister Thomas Kemp; and the woolen draper Matthew Brickdale. Other "merchants" in clothing included William Hussey of Salisbury; Henry Jones of London; James Morrison, the railway reformer; John Patteson of Norwich; and Joseph Windham-Ashe of London and Norfolk. In addition, the banker Sir Samuel Fludyer, a lord mayor of London, made a fortune in the clothing trade.

Ten or more "merchants" in the House dealt in food staples, such as Henry Parsons, a baker; Thomas Brayen, a grocer; David Callaghan in the Irish provision trade; the brothers Thomas and William Carter, who operated a grain mill in Liverpool; Frederick Bull, a lord mayor of London, who was a dealer in tea; also four traders in grain: Robert Farrand of Norfolk; Henry Maister of Holderness; Sir Samuel Scott, a corn dealer in Kent; and Christopher Savile, sometime corn factor to the Navy Victualing Board, who was expelled from the House for perjury and was jailed. In addition, the banker Sir William Curtis, a lord mayor of London and friend of George IV, was for some years a baker for the navy.

The other "merchants" engaged in a wide variety of commercial pursuits. Members interested in mining included Ralph Thicknesse, in the Wigan coal trade; Owen Williams, a proprietor of copper mines; and Robert Hoblyn, the book collector, who augmented his inherited wealth by tin mining in Cornwall. A half dozen or so M.P.'s participated in the railway boom of the early Victorian period, such as the promoters John Beckett and Benjamin Hall, and Charles Russell, formerly in the Bengal naval service, who was for many years chairman of the Great Western Railroad. Six M.P.'s found a livelihood in the publishing business: Andrew Strahan, and his father William, the publisher of Hume, Gibbon, and Robertson; Daniel Whittle Harvey, founder of the Sunday *Times;* the barrister Joseph Richardson, who became a proprietor of the *Morning Post;* Andrew Spottiswoode, head of the firm of Eyre & Spottiswoode; and Robert Torrens, former army officer and friend of both Peel and Ricardo, who became an editor in his later years. Joseph Butterworth sold law books; Frederick Gye operated Vauxhall Gardens; and both Nathaniel Jefferys and James Kerr were jewelers.

Finally, among the "merchants" twenty or more were primarily interested in trade with Europe and continental America. John Morison traded with Russia, and Thomas Pelham of Stanmer was in the Turkey trade; William Bouverie (later Earl of Radnor) was governor of the Levant Company; and Joseph Mellish was governor of the Hamburg Company. Robert Godschall, a lord mayor of London, was interested in the Portuguese trade, along with William Mayne (later Baron Newhaven), who lived many years in Lisbon; Daniel Sykes of Hull, a barrister and East India proprietor, also imported iron from Sweden. Mention has already been made of the M.P.'s trading to continental North America.[24] Trade with South America appears in the person of William Jacob, an alderman of London and fellow of the Royal Society.

Much work in the unpublished records of business firms remains to be done before any definitive analysis of the commercial representation can be made. But at least it appears that the "merchants" in the House engaged in a broad range of activities, from weaving and brewing to coal mining and the import-export trade, all the way from Moscow west to the new world. The diversity of their business interests, both in kind and in geographical location, stands out as their single most prominent characteristic.

It is impossible to draw a firm line between the "merchants" and the 230 M.P.'s classified as bankers, because many bankers of the old regime combined their financial activities with other forms of commerce.[25] For example, the bankers John Baker and Sir James Sanderson were former hop merchants; Nathaniel Polhill had been a tobacco merchant; and Abraham Robarts combined banking with enterprises both in the West Indies and in India. But after about 1750 banking in Britain underwent a sudden and rapid growth, which found expression after some delay in the House of Commons. The "merchants" outnumbered the bankers at every general election between 1734 and 1790, but at the next eleven general elections 1790–1831 the bankers outnumbered the merchants three to two.

Nine-tenths of the bankers in the House operated in London, but toward the end of the period an increasing number of country bankers were elected. This shift in locale reflects a nationwide movement, for in the last third of the eighteenth century country banking developed in unprecedented fashion in England and Scotland alike.[26] Among the first of the country bankers in the House was Abel Smith of Nottingham, in 1774; four other members of his family entered the House before 1800; and Richard Ellison, a banker of Lincoln, was elected in 1796.

Nine bankers in the House and 12 other M.P.'s in the commercial interest are known to have participated in the insurance business, which was coming into prominence as an adjunct of banking proper.[27] Five M.P.'s were active in marine underwriting, the

24. See above, p. 15.
25. John H. Clapham, *The Bank of England* (Cambridge, Eng., University Press; New York, Macmillan, 1945), *1*, 6–7, 158.
26. Clapham, *Bank of England, 1*, 163; Graham, *Social Life of Scotland*, p. 206.
27. John H. Clapham, *An Economic History of Modern Britain* (Cambridge, Eng., University Press, 1939–), *1*, 284.

oldest established form of insurance in the kingdom. Of these three were in Lloyd's: William Thompson, a lord mayor of London, and George Richard Robinson, who made a fortune in the Newfoundland trade, both chairmen of Lloyd's; and the Russian-born John Julius Angerstein, a leading figure in the development of Lloyd's in mid-century. The two remaining M.P.'s were associated with the Alliance Insurance Company, which underwrote marine insurance as well as fire and life: John Irving, a banker and former army contractor, the company's first president; and a director, Robert Townsend Townsend-Farquhar, who was also governor of the East India Company. Fifteen additional M.P.'s were interested in fire insurance, which became popular after about 1720, including William Duff-Gordon, a former merchant at Cadiz, who was chairman of the Atlas Fire and Life. Only four M.P.'s were connected with life insurance firms, doubtless because in the old regime life insurance had not developed so extensively as marine or fire underwriting: Irving, Townsend-Farquhar, and Duff-Gordon aforementioned, as well as John Stewart (ca 1789–1860), a West Indies proprietor, who was chairman of the Universal Life Assurance Company.

The presence in the House of Commons of 21 men associated with insurance illustrates once again how sensitive the representation was to changing economic conditions. Of the 21, only four first entered the House before 1796, for insurance did not become a large-scale business enterprise until the latter years of the eighteenth century. But after 1796, as the insurance business rapidly expanded, an average of five M.P.'s in insurance appeared at the general elections, with as many as seven in 1831.

A number of near-dynasties founded on banking rivaled the landed families in the House. Heading the list, ten members of the London Barings and ten members of the Smith family of Nottingham were elected 1734–1832. The London banking families of Drummond and Martin each sent six members to the Commons, as did the Huguenot banking family of Latouche in Ireland. Four M.P.'s apiece came from the families of Child, Mackworth-Praed, and Williams, and three apiece from the families of Colebrooke, Roberts, Stephenson, and Thornton. The following banking families sent two members each: Caswall, Crickitt, Everett, Gleadowe-Newcomen, Glyn, Hammett, Hankey, Herries, Ladbroke, and Lubbock.

Participation in the affairs of the Bank of England served further to unify the bankers in the House. A clause in the Bank's charter specifically permitted members of Parliament to be of the corporation, and ten of the original 24 directors were M.P.'s.[28] From its inception the Bank took a prominent part in national politics, and 32 of the 230 bankers in the House 1734–1832, or one in seven, were Bank directors.[29]

Relations between bankers—particularly Bank directors—and the East India Company remained close, particularly as the Bank consistently lent the company large sums of money.[30] Of the 230 bankers in the House 1734–1832, 48, or about one in five, had been active in the East India Company, nine as nabobs and the remainder in the Indian interest at home.

Historical tradition has made much of the entrance of the nabobs into British political life.[31] Upholders of this tradition are fond of citing Chatham's speech of 22 January 1770 as evidence that the nabobs were inordinately rich and shamelessly corrupt: "The riches of Asia have been poured in upon us, and have brought with them not only Asiatic luxury, but, I fear, Asiatic principles of government. Without connections, without any natural interest in the soil, the importers of foreign gold have forced their way into Parliament, by such a torrent of private corruption, as no private hereditary fortune could resist." [32]

A few nabobs made spectacular fortunes, including Chatham's own grandfather, Thomas ("Diamond") Pitt, but contemporary opinion exaggerated to the point of myth making not only the number of wealthy nabobs but also the amount of wealth which they had accumulated overseas.[33] Particularly toward the end of the eighteenth century, Englishmen going to India sought little more than the security of a modest competence and the chance to rise a little in the social scale, and few exceeded their expectations.[34]

28. Clapham, *Bank of England, 1,* 18; Wilfrid Marston Acres, *The Bank of England from Within, 1694–1900* (London, Oxford University Press, 1931), *1,* 24.

29. For a list of Bank directors see Acres, *Bank of England, 2,* 613. I have not included M.P.'s who were Bank directors only before 1734 or who became directors after 1832.

30. Clapham, *Bank of England, 1,* 116.

31. E.g., George M. Trevelyan, *English Social History* (New York and London, Longmans, Green, 1942), p. 391.

32. *Parliamentary History of England,* ed. Cobbett, *16,* 752.

33. Holden Furber, *John Company at Work* (Cambridge, Mass., Harvard University Press, 1948), p. 27; James M. Holzman, *The Nabobs in England* (New York, 1926), p. 27; *Bengal Past and Present, 13* (1916), 73.

34. Furber, *John Company,* pp. 310–13, 321–22, 338–39.

Not all of the nabobs in the House were successful businessmen. Dundas' son-in-law James Charles Stuart Strange, for example, after 22 years in India became a partner in the bank of Strange, Dashwood, and Company, which failed; and in order to recoup his lost fortune he left the House to return to India. Similarly George Templer, another former nabob, failed as a London banker in 1816, and died three years later in India, where he was trying to make a fresh start. Clearly, the romance inherent in the nabob's journey to the East lured not a few contemporary observers into the realm of fantasy. Equally clearly, historians using such uncritical contemporary reports have vastly exaggerated the impact of the nabobs on British political life.

With a nabob defined as a British citizen who had lived in the Orient, usually but not always in the East India Company's service and mainly for profit (and excluding a few high governmental officials and army or naval officers on temporary duty there), 144 nabobs sat in the House of Commons 1734–1832. In view of the extravagant talk of many observers, 144 seems a small number indeed, well under 3 per cent of the total representation. Measured by length of service rather than by numbers, the proportional weight of the nabobs drops still further, since they served an average of almost three years less than the other members.

At the general elections of 1734 and 1747 only two nabobs entered the House. There were three in 1741, four in 1754, and five in 1761. In all, between 1734 and 1761 (including the general election of the latter year), only eleven nabobs entered the Commons: Clive; George Morton Pitt (a relative of Chatham); Harry Gough (who had pioneered the China trade); Matthew Martin (who had successfully defended his ship against French raiders); the ship captains William Mabbott and Robert Haldane; Gabriel Hanger (later created Baron Coleraine); the former wine merchant Robert Jones; James Peachey (later created Baron Selsey); John Stephenson; and John Walsh. After 1761, 133 nabobs entered the House, with an average of 18 per general election 1768–90 and 25 per general election 1796–1812, and with a high of 30 nabobs in 1802. But thereafter the number of nabobs declined to an average of 17 per general election 1818–31, as a reflection of the diminishing rewards which the Indian adventure offered in the early years of the nineteenth century.

As a general rule the nabobs in the House were self-made men. Fourteen in their number had been ship captains, and 24 had risen by service in the Indian army. They first received election to the House eight years later in life than the national average. Only 21 in their number had attended a public school and only 18 had attended a university. Only three were sons of peers, and only 24 ended their parliamentary careers as baronets. Nevertheless their backgrounds were far from being universally lowly. Aside from the three sons of peers, aforementioned, the nabobs Charles and John Buller came from a prominent parliamentary family, and William Frankland derived from the landed gentry of Yorkshire. Even among the nabobs there is evidence that young men from old established families did not hesitate to engage in new forms of wealth-producing enterprise.

In addition to the nabobs in the House, who had lived in the Orient, another 144 M.P.'s who stayed at home belonged to the East India "interest." These include, to begin with, 48 M.P.'s who were directors of the East India Company 1734–1832 (in addition to 26 nabobs who became directors).[35] A second group consisted of 19 shipowners in the India trade (in addition to two nabobs, John Innes and John Woolmore, who became shipowners), for the company had long since adopted the policy of chartering and not owning ships.[36] The remainder were mostly proprietors, that is, large shareholders as opposed to small investors,[37] and a few M.P.'s, such as John Smith, a company solicitor, and Richard Hussey, a barrister retained as the company's counsel, appear in the India "interest" because of their close association with company affairs.

Up to 1761, and including the general election of that year, the strength of the India "interest" in the House was negligible, amounting to only 22 M.P.'s in all. These 22 M.P.'s, in addition to eleven nabobs, were the only representatives in the East India

35. For a list of East India Company directors after 1758, see C. H. and D. Philips, "Alphabetical List of Directors of the East India Company from 1758 to 1858," *Journal of the Royal Asiatic Society* (October 1941), pp. 325–36; for a less accurate list before 1758 see C. C. Prinsep, *Record of . . . Civil Servants in the Madras Presidency* (London, 1885). I have not included in the totals M.P.'s who were company directors only before 1734 or who became directors after 1832.

36. Furber, *John Company*, p. 12.

37. The *Edinburgh Advertiser* of 9–19 June 1786 named well over one hundred M.P.'s who held some company stock (see David S. Reid, "An Analysis of British Parliamentary Opinion on American Affairs at the Close of the War of Independence," *Journal of Modern History, 18* [1946], 215). But to include all shareholders, large and small alike, as belonging to the Indian interest, seems a *reductio ad absurdum.*

group to enter the House 1734–61, but after 1761 their numbers increased steadily, although the nabobs in the group began to decline. They were 57 (30 nabobs and 27 "interest") in 1802, and they reached their peak in 1830 with a total of 68 M.P.'s (17 nabobs and 51 "interest"). Taken together, the nabobs and the East India "interest" accounted for 288 M.P.'s 1734–1832, about 6 per cent of the total representation and one-third of the commercial men in the House.

A high proportion of M.P.'s in the India "interest" also engaged in other forms of business. The company director, William Baker, was also governor of the Hudson's Bay Company; a second director, Stephen Bisse, was active in the Lisbon trade; and a third, Samuel Smith. was also a banker and treasurer of the Turkey Company. Of the East India proprietors, James Brogden traded to Russia and Daniel Sykes was an importer of Swedish iron. Among the shipowners in the India trade, John Atkins, a lord mayor of London, was also a West Indies merchant; Richardson Borradaile was a furrier; and William Mellish was a director of the Bank of England.

In effect, the shipowners within the East India "interest" themselves belonged to a larger "shipping interest" which cut across a number of related commercial activities. James Mangles, for example, who was a shipowner in the India "interest" also inherited a ship's chandlery from his father. Mangles certainly had much in common with two M.P.'s unconnected with India: John Wells of Kent, a shipbuilder, and the manufacturer, Arthur Howe Holdsworth, who invented a number of mechanical devices for merchant ships. John Julius Angerstein, in the shipping interest of the East India trade, was also active in Lloyd's, and therefore shared a set of special economic "interests" with the M.P.'s in marine and other forms of insurance. Anthony Bacon, a merchant trading to North America, also owned ships, and Slingsby Bethell was president of the British Herring Fishery. Without too much special pleading, the shipping "interest" could be extended to include almost all merchants trading overseas, not only to India, but also to Europe, the Americas, and the West Indies.

Considering the complexity of the business world, it is a misnomer to speak of an East India "interest" in the sense of a well-defined and more or less permanent group. The East India M.P.'s were not a well-organized economic unit, and they rarely acted together except when Indian affairs came under discussion in the House.[38]

While the nabobs were opening the Orient to British trade, another group of commercial adventurers were developing a new source of wealth across the globe, in the rich sugar islands of the West Indies. On the plantations slave labor and absentee landownership led to dreadful social conditions,[39] but sugar, the white gold of the Caribbean, provided the mother country with immense wealth, and this new wealth soon found representation in the House of Commons. As early as 1699 Sir Robert Davers, born in Barbados, became a member of Parliament, and in the period 1734–1832 no less than 169 men associated with the West Indies entered the House.

As in the East India group, there were two main categories of West Indians, 45 merchants trading to the Caribbean, and 124 M.P.'s in the West Indies "interest," mainly absentee owners of Caribbean estates. Like the nabobs, the 45 West Indian merchants were mostly self-made men. They first entered the House at the average age of 42 and sat there three years less than the national average; only five had attended a public school; only nine had studied at a university; and only two ended their parliamentary careers in a formally privileged social status: the baronets Sir John Rae Reid and Sir John Gladstone, the father of the Victorian statesman. As a group the West Indian merchants in the House partook of few upper-class characteristics.

On the other hand, the 124 M.P.'s in the West Indian "interest" were to a great extent patrician. Their age on first election was the lowest in the commercial group and approximated the national average; 45, or more than a third, had received a public-school education; and 66, or over half, had attended a university. Only eight in their number participated directly in trade, and only 17 were professional men. Such characteristics point to the conclusion that in effect the M.P.'s in the West Indies "interest" were country gentlemen whose estates lay overseas.

Although the West Indian merchants and "interest" in the House differed in social character, they shared the same basic

38. Cyril H. Philips, *The East India Company 1784–1834* (Manchester, Manchester University Press, 1940), p. 299.

39. See Lowell J. Ragatz, *The Fall of the Planter Class in the British Caribbean 1763–1833* (New York, 1928), pp. 3, 42–44.

source of wealth, and as time passed their economic interests tended to merge. When in 1740 the Planters Club of London was founded, it admitted only West Indian plantation owners (or proprietors) and excluded merchants, but in the next generation, as Caribbean estates passed to creditor merchants and as plantation owners took an active part in the sugar trade, the agrarian and trading interests fused, until in 1780 the Society of West Indian Planters and Merchants included both groups under one roof.[40] Insofar as the West Indians in the House operated as a pressure group, little distinction can be made between the active merchants and the plantation owners, many of whom disdained to live on their tropical estates.

Jamaica, the largest British possession in the West Indies, accounted for more M.P.'s than any other Caribbean island. Six Beckfords in the House 1734–1832 owned profitable trading and sugar-producing interests there. Two West Indian merchants in the House, George Heathcote and Benjamin Vaughan, were born in Jamaica, as was the barrister Sir Edward Hyde East. Edward Morant and John Rock Grosset were at one time members of the Jamaica legislature; Lovell Stanhope was agent for Jamaica, and Robert Sewell was not only the island's agent but also its attorney general. Seven other M.P.'s had close ties with Jamaica, mainly in land, including three members of the Ellis family and the humanitarian Matthew ("Monk") Lewis.

At least seven M.P.'s had economic roots in Antigua. These included William Matthew Burt, a governor of the island; two agents, John Sharpe and the banker Anthony Browne; Wilkes' supporter, Alderman Richard Oliver; and Wilkes' antagonist, the Antigua-born Samuel Martin.

M.P.'s connected with St. Christophers included Charles Barrow and Crisp Molineux, who were born there, as well as Patrick Blake, John St. Leger Douglas, and Samuel Greatheed, who had estates there. Wealth from Barbados established the Lascelles family, which sent eight of its members to the House 1734–1832. Other Barbadians included Sir Francis Ford, who was born on the island; Samuel Estwick, the island's agent; and James Edward Colleton, who owned estates there. James Wilson had been a member of the council at St. Vincent, and William Manning (father of the cardinal) was for a time the island's agent. Arthur Leary Pigott was attorney general at Grenada, and Joseph Marryat had

40. *Ibid.*, p. 51.

lived there. Charles Henry Bouverie was agent for St. Lucia, and William Holmes was agent for Demerara. Martin Madan had estates at Nevis, as did Nathaniel Webb at Montserrat, Paul Wentworth at Surinam, and Francis Blake at San Domingo. In territorial distribution the West Indian M.P.'s touched virtually all the important areas in Britain's Caribbean empire.

Up to and including the general election of 1780, the West Indians in the House equaled the East Indians in numerical strength, but thereafter the East Indians took the lead. Over the entire period, and excluding 16 M.P.'s interested in both areas, the East Indians outnumbered the Caribbean M.P.'s about five to three. Nevertheless, the West Indian group actually grew in number, from an average of 24 at the elections 1796–1812 to 34 at the elections 1818–31. In 1792 the West Indians were able to block an attempt on the part of the East India Company to obtain special privileges in the sugar trade, but the Act of 1807 abolishing the slave trade came as a crushing defeat to the Caribbean interests, and the next decades brought increasing economic distress.[41] Yet the coming blight did not have an immediate effect in the House of Commons. For the time being the West Indians more than maintained their numerical strength.

The manufacturers in the House form the smallest segment of the commercial interest, with only 29 M.P.'s in this period. Of these, eight first entered before 1800: two M.P.'s in munitions, Anthony Bacon in 1764, a government contractor and gunmaker, also Miles Peter Andrews in 1796, who owned a powder magazine at Dartford; two M.P.'s in heavy industry, Charles Boone in 1757, a proprietor of Crawley's iron forge, and the banker Sir John Call in 1784, who operated a copper smelting plant; one paper maker, Clement Taylor, in 1780; one porcelain manufacturer, Christopher Potter in 1781; and two representatives of the textile industry, John Cockburn, M.P. 1708–41, who operated a linen factory, and Sir Robert Peel, the elder, in 1790, the first representative of the new powered-machine cotton industry of the north.

After 1800, 21 more manufacturing M.P.'s entered the House: a second porcelain manufacturer, William Taylor Copeland, in 1831; two more paper makers, the banker Arthur Howe Holdsworth in 1802, and William Venables, a lord mayor of London in 1831; five more M.P.'s in heavy industry, Samuel Stephens in 1802, a barrister who was a partner in the copper smelting firm of Williams

41. *Ibid.*, pp. 212, 260, 276, 286, 347.

Foster Company; Samuel Homfray in 1818, chief proprietor of the Tredegar Iron Works; Joshua Walker in 1818, an ironmaster at Rotheram; Sir Josiah John Guest in 1826, who made a number of improvements in iron making; and James Foster, the ironmaster, in 1831. Nine M.P.'s elected after 1800 were in the textile industry: Charles Brooke, a woolen manufacturer, in 1802; the brothers John and Samuel Horrocks, cotton manufacturers, in 1802 and 1804 respectively; Joseph Cripps, who owned cloth mills, in 1806; Sir George Philips, a Lancashire cotton magnate, in 1812; John Maberly, a partner in the Broadfield Linen Works of Aberdeen, in 1816; Thomas Houldsworth, of Manchester, in 1818; Henry Monteith, a Scottish calico manufacturer, in 1820; and John Marshall, a linen manufacturer, in 1826. Four other M.P.'s complete the roster: John Rawlinson Harris, a manufacturing and retailing hatter, in 1830; John Hodson, in 1802; Kirkman Finlay, in 1812; and William Evans, in 1818. In all, over the period 1734–1832 eleven M.P.'s were in textiles; seven in heavy industry; three in paper; two each in munitions and ceramics; and four in a miscellaneous or unspecified category.

As a group the manufacturers in the House of Commons exhibited few upper-class characteristics. They first entered the House seven years later in life than the national average. Three only had had ancestors in the House before them: Arthur Howe Holdsworth, an old Etonian; Samuel Stephens, who had studied at Cambridge; and Charles Boone, who was a product of both Eton and Cambridge.[42] Kirkman Finlay and Henry Monteith had studied at Glasgow. John Call, Robert Peel, and George Philips were created baronets before 1832 and Josiah John Guest thereafter, but no sons of peers or Irish peers appear among the manufacturing M.P.'s. By birth and education, only Boone, Holdsworth, and Stephens belonged to the elite, for Glasgow conferred little distinction in comparison to Eton or Cambridge, and the four baronets did not inherit their honors.

Probably the single most remarkable characteristic of the manufacturing M.P.'s was the smallness of their numbers—only 29 in the years 1734–1832, when as a whole the factory operators were attaining considerable prominence in the business world. No manufacturer entered the House at the three general elections 1741–54,

42. Only one other manufacturer may claim a blood relative previously in the House, Samuel Horrocks, M.P. in 1804, who was preceded by his brother John in 1802.

and no more than four at any general election between 1761 and 1796. In the succeeding elections up to 1832 they never exceeded a high of 13 in 1818. Before the Reform Act of 1832 the industrial revolution had little direct effect upon the pattern of British politics.[43]

Taking the 897 members in the commercial interest, adding the 1,753 professional men, and deducting the 95 M.P.'s active in both categories, yields a net total of 2,555 members in the professions and in trade, and leaves 2,479 with no stated occupation. Here one may follow a contemporary handbook, which concludes that "all members not described as of some profession or business, may be presumed to be landed proprietors." [44] About half of the representation, then, were country gentlemen, but it is impossible to determine how many of the remaining members had important landed interests. Doubtless a majority of the West Indian proprietors and the army officers on temporary service had their economic roots in the soil. Altogether, probably at least half of the 2,555 M.P.'s classified as professional or commercial had substantial agrarian investments, particularly in view of the interpenetration of the landed gentry with the professional and commercial groups. In consequence, it appears reasonable to assume that about three-quarters of the 5,034 M.P.'s 1734–1832 were mainly concerned with land rather than with other forms of wealth. Contemporary analyses, which take no account of members with more than one economic interest, tend to substantiate this estimate.[45]

The relationship between the landed and the moneyed men touches close to the heart of British political life in the old regime, and provides one key to understanding not only some of the conflicting ideologies of the period but also some of the forces which were changing the structure of British society. In many ways the old regime retained a quasi-feudal character, particularly as land still formed the theoretical basis of political representation.[46] Land,

43. See Witt Bowden, *Industrial Society in England towards the End of the Eighteenth Century* (New York, 1925), pp. 161–64; Gwen Whale, "The Influence of the Industrial Revolution (1760–1790) on the Demand for Parliamentary Reform," Royal Historical Society *Transactions*, 4th Ser., *5* (1922), 130–31.

44. *Dod's Parliamentary Companion* (1834), p. 83.

45. S. F. Woolley, "The Personnel of the Parliament of 1833," *English Historical Review, 53* (1938), 246.

46. Robson, *Oxfordshire Election of 1754*, pp. 44, 54; MacIver, *Web of Government*, pp. 137–39; Kingsley, *Representative Bureaucracy*, p. 25; Helen E. Witmer, *The Property Qualifications of Members of Parliament* (New York, Columbia University Press; London, King & Staples, 1943), pp. 52–57, 80–81, 89–90, 218.

as the older form of wealth, remained "the most potent and impressive" kind of riches,[47] just as men habitually consider the historically old occupations, farming in this instance, to be more honorable than the new ones.[48] In 1722 Swift wrote, "There could not be a truer maxim in our government than this, that the possessors of the soil are the best judges of what is for the advantage of the kingdom." [49] In 1832, during the heated debates on parliamentary reform, Lord Mahon stated, "I believe the landed interest to be the firmest basis of a constitutional government." [50] And Dr. Johnson, with characteristic bluntness, defended this stake-in-the-country theory of representation, "Influence must ever be in proportion to property, and it is right it should." [51] Here as in other similar statements property usually meant property in land,[52] but occasionally, as in the debates on parliamentary reform, speakers used the term in its broader sense, as "property, whether commercial or landed." [53] And Perceval carried the argument to a plutocratic extreme: "All the interests in society were represented in money, the general representative of value: and as these [rotten] boroughs could be obtained for money, all interests became by these means represented in society. They all found access to Parliament." [54]

Contemporaries were well aware of the conflict, which Swift had deplored,[55] between landed and commercial wealth. In 1798 during a debate on the income tax William Smith spoke contemptuously of the country gentlemen as drones in contrast to the bees in the mercantile interest.[56] The food riots of 1815 accentuated the conflict between the landlords and the business community, and in the following year the livery men of London resolved in favor of tax

47. E. S. Roscoe, *The English Scene in the Eighteenth Century* (New York, 1912), p. 129.

48. Gorer, "Society as Viewed by the Anthropologist," *The Cultural Approach to History*, ed. Ware, p. 24.

49. Swift to Pope 10 January 1721/22, *The Correspondence of Jonathan Swift*, ed. Ball, *3*, 121.

50. *Parliamentary Debates*, ed. T. C. Hansard, 3d Ser., *11*, 419.

51. *Boswell's Life of Johnson*, ed. G. B. Hill, rev. L. F. Powell (Oxford, Clarendon Press, 1934–50), *5*, 56.

52. Jennings, *Parliament*, p. 365.

53. Hansard, *11*, 420.

54. *Ibid.*, *3*, 266.

55. Swift to Pope 10 January 1721/22, *Correspondence*, ed. Ball, *3*, 121.

56. Earl Stanhope, *Life of . . . Pitt* (London, 1861), *3*, 165; *Parliamentary History*, ed. Cobbett, *34*, 96.

reduction and parliamentary reform.[57] As early as 1768 Lady Sarah Osborn wrote, "The landed interest is beat out, and merchants, nabobs, and those who have gathered riches from the East and West Indies stand the best chance of governing this country." [58] In 1826 Creevey commented, "The charm of the power of the landed interest is gone; and in a new Parliament Canning and Huskisson may effect whatever revolution they like in the Corn Laws." [59] Such comments, of course, were premature, for the landlords continued to enjoy preferential taxation,[60] and the real test of strength between land and commerce lay in the future.

The continuing interassimilation of the men of land and the men of trade doubtless blurred the contending issues. Also, land outnumbered trade in the House by about three to one, and as a group the commercial members lacked the cultural unity of the older elite. Bagehot observed: "The merchants and manufacturers in Parliament are a motley race—one educated here, another there, and a third not educated at all; some are of the second generation of traders . . . Others are self-made . . . Traders have no bond of union, no habits of intercourse." [61] Before 1832 at least, the landed interest remained the strongest part of the ruling class in the House of Commons, enjoying for the time being a preponderance though not a monopoly of political power. But already strong signs had appeared that nonlanded economic groups would soon obtain a progressively larger share of the representation.

57. Kingsley, *Representative Bureaucracy*, p. 45.
58. *Ibid.*, p. 44.
59. Creevey to Miss Ord 13 May 1826, *The Creevey Papers*, ed. Herbert Maxwell (new ed. London, Murray, 1933), p. 443.
60. Larkin, *Property in the Eighteenth Century*, p. 117.
61. Walter Bagehot, *The English Constitution* (Boston, 1873), pp. 225–26.

10. Conclusion

THE BRITISH RULING CLASS of the old regime, as it appeared in the House of Commons 1734–1832, was a remarkably cohesive yet cosmopolitan group—cohesive in its similarity of descent, education, and professional occupation, yet cosmopolitan not only geograpically but also in its economic interests. As such, the ruling class was toughly knit without the danger of atrophy and flexible without the equal danger of disintegration.

A number of forces worked together to mold the M.P.'s into a cohesive and therefore effective elite corps. Their social backgrounds were mostly homogeneous; their cultural values were harmonious and bolstered by a common educational tradition; they shared a community of professional interests; they derived much of their wealth from a single source, the land; they entered the House early enough in life to adapt themselves easily to its customs and procedures; and they served long enough together to acquire that habit of cooperation which is born only of long continued association.

At the same time the representation was extremely cosmopolitan. In an era of empire building, planters from Jamaica rubbed shoulders with nabobs from Calcutta; army officers with service in Canada sat next to naval officers with service in the Far East; and the diplomatists present rivaled the merchant adventurers in their intimate knowledge of every city of the civilized world. Increasing numbers of Irishmen filed into the lobbies with former Huguenots and North Americans, and more and more Scots took the high road to England and opportunity. For the theme of diversity played loudly, as new blood and broad experience poured in to refresh the older ruling elite.

In particular, more and more representatives of the new wealth made their way into the House. Merchants in liquor, clothing, and food staples took their seats with printers, mine owners, and shipbuilders, and as the financial world matured the M.P.'s in banking and insurance increased in number. The East India group rose to parliamentary prominence and then declined, but still managed to outnumber the planters and merchants from the Caribbean. Toward the end of the period a tiny cell of manufacturers appeared.

All of these economic forces flowed freely through the obsolete electoral machinery. It has been contended that the commercial interests entered the House mainly through the rotten boroughs,[1] but such was not the case, for the rotten borough representation showed characteristics which so closely approximate the national average that the members holding this type of seat can be called typical of the House's membership as a whole.[2] Far from being the stronghold of the "new" men, the rotten boroughs attracted members generally similar in characteristics to the entire representation, and if anything a little more privileged. A far greater proportion of the "new" men found seats in English open boroughs.[3] Clearly, the majority of the commercial members sat, not as the nominees and servants of borough patrons, but as bona fide representatives of the social and economic forces at work in the nation.

Throughout, the ruling class adapted itself to the basic social and economic pressures which were refashioning the structure of British society. As wealth from trade seriously rivaled wealth from land, aristocrats and their sons did not disdain to enter trade, and after a probationary period they welcomed into their midst the newly rich businessmen. Such interpenetration kept the ruling class flexible, but the probationary period prevented the social disintegration which might have followed too swift a change.

Inertia also checked change.[4] By way of illustration, the nabobs reached their peak strength in the House when the prosperity of the India trade was already declining; the West Indians continued to grow in number after the West Indies had entered their long decline; the banking M.P.'s did not appear in strength until some time after the banking business had undergone a phenomenal

1. Namier, *England in the Age of the American Revolution,* p. 5; *Parliamentary Debates,* ed. Hansard, 3d Ser., *3,* 224.

2. The 1,966 M.P.'s who represented rotten boroughs first received election at the average age of 33; 1,020 had had parliamentary ancestors; 1,246 belonged to parliamentary family groups; 690 had privileged social status as baronets, Irish peers, or sons of peers; 799 had attended public schools; 1,010 had attended universities; and 355 belonged to the commercial interest. In each respect this group of 1,966 M.P.'s approximates the national average. In classifying the boroughs for purposes of analysis, I have followed the *Parliamentary Papers of John Robinson,* ed. William T. Laprade (Camden Society, 3d Ser., 1922). Although some changes occurred over the entire period 1734–1832, Robinson's designations seem accurate enough for the present purpose.

3. Of the 2,348 open-borough members 581 belonged to the commercial interest. Of course, some commercial M.P.'s sat for both rotten and open boroughs.

4. The brake of inertia on social-economic forces can lead to a phenomenon which the anthropologists call "culture lag," that is, the tendency for a cultural response to lag behind a cultural stimulus.

growth; and only a handful of manufacturers entered the House before 1832, although nationwide they were already outstripping the men in older forms of business. In each instance it took about a generation for a stimulus at work in the nation to make itself felt in the personnel of the House.

It has been observed that the old regime was plutocratic in character.[5] In support of this view it is true that the ruling class tended to worship wealth, that the aristocracy and gentry freely entered trade, and that a number of M.P.'s were extremely rich men. William Beckford, author of *Vathek*, had an annual income of £100,000; Stephens Lyne-Stephens was said to be the richest commoner in England; John Gordon (ca 1773–1858) was reported to be the richest commoner in Scotland; and Luke White, the former itinerant bookseller, was stated to be the richest man in all Ireland. Moreover, the members received no pay, and the price of rotten boroughs as well as election expenses in the open constituencies were steadily rising.[6] Thus far the argument for plutocracy appears convincing.

On the other hand, although complete evidence is lacking, many members were far from wealthy, particularly as younger sons without fortunes and a number of professional men in moderate circumstances found their way into the House.[7] Upon occasion a borough patron or the government itself paid a member's election expenses.[8] The younger Pitt, Sheridan, Burke, and Fox lacked the legal qualification in land, and contemporary estimates placed the unqualified members at one-third of the House in 1783, 100 in 1806, and one-half in 1837.[9] The presence of such members mitigated the plutocratic cast of the House, but at the same time they doubtless tended to identify themselves with the economic interests which made possible their election. In view of the known wealth in the House of Commons, and in view of the critical importance of wealth in the structure of British society in the old regime, the unreformed House appears to have represented, as Namier has

5. Albert von Ruville, *William Pitt Earl of Chatham*, trans. H. J. Chaytor (London, 1907), *1*, 16, 170; Carl J. Friedrich, "Plutocracy" in the *Encyclopedia of the Social Sciences* (New York, Macmillan, 1935), *12*, 175–76; Andrews, *The Colonial Background of the American Revolution*, p. 189.

6. Porritt, *The Unreformed House of Commons*, *1*, 151–203; Butler, *The Passing of the Great Reform Bill*, p. 176.

7. Thomson, *A Constitutional History of England, 1642 to 1801*, p. 467.

8. Roscoe, *The English Scene in the Eighteenth Century*, p. 130.

9. Witmer, *The Property Qualifications of Members of Parliament*, esp. pp. 52–57, 80–81, 89–90, 218.

suggested, "not so much the sense of the community, as the distribution of power within it." [10]

During the old regime the people at large remained for the most part apathetic to political issues; and the ruling class had reason to fear popular demonstrations, which often ended in destructive rioting.[11] In the absence of an informed electorate, even reformers agreed that the House should represent interests rather than persons.[12]

But despite its outmoded electoral system, the unreformed House of Commons responded quickly to such public opinion as then existed, and its membership reflected fairly accurately the dominant social and economic forces within the state.[13] It at least provided an instrument through which the ruling class could operate as the trustee of the nation, until such time as the people at large could assume a larger share of political power and political responsibility.

10. Namier, *England,* p. 3; cf. Arnold J. Toynbee, *A Study of History,* abridged by D. C. Somervell (New York and London, Oxford University Press, 1947), p. 323.

11. Herbert Butterfield, *George III, Lord North, and the People, 1779–80* (London, Bell, 1949), p. 379; Cecil S. Emden, *The People and the Constitution* (Oxford, Clarendon Press, 1933), p. 183; Robson, *The Oxfordshire Election of 1754,* p. 97.

12. Butler, *Great Reform Bill,* p. 242; Eric G. Forrester, *Northamptonshire County Elections and Electioneering 1695–1832* (London, Oxford University Press, 1941), p. 3.

13. See Gibbons, *Ideas of Political Representation in Parliament 1651–1832,* pp. 8, 10; David L. Keir, *The Constitutional History of Modern Britain, 1485–1937* (2d ed. London, Black, 1943), p. 394; Taine, *Notes on England,* p. 201.

Table Showing Average Age on First Election, Average Length of Service, and the Number of M.P.'s Born before and after 1750, by Ancestry, Status, Education, and Occupation

	Av. Age on First Election	Av. Service (yrs.)	Date of Birth before 1750	Date of Birth 1750 and after	Total, Age Known	Age Not Known	Grand Total
Total	34.6	13.4	2217	2323	4540	494	5034
With ancestor M.P.'s	31.0	14.6	1286	1390	2676	137	2813
Without ancestor M.P.'s	39.8	11.8	931	933	1864	357	2221
In family groups	30.6	14.5	1412	1483	2895	150	3045
Not in family groups	38.8	11.5	805	840	1645	344	1989
Status on first election							
Baronets	35.3	14.3	264	166	430	22	452
Irish peers	32.9	13.0	40	23	63	1	64
Eld. sons Eng. peers	23.7	10.7	84	206	290	—	290
Ygr. sons Eng. peers	27.3	15.8	140	195	335	6	341
Sons of Scots peers	31.3	12.2	44	36	80	5	85
Sons of Irish peers	30.4	11.3	38	104	142	5	147
Sons of peeresses	29.2	10.7	4	16	20	—	20
Other	36.6	12.7	1603	1577	3180	455	3635
Nationality							
English	34.5	14.2	—	—	3501	355	3856
Scotch	35.6	10.7	—	—	545	102	647
Irish	37.3	10.5	—	—	476	36	512
North America	40.7	9.8	—	—	16	1	17
Other	45.5	10.4	—	—	2	—	2
Public Schools							
Charterhouse	34.4	12.2	9	21	30	2	32
Eton	29.3	14.3	277	498	775	10	785
Harrow	29.3	13.7	20	247	267	3	270
Rugby	33.8	14.1	15	36	51	—	51
Shrewsbury	37.5	15.6	10	5	15	—	15
Westminster	30.7	16.0	307	235	542	2	544
Winchester	31.2	16.4	28	42	70	—	70
Total	—	—	666	1084	1750	17	1767
More than one school	—	—	21	32	53	—	53
Net total	30.2	14.8	645	1052	1697	17	1714
Nonpublic school	37.3	12.6	1572	1271	2843	477	3320
Universities							
Oxford	31.1	15.2	631	655	1286	—	1286
Cambridge	32.2	14.6	379	492	871	2	873

Table Showing Average Age on First Election, Average Length of Service, and the Number of M.P.'s Born before and after 1750, by Ancestry, Status, Education, and Occupation (continued)

	Av. Age on First Election	Av. Service (yrs.)	Date of Birth before 1750	Date of Birth 1750 and after	Total, Age Known	Age Not Known	Grand Total
Universities (continued)							
Dublin	39.9	9.8	33	142	175	1	176
Scots universities	35.8	11.6	51	74	125	—	125
Foreign universities	32.6	15.0	28	10	38	1	39
Total	—	—	1122	1373	2495	4	2499
More than one university	—	—	40	42	82	1	83
Net total	32.4	14.4	1082	1331	2413	3	2416
Nonuniversity	37.1	12.3	1135	992	2127	491	2618
Professions							
Army (career)	33.8	12.7	204	248	452	58	510
Army (temporary)	31.3	13.6	95	204	299	18	317
Navy (career)	39.6	10.1	97	95	192	15	207
Navy (temporary)	36.7	11.9	12	15	27	—	27
Law	38.9	13.0	321	343	664	36	700
Medicine	48.3	12.5	4	4	8	3	11
Total	—	—	733	909	1642	130	1772
More than one profession	—	—	8	11	19	—	19
Net total	36.2	12.7	725	898	1623	130	1753
Nonprofessional	33.7	13.7	1492	1425	2917	364	3281
Commerce							
Bankers	40.4	13.3	84	121	205	25	230
Manufacturers	41.5	15.4	5	21	26	3	29
Nabobs	42.2	10.7	62	61	123	21	144
India interest	39.5	15.4	40	85	125	19	144
West Indies merchants	42.1	10.3	18	20	38	7	45
West Indies interest	34.8	14.6	52	61	113	11	124
"Merchants"	41.1	12.7	111	88	199	58	257
Total	—	—	372	457	829	144	973
More than one *	—	—	22	48	70	6	76
Net total	40.1	13.1	350	409	759	138	897
Noncommercial	33.5	13.5	1867	1914	3781	356	4137

* I have not made multiple entries for men stated to be "merchants" in addition to another form of trade. That is, if a man is stated to be a banker and a merchant, he appears only once, as a banker.

	Av. Age on First Election	Av. Service (yrs.)	Date of Birth before 1750	Date of Birth 1750 and after	Total, Age Known	Age Not Known	Grand Total
Commercial men	40.1	13.1	350	409	759	138	897
Professional men	36.2	12.7	725	898	1623	130	1753
Total	—	—	1075	1307	2382	268	2650
In professions and trade	—	—	23	63	86	9	95
Net total	37.3	12.8	1052	1244	2296	259	2555
No stated occupation	31.9	14.0	1165	1079	2244	235	2479

Appendix 2

Members of French Huguenot Descent

(The numbers are keyed to the check list of members at the end of the work.)

80	1274	1712	2682	3590
81	1280	1713	2683	3595
82	1284	1830	2684	3710
165	1285	1832	2685	3711
258	1288	1846	2720	3713
398	1299	2172	2722	3812
779	1304	2494	2723	3813
847	1331	2639	2734	3901
1068	1332	2666	2747	3906
1267	1439	2670	2759	4455
1270	1443	2671	2786	4456
1271	1710	2680	3064	4457
1272	1711	2681	3442	4548

Appendix 3

Table Showing Age Groupings at General Elections

	1734	1741	1747	1754	1761	1768	1774	1780	1784	1790	1796†	1802	1806	1807	1812	1818	1820	1826	1830	1831
Under 21	2	6	4	—	—	4	6	2	—	3	5	1	4	3	3	1	1	—	—	—
21–24 *	25	32	32	22	30	36	40	34	22	33	43	32	35	37	31	34	24	20	31	33
25–29	63	48	64	50	36	47	45	61	61	48	69	52	65	80	62	62	63	79	61	55
30–34	49	64	51	64	62	63	62	68	78	77	78	71	69	65	79	80	80	66	78	103
35–39	76	53	69	68	80	73	60	66	83	81	87	92	88	77	88	74	86	80	79	65
40–44	64	69	69	72	66	89	73	66	63	69	82	81	87	99	70	77	76	79	87	102
45–49	67	71	56	70	67	66	78	62	56	57	68	98	81	77	98	73	82	73	71	72
50–54	42	34	65	54	56	51	64	66	56	53	70	71	76	78	67	80	73	76	68	66
55–59	37	42	29	43	44	43	44	45	48	46	48	52	51	52	55	60	61	63	72	62
60–64	29	28	30	28	32	21	27	25	32	38	38	36	42	30	32	40	38	54	42	43
65–69	14	12	15	17	22	12	9	11	11	16	23	19	15	13	18	26	27	28	27	25
70 and over	7	10	10	15	18	9	10	14	12	13	16	17	15	17	16	17	16	22	25	18
Age unknown	83	89	64	55	45	44	40	38	36	24	31	36	30	30	39	34	31	18	17	14
Total	558	558	558	558	558	558	558	558	558	558	658	658	658	658	658	658	658	658	658	658
Average	42.3	42.2	42.3	43.7	44.2	42.0	42.5	42.3	42.3	42.7	42.6	44.0	43.3	42.8	43.4	44.1	44.1	45.0	44.6	43.9

* That is, from 21 years 0 months through 24 years 11 months.

† Includes 100 Irish members returned in 1801.

N.B. In making this and other tabulations by general elections, I have disregarded hedgers, i.e., M.P.'s returned for two or more seats at the same election. In each case, when the hedger gave up his superfluous seat(s), I have considered his successor as the originally returned member. In this respect I have followed the practice of L. B. Namier (*England in the Age of the American Revolution*, pp. 248–49).

APPENDIX 4

Members under Age on First Election

86	971	2191	3228	4077
285	1076	2314	3255	4084
306	1077	2468	3353	4135
458	1165	2508	3465	4229
499	1320	2519	3469	4235
532	1373	2535	3581	4379
541	1433	2770	3585	4489
588	1603	2774	3600	4530
594	1632	2859	3917	4564
636	1653	2862	3948	4633
700	1660	2867	3952	4677
705	1743	2872	3971	4741
748	1754	2915	3975	4811
825	1762	2997	3977	
839	2083	3000	3987	
929	2090	3005	4018	
952	2156	3192	4075	

APPENDIX 5

Members Serving over 50 Years

49	1472	2857	4533
163	1514	3017	4578
283	2049	3456	4721
655	2136	3666	4898
692	2750	3943	4972
813	2856	4447	

Note on fathers of the House of Commons:

The following additions and corrections may be made to A. B. Beaven's list of fathers of the House of Commons in *Notes and Queries*, 12th Ser., 7. 272:

1. For *Richard Shuttleworth, M.P. 1705–49*, read *Horatio Walpole, M.P. 1702–56*.

2. Insert *William Edwardes, M.P. 1747–84, 1786–1801*, before *Philip Stephens, M.P. 1759–1806*; presumably a "father's" service need not have been continuous, and Edwardes' service, although broken 1784–86, antedated and exceeded that of Stephens in 1796.

3. Insert *George Augustus Henry Cavendish, M.P. 1775–1831* before *Samuel Smith, M.P. 1788–1832*.

Table Showing Social Status by General Elections

	1734	1741	1747	1754	1761	1768	1774	1780	1784	1790	1796 *	1802	1806	1807	1812	1818	1820	1826	1830	1831
Baronets	93	77	65	61	68	64	78	75	83	73	85	84	73	70	78	72	69	67	84	76
Irish peers	7	12	12	16	18	24	18	20	19	19	16	7	9	10	6	4	6	7	3	2
Eld. sons Eng. peers	10	17	23	25	27	25	20	25	27	42	38	40	45	47	38	50	46	57	66	56
Yr. sons Eng. peers	40	49	57	54	51	46	44	44	37	40	51	57	60	61	58	71	62	66	57	54
Sons of Scots peers	15	15	13	12	11	10	13	10	10	7	11	8	10	7	4	2	5	6	5	3
Sons of Irish peers	3	7	6	7	7	7	15	14	11	12	28	28	34	30	31	26	25	25	23	20
Sons of peeresses	—	2	2	2	3	3	1	—	—	1	—	3	4	4	6	4	3	4	1	2
Other	390	379	380	381	373	379	369	370	371	364	429	431	423	429	437	429	442	426	419	445
Total	558	558	558	558	558	558	558	558	558	558	658	658	658	658	658	658	658	658	658	658

* Includes 100 Irish members returned in 1801.

84

Table Showing Members with Blood Relatives in the Male Line
Previously in the House, by General Elections

	1734	1741	1747	1754	1761	1768	1774	1780	1784	1790	1796 *	1802	1806	1807	1812	1818	1820	1826	1830	1831
Father	118	125	142	145	150	132	126	112	105	107	117	129	136	151	146	157	140	165	168	162
Father and grandfather	94	90	99	111	99	109	109	112	105	115	106	99	112	108	106	120	124	132	129	123
Grandfather only	47	62	43	48	52	51	50	45	40	53	48	40	45	42	45	41	40	38	43	37
Other relative	67	67	68	71	75	69	63	67	76	72	79	87	86	83	72	66	66	78	74	72
Total	326	344	352	375	376	361	348	336	326	347	350	355	379	384	369	384	370	413	414	394
"New" men	232	214	206	183	182	197	210	222	232	211	308	303	279	274	289	274	288	245	244	264
Grand total	558	558	558	558	558	558	558	558	558	558	658	658	658	658	658	658	658	658	658	658

* Includes 100 Irish members returned in 1801.

Table Showing Members belonging to Family Groups, by General Elections

	1734	1741	1747	1754	1761	1768	1774	1780	1784	1790	1796 *	1802	1806	1807	1812	1818	1820	1826	1830	1831
In family groups	336	355	374	388	387	391	387	383	382	397	436	434	443	441	427	428	406	419	416	392
Not in family groups	222	203	184	170	171	167	171	175	176	161	222	224	215	217	231	230	252	239	242	266
Total	558	558	558	558	558	558	558	558	558	558	658	658	658	658	658	658	658	658	658	658

* Includes 100 Irish members returned in 1801.

Appendix 9

Members of Illegitimate Birth

322	909	1691	2833	3379
352	1399	1755	3001	3518
354	1595	2463	3078	4255
361	1630	2620	3369	4466
908	1678	2628	3371	4797

Appendix 10

Table Showing the M.P.'s with a Public-school Education, by General Elections

	1734	1741	1747	1754	1761	1768	1774	1780	1784	1790	1796 *	1802	1806	1807	1812	1818	1820	1826	1830	1831
Charterhouse	1	2	2	2	3	3	3	1	2	3	6	8	4	5	8	7	8	3	2	6
Eton	43	62	63	72	79	86	105	108	112	115	100	113	123	126	131	135	137	133	144	135
Harrow	2	2	1	2	4	6	9	21	26	37	47	55	54	58	60	66	65	86	87	76
Rugby	3	5	4	4	6	3	3	3	2	2	4	5	8	10	9	11	9	12	8	10
Shrewsbury	1	2	2	1	1	—	2	4	5	6	2	3	2	2	2	2	4	2	3	2
Westminster	46	61	83	90	111	100	90	82	74	87	85	72	75	72	69	88	92	78	71	65
Winchester	4	4	7	6	6	4	9	9	8	12	14	14	11	11	8	11	11	19	19	11
Total	100	138	162	177	210	202	221	228	229	262	258	270	277	284	287	320	326	333	334	305
More than one	1	2	2	2	7	3	6	12	12	11	12	16	12	12	10	10	12	12	10	6
Net total	99	136	160	175	203	199	215	216	217	251	246	254	265	272	277	310	314	321	324	299

* Includes 100 Irish members returned in 1801.

APPENDIX 11

Table Showing the M.P.'s with a University Education by General Election

	1734	1741	1747	1754	1761	1768	1774	1780	1784	1790	1796 *	1802	1806	1807	1812	1818	1820	1826	1830	1831
Oxford (Christ Ch.)	32	43	45	38	40	43	43	50	47	61	73	80	86	100	111	129	136	132	137	119
Oxford (other)	119	116	118	116	115	111	109	101	107	98	88	87	72	74	71	61	62	68	66	68
Cambridge (Trinity)	12	8	9	11	13	25	34	35	32	38	36	39	48	45	52	55	61	69	80	87
Cambridge (other)	88	64	74	76	81	88	75	89	71	81	94	89	77	77	69	72	73	61	65	62
Aberdeen	—	—	—	—	—	—	—	3	2	2	3	2	1	1	2	4	4	3	4	4
Edinburgh	2	1	3	2	4	7	6	6	5	6	4	9	9	9	7	10	11	14	12	12
Glasgow	—	3	3	5	6	11	11	7	11	7	7	7	7	10	6	9	9	7	7	11
St. Andrews	—	—	—	—	2	2	3	2	1	1	1	1	—	—	—	—	—	—	1	1
Dublin	2	3	3	4	5	8	8	7	5	4	47	38	34	31	38	37	39	41	40	39
Brunswick	—	—	—	—	—	—	—	—	—	—	—	—	—	—	—	—	—	—	—	—
Freiburg	—	—	—	—	—	—	—	—	—	—	—	—	—	1	—	1	—	—	—	—
Göttingen	—	—	—	—	—	1	1	—	1	1	1	1	1	2	—	—	—	1	1	1
Leipzig	—	—	—	1	—	1	2	—	—	1	—	—	—	—	—	—	—	—	—	1
Leyden	4	2	8	8	12	8	7	4	3	1	2	2	1	—	—	—	—	—	—	—
Neuchâtel	—	—	—	—	—	—	—	1	—	—	—	—	—	1	—	—	—	—	—	—
Paris	—	—	—	—	—	—	—	1	1	1	1	1	—	—	—	—	—	—	—	—
Turin	—	—	—	—	—	—	—	—	—	1	—	—	—	—	—	—	—	—	—	—
Utrecht	1	1	1	2	1	—	1	—	1	—	—	—	—	—	—	—	—	—	—	—
King's (N.Y.)	—	—	—	—	—	—	—	—	—	—	—	—	—	—	—	—	—	—	—	—
Ft. William (Bengal)	—	—	—	—	—	—	—	—	—	—	—	—	—	—	—	—	—	—	1	1
Total	260	241	264	263	279	305	300	306	287	303	352	356	336	351	356	378	395	396	414	406
More than one	6	5	11	9	12	11	13	13	10	11	14	18	13	19	9	13	15	16	18	19
Net total	254	236	253	254	267	294	287	293	277	292	338	338	323	332	347	365	380	380	396	387

* Includes 100 Irish members returned in 1801.

Appendix 12

Table Showing Professional Men in the House of Commons, by General Elections

	1734	1741	1747	1754	1761	1768	1774	1780	1784	1790	1796*	1802	1806	1807	1812	1818	1820	1826	1830	1831
Army (career)	49	49	52	57	59	64	60	50	57	65	65	60	79	71	74	65	63	71	64	47
Army (temporary)	20	16	23	20	27	30	34	38	36	37	43	43	46	50	55	59	55	69	71	74
Navy (career)	9	11	12	15	21	19	15	17	25	20	12	24	30	26	16	21	23	25	24	24
Navy (temporary)	1	—	1	1	1	2	5	4	5	4	4	6	4	5	5	2	3	4	2	5
Law	65	64	79	71	70	68	62	71	76	72	89	96	113	109	106	105	112	96	96	108
Medicine	1	1	—	—	1	2	1	1	1	1	1	—	1	—	1	4	3	2	3	2
Total	145	141	167	164	179	185	177	181	200	199	214	229	273	261	257	256	259	267	260	260
More than one	2	2	1	—	2	2	2	3	2	3	3	4	3	2	1	3	4	4	1	3
Net Total	143	139	166	164	177	183	175	178	198	196	211	225	270	259	256	253	255	263	259	257

* Includes 100 Irish members returned in 1801.

Appendix 13

Physicians in the House of Commons 1734–1832

1083	2433
1325	2944
1326	2946
1684	2955
1798	3063
2409	

Table Showing Commercial Interests, by General Elections

	1734	1741	1747	1754	1761	1768	1774	1780	1784	1790	1796*	1802	1806	1807	1812	1818	1820	1826	1830	1831
Bankers	13	9	7	13	13	10	17	26	26	27	46	45	47	44	43	47	41	42	46	47
Manufacturers	1	—	—	—	1	2	2	3	4	4	3	6	8	7	8	13	9	8	8	7
Nabobs	2	3	2	4	5	15	15	17	22	23	27	30	25	18	26	17	21	15	17	16
India interest	8	4	9	9	10	8	11	12	10	12	14	27	30	31	29	29	29	44	51	48
West Indies merchants	1	1	3	4	4	3	3	3	4	3	6	6	6	6	9	7	8	8	8	5
West Indies interest	4	3	8	16	20	19	17	21	16	14	18	17	13	17	20	26	27	31	27	23
"Merchants"	39	40	31	24	23	29	31	28	32	20	30	31	26	27	25	28	31	31	29	39
Total	68	60	60	70	76	86	96	110	114	103	144	162	155	150	160	167	166	179	186	185
More than one†	5	1	2	2	2	1	2	2	5	6	13	22	23	20	20	20	16	25	33	25
Net total	63	59	58	68	74	85	94	108	109	97	131	140	132	130	140	147	150	154	153	160

* Includes 100 Irish members returned in 1801.

† I have not made multiple entries for men stated to be "merchants" in addition to another form of trade. That is, if a man is stated to be a banker and a merchant, he appears only once, as a banker.

APPENDIX 15

Merchants in the House of Commons 1734–1832

82	724	1656	2427	3017	4042	4773
85	790	1696	2447	3029	4043	4800
142	792	1712	2451	3030	4092	4813
147	805	1791	2473	3068	4095	4822
165	847	1801	2474	3079	4118	4829
228	850	1818	2477	3082	4125	4830
240	907	1830	2483	3085	4165	4831
241	1001	1832	2489	3091	4186	4832
249	1003	1837	2490	3097	4202	4873
318	1012	1850	2494	3098	4240	4886
327	1023	1853	2497	3237	4242	4904
342	1064	1860	2549	3244	4245	4921
379	1082	1869	2561	3316	4282	4926
398	1105	1873	2572	3406	4304	4927
442	1157	1875	2573	3409	4344	4930
475	1159	1908	2580	3422	4345	4957
477	1162	1909	2589	3479	4357	4982
483	1173	1971	2607	3482	4424	
513	1267	1974	2611	3504	4432	
515	1313	1977	2613	3505	4439	
516	1316	2039	2654	3512	4455	
520	1329	2050	2667	3547	4458	
527	1332	2065	2669	3557	4469	
531	1393	2071	2757	3616	4471	
562	1401	2111	2771	3680	4483	
599	1424	2114	2772	3713	4484	
600	1438	2148	2787	3773	4485	
602	1457	2158	2792	3821	4507	
612	1491	2177	2793	3831	4511	
657	1515	2193	2794	3833	4516	
686	1521	2217	2822	3838	4518	
689	1556	2228	2826	3842	4572	
704	1557	2312	2827	3852	4634	
709	1558	2313	2828	3858	4636	
710	1571	2317	2842	3859	4637	
711	1584	2363	2920	3920	4658	
716	1590	2417	2945	3973	4691	
718	1595	2418	2947	3995	4731	
719	1612	2420	2975	4013	4737	
722	1645	2426	2983	4021	4768	

APPENDIX 16

Bankers in the House of Commons 1734–1832

40	954	1858	2682	3758	4261 *
46	969	1859	2683	3762	4290
59	973	1862	2847	3820	4291
81	998	1863	2868	3832	4299
156	999	1865	2869	3837 *	4326
162	1052	1896	2870	3856	4335
168	1102	1903	2884	3860	4346
188	1149	1912	2914	3865	4351 *
192	1150	2046	2950	3866	4403
193	1151	2055 *	2952	3868 *	4451
197	1179	2069	2981	3871	4457 *
215 *	1183	2070	3014 *	3881	4474 *
227 *	1248	2105	3019	3901	4475
232 *	1250	2106	3027	3909	4477 *
233	1291	2123	3037	3921	4502
238	1296	2126	3038	3924	4513 *
257	1304	2127	3039	3998	4727
326	1339	2172	3041	4003 *	4729
351	1379	2194	3042	4009	4736
369	1380	2212 *	3081	4030	4744 *
432	1381	2268	3093 *	4098	4761 *
476	1382	2269	3122	4099	4789
488	1385	2280	3134	4110	4840 *
512	1474	2281	3151	4133	4843
514	1518	2305	3238	4137	4872
532	1546	2326 *	3242	4141	4889
556 *	1553	2328	3248	4161	4891
563	1554	2348	3328	4162	4892
581	1559 *	2362	3330	4163	4895
641	1560	2369 *	3468	4167	4985
656 *	1562	2379	3476	4168	
666 *	1586	2444	3515	4172	
708	1683 *	2479	3531 *	4174	
801	1694 *	2525	3591	4178	
802	1697	2545 *	3594	4181	
844	1710 *	2609	3651	4183	
884	1765 *	2610	3682	4184	
885	1784	2641	3687	4197	
886	1797	2642	3710 *	4241	
887	1841	2681	3726	4243	

* Directors of the Bank of England in these years.

APPENDIX 17

Nabobs in the House of Commons 1734–1832

7	855	1715	2525	3514	4289 *
46	866	1764	2532	3515	4343
54	957	1769	2536	3524	4346
57	969	1793	2552 *	3597	4350
60 *	992	1877	2691	3598	4363
83	1048	1920 *	2821 *	3648	4365 *
191 *	1072	1938	2880 *	3708	4389
207	1086	1942 *	2883	3709	4390
224 *	1166	1948	2913 *	3711	4405
239	1202	1968	2944	3756	4433 *
242	1203	1975 *	2955	3757	4451
269	1227 *	2054	2957	3761	4537 *
331	1358	2062	2969	3777	4544
416	1362	2124	2992	3854	4624
435	1368	2304	3043	3855	4641
538	1383	2344	3099 *	3880 *	4642 *
581	1426	2409	3162	3929	4732
615	1440	2419 *	3199	3940 *	4760
626	1510	2433	3213	3946	4854
628	1594	2441 *	3299	4032 *	4868
648	1598	2465 *	3368	4051	4955
708	1658	2472	3389	4180	4963
723	1687 *	2491 *	3475	4182	4975
779	1688	2503 *	3476	4277	4987

* Directors of the East India Company in these years.

The above list of nabobs and the succeeding list of M.P.'s in the East India "interest" differ somewhat from the lists in the appendixes of C. H. Philips, *The East India Company 1784–1834* (Manchester, 1940). Correspondence with Mr. Philips indicates that his lists are probably too comprehensive, while my own lists doubtless err the other way, in that they exclude some M.P.'s only because the genealogical evidence at my disposal appears inconclusive.

Appendix 18

Members in the India Interest 1734–1832

26	456	1621 *	2676 *	3516	4179 *
47	469 *	1713 *	2747 *	3535	4184
56 *	502	1719 *	2788 *	3591	4261
58 *	532	1804	2820	3710	4281 *
81 *	539	1845 *	2845	3771	4387 *
92	543	1893	2869	3798 *	4404
149 *	646	1943	2881 *	3837	4456 *
158	768	1952	2900	3865 *	4476 *
159 *	884	2131	2943	3866	4520 *
161	959	2161	2968	3872	4570
188	967 *	2212	2993	3881	4744
193	973	2269	2994	3925	4748
199 *	998 *	2311	3022	3928 *	4756
215 *	1139 *	2422	3027	3999	4787
232	1151	2431	3041	4029	4833
233 *	1183	2432 *	3093	4033 *	4836
234	1199 *	2446	3132 *	4097	4855 *
237	1246	2449	3136 *	4112	4872 *
317	1287 *	2462	3151	4137	4891
332	1299	2479	3168 *	4167 *	4911 *
396	1304 *	2486 *	3209	4171	4948
399 *	1310	2531 *	3314	4172	4950 *
404	1498	2565	3327 *	4174	4961
450	1562	2592	3488 *	4178 *	4985

* Directors of the East India Company in these years.

Appendix 19

West Indies Merchants in the House of Commons 1734–1832

158	385	1474	2900	3668
186	396	1560	2929	3669
188	528	1854	3014	3788
189	534	1940	3026	3837
190	563	2204	3122	4504
321	1237	2208	3260	4549
322	1248	2283	3317	4590
323	1357	2676	3318	4644
341	1442	2884	3403	4807

Members in the West Indies Interest 1734–1832

66	1498	2674	3865
115	1499	2675	3911
264	1506	2677	3919
293	1507	2678	4026
319	1508	2679	4070
320	1538	2774	4093
324	1539	2844	4094
343	1720	2907	4102
363	1742	2972	4154
415	1744	2993	4254
417	1788	3027	4265
418	1796	3035	4272
471	1798	3045	4273
665	1804	3106	4323
855	1839	3147	4326
979	1847	3155	4342
980	1887	3207	4401
981	1888	3216	4463
1002	1893	3257	4464
1175	1895	3284	4577
1195	1924	3311	4578
1242	1941	3372	4579
1251	1965	3478	4617
1254	2024	3480	4730
1255	2337	3519	4769
1257	2479	3532	4778
1314	2486	3560	4838
1315	2492	3593	4864
1351	2540	3630	4865
1377	2672	3640	4917
1455	2673	3793	4962

Manufacturers in the House of Commons 1734–1832

90	1056	2167	2386	3719
170	1151	2320	2914	4286
452	1546	2328	3031	4429
550	1642	2343	3193	4654
708	1738	2376	3536	4700
968	2035	2377	3614	

Check List of Members

Authorities Most Frequently Cited in Abbreviated Form

Admissions to St. John, Cambridge   *Admissions to the College of St. John the Evangelist in the University of Cambridge,* ed. J. E. B. Mayor and R. F. Scott, 4 vols., Cambridge, 1882–1931.

Alumni Cantab.   *Alumni Cantabrigienses,* ed. John and J. A. Venn, pt. 1, to 1751, 4 vols., Cambridge, 1922–27; pt. 2, 1752–1900, 3 vols., Cambridge, 1940–.

Alumni Carthusiani   *Alumni Carthusiani,* ed. Bower Marsh and Frederick A. Crisp, London, 1913.

Alumni Dublin.   *Alumni Dublinenses,* ed. George D. Burtchaell and Thomas U. Sadleir, new ed. Dublin, 1935.

Alumni Felsted.   *Alumni Felstedienses,* ed. F. S. Moller, London, 1931.

Alumni Oxon.   *Alumni Oxonienses,* ed. Joseph Foster, *1500–1714,* 4 vols., Oxford, 1891–92; *1715–1886,* 4 vols., London, 1887–88.

Bates Harbin   Bates Harbin, Sophia W., *Members of Parliament for the County of Somerset,* Taunton, 1939.

Bean   Bean, William W., *The Parliamentary Representation of the Six Northern Counties of England,* Hull, 1890.

Boase   Boase, Frederick, *Modern English Biography,* 6 vols., Truro, 1892–1921.

Burke's *Peerage*   Burke, Sir John B., *Peerage and Baronetage.*

Burke's *LG*   Burke, Sir John B., *Landed Gentry.*

Burtchaell's *Kilkenny M.P.'s*   Burtchaell, George D., *Genealogical Memoirs of the Members of Parliament for the County and City of Kilkenny,* Dublin, 1888.

Collins' *Peerage*   Collins, Arthur, *Peerage of England,* ed. Samuel E. Brydges, 9 vols., London, 1812.

Courtney's *Cornwall M.P.'s*   Courtney, William P., *The Parliamentary Representation of Cornwall to 1832,* 1889.

DNB   *Dictionary of National Biography.*

Eton Coll. Reg.   *Eton College Register,* ed. Richard A. Austen-Leigh, *1698–1752,* Eton, 1927; *1753–1790,* Eton, 1921.

Eton Lists   *Eton School Lists, from 1791 to 1850,* ed. H. E. C. Stapylton, 2d ed. London, 1864.

Ferguson   Ferguson, Richard S., *Cumberland and Westmorland M.P.'s,* Carlisle, 1871.

Foster's *Scots M.P.'s*   Foster, Joseph, *Members of Parliament, Scotland,* 2d ed. London, 1882.

GEC   Cokayne, George Edward, *Complete Baronetage,* 6 vols., Exeter,

1900–9; *Complete Peerage,* 8 vols., London, 1887–98, and new ed.,
ed. Vicary Gibbs et al, 11 vols., London, 1910–.

Gent. Mag.   The Gentleman's Magazine. Unless a year is cited, reference is to the obituary notice appearing in the same year as the
death of the member in question.

Gooder   Gooder, Arthur, *The Parliamentary Representation of the
County of York, 1258–1832,* 2 vols., Wakefield, 1935–38.

Harrow Reg.   The Harrow School Register, 1571–1800, ed. William
T. J. Gun, London and New York, 1934; *1800–1911,* ed. M. G.
Dauglish and P. K. Stephenson, London, 1911.

Lists, 1806, 1812, etc.   *1806:* Wilson, Joshua, *A Biographical Index to
the Present House of Commons,* London, 1806; *1812: A Biographical List of the House of Commons Elected in October, 1812,* London, 1813; *1821: A Full View of the House of Commons,* London,
1821; *1832: Key to Both Houses of Parliament,* London, 1832.

Musgrave's *Obituary*   Musgrave, Sir William, *Obituary,* ed. Sir George
J. Armytage, Harleian Society, 6 vols., 1899–1901.

Old Westminsters   The Record of Old Westminsters, ed. G. F. Russell
Barker and Alan H. Stenning, 2 vols., London, 1928; *A Supple-
mentary Volume,* ed. J. B. Whitmore and G. R. Y. Radcliffe, London [1938?].

Park   Park, Godfrey Richard, *Parliamentary Representation of Yorkshire,* Hull, 1886.

Pink   Pink, William D., and Beaven, Alfred B., *The Parliamentary
Representation of Lancashire,* London, 1889.

Scots Peerage   Scots Peerage, ed. James B. Paul, 9 vols., Edinburgh,
1904–14.

Venn MS   Unpublished portions of *Alumni Cantabrigienses,* by cour-
tesy of J. A. Venn.

Wedgwood   Wedgwood, Josiah C., "Staffordshire Parliamentary History," *William Salt Archaeological Society,* 1922 and 1933.

Whitley's *Coventry M.P.'s*   Whitley, T. W., *The Parliamentary Representation of the City of Coventry,* Coventry, 1894.

Williams' *Gloucester M.P.'s*   Williams, William R., *The Parliamentary
History of the County of Gloucester,* Hereford, 1898.

Williams' *Hereford M.P.'s*   Williams, William R., *The Parliamentary
History of the County of Hereford,* Brecknock, 1896.

Williams' *Oxford M.P.'s*   Williams, William R., *The Parliamentary
History of the County of Oxford,* Brecknock, 1899.

Williams' *Wales M.P.'s*   Williams, William R., *The Parliamentary History of the Principality of Wales,* Brecknock, 1895.

Williams' *Worcester M.P.'s*   Williams, William R., *The Parliamentary
History of the County of Worcester,* Hereford, 1897.

Abbreviations

Bn	Baron
Bt	Baronet
Ca	Circa
D.	Duke
E.	Earl
M.	Marquess
Vct	Viscount

1. ABBOTT, Charles (1757–1829), 1st Bn Colchester, M.P. Helston 1795–1802, Woodstock 1802–6, Oxford Univ. 1806–17 (GEC; DNB; *Old Westminsters*).
2. ABDY, Anthony Thomas (ca 1721–75), 5th Bt, M.P. Knaresborough 1763–75 (GEC; *Alumni Cantab.; Alumni Felsted.*).
3. ABDY, John (ca 1714–59), 4th Bt, M.P. Essex 1748–59 (GEC).
4. ABDY, Robert (1688–1748), 3d Bt, M.P. Essex 1727–48 (GEC).
5. ABDY, William (ca 1779–1868), 7th Bt, M.P. Malmesbury 1817–18 (GEC; *Eton Lists*).

ABERCORN, 1st M. of, *see* HAMILTON, John James.

6. ABERCROMBY, Alexander (1784–1853), M.P. Clackmannanshire 1817–18 (DNB).
7. ABERCROMBY, Burnet (ca 1738–92), M.P. Clackmannanshire 1788–90 (Burke's *Peerage;* Foster's *Scots M.P.'s*).
8. ABERCROMBY, George (1770–1843), 2d Bn Abercromby, M.P. Edinburgh City 1805–6, Clackmannanshire 1806–7, 1812–15 (GEC).
9. ABERCROMBY, George Ralph (1800–52), 3d Bn Abercromby, M.P. Clackmannanshire 1824–26, 1830–31, Stirlingshire 1838–41, Clackmannan and Kinross-shire 1841–42 (GEC).
10. ABERCROMBY, James (ca 1706–81), M.P. Banffshire 1734–54 (*Dict. Am. Biog.*).
11. ABERCROMBY, James, M.P. Clackmannanshire 1761–68 (Foster's *Scots M.P.'s*).
12. ABERCROMBY, James (1776–1858), 1st Bn Dunfermline, M.P. Midhurst 1807–12, Calne 1812–30, Edinburgh City 1832–39 (GEC; DNB).
13. ABERCROMBY, John (1772–1817), M.P. Clackmannanshire 1815–17 (DNB).
14. ABERCROMBY, Ralph (1734–1801), M.P. Clackmannanshire 1774–80, 1796–98 (DNB).
15. ABERCROMBY, Robert (1740–1827), M.P. Clackmannanshire 1798–1802 (DNB).
16. ABERCROMBY, Robert (1784–1855), 5th Bt, M.P. Banffshire 1812–18 (GEC).

ABERGAVENNY, 2d E. of, *see* NEVILL, Henry.

ABINGDON, 6th E. of, *see* BERTIE, Montagu.

ABINGER, 1st Bn, *see* SCARLETT, James.

17. ABNEY-HASTINGS, Charles (1792–1858), 2d Bt, M.P. Leicester borough 1826–31 (Boase; *Eton Lists*).
18. ACHESON, Archibald (1776–1849), 1st Bn Worlingham, M.P. Armagh Co. 1801–7 (GEC; DNB).
19. ACHESON, Archibald (1806–64), 1st Bn Acheson, M.P. Armagh Co. 1830–47 (GEC; *Harrow Reg.*).

ACLAND, *see* DYKE-ACLAND.

20. ACLAND-PALMER, John (1756–1831), 1st Bt, M.P. Bridgwater 1781–84 (Burke's *Colonial Gentry; Alumni Oxon.*).

A'COURT, Pierce Ashe, *see* ASHE-A'COURT, Pierce.

21. A'COURT, William (1779–1860), 1st Bn Heytesbury, M.P. Dorchester 1812–14 (GEC; DNB).

A'COURT, William Pierce Ashe, *see* ASHE-A'COURT, William Pierce.

22. A'COURT-ASHE, William (ca 1709–81), M.P. Heytesbury 1751–81 (Burke's *Peerage;* Foster's *Collect. Geneal.*).

23. A'COURT-REPINGTON, Charles Ashe (1785–1861), M.P. Heytesbury 1820–20 (Burke's *Peerage;* Foster's *Collect. Geneal.;* Boase).

24. A'COURT-REPINGTON, Edward Henry (1783–1855), M.P. Heytesbury 1820–32, Tamworth 1837–47 (Burke's *Peerage;* Foster's *Collect. Geneal.*).

25. ADAIR, James (ca 1743–98), M.P. Cockermouth 1775–80, Higham Ferrers 1793–98 (DNB; *Alumni Cantab.; Eton Coll. Reg.*).

26. ADAIR, Robert (1763–1855), M.P. Appleby 1799–1802, Camelford 1802–12 (DNB; *Old Westminsters*).

27. ADAM, Charles (1780–1853), M.P. Kinross-shire 1831–32, Clackmannan and Kinross-shire 1832–41 (DNB).

28. ADAM, Robert (1728–92), M.P. Kinross-shire 1768–74 (DNB).

29. ADAM, William (1751–1839), M.P. Gatton 1774–80, Wigtown burghs 1780–84, Aberdeen burghs 1784–90, Ross-shire 1790–94, Kincardineshire 1806–12 (DNB).

30. ADAMS, Charles (ca 1753–1821), M.P. Weymouth and Melcombe Regis 1801–12 (Foster's *Collect. Geneal.*).

31. ADAMS, James (ca 1752–1816), M.P. West Looe 1784–90, Hindon 1790–96, Bramber 1796–1802, Harwich 1803–6, 1807–7 (Foster's *Collect. Geneal.; Alumni Oxon.*).

32. ADAMS, John (ca 1746–1817), M.P. Carmarthen borough 1774–80 (Williams' *Wales M.P.'s*).

ADAMS, Thomas, *see* ANSON, Thomas.

33. ADAMS, William (ca 1752–1811), M.P. Plympton Erle 1796–1801, Totnes 1801–11 (Burke's *LG* [ed. 1849]; Foster's *Collect. Geneal.*).

34. ADAMSON, Robert (ca 1753–1817), M.P. Cricklade 1784–85 (*Eton Coll. Reg.*).

ADARE, Vct, *see* WYNDHAM-QUIN, Windham Henry.

35. ADDAMS-WILLIAMS, William (1787–1861), M.P. Monmouthshire 1831–41 (Burke's *LG;* Williams' *Wales M.P.'s*).

36. ADDINGTON, Henry (1757–1844), 1st Vct Sidmouth, M.P. Devizes 1784–1805 (GEC; DNB).

37. ADDINGTON, John Hiley (1759–1818), M. P. Truro 1787–90, Winchelsea 1794–96, Wendover 1796–1802, Bossiney 1802–3, Har-

wich 1803–18 (Burke's *Peerage; Alumni Oxon.;* Pellew's *Sidmouth, passim*).

38. ADEANE, Henry John (1789–1847), M.P. Cambridgeshire 1830–32 (*Alumni Cantab.*).

39. ADEANE, James Whorwood (ca 1740–1802), M.P. Cambridge borough 1780–89, Cambridgeshire 1789–1802 (M. Deane, *Book of Dene,* p. 139).

40. ADEY, Stephen Thurston (d. 1801), M. P. Higham Ferrers 1798–1801 (Foster's *Collect Geneal.; Royal Kalendar* [1799], p. 35).

41. AFFLECK, Edmund (1725–88), 1st Bt, M.P. Colchester 1782–88 (DNB; GEC).

42. AFFLECK, Gilbert (ca 1685–1764), M.P. Cambridge borough 1722–27, 1737–41 (*Alumni Oxon.*).

43. AFFLECK, John (1710–76), M.P. Suffolk 1743–61, Agmondesham 1767–68 (GEC; *Old Westminsters*).

44. AGAR, Emanuel Felix (ca 1781–1866), M.P. Sudbury 1807–12 (Boase).

45. AGNEW, Andrew (1793–1849), 7th Bt, M.P. Wigtownshire 1830–37 (DNB; GEC).

46. AGNEW, John (ca 1759–1812), M.P. Stockbridge 1799–1802 (Foster's *Collect. Geneal.*).

AILESBURY, M. of, *see* BRUDENELL-BRUCE, Charles and George William Frederick.

47. AINSLIE, Robert (ca 1730–1812), 1st Bt, M.P. Milborne Port 1796–1802 (DNB).

48. AINSLIE, Robert Sharpe (1777–1858), 2d Bt, M.P. St. Michael 1802–6 (*Alumni Cantab.*).

49. AISLABIE, William (ca 1700–81), M.P. Ripon 1721–81 (Musgrave's *Obituary;* Foster's *Collect. Geneal.;* Bean).

ALBEMARLE, Earls of, *see* KEPPEL, Augustus Frederick and George.

50. ALCOCK, Thomas (ca 1801–66), M.P. Newton 1826–30, Ludlow 1839–40, East Surrey 1847–65 (Boase).

51. ALCOCK, William Congreve (ca 1771–1813), M.P. Waterford City 1801–3, Wexford Co. 1807–12 (Burke's *Irish LG; Alumni Dublin.*).

ALDBOROUGH, 2d E. of, *see* STRATFORD, Edward.

52. ALDRIDGE, John Clater (ca 1737–95), M.P. Queenborough 1784–90, Shoreham 1790–95 (Burke's *LG; Alumni Oxon.;* Comber's *Sussex Geneal., Horsham*).

53. ALDWORTH-NEVILLE, Richard (1717–93), M.P. Reading 1747–54, Wallingford 1754–61, Tavistock 1761–74 (DNB; *Eton Coll. Reg.*).

54. ALEXANDER, Boyd (1758–1825), M.P. Renfrewshire 1796–1802, Glasgow burghs 1803–6 (Burke's *Peerage;* Foster's *Scots M.P.'s;* Addison's *Glasgow Matric. Albums*).

55. ALEXANDER, Henry (ca 1763–1818), M.P. Londonderry Co. 1801–2, Old Sarum 1802–6 (*Alumni Cantab.; Alumni Dublin.*).

56. ALEXANDER, Henry (1787–1861), M.P. Barnstable 1826–30 (Foster's *Baronetage;* Boase).

57. ALEXANDER, James (ca 1769–1848), M.P. Old Sarum 1812–32 (Burke's *Irish LG;* Foster's *Collect. Geneal.; 1832 List*).

58. ALEXANDER, Josias Du Pré (ca 1771–1839), M.P. Old Sarum 1820–28, 1830–32 (Burke's *Irish LG;* Prinsep's *Madras Civilians,* p. 2).

59. ALEXANDER, William (d. 1761), M.P. Edinburgh City 1754–61 (Burke's *Peerage;* Foster's *Scots M.P.'s*).

60. ALLAN, Alexander (ca 1764–1820), 1st Bt, M.P. Berwick-on-Tweed 1803–6, 1807–20 (Foster's *Collect. Geneal.;* Bean; *1812 List*).

61. ALLAN, George (1767–1828), M.P. Durham City 1813–18 (*Alumni Cantab.*).

62. ALLANSON, Charles (ca 1721–75), M.P. Ripon 1768–75 (Hunter's *Familiae Min. Gent.; Alumni Oxon.; Genealogist,* N.S., *15,* 48; Bean).

63. ALLANSON-WINN, George (ca 1725–98), 1st Bn Headley, M.P. Ripon 1789–98 (GEC).

64. ALLANSON-WINN, George Mark Arthur Way (1785–1827), M.P. Maldon 1826–27 (Burke's *Peerage* sub Headley; *Gent. Mag., 2, 559*).

65. ALLARDICE, Alexander (ca 1743–1801), M.P. Aberdeen burghs 1792–1801 (*Scottish Notes and Queries, 1,* 50).

66. ALLEN, Benjamin (ca 1732–91), M.P. Bridgwater 1768–81 (*Alumni Cantab.*).

67. ALLEN, Jefferys (ca 1760–1844), M.P. Bridgwater 1796–1804 (*Alumni Cantab.*).

68. ALLEN, John Hensleigh (1769–1843), M.P. Pembroke borough 1818–26 (*Alumni Cantab.;* Williams' *Wales M.P.'s; Old Westminsters*).

69. ALLEN, Joshua (1728–1816), 5th Vct Allen, M.P. Eye 1762–70 (GEC).

70. ALLGOOD, Lancelot (1711–82), M.P. Northumberland 1749–54 (Burke's *LG; New Hist. of Northumberland, 15,* 201; *Alumni Oxon.*).

71. ALLSOPP-LOWDHAM, Lewis (d. 1835), M.P. Camelford 1819–20 (Foster's *Collect. Geneal.*).

72. ALSTON, Rowland (ca 1679–1759), 4th Bt, M.P. Bedfordshire 1722–41 (GEC).

73. ALSTON, Thomas (ca 1725–74), 5th Bt, M.P. Bedfordshire 1747–61 (GEC; *Alumni Cantab.; Old Westminsters*).

ALTHORP, Vct, *see* SPENCER, George John and John Charles.

ALVANLEY, 1st Bn, *see* ARDEN, Richard Pepper.

74. AMBLER, Charles (1721–94), M.P. Bramber 1769–74, Newton 1775–80, Boroughbridge 1780–84, Saltash 1784–90 (L. Ambler, *Ambler Family*, p. 82).

75. AMCOTTS, Charles (ca 1730–77), M.P. Boston 1754–61, 1766–77 (*Alumni Cantab.;* Maddison's *Lincs Pedigrees;* Thompson's *Boston*, pp. 453, 503).

76. AMCOTTS, Wharton (1740–1807), 1st Bt, M.P. East Retford 1780–90, 1796–1802 (GEC; Maddison's *Lincs Pedigrees*).

77. AMCOTTS-INGILBY, William (1783–1854), 2d Bt, M.P. East Retford 1807–12, Lincolnshire 1823–32, Lincolnshire (part of Lindsey) 1832–34 (GEC; Maddison's *Lincs Pedigrees*).

AMESBURY, Bn, *see* DUNDAS, Charles.

78. AMHERST, William (1732–81), M.P. Hythe 1766–68, Launceston 1768–74 (Burke's *Peerage;* Foster's *Collect. Geneal.*).

79. AMHERST, William Pitt (1805–86), 2d E. Amherst, M.P. East Grinstead 1829–32 (GEC; *Old Westminsters*).

80. AMYAND, Claudius (1718–74), M.P. Tregony 1747–54, Sandwich 1754–56 (*Old Westminsters*).

AMYAND, George, *see* CORNEWALL, George.

81. AMYAND, George (1720–66), 1st Bt, M.P. Barnstable 1754–66 (GEC; *Old Westminsters*).

82. AMYAND, John (1751–80), M.P. Camelford 1774–80 (*Eton Coll. Reg.;* Misc. Geneal. et Herald., N.S., 4).

83. AMYATT, James (1734–1813), M.P. Totnes 1774–80, Southampton borough 1784–1806 (Foster's *Collect. Geneal.*).

ANCASTER, 5th D. of, *see* BERTIE, Brownlow.

ANCRAM, E. of, *see* KERR, John William and William Henry.

84. ANDERSON, Francis Evelyn (1752–1821), M.P. Great Grimsby 1774–80, Beverley 1780–84 (*Eton Coll. Reg.*).

85. ANDERSON, John William (ca 1736–1813), 1st Bt, M.P. London 1793–1806 (GEC; Beaven's *Aldermen of London*).

86. ANDERSON-PELHAM, Charles (1749–1823), 1st Bn Yarborough, M.P. Beverley 1768–74, Lincolnshire 1774–94 (GEC; *Eton Coll. Reg.*).

87. ANDERSON-PELHAM, Charles (1781–1846), 1st E. of Yarborough, M.P. Great Grimsby 1803–7, Lincolnshire 1807–23 (GEC).

88. ANDERSON-PELHAM, Charles Anderson Worsley (1809–62), 2d E. of Yarborough, M.P. Newtown 1830–31, Lincolnshire 1831–32, Lincolnshire (part of Lindsey) 1832–46 (GEC).

89. ANDERSON-PELHAM, George (1785–1835), M.P. Great Grimsby 1806–7, Newtown 1808–20 (Burke's *Peerage* sub Yarborough; Foster's *Collect. Geneal.*).

ANDOVER, Vct, *see* HOWARD, Thomas and William.

90. ANDREWS, Miles Peter (ca 1742–1814), M.P. Bewdley 1796–1814 (DNB; Williams' *Worcester M.P.'s*).

91. ANDREWS, Townshend (1702–37), M.P. Hindon 1727–34, Bossiney 1734–37 (*Alumni Cantab.; Merchant Taylor School Reg.; Calendar Inner Temple Records, 5,* 47).

92. ANGERSTEIN, John Julius (ca 1735–1823), M.P. Camelford 1796–1802 (DNB).

ANGLESEY, 2d M. of, *see* PAGET, Henry.

ANNALY, 1st Bn, *see* WHITE, Henry.

93. ANNESLEY, Arthur (ca 1760–1841), M.P. Oxford City 1790–96 (Burke's *Peerage* sub Valentia; Williams' *Oxford M.P.'s*).

94. ANNESLEY, Francis (1734–1812), M.P. Reading 1774–1806 (*Alumni Cantab.*).

95. ANNESLEY, George (1771–1844), 2d E. of Mountnorris, M.P. Yarmouth (Hants) 1808–10 (GEC; *Rugby Reg.*).

96. ANNESLEY, George Arthur (1793–1841), M.P. Wexford Co. 1830–31 (GEC sub Mountnorris; *Alumni Oxon.*).

97. ANNESLEY, William Richard (1772–1838), 3d E. of Annesley, M.P. Downpatrick 1815–20 (GEC; *Alumni Dublin.*).

98. ANSON, George (1697–1762), 1st Bn Anson, M.P. Hedon 1744–47 (DNB; GEC).

99. ANSON, George (1731–89), M.P. Saltash 1761–68, Lichfield 1770–89 (Burke's *Peerage* sub Lichfield; Wedgwood).

100. ANSON, George (1769–1849), M.P. Lichfield 1806–41 (*Eton Coll. Reg.*).

101. ANSON, George (1797–1857), M.P. Great Yarmouth 1819–34, Stoke 1836–37, South Staffordshire 1837–53 (DNB; *Eton Lists*).

102. ANSON, Thomas (ca 1695–1773), M.P. Lichfield 1747–70 (*Alumni Oxon.;* Wedgwood).

103. ANSON, Thomas (1767–1818), 1st Vct Anson, M.P. Lichfield 1789–1806 (GEC; *Eton Coll. Reg.*).

104. ANSON, Thomas William (1795–1854), 1st E. of Lichfield, M.P. Great Yarmouth 1818–18 (GEC).

ANSTRUTHER, John, *see* CARMICHAEL-ANSTRUTHER, John.

105. ANSTRUTHER, John (ca 1678–1753), 1st Bt, M.P. Anstruther Easter burghs 1708–12, 1713–15, Fifeshire 1715–41 (GEC).

106. ANSTRUTHER, John (1718–99), 2d Bt, M.P. Anstruther Easter burghs 1766–74, 1780–82, 1790–93 (GEC).

107. ANSTRUTHER, John (1753–1811), 1st and 4th Bt, M.P. Anstruther Easter burghs 1783–90, 1796–97, 1806–11, Cockermouth 1790–96 (DNB; GEC).

108. ANSTRUTHER, Philip (ca 1678–1760), M.P. Anstruther Easter burghs 1715–41, 1747–54 (W. Wood, *East Neuk of Fife,* p. 403).

109. ANSTRUTHER, Robert (b. 1757), M.P. Anstruther Easter burghs 1793–94 (Burke's *Peerage; Harrow Reg.; Notes and Queries,* 11th Ser., *4,* 494).

110. ANSTRUTHER-PATERSON, Philip (1752–1808), 4th Bt, M.P. Anstruther Easter burghs 1774–77 (GEC).

ANTONIE, William Lee, see LEE-ANTONIE, William.

111. ANTROBUS, Gibbs Crawford (1793–1861), M.P. Aldborough 1820–26, Plympton Erle 1826–32 (*Alumni Cantab*.).

APSLEY, Bn, see BATHURST, Henry and Henry George.

112. ARBUTHNOT, Charles (1767–1850), M.P. East Looe 1795–96, Eye 1809–12, Orford 1812–18, St. Germans 1818–27, St. Ives 1828–30, Ashburton 1830–31 (DNB; *Old Westminsters*).

113. ARBUTHNOT, Charles George James (ca 1801–70), M.P. Tregony 1831–32 (Boase; *Old Westminsters*).

114. ARBUTHNOTT, Hugh (ca 1780–1868), M.P. Kincardineshire 1826–65 (*Scots Peerage*).

115. ARCEDECKNE, Andrew (ca 1780–1849), M.P. Dunwich 1826–31 (*Alumni Oxon.; Eton Lists; 1832 List; Gent. Mag., 1,* 430).

116. ARCEDECKNE, Chaloner (ca 1743–1809), M.P. Wallingford 1780–84, Westbury 1784–86 (*Eton Coll. Reg.*).

117. ARCHDALL, Mervyn (1763–1839), M.P. Fermanagh 1801–34 (Burke's *Irish LG; Gent. Mag., 2,* 315).

118. ARCHDALL, Richard (ca 1746–1824), M.P. Kilkenny City 1801–2, Dundalk 1802–6 (*Alumni Dublin.; Harrow Reg.;* Glover's *Derbyshire, 2,* 477).

119. ARCHER, Andrew (1736–78), 2d Bn Archer, M.P. Coventry 1761–68 (GEC; *Eton Coll. Reg.*).

120. ARCHER, Henry (1700–68), M.P. Warwick borough 1735–68 (*Eton Coll. Reg.; Notes and Queries,* 9th Ser., *11,* 313).

121. ARCHER, Thomas (1695–1768), 1st Bn Archer, M.P. Warwick borough 1735–41, Bramber 1741–47 (GEC).

122. ARCHER, William (ca 1680–1739), M.P. Berks 1734–39 (Musgrave's *Obituary; Misc. Geneal. et Herald.,* N.S., *1*).

123. ARCHER–HOUBLON, John (1773–1831), M.P. Essex 1810–20 (Burke's *LG; Alumni Felsted.*).

ARDEE, Bn, see BRABAZON, William.

ARDEN, 1st Bn, see PERCEVAL, Charles George.

124. ARDEN, Richard Pepper (1744–1804), 1st Bn Alvanley, M.P. Newtown 1783–84, Aldborough 1784–90, Hastings 1790–94, Bath 1794–1801 (GEC; DNB; *Alumni Cantab*.).

ARGYLL, Dukes of, see CAMPBELL, George, John, and John Douglas Edward Henry.

125. ARKWRIGHT, Richard (1781–1832), M.P. Rye 1813–18, 1826–30 (*Alumni Cantab*.).

126. ARMYTAGE, George (1734–83), 3d Bt, M.P. York City 1761–68 (GEC).

ARMYTAGE, Godfrey Wentworth, see WENTWORTH-ARMYTAGE, Godfrey.

127. ARMYTAGE, John (1732–58), 2d Bt, M.P. York City 1754–58 (GEC; *Alumni Cantab.; Eton Coll. Reg.*).

ARRAN, 3d E. of, *see* GORE, Arthur Saunders.

128. ARSCOTT, Arthur (1683–1763), M. P. Tiverton 1722–47 (*Notes and Queries, 170,* 22; Vivian's *Visitation of Devon,* p. 21).

129. ARSCOTT, John (ca 1718–88), M.P. Ashburton 1741–54 (Vivian's *Visitation of Devon,* p. 21).

130. ARUNDEL, Richard (d. 1758), M.P. Knaresborough 1720–58 (DNB; Boase and Courtney, *Biblio. Cornub.*).

ARUNDELL, *see* MONCKTON-ARUNDELL.

ASH, William Wyndham, *see* WINDHAM, William.

131. ASHBURNHAM, George (1785–1813), M.P. New Romney 1807–12, Weobley 1812–13 (GEC; *Alumni Cantab.*).

132. ASHBURNHAM, Percy (1799–1881), M.P. Berealston 1825–30 (Burke's *Peerage*).

133. ASHBURNHAM, William (ca 1677–1755), 2d Bt, M.P. Hastings 1710–13, 1722–41, Seaford 1715–17 (GEC).

134. ASHBURNHAM, William (1739–1823), 5th Bt, M.P. Hastings 1761–74 (GEC; *Alumni Cantab.*).

ASHBURTON, Bn, *see* DUNNING, John; *also* BARING, Alexander, Francis, and William Bingham.

135. ASHBY, Shukbrugh (1724–92), M.P. Leicester borough 1784–84 (*Alumni Oxon.;* Fletcher's *Leicester Pedigrees*).

136. ASHBY, Thomas (ca 1695–1743), M.P. St. Albans 1734–43 (*Alumni Cantab.*).

137. ASHE, Edward (ca 1674–1748), M.P. Heytesbury 1695–1747 (*Alumni Oxon.;* Musgrave's *Obituary*).

ASHE, Joseph Wyndham, *see* WINDHAM-ASHE, Joseph.

138. ASHE, William (d. 1750), M.P. Heytesbury 1747–50 (Musgrave's *Obituary;* MS, *ex inform.* Hon. H. A. Wyndham).

139. ASHE-A'COURT, Pierce (ca 1707–68), M.P. Heytesbury 1734–68 (GEC).

140. ASHE-A'COURT, William Pierce (ca 1747–1817), 1st Bt, M.P. Heytesbury 1781–90, 1806–7 (GEC; *Eton Coll. Reg.*).

141. ASHURST, William Henry (1778–1846), M.P. Oxfordshire 1815–30 (Burke's *LG;* Williams' *Oxford M.P.'s*).

ASHLEY, Cropley, *see* COOPER, Cropley Ashley.

142. ASHLEY, Solomon (d. 1775), M.P. Bridport 1734–41 (*Genealogist,* 1st Ser., *1*).

143. ASHLEY-COOPER, Anthony (1801–85), 7th E. of Shaftesbury, M.P. Woodstock 1826–30, Dorchester 1830–31, Dorset 1831–46, Bath 1847–51 (GEC; DNB).

144. ASHLEY-COOPER, Anthony Henry (1807–58), M.P. Dorchester 1831–47 (Boase; *Eton Lists*).

145. ASHLEY-COOPER, Anthony John (1808–67), M.P. Gatton 1831–32 (Burke's *Peerage* sub Shaftesbury; *Alumni Oxon.*).

146. ASHLEY-COOPER, Anthony William (1803–77), M.P. Dorchester 1826–30 (Burke's *Peerage* sub Shaftesbury; *Alumni Oxon.*). ASHTOWN, 1st Bn, *see* TRENCH, Frederick.

147. ASSHETON-SMITH, Thomas (ca 1752–1828), M.P. Carnarvonshire 1774–80, Andover 1797–1821 (Williams' *Wales M.P.'s; Eton Coll. Reg.*).

148. ASSHETON-SMITH, Thomas (1776–1858), M.P. Andover 1821–31, Carnarvonshire 1832–37 (DNB; *Eton Coll. Reg.*).

149. ASTELL, William (1774–1847), M.P. Bridgwater 1807–32, Bedfordshire 1841–47 (DNB).

150. ASTLEY, Edward (1729–1802), 4th Bt, M.P. Norfolk 1768–90 (GEC; *Alumni Cantab.*).

151. ASTLEY, Jacob Henry (1756–1817), 5th Bt, M.P. Norfolk 1797–1806, 1807–17 (GEC; *Alumni Cantab.; Old Westminsters; Harrow Reg.*).

152. ASTLEY, John (1687–1772), 2d Bt, M.P. Shrewsbury 1727–34, Salop 1734–72 (GEC).

153. ASTLEY, John Dugdale (1778–1842), 1st Bt, M.P. Wilts 1820–32, North Wilts 1832–34 (Burke's *Peerage; Alumni Oxon.*).

154. ASTON, Thomas (ca 1705–44), 4th Bt, M.P. Liverpool 1729–34, St. Albans 1734–41 (GEC).

155. ASTON, Willoughby (1714–72), 5th Bt, M.P. Nottingham borough 1754–61 (GEC; *Misc. Geneal. et Herald,* 4th Ser., 2).

156. ATHERLEY, Arthur (ca 1772–1844), M.P. Southampton borough 1806–7, 1812–18, 1831–34 (*Alumni Cantab.; Eton Coll. Reg.*).

157. ATHERTON-GWILLYM, Robert Vernon (ca 1741–83), M.P. Newton 1774–80 (Pink; Bean). ATHOLL, 3d D. of, *see* MURRAY, John.

158. ATKINS, John (ca 1760–1838), M.P. Arundel 1802–6, 1826–32, London 1812–18 (Beaven's *Aldermen of London; Gent. Mag., 2,* 663; *1832 List*). ATKINSON, Christopher, *see* SAVILE, Christopher.

159. ATKINSON, Richard (1738–85), M.P. New Romney 1784–85 (Burke's *LG;* Beaven's *Aldermen of London*).

160. ATKYNS-WRIGHT, John (d. 1822), M.P. Oxford City 1802–7, 1812–20 (*Alumni Oxon.;* Williams' *Oxford M.P.'s;* Davenport's *Oxfordshire,* p. 139).

161. ATTERSOLL, John, M.P. Wootton Bassett 1812–13 (*1812 List*).

162. ATTWOOD, Mathias (1779–1851), M.P. Fowey 1819–19, Callington 1820–30, Boroughbridge 1830–32, Whitehaven 1832–47 (Burke's *Family Records; Gent. Mag., 1* [1852], 192; Ferguson; Bean).

163. AUBREY, John (1739–1826), 6th Bt, M.P. Wallingford 1768–74, 1780–84, Aylesbury 1774–80, Bucks 1784–90, Clitheroe 1790–96,

Aldeburgh 1796–1812, Steyning 1812–20, Horsham 1820–26 (GEC; *Old Westminsters*).

164. AUBREY, Thomas (ca 1740–1814), M.P. Wallingford 1784–90 (*Old Westminsters*).

AUCKLAND, 1st Bn and 1st E. of, see EDEN, William and George.

165. AUFRERE, George René (1715–1801), M.P. Stamford 1765–74 (Oliver's *Antigua, 4*, 417; Huguenot Soc. *Proceedings, 9*, 154; Agnew's *Protestant Exiles, 2*, 242).

166. AUSTEN, Robert (1697–1743), 4th Bt, M.P. New Romney 1728–34, 1736–41 (GEC).

AVELAND, 1st Bn, see HEATHCOTE, Gilbert John.

AYLESFORD, Earls of, see FINCH, Heneage.

167. BABINGTON, Thomas (1758–1837), M.P. Leicester borough 1800–18 (*Alumni Cantab.; Rugby Reg.*).

168. BACKWELL, Barnaby (d. 1754), M.P. Bishop's Castle 1754–54 (Lipscomb's *Bucks, 4*, 376).

169. BACKWELL, Richard (ca 1695–1765), M.P. Northampton borough 1755–61 (*Gray's Inn Reg.; Lloyd's Evening Post*, 15–18 Feb. 1765).

170. BACON, Anthony (ca 1717–ca 1786), M.P. Aylesbury 1764–84 (*Jour. of Econ. and Business Hist., 2* [1929], 20–70).

171. BACON, Edmund (1693–1738), 5th Bt, M.P. Thetford 1722–38 (GEC; *Alumni Cantab.*).

172. BACON, Edmund (ca 1680–1755), 6th Bt, M.P. Thetford 1710–13, Norfolk 1713–15, 1728–41 (GEC; *Alumni Cantab.*).

173. BACON, Edward (ca 1713–86), M.P. Lynn 1742–47, Callington 1748–54, Newport 1754–56, Norwich 1756–84 (*Notes and Queries*, 8th Ser., *7*, 53; Foster's *Collect. Geneal., 2*, 29).

174. BACON, Thomas Sclater (ca 1664–1736), M.P. Cambridge borough 1722–36 (*Walpole-Cole Corr.* [Yale ed.], *1*, 19 n.).

175. BACON, Waller (ca 1670–1734), M.P. Norwich 1705–10, 1715–34 (*Alumni Oxon.; East Anglian, 2*, 238; Foster's *Collect. Geneal., 2*, 32).

176. BAGENAL, Walter (ca 1762–1814), M.P. Carlow Co. 1802–12 (P. H. D. Bagenal, *Vicissitudes of an Anglo-Irish Family*, app., p. xiv).

177. BAGOT, Charles (1781–1843), M.P. Castle Rising 1807–8 (DNB; *Alumni Oxon.; Rugby Reg.*).

178. BAGOT, Walter Wagstaffe (1702–68), 5th Bt, M.P. Newcastle-under-Lyme 1724–27, Staffordshire 1727–54, Oxford University 1762–68 (GEC; Williams' *Oxford M.P.'s;* Wedgwood).

179. BAGOT, William (1728–98), 1st Bn Bagot, M.P. Staffordshire 1754–80 (GEC; *Old Westminsters;* Wedgwood).

180. BAGOT-CHESTER, Charles (1770–1838), M.P. Castle Rising 1794–1807 (*Old Westminsters*).

181. BAGWELL, John (ca 1745–1816), M.P. Tipperary 1801–6 (*Cork Archaeol. Jour.* [1895], pp. 41–42; Foster's *Collect. Geneal.*).

182. BAGWELL, John (d. 1806), M.P. Cashel 1801–2 (Foster's *Collect. Geneal.*).

183. BAGWELL, Richard (ca 1778–1826), M.P. Cashel 1801–1 (Foster's *Collect. Geneal.; Alumni Dublin.;* Burke's *LG* [ed. 1849]).

184. BAGWELL, William (ca 1776–1826), M.P. Clonmel 1801–19, Tipperary 1819–26 (*Old Westminsters; Cornwallis Corr., 3,* 180 n.).

185. BAIKIE, Robert (d. 1817), M.P. Orkney and Shetland 1780–81 (Foster's *Scots M.P.'s*).

186. BAILLIE, Evan (ca 1742–1835), M.P. Bristol 1802–12 (Burke's *LG;* Williams' *Gloucester M.P.'s;* Bulloch's *Baillie of Dunain,* p. 37).

187. BAILLIE, George (1763–1841), M.P. Berwickshire 1796–1818 (*Scots Peerage* sub Haddington; *Alumni Cantab.*).

188. BAILLIE, Hugh Duncan (1777–1866), M.P. Rye 1830–31, Honiton 1835–47 (Burke's *LG;* Boase; *1832 List*).

189. BAILLIE, James (ca 1737–93), M.P. Horsham 1792–93 (Burke's *LG;* Albery's *Horsham*).

190. BAILLIE, James Evan (ca 1781–1863), M.P. Tralee 1813–18, Bristol 1830–34 (Burke's *LG;* Williams' *Gloucester M.P.'s;* Boase).

191. BAILLIE, John (1772–1833), M.P. Hedon 1820–30, Inverness burghs 1830–31, 1832–33 (DNB; Hodson's *Bengal Army List*).

192. BAILLIE, Peter (d. 1811), M.P. Inverness burghs 1807–11 (Burke's *LG;* Foster's *Scot's M.P.'s; Gent. Mag., 2,* 292).

193. BAINBRIDGE, Edward Thomas, M.P. Taunton 1830–42 (Dod's *Parl. Companion* [1834], p. 87; query *Gent. Mag., 2* [1858], 540).

194. BAIRD, Robert (d. 1828), M.P. Haddington burghs 1796–1802 (Foster's *Baronetage;* Burke's *Peerage*).

195. BAKER, Edward (ca 1775–1862), M.P. Wilton 1823–30, 1837–41 (*Alumni Cantab.;* Boase; Wiltshire *Notes and Queries, 6,* 573).

196. BAKER, Hercules (ca 1689–1744), M.P. Hythe 1722–44 (DNB sub John Baker; Charnock's *Biog. Naval., 4,* 38; Suckling's *Forgotten Past,* p. 85).

197. BAKER, John (ca 1755–1831), M.P. Canterbury 1796–97, 1802–18 (*Gent. Mag., 1,* 176; *Annual Register,* p. 222).

198. BAKER, Peter William (ca 1756–1815), M.P. Arundel 1781–84, Wootton Bassett 1802–6, Corfe Castle 1807–15 (*Alumni Cantab.; Eton Coll. Reg.*).

199. BAKER, William (1705–70), M.P. Plympton Erle 1747–68 (Burke's *LG;* Beaven's *Aldermen of London*).

200. BAKER, William (1743–1824), M.P. Plympton Erle 1768–74, Aldborough 1777–80, Hertford borough 1780–84, Herts 1790–1802, 1805–7 (*Alumni Cantab.; Eton Coll. Reg.;* Martin's *Masters of the Bench, Inner Temple*).

201. BAKER, William (ca 1772–1858), M.P. Bodmin 1806–7 (*Alumni Oxon.;* Boase; Williams' *Great Sessions in Wales*).

202. BAKER-HOLROYD, John (ca 1735–1821), 1st E. of Sheffield, M.P. Coventry 1780–80, 1781–84, Bristol 1790–1802 (DNB; GEC).

203. BALCH, Robert (1725–79), M.P. Bridgwater 1753–61 (T. W. Balch, *Balch Genealogica,* p. 64).

204. BALDWIN, Charles Barry (ca 1789–1859), M.P. Totnes 1830–32, 1840–52 (Boase).

205. BALDWIN, William (ca 1737–1813), M.P. Malton 1795–98, Westbury 1802–6 (Esdaile's *Temple Church Monuments,* p. 147; *Royal Kalendar* [1796], p. 40 and [1803], p. 64).

206. BALDWYN, Charles (1729–1801), M.P. Salop 1766–80 (Burke's *LG* sub Childe; *Alumni Oxon.;* Shrop. Archaeol. Soc. *Trans.,* 4th Ser., *2,* 380).

207. BALFOUR, James (d. 1845), M.P. Anstruther Easter burghs 1826–31, Haddingtonshire 1831–34 (Burke's *LG; Dod's Parl. Companion* [1834], p. 87).

208. BALFOUR, John (1750–1842), M.P. Orkney and Shetland 1790–96, 1820–26 (Burke's *LG;* Foster's *Scot's M.P.'s*).

209. BALFOUR, Nisbet (ca 1743–1823), M.P. Wigtown burghs 1790–96, Arundel 1797–1802 (DNB).

210. BALFOUR-RAMSAY, Robert (ca 1698–1767), M.P. Edinburghshire 1751–54 (Burke's *LG* sub Balfour).

211. BALLE, Thomas (ca 1671–1749), M.P. Exeter 1734–41 (Devonshire Assoc. *Trans., 62,* 213).

BALTIMORE, 6th Bn, *see* CALVERT, Charles.

212. BAMPFYLDE, Charles Warwick (1753–1823), 5th Bt, M.P. Exeter 1774–90, 1796–1812 (GEC).

213. BAMPFYLDE, John (ca 1691–1750), M.P. Exeter 1715–22, Devon 1736–41 (Burke's *Peerage* sub Poltimore; *Alumni Oxon.*).

214. BAMPFYLDE, Richard Warwick (1722–76), 4th Bt, M.P. Exeter 1743–47, Devon 1747–76 (GEC; *Alumni Oxon.*).

215. BANCE, John (ca 1694–1755), M.P. Westbury 1734–41, 1747–48, Wallingford 1741–47 (Mordaunt's *Obituary; Notes and Queries, 179,* 96; *Misc. Geneal. et Herald.,* 1st Ser., *3,* 211, 215).

216. BANCKS, Jacob (ca 1702–38), M.P. Shaftesbury 1734–38 (Burke's *LG* [ed. 1849]; Musgrave's *Obituary;* Hutchins' *Dorset, 4,* 385, 401).

BANDON, Earls of, *see* BERNARD, Francis and James.

217. BANKES, George (ca 1788–1856), M.P. Corfe Castle 1816–23, 1826–32, Dorset 1841–56 (DNB; *Alumni Cantab.; Old Westminsters*).

218. BANKES, Henry (1700–76), M.P. Corfe Castle 1741–62 (*Alumni Cantab.; Eton Coll. Reg.*).

219. BANKES, Henry (ca 1757–1834), M.P. Corfe Castle 1780–1826, Dorset 1826–31 (DNB; *Alumni Cantab.; Old Westminsters*).

220. BANKES, John (d. 1772), M.P. Corfe Castle 1718–19, 1722–41 (Burke's *LG*).

221. BANKES, William John (ca 1787–1855), M.P. Truro 1810–12, Cambridge Univ. 1822–26, Marlborough 1829–32, Dorset 1832–34 (DNB; *Alumni Cantab.; Old Westminsters*).

222. BANKS, William (ca 1719–61), M.P. Grampound 1741–47 (*Old Westminsters*).

223. BANKS-HODGKINSON, Robert (ca 1722–92), M.P. Wareham 1748–54 (*Alumni Oxon.*).

224. BANNERMAN, John Alexander, M.P. Bletchingley 1807–7 (Dodwell and Miles, *Indian Army Officers;* Philips' *East India Co.*, pp. 335, 341).

225. BARBOR, Robert (d. 1761), M.P. Stamford 1747–61 (Musgrave's *Obituary; Parl. Hist., 15,* 304; W. Salt Archaeol. Soc. *Trans.*, N.S. 6, *2,* 343; *Calendar Inner Temple Records, 4,* 122).

226. BARCLAY, Charles (1780–1855), M.P. Southwark 1815–18, Dundalk 1826–30, West Surrey 1835–37 (Burke's *LG;* Boase; *Gent. Mag., 1,* 189).

227. BARCLAY, David (1784–1861), M.P. Penryn 1826–30, Sunderland 1835–37, 1841–47 (Burke's *LG;* Boase; *Notes and Queries, 179,* 149).

228. BARCLAY, George (ca 1759–1819), M.P. Bridport 1795–1807 (Brayley and Britton, *Surrey, 4,* 467; *1806 List*).

229. BARCLAY, Robert (1732–97), M.P. Kincardineshire 1788–97 (C. W. Barclay, *Barclay Family, 3,* 215).

230. BARCLAY, Robert (1755–1839), 8th Bt, M.P. Newtown 1802–7 (GEC).

BARHAM, Bns, see MIDDLETON, Charles; *also* NOEL, Charles Noel.

231. BARHAM, Charles Henry (ca 1809–78), M.P. Appleby 1832–32 (*Alumni Oxon.;* Ferguson; Parish's *List of Carthusians*).

BARHAM, John Foster and Joseph Foster, see FOSTER-BARHAM, John and Joseph.

232. BARING, Alexander (1774–1848), 1st Bn Ashburton, M.P. Taunton 1806–26, Callington 1826–31, Thetford 1831–32, North Essex 1832–35 (GEC; DNB; *1832 List*).

233. BARING, Francis (1740–1810), 1st Bt, M.P. Grampound 1784–90, Wycombe 1794–96, 1802–6, Calne 1796–1802 (DNB; GEC).

234. BARING, Francis (1800–68), 3d Bn Ashburton, M.P. Thetford 1830–31, 1832–41, 1848–57 (GEC; *Harrow Reg.;* Dod's *Parl. Companion* [1834], p. 87).

235. BARING, Francis Thornhill (1796–1866), 1st Bn Northbrook, M.P. Portsmouth 1826–65 (DNB; GEC).

236. BARING, Henry (1777–1848), M.P. Bossiney 1806–7, Colchester 1820–26 (Burke's *Peerage* sub Northbrook).

237. BARING, Henry Bingham (1804–69), M.P. Callington 1831–32,

Marlborough 1832–68 (Burke's *Peerage* sub Northbrook; *Alumni Oxon.;* Dod's *Parl. Companion* [1834], p. 88).

238. BARING, John (ca 1730–1816), M.P. Exeter 1776–1802 (Burke's *Peerage* sub Northbrook; Devonshire Assoc. *Trans., 62,* 216; *Gent. Mag., 1,* 278).

239. BARING, Thomas (1772–1848), 2d Bt, M.P. Wycombe 1806–32, Hampshire 1832–32 (GEC).

240. BARING, William Bingham (1799–1864), 2d Bn Ashburton, M.P. Thetford 1826–30, 1842–48, Callington 1830–31, Winchester 1832–37, North Staffordshire 1837–41 (GEC; DNB; *Eton Lists; 1832 List*).

241. BARING-WALL, Charles (ca 1795–1853), M.P. Guildford 1819–26, 1830–31, 1832–47, Wareham 1826–30, Weymouth and Melcombe Regis 1831–32, Salisbury 1847–53 (Burke's *Peerage* sub Northbrook; *Alumni Oxon.; 1832 List*).

242. BARKER, Robert (ca 1732–89), 1st Bt, M.P. Wallingford 1774–80 (DNB; Holzman's *Nabobs in Eng.*).

243. BARLOW, Francis William (d. 1805), M.P. Coventry 1802–5 (Whitley's *Coventry M.P.'s*).

244. BARLOW, George (d. ca 1775), 3d Bt, M.P. Haverfordwest 1743–47 (GEC; Williams' *Wales M.P.'s*).

245. BARLOW, Hugh (d. 1763), M.P. Pembroke borough 1747–61 (M. Barlow, *Barlow Family Records,* p. 49; Williams' *Wales M.P.'s*).

246. BARLOW, Hugh (ca 1729–1809), M.P. Pembroke borough 1774–1809 (Williams' *Wales M.P.'s*).

247. BARLOW, Lewis (d. 1737), M.P. Orford 1734–37 (M. Barlow, *Barlow Family Records,* p. 49).

248. BARLOW-HOY, James (d. 1843), M.P. Southhampton borough 1830–31, 1832–33, 1835–37 (*Gent. Mag., 2,* 547).

BARNARD, Vct, *see* VANE, Henry and William Harry.

249. BARNARD, John (ca 1685–1764), M.P. London 1722–61 (DNB; Beaven's *Aldermen of London*).

250. BARNE, Barne (1754–1828), M.P. Dunwich 1777–91 (*Alumni Cantab.; Old Westminsters*).

251. BARNE, Frederick (1801–86), M.P. Dunwich 1830–32 (*Alumni Cantab.; Old Westminsters*).

252. BARNE, Michael (ca 1759–1837), M.P. Dunwich 1812–30 (*Alumni Cantab.; Old Westminsters*).

253. BARNE, Miles (ca 1718–80), M.P. Dunwich 1747–54, 1764–77 (Burke's *LG*).

254. BARNE, Miles (1746–1825), M.P. Dunwich 1791–96 (*Alumni Cantab.*).

255. BARNE, Snowdon (1756–1825), M.P. Dunwich 1796–1812 (*Alumni Cantab.; Old Westminsters*).

256. BARNETT, Charles James (ca 1798–1882), M.P. Maidstone 1831–34

(Boase; Prinsep's *Madras Civilians,* p. 8; Dod's *Parl. Companion* [1834], p. 88).

257. BARNETT, James (ca 1760–1836), M.P. Rochester 1806–7, 1816–20 (*Old Westminsters;* Smith's *Rochester in Parl.*).

258. BARRÉ, Isaac (ca 1726–1802), M.P. Wycombe 1761–74, Calne 1774–90 (DNB; *Alumni Dublin.*).

BARRELS, Vct, *see* KNIGHT, Henry.

BARRETT, Samuel Barrett Moulton, *see* MOULTON-BARRETT, Samuel Barrett.

259. BARRETT, Thomas (ca 1744–1803), M.P. Dover 1773–74 (*Alumni Cantab.*).

260. BARRETT-LENNARD, Thomas (1788–1856), M.P. Ipswich 1820–26, Maldon 1826–37, 1847–52 (Burke's *Peerage; Harl. Soc., 14,* 674).

261. BARRINGTON, John (d. 1776), 7th Bt, M.P. Newtown 1729–34, 1741–75 (GEC).

262. BARRINGTON, John (1752–1818), 9th Bt, M.P. Newtown 1780–96 (GEC; *Alumni Cantab.; Eton Coll. Reg.*).

263. BARRINGTON-SHUTE, William Wildman (1717–93), 2d Vct Barrington, M.P. Berwick-on-Tweed 1740–54, Plymouth 1754–78 (GEC; DNB).

264. BARROW, Charles (1707–89), 1st Bt, M.P. Gloucester City 1751–89 (GEC; Williams' *Gloucester M.P.'s; Genealogist,* N.S., *30,* 75).

265. BARRY, James (ca 1667–1748), 4th E. of Barrymore, M.P. Stockbridge 1710–13, 1714–15, Wigan 1715–27, 1734–47 (GEC).

BARRY, John Maxwell, *see* MAXWELL-BARRY, John.

266. BARRY, Richard (d. 1787), M.P. Wigan 1747–61 (Burke's *Ext. Peerage;* Pink; Bean).

267. BARRY, Richard (1769–93), 7th E. of Barrymore, M.P. Heytesbury 1791–93 (GEC; *Eton Coll. Reg.*).

BARRYMORE, Earls of, *see* BARRY, James and Richard.

268. BARTON, Nathaniel (ca 1764–1828), M.P. Westbury 1820–20 (*Wiltshire Notes and Queries, 7,* 96).

269. BARWELL, Richard (1741–1804), M.P. Helston 1781–84, St. Ives 1784–90, Winchelsea 1790–96 (DNB; *Old Westminsters; Genealogists Mag., 6,* 19).

270. BASSET, Francis (ca 1716–69), M.P. Penryn 1766–69 (Burke's *LG; Alumni Oxon.*).

271. BASSET, Francis (ca 1740–1802), M.P. Barnstable 1780–84 (Burke's *LG; Alumni Oxon.;* Devonshire Assoc. *Trans., 73,* 187).

272. BASSET, Francis (1757–1835), 1st Bn Basset, M.P. Penryn 1780–96 (DNB; GEC; *Alumni Cantab.; Eton Coll. Reg.; Harrow Reg.*).

273. BASSET, John (ca 1715–57), M.P. Barnstable 1740–41 (*Alumni Oxon.;* Devonshire Assoc. *Trans., 73,* 184; Vivian's *Visitation of Devon,* p. 48).

274. BASTARD, Edmund (1758–1816), M.P. Dartmouth 1787–1812 (*Eton Coll. Reg.*).

275. BASTARD, Edmund Pollexfen (1784–1838), M.P. Dartmouth 1812–16, Devon 1816–30 (Burke's *LG; Alumni Oxon.; Eton Lists*).

276. BASTARD, John (ca 1787–1835), M.P. Dartmouth 1816–32 (Burke's *LG; Gent. Mag., 1,* 661).

277. BASTARD, John Pollexfen (ca 1756–1816), M.P. Truro 1783–84, Devon 1784–1816 (DNB; *Eton Coll. Reg.*).

278. BATEMAN, John (1721–1802), 2d Vct Bateman, M.P. Orford 1746–47, Woodstock 1747–68, Leominster 1768–84 (GEC).

279. BATEMAN, William (d. 1783), M.P. Gatton 1752–54 (Lodge and Archdall's *Irish Peerage;* Charnock's *Biog. Naval., 5,* 362).

280. BATEMAN-HANBURY, William (1780–1845), 1st Bn Bateman, M.P. Northampton borough 1810–18 (GEC; *Eton Lists*).

281. BATEMAN-ROBSON, Richard (d. 1827), M.P. Okehampton 1796–1802, 1806–7, Honiton 1806–6, Shaftesbury 1812–13 (Devonshire Assoc. *Trans., 66,* 267; Wright's *Oakhampton,* p. 143).

282. BATESON, Robert (1782–1863), 1st Bt, M.P. Londonderry Co. 1830–42 (*Alumni Cantab.*).

BATH, 1st E. of, *see* PULTENEY, William.

BATH, M. of, see THYNNE, Henry Frederick and Thomas.

283. BATHURST, Benjamin (ca 1693–1767), M.P. Cirencester 1713–27, Gloucester City 1727–54, Monmouth borough 1754–67 (*Eton Coll. Reg.;* Williams' *Wales M.P.'s*).

284. BATHURST, Benjamin (1711–67), M.P. Gloucestershire 1734–41, Cirencester 1754–61 (GEC; Williams' *Oxford M.P.'s*).

BATHURST, Charles Bragge, *see* BRAGGE-BATHURST, Charles.

285. BATHURST, Henry (1714–94), 1st Bn Apsley and 2d E. Bathurst, M.P. Cirencester 1735–54 (GEC; DNB; *Eton Coll. Reg.*):

286. BATHURST, Henry (1762–1834), 3d E. Bathurst, M.P. Cirencester 1783–94 (GEC; DNB; *Eton Coll. Reg.*).

287. BATHURST, Henry George (1790–1866), 4th E. Bathurst, M.P. Weobley 1812–12, Cirencester 1812–34 (GEC; *Eton Lists;* Addison's *Glasgow Matric. Albums*).

288. BATHURST, Peter (1687–1748), M.P. Wilton 1711–13, Cirencester 1727–34, Salisbury 1734–41 (*Eton Coll. Reg.;* Williams' *Gloucester M.P.'s*).

289. BATHURST, Peter (ca 1724–1801), M.P. Eye 1784–90, 1792–95 (*Alumni Oxon.;* Collins' *Peerage*).

290. BATHURST, Seymour Thomas (1793–1834), M.P. St. Germans 1818–26 (Burke's *Peerage;* Collins' *Peerage*).

291. BATHURST, William Lennox (1791–1878), 5th E. Bathurst, M.P. Weobley 1812–16 (GEC; *Eton Lists;* Addison's *Glasgow Matric. Albums*).

BATLEY, Charles Harrison, *see* HARRISON-BATLEY, *Charles.*

292. BATTIE-WRIGHTSON, William (1789–1879), M.P. East Retford 1826–27, Hull 1830–32, Northallerton 1835–65 (Burke's *LG;* Ball and Venn's *Admissions to Trinity College; Genealogist,* N.S., *14,* 47; Bean; Hardwicke's *House of Commons* [1858], p. 156).

BAYHAM, Vct, *see* PRATT, John Jeffries.

293. BAYLY, Nathaniel (ca 1726–98), M.P. Abingdon 1770–74, Westbury 1774–79 (Oliver's *Antigua, 1,* 235; *Notes and Queries, 192,* 16).

294. BAYLY, Nicholas (ca 1709–82), 2d Bt, M.P. Anglesey 1734–41, 1747–61, 1770–74 (GEC; Williams' *Wales M.P.'s*).

295. BAYLY, Nicholas (ca 1749–1814), M.P. Anglesey 1784–90 (Williams' *Wales M.P.'s*).

296. BAYLY–WALLIS, Lewis (ca 1775–1848), M.P. Ilchester 1799–1802 (*Notes and Queries,* 12th Ser., *3,* 74, 155; *Gent. Mag., 2,* 445).

297. BAYNES-GARFORTH, John (ca 1722–1808), M.P. Cockermouth 1780–84, 1790–1802, Haslemere 1784–90 (*Gent. Mag., 2,* 1040; Whitaker's *Craven,* p. 215; Bean; Ferguson).

BAYNING, Bns, *see* POWLETT-TOWNSHEND, Charles; *also* TOWNSHEND, Charles Frederick Powlett.

298. BAYNTUN, Samuel Adlam (1804–33), M.P. York City 1830–33 (*Old Westminsters*).

299. BAYNTUN-ROLT, Andrew (ca 1745–1816), 2d Bt, M.P. Weobley 1780–86 (GEC; Williams' *Hereford M.P.'s*).

300. BAYNTUN-ROLT, Edward (ca 1710–1800), 1st Bt, M.P. Chippenham 1737–80 (GEC; Clutterbuck's *Herts, 2,* 427; *Annual Register,* p. 56).

BEACH, Michael Hicks, *see* HICKS-BEACH, Michael.

301. BEACH, William (1783–1856), M.P. Malmesbury 1812–17 (Burke's *LG; Alumni Oxon.*).

302. BEAGHAN, Edmund Hungate (1703–55), M.P. Winchelsea 1734–41, Weymouth and Melcombe Regis 1747–54 (Carthew's *East and West Bradenham,* pp. 108, 119; *Calendar Inner Temple Records, 4,* 87).

303. BEAKE, Gregory (d. 1749), M.P. St. Ives 1741–47 (Musgrave's *Obituary*).

304. BEARCROFT, Edward (ca 1737–96), M.P. Hindon 1784–90, Saltash 1790–96 (*Alumni Cantab.;* Williams' *Worcester M.P.'s*).

BEAUCHAMP, Vct, *see* INGRAM-SEYMOUR-CONWAY, Francis; *also* SEYMOUR-CONWAY, Richard.

BEAUCHAMP, Earls, *see* LYGON, Henry Beauchamp, William and William Beauchamp.

305. BEAUCHAMP-PROCTOR, William (1722–73), 1st Bt, M.P. Middlesex 1747–68 (GEC).

306. BEAUCLERK, Aubrey (1740–1802), 5th D. of St. Albans, M.P. Thetford 1761–68, Aldborough 1768–74 (GEC; *Old Westminsters*).

307. BEAUCLERK, Aubrey (1765–1815), 6th D. of St. Albans, M.P. Hull 1790–96 (GEC).

308. BEAUCLERK, Charles George (1774–1846), M.P. Richmond 1796–98 (Burke's *Peerage* sub St. Albans; *Alumni Oxon.; Etoniana, 94*, 694).

309. BEAUCLERK, George (1704–68), M.P. Windsor 1744–54, 1768–68 (Burke's *Peerage* sub St. Albans; *Notes and Queries*, 12th Ser., *3*, 11).

310. BEAUCLERK, Henry (1701–61), M.P. Plymouth 1740–41, Thetford 1741–61 (Burke's *Peerage* sub St. Albans; *Notes and Queries*, 12th Ser., *3*, 11).

311. BEAUCLERK, Sidney (1703–44), M.P. Windsor 1733–44 (*Eton Coll. Reg.*).

312. BEAUCLERK, Vere (1699–1781), 1st Bn Vere, M.P. Windsor 1726–41, Plymouth 1741–50 (GEC).
BEAUFORT, Dukes of, *see* SOMERSET, Charles Noel, Henry, and Henry Charles.

313. BEAUFOY, Henry (ca 1751–95), M.P. Minehead 1783–84, Great Yarmouth 1784–95 (DNB; Faulkner's *Brentford*, p. 190).
BEAULIEU, 1st E., *see* HUSSEY-MONTAGU, Edward.

314. BEAUMONT, George (ca 1665–1737), 4th Bt, M.P. Leicester borough 1702–37 (GEC; Kirby's *Winchester Scholars*, p. 201).

315. BEAUMONT, George Howland (1753–1827), 7th Bt, M.P. Berealston 1790–96 (DNB; GEC; *Eton Coll. Reg.*).

316. BEAUMONT, Thomas Richard (1758–1829), M.P. Northumberland 1795–1818 (*Alumni Oxon.;* Burke's *LG* [ed. 1849]; Hunter's *Deanery of Doncaster, 2*, 249).

317. BEAUMONT, Thomas Wentworth (1792–1848), M.P. Northumberland 1818–26, 1830–32, Stafford borough 1826–30, South Northumberland 1832–37 (DNB; *Alumni Cantab.; Eton Lists; 1832 List*).
BECHER, William Wrixon, *see* WRIXON-BECHER, William.

318. BECKETT, John (1775-1847), 2d Bt, M.P. Cockermouth 1818–21, Haslemere 1826–32, Leeds 1835–37 (*Alumni Cantab.;* Foster's *Baronetage;* Martin's *Masters of the Bench, Inner Temple*).

319. BECKFORD, Julines (ca 1718–64), M.P. Salisbury 1754–64 (*Old Westminsters*).

320. BECKFORD, Peter (ca 1740–1811), M.P. Morpeth 1768–74 (DNB; *Old Westminsters*).

321. BECKFORD, Richard (ca 1712–56), M.P. Bristol 1754–56 (*Old Westminsters;* Williams' *Gloucester M.P.'s;* Beaven's *Aldermen of London*).

322. BECKFORD, Richard (d. 1796), M.P. Bridport 1780–84, Arundel

1784–90, Leominster 1791–96 (Williams' *Hereford M.P.'s; Notes and Queries,* 8th Ser., *9,* 193).

323. BECKFORD, William (1709–70), M.P. Shaftesbury 1747–54, London 1754–70 (DNB; *Old Westminsters;* Beaven's *Aldermen of London*).

324. BECKFORD, William (1759–1844), M.P. Wells 1784–90, Hindon 1790–94, 1806–20 (DNB).

BECTIVE, Bn, *see* TAYLOUR, Thomas.

BEDFORD, 7th D. of, *see* RUSSELL, Francis.

325. BELAYSE, Henry (1743–1802), 2d E. Fauconberg, M.P. Peterborough 1768–74 (GEC; *Eton Coll. Reg.*).

326. BELCHIER, William (d. 1772), M.P. Southwark 1747–61 (Musgrave's *Obituary*).

BELFAST, E. of, *see* CHICHESTER, George Hamilton.

BELGRAVE, Vct, *see* GROSVENOR, Richard and Robert.

327. BELL, Matthew (1793–1871), M.P. Northumberland 1826–31, South Northumberland 1832–52 (Burke's *LG; Alumni Oxon.;* Welford's *Men of Mark*).

328. BELLAS-GREENOUGH, George (1778–1855), M.P. Gatton 1807–12 (DNB; *Eton Coll. Reg.*).

329. BELLEW, Patrick (1798–1866), 1st Bn Bellew, M.P. Louth 1831–32, 1834–37 (GEC).

330. BELLINGHAM, William (ca 1755–1826), 1st Bt, M.P. Reigate 1784–89 (GEC; *Alumni Dublin.*).

BELMORE, Earls, *see* CORRY, Armar Lowry; *also* LOWRY-CORRY, Somerset.

BELPER, 1st Bn, *see* STRUTT, Edward.

BELSHES-WISHART, John, *see* STUART, John.

331. BENFIELD, Paul (ca 1740–1810), M.P. Cricklade 1780–84, Malmesbury 1790–92, Shaftesbury 1793–1802 (DNB; Holzman's *Nabobs in Eng.*).

332. BENN-WALSH, John (1759–1825), 1st Bt, M.P. Bletchingley 1802–6 (Burke's *Peerage* sub Ormathwaite).

333. BENNET, Charles (1716–67), 3d E. of Tankerville, M.P. Northumberland 1748–49 (GEC).

334. BENNET, Charles Augustus (1776–1859), 5th E. of Tankerville, M.P. Steyning 1803–6, Knaresborough 1806–18, Berwick-on-Tweed 1820–22 (GEC; *Eton Coll. Reg.*).

335. BENNET, Henry Grey (1777–1836), M.P. Shrewsbury 1806–7, 1811–26 (*Alumni Cantab.; Eton Coll. Reg.*).

336. BENNET, Philip, M.P. Shaftesbury 1734–35, 1738–41, Bath 1741–47.

337. BENNET, Richard Henry Alexander (ca 1744–1814), M.P. Newport 1770–74 (*Notes and Queries,* 11th Ser., *1,* 370).

338. BENNET, Richard Henry Alexander (ca 1771–1818), M.P. Laun-

ceston 1802–6, 1807–12, Enniskillen 1807–7 (*Notes and Queries,* 11th Ser., *1,* 370).

339. BENNETT, John (1773–1852), M.P. Wilts 1819–32, South Wilts 1832–52 (Burke's *LG;* Boase; *Eton Lists*).

340. BENNETT, Thomas (d. 1738), M.P. Notts 1732–38 (Musgrave's *Obituary*).

341. BENSON, Ralph (ca 1773–1845), M.P. Stafford borough 1812–18, 1826–30 (Burke's *LG;* Wedgwood; Pink; Bean).

342. BENSON, Thomas (1708–72), M.P. Barnstable 1747–54 (Devonshire Assoc. *Trans., 73,* 185).

343. BENT, John, M.P. Sligo borough 1818–20, Totnes 1820–26.

344. BENT, Robert, M.P. Aylesbury 1802–4.

BENTINCK, *see* CAVENDISH-BENTINCK.

345. BENTINCK, George (1715–59), M.P. Droitwich 1742–47, Grampound 1747–54, Malmesbury 1754–59 (Williams' *Worcester M.P.'s;* Burke's *Peerage* sub Portland).

346. BETINCK, John Albert (ca 1737–75), M.P. Rye 1761–68 (DNB).

347. BENYON, Benjamin (ca 1765–1834), M.P. Stafford borough 1818–26 (Wedgwood).

348. BENYON, Richard (1746–96), M.P. Peterborough 1774–96 (*Eton Coll. Reg.; Admissions to St. John, Cambridge*).

BENYON, Richard, *see* DE BEAUVOIR, Richard Benyon.

349. BERESFORD, George Thomas (1781–1839), M.P. Londonderry City 1802–12, Coleraine 1812–14, Waterford Co. 1814–26, 1830–31 (*Eton Coll. Reg.*).

350. BERESFORD, John (1738–1805), M.P. Waterford Co. 1801–5 (DNB; *Alumni Dublin.*).

351. BERESFORD, John Claudius (1766–1846), M.P. Dublin City 1801–4, Waterford Co. 1806–11 (*Alumni Dublin.; Genealogical Mag., 2,* 110).

352. BERESFORD, John Poo (ca 1766–1844), 1st Bt, M.P. Coleraine 1809–12, 1814–23, 1832–33, Berwick-on-Tweed 1823–26, Northallerton 1826–32, Chatham 1835–37 (DNB; Foster's *Baronetage*).

353. BERESFORD, Marcus (1800–76), M.P. Northallerton 1824–26, Berwick-on-Tweed 1826–32 (*Alumni Dublin.;* Burke's *Peerage* sub Decies).

354. BERESFORD, William Carr (1768–1854), 1st Vct Beresford, M.P. Waterford Co. 1811–14 (DNB; GEC).

355. BERKELEY, George (1692–1746), M.P. Dover 1720–34, Hedon 1734–41, 1742–46 (DNB; *Alumni Cantab.; Old Westminsters*).

356. BERKELEY, George Cranfield (1753–1818), M.P. Gloucestershire 1783–1810 (DNB; *Eton Coll. Reg.;* Williams' *Gloucester M.P.'s*).

357. BERKELEY, John (ca 1697–1773), 5th Bn Berkeley, M.P. Stockbridge 1735–41 (GEC).

358. BERKELEY, Maurice Frederick Fitzhardinge (1788–1867), 1st Bn
Fitzhardinge, M.P. Gloucester City 1831–33, 1835–37, 1841–57
(DNB; GEC).

359. BERKELEY, Norborne (ca 1717–70), 4th Bn Botetourt, M.P. Gloucestershire 1741–63 (GEC; *Old Westminsters; Dict. Am. Biog.*)

360. BERKELEY, Rowland (ca 1733–1805), M.P. Droitwich 1774–74
(Burke's *LG;* Williams' *Worcester M.P.'s; Alumni Oxon.*).

361. BERKELEY, William Fitzhardinge (1786–1857), 1st E. Fitzhardinge,
M.P. Gloucestershire 1810–10 (GEC).

362. BERKELEY-PORTMAN, Henry William (ca 1709–61), M.P. Taunton
1734–41, Somerset 1741–47 (Burke's *Peerage;* Bates Harbin;
Hutchins' *Dorset, 1,* 256).

363. BERNAL, Ralph (ca 1785–1854), M.P. Lincoln City 1818–20, Rochester 1820–41, 1847–52, Weymouth and Melcombe Regis 1842–47
(DNB; *Alumni Cantab.*).

364. BERNARD, Francis (1810–77), 3d E. of Bandon, M.P. Bandon
1831–31, 1842–56 (GEC).

365. BERNARD, James (1785–1856), 2d E. of Bandon, M.P. Youghal
1806–7, 1818–20, Cork Co. 1807–18, Bandon 1820–26, 1830–30
(*Alumni Cantab.;* GEC).

366. BERNARD, Richard Boyle (1787–1850), M.P. Bandon 1812–15
(*Alumni Cantab.;* Burke's *Peerage* sub Bandon; *Linc. Inn Reg.*).

367. BERNARD, Robert (ca 1740–89), 5th Bt, M.P. Hunts 1765–68,
Westminster 1770–74 (GEC; *Old Westminsters*).

368. BERNARD, Thomas (ca 1769–1834), M.P. Kings 1802–32 (Burke's
Irish LG).

369. BERNARD-MORLAND, Scrope (1758–1830), 4th Bt, M.P. Aylesbury
1789–1802, St. Mawes 1806–8, 1809–30 (GEC).

370. BERTIE, Albemarle (ca 1669–1742), M.P. Lincolnshire 1705–8,
Cockermouth 1708–10, Boston 1734–41 (Burke's *Peerage* sub
Lindsey; *Alumni Oxon.*).

371. BERTIE, Albemarle (1744–1818), 9th E. of Lindsey, M.P. Stamford 1801–9 (GEC).

372. BERTIE, Brownlow (1729–1809), 5th D. of Ancaster, M.P. Lincolnshire 1761–79 (GEC; *Old Westminsters*).

373. BERTIE, Montagu (1808–84), 6th E. of Abingdon, M.P. Oxfordshire 1830–52, Abingdon 1852–54 (*Alumni Cantab.;* GEC).

374. BERTIE, Norreys (ca 1718–66), M.P. Oxfordshire 1743–54 (Williams' *Oxford M.P.'s*).

375. BERTIE, Peregrine (ca 1723–86), M.P. Westbury 1753–74 (*Alumni
Oxon.;* Maddison's *Lincs Pedigrees*).

376. BERTIE, Peregrine (1741–90), M.P. Oxford City 1774–90 (Charnock's *Biog. Naval., 6,* 515; *Old Westminsters;* Williams' *Oxford
M.P.'s*).

377. BERTIE, Robert (1721–82), M.P. Whitchurch 1751–54, Boston 1754–

82 (Collins' *Peerage* sub Ancaster; *Notes and Queries;* 12th Ser., *3*, 305).

378. BERTIE, Vere (ca 1712–68), M.P. Boston 1741–54 (Lipscomb's *Bucks, 1,* 236; *Old Westminsters*).

BERWICK, Bns, *see* HILL, Noel; *also* NOEL-HILL, William.

BESSBOROUGH, Earls of, *see* PONSONBY, Frederick, John George Brabazon, John William, and William.

379. BEST, George (ca 1760–1818), M.P. Rochester 1790–96 (Berry's *County Geneal.: Kent,* p. 383; *Eton Coll. Reg.;* Smith's *Rochester in Parl.*).

380. BEST, Thomas (ca 1713–95), M.P. Canterbury 1741–54, 1761–68 (*Alumni Oxon.;* Burke's *LG*).

381. BEST, William Draper (1767–1845), 1st Bn Wynford, M.P. Petersfield 1802–6, Bridport 1812–17, Guildford 1818–18 (DNB; GEC).

382. BEST, William Samuel (1798–1869), 2d Bn Wynford, M.P. St. Michael 1831–32 (*Eton Lists; GEC*).

BETHELL, Christopher Codrington, *see* CODRINGTON-BETHELL, Christopher.

383. BETHELL, Hugh (1727–72), M.P. Beverley 1768–72 (*Alumni Cantab.;* Foster's *Yorkshire Pedigrees*).

384. BETHELL, Richard (1772–1864), M.P. Yorkshire 1830–31, Yorkshire (East Riding) 1832–41 (*Alumni Cantab.; Eton Coll. Reg.;* Gooder).

385. BETHELL, Slingsby (d. 1758), M.P. London 1747–58 (Beaven's *Aldermen of London;* Oliver's *Antigua, 1,* 42, 44).

386. BETTESWORTH-TREVANION, John Trevanion Purnell (ca 1780–1840), M.P. Penryn 1807–7 (Boase and Courtney, *Biblio Cornub.;* Burke's *LG* [ed. 1849]; *Eton Lists*).

387. BEVAN, Arthur (ca 1688–1743), M.P. Carmarthen 1727–41 (*Alumni Oxon.;* Musgrave's *Obituary;* Williams' *Wales M.P.'s*).

BEVERLEY, Earls of, *see* PERCY, Algernon and George.

388. BEWICKE, Calverley (ca 1755–1815), M.P. Winchelsea 1806–15 (*Alumni Oxon.;* Burke's *LG*).

BEXLEY, 1st Bn, *see* VANSITTART, Nicholas.

389. BICKERTON, Richard (1727–92), 1st Bt, M.P. Rochester 1790–92 (DNB; GEC).

BICKERTON, Richard Hussey, *see* HUSSEY-BICKERTON, Richard.

BIDDULPH, Robert Myddleton, *see* MYDDLETON-BIDDULPH, Robert.

390. BILSON-LEGGE, Henry (1708–64), M.P. East Looe 1740–41, Orford 1741–59, Hampshire 1759–64 (DNB; GEC).

391. BINDLEY, John (d. 1786), M.P. Dover 1766–68 (Musgrave's *Obituary*).

392. BINGHAM, Charles (1735–99), 1st E. of Lucan, M.P. Northampton borough 1782–84 (GEC).

393. BINGHAM, George Charles (1800–88), 3d E. of Lucan, M.P. Mayo 1826–30 (DNB; GEC; *Old Westminsters*).

394. BINGHAM, Richard (1764–1839), 2d E. of Lucan, M.P. St. Albans 1790–1800 (GEC; *Old Westminsters*).

BINGLEY, 1st Bn, *see* Fox-LANE, George.

BINNING, Bn, *see* HAMILTON, Thomas.

395. BIRCH, John (d. 1735), M.P. Weobley 1691–91, 1701–2, 1705–35 (Booker's *Chapel of Birch,* p. 120; Williams' *Great Sessions in Wales*).

396. BIRCH, Joseph (1755–1833), 1st Bt, M.P. Nottingham borough 1802–3, 1818–30, Ludgershall 1812–18 (Bean; Foster's *Baronetage;* Pink).

397. BIRD, John, M.P. Coventry 1734–37.

398. BIRD, William Wilberforce (ca 1759–1836), M.P. Coventry 1796–1802 (*Gent. Mag., 2,* 222, 433; *Genealogists Mag., 6,* 20; Whitley's *Coventry M.P.'s*).

399. BISSE, Stephen (ca 1672–1741), M.P. New Romney 1734–41 (*Geneal. Queries and Memoranda, 1,* 17; *Misc. Geneal. et Herald.,* 2d Ser., *1,* 344, and *2,* 127; Prinsep's *Madras Civilians,* p. x).

400. BISSHOPP, Cecil (d. 1778), 6th Bt, M.P. Penryn 1727–34, Boroughbridge 1755–68 (GEC).

401. BISSHOPP, Cecil (1753–1828), 12th Bn Zouche, M.P. Shoreham 1780–90, 1796–1806 (GEC).

402. BISSHOPP, Cecil (ca 1783–1813), M.P. Newport (Hants) 1811–12 (*Eton Lists;* GEC).

403. BLACHFORD, Barrington Pope (d. 1816), M.P. Newtown 1807–16 (*Eton Lists; Gent. Mag. 1,* 478, 568; *1812 List*).

404. BLACKBURN, John (d. 1824), M.P. Aldborough 1797–1802, Newport (Hants) 1802–6 (*Harrow Reg.; 1806 List*).

405. BLACKBURNE, John (1754–1833), M.P. Lancashire 1784–1830 (*Alumni Oxon.;* Bean; Burke's *LG; Harrow Reg.;* Pink).

BLACKBURNE, John Ireland, *see* IRELAND-BLACKBURNE, John.

406. BLACKETT, Christopher (1787–1847), M.P. Berealston 1830–31, South Northumberland 1837–41 (Burke's *LG; New Hist. of Northumberland, 12,* 232; Bean).

407. BLACKETT, Edward (1719–1804), 4th Bt, M.P. Northumberland 1768–74 (*Archaeol. Aeliana,* 4th Ser., *23;* GEC; *Linc. Inn Reg.*).

BLACKETT, Walter Calverley, *see* CALVERLEY-BLACKETT, Walter.

408. BLACKNEY, Walter (d. 1842), M.P. Carlow Co. 1831–34 (*Gent. Mag., 1* [1843], 91).

409. BLACKSTONE, William (1723–80), M.P. Hindon 1761–68, Westbury 1768–70 (*Alumni Carthusiani;* DNB).

410. BLACKWELL, Samuel (d. 1785), M.P. Cirencester 1774–85 (Williams' *Gloucester M.P.'s*).

411. BLACKWOOD, James Stevenson (1755–1836), 2d Bn Dufferin, M.P. Helston 1807–12, Aldeburgh 1812–18 (GEC).

412. BLADEN, Martin (ca 1680–1746), M.P. Stockbridge 1715–34, Maldon 1734–41, Portsmouth 1741–46 (*Alumni Cantab.;* DNB; *Old Westminsters*).

413. BLADEN, Thomas (ca 1698–1780), M.P. Steyning 1727–34, Ashburton 1735–41 (*Old Westminsters*).

414. BLAGRAVE, John (b. ca 1713), M.P. Reading 1739–47 (*Alumni Oxon.;* Beatson's *Chron. Reg., ex inform* John Bean King).

BLAIR, James Hunter, *see* HUNTER-BLAIR, James.

415. BLAIR, James (d. 1841), M.P. Saltash 1818–20, Aldeburgh 1820–26, Minehead 1826–30, Wigtownshire 1837–41 (Burke's *Peerage* sub Courtoun; Foster's *Scots M.P.'s;* Ragatz, *Fall of the Planter Class,* p. 52).

416. BLAIR, William (d. 1841), M.P. Ayrshire 1829–32 (Burke's *LG;* Foster's *Scots M.P.'s*).

417. BLAKE, Francis (1774–1860), 3d Bt, M.P. Berwick-on Tweed 1820–26, 1827–34 (*Alumni Cantab.;* Dod's *Parl. Companion* [1834], p. 92; GEC; *Old Westminsters*).

418. BLAKE, Patrick (ca 1742–84), 1st Bt, M.P. Sudbury 1768–74, 1775–84 (*Alumni Cantab. Eton Coll. Reg.;* GEC; Oliver's *Antigua, 1,* 54).

419. BLAKE, Robert (d. 1823), M.P. Arundel 1819–23 (*Gent. Mag., 1,* 475; *Royal Kalendar* [1821], p. 49).

420. BLAKE, Valentine John (1780–1847), 12th Bt, M.P. Galway town 1813–20, 1841–47 (*Alumni Dublin.;* GEC).

421. BLAKE, William, M.P. Chippenham 1807–8.

422. BLAKE-DELAVAL, Francis (1727–71), M.P. Hindon 1751–54, Andover 1754–68 (*Old Westminsters*).

423. BLAMIRE, William (1790–1862), M.P. Cumberland 1831–32, East Cumberland 1832–36 (DNB; *Old Westminsters*).

424. BLAND, John (1722–55), 6th Bt, M.P. Ludgershall 1754–55 (GEC; *Genealogist,* N.S., *18,* 259; *Old Westminsters*).

BLANDFORD, M. of, *see* SPENCER, George; *also* SPENCER-CHURCHILL, George.

BLAQUIERE, John, *see* DE BLAQUIERE, John.

425. BLAYNEY, Andrew Thomas (1770–1834), 11th Bn Blayney, M.P. Old Sarum 1806–7 (DNB; GEC).

426. BLAYNEY, Cadwallader Davis (1802–74), 12th Bn Blayney, M.P. Monaghan 1830–34 (*Eton Lists;* GEC).

427. BLIGH, Edward (1795–1835), 5th E. of Darnley, M.P. Canterbury 1818–30 (GEC).

428. BLIGH, John (1719–81), 3d E. of Darnley, M.P. Maidstone 1741–47 (GEC; *Old Westminsters*).

429. BLIGH, Thomas Cherburgh (ca 1761–1830), M.P. Meath 1802–12 (*Alumni Cantab.;* Burke's *Irish LG*).

BLONDEAU, William Nevill, *see* HART, William Nevill.

430. BLOOMFIELD, Benjamin (1762–1846), 1st Bn Bloomfield, M.P. Plymouth 1812–17 (DNB; GEC).

431. BLOUNT, Edward (1769–1843), M.P. Steyning 1830–32 (Burke's *Peerage;* Foster's *Baronetage*).

432. BLOXHAM, Matthew (ca 1744–1822), M.P. Maidstone 1788–1806 (Beaven's *Aldermen of London; Gent. Mag., 2*, 374; *1806 List*).

433. BLUDWORTH, Thomas, M.P. Bodmin 1741–47.

434. BLUNDEN, Overington (1767–1837), M.P. Kilkenny City 1812–14 (Burke's *Peerage;* Burtchaell's *Kilkenny M.P.'s*).

435. BLUNT, Charles Richard (1775–1840), 4th Bt, M.P. Lewes 1831–40 (GEC).

436. BOCLAND, Maurice (ca 1695–1765), M.P. Yarmouth (Hants) 1733–34, 1741–47, Lymington 1734–41, Newtown 1747–54 (*Misc. Geneal. et Herald.,* 2d Ser., *1; Notes and Queries,* 12th Ser., *3,* 191).

437. BODDINGTON, Samuel (ca 1767–1843), M.P. Tralee 1807–7 (*Gent. Mag., 1,* 665).

438. BODKIN, John James (ca 1801–82), M.P. Galway town 1831–32, Galway Co. 1835–47 (Boase).

439. BODVELL, William (ca 1689–1759), M.P. Carnarvonshire 1741–54, Montgomery 1754–59 (Williams' *Wales M.P.'s*).

440. BOLD, Peter (ca 1706–62), M.P. Wigan 1727–34, Lancashire 1736–41, 1750–61 (*Alumni Oxon.;* Bean; Pink).

BOLD, Peter Patten, *see* PATTEN-BOLD, Peter.

441. BOLDERO, Henry George (ca 1797–1873), M.P. Chippenham 1831–32, 1835–59 (Boase).

BOLINGBROKE, 3d Vct, *see* ST. JOHN, George Richard.

442. BOLLAND, John (ca 1742–1829), M.P. Bletchingley 1814–18 (*Gent. Mag., 1,* 572).

BOLTON, Bns, *see* ORDE, Thomas; *also* ORDE-POWLETT, William.

BOLTON, Dukes of, *see* POWLETT, Charles and Harry.

443. BOND, John (1678–1744), M.P. Corfe Castle 1721–22, 1727–44 (Burke's *LG;* Hutchins' *Dorset, 1,* 463).

444. BOND, John (1717–84), M.P. Corfe Castle 1747–61, 1764–80 (*Alumni Oxon.;* Burke's *LG;* Hutchins' *Dorset, 1,* 463).

445. BOND, John (1753–1824), M.P. Corfe Castle 1780–1801 (*Alumni Cantab.*).

446. BOND, John (1802–44), M.P. Corfe Castle 1823–28 (*Alumni Oxon.;* Burke's *LG;* Hutchins' *Dorset, 1,* 463).

447. BOND, Nathaniel (1754–1823), M.P. Corfe Castle 1801–7 (*Alumni Cantab.*).

448. BOND-HOPKINS, Benjamin (ca 1746–94), M.P. Ilchester 1784–90,

Malmesbury 1790–94 (*Gent. Mag.*, p. 183; Manning and Bray's *Surrey, 3,* 278–79).

449. BONHAM, Francis Robert (b. ca 1786), M.P. Rye 1830–31, Harwich 1835–37 (*Alumni Oxon.*).

450. BONHAM, Henry (d. 1830), M.P. Leominster 1806–12, Sandwich 1824–26, Rye 1826–30 (Williams' *Hereford M.P.'s*).

451. BONHAM-CARTER, John (ca 1788–1838), M.P. Portsmouth 1816–38 (*Alumni Cantab.;* Burke's *LG;* *Linc. Inn Reg.*).

BONTINE, William Cunningham, *see* CUNNINGHAM-GRAHAM-BONTINE, William.

452. BOONE, Charles (ca 1730–1819), M.P. Castle Rising 1757–68, 1784–96, Ashburton 1768–84 (*Alumni Cantab.; Eton Coll. Reg.; Royal Kalendar* [1769], p. 23).

453. BOONE, Daniel (ca 1710–70), M.P. Ludgershall 1734–41, Grampound 1741–47, Stockbridge 1747–54, Minehead 1754–61 (*Alumni Cantab.; Eton Coll. Reg.; Misc. Geneal. et Herald.*, 2d Ser., *4*).

BOOTLE, Richard Wilbraham, *see* WILBRAHAM-BOOTLE, Richard.

454. BOOTLE, Thomas (ca 1685–1753), M.P. Liverpool 1724–34, Midhurst 1734–53 (Bean; Martin's *Masters of the Bench, Inner Temple;* Pink).

455. BOOTLE-WILBRAHAM, Edward (1771–1853), 1st Bn Skelmersdale, M.P. Westbury 1795–96, Newcastle-under-Lyme 1796–1812, Clitheroe 1812–18, Dover 1818–28 (*Eton Coll. Reg.;* GEC).

BORINGDON, 1st Bn, *see* PARKER, John.

456. BORRADAILE, Richardson (ca 1763–1835), M.P. Newcastle-under-Lyme 1826–31 (Wedgwood; *1832 List*).

457. BOSCAWEN, Edward (1711–61), M.P. Truro 1742–61 (DNB).

458. BOSCAWEN, Edward (1787–1841), 1st E. of Falmouth, M.P. Truro 1807–8 (DNB; GEC).

459. BOSCAWEN, Edward Hugh (1744–74), M.P. Truro 1767–74 (*Eton Coll. Reg.;* GEC sub Falmouth).

460. BOSCAWEN, George (1712–75), M.P. Penryn 1743–61, Truro 1761–74 (*Eton Coll. Reg.*).

461. BOSCAWEN, George (b. 1745), M.P. St. Mawes 1768–74, Truro 1774–80 (*Eton Coll. Reg.*).

462. BOSCAWEN, Hugh (1750–95), M.P. St. Mawes 1774–90 (Burke's *Peerage* and Debrett's *Peerage* [1834] sub Falmouth).

463. BOSCAWEN, John (1714–67), M.P. Truro 1747–67 (*Eton Coll. Reg.*).

464. BOSCAWEN, William Augustus Spencer (1750–1828), M.P. Truro 1784–92 (Burke's *Peerage* and Collins' *Peerage* sub Falmouth; *Gent. Mag., 1,* 573).

BOSTON, 1st Bn, *see* IRBY, William.

465. BOSWELL, Alexander (1775–1822), 1st Bt, M.P. Plympton Erle 1816–21 (DNB; *Eton Coll. Reg.*).

466. BOTELER, John (ca 1684–1774), M.P. Wendover 1734–35 (Clutterbuck's *Herts, 2,* 477, 490).

467. BOUCHERETT, Ayscoghe (1755–1815), M.P. Great Grimsby 1796–
1803 (*Alumni Cantab.*).

468. BOUGHEY-FLETCHER, John Fenton (1784–1823), 2d Bt, M.P. Newcastle-under-Lyme 1812–18, Staffordshire 1820–23 (GEC).

BOUGHTON, *see* ROUSE-BOUGHTON.

469. BOULTON, Henry Crabb (d. 1773), M.P. Worcester City 1754–73
(Williams' *Worcester M.P.'s*).

BOURNE, William Sturges, *see* STURGES-BOURNE, William.

470. BOUVERIE, Bartholomew (1753–1835), M.P. Downton 1790–96,
1806–12, 1819–26, 1826–30 (GEC sub Folkestone; *Harrow Reg.*).

471. BOUVERIE, Charles Henry (1782–1836), M.P. Dorchester 1811–12,
Downton 1812–13 (Burke's *Peerage* sub Radnor; Hoare's *Modern
Wiltshire, 3,* 37).

472. BOUVERIE, Duncombe Pleydell (1780–1850), M.P. Downton 1806–7,
Salisbury 1828–32, 1833–34 (Burke's *Peerage* sub Radnor; *Harrow Reg.*).

473. BOUVERIE, Edward (1738–1810), M.P. Salisbury 1761–71, Northampton borough 1790–1810 (*Alumni Oxon.; Eton Coll. Reg.*).

474. BOUVERIE, Edward (1760–1824), M.P. Downton 1796–1803
(Burke's *Peerage* sub Radnor; *Harrow Reg.*).

475. BOUVERIE, Jacob (1694–1761), 1st Vct Folkestone, M.P. Salisbury
1741–47 (GEC).

BOUVERIE, Jacob Pleydell, *see* PLEYDELL-BOUVERIE, Jacob.

476. BOUVERIE, Philip Pleydell (1788–1872), M.P. Cockermouth 1830–
31, Downton 1831–32, Berks 1857–65 (Bean; Burke's *Peerage*
sub Radnor; Ferguson; *Harrow Reg.*).

477. BOUVERIE, William (1725–76), 1st E. of Radnor, M.P. Salisbury
1747–61 (GEC).

478. BOUVERIE, William Henry (1752–1806), M.P. Salisbury 1776–1802
(Burke's *Peerage* sub Radnor; *Harrow Reg.*).

BOUVERIE, William Pleydell, *see* PLEYDELL-BOUVERIE, William.

479. BOWES, Andrew Robinson (ca 1745–1810), M.P. Newcastle-upon-
Tyne 1780–84 (Bean; DNB; *Gent. Mag., 1,* 183).

480. BOWES, George (1701–60), M.P. Durham Co. 1727–60 (Bean;
Foster's *Collect. Geneal., 2,* 87; Surtees' *Durham, 4,* 108).

481. BOWLBY, Thomas (1721–95), M.P. Launceston 1780–83 (*Alumni
Cantab.*).

482. BOWLES, Phineas (1690–1749), M.P. Bewdley 1735–41 (W. H.
Bowles, *Bowles Family,* pp. 65, 73–74; DNB).

483. BOWLES, William (1686–1748), M.P. Bridport 1727–41, Bewdley
1741–48 (W. H. Bowles, *Bowles Family,* p. 65; Williams' *Worcester M.P.'s*).

484. BOWYER, George (ca 1739–1800), 1st and 5th Bt, M.P. Queenborough 1784–90 (DNB; GEC).
485. BOWYER, George (1783–1860), 2d and 6th Bt, M.P. Malmesbury 1807–10, Abingdon 1811–18 (*Eton Lists;* GEC).
486. BOWYER, Henry (1786–1853), M.P. Abingdon 1809–11 (*Alumni Oxon.;* Burke's *Peerage*).
487. BOYD, John (1750–1815), 2d Bt, M.P. Wareham 1780–84 (GEC).
488. BOYD, Walter (ca 1754–1837), M.P. Shaftesbury 1796–1802, Lymington 1823–30 (DNB).
489. BOYLE, Courtenay (1769–1844), M.P. Bandon 1806–7 (Burke's *Peerage* sub Cork; Collins' *Peerage* sub Boyle).
490. BOYLE, David (1772–1853), M.P. Ayrshire 1807–11 (Addison's *Glasgow Matric. Albums;* DNB).
491. BOYLE, Hamilton (1730–64), 6th E. of Cork, M.P. Warwick borough 1761–62 (GEC; *Old Westminsters*).
492. BOYLE, Henry (1771–1842), 3d E. of Shannon, M.P. Cork Co. 1801–7, Bandon 1807–7 (GEC).
493. BOYLE, John (1803–74), M.P. Cork Co. 1827–30, Cork City 1830–32 (*Alumni Oxon.;* Burke's *Peerage* sub Cork).
494. BOYLE, Richard (1809–68), 4th E. of Shannon, M.P. Cork Co. 1830–32 (GEC; *Harrow Reg.*).
495. BOYLE-WALSINGHAM, Robert (1736–80), M.P. Knaresborough 1758–61, 1768–80, Fowey 1761–68 (Burke's *Peerage* sub Shannon).
BOYNE, 2d Vct, *see* HAMILTON, Gustavus.
496. BOYNTON, Francis (1677–1739), 4th Bt, M.P. Hedon 1734–39 (*Alumni Cantab.;* GEC).
497. BOYNTON, Griffith (1745–78), 6th Bt, M.P. Beverley 1772–74 (*Alumni Cantab.;* GEC).
498. BRABAZON, William (1803–87), 11th E. of Meath, M.P. Dublin Co. 1830–32, 1837–41 (GEC).
BRADDYLL, *see* GALE-BRADDYLL.
BRADFORD, 1st E. of, *see* BRIDGEMAN, Orlando.
499. BRADSHAIGH, Roger (ca 1675–1747), 3d Bt, M.P. Wigan 1695–1747 (GEC).
BRADSHAW, Augustus Cavendish, *see* CAVENDISH-BRADSHAW, Augustus.
500. BRADSHAW, Ellerker (1680–1742), M.P. Beverley 1727–29, 1734–41 (Bean; Hall's *South Cave,* p. 185).
501. BRADSHAW, James (d. 1847), M.P. Brackley 1825–32, Berwick-on-Tweed 1835–37, Canterbury 1837–47 (Marshall's *Naval Biog., 9,* 308; Bean; cf. *Harrow Reg.*).
502. BRADSHAW, Robert Haldane (ca 1760–1835), M.P. Brackley 1802–32 (*Gent. Mag., 1,* 556; Palmer's *Perlustration of Great Yarmouth, 1,* 362; *1832 List*).

503. BRADSHAW, Thomas (d. 1774), M.P. Harwich 1767–68, Saltash 1768–74 (Musgrave's *Obituary*).
504. BRAGGE-BATHURST, Charles (ca 1754–1831), M.P. Monmouth borough 1790–96, Bristol 1796–1812, Bodmin 1812–18, Harwich 1818–23 (Burke's *LG;* Williams' *Wales M.P.'s*).
505. BRAMSTON, Thomas (ca 1690–1765), M.P. Maldon 1712–34, Essex 1734–47 (*Alumni Cantab.;* Williamson's *Middle Temple Bench Book*).
506. BRAMSTON, Thomas Berney (1733–1813), M.P. Essex 1779–1802 (*Alumni Felsted.; Alumni Oxon.;* Burke's *LG*).
507. BRAMSTON, Thomas Gardiner (1770–1831), M.P. Essex 1830–30 (*Alumni Felsted.; Alumni Oxon.;* Burke's *LG*).
508. BRAND, Thomas (d. 1770), M.P. Shoreham 1741–47, Tavistock 1747–54, Gatton 1754–68, Okehampton 1768–70 (Clutterbuck's *Herts, 3, 74;* Eton. *Coll. Reg.*).
509. BRAND, Thomas (ca 1750–94), M.P. Arundel 1774–80 (*Alumni Cantab.; Old Westminsters;* GEC).
510. BRAND, Thomas (1774–1851), 20th Bn Dacre, M.P. Helston 1807–7, Herts 1807–19 (GEC).
511. BRAND-HOLLIS, Thomas (ca 1719–1804), M.P. Hindon 1774–76 (*Alumni Cantab.;* Addison's *Glasgow Matric. Albums;* Warrand's *Herts Families,* p. 43).
512. BRANDLING, Charles (1733–1802), M.P. Newcastle-upon-Tyne 1784–97 (*Alumni Cantab.; New Hist. of Northumberland, 13, 352; 1806 List*).
513. BRANDLING, Charles John (1769–1826), M.P. Newcastle-upon-Tyne 1798–1812, Northumberland 1820–26 (*Alumni Cantab.*).
   BRANDON, Dukes of, *see* HAMILTON, Alexander and Archibald.
514. BRASSEY, Nathaniel (ca 1697–1765), M.P. Hertford borough 1734–61 (Clutterbuck's *Herts, 2, 208;* Misc. *Geneal. et Herald.,* N.S., *2*).
   BRAYBROOKE, Bns, *see* GRIFFIN, John Griffin and Richard.
515. BRAYEN, Thomas (1800–64), M.P. Leominster 1831–31 (Williams' *Hereford M.P.'s*).
   BREADALBANE, Earls of, *see* CAMPBELL, John.
   BRECKNOCK, E. of, *see* PRATT, George Charles.
   BRERETON, Charles Trelawny, *see* TRELAWNY-BRERETON, Charles.
   BRERETON, Owen Salusbury, *see* SALUSBURY-BRERETON, Owen.
516. BRERETON-SALUSBURY, Thomas (d. 1756), M.P. Liverpool 1724–29, 1734–56 (Bean; Pink).
517. BRETON, William (d. 1773), M.P. Bossiney 1746–47 (Walpole-Montagu *Corr.* [Yale ed.], *2,* 119 n.).
518. BRETT, Charles (d. 1799), M.P. Lostwithiel 1768–76, Sandwich 1776–80, 1784–90, Dartmouth 1782–84 (*Gent. Mag.,* pp. 173, 250; *Notes and Queries,* 3d Ser., *2,* 63).

519. BRETT, Peircy (ca 1709–81), M.P. Queenborough 1754–74 (DNB).
BRICE, Robert, see KINGSMILL, Robert.

520. BRICKDALE, Matthew (1735–1831), M.P. Bristol 1768–74, 1780–90 (Williams' *Gloucester M.P.'s*).

521. BRIDGEMAN, Henry (1725–1800), 1st Bn Bradford, M.P. Ludlow 1748–68, Wenlock 1768–94 (*Alumni Cantab.;* GEC).

522. BRIDGEMAN, Henry Simpson (1757–82), M.P. Wigan 1780–82 (*Alumni Cantab.;* Bean; *Harrow Reg.;* Pink).
BRIDGEMAN, John, see SIMPSON, John.

523. BRIDGEMAN, Orlando (ca 1679–1738), 2d Bt, M.P. Coventry 1707–10, Calne 1715–22, Lostwithiel 1724–27, Bletchingley 1727–34, Dunwich 1734–38 (GEC).

524. BRIDGEMAN, Orlando (1762–1825), 1st E. of Bradford, M.P. Wigan 1784–1800 (*Alumni Cantab.;* GEC).

525. BRIDGES, Brook (1733–91), 3d Bt, M.P. Kent 1763–74 (*Alumni Cantab.; Eton Coll. Reg.;* GEC).

526. BRIDGES, George (ca 1679–1751), M.P. Winchester 1714–51 (*British Topographer* [1789], p. 162; Collins' *Peerage* sub Chandos; Musgrave's *Obituary*).

527. BRIDGES, George (ca 1763–1840), M.P. London 1820–26 (Beaven's *Aldermen of London; Gent. Mag., 1,* 446; Taylor's *Biog. Leodiensis,* p. 380).
BRIDPORT, Bns and Vct, see HOOD, Alexander and Samuel.
BRIDGWATER, 7th E. of, see EGERTON, John William.

528. BRIGHT, Henry (1784–1869), M.P. Bristol 1820–30 (Boase; *Alumni Cantab.;* Williams' *Gloucester M.P.'s*).

529. BRINCKMAN, Theodore Henry Lavington (1798–1880), 1st Bt, M.P. Yarmouth (Hants) 1821–26 (*Alumni Cantab.;* Foster's *Baronetage*).

530. BRISCOE, John Ivatt (1791–1870), M.P. Surrey 1830–32, East Surrey 1832–34, Westbury 1837–41, West Surrey 1857–70 (*Alumni Oxon.;* Boase; Cobbett's *Twickenham,* p. 53).
BRISTOL, E. and M. of, see HERVEY, Augustus John and Frederick William.

531. BRISTOW, John (ca 1701–68), M.P. Berealston 1734–41, 1754–61, St. Ives 1741–54, Arundel 1761–68 (Hoare's *Modern Wiltshire, 5,* 34; *Misc. Geneal. et Herald.,* 5th Ser., 7).

532. BRISTOW, Robert (1688–1737), M.P. Winchelsea 1708–37 (*Misc. Geneal. et Herald.,* 5th Ser., 7; *Notes and Queries, 179,* 80).

533. BRISTOW, Robert (ca 1712–76), M.P. Winchelsea 1738–41, Shoreham 1747–61 (*Misc. Geneal. et Herald.,* 5th Ser., 7; Musgrave's *Obituary*).

534. BROADHEAD, Theodore Henry (1767–1820), M.P. Wareham 1812–18, Yarmouth (Hants) 1820–20 (*Alumni Cantab.; Eton Coll. Reg.; 1821 List*).

BROADHEAD, Theodore Henry Lavington, *see* BRINCKMAN, Theodore Henry Lavington.

535. BROADHURST, John, M.P. Weymouth and Melcombe Regis 1812–13, Hedon 1813–18, Sudbury 1818–20.

536. BRODIE, Alexander (1697–1754), M.P. Elginshire 1720–41, Caithness-shire 1741–47, Inverness burghs 1747–54 (Burke's *LG;* Tayler's *Morayshire M.P.'s*).

537. BRODIE, Alexander (d. 1770), M.P. Nairnshire 1735–41 (Burke's *LG;* Foster's *Scots M.P.'s*).

538. BRODIE, Alexander (1748–1812), M.P. Nairnshire 1785–90, Elgin burghs 1790–1802 (Foster's *Scots M.P.'s*).

539. BRODIE, James (1744–1824), M.P. Elginshire 1796–1807 (Burke's *LG;* Foster's *Scots M.P.'s;* Tayler's *Morayshire M.P.'s*).

BRODNAX, Thomas, *see* KNIGHT, Thomas.

540. BRODRICK, George (1730–65), 3d Vct Midleton, M.P. Ashburton 1754–61, Shoreham 1761–65 (*Eton Coll. Reg.;* GEC).

541. BRODRICK, George (1754–1836), 4th Vct Midleton, M.P. Whitchurch 1774–96 (*Alumni Cantab.; Eton. Coll. Reg.;* GEC).

542. BRODRICK, William (1763–1819), M.P. Whitchurch 1796–1818 (*Alumni Cantab.; Eton. Coll. Reg.*).

543. BROGDEN, James (ca 1765–1842), M.P. Launceston 1796–1832 (*Eton Coll. Reg.; 1832 List*).

BROME, Vct, *see* CORNWALLIS, Charles.

544. BROMLEY, Henry (1705–55), 1st Bn Montfort, M.P. Cambridgeshire 1727–41 (GEC; *Alumni Cantab.; Eton Coll. Reg.*).

545. BROMLEY, Henry (ca 1761–1837), M.P. Worcester 1806–7 (Williams' *Worcester M.P.'s;* MS, *ex inform.* Canon J. G. Richardson).

546. BROMLEY, Thomas (1733–99), 2d Bn Montfort, M.P. Cambridge borough 1754–55 (*Eton Coll. Reg.;* GEC).

547. BROMLEY, William (1699–1737), M.P. Fowey 1725–27, Warwick borough 1727–35, Oxford Univ. 1737–37 (DNB; *Old Westminsters*).

548. BROMLEY, William Throckmorton (ca 1727–69), M.P. Warwickshire 1765–69 (*Old Westminsters*).

549. BROMLEY-CHESTER, William (1738–80), M.P. Gloucestershire 1776–80 (*Old Westminsters;* Williams' *Gloucester M.P.'s*).

BROOKE, Bn, *see* GREVILLE, Henry Richard.

550. BROOKE, Charles, M.P. Chippenham 1802–3, 1806–7, 1812–18, Ilchester 1803–6 (*1806 List*).

551. BROOKE, Henry Vaughan (ca 1743–1807), M.P. Donegal 1801–2, 1806–7 (*Alumni Dublin.; Gent. Mag., 2,* 1178; cf. Foster's *Collect. Geneal., 2,* 105).

552. BROOKE, Thomas (ca 1754–1820), M.P. Newton 1786–1807 (Bean; Omerod's *Chester, 1,* 677, 685; Pink).

553. BROOKE, Thomas Langford (ca 1770–1815), M.P. Newton 1797–97 (*Alumni Oxon.;* Omerod's *Chester, 1,* 465).

554. BROOKE-PECHELL, Samuel John (1785–1849), 3d Bt, M.P. Helston 1830–31, Windsor 1832–34 (DNB; GEC).

555. BROOKE-PECHELL, Thomas (1753–1826), 2d Bt, M.P. Downton 1813–18, 1819–26 (GEC; *Old Westminsters*).

556. BROOKSBANK, Stamp (1694–1756), M.P. Colchester 1727–34, Saltash 1743–54 (Burke's *LG; Notes and Queries, 179,* 82).

557. BROUGHAM, Henry (1778–1868), 1st Bn Brougham, M.P. Camelford 1810–12, Winchelsea 1815–30, Knaresborough 1830–30, Yorkshire 1830–30 (DNB; GEC; Gooder).

558. BROUGHAM, James (1780–1833), M.P. Tregony 1826–30, Downton 1830–31, Winchelsea 1831–32, Kendal 1832–33 (Bean; Burke's *Peerage;* Pink).

559. BROUGHAM, William (1795–1886), 2d Bn Brougham, M.P. Southwark 1831–34 (*Alumni Cantab.;* DNB; GEC).

BROUGHTON, 1st Bn, *see* HOBHOUSE, John Cam.

560. BROUGHTON-DELVES, Brian (1718–44), 4th Bt, M.P. Wenlock 1741–44 (GEC; Shrop. Archaeol. Soc. *Trans.,* 3d Ser., *2,* 340).

561. BROWN, Lancelot (ca 1749–1802), M.P. Totnes 1780–84, Huntingdon borough 1784–87, Hunts 1792–94 (*Eton Coll. Reg.*).

562. BROWN, Robert (d. 1760), 1st Bt, M.P. Ilchester 1734–47 (DNB; GEC).

563. BROWNE, Anthony (1769–1840), M.P. Hedon 1806–18 (*Gent. Mag., 1,* 442; Oliver's *Antigua, 1,* 74, and *3,* 413; *1812 List*).

564. BROWNE, Denis (ca 1763–1828), M.P. Mayo 1801–18, Kilkenny City 1820–26 (Burke's *Peerage* sub Sligo; Collins' *Peerage* sub Mounteagle).

565. BROWNE, Dominick (1787–1860), 1st Bn Oranmore, M.P. Mayo 1814–26, 1830–36 (*Alumni Cantab.;* GEC).

566. BROWNE, Francis John (1754–1833), M.P. Dorset 1784–1806 (Hutchins' *Dorset, 2,* 298).

567. BROWNE, Isaac Hawkins (1706–60), M.P. Wenlock 1744–54 (*Alumni Cantab.;* DNB; *Old Westminsters*).

568. BROWNE, Isaac Hawkins (1745–1818), M.P. Bridgnorth 1784–1812 (DNB; *Misc. Geneal. et Herald.,* 1st Ser., *3; Old Westminsters*).

569. BROWNE, James (1793–1854), M.P. Mayo 1818–31 (*Alumni Cantab.; Alumni Dublin.; Eton Lists*).

570. BROWNE, John (1696–1750), M.P. Dorchester 1727–50 (Hutchins' *Dorset, 2,* 298, 301; *Linc. Inn Reg.*).

571. BROWNE, John Denis (ca 1799–1862), M.P. Mayo 1831–34 (*Annual Register,* p. 333; Burtchaell's *Kilkenny M.P.'s*).

572. BROWNE, Peter Denis (ca 1794–1872), M.P. Rye 1818–26 (*Alumni Dublin.;* Burke's *Peerage* sub Sligo).

573. BROWNE, Robert (b. ca 1695), M.P. Dorchester 1737–41 (*Alumni Oxon.*).

574. BROWNE, William (1791–1876), M.P. Kerry 1830–31, 1841–47 (Boase).

BROWNLOW, Bns and E., *see* CUST, Brownlow and John.

575. BROWNLOW, Charles (1795–1847), 1st Bn Lurgan, M.P. Armagh Co. 1818–32 (*Alumni Cantab.; Alumni Dublin.;* GEC).

576. BROWNLOW, John (ca 1691–1754), 1st Vct Tyrconnel, M.P. Lincoln-shire 1715–22, Grantham 1722–41 (GEC; Maddison's *Lincs Pedigrees*).

577. BROWNLOW, William (ca 1755–1815), M.P. Armagh Co. 1807–15 (Burke's *Peerage* sub Lurgan; *Gent. Mag., 2,* 185).

BRUCE, E., *see* BRUDENELL-BRUCE, Charles and George William Frederick.

BRUCE, Charles Brudenell, *see* BRUDENELL-BRUCE, Charles.

BRUCE, Charles Lennox Cumming, *see* CUMMING-BRUCE, Charles Lennox.

BRUCE, George William Frederick Brudenell, *see* BRUDENELL-BRUCE, George William Frederick.

578. BRUCE, James (1769–98), M.P. Marlborough 1796–97 (*Old West-minsters; Scots Peerage* sub Elgin).

BRUCE, James Lewis Knight, *see* KNIGHT–BRUCE, James Lewis.

579. BRUCE, John (ca 1745–1826), M.P. St. Michael 1809–14 (DNB).

580. BRUCE, Michael (1787–1861), M.P. Ilchester 1830–31 (*Alumni Cantab.; Eton Lists*).

581. BRUCE, Patrick Craufurd (d. 1820), M.P. Evesham 1802–6, Rye 1806–7, Dundalk 1807–8 (Williams' *Worcester M.P.'s; Alumni Oxon.*).

582. BRUCE, Robert (1795–1864), M.P. Clackmannanshire 1820–24 (*Alumni Cantab.;* GEC and *Scots Peerage* sub Balfour).

583. BRUCE, Thomas (ca 1738–97), M.P. Marlborough 1790–96, Great Bedwin 1796–97 (Debrett's *Peerage* [1834] sub Elgin; *Rugby Reg.*).

584. BRUCE-HOPE, John (ca 1684–1766), 7th Bt, M.P. Kinross-shire 1727–34, 1741–47 (DNB; GEC).

585. BRUDENELL, George Bridges (ca 1726–1801), M.P. Rutland 1754–61, 1768–90, Stamford 1761–68 (*Alumni Cantab.*).

586. BRUDENELL, James (d. 1746), M.P. Chichester 1713–15, 1734–46, Andover 1715–34 (Collins' *Peerage* sub Cardigan; Musgrave's *Obituary*).

587. BRUDENELL, James (1725–1811), 5th E. of Cardigan, M.P. Shaftes-bury 1754–61, Hastings 1761–68, Marlborough 1768–80 (GEC).

588. BRUDENELL, James Thomas (1797–1868), 7th E. of Cardigan, M.P. Marlborough 1818–29, Fowey 1830–32, North Northamptonshire 1832–37 (DNB; GEC; *Harrow Reg.*).

BRUDENELL, John, *see* MONTAGU, John.

589. BRUDENELL, Robert (ca 1727–68), M.P. Great Bedwin 1756–61, Marlborough 1761–68 (*Alumni Oxon.;* Collins' *Peerage* sub Cardigan).

590. BRUDENELL, Robert (1769–1837), 6th E. of Cardigan, M.P. Marlborough 1797–1802 (GEC; *Harrow Reg.*).

591. BRUDENELL-BRUCE, Charles (1773–1856), 1st M. of Ailesbury, M.P. Marlborough 1796–1814 (GEC).

592. BRUDENELL–BRUCE, George William Frederick (1804–78), 2d M. of Ailesbury, M.P. Marlborough 1826–29 (GEC).

593. BRUEN, Henry (ca 1789–1852), M.P. Carlow Co. 1812–31, 1835–37, 1840–52 (*Alumni Oxon.;* Boase).

594. BRYDGES, Henry (1708–71), 2d D. of Chandos, M.P. Hereford City 1727–34, Steyning 1734–41, Bishop's Castle 1741–44 (*Alumni Cantab.;* GEC; *Old Westminsters*).

595. BRYDGES, James (1731–89), 3d D. of Chandos, M.P. Winchester 1754–61, Radnorshire 1761–68 (GEC; *Old Westminsters*).

596. BRYDGES, John William Head (1764—1839), M.P. Coleraine 1823–31, Armagh borough 1831–32 (*Alumni Cantab.;* Collins' *Peerage* sub Chandos).

597. BRYDGES, Samuel Egerton (1762–1837), 1st Bt, M.P. Maidstone 1812–18 (*Alumni Cantab.;* DNB).

598. BUBB-DODINGTON, George (ca 1691–1762), 1st Bn Melcombe, M.P. Winchelsea 1715–22, Bridgwater 1722–54, Weymouth and Melcombe Regis 1754–61 (DNB; GEC).

BUCCLEUCH, 4th D. of, *see* MONTAGU-SCOTT, Charles William Henry.

599. BUCHANAN, John (1761–1839), M.P. Dumbartonshire 1821–26 (Burke's *LG;* Addison's *Glasgow Matric. Albums*).

600. BUCHANAN, Neil (d. 1744), M.P. Glasgow burghs 1741–44 (Foster's *Scots M.P.'s*).

601. BUCHANAN-RIDDELL, John (ca 1768–1819), 9th Bt, M.P. Linlithgow burghs 1812–19 (Foster's *Scots M.P.'s;* GEC).

602. BUCK, John (ca 1704–45), M.P. Taunton 1741–45 (Burke's *Peerage* sub Stucley; Watkins' *Bideford,* p. 88).

603. BUCK, Lewis William (1784–1858), M.P. Exeter 1826–32, North Devon 1839–57 (*Alumni Cantab.;* Howard and Crisp's *Visitation of Eng. and Wales, 2,* 148).

BUCKINGHAM, M. and D. of, *see* NUGENT-TEMPLE-GRENVILLE, George; *also* TEMPLE-NUGENT-BRYDGES-CHANDOS-GRENVILLE, Richard.

BUCKINGHAM and CHANDOS, 2d D. of, *see* TEMPLE-NUGENT-BRYDGES-CHANDOS-GRENVILLE, Richard Plantaganet.

BUCKINGHAMSHIRE, E. of, *see* HOBART, George, John, and Robert; *also* HAMPDEN, George Robert.

604. BUCKLER-LETHBRIDGE, Thomas (1778–1849), 2d Bt, M.P. Somerset

1806–12, 1820–30 (Bates Harbin; Foster's *Baronetage; Alumni Oxon.*).

605. BUCKNALL, Thomas Skip Dyot (d. 1804), M.P. St. Albans 1796–1802 (*Gent. Mag., 1,* 92).

606. BUCKNALL-GRIMSTON, William (1750–1814), M.P. St. Albans 1784–90, Appleby 1791–96 (Bean; *Eton Coll. Reg.;* Ferguson; Peile's *Biog. Reg. of Christ's College*).

607. BUCKWORTH, John (1704–59), 2d Bt, M.P. Weobley 1734–41 (*Eton Coll. Reg.;* GEC).

608. BUDGEN, Thomas (d. 1772), M.P. Surrey 1751–61 (Burke's *Irish LG*).

BULKELEY, 7th Vct, *see* WARREN-BULKELEY, Thomas James.

609. BULKELEY, James (1717–52), 6th Vct Bulkeley, M.P. Beaumaris 1739–52 (GEC; *Old Westminsters*).

BULKELEY, John Bulkeley Coventry, *see* COVENTRY-BULKELEY, John Bulkeley.

610. BULKELEY, Richard (1707–39), 5th Vct Bulkeley, M.P. Beaumaris 1730–39 (GEC; *Old Westminsters*).

BULKELEY, Richard Bulkeley Williams, *see* WILLIAMS-BULKELEY, Richard Bulkeley.

BULKELEY, Thomas James, *see* WARREN-BULKELEY, Thomas James.

611. BULL, Daniel (ca 1727–91), M.P. Calne 1761–62 (*Genealogist, N.S., 14,* 40, 93; *Wilts Archaeol. and Nat. Hist. Mag., 44,* 106).

612. BULL, Frederick (d. 1784), M.P. London 1773–84 (Beaven's *Aldermen of London;* Orridge's *Citizens of London,* p. 248).

613. BULL, Richard (ca 1725–1805), M.P. Newport 1756–80 (*Alumni Cantab.; Gent. Mag.,* p. 1179; *Old Westminsters;* Namier).

614. BULLER, Anthony (1780–1866), M.P. West Looe 1812–16, 1831–32 (Burke's *LG* sub Champernowne; *Linc. Inn Reg.*).

615. BULLER, Charles (1774–1848), M.P. West Looe 1812–16, 1826–30 (*Old Westminsters*).

616. BULLER, Charles (1806–48), M.P. West Looe 1830–31, Liskeard 1832–48 (*Alumni Cantab.;* DNB; Dod's *Parl. Companion* [1834], p. 95; *Harrow Reg.*).

617. BULLER, Edward (1764–1824), 1st Bt, M.P. East Looe 1802–20 (*Old Westminsters*).

618. BULLER, Francis (1723–64), M.P. West Looe 1761–64 (*Alumni Oxon.;* Burke's *LG*).

619. BULLER, Frederick William (ca 1772–1855), M.P. East Looe 1798–1802 (Burke's *LG;* Boase).

620. BULLER, James (1717–65), M.P. East Looe 1741–47, Cornwall 1748–65 (*Alumni Oxon.;* Burke's *LG*).

621. BULLER, James (1766–1827), M.P. Exeter 1790–96, 1802–18, East Looe 1802–2 (Burke's *LG; Harrow Reg.*).

622. BULLER, James (1772–1830), M.P. West Looe 1802-5, 1806–12 (*Old Westminsters*).

623. BULLER, James Wentworth (1798–1865), M.P. Exeter 1830–34, North Devon 1857–65 (*Alumni Oxon.;* Boase; Burke's *LG; Harrow Reg.*).

624. BULLER, John (1721–86), M.P. East Looe 1747–86 (*Alumni Oxon.;* Burke's *LG*).

625. BULLER, John (1744–90), M.P. Exeter 1768–74, Launceston 1774–80, West Looe 1780–82, 1784–84 (*Alumni Oxon.;* Burke's *LG*).

626. BULLER, John (ca 1762–1807), M.P. East Looe 1796–99, 1802–7 (*Old Westminsters*).

627. BULLER, John (1771–1849), M.P. West Looe 1796–96, 1826–27 (*Old Westminsters*).

628. BULLER-ELPHINSTONE, James Drummond (1788–1857), M.P. East Looe 1826–29 (Boase; *Harrow Reg.; Scots Peerage*).

629. BULLER-YARDE-BULLER, Francis (1767–1833), 2d Bt, M.P. Totnes 1790–96 (Burke's *Peerage* sub Churston).

630. BULLOCK, John (1731–1809), M.P. Maldon 1754–74, Steyning 1780–84, Essex 1784–1809 (*Alumni Cantab.; Alumni Felsted.*).

631. BULLOCK, Joseph (1732–1808), M.P. Wendover 1770–75 (*Alumni Oxon.;* Lipscomb's *Bucks, 2,* 600; *Royal Kalendar* [1772], p. 48).

632. BULWER, William Henry Lytton Earle (1801–72), 1st Bn Dalling and Bulwer, M.P. Wilton 1830–31, Coventry 1831–34, Marylebone 1835–37, Tamworth 1868–71 (DNB; GEC; *Harrow Reg.*).

633. BULWER-LYTTON, Edward George Earle Lytton (1803–73), 1st Bn Lytton, M.P. St. Ives 1831–32, Lincoln City 1832–41, Herts 1852–66 (*Alumni Cantab.;* DNB; GEC).

634. BUNBURY, Charles (1708–42), 4th Bt, M.P. Chester City 1733–42 (GEC).

635. BUNBURY, Henry Edward (1778–1860), 7th Bt, M.P. Suffolk 1830–32 (DNB; GEC; *Old Westminsters*).

636. BUNBURY, Thomas Charles (1740–1821), 6th Bt, M.P. Suffolk 1761–84, 1790–1812 (*Alumni Cantab.;* GEC; *Old Westminsters*).

BUNNEY, Edmund, *see* CRADOCK-HARTOPP, Edmund.

637. BURCH, Joseph Randyll (ca 1757–1826), M.P. Thetford 1790–1802 (*Gent. Mag., 1,* 477).

638. BURCHETT, Josiah (ca 1666–1746), M.P. Sandwich 1705–13, 1722–41 (DNB; *Notes and Queries, 176,* 56).

639. BURDETT, Francis (1770–1844), 5th Bt, M.P. Boroughbridge 1796–1802, Middlesex 1802–4, 1805–6, Westminster 1807–37, North Wilts 1837–44 (DNB; GEC; *Old Westminsters*).

640. BURDETT, Robert (1716–97), 4th Bt, M.P. Tamworth 1748–68 (GEC; *Old Westminsters;* Wedgwood).

641. BURDON, Rowland (ca 1757–1838), M.P. Durham Co. 1790–1806 (*Alumni Oxon.;* Burke's *LG; Gent. Mag., 2,* 553).

BURFORD, E. of, *see* BEAUCLERK, Aubrey.

642. BURGE, William (ca 1786–1849), M.P. Eye 1831–32 (*Alumni Oxon.;* Martin's *Masters of the Bench, Inner Temple;* Pink).

BURGES, James Bland, *see* LAMB, James Bland.

BURGH, Ulysses, *see* DE BURGH, Ulysses.

643. BURGOYNE, John (1723–92), M.P. Midhurst 1761–68, Preston 1768–92 (DNB; *Old Westminsters*).

644. BURGOYNE, Roger (ca 1710–80), 6th Bt, M.P. Bedfordshire 1735–47 (*Alumni Cantab.; Eton Coll. Reg.;* GEC).

645. BURKE, Edmund (1729–97), M.P. Wendover 1765–74, Bristol 1774–80, Malton 1780–94 (*Alumni Dublin.;* DNB).

646. BURKE, John (ca 1782–1847), 2d Bt, M.P. Galway Co. 1830–32 (*Alumni Cantab.; Alumni Dublin.;* GEC; *1832 List*).

647. BURKE, Richard (1758–94), M.P. Malton 1794–94 (*Old Westminsters*).

648. BURKE, William (ca 1729–98), M.P. Great Bedwin 1766–74 (DNB; *Old Westminsters*).

649. BURLAND, John Berkeley (1754–1804), M.P. Totnes 1802–4 (Collinson's *Somerset, 1,* 257; *Old Westminsters*).

BURLINGTON, E. of, *see* CAVENDISH, George Augustus.

650. BURRARD, George (1805–70), 4th Bt, M.P. Lymington 1828–32 (*Eton Lists;* GEC).

651. BURRARD, Harry (ca 1707–91), 1st Bt, M.P. Lymington 1741–78 (GEC).

652. BURRARD, Harry (1755–1813), 1st Bt, M.P. Lymington 1780–88, 1790–91, 1802–2 (DNB; GEC).

653. BURRARD, Paul (1678–1735), M.P. Lymington 1705–13, 1719–27, Yarmouth (Hants) 1727–35 (Burke's *Peerage;* DNB sub Harry Burrard).

654. BURRARD–NEALE, Harry (1765–1840), 2d Bt, M.P. Lymington 1790–1802, 1806–7, 1812–23, 1832–34 (DNB; GEC).

655. BURRELL, Charles Merrik (1774–1862), 3d Bt, M.P. Shoreham 1806–62 (*Alumni Cantab.;* GEC; *Old Westminsters*).

656. BURRELL, Merrick (1699–1787), 1st Bt, M.P. Great Marlow 1747–54, Grampound 1754–68, Haslemere 1774–80, Great Bedwin 1780–84 (Comber's *Sussex Geneal.: Ardingly;* GEC; *Merchant Taylor School Reg.*).

657. BURRELL, Peter (1692–1756), M.P. Haslemere 1722–54, Dover 1755–56 (*Comber's Sussex Geneal.: Ardingly; Merchant Taylor School Reg.*).

658. BURRELL, Peter (1723–75), M.P. Launceston 1759–68, Totnes 1768–74 (*Alumni Cantab.; Merchant Taylor School Reg.*).

659. BURRELL, Peter (1754–1820), 1st Bn Gwydir, M.P. Haslemere

1776–80, Boston 1782–96 (*Alumni Cantab.; Eton Coll. Reg.;* GEC).

BURRELL, Peter Robert, *see* DRUMMOND-BURRELL, Peter Robert.

660. BURRELL, Walter (1777–1831), M.P. Sussex 1812–31 (Comber's *Sussex Geneal.: Ardingly; Old Westminsters*).

661. BURRELL, William (1732–96), 2d Bt, M.P. Haslemere 1768–74 (*Alumni Cantab.;* DNB; GEC; *Old Westminsters*).

662. BURROUGHES, William (ca 1753–1829), 1st Bt, M.P. Enniskillen 1802–6, Colchester 1817–18, Taunton 1818–19 (*Alumni Dublin.; Gent. Mag., 2,* 82).

663. BURROUGHES-PAULET, Charles Ingoldsby (1764–1843), 13th M. of Winchester, M.P. Truro 1792–96 (*Eton Coll. Reg.;* GEC).

664. BURROW, Edward (d. 1800), M.P. Cockermouth 1796–1800 (Bean; Ferguson).

665. BURT, William Matthew (d. 1781), M.P. Great Marlow 1761–68 (Oliver's *Antigua, 1,* 88).

666. BURTON, Bartholomew (ca 1695–1770), M.P. Camelford 1759–68 (*Notes and Queries, 179, 98*).

667. BURTON, Francis (ca 1744–1832), M.P. Heytesbury 1780–84, Woodstock 1784–90, Oxford City 1790–1812 (*Old Westminsters;* Williams' *Oxford M.P.'s*).

668. BURTON, Francis Nathaniel (1766–1832), M.P. Clare 1801–8 (GEC and Burke's *Peerage* sub Conyngham).

BURTON, Napier Christie, *see* CHRISTIE-BURTON, Napier.

669. BURTON, Ralph (d. 1768), M.P. Wareham 1768–68 (Musgrave's *Obituary*).

670. BURTON, Robert (ca 1739–1810), M.P. Wendover 1784–90 (*Gent. Mag., 1,* 388; Foster's *Collect. Geneal., 2,* 117).

BURTON, Robert Christie, *see* CHRISTIE-BURTON, Robert.

671. BURTON, William Henry (1739–1818), M.P. Carlow borough 1801–2 (*Alumni Dublin.;* Burke's *Irish LG;* Burtchaell's *Kilkenny M.P.'s*).

672. BURTON-PETERS, Henry (ca 1792–1875), M.P. Beverley 1830–37 (Bean; Burke's *LG* sub Christie; *Harrow Reg.; Linc. Inn. Reg.*).

673. BURTON-PHILLIPSON, Richard (ca 1724–92), M.P. Eye 1762–68, 1770–92 (*Alumni Cantab.; Eton Coll. Reg.; East Anglian,* N.S., *9,* 128).

BURY, Vct, *see* KEPPEL, Augustus Frederick.

674. BURY, Charles William (1801–51), 2d E. of Charleville, M.P. Carlow borough 1826–32, Penryn 1832–34 (GEC).

675. BURY, Thomas, M.P. Newport 1741–54.

676. BUSHBY-MAITLAND, John (d. 1822), M.P. Camelford 1818–19 (Grant's *Faculty of Advocates; Misc. Geneal. et Herald.,* 1st Ser., *2,* 208).

677. Busk, William (ca 1769–1849), M.P. Barnstable 1812–12 (Burke's
      LG [ed. 1886]; *Notes and Queries, 178,* 391).
      Bute, E. and M. of, *see* Stuart, John.

678. Butler, Edward (ca 1686–1745), M.P. Oxford Univ. 1737–45
      (*Alumni Oxon.;* Williams' *Oxford M.P.'s*).

679. Butler, James (ca 1680–1741), M.P. Arundel 1705–8, Sussex
      1715–22, 1728–41 (*Alumni Cantab.;* Berry's *County Geneal.:
      Sussex,* p. 176).

680. Butler, James Wandesford (1774–1838), 1st M. of Ormonde, M.P.
      Kilkenny Co. 1801–20 (*Eton Coll. Reg.;* GEC).

681. Butler, John (1707–66), M.P. East Grinstead 1742–47, Sussex
      1747–66 (*Alumni Cantab.;* Berry's *County Geneal.: Sussex,*
      p. 176).

682. Butler, John (1808–54), 2d M. of Ormonde, M.P. Kilkenny Co.
      1830–32 (GEC; *Harrow Reg.*).

683. Butler, Richard (1761–1817), 7th Bt, M.P. Carlow Co. 1801–2
      (*Alumni Dublin.;* GEC).

684. Butler, Richard (1794–1858), 2d E. of Glengall, M.P. Tipperary
      1818–19 (GEC).

685. Butler-Clarke-Southwell-Wandesford,   Charles   Harward
      (1780–1860), M.P. Kilkenny City 1802–9, 1814–20, Kilkenny
      Co. 1820–30 (*Alumni Cantab.;* Boase; Burtchaell's *Kilkenny
      M.P.'s; Eton Coll. Reg.*).

686. Butterworth, Joseph (ca 1770–1826), M.P. Coventry 1812–18,
      Dover 1820–26 (DNB).

687. Buxton, John Jacob (1788–1842), 2d Bt, M.P. Great Bedwin
      1818–32 (GEC; *Harrow Reg.*).

688. Buxton, Robert John (1753–1839), 1st Bt, M.P. Thetford 1790–96,
      Great Bedwin 1797–1806 (GEC).

689. Buxton, Thomas Fowell (1786–1845), 1st Bt, M.P. Weymouth
      and Melcombe Regis 1818–37 (DNB; Foster's *Baronetage; Linc.
      Inn Reg.*).

690. Byde, Thomas Plumer (ca 1721–89), M.P. Herts 1761–68 (*Alumni
      Cantab.; Old Westminsters*).

691. Byng, George (ca 1735–89), M.P. Wigan 1768–80, Middlesex
      1780–84 (*Old Westminsters*).

692. Byng, George (1764–1847), M.P. Newport (Hants) 1790–90, Mid-
      dlesex 1790–1847 (*Old Westminsters*).

693. Byng, George Stevens (1806–86), 2d E. of Strafford, M.P. Mil-
      borne Port 1830–31, 1831–32, Chatham 1834–34, 1837–52, Poole
      1835–37 (GEC).

694. Byng, John (ca 1704–57), M.P. Rochester 1751–57 (DNB).

695. Byng, John (ca 1772–1860), 1st E. of Strafford, M.P. Poole 1831–
      35 (DNB; GEC).

696. BYNG, Robert (ca 1703–40), M.P. Plymouth 1728–39 (Collins' *Peerage* sub Torrington; Musgrave's *Obituary*).

697. BYRNE, Michael (ca 1744–72), M.P. St. Mawes 1770–72 (*Eton Coll. Reg.*).

698. BYRON, Thomas (ca 1772–1845), M.P. Hertford borough 1823–30 (*Gent. Mag., 1* [1845], 560 and *2* [1849], 671; Parish's *List of Carthusians*).

699. BYRON, William (1749–76), M.P. Morpeth 1775–76 (GEC; *Eton Coll. Reg.*).

700. CADOGAN, Charles Sloane (1728–1807), 1st E. Cadogan, M.P. Cambridge borough 1749–76 (GEC).

701. CAESAR, Charles (1673–1741), M.P. Hertford borough 1701–8, 1710–15, 1722–23, Herts 1727–34, 1736–41 (*Alumni Cantab.*).

702. CALCRAFT, Granby Hales (1800–55), M.P. Wareham 1831–32 (*Alumni Oxon.;* Boase; Hutchins' *Dorset, 1,* 534).

703. CALCRAFT, Granby Thomas (ca 1770–1820), M.P. Wareham 1807–8 (DNB; *Eton Coll. Reg.; Harrow Reg.*).

704. CALCRAFT, John (ca 1726–72), M.P. Calne 1766–68, Rochester 1768–72 (DNB).

705. CALCRAFT, John (1765–1831), M.P. Wareham 1786–90, 1800–6, 1818–31, Rochester 1806–18, Dorset 1831–31 (DNB; *Eton Coll. Reg.; Harrow Reg.*).

706. CALCRAFT, John Hales (1796–1880), M.P. Wareham 1820–26, 1832–41, 1857–59 (*Alumni Oxon.; Eton Lists;* Hutchins' *Dorset, 1,* 534).

707. CALCRAFT, Thomas, M.P. Poole 1761–74.

708. CALL, John (1732–1801), 1st Bt, M.P. Callington 1784–1801 (DNB; GEC).

709. CALLAGHAN, Daniel (1786–1849), M.P. Cork City 1830–34, 1835–49 (Burke's *LG* [ed. 1849]; Dod's *Parl. Companion* [1834], p. 97; *Gent. Mag., 2,* 653).

710. CALLAGHAN, Gerard (d. 1833), M.P. Dundalk 1818–20, Cork City 1829–30 (Burke's *LG* [ed. 1849]; *Royal Kalendar* [1830], p. 72).

711. CALLANDER, Alexander (1741–92), M.P. Aberdeen burghs 1790–92 (Burke's *LG;* Foster's *Scots M.P.'s*).

712. CALLANDER, John (1739–1812), 1st Bt, M.P. Berwick-on-Tweed 1795–1802, 1806–7 (GEC).

713. CALLEY, Thomas (1780–1836), M.P. Cricklade 1812–18, 1831–34 (*Alumni Cantab.;* Burke's *LG*).

CALTHORPE, 1st Bn, *see* GOUGH-CALTHORPE, Henry.

CALTHORPE, 4th Bn, *see* GOUGH, Frederick.

CALTHORPE, Arthur Gough and Frederick Gough, *see* GOUGH-CALTHORPE, Arthur and Frederick.

714. CALTHORPE, Henry (ca 1717–88), M.P. Hindon 1741–47 (Burke's
      LG; Musgrave's Obituary).

715. CALTHORPE, James (ca 1699–1784), M.P. Hindon 1758–61 (*Alumni
      Cantab.*).

716. CALVERLEY-BLACKETT, Walter (1707–77), 2d Bt, M.P. Newcastle-
      upon-Tyne 1734–77 (GEC; *Old Westminsters;* Welford's *Men
      of Mark*).

717. CALVERT, Charles (1699–1751), 5th Bn Baltimore, M.P. St. Ger-
      mans 1734–41, Surrey 1741–51 (GEC).

718. CALVERT, Charles (1768–1832), M.P. Southwark 1812–30, 1830–
      32 (Burke's *LG; Harrow Reg.*).

719. CALVERT, John (1726–1804), M.P. Wendover 1754–61, Hertford
      borough 1761–80, 1784–1802, Tamworth 1780–84 (*Admissions to
      St. John, Cambridge* sub Edward Calvert; Clutterbuck's *Herts,
      3, 335*; Lipscomb's *Bucks, 1,* 185; Wedgwood).

720. CALVERT, John (ca 1758–1844), M.P. Malmesbury 1780–84, Tam-
      worth 1784–90, St. Albans 1790–96, Huntingdon borough 1796–
      1831 (*Alumni Cantab.; Eton Coll. Reg.*).

721. CALVERT, Nicolson (ca 1725–93), M.P. Tewkesbury 1754–74
      (*Alumni Cantab.;* Williams' *Gloucester M.P.'s*).

722. CALVERT, Nicolson (1764–1841), M.P. Hertford borough 1802–26,
      Herts 1826–34 (*Alumni Cantab.;* Burke's *LG; Harrow Reg.*).

723. CALVERT, Thomas (b. ca 1759), M.P. St. Mawes 1792–95 (War-
      rand's *Herts Families,* p. 66).

724. CALVERT, William (ca 1704–61), M.P. London 1742–54, Old Sarum
      1755–61 (*Alumni Cantab.;* Warrand's *Herts Families,* p. 58).

      CAMDEN, Bn, E., and M., *see* PRATT, Charles, George Charles, and
      John Jeffries.

      CAMELFORD, 1st Bn, *see* PITT, Thomas.

725. CAMPBELL, Alexander (d. 1785), M.P. Nairnshire 1784–85 (Burke's
      Peerage sub Cawdor; Foster's *Scots M.P.'s*).

726. CAMPBELL, Alexander (d. 1832), M.P. Anstruther Easter burghs
      1797–1806, Stirling burghs 1807–18 (Foster's *Scots M.P.'s; Gent.
      Mag., 1,* 273).

      CAMPBELL, Alexander Glynn, *see* GLYNN-CAMPBELL, Alexander.

727. CAMPBELL, Alexander Hume (1708–60), M.P. Berwickshire 1734–
      60 (Foster's *Scots M.P.'s; Scots Peerage* sub Marchmont).

728. CAMPBELL, Archibald (1739–91), M.P. Stirling burghs 1774–80,
      1789–91 (Addison's *Glasgow Matric. Albums;* DNB).

729. CAMPBELL, Archibald (ca 1763–1838), M.P. Glasgow burghs
      1806–9, 1820–31, Elgin burghs 1812–12, Perth burghs 1818–20
      (Foster's *Scots M.P.'s*).

730. CAMPBELL, Charles (d. 1741), M.P. Argyllshire 1736–41 (Foster's
      Scots M.P.'s; Notes and Queries, 12th Ser., *6,* 70).

731. CAMPBELL, Daniel (d. 1777), M.P. Lanarkshire 1760–68 (Burke's *LG;* Foster's *Scots M.P.'s*).
732. CAMPBELL, DUGALD (d. 1764), M.P. Argyllshire 1754–61, Ayrshire 1761–64 (Foster's *Scots M.P.'s*).
733. CAMPBELL, Duncan (d. 1765), M.P. Argyllshire 1747–54 (Foster's *Scots M.P.'s*).
734. CAMPBELL, Duncan (ca 1763–1837), M.P. Ayr burghs 1809–18 (Addison's *Glasgow Matric. Albums;* Foster's *Scots M.P.'s*).
735. CAMPBELL, Frederick (ca 1729–1816), M.P. Glasgow burghs 1761–80, Argyllshire 1780–99 (DNB; *Old Westminsters; St. Paul's School Reg.*).
736. CAMPBELL, George (1759–1821), M.P. Carmarthen borough 1806–13 (Williams' *Wales M.P.'s*).
737. CAMPBELL, George Pryse (ca 1793–1858), M.P. Nairnshire 1820–26, 1830–31 (Burke's *Peerage* sub Cawdor; Foster's *Scots M.P.'s*).
738. CAMPBELL, George William (1768–1839), 6th D. of Argyll, M.P. St. Germans 1790–96 (GEC; *Scots Peerage*).
739. CAMPBELL, Henry Frederick (1769–1856), M.P. Nairnshire 1796–1802, 1806–7 (Foster's *Scots M.P.'s*).
CAMPBELL, Hugh Hume, *see* HUME-CAMPBELL, Hugh.
740. CAMPBELL, Ilay (1734–1823), 1st Bt, M.P. Glasgow burghs 1784–89 (Addison's *Glasgow Matric. Albums;* DNB).
741. CAMPBELL, James (ca 1666–1752), 2d Bt, M.P. Argyllshire 1707–34, Stirlingshire 1734–41 (Foster's *Scots M.P.'s;* GEC).
742. CAMPBELL, James (ca 1677–1745), M.P. Ayrshire 1727–41 (DNB; Foster's *Scots M.P.'s*).
743. CAMPBELL, James (1737–1805), M.P. Stirling burghs 1780–89 (Addison's *Glasgow Matric. Albums;* Foster's *Scots M.P.'s*).
744. CAMPBELL, James (d. 1788), 3d Bt, M.P. Stirlingshire 1747–68 (GEC; Foster's *Scots M.P.'s*).
CAMPBELL, James Mure, *see* MURE-CAMPBELL, James.
745. CAMPBELL, John (ca 1693–1770), 4th D. of Argyll, M.P. Buteshire 1713–15, Elgin burghs 1715–22, 1725–27, Dumbartonshire 1727–61 (GEC; *Scots Peerage*).
746. CAMPBELL, John (ca 1695–1777), M.P. Pembrokeshire 1727–47, Nairnshire 1747–54, Inverness burghs 1754–61, Corfe Castle 1762–68 (Burke's *Peerage* sub Cawdor; Foster's *Scots M.P.'s*).
747. CAMPBELL, John (1696–1782), 3d E. of Breadalbane, M.P. Saltash 1727–41, Orford 1741–45 (DNB; GEC; *Scots Peerage*).
748. CAMPBELL, John (1723–1806), 5th D. of Argyll, M.P. Glasgow burghs 1744–61, Dover 1765–66 (GEC; *Scots Peerage*).
749. CAMPBELL, John (d. 1809), M.P. Ayr burghs 1807–9 (Burke's *LG;* Foster's *Scots M.P.'s*).
750. CAMPBELL, John (1755–1821), 1st Bn Cawdor, M.P. Nairnshire

1777–80, Cardigan borough 1780–96 (*Eton Coll. Reg.;* GEC; MS, *ex inform.* E. H. Stuart Jones).

751. CAMPBELL, John (d. 1826), M.P. Ayr burghs 1794–1807 (Burke's *Peerage* sub Argyll; Foster's *Scots M.P.'s*).

752. CAMPBELL, John (1779–1861), 1st Bn Campbell, M.P. Stafford borough 1830–32, Dudley 1832–34, Edinburgh City 1834–41 (DNB; GEC).

753. CAMPBELL, John (1796–1862), 2d M. of Breadalbane, M.P. Oke-hampton 1820–26, Perthshire 1832–34 (Addison's *Glasgow Matric. Albums;* DNB; GEC).

754. CAMPBELL, John, M.P. Stirling burghs 1818–19.

755. CAMPBELL, John (1798–1830), M.P. Dumbartonshire 1826–30 (Foster's *Scots M.P.'s; Harrow Reg.;* Grant's *Faculty of Advocates*).

756. CAMPBELL, John Douglas Edward Henry (1777–1847), 7th D. of Argyll, M.P. Argyllshire 1799–1822 (GEC; *Scots Peerage*).

757. CAMPBELL, John Frederick (1790–1860), 1st E. of Cawdor, M.P. Carmarthen borough 1813–21 (*Eton Lists;* GEC).

758. CAMPBELL, Peter (d. 1751), M.P. Buteshire 1722–27, 1734–41, Elgin burghs 1728–34 (Musgrave's *Obituary*).

759. CAMPBELL, Pryse (ca 1727–68), M.P. Inverness-shire 1754–61, Nairnshire 1761–68, Cardigan borough 1768–68 (*Alumni Cantab.;* Williams' *Wales M.P.'s*).

760. CAMPBELL, Robert (d. 1790), M.P. Argyllshire 1766–72 (Foster's *Scots M.P.'s*).

761. CAMPBELL, Walter Frederick (1798–1855), M.P. Argyllshire 1822–32, 1835–41 (Boase; *Eton Lists;* Foster's *Scots M.P.'s*).

762. CAMPBELL, William, M.P. Glasgow burghs 1734–41.

763. CAMPBELL, William (d. 1778), M.P. Argyllshire 1764–66 (*Dict. Am. Biog.; Scots Peerage*).

764. CAMPBELL-COLQUHOUN, Archibald (d. 1820), M.P. Elgin burghs 1807–10, Dumbartonshire 1810–20 (DNB).

765. CANNING, George (1770–1827), M.P. Newtown 1793–96, 1806–7, Wendover 1796–1802, Tralee 1802–6, Hastings 1807–12, Liverpool 1812–22, Harwich 1823–26, Newport (Hants) 1826–27, Seaford 1827–27 (DNB; *Eton Coll. Reg.*).

766. CANNING, George (1778–1840), 1st Bn Garvagh, M.P. Sligo borough 1806–12, Petersfield 1812–20 (GEC).

767. CANNING, Stratford (1786–1880), 1st Vct Stratford, M.P. Old Sarum 1828–30, Stockbridge 1831–32, Lynn 1835–42 (*Alumni Cantab.;* DNB; GEC).

CANTERBURY, 1st Vct, *see* MANNERS-SUTTON, Charles.

768. CAPEL, John (ca 1767–1846), M.P. Queenborough 1826–32 (*Gent. Mag., 1* [1847], 214; *1832 List*).

769. CAPEL-CONINGSBY, George (1757–1839), 5th E. of Essex, M.P.

Westminster 1779–80, Lostwithiel 1781–84, Okehampton 1785–
90, New Radnor 1794–99 (*Alumni Cantab.;* GEC; *Old Westminsters*).

770. CARADOC, John Hobart (1799–1873), 2d Bn Howden, M.P. Dundalk 1830–31 (DNB; GEC).

CARBERY, Bns, *see* EVANS, George.

CARDIFF, 1st Bn, *see* STUART, John.

CARDIGAN, Earls of, *see* BRUDENELL, James and James Thomas.

CARDONNEL, George, *see* TALBOT-RICE, George.

771. CAREW, Coventry (ca 1717–48), 6th Bt, M.P. Cornwall 1744–48
(GEC).

CAREW, Reginald Pole, *see* POLE-CAREW, Reginald.

772. CAREW, Robert Shapland (1752–1829), M.P. Wexford Co. 1806–7
(*Alumni Dublin.; Eton Coll. Reg.*).

773. CAREW, Robert Shapland (1787–1856), 1st Bn. Carew, M.P. Wexford Co. 1812–30, 1831–34 (*Eton Lists;* GEC).

774. CAREW, Thomas (ca 1702–66), M.P. Minehead 1739–47 (Burke's
LG sub Trollope; Collinson's *Somerset, 3,* 517).

775. CAREW, William (ca 1689–1744), 5th Bt, M.P. Saltash 1711–13,
Cornwall 1713–44 (*Alumni Oxon.;* GEC).

776. CAREY, Walter (ca 1686–1757), M.P. Helston 1722–27, Dartmouth 1727–57 (*Alumni Oxon.;* Devonshire Assoc. *Trans., 43,*
366).

CARHAMPTON, Vct and E. of, *see* LUTTRELL, Henry Lawes, John,
and Simon.

CARLETON, Bn, *see* BOYLE, Henry and Richard.

CARLINGFORD, Vct, *see* CARPENTER, George.

CARLISLE, E. of, *see* HOWARD, George, George William Frederick,
and Henry.

CARMARTHEN, M. of, *see* D'ARCY-OSBORNE, Francis Godolphin.

777. CARMICHAEL, James (d. 1754), M.P. Linlithgow burghs 1734–42,
1748–54 (*Eton Coll. Reg.*).

778. CARMICHAEL-ANSTRUTHER, John (1785–1818), 2d and 5th Bt, M.P.
Anstruther Easter burghs 1811–18 (*Eton Lists;* Foster's *Scots
M.P.'s;* GEC).

779. CARNAC, John (ca 1716–1800), M.P. Leominster 1768–74 (*Alumni
Dublin.;* DNB; Huguenot Soc. *Proceedings, 10,* 141).

CARNARVON, E. and M. of, *see* BRYDGES, Henry and James; *also*
HERBERT, Henry, Henry George, and Henry John George.

780. CARNEGIE, David (1753–1805), 4th Bt, M.P. Aberdeen burghs
1784–90, Forfarshire 1796–1805 (*Eton Coll. Reg.;* GEC; Foster's
Scots M.P.'s).

781. CARNEGIE, James (ca 1715–65), 3d Bt, M.P. Kincardineshire 1741–
65 (Addison's *Glasgow Matric. Albums;* Foster's *Scots M.P.'s;*
GEC).

782. CARNEGIE, James (1799–1849), 5th Bt, M.P. Aberdeen burghs 1830–31 (*Eton Lists;* Foster's *Scots M.P.'s;* GEC).

783. CARPENTER, Charles (ca 1757–1803), M.P. Berwick-on-Tweed 1790–96 (GEC sub Tyrconnell; Bean).

784. CARPENTER, George (ca 1695–1749), 2d Bn Carpenter, M.P. Morpeth 1717–27, Weobley 1741–47 (GEC).

785. CARPENTER, George (1723–62), 1st E. of Tyrconnell, M.P. Taunton 1754–62 (GEC).

786. CARPENTER, George (1750–1805), 2d E. of Tyrconnell, M.P. Scarborough 1772–96, Berwick-on-Tweed 1796–1802 (GEC; *Old Westminsters*).

CARRINGTON, Bn, *see* CARRINGTON, Robert John; *also* SMITH, Robert.

787. CARRINGTON, Codrington Edmund (1769–1849), M.P. St. Mawes 1826–31 (DNB).

788. CARRINGTON, Robert John (1796–1868), 2d Bn Carrington, M.P. Wendover 1818–20, Bucks 1820–31, Wycombe 1831–38 (GEC).

789. CARROLL, John (b. ca 1791), M.P. New Ross 1818–21 (*Alumni Dublin.*).

CARTER, John, *see* BONHAM-CARTER, John.

790. CARTER, Thomas (d. 1767), M.P. Hull 1747–54 (Gunnell's *Hull Celebrities,* p. 376; Musgrave's *Obituary*).

791. CARTER, Thomas (ca 1761–1835), M.P. Tamworth 1796–1802, Callington 1807–10 (Baker's *Northampton, 1,* 495; *Gent. Mag., 2, 205; Old Westminsters;* Wedgwood).

792. CARTER, William (ca 1701–44), M.P. Hull 1741–44 (Gunnell's *Hull Celebrities, p.* 362; Monson's *Lincs Church Notes,* p. 299).

CARTERET, Bn, *see* THYNNE, George and John.

793. CARTERET, Henry Frederick (1735–1826), 1st Bn Carteret, M.P. Staffordshire 1757–61, Weobley 1761–70 (GEC).

794. CARTERET, Robert (1721–76), 2d E. of Granville, M.P. Yarmouth (Hants) 1744–47 (GEC; *Old Westminsters*).

795. CARTWRIGHT, Thomas (ca 1671–1748), M.P. Northamptonshire 1695–98, 1701–48 (*Alumni Cantab.*).

796. CARTWRIGHT, William (ca 1705–68), M.P. Northamptonshire 1754–68 (*Alumni Oxon.;* Burke's *LG; Rugby Reg.*).

797. CARTWRIGHT, William Ralph (1771–1847), M.P. Northamptonshire 1797–1831, South Northamptonshire 1832–46 (*Eton Coll. Reg.*).

798. CARUS-WILSON, William Wilson (1764–1851), M.P. Cockermouth 1821–27 (*Alumni Cantab.*).

799. CARY, Lucius Ferdinand (ca 1736–80), M.P. Bridport 1774–80 (*Old Westminsters;* GEC and *Scots Peerage* sub Falkland).

CARY, Walter, *see* CAREY, Walter.

CARYSFORT, Bn and E. of, *see* PROBY, Granville Levenson and John.

800. CASBERD, Robert Matthew (1772–1842), M.P. Milborne Port 1812–

20 (Burke's *LG* [ed. 1849]; Williams' *Great Sessions in Wales;* Williamson's *Middle Temple Bench Book*).

CASHELL, 7th Vct, *see* WARREN-BULKELEY, Thomas James.

CASSILIS, E. of, *see* KENNEDY, Archibald and David.

CASTLECOOTE, 2d Bn, *see* COOTE, Charles Henry.

CASTLE-CUFFE, Vct, *see* CUFFE, John Otway.

CASTLEMAINE, Bn and Vct, *see* HANDCOCK, Richard and William.

CASTLEREAGH, Vct, *see* STEWART, Frederick William Robert and Robert.

801. CASWALL, George (d. 1742), M.P. Leominster 1717–21, 1722–41 (*Misc. Geneal. et Herald.*, N.S., *2;* Williams' *Hereford M.P.'s*).

802. CASWALL, John (ca 1701–42), M.P. Leominster 1741–42 (*Notes and Queries*, 12th Ser., *3*, 255; Williams' *Hereford M.P.'s*).

803. CASWALL, Timothy (d. 1802), M.P. Hertford borough 1761–68, Brackley 1771–89 (Cussans' *Herts, 2*, pt. 3, 161; *Gent. Mag., 2*, 880).

804. CATHCART, Charles Allan (1759–88), M.P. Clackmannanshire 1784–88 (*Eton Coll. Reg.; Scots Peerage*).

CATHERLOUGH, 1st Bn, *see* KNIGHT, Robert.

805. CATOR, John (1728–1806), M.P. Wallingford 1772–80, Ipswich 1784–84 (Burke's *LG; Gent. Mag., 1*, 285).

806. CAULFEILD, Henry (1779–1862), M.P. Armagh Co. 1802–7, 1815–18, 1820–30 (*Alumni Dublin.;* Burke's *Peerage* sub Charlemont).

CAVE, Robert Otway, see OTWAY-CAVE, Robert.

807. CAVE, Thomas (1712–78), 5th Bt, M. P. Leicestershire 1741–47, 1762–74 (GEC; *Rugby Reg.*).

808. CAVE, Thomas (1766–92), 7th Bt, M.P. Leicestershire 1790–92 (GEC).

809. CAVENDISH, Charles (ca 1693–1783), M.P. Heytesbury 1725–27, Westminster 1727–34, Derbyshire 1734–41 (*Eton Coll. Reg.;* Musgrave's *Obituary*).

810. CAVENDISH, Charles Compton (1793–1863), 1st Bn Chesham, M.P. Aylesbury 1814–18, Newtown 1821–30, Yarmouth (Hants) 1831–32, East Sussex 1832–41, Youghal 1841–47, Bucks 1847–57 (GEC).

811. CAVENDISH, Frederick (1729–1803), M.P. Derbyshire 1751–54, Derby borough 1754–80 (DNB).

812. CAVENDISH, George Augustus (ca 1727–94), M.P. Weymouth and Melcombe Regis 1751–54, Derbyshire 1754–80, 1781–94 (*Alumni Cantab.*).

813. CAVENDISH, George Augustus Henry (1754–1834), 1st E. of Burlington, M.P. Knaresborough 1775–80, Derby borough 1780–97, Derbyshire 1797–1831 (*Alumni Cantab.;* GEC).

814. CAVENDISH, George Henry Compton (1784–1809), M.P. Aylesbury 1806–9 (Burke's *Peerage* and Collins' *Peerage* sub Devonshire).

815. CAVENDISH, Henry (1732–1804), 2d Bt, M.P. Lostwithiel 1768–74 (*Alumni Dublin.; Eton Coll. Reg.;* DNB; GEC).

816. CAVENDISH, Henry Frederick Compton (1789–1873), M.P. Derby borough 1812–34 (*Alumni Cantab.;* Burke's *Peerage* sub Devonshire).

817. CAVENDISH, Henry Manners (1793–1863), 3d Bn Waterpark, M.P. Knaresborough 1830–32, South Derbyshire 1832–34, Lichfield 1854–56 (GEC; *Harrow Reg.*).

818. CAVENDISH, James (d. 1741), M.P. Malton 1741–41 (Burke's *Peerage* sub Devonshire; Musgrave's *Obituary*).

819. CAVENDISH, James (d. 1751), M.P. Derby borough 1701–2, 1705–10, 1715–42 (Burke's *Peerage* sub Devonshire; Musgrave's *Obituary*).

820. CAVENDISH, John (1732–96), M.P. Weymouth and Melcombe Regis 1754–61, Knaresborough 1761–68, York City 1768–84, Derbyshire 1794–96 (*Alumni Cantab.;* DNB).

821. CAVENDISH, Philip (d. 1743), M.P. St. Germans 1722–27, Portsmouth 1734–43 (Charnock's *Biog. Naval., 3, 215;* Musgrave's *Obituary*).

822. CAVENDISH, Richard (ca 1703–69), M.P. Andover 1761–68 (*Eton Coll. Reg.;* Surtees' *Durham, 1,* cxxi).

823. CAVENDISH, Richard (1751–81), M.P. Lancaster borough 1773–80, Derbyshire 1780–81 (*Alumni Cantab.*).

824. CAVENDISH, William (ca 1720–64), 4th D. of Devonshire, M.P. Derbyshire 1741–51 (DNB; GEC).

825. CAVENDISH, William (1783–1812), M.P. Knaresborough 1804–4, Aylesbury 1804–6, Derby borough 1806–12 (*Alumni Cantab.;* GEC sub Devonshire).

826. CAVENDISH, William (1808–91), 7th D. of Devonshire, M.P. Cambridge Univ. 1829–31, Malton 1831–31, Derbyshire 1831–32, North Derbyshire 1832–34 (*Alumni Cantab.;* DNB; GEC).

827. CAVENDISH-BENTINCK, Edward Charles (1744–1819), M.P. Lewes 1766–68, Carlisle 1768–74, Notts 1775–96, Clitheroe 1796–1802 (*Old Westminsters*).

828. CAVENDISH-BENTINCK, Frederick (1781–1828), M.P. Weobley 1816–24, Queenborough 1824–26 (*Old Westminsters*).

829. CAVENDISH-BENTINCK, William Charles Augustus (1780–1826), M.P. Ashburton 1807–12 (*Old Westminsters*).

830. CAVENDISH-BENTINCK, William George Frederick (1802–48), M.P. Lynn 1828–48 (DNB).

831. CAVENDISH-BENTINCK, William Henry (1738–1809), 3d D. of Portland, M.P. Weobley 1761–62 (DNB; GEC; *Old Westminsters*).

832. CAVENDISH-BENTINCK, William Henry (1774–1839), M.P. Camelford 1796–96, Notts 1796–1802, 1812–14, 1816–26, Lynn 1826–28, Glasgow City 1836–39 (DNB; Foster's *Scots M.P.'s*).

833. CAVENDISH-BRADSHAW, Augustus (1768–1832), M.P. Honiton 1805–12, Castle Rising 1812–17 (*Alumni Cantab.*).

834. CAVENDISH-SCOTT-BENTINCK, William Henry (1768–1854), 4th D. of Portland, M.P. Petersfield 1790–91, Bucks 1791–1809 (GEC; *Old Westminsters*).

835. CAVENDISH-SCOTT-BENTINCK, William Henry (1796–1824), M.P. Bletchingley 1819–21, Lynn 1822–24 (GEC sub Portland).

836. CAVENDISH-SCOTT-BENTINCK, William John (1800–79), 5th D. of Portland, M.P. Lynn 1824–26 (DNB; GEC).

CAWDOR, Bn and E., *see* CAMPBELL, John and John Frederick.

CAWTHORNE, John Fenton, *see* FENTON-CAWTHORNE, John.

837. CAYLEY, William (d. 1768), M.P. Dover 1752–55 (Foster's *Yorkshire Pedigrees;* Musgrave's *Obituary*).

838. CECIL, Brownlow (1725–93), 9th E. of Exeter, M.P. Rutland 1747–54 (*Alumni Cantab.;* GEC).

839. CECIL, Henry (1754–1804), 1st M. of Exeter, M.P. Stamford 1774–90 (*Eton Coll. Reg.;* GEC).

840. CECIL, James (1748–1823), 1st M. of Salisbury, M.P. Great Bedwin 1774–80, Launceston 1780–80 (GEC).

CECIL, James Brownlow William, *see* GASCOYNE-CECIL, James Brownlow William.

841. CECIL, Thomas (1797–1873), M.P. Stamford 1818–32 (*Alumni Cantab.*).

842. CECIL, Thomas Chambers (1728–78), M.P. Rutland 1761–68 (GEC sub Exeter).

843. CHAFIN, George (1689–1766), M.P. Dorset 1713–54 (*Alumni Oxon.;* Hutchins' *Dorset, 3, 565*).

844. CHALONER, Robert (1776–1842), M.P. Richmond 1810–18, York City 1820–26 (Burke's *LG,* [ed. 1849]; *Harrow Reg.; 1821 List*).

CHAMBERLAYNE, George, *see* DENTON, George.

845. CHAMBERLAYNE, William (ca 1761–1829), M.P. Christchurch 1800–2, Southampton borough 1818–29 (Burke's *LG;* Kirby's *Winchester Scholars; Gent. Mag., 1* [1830], 87; cf. *Alumni Cantab.*).

846. CHAMBERS, George, M.P. Honiton 1796–1802.

847. CHAMIER, Anthony (1725–80), M.P. Tamworth 1778–80 (Agnew's *Protestant Exiles, 2,* 246, 294–95; DNB; Wedgwood).

848. CHAMPERNOWNE, Arthur (ca 1769–1819), M.P. Saltash 1806–7 (Vivian's *Visitation of Devon,* p. 164).

849. CHAMPION, Anthony (1725–1801), M.P. St. Germans 1754–61, Liskeard 1761–68 (*Eton Coll. Reg.;* DNB).

850. CHAMPION, George (d. 1754), M.P. Aylesbury 1734–41 (Beaven's *Aldermen of London*).

CHANDLER, Richard, *see* CAVENDISH, Richard.

CHANDOS, M. of, *see* TEMPLE-NUGENT-BRYDGES-CHANDOS-GRENVILLE, Richard Plantaganet.

CHANDOS, Dukes of, *see* BRYDGES, Henry and James.

851. CHAPLIN, Charles (1759–1816), M.P. Lincolnshire 1802–16 (*Alumni Cantab.*).

852. CHAPLIN, Charles (1786–1859), M.P. Stamford 1809–12, Lincolnshire 1818–31 (*Alumni Oxon.; Burke's LG; Harrow Reg.*).

853. CHAPLIN, John (ca 1729–64), M.P. Lincoln City 1754–61, Stamford 1761–64 (*Old Westminsters*).

854. CHAPLIN, Thomas (1794–1863), M.P. Stamford 1826–31, 1832–38 (Burke's *LG; Harrow Reg.*).

855. CHAPMAN, Charles (ca 1754–1809), M.P. Newtown 1802–5 (*Gent. Mag., 1*, 286, 388; *1806 List*).

856. CHAPMAN, John (ca 1710–81), 2d Bt, M.P. Taunton 1741–47 (GEC; *Misc. Geneal. et Herald.*, N.S., *1*, 6).

857. CHAPMAN, Montagu Lowther (1808–52), 3d Bt, M.P. Westmeath 1830–41 (*Alumni Dublin.;* Foster's *Collect. Geneal., 2*, 144; GEC).

858. CHAPPLE, William (ca 1677–1745), M.P. Dorchester 1723–37 (DNB).

CHARLEVILLE, 2d E. of, *see* BURY, Charles William.

859. CHARLTON, Job Staunton (ca 1701–78), M.P. Newark 1741–61 (*Alumni Cantab.; London Chronicle,* 28 Feb. to 3 Mar. 1778).

CHARLTON, Nicholas Lechmere, *see* LECHMERE-CHARLTON, Nicholas.

860. CHARTERIS–WEMYSS, Francis (1749–1808), M.P. Haddington burghs 1780–87 (*Scots Peerage*).

CHATHAM, 1st E. of, *see* PITT, William.

CHAWORTH, 2d Bn, *see* BRABAZON, William.

861. CHAYTOR, William (1732–1819), M.P. Penryn 1774–80, Hedon 1780–90 (*Alumni Cantab.;* Foster's *Yorkshire Pedigrees*).

862. CHAYTOR, William Richard Carter (1805–71), 2d Bt, M.P. Durham City 1831–34 (*Alumni Oxon.;* Burke's *Peerage; Harrow Reg.*).

CHEDWORTH, 1st Bn, *see* HOWE, John.

863. CHEERE, Charles Madryll (ca 1773–1825), M.P. Cambridge borough 1820–25 (*Bury Grammar School List,* p. 69).

864. CHEESMENT-SEVERN, John (1781–1875), M.P. Wootton Bassett 1807–8, Fowey 1830–32 (*Alumni Oxon.;* Burke's *LG* [ed. 1849]).

865. CHERNOCK, Boteler (1696–ca 1756), 4th Bt, M.P. Bedfordshire 1740–47 (GEC).

866. CHERRY, George Henry (1793–1848), M.P. Dunwich 1820–26 (*Alumni Oxon.;* Burke's *LG; 1821 List*).

CHESHAM, 1st Bn, *see* CAVENDISH, Charles Compton.

CHESTER, Charles Bagot, *see* BAGOT-CHESTER, Charles.

867. CHESTER, John (1693–1748), 6th Bt, M.P. Bedfordshire 1741–47 (*Alumni Cantab.;* GEC).

868. CHESTER, Thomas (1696–1763), M.P. Gloucester 1727–28, Gloucestershire 1734–63 (Williams' *Gloucester M.P.'s*).

CHESTER, William Bromley, *see* BROMLEY-CHESTER, William.

869. CHETWODE, John (1764–1845), 4th Bt, M.P. Newcastle-under-Lyme 1815–18, Buckingham borough 1841–45 (*Alumni Cantab.;* GEC).

870. CHETWYNDE, George (1783–1850), 2d Bt, M.P. Stafford borough 1820–26 (GEC; *Harrow Reg.*).

871. CHETWYND, John (ca 1680–1767), 2d Vct Chetwynd, M.P. St. Mawes 1715–22, Stockbridge 1722–34, Stafford borough 1738–47 (GEC; Wedgwood).

872. CHETWYND, William (1721–91), 4th Vct Chetwynd, M.P. Stockbridge 1747–54 (GEC; *Old Westminsters*).

873. CHETWYND, William Richard (ca 1684–1770), 3d Vct Chetwynd, M.P. Stafford borough 1715–22, 1734–70, Plymouth 1722–27 (DNB; GEC; *Old Westminsters;* Wedgwood).

874. CHETWYND, William Richard (ca 1732–65), M.P. Stafford borough 1754–65 (GEC; *Eton Coll. Reg.;* Wedgwood).

875. CHETWYND-TALBOT, Henry John (1803–68), 3d E. Talbot, M.P. Hertford borough 1830–31, 1832–34, Armagh borough 1831–31, Dublin City 1831–32, South Staffordshire 1837–49 (GEC).

876. CHETWYND-TALBOT, John (1749–93), 1st E. Talbot, M.P. Castle Rising 1777–82 (*Eton Coll. Reg.;* GEC).

CHEWTON, Vct, *see* WALDEGRAVE, John.

CHICHESTER, E. of, *see* PELHAM, Thomas.

877. CHICHESTER, Arthur (1739–99), 1st M. of Donegal, M.P. Malmesbury 1768–74 (GEC; *Old Westminsters*).

878. CHICHESTER, Arthur (d. 1847), 1st Bt, M.P. Carrickfergus 1812–18, 1820–30, Belfast 1818–20, 1830–32 (Burke's *Peerage* sub O'Neill; *Linc. Inn Reg.*) .

879. CHICHESTER, Arthur (1797–1837), 1st Bn Templemore, M.P. Milborne Port 1826–30, Wexford Co. 1830–31 (GEC; *Harrow Reg.*).

880. CHICHESTER, George Hamilton (1797–1883), 3d M. of Donegal, M.P. Carrickfergus 1818–20, Belfast 1820–30, 1837–38, Antrim 1830–37 (GEC).

881. CHICHESTER, John (1689–1740), 4th Bt, M.P. Barnstable 1734–40 (*Alumni Oxon.;* GEC).

882. CHICHESTER, John Palmer Bruce (ca 1794–1851), 1st Bt, M.P. Barnstable 1831–41 (Boase; Foster's *Baronetage*).

883. CHICHESTER, Spencer Stanley (1775–1819), M.P. Carrickfergus 1802–7 (Burke's *Peerage* sub Templemore).

884. CHILD, Francis (ca 1684–1740), M.P. London 1722–27, Middlesex 1727–40 (DNB; Price's *Temple Bar,* p. 24).

885. CHILD, Francis (ca 1736–63), M.P. Bishop's Castle 1761–63 (*Old Westminsters*).

886. CHILD, Robert (ca 1739–82),. M.P. Wells 1766–82 (*Old West-minsters*).

887. CHILD, Samuel (ca 1694–1752), M.P. Bishop's Castle 1747–52 (Shrop. Archaeol. Soc. *Trans.*, 2d Ser., *10;* Wiltshire *Notes and Queries, 2,* 209; MS, *ex inform.* the Reverend G. Craggs).

888. CHILD-TYLNEY, John (1712–84), 2d E. Tylney, M.P. Malmesbury 1761–68 (*Eton Coll. Reg.;* GEC; *Old Westminsters*).

889. CHILD-VILLIERS, George Augustus Frederick (1808–59), 6th E. of Jersey, M.P. Rochester 1830–31, Minehead 1831–32, Honiton 1832–34, Weymouth 1837–42, Cirencester 1844–52 (GEC).

890. CHILDE, William Lacon (1786–1880), M.P. Wenlock 1820–26 (*Alumni Oxon.;* Burke's *LG; Harrow Reg.;* Boase; *Shrewsbury School Reg.;* Shrop. Archaeol. Soc. *Trans.*, 4th Ser., *2,* 382).

891. CHINNERY, Broderick (ca 1740–1808), 1st Bt, M.P. Bandon 1801–6 (*Cork Archaeol. Jour.* [1895], p. 230; GEC).

CHISWELL, Richard Muilman Trench, *see* MUILMAN-TRENCH-CHISWELL, Richard.

892. CHOLMELEY, Montague (1772–1831), 1st Bt, M.P. Grantham 1820–26 (Burke's *Peerage;* Foster's *Baronetage*).

893. CHOLMELEY, Montague John (1802–74), 2d Bt, M.P. Grantham 1826–31, North Lincolnshire 1847–52, 1857–74 (*Alumni Oxon.;* Burke's *Peerage; Harrow Reg.*).

894. CHOLMLEY, George (1782–1874), 7th Bt, M.P. Yorkshire 1831–32, Yorkshire (West Riding) 1832–41, Preston 1841–57 (GEC; Gooder).

895. CHOLMLEY, Nathaniel (1721–91), M.P. Aldborough 1756–68, Boroughbridge 1768–74 (Burke's *LG* [ed. 1849]; Bean; *Etoniana, 65,* 232; *Genealogist,* N.S., *19,* 252; *Misc. Geneal. et Herald.,* 1st Ser., *2,* 218–28).

896. CHOLMONDELEY, Charles (1685–1756), M.P. Cheshire 1710–15, 1722–56 (*Alumni Cantab.;* Omerod's *Chester,, 2,* 158).

897. CHOLMONDELEY, George (1724–64), M.P. Bramber 1754–61, Corfe Castle 1761–64 (GEC).

898. CHOLMONDELEY, George Horatio (1792–1870), 2d M. of Cholmondeley, M.P. Castle Rising 1817–21 (GEC).

899. CHOLMONDELEY, James (1708–75), M.P. Bossiney 1731–34, Camelford 1734–41, Montgomery borough 1741–47 (Burke's *Peerage;* Williams' *Wales M.P.'s*).

900. CHOLMONDELEY, Thomas (1726–79), M.P. Cheshire 1756–68 (*Alumni Cantab.; Old Westminsters*).

901. CHOLMONDELEY, Thomas (1767–1855), 1st Bn Delamere, M.P. Cheshire 1796–1812 (*Alumni Cantab.;* GEC).

902. CHOLMONDELEY, William Henry Hugh (1800–84), 3d M. of Cholmondeley, M.P. Castle Rising 1822–32, South Hampshire 1852–57 (*Eton Lists;* GEC).

903. CHRISTIAN-CURWEN, John (ca 1756–1828), M.P. Carlisle 1786–90, 1791–1812, 1816–20, Cumberland 1820–28 (Burke's *LG;* Bean; *Gent. Mag., 1* [1829], 178).

904. CHRISTIE-BURTON, Napier (1758–1835), M.P. Beverley 1796–1806 (Burke's *LG; Gent Mag., 2,* 204).

905. CHRISTIE-BURTON, Robert (d. 1822), M.P. Beverley 1818–20 (Burke's *LG*).

906. CHRISTOPHER-NISBET-HAMILTON, Robert Adam (1804–77), M.P. Ipswich 1827–31, 1835–35, Edinburgh City 1831–32, North Lincolnshire 1837–57 (Foster's *Scots M.P.'s;* Grant's *Faculty of Advocates;* Williams' *Worcester M.P.'s*).

907. CHURCH, John Barker (ca 1746–1818), M.P. Wendover 1790–96 (Palmer's *Perlustration of Great Yarmouth, 2,* 322; Schuyler's *Colonial New York, 2, 274, 280*).

CHURCHILL, 1st Bn, *see* SPENCER, Francis Almeric.

908. CHURCHILL, Charles (ca 1679–1745), M.P. Weymouth and Melcombe Regis 1701–10, Castle Rising 1715–45 (DNB sub Charles Churchill [1656–1714]; J. Harrington, *Bath Abbey* [1778], p. 41).

909. CHURCHILL, Charles (ca 1721–1812), M.P. Stockbridge 1741–47, Milborne Port 1747–54, Great Marlow 1754–61 (*Gent. Mag., 1,* 398; *Notes and Queries,* 12th Ser., *3,* 304; *Old Westminsters*).

CHURCHILL, Charles Spencer and George Spencer, *see* SPENCER-CHURCHILL, Charles and George.

910. CHURCHILL, Horatio (1759–1817), M.P. Castle Rising 1796–1802 (Hasted's *Kent,* ed. Drake, p. 265; *Notes and Queries,* 3d Ser., *6,* 318).

911. CHUTE, Anthony (1691–1754), M.P. Yarmouth (Hants) 1737–41, Newport (Hants) 1741–47 (Chute's *Hist. of the Vyne*).

912. CHUTE, Francis (d. 1745), M.P. Hedon 1741–42 (Bean; Chute's *Hist. of the Vyne; Linc. Inn Reg.*).

913. CHUTE, William John (1757–1824), M.P. Hampshire 1790–1806, 1807–20 (*Alumni Cantab.;* Burke's *LG; Harrow Reg.*).

CLANBRASSIL, Bn and E. of, *see* HAMILTON, James and John; *also* JOCELYN, Robert.

CLANCARTY, 1st Vct, *see* TRENCH, Richard Power.

CLARE, 3d. E. of, *see* FITZGIBBON, Richard Hobart.

CLARENDON, E. of, *see* VILLIERS, John Charles and Thomas.

914. CLARGES, Thomas (1751–82), 3d Bt, M.P. Lincoln City 1780–82 (*Eton Coll. Reg.;* GEC).

915. CLARKE, Charles (ca 1702–50), M.P. Hunts 1739–41, Whitchurch 1743–43 (*Alumni Cantab.;* DNB; *Eton Coll. Reg.*).

CLARKE, Charles Harward Butler, *see* BUTLER-CLARKE-SOUTHWELL-WANDESFORD, Charles Harward.

916. CLARKE, Edward (b. 1770), M.P. Wootton Bassett 1796–1802 (*Alumni Cantab.*).

917. CLARKE, George (ca 1661–1736), M.P. Winchelsea 1702–5, East Looe 1705–8, Launceston 1711–13, Oxford Univ. 1717–36 (*Alumni Oxon.;* DNB; *Notes and Queries,* 7th Ser., *12,* 115; Williams' *Gloucester M.P.'s*).

918. CLARKE, Godfrey Bagnall (ca 1742–74), M.P. Derbyshire 1768–74 (Hunter's *Familiae Min. Gent.*).

919. CLARKE, Thomas (ca 1671–1754), M.P. Hertford borough 1705–10, 1715–22, 1723–41 (*Whitehall Evening Post* 31 Oct. to 2 Nov. 1754).

920. CLARKE, Thomas (ca 1703–64), M.P. St. Michael 1747–54, Lost-withiel 1754–61 (*Alumni Cantab.;* DNB; *Old Westminsters*).

921. CLARKE–JERVOISE, Jervoise (ca 1734–1808), M.P. Yarmouth (Hants) 1768–69, 1774–79, 1791–1808, Hampshire 1779–90 (Foster's *Baronetage*).

922. CLARKE-JERVOISE, Thomas (ca 1764–1809), M.P. Yarmouth (Hants) 1787–90 (Hunter's *Familiae Min. Gent.; The Ancestor, 3,* 8).

923. CLAUGHTON, Thomas (ca 1775–1842), M.P. Newton 1818–25 (Bean; *Gent. Mag., 1,* 452; Pink; *Rugby Reg.*).

924. CLAVELL, George (1725–74), M.P. Dorchester 1752–54 (Hutchins' *Dorset, 1,* 570).

925. CLAVERING, John (d. 1762), M.P. Great Marlow 1727–31, Penryn 1734–41 (Lipscomb's *Bucks, 3,* 599; Musgrave's *Obituary*).

926. CLAVERING, Thomas (1719–94), 7th Bt, M.P. St. Mawes 1753–54, Shaftesbury 1754–61, Durham Co. 1768–90 (Bean; GEC; Burke's *LG*).

927. CLAVERING-COWPER, George Nassau (1738–89), 3d E. Cowper, M.P. Hertford borough 1759–61 (*Eton Coll. Reg.;* GEC).

928. CLAYTON, Courthope (d. 1762), M.P. Eye 1749–61 (*Cork Archaeol. Jour.* [1895], p. 231; Hist. Soc. of Lancs. and Cheshire *Trans., 32,* 43; *Notes and Queries,* 12th Ser., *2,* 191).

929. CLAYTON, Kenrick (ca 1713–69), 2d Bt, M.P. Bletchingley 1734–69 (GEC; Manning and Bray's *Surrey, 2,* 294).

930. CLAYTON, Richard (ca 1703–70), M.P. Wigan 1747–54 (*Alumni Oxon.;* Burke's *LG* [ed. 1849]; Martin's *Masters of the Bench, Inner Temple*).

931. CLAYTON, Robert (ca 1740–99), 3d Bt, M.P. Bletchingley 1768–83, 1787–96, Surrey 1783–84, Ilchester 1796–99 (*Alumni Cantab.; Eton Coll. Reg.;* GEC).

932. CLAYTON, William (d. 1744), 1st Bt, M.P. Bletchingley 1715–44 (GEC).

933. CLAYTON, William (d. 1783), M.P. Bletchingley 1745–61, Great Marlow 1761–83 (Burke's *Peerage;* Musgrave's *Obituary*).

934. CLAYTON, William (1671–1752), 1st Bn Sundon, M.P. Woodstock 1716–22, St. Albans 1722–27, Westminster 1727–41, Plympton 1742–47, St. Mawes 1747–52 (GEC; *Genealogist,* N.S., *26,* 135).

935. CLAYTON, William (1762–1834), 4th Bt, M.P. Great Marlow 1783–90 (GEC).

936. CLAYTON, William Robert (1786–1866), 5th Bt, M.P. Great Marlow 1832–42 (Boase; *Eton Lists;* GEC).

937. CLEMENTS, Henry John (1781–1843), M.P. Leitrim 1805–18, Cavan 1840–43 (Burke's *Irish LG*).

938. CLEMENTS, John Marcus (1789–1833), M.P. Leitrim 1820–26, 1830–32 (Burke's *Irish LG*).

939. CLEMENTS, Nathaniel (1768–1854), 2d E. of Leitrim, M.P. Leitrim 1801–4 (GEC).

940. CLEMENTS, Robert Bemingham (1805–39), M.P. Leitrim 1826–30, 1832–39 (*Alumni Oxon.;* GEC sub Leitrim).

941. CLEPHANE, David, M.P. Kinross-shire 1803–6, 1807–11.

CLEPHANE, William Douglas McLean, *see* MCLEAN-CLEPHANE, William Douglas.

942. CLERK, George (1787–1867), 6th Bt, M.P. Edinburghshire 1811–32, 1835–37, Stamford 1838–47, Dover 1847–52 (DNB; GEC).

CLERKE, Philip Jennings, *see* JENNINGS-CLERKE, Philip.

CLERMONT, 2d Vct, *see* FORTESCUE, William Charles.

CLEVELAND, D. of, *see* VANE, Henry and William John Frederick.

943. CLEVLAND, John (ca 1707–63), M.P. Saltash 1741–43, 1761–63, Sandwich 1747–61 (*Old Westminsters*).

944. CLEVLAND, John (ca 1734–1817), M.P. Barnstable 1766–1802 (Burke's *LG* sub Christie; *Gent. Mag., 1,* 643).

CLIFDEN, 2d Vct, *see* ELLIS, Henry Welbore.

CLIFFORD, Bn, *see* SOUTHWELL, Edward.

945. CLIFFORD, Augustus William James (1788–1877), 1st Bt, M.P. Bandon 1818–20, 1831–32, Dungarvan 1820–22 (DNB; *Harrow Reg.*).

CLIFTON, Bn, *see* BLIGH, Edward and John.

946. CLIFTON, Robert (ca 1690–1762), 5th Bt, M.P. East Retford 1727–41 (GEC).

CLINTON, 19th Bn, *see* TREFUSIS, Charles Rodolph.

CLINTON, Clinton James Fynes, *see* FYNES-CLINTON, Clinton James.

947. CLINTON, George (ca 1685–1761), M.P. Saltash 1754–61 (Charnock's *Biog. Naval., 4,* 59).

948. CLINTON, Henry (ca 1738–95), M.P. Boroughbridge 1772–74, Newark 1774–84, Launceston 1790–94 (DNB).

949. CLINTON, Henry (1771–1829), M.P. Boroughbridge 1808–18 (DNB; *Eton Coll. Reg.*).

CLINTON, Henry Fynes, *see* FYNES-CLINTON, Henry.

CLINTON, Henry Fiennes Pelham, John Pelham and Thomas Pelham, *see* PELHAM-CLINTON, Henry Fiennes, John, and Thomas.

950. CLINTON, William Henry (1769–1846), M.P. East Retford 1794–96, Boroughbridge 1806–18, Newark 1818–29 (DNB; *Eton Coll. Reg.*).

951. CLIVE, Edward (1703–71), M.P. St. Michael 1741–45 (DNB; Robinson's *Hereford,* p. 313; Williams' *Great Sessions in Wales*).

952. CLIVE, Edward (1754–1839), 1st E. of Powis, M.P. Ludlow 1774–94 (GEC; DNB; *Eton Coll. Reg.*).

CLIVE, Edward, *see* HERBERT, Edward.

953. CLIVE, Edward Bolton (ca 1765–1845), M.P. Hereford City 1826–45 (Burke's *LG;* Wiliams' *Hereford M.P.'s*).

954. CLIVE, George (d. 1779), M.P. Bishop's Castle 1763–79 (Burke's *LG; Lloyd's Evening Post,* 24–26 Mar. 1779).

955. CLIVE, Henry (ca 1778–1848), M.P. Ludlow 1807–18, Montgomery borough 1818–32 (*Gent. Mag., 1, 550; Old Westminsters;* Williams' *Wales M.P.'s*).

956. CLIVE, Richard (1694–1771), M.P. Montgomery borough 1759–71 (Robinson's *Hereford,* p. 313; Williams' *Wales M.P.'s*).

957. CLIVE, Robert (1725–74), 1st Bn Clive, M.P. St. Michael 1754–55, Shrewsbury 1761–74 (DNB; GEC).

958. CLIVE, Robert (1769–1833), M.P. Ludlow 1794–1807 (*Eton Coll. Reg.*).

959. CLIVE, Robert Henry (1789–1854), M.P. Ludlow 1818–32, South Salop 1832–54 (*Alumni Cantab.;* Dod's *Parl. Companion* [1834], p. 102; *Eton Lists*).

960. CLIVE, William (1745–1825), M.P. Bishop's Castle 1768–70, 1779–1820 (*Eton Coll. Reg.*).

CLONMELL, 2d E. of, *see* SCOTT, Thomas.

961. CLUTTERBUCK, Thomas (ca 1671–1742), M.P. Liskeard 1722–34, Plympton Erle 1734–42 (*Alumni Cantab.; Old Westminsters*).

COBHAM, Vct, *see* GRENVILLE-TEMPLE, Richard.

962. COCHRANE, Alexander Forrester Inglis (1758–1832), M.P. Stirling burghs 1800–2, 1803–6 (DNB).

963. COCHRANE, George Augustus Frederick (b. 1762), M.P. Grampound 1807–8, 1808–12 (*Scots Peerage* sub Dundonald).

964. COCHRANE, Thomas (1775–1860), 10th E. of Dundonald, M.P. Honiton 1806–7, Westminster 1807–18 (DNB; GEC).

965. COCHRANE-JOHNSTONE, Andrew James (b. 1767), M.P. Stirling burghs 1791–97, Grampound 1807–8, 1812–14 (DNB).

966. COCKBURN, George (1772–1853), 10th Bt, M.P. Portsmouth 1818–20, Weobley 1820–28, Plymouth 1828–32, Ripon 1841–47 (DNB; GEC).

967. COCKBURN, James (ca 1729–1804), 8th Bt, M.P. Linlithgow burghs 1772–84 (GEC).

968. Cockburn, John (? 1678–1758), M.P. Haddingtonshire 1708–41 (Cockburn-Hood, *House of Cockburn,* pp. 156–58; Foster's *Scots M.P.'s*).

969. Cockerell, Charles (1755–1837), 1st Bt, M.P. Tregony 1802–6, Lostwithiel 1807–7, Bletchingley 1809–12, Seaford 1816–18, Evesham 1819–37 (Foster's *Baronetage; Western Antiquary, 6, 31;* Williams' *Worcester M.P.'s*).

970. Cocks, Charles (1725–1806), 1st Bn Somers, M.P. Reigate 1747–84 (GEC).

971. Cocks, Edward Charles (1786–1812), M.P. Reigate 1806–12 (GEC sub Somers).

972. Cocks, James (ca 1685–1750), M.P. Reigate 1707–10, 1713–47 (Collins' *Peerage* sub Somers; Clutterbuck's *Herts, 1,* 457).

973. Cocks, James Somers (1773–1854), M.P. Reigate 1808–18, 1823–31 (*Alumni Oxon.;* Lodge's *Peerage* sub Somers; Manning and Bray's *Surrey, 3,* clxvii; Namier; *1832 List*).

974. Cocks, James Somers (1790–1856), M.P. Reigate 1818–23 (*Alumni Oxon.;* Burke's *Peerage* sub Somers; *Gent. Mag., 2, 254; Linc. Inn Reg.; Royal Kalendar* [1823]; Namier).

975. Cocks, John Somers (1760–1841), 1st E. Somers, M.P. West Looe 1782–84, Grampound 1784–90, Reigate 1790–1806 (GEC; *Harrow Reg.; Old Westminsters*).

976. Cocks, John Somers (1788–1852), 2d E. Somers, M.P. Reigate 1812–18, 1832–41, Hereford City 1818–32 (GEC; *Old Westminsters*).

977. Cocks, Philip James (1774–1857), M.P. Reigate 1806–6 (Burke's *Peerage* sub Somers; *Harrow Reg.*).

978. Codrington, John (ca 1678–1754), M.P. Bath 1710–27, 1734–41 (*Alumni Oxon.;* Bristol and Glouc. Archaeol. Soc. *Trans., 21,* 331; Oliver's *Antigua, 1,* 147).

979. Codrington, William (d. 1738), 1st Bt, M.P. Minehead 1737–38 (GEC; Oliver's *Antigua, 1,* 145).

980. Codrington, William (1719–92), 2d Bt, M.P. Beverley 1747–61, Tewkesbury 1761–92 (GEC; *Jour. Mod. Hist., 18* [1946], 215; *Old Westminsters*).

981. Codrington-Bethell, Christopher (1764–1843), M.P. Tewkesbury 1797–1812 (Foster's *Baronetage; Harrow Reg.;* Ragatz, *Fall of the Planter Class,* p. 52).

982. Coffin, Isaac (1759–1839), 1st Bt, M.P. Ilchester 1818–26 (Burke's *Colonial Gentry;* DNB).

983. Coghill, John (1732–85), 1st Bt, M.P. Newport 1780–85 (GEC).

984. Coke, Daniel Parker (1745–1825), M.P. Derby borough 1776–80, Nottingham borough 1780–1802, 1803–12 (DNB; Williamson's *Middle Temple Bench Book*).

985. COKE, Edward (1719–53), M.P. Norfolk 1741–47, Harwich 1747–53 (GEC sub Leicester; *Old Westminsters*).

986. COKE, Edward (ca 1758–1837), M.P. Derby borough 1780–1807, 1807–18 (*Harrow Reg.*; Stirling's *Coke of Norfolk*, p. 577).

987. COKE, Thomas William (1754–1842), 1st E. of Leicester, M.P. Norfolk 1776–84, 1790–1807, 1807–32, Derby borough 1807–7 (DNB; GEC; *Eton Coll. Reg.*).

988. COKE, Thomas William (b. 1793), M.P. Derby borough 1818–26 (*Alumni Oxon.*; *Eton Lists*; Howard and Crisp's *Visitation of Eng. and Wales, 8,* 155).

989. COKE, Wenman (ca 1717–76), M.P. Harwich 1753–61, Okehampton 1761–68, Derby borough 1772–74, Norfolk 1774–76 (Lipscomb's *Bucks, 3,* 18; Stirling's *Coke of Norfolk*, p. 619).

COLBORNE, *see* RIDLEY-COLBORNE.

COLCHESTER, 1st Bn, *see* ABBOTT, Charles.

990. COLCLOUGH, Caesar (1766–1824), M.P. Wexford Co. 1806–6, 1818–20 (*Alumni Dublin.*; Burke's *Irish LG*).

991. COLCLOUGH, John (1767–1807), M.P. Wexford Co. 1806–7 (Burke's *Irish LG*).

992. COLE, Arthur Henry (1780–1844), M.P. Enniskillen 1828–44 (*Alumni Dublin.*; Burke's *Peerage* sub Enniskillen; *Gent. Mag., 1,* 204; Prinsep's *Madras Civilians*, p. 32).

993. COLE, Christopher (ca 1770–1836), M.P. Glamorgan 1817–18, 1820–30 (*Alumni Oxon.*; *Ann. Biog. and Obit.* [1837], p. 110; DNB).

994. COLE, Galbraith Lowry (1772–1842), M.P. Fermanagh 1803–23 (DNB; Burke's *Peerage* sub Enniskillen).

995. COLE, John Willoughby (1768–1840), 2d E. of Enniskillen, M.P. Fermanagh 1801–3 (*Alumni Dublin.*; GEC).

996. COLE, William Willoughby (1807–86), 3d E. of Enniskillen, M.P. Fermanagh 1831–40 (GEC; *Harrow Reg.*).

997. COLE-HAMILTON, Arthur (1756–1822), M.P. Enniskillen 1801–2 (*Cornwallis Corr., 3,* 45 n.; *Misc. Geneal. et Herald.*, 1st Ser., *2,* 244).

998. COLEBROOKE, George (1729–1809), 2d Bt, M.P. Arundel 1754–74 (GEC).

999. COLEBROOKE, James (1722–61), 1st Bt, M.P. Gatton 1751–61 (GEC).

1000. COLEBROOKE, Robert (1718–84), M.P. Maldon 1741–61 (Foster's *Baronetage;* Lipscomb's *Bucks, 1,* 134).

COLERAINE, Bn, *see* HANGER, Gabriel and William.

1001. COLHOUN, William, M.P. Bedford borough 1784–1802 (O'Byrne's *Rep. Hist. of Gt. Brit.*; *Royal Kalendar* [1785], p. 25).

1002. COLLETON, James Edward (ca 1710–90), M.P. Lostwithiel 1747–68, St. Mawes 1772–74 (*Alumni Cantab.*; *Eton Coll. Reg.*).

1003. COLLETT, Ebenezer John (ca 1754–1833), M.P. Grampound 1814–18, Cashel 1819–30 (*Gent. Mag., 2*, 476; *1821 List*).

1004. COLLIER, George (1732–95), M.P. Honiton 1784–90 (DNB; Burke's *Family Records*).

1005. COLLINS, Henry Powell (ca 1776–1854), M.P. Taunton 1811–18, 1819–20 (Burke's *LG* [ed. 1849]; Boase).

1006. COLMAN, Edward, M.P. Orford 1768–71 (*Army Lists* 1772–75).

COLQUHOUN, Archibald, *see* CAMPBELL-COLQUHOUN, Archibald.

COLQUHOUN, James, *see* GRANT, James.

1007. COLQUHOUN, James (1774–1836), 3d Bt, M.P. Dumbartonshire 1799–1806 (GEC).

COLQUHOUN, Ludovic, *see* GRANT, Ludovic.

1008. COLT, Robert (1756–97), M.P. Lymington 1784–90 (Burke's *LG;* Grant's *Faculty of Advocates*).

1009. COLTHURST, Nicholas Conway (1789–1829), 4th Bt, M.P. Cork City 1812–29 (*Alumni Cantab.;* GEC; *Eton Lists*).

1010. COLVILE, Robert, M.P. Kinross-shire 1754–61.

COLYEAR, James Dawkins, *see* DAWKINS-COLYEAR, James.

1011. COLYEAR, Thomas Charles (1772–1835), 4th E. of Portmore, M.P. Boston 1796–1802 (GEC).

1012. COMBE, Harvey Christian (ca 1752–1818), M.P. London 1796–1817 (Burke's *LG;* Beaven's *Aldermen of London;* Bayley's *Surrey, 2*, 150).

1013. COMBE, Richard (ca 1728–80), M.P. Milborne Port 1772–72, Aldeburgh 1774–80 (*Alumni Oxon.;* Musgrave's *Obituary*).

COMBERMERE, 1st Vct, *see* COTTON, Stapleton.

1014. COMPTON, Charles (ca 1697–1755), M.P. Northampton borough 1754–55 (*Eton Coll. Reg.*).

1015. COMPTON, Charles (1760–1828), 1st M. of Northampton, M.P. Northampton borough 1784–96 (*Alumni Cantab.;* GEC; *Old Westminsters*).

1016. COMPTON, George (ca 1692–1758), 6th E. of Northampton, M.P. Tamworth 1727–27, Northampton borough 1727–54 (GEC; *Eton Coll. Reg.;* Wedgwood).

1017. COMPTON, Spencer (1738–96), 8th E. of Northampton, M.P. Northampton borough 1761–63 (GEC; *Old Westminsters*).

1018. COMPTON, Spencer Joshua Alwyne (1790–1851), 2d M. of Northampton, M.P. Northampton borough 1812–20 (*Alumni Cantab.;* DNB; GEC).

1019. COMYN, Valens (d. 1751), M.P. Hindon 1747–51 (Cobbett's *Twickenham*, p. 68; Musgrave's *Obituary*).

1020. CONCANNON, Lucius (d. 1823), M.P. Appleby 1818–20, Winchelsea 1820–23 (Bean; *Eton Coll. Reg.;* Ferguson; *Notes and Queries, 157*, 301).

1021. CONDUITT, John (1688–1737), M.P. Whitchurch 1721–34, South-ampton borough 1735–37 (*Alumni Cantab.;* DNB; *Old Westminsters*).

CONGLETON, 1st Bn, *see* PARNELL, Henry Brooke.

1022. CONGREVE, Ralph (ca 1721–75), M.P. Cardigan borough 1769–74 (Berry's *County Geneal.: Berks,* p. 30; Williams' *Wales M.P.'s*).

1023. CONGREVE, William (1772–1828), 2d Bt, M.P. Gatton 1812–16, Plymouth 1818–28 (DNB).

CONINGSBY, George Capel, *see* CAPEL-CONINGSBY, George.

1024. CONOLLY, Edward Michael (1786–1848), M.P. Donegal 1831–48 (Burke's *Irish LG; Gent. Mag., 1* [1849], 204).

1025. CONOLLY, Thomas (ca 1738–1803), M.P. Malmesbury 1759–68, Chichester 1768–80 (Burke's *Irish LG;* DNB; *Old Westminsters*).

1026. CONOLLY, William (d. 1754), M.P. Aldeburgh 1734–47, Petersfield 1747–54 (Burke's *Irish LG*).

1027. CONSTABLE, Thomas Aston Clifford (1807–70), 2d Bt, M.P. Hedon 1830–32 (Burke's *Peerage* sub Clifford).

CONWAY, *see* SEYMOUR, SEYMOUR-CONWAY and INGRAM-SEYMOUR-CONWAY.

1028. CONWAY, Henry Seymour (1719–95), M.P. Higham Ferrers 1741–47, Penryn 1747–54, St. Mawes 1754–61, Thetford 1761–74, Bury 1775–84 (DNB; *Eton Coll. Reg.*).

1029. CONYERS, Edward (ca 1693–1742), M.P. East Grinstead 1725–27, 1734–41 (*Alumni Oxon.;* Nichols' *Leicester, 2,* pt. 2, 457).

1030. CONYERS, John (1717–75), M.P. Reading 1747–54, Essex 1772–75 (Nichols' *Leicester, 2,* pt. 2, 457; cf. *Alumni Cantab.*).

1031. CONYNGHAM, Francis Nathaniel (1797–1876), 2d M. Conyngham, M.P. Westbury 1818–20, Donegal 1825–31 (GEC).

1032. CONYNGHAM, Henry (ca 1705–81), 1st E. of Conyngham, M.P. Tiverton 1747–54, Sandwich 1756–74 (GEC).

1033. CONYNGHAM, Henry Joseph (1795–1824), M.P. Donegal 1818–24 (GEC; *Old Westminsters*).

1034. COOKE, Bryan (1756–1821), M.P. Malton 1798–1807, 1808–12 (*Eton Coll. Reg.;* Foster's *Baronetage*).

1035. COOKE, George (ca 1709–68), M.P. Tregony 1742–47, Middlesex 1750–68 (Burke's *LG* sub Vernon; Martin's *Masters of the Bench, Inner Temple*).

1036. COOKE, Henry Frederick (ca 1784–1837), M.P. Orford 1826–32 (Burke's *LG; Gent. Mag., 1,* 657).

COOKE, Sambroke, *see* FREEMAN, Sambroke.

COOPER, *see* ASHLEY-COOPER.

1037. COOPER, Cropley Ashley (1768–1851), 6th E. of Shaftesbury, M.P. Dorchester 1790–90, 1791–1811 (GEC).

1038. COOPER, Edward Joshua (1798–1863), M.P. Sligo Co. 1830–41, 1857–59 (*Alumni Oxon.;* Burke's *Irish LG;* DNB).

1039. COOPER, Edward Synge (ca 1763–1830), M.P. Sligo Co. 1806–30 (*Alumni Dublin.;* Burke's *Irish LG*).

1040. COOPER, Grey (ca 1726–1801), 3d Bt, M.P. Rochester 1765–68, Grampound 1768–74, Saltash 1774–84, Richmond 1786–90 (*Alumni Cantab.;* DNB; GEC).

1041. COOPER, John (ca 1717–79), M.P. Downton 1775–79 (Musgrave's *Obituary; Wiltshire Notes and Queries, 7,* 44).

1042. COOPER, John Hutton (1765–1828), 1st Bt, M.P. Dartmouth 1825–28 (Burke's *Ext. Baronetcies; Gent. Mag., 1* [1829], 178).

1043. COOPER, Joshua Edward (ca 1762–1837), M.P. Sligo Co. 1801–6 (*Alumni Dublin.;* Burke's *Irish LG*).

1044. COOPER, Robert Bransby (1762–1845), M.P. Gloucester City 1818–30 (*Alumni Cantab.;* Williams' *Gloucester M.P.'s*).

1045. COOTE, Algernon (1689–1744), 6th E. of Mountrath, M.P. Castle Rising 1724–34, Hedon 1742–44 (*Alumni Cantab.;* GEC).

1046. COOTE, Charles Henry (1754–1823), 2d Bn Castle Coote, M.P. Queens 1801–2 (*Alumni Dublin.;* GEC).

1047. COOTE, Charles Henry (1792–1864), 9th Bt, M.P. Queens 1821–47, 1852–59 (GEC; *Eton Lists*).

1048. COOTE, Eyre (ca 1726–83), M.P. Leicester borough 1768–74, Poole 1774–80 (DNB).

1049. COOTE, Eyre (ca 1762–1823), M.P. Queens 1802–5, Barnstable 1812–18 (*Alumni Dublin.;* DNB; *Eton Coll. Reg.*).

1050. COOTE, Eyre (ca 1806–34), M.P. Clonmel 1830–32 (*Alumni Oxon.;* Burke's *Peerage*).

1051. COPE, James (ca 1709–56), M.P. Downton 1754–56 (Musgrave's *Obituary; Notes and Queries, 175,* 60).

1052. COPE, John (1673–1749), 6th Bt, M.P. Plympton Erle 1705–8, Tavistock 1708–27, Hampshire 1727–34, Lymington 1734–41 (*Notes and Queries, 179,* 60; GEC).

1053. COPE, John (d. 1760), M.P. Queensborough 1722–27, Liskeard 1727–34, Orford 1738–41 (DNB).

1054. COPE, Monnoux (ca 1696–1763), 7th Bt, M.P. Banbury 1722–27, Newport (Hants) 1741–47 (*Alumni Cantab.;* GEC).

1055. COPE, Robert Camden (ca 1771–1819), M.P. Armagh Co. 1801–2 (*Alumni Cantab.;* Burke's *Irish LG*).

1056. COPELAND, William Taylor (1797–1868), M.P. Coleraine 1831–32, 1833–37, Stoke 1837–52, 1857–65 (DNB).

1057. COPLESTON, Thomas (d. 1748), M.P. Callington 1719–48 (Musgrave's *Obituary*).

1058. COPLEY, John Singleton (1772–1863), 1st Bn Lyndhurst, M.P. Yarmouth (Hants) 1818–18, Ashburton 1818–26, Cambridge Univ. 1826–27 (*Alumni Cantab.;* DNB; GEC).

1059. Copley, Lionel (ca 1767–1806), 2d Bt, M.P. Tregony 1796–1802 (GEC; *Harrow Reg.*).

1060. Corbet, John (ca 1752–1817), M.P. Shrewsbury 1775–80 (*Alumni Oxon.;* Burke's *LG*).

1061. Corbett, Panton (1785–1855), M.P. Shrewsbury 1820–30 (*Alumni Oxon.;* Boase).

1062. Corbett, Richard (1696–1774), 4th Bt, M.P. Shrewsbury 1723–27, 1734–54 (GEC).

1063. Corbett, Thomas (d. 1751), M.P. Saltash 1734–51 (DNB; *Old Westminsters*).

1064. Corbett, William (1702–48), 5th Bt, M.P. Montgomery borough 1728–41, Ludlow 1741–48 (GEC; *Parish Reg. Adderley, Salop,* p. 8; Williams' *Wales M.P.'s*).

Cork, 6th E. of, *see* Boyle, Hamilton.

Cornbury, Vct, *see* Hyde, Henry.

1065. Cornwall, Charles Wolfran (1735–89), M.P. Grampound 1768–74, Winchelsea 1774–84, Rye 1784–89 (DNB; Robinson's *Hereford,* p. 116).

1066. Cornewall, Frederick (1706–88), M.P. Montgomery borough 1771–74 (Charnock's *Biog. Naval., 5, 288;* Reade's *House of Cornewall,* pp. 125–29; Williams' *Wales M.P.'s*).

1067. Cornewall, Frederick Hamilton (1791–1845), M.P. Bishop's Castle 1830–31 (*Alumni Cantab.;* Shrop. Archaeol. Soc. *Trans.,* 2d Ser., *10*).

Cornewall, Frederick Walker, *see* Walker-Cornewall, Frederick.

1068. Cornewall, George (1748–1819), 2d Bt, M.P. Herefordshire 1774–96, 1802–7 (GEC; *Eton Coll. Reg.; Misc. Geneal. et Herald.,* N.S., *4*).

1069. Cornewall, Henry (1685–1756), M.P. Hereford City 1747–54 (Reade's *House of Cornewall,* p. 105; Williams' *Hereford M.P.'s*).

1070. Cornewall, James (ca 1699–1744), M.P. Weobley 1732–34, 1737–41 (DNB).

1071. Cornewall, Velters (ca 1696–1768), M.P. Herefordshire 1722–68 (*Alumni Oxon.;* Burke's *Peerage*).

1072. Cornish, Samuel (d. 1770), 1st Bt, M.P. Shoreham 1765–70 (DNB; GEC).

Cornwallis, 5th E., *see* Mann, James.

1073. Cornwallis, Charles (1738–1805), 1st M. Cornwallis, M.P. Eye 1760–62 (*Alumni Cantab.;* DNB; GEC; *Eton Coll. Reg.*).

1074. Cornwallis, Charles (1774–1823), 2d M. Cornwallis, M.P. Eye 1795–96, Suffolk 1796–1805 (*Alumni Cantab.;* DNB; GEC; *Eton Coll. Reg.*).

1075. Cornwallis, Edward (1713–76), M.P. Eye 1743–49, Westminster 1753–62 (*Eton Coll. Reg.*).

1076. CORNWALLIS, Henry (1740–61), M.P. Eye 1761–61 (*Eton Coll. Reg.*).

CORNWALLIS, James, *see* MANN, James.

1077. CORNWALLIS, John (1706–68), M.P. Eye 1727–47 (*Eton Coll. Reg.*).

1078. CORNWALLIS, Stephen (1703–43), M.P. Eye 1727–43 (Collins' *Peerage; Harrow Reg.*).

1079. CORNWALLIS, William (1744–1819), M.P. Eye 1768–74, 1782–84, 1790–1807, Portsmouth 1784–90 (DNB; *Eton Coll. Reg.*).

CORRY, *see* LOWRY-CORRY.

1080. CORRY, Isaac (ca 1755–1813), M.P. Dundalk 1801–2, Newry 1802–6, Newport (Hants) 1806–7 (*Alumni Dublin.;* DNB).

1081. CORRY, Thomas Charles Stewart (ca 1785–1844), M.P. Monaghan 1807–12, 1813–18 (*Alumni Oxon.*).

1082. COSTER, Thomas (1684–1739), M.P. Bristol 1734–39 (Williams' *Gloucester M.P.'s*).

1083. COTES, Charles (ca 1686–1748), M.P. Tamworth 1735–47 (*Alumni Oxon.;* Munk's *Roll, 2,* 137).

1084. COTES, John (ca 1750–1821), M.P. Wigan 1782–1802, Salop 1806–21 (Burke's *LG; Eton Coll. Reg.*).

1085. COTES, Thomas (1712–67), M.P. Great Bedwin 1761–67 (Burke's *LG;* Charnock's *Biog. Naval., 5,* 12).

1086. COTSFORD, Edward (1740–1810), M.P. Midhurst 1784–90 (Holzman's *Nabobs in Eng.*).

COTTENHAM, 1st E. of, *see* PEPYS, Charles Christopher.

1087. COTTER, James Laurence (ca 1780–1834), 3d Bt, M.P. Mallow 1812–18 (*Alumni Dublin.;* GEC).

COTTERELL, John Geers, *see* GEERS-COTTERELL, John.

COTTESLOE, 1st Bn, *see* FREMANTLE, Thomas Francis.

1088. COTTON, John Hynde (ca 1688–1752), 3d Bt, M.P. Cambridge borough 1708–22, 1727–41, Cambridgeshire 1722–27, Marlborough 1741–52 (*Alumni Cantab.;* DNB; GEC; *Old Westminsters*).

1089. COTTON, John Hynde (ca 1717–95), 4th Bt, M.P. St. Germans 1741–47, Marlborough 1752–61, Cambridgeshire 1764–80 (*Alumni Cantab.;* GEC).

1090. COTTON, Lynch Salusbury (ca 1705–75), 4th Bt, M.P. Denbighshire 1749–74 (GEC).

1091. COTTON, ROBERT Salusbury (1695–1748), 3d Bt, M.P. Cheshire 1727–34, Lostwithiel 1741–47 (*Alumni Oxon.;* GEC).

1092. COTTON, Robert Salusbury (ca 1739–1809), 5th Bt, M.P. Cheshire 1780–96 (*Alumni Cantab.;* GEC; *Old Westminsters*).

1093. COTTON, Stapleton (1773–1865), 1st Vct Combermere, M.P. Newark 1806–14 (DNB; GEC; *Old Westminsters*).

1094. COURTENAY, Henry Reginald (1714–63), M.P. Honiton 1741–47, 1754–63 (*Old Westminsters*).

1095. COURTENAY, John (1738–1816), M.P. Tamworth 1780–96, Appleby 1796–1807, 1812–12 (DNB; *Notes and Queries,* 10th Ser., *9,* 313).

1096. COURTENAY, Kelland (ca 1708–48), M.P. Truro 1734–41, Huntingdon borough 1747–48 (*Alumni Oxon.;* Boase and Courtney, *Biblio. Cornub.; Calendar Inner Temple Records, 4,* 99).

1097. COURTENAY, Thomas Peregrine (1782–1841), M.P. Totnes 1811–32 (DNB; *Old Westminsters*).

1098. COURTENAY, William (1676–1735), 2d Bt, M.P. Devon 1701–10, 1712–35 (GEC).

1099. COURTENAY, William (1710–62), 1st Vct Courtenay, M.P. Honiton 1734–41, Devon 1741–62 (GEC; *Old Westminsters*).

1100. COURTENAY, William (1777–1859), 10th E. of Devon, M.P. Exeter 1812–26 (GEC; *Old Westminsters*).

COURTOWN, E. of, *see* STOPFORD, James, James George, and James Thomas.

1101. COUSSMAKER, George (ca 1797–1821), M.P. Kinsale 1818–21 (*Alumni Oxon.; Old Westminsters*).

1102. COUTTS, James (1733–78), M.P. Edinburgh City 1762–68 (Foster's *Scots M.P.'s*).

1103. COVENTRY, George William (1722–1809), 6th E. of Coventry, M.P. Bridport 1744–47, Worcestershire 1747–51 (GEC).

1104. COVENTRY, George William (1784–1843), 8th E. of Coventry, M.P. Worcester City 1816–26 (GEC; *Old Westminsters*).

1105. COVENTRY, Thomas (ca 1713–97), M.P. Bridport 1754–80 (*Alumni Oxon.;* Martin's *Masters of the Bench, Inner Temple*).

1106. COVENTRY, Thomas Henry (1721–44), M.P. Bridport 1742–44 (*Alumni Oxon.;* GEC).

1107. COVENTRY-BULKELEY, John Bulkeley (1724–1801), M.P. Worcestershire 1751–61 (*Alumni Oxon.;* Williams' *Worcester M.P.'s*).

1108. COWAN, Robert (d. 1737), M.P. Tregony 1737–37 (*Gent. Mag.,* p. 125).

COWLEY, 1st Bn, *see* WELLESLEY, Henry.

COWPER, 3d E. of, *see* CLAVERING-COWPER, George Nassau.

1109. COWPER, Edward Spencer (1779–1823), M.P. Hertford borough 1802–17 (*Alumni Cantab.*).

1110. COWPER, George Augustus Frederick (1806–56), 6th E. Cowper, M.P. Canterbury 1830–34 (GEC).

1111. COWPER, William (ca 1722–69), M.P. Hertford borough 1768–69 (*Alumni Oxon.;* Clutterbuck's *Herts, 2,* 195, 208).

COX, James, *see* COCKS, James.

1112. COX, Lawrence (d. 1792), M.P. Honiton 1774–80, Berealston 1781–84 (Devonshire Assoc. *Trans., 66,* 265; Hutchins' *Dorset, 4,* 434).

1113. COXE, Charles Westley (d. 1806), M.P. Cricklade 1784–85 (Bristol and Glouc. Archaeol. Soc. *Trans., 50,* 180; *Wiltshire Notes and Queries, 7,* 191).

1114. Coxe, Henry Hippisley (ca 1748–95), M.P. Somerset 1792–95 (Burke's *LG;* Bates Harbin).

1115. Coxe, John (ca 1695–1783), M.P. Cirencester 1749–54 (*Alumni Oxon.;* Williams' *Gloucester M.P.'s*).

1116. Coxe, Richard Hippisley (ca 1742–86), M.P. Somerset 1768–84 (Bates Harbin; *Old Westminsters*).

1117. Coxhead, Thomas (ca 1734–1811), M.P. Bramber 1790–96 (*Gent. Mag., 2,* 590).

Cradock, John Hobart, *see* Caradoc, John Hobart.

1118. Cradock, Sheldon (1777–1852), M.P. Camelford 1822–32 (*Alumni Cantab.*).

1119. Cradock-Hartopp, Edmund (1749–1833), 1st Bt, M.P. Leicestershire 1798–1806 (GEC).

1120. Craggs, James Newsham (1715–69), M.P. St. Germans 1741–47, St. Mawes 1754–61 (*Misc. Geneal et Herald.,* 1st Ser., *2,* 39; Musgrave's *Obituary*).

1121. Craggs-Eliot, Edward (1727–1804), 1st Bn Eliot, M.P. St. Germans 1748–68, 1774–75, Liskeard 1768–74, Cornwall 1775–84 (DNB; GEC).

1122. Craggs-Nugent, Robert (ca 1702–88), 1st E. Nugent, M.P. St. Mawes 1741–54, 1774–84, Bristol 1754–74 (DNB; GEC).

1123. Craig, James, M.P. Carrickfergus 1807–12.

1124. Craigie, Robert (ca 1685–1760), M.P. Tain burghs 1742–47 (DNB; Foster's *Scots M.P.'s*).

1125. Crampton, Philip Cecil (1782–1862), M.P. Saltash 1831–31, Milborne Port 1831–32 (*Alumni Dublin.;* Boase).

Cranley, 1st Bn, *see* Onslow, George.

1126. Craster, John (ca 1697–1763), M.P. Weobley 1754–61 (*Alumni Oxon.;* Burke's *LG;* Williams' *Hereford M.P.'s*).

Craufurd, Charles Gregan, *see* Gregan-Craufurd, Charles.

1127. Craufurd, Gibbs (ca 1732–93), M.P. Queenborough 1790–93 (Burke's *Family Records; Eton Coll. Reg.; Misc. Geneal. et Herald.,* 5th Ser., *6*).

1128. Craufurd, James (d. 1811), M.P. Horsham 1783–84 (Burke's *LG; Eton Coll. Reg.*).

1129. Craufurd, John (d. 1764), M.P. Berwick-on-Tweed 1761–64 (Burke's *LG;* Bean).

1130. Craufurd, John (ca 1742–1814), M.P. Old Sarum 1768–74, Renfrewshire 1774–80, Glasgow burghs 1780–84, 1790–90 (*Eton Coll. Reg.*).

1131. Craufurd, Patrick (d. 1778), M.P. Ayrshire 1741–54, Renfrewshire 1761–68 (Burke's *LG;* Foster's *Scots M.P.'s*).

1132. Craufurd, Patrick, M.P. Arundel 1780–81.

1133. CRAUFURD, Robert (1764–1812), M.P. East Retford 1802–6 (DNB; *Harrow Reg.*).

1134. CRAVEN, Thomas (1714–72), M.P. Berks 1766–72 (Foster's *Peerage;* Collins' *Peerage*).

1135. CRAVEN, William (1705–69), 5th Bn Craven, M.P. Warwickshire 1746–64 (*Alumni Cantab.;* GEC).

CRAWFORD, E. of, *see* LINDSAY, James.

1136. CRAWFORD, Arthur Johnston (b. ca 1786), M.P. Old Sarum 1818–20 (*Alumni Dublin.;* Burke's *Irish LG; Linc. Inn Reg.*).

1137. CRAWLEY, John (ca 1700–67), M.P. Marlborough 1737–47 (W. Austin, *Luton, 2,* 60, 67; Crawley-Boevey, *Perverse Widow,* p. 301; Nichols' *Leicester, 3,* pt. 1, 218).

1138. CRAWLEY, Samuel (1790–1852), M.P. Honiton 1818–26, Bedford borough 1832–37, 1838–41 (*Alumni Oxon.;* Burke's *LG; Bedfordshire Notes and Queries, 2,* 323; Eton Lists).

1139. CREED, James (ca 1695–1762), M.P. Canterbury 1754–61 (Hasted's *Kent,* ed. Drake, p. 102; Musgrave's *Obituary;* Shaw's *Knights, 2,* 286).

1140. CREEVY, Thomas (1768–1838), M.P. Thetford 1802–6, 1807–18, Appleby 1820–26, Downton 1831–32 (*Alumni Cantab.; Creevy Papers;* Gore's *Life*).

CREMORNE, 2d Bn, *see* DAWSON, Richard Thomas.

CRESPIGNY, *see* DE CRISPIGNY.

1141. CRESSETT-PELHAM, Henry (ca 1729–ca 1803), M.P. Bramber 1751–54, Tiverton 1754–58 (*Alumni Cantab.;* Burke's *LG*).

1142. CRESSETT-PELHAM, John (d. 1838), M.P. Lewes 1796–1802, Salop 1822–32, Shrewsbury 1835–37 (Burke's *LG*).

1143. CRESSWELL, Estcourt (d. 1823), M.P. Cirencester 1768–74 (Williams' *Gloucester M.P.'s*).

1144. CRESSWELL, Thomas Estcourt (d. 1788), M.P. Wootton Bassett 1754–74 (Burke's *LG* [ed. 1849]).

1145. CREWE, Charles (b. ca 1710), M.P. Cheshire 1753–54 (*Alumni Oxon.*).

1146. CREWE, John (ca 1709–52), M.P. Cheshire 1734–52 (*Alumni Oxon.;* GEC; Omerod's *Chester, 3,* 314; Wedgwood).

1147. CREWE, John (1742–1829), 1st Bn Crewe, M.P. Stafford borough 1765–68, Cheshire 1768–1802 (DNB; GEC; *Old Westminsters*).

1148. CRICHTON-STUART, Patrick James Herbert (1794–1859), M.P. Cardiff 1818–20, 1826–32, Buteshire 1820–26, Ayr burghs 1834–52, Ayrshire 1857–59 (Foster's *Scots M.P.'s;* Peile's *Biog. Reg. of Christ's College;* Williams' *Wales M.P.'s*).

1149. CRICKITT, Charles Alexander (1736–1803), M.P. Ipswich 1784–1803 (*Gent. Mag., 1,* 92; *Merchant Taylor School Reg.*).

1150. CRICKITT, Robert Alexander (ca 1785–1832), M.P. Ipswich 1807–20

(*Eton Lists; Gent. Mag.*, *1*, 81; *Parish Reg. Dutch Church, Colchester*, p. 78).

1151. CRIPPS, Joseph (1765–1847), M.P. Cirencester 1806–12, 1818–41 (Howard and Crisp's *Visitation of Eng. and Wales*, *2*, 119; Williams' *Gloucester M.P.'s*).

1152. CROFTES, Richard (ca 1740–83), M.P. Petersfield 1767–68, Downton 1768–71, Cambridge Univ. 1771–80 (*Alumni Cantab.; Eton Coll. Reg.; Parish Reg. Little Saxham, Suffolk*, pp. 211, 237).

1153. CROKER, John Wilson (1780–1857), M.P. Downpatrick 1807–12, Athlone 1812–18, Yarmouth (Hants) 1819–20, Bodmin 1820–26, Aldeburgh 1826–27, 1830–32, Dublin Univ. 1827–30 (DNB; *Alumni Dublin.*).

1154. CROMPTON, Samuel (1786–1849), 1st Bt, M.P. East Retford 1818–26, Derby borough 1826–30, Thirsk 1834–41 (*Alumni Cantab.*; Burke's *LG*).

1155. CROSBIE, James (d. 1836), M.P. Kerry 1801–6, 1812–26 (Foster's *Baronetage; Harrow Reg.*).

1156. CROSBIE, William (d. 1798), M.P. Newark 1790–96 (*Army Lists; Gent. Mag.*, *1*, 543).

1157. CROSBY, Brass (1725–93), M.P. Honiton 1768–74 (Beaven's *Aldermen of London;* DNB).

1158. CROSSE, John (ca 1701–62), 2d Bt, M.P. Wootton Bassett 1727–34, Lostwithiel 1735–47, Westminster 1754–61 (GEC; *Genealogists Mag.*, *6*, 186; *Old Westminsters*).

1159. CROWLE, George (d. 1754), M.P. Hull 1724–47 (Gunnell's *Hull Celebrities*, p. 337; *Six North Country Diaries* [Surtees Soc.], p. 180 n.).

1160. CROWLE, John Charles (ca 1738–1811), M.P. Richmond 1769–74 (*Alumni Cantab.; Notes and Queries*, 12th Ser., *3*, 183).

1161. CROWLE, Richard (ca 1700–57), M.P. Hull 1754–57 (*Alumni Cantab.*).

1162. CRUGER, Henry (1739–1827), M.P. Bristol 1774–80, 1784–90 (*Dict. Am. Biog.;* Williams' *Gloucester M.P.'s*).

1163. CRUTCHLEY, Jeremiah (1745–1805), M.P. Horsham 1784–90, Grampound 1790–96, St. Mawes 1796–1802 (Burke's *LG*).

1164. CUFFE, James (d. 1828), M.P. Tralee 1819–28 (*Gent. Mag.*, *2*, 188).

1165. CUFFE, John Otway (1788–1820), 2d E. of Desart, M.P. Bossiney 1808–17 (*Alumni Oxon.;* GEC; *Eton Lists*).

1166. CUMMING, George (ca 1753–1834), M.P. Inverness burghs 1803–6, 1818–26 (Foster's *Scots M.P.'s*).

CUMMING, William Gordon Gordon, *see* GORDON-CUMMING, William Gordon.

1167. CUMMING-BRUCE, Charles Lennox (1790–1875), M.P. Inverness burghs 1831–32, 1833–37, Elginshire 1840–68 (*Alumni Oxon.;* Tayler's *Morayshire M.P.'s*).

1168. CUMMING-GORDON, Alexander Penrose (d. 1806), 1st Bt, M.P. Inverness burghs 1802–3 (Burke's *Peerage;* Foster's *Scots M.P.'s*).

1169. CUNINGHAME, Alexander (d. 1742), M.P. Renfrewshire 1734–42 (Foster's *Scots M.P.'s*).

1170. CUNINGHAME, James (d. 1788), M.P. East Grinstead 1786–88 (Burke's *Irish LG;* Musgrave's *Obituary*).

1171. CUNINGHAME, Robert (d. 1801), 1st Bn Rossmore, M.P. East Grinstead 1788–89 (GEC).

1172. CUNINGHAME-FAIRLIE, William (d. 1837), 7th Bt, M.P. Leominster 1818–19, 1820–26 (GEC).

1173. CUNLIFFE, Ellis (1717–67), 1st Bt, M.P. Liverpool 1755–67 (GEC; Foster's *Baronetage*).

1174. CUNLIFFE-OFFLEY, Foster (1782–1832), M.P. Chester City 1831–32 (Burke's *Peerage; Gent. Mag., 1,* 477).

1175. CUNNINGHAM-GRAHAM, Robert (ca 1735–97), M.P. Stirlingshire 1794–96 (Addison's *Glasgow Matric. Albums;* Burke's *LG;* DNB).

1776. CUNNINGHAM-GRAHAM-BONTINE, William (ca 1772–1845), M.P. Dumbartonshire 1796–97 (Addison's *Glasgow Matric. Albums;* Foster's *Scots M.P.'s*).

1177. CUNYNGHAME, William Augustus (ca 1747–1828), 4th Bt, M.P. Linlithgowshire 1774–90 (*Alumni Oxon.;* GEC).

1178. CURRIE, John (1797–1873), M.P. Hertford borough 1831–32 (Boase; Burke's *Peerage*).

1179. CURRIE, William (1756–1829), M.P. Gatton 1790–96, Winchelsea 1796–1802 (Burke's *Peerage;* Foster's *Baronetage*).

1180. CURTEIS, Edward Jeremiah (1762–1835), M.P. Sussex 1820–30 (*Old Westminsters*).

1181. CURTEIS, Herbert Barrett (1793–1847), M.P. Sussex 1830–32, East Sussex 1832–37, Rye 1841–47 (*Old Westminsters*).

1182. CURTIS, John (ca 1751–1813), M.P. Wells 1782–84, Steyning 1791–94 (*Gent. Mag., 2,* 627; Palmer's *Perlustration of Great Yarmouth, 1,* 218).

1183. CURTIS, William (1752–1829), 1st Bt, M.P. London 1790–1818, 1820–26, Bletchingley 1819–20, Hastings 1826–26 (Beaven's *Aldermen of London;* DNB).

1184. CURWEN, Eldred (1692–1745), M.P. Cockermouth 1738–41 (Bean; Burke's *LG;* Ferguson).

1185. CURWEN, Henry (1728–78), M.P. Carlisle 1761–68, Cumberland 1768–74 (*Alumni Cantab.; Eton Coll. Reg.*).

CURWEN, John Christian, *see* CHRISTIAN-CURWEN, John.

1186. CURZON, Assheton (1730–1820), 1st Vct Curzon, M.P. Clitheroe 1754–80, 1792–94 (GEC; *Old Westminsters*).

1187. CURZON, Nathaniel (ca 1676–1758), 4th Bt, M.P. Derby borough 1713–15, Clitheroe 1722–27, Derbyshire 1727–54 (GEC).

1188. CURZON, Nathaniel (1727–1804), 1st Bn Scarsdale, M.P. Clitheroe 1748–54, Derbyshire 1754–61 (GEC; *Old Westminsters*).

1189. CURZON, Nathaniel (1751–1837), 2d Bn Scarsdale, M.P. Derbyshire 1775–84 (GEC; *Old Westminsters*).

1190. CURZON, Penn Assheton (1757–97), M.P. Leominster 1784–90, Clitheroe 1790–92, Leicestershire 1792–97 (GEC sub Howe; *Old Westminsters*).

1191. CURZON, Robert (1774–1863), M.P. Clitheroe 1796–1831 (*Linc. Inn Reg.; Old Westminsters*).

1192. CURZON, Robert (1810–73), 14th Bn Zouche, M.P. Clitheroe 1831–32 (DNB; GEC).

1193. CURZON, William (ca 1681–1749), M.P. Clitheroe 1734–47 (*Alumni Oxon.*).

1194. CUST, Brownlow (1744–1807), 1st Bn Brownlow, M.P. Ilchester 1768–74, Grantham 1774–76 (*Alumni Cantab.;* GEC; *Eton Coll. Reg.*).

1195. CUST, Edward (1794–1878), M.P. Grantham 1818–26, Lostwithiel 1826–32 (DNB; *1832 List*).

1196. CUST, Francis Cokayne (1721–91), M.P. Grantham 1770–74, 1780–91, Helston 1775–80 (*Alumni Cantab.; Eton Coll. Reg.*).

1197. CUST, John (1718–70), 3d Bt, M.P. Grantham 1743–70 (*Alumni Cantab.;* DNB; GEC; *Eton Coll. Reg.*).

1198. CUST, John (1779–1853), 1st E. of Brownlow, M.P. Clitheroe 1802–7 (*Alumni Cantab.;* GEC; *Eton Coll. Reg.*).

1199. CUST, Peregrine (ca 1724–85), M.P. Bishop's Castle 1761–68, Shoreham 1768–74, Ilchester 1774–75, 1780–85, Grantham 1776–80 (*Alumni Oxon.;* Shrop. Archaeol. Soc. *Trans.*, 2d Ser., *10; The Reliquary, 8,* 221).

1200. CUST, Peregrine Francis (1791–1873), M.P. Honiton 1818–26, Clitheroe 1826–32 (Boase; *1832 List*).

1201. CUST, William (1787–1845), M.P. Lincolnshire 1816–18, Clitheroe 1818–22 (*Alumni Cantab.*).

1202. CUTHBERT, James Ramsay, M.P. Appleby 1807–12 (Bean; Ferguson).

DACRE, 20th Bn, *see* BRAND, Thomas.

DALKEITH, E. of, *see* SCOTT, Francis, *also* MONTAGU-SCOTT, Charles William Henry.

1203. DALLAS, George (1758–1833), 1st Bt, M.P. Newport (Hants) 1800–2 (DNB; GEC).

1204. DALLAS, Robert (1756–1824), M.P. St. Michael 1802–5, Dysart burghs 1805–6 (DNB).

DALLING and BULWER, 1st Bn, see BULWER, William Henry Lytton Earle.

1205. DALRYMPLE, Adolphus John (1784–1866), 2d Bt, M.P. Weymouth and Melcombe Regis 1817–18, Appleby 1819–26, Haddington burghs 1826–31, 1831–32, Brighton 1837–41 (Boase; *Scots Peerage*).

1206. DALRYMPLE, Hew (1712–90), 2d Bt, M.P. Haddington burghs 1742–47, 1761–68, Haddingtonshire 1747–61 (GEC; *Scots Peerage*).

DALRYMPLE, Hew Hamilton, see HAMILTON-DALRYMPLE, Hew.

DALRYMPLE, John, see HAMILTON, John.

1207. DALRYMPLE, William (1678–1744), M.P. Ayrshire 1707–8, Clackmannanshire 1708–10, Wigtown burghs 1722–27, Wigtownshire 1727–41 (*Scots Peerage* sub Stair).

1208. DALRYMPLE, William (ca 1735–1807), M.P. Wigtown burghs 1784–90 (Addison's *Glasgow Matric. Albums; Scots Peerage* sub Stair).

1209. DALRYMPLE-HAMILTON, Hew (1774–1834), 4th Bt, M.P. Haddingtonshire 1795–1800, Ayrshire 1803–7, 1811–18, Haddington burghs 1820–26 (*Alumni Oxon.;* GEC; *Scots Peerage*).

1210. DALSTON, George (1718–65), 4th Bt, M.P. Westmorland 1754–61 (GEC; *Old Westminsters*).

1211. DALSTON, John (ca 1707–59), M.P. Westmorland 1747–59 (*Alumni Oxon.;* Burke's *Ext. Baronetcies;* Bean; Ferguson).

1212. DALWAY, Noah (d. 1820), M.P. Carrickfergus 1801–2 (*Notes and Queries,* 7 Aug. 1948).

1213. DALY, Denis Bowes (ca 1745–1821), M.P. Kings 1801–2, Galway town 1802–5, Galway Co. 1805–18 (*Alumni Dublin.;* Burke's *Irish LG*).

1214. DALY, James (1782–1847), 1st Bn Dunsandle, M.P. Galway town 1805–11, Galway Co. 1812–30, 1832–34 (*Alumni Dublin.;* GEC).

1215. DALY, St. George (ca 1758–1829), M.P. Galway town 1801–1 (*Alumni Dublin.;* Burke's *Peerage* sub Dunsandle; Ball's *Judges in Ireland, 2, 332*).

1216. DAMER, George (1727–52), M.P. Dorchester 1751–52 (Burke's *Peerage* sub Portarlington; Hutchins' *Dorset, 4,* 387).

1217. DAMER, George (1746–1808), 2d E. of Dorchester, M.P. Cricklade 1768–74, Anstruther Easter burghs 1778–80, Dorchester 1780–91, Malton 1792–98 (*Alumni Cantab.;* GEC; *Eton Coll. Reg.*).

1218. DAMER, John (1720–83), M.P. Dorchester 1762–80 (Burke's *Peerage* sub Portarlington; Hutchins' *Dorset, 4,* 387).

1219. DAMER, John (1744–76), M.P. Gatton 1768–74 (*Alumni Cantab.;* *Eton Coll. Reg.;* Hutchins' *Dorset, 4,* 387).

1220. DAMER, Joseph (1718–98), 1st E. of Dorchester, M.P. Weymouth and Melcombe Regis 1741–47, Bramber 1747–54, Dorchester 1754–62 (*Alumni Dublin.;* GEC).

1221. DAMER, Lionel (1748–1807), M.P. Peterborough 1786–1802 (*Alumni Cantab.;* Burke's *Peerage* sub Portarlington; *Eton Coll. Reg.;* Hutchins' *Dorset, 4,* 387).

DANCE, Nathaniel, *see* HOLLAND, Nathaniel.

1222. DANIELL, Ralph Allen (1762–1823), M.P. West Looe 1805–12 (*Notes and Queries, 148,* 320; *Parish Reg. St. Mary's Truro,* p. 715).

1223. DANVERS, Joseph (ca 1697–1753), 1st Bt, M.P. Boroughbridge 1722–27, Bramber 1727–34, Totnes 1734–47 (GEC; *Linc. Inn Reg.*).

1224. DARBY, George (d. 1790), M.P. Plymouth 1780–84 (DNB).

1225. DARCY, Conyers (ca 1685–1758), M.P. Yorkshire 1707–8, 1747–58, Newark 1715–22, Richmond 1722–27, 1728–47 (*Alumni Cantab.; Eton Coll. Reg.;* Gooder).

1226. D'ARCY-OSBORNE, Francis Godolphin (1798–1859), 7th D. of Leeds, M.P. Helston 1826–30 (GEC).

1227. DARELL, Lionel (1742–1803), 1st Bt, M.P. Hedon 1784–1802 (GEC; Holzman's *Nabobs in Eng.*).

1228. DARKER, John (ca 1722–84), M.P. Leicester borough 1766–68, 1774–84 (Musgrave's *Obituary;* Nichols' *Leicester, 3,* pt. 1, 376).

1229. DARLING, Robert (d. 1770), M.P. Wendover 1768–70 (Musgrave's *Obituary;* Namier's *England,* p. 43; *Notes and Queries,* 8th Ser., *2,* 387; Shaw's *Knights, 2,* 292).

DARLINGTON, E. of, *see* VANE, Henry and William Henry.

DARNLEY, E. of, *see* BLIGH, Edward and John.

DARTMOUTH, E. of, *see* LEGGE, George and William.

1230. DASHWOOD, Francis (1708–81), 15th Bn Le Despencer, M.P. New Romney 1741–61, Weymouth and Melcombe Regis 1761–63 (DNB; GEC; *Eton Coll. Reg.*).

1231. DASHWOOD, George (1786–1861), 4th Bt, M.P. Truro 1814–18 (GEC; *Harrow Reg.*).

DASHWOOD, Henry, *see* PEYTON, Henry.

1232. DASHWOOD, Henry Watkin (1745–1828), 3d Bt, M.P. Wigtown burghs 1775–80, Woodstock 1784–1820 (GEC; Williams' *Oxford M.P.'s*).

1233. DASHWOOD, James (ca 1715–79), 2d Bt, M.P. Oxfordshire 1740–55, 1761–68 (GEC).

1234. DASHWOOD, James (ca 1759–1840), M.P. Gatton 1802–3 (Burke's *Peerage; Gent. Mag., 1* [1841], 106).

1235. DASHWOOD-KING, John (1716–93), 3d Bt, M.P. Bishop's Castle 1753–61 (GEC; *Eton Coll. Reg.*).

1236. DASHWOOD-KING, John (ca 1765-1849), 4th Bt, M.P. Wycombe 1796-1831 (*Alumni Oxon.;* GEC).

1237. DAUBENY, George (1742-1806), M.P. Bristol 1781-84 (Burke's *LG; Genealogical Mag., 8,* 100; Williams' *Gloucester M.P.'s*).

1238. DAVENPORT, Davies (1757-1837), M.P. Cheshire 1806-30 (Burke's *LG; Alumni Oxon.; Gent. Mag., 1,* 430).

1239. DAVENPORT, Edward Davies (1778-1847), M.P. Shaftesbury 1826-30 (*Alumni Oxon.;* Burke's *LG;* Pink; *Rugby Reg.; 1812 List*).

1240. DAVENPORT, Thomas (1734-86), M.P. Newton 1780-86 (*Alumni Oxon.; Old Westminsters; Yorkshire Archaeol. Jour., 1,* 307).

1241. DAVERS, Charles (1737-1806), 6th Bt, M.P. Weymouth and Melcombe Regis 1768-74, Bury 1774-1802 (*Alumni Cantab.,* GEC).

1242. DAVERS, Jermyn (ca 1686-1743), 4th Bt, M.P. Bury 1722-27, Suffolk 1727-43 (*Alumni Oxon.;* GEC).

1243. DAVIDSON, Duncan (ca 1733-99), M.P. Cromartyshire 1790-96 (Burke's *LG*).

1244. DAVIDSON, Duncan (ca 1800-81), M.P. Cromartyshire 1826-30, 1831-32 (Burke's *LG; Harrow Reg.; Linc. Inn Reg.;* Boase).

1245. DAVIES, Somerset (1754-1817), M.P. Ludlow 1783-84 (*Alumni Cantab.; Eton Coll. Reg.*).

1246. DAVIES, Thomas Henry Hastings (1789-1846), M.P. Worcester City 1818-34, 1837-41 (Burke's *LG;* Dod's *Parl. Companion* [1834], p. 106; Williams' *Worcester M.P.'s*).

1247. DAVIS, Hart (1791-1854), M.P. Colchester 1812-18 (Howard and Crisp's *Visitation of Eng. and Wales, 9,* 28; Williams' *Gloucester M.P.'s*).

1248. DAVIS, Richard Hart (1766-1842), M.P. Colchester 1807-12, Bristol 1812-31 (Howard and Crisp's *Visitation of Eng. and Wales, 9,* 28; *Essex Review, 8,* 235; Williams' *Gloucester M.P.'s*).

1249. DAVIS-PROTHEROE, Edward (ca 1798-1852), M.P. Evesham 1826-30, Bristol 1831-32, Halifax 1837-47 (*Alumni Oxon.;* Williams' *Worcester M.P.'s*).

1250. DAWES, John, M.P. Tregony 1780-84, Hastings 1784-90 (*Royal Kalendar* [1782], p. 47; query Foster's *Lancashire Pedigrees* and *Gent. Mag., 1* [1822], 378).

1251. DAWKINS, Henry (1728-1814), M.P. Southampton borough 1760-68, Chippenham 1769-74, 1780-84, Hindon 1776-80 (*Alumni Oxon.;* Burke's *LG*).

1252. DAWKINS, Henry (ca 1765-1852), M.P. Boroughbridge 1806-8, Aldborough 1812-14 (Boase; Burke's *LG; Linc. Inn Reg.*).

1253. DAWKINS, Henry (1788-1864), M.P. Boroughbridge 1824-30 (Boase; Burke's *LG; Harrow Reg.*).

1254. DAWKINS, James (ca 1695-1766), M.P. Woodstock 1734-47 (Burke's *LG;* Williams' *Oxford M.P.'s*).

1255. DAWKINS, James (ca 1722–57), M.P. Hindon 1754–57 (DNB).
1256. DAWKINS-COLYEAR, James (ca 1760–1843), M.P. Chippenham 1784–1806, 1807–12, Hastings 1812–26, Wilton 1831–32 (*Alumni Oxon.;* Burke's *LG*).
1257. DAWKINS-PENNANT, George Hay (ca 1764–1840), M.P. Newark 1814–18, New Romney 1820–30 (Burke's *LG* [ed. 1849]; *Gent. Mag., 1* [1841], 318).
1258. DAWNAY, Henry Pleydell (1727–60), 3d Vct Downe, M.P. Yorkshire 1750–60 (GEC; *Eton Coll. Reg.;* Gooder).
1259. DAWNAY, John (1728–80), 4th Vct Downe, M.P. Cirencester 1754–68, Malton 1768–74 (GEC; *Eton Coll. Reg.*).
1260. DAWNAY, John Christopher Burton (1764–1832), 5th Vct Downe, M.P. Petersfield 1787–90, Wootton Bassett 1790–96 (GEC; *Eton Coll. Reg.*).
1261. DAWSON, Alexander (ca 1771–1831), M.P. Louth 1826–31 (*Alumni Dublin.; Gent. Mag., 2,* 282).
1262. DAWSON, George Robert (1790–1856), M.P. Londonderry Co. 1815–30, Harwich 1830–32 (*Alumni Oxon.;* Burke's *LG; Harrow Reg.*).
DAWSON, James Hewitt Massy, *see* MASSY-DAWSON, James Hewitt.
1263. DAWSON, Richard (ca 1761–1807), M.P. Monaghan 1801–7 (*Alumni Oxon.; Alumni Dublin.;* GEC sub Cremorne).
1264. DAWSON, Richard Thomas (1788–1827), 2d Bn Cremorne, M.P. Monaghan 1812–13 (*Alumni Cantab.;* GEC).
1265. DEANE, Jocelyn (ca 1749–80), M.P. Helston 1780–80 (Debrett's *Peerage* [1834] sub Muskerry).
1266. DE BEAUVOIR, Richard Benyon (1770–1854), M.P. Pontefract 1802–6, Wallingford 1806–12 (*Alumni Cantab.;* Burke's *LG*).
1267. DE BLAQUIERE, John (1732–1812), 1st Bn De Blaquiere, M.P. Rye 1801–2, Downton 1803–6 (DNB; GEC).
1268. DE BURGH, Ulysses (1788–1863), 2d Bn Downes, M.P. Carlow Co. 1818–26, Queenborough 1826–30 (*Alumni Dublin.;* DNB; GEC).
DE CLIFFORD, 20th Bn, *see* SOUTHWELL, Edward.
1269. DE CORNEWALL, Robert (1700–56), 1st Bt, M.P. Leominster 1747–54 (GEC appendix; Reade's *House of Cornewall,* p. 99).
1270. DE CRESPIGNY, Philip Champion (d. 1803), M.P. Sudbury 1774–75, Aldeburgh 1780–90 (*Gent. Mag., 1,* 89; *Notes and Queries,* 8th Ser., *8,* 196).
1271. DE CRESPIGNY, Thomas Champion (ca 1762–99), M.P. Sudbury 1790–96 (*Alumni Cantab.*).
1272. DE CRESPIGNY, William Champion (1765–1829), 2d Bt, M.P. Southampton borough 1818–26 (*Alumni Cantab.; Eton Coll. Reg.*).
DE DUNSTANVILLE, 1st Bn, *see* BASSET, Francis.

1273. DEEDES, William (1761–1834), M.P. Hythe 1807–12 (*Alumni Oxon.;* Burke's *LG*).

DEERHURST, Vct, *see* COVENTRY, George William and Thomas Henry.

DE FREYNE, 1st Bn, *see* FRENCH, Arthur.

1274. DE GRENIER-FONBLANQUE, John (ca 1760–1837), M.P. Camelford 1802–6 (DNB).

1275. DE GREY, Thomas (1719–81), M.P. Norfolk 1764–74 (*Alumni Cantab.;* Collins' *Peerage* sub Walsingham).

1276. DE GREY, Thomas (1748–1818), 2d Bn Walsingham, M.P. Wareham 1774–74, Tamworth 1774–80, Lostwithiel 1780–81 (*Alumni Cantab.;* GEC; *Eton Coll. Reg.*).

1277. DE GREY, William (1719–81), 1st Bn Walsingham, M.P. Newport 1761–70, Cambridge Univ. 1770–71 (DNB; GEC).

1278. DEHANY, Philip (ca 1734–1809), M.P. St. Ives 1778–80 (*Alumni Cantab.; Old Westminsters*).

1279. DE HORSEY, Spencer Horsey (1790–1860), M.P. Aldeburgh 1829–30, Orford 1830–32, Newcastle-under-Lyme 1837–41 (*Alumni Oxon.;* Boase; Burke's *Family Records*).

DELAMERE, 1st Bn, *see* CHOLMONDELEY, Thomas.

1280. DE LANCEY, Oliver (ca 1749–1822), M.P. Maidstone 1796–1802 (DNB).

1281. DE LA POLE, John William (1757–99), 6th Bt, M.P. West Looe 1790–96 (GEC).

DELAVAL, Francis Blake, *see* BLAKE-DELAVAL, Francis.

1282. DELAVAL, George (1703–82), M.P. Northumberland 1757–74 (*New Hist. of Northumberland, 4,* 418).

DELAVAL, John Hussey, *see* HUSSEY-DELAVAL, John.

1283. DELGARNO, John (ca 1751–1818), M.P. Yarmouth (Hants) 1804–4, 1808–8, Newport 1814–16 (*Gent. Mag., 1,* 475).

DE L'ISLE and DUDLEY, 1st Bn, *see* SIDNEY, Philip Charles.

1284. DELME, Peter (1710–70), M.P. Ludgershall 1734–41, Southampton borough 1741–54 (Agnew's *Protestant Exiles, 3,* 88; Cussans' *Herts, 2,* pt. 1, 45).

1285. DELME, Peter (1748–89), M.P. Morpeth 1774–89 (Burke's *LG* sub Radcliffe; Cussans' *Herts, 2,* pt. 1, 45).

DELVES, Brian Broughton, *see* BROUGHTON-DELVES, Brian.

DE MAULEY, 1st Bn, *see* PONSONBY, William Francis Spencer.

1286. DE MOLEYNS, Frederick William Beaufort (1804–54), M.P. Kerry 1831–37 (*Alumni Dublin.;* Boase).

1287. DEMPSTER, George (1732–1818), M.P. Perth burghs 1761–68, 1769–90 (DNB; Grant's *Faculty of Advocates*).

DENHAM, James, *see* STEUART-DENHAM, James.

1288. DENIS, Peter (ca 1713–78), 1st Bt, M.P. Hedon 1754–68 (DNB; GEC).

1289. DENISON, John (ca 1758–1820), M.P. Wootton Bassett 1796–1802,

Colchester 1802–6, Minehead 1807–12 (Burke's *LG; Essex Review, 8,* 234).

1290. DENISON, John Evelyn (1800–73), 1st Vct Ossington, M.P. Newcastle-under-Lyme 1823–26, Hastings 1826–30, Notts 1831–32, South Notts 1832–37, Malton 1841–57, North Notts 1857–72 (DNB; GEC).

1291. DENISON, William Joseph (1770–1849), M.P. Camelford 1796–1802, Hull 1806–7, Surrey 1818–32, West Surrey 1832–49 (DNB).

1292. DENMAN, Thomas (1779–1854), 1st Bn Denman, M.P. Wareham 1818–20, Nottingham borough 1820–26, 1830–32 (*Alumni Cantab.;* DNB; GEC; *Eton Coll. Reg.*).

1293. DENNIS, George (d. 1740), M.P. Liskeard 1734–40 (Musgrave's *Obituary*).

1294. DENNY, Edward (ca 1773–1831), 3d Bt, M.P. Tralee 1828–29 (*Alumni Dublin.;* GEC).

1295. DENNY, Edward (1796–1889), 4th Bt, M.P. Tralee 1818–19 (Boase; GEC).

1296. DENT, John (ca 1760–1826), M.P. Lancaster borough 1790–1812, Poole 1818–26 (Bean; Burke's *LG; Notes and Queries,* 8th Ser., 7, 117; Pink).

1297. DENTON, George (d. 1757), M.P. Buckingham borough 1728–47 (Lipscomb's *Bucks, 3,* 18; Musgrave's *Obituary*).

1298. DENYS, George William (1788–1857), 1st Bt, M.P. Hull 1812–18 (*Alumni Cantab.;* Baker's *Northampton, 2,* 144; Foster's *Baronetage*).

1299. DE PONTHIEU, John (d. 1813), M.P. Helston 1806–7, Westbury 1810–12 (*Gent. Mag., 1* [1813], 495 and *2* [1817], 379).

DERBY, Earls of, *see* STANLEY, Edward; *also* SMITH-STANLEY, Edward and Edward George Geoffrey.

1300. DERING, Cholmeley (ca 1775–1858), M.P. New Romney 1817–18 (*Alumni Oxon.;* Burke's *Peerage*).

1301. DERING, Edward (1705–62), 5th Bt, M.P. Kent 1733–54 (GEC; *Old Westminsters*).

1302. DERING, Edward (1732–98), 6th Bt, M.P. New Romney 1761–70, 1774–87 (*Alumni Cantab.;* GEC; *Old Westminsters*).

1303. DERING, Edward Cholmeley (1807–96), 8th Bt, M.P. Wexford town 1830–30, 1831–31, New Romney 1831–32, East Kent 1852–57, 1863–68 (GEC; *Harrow Reg.*).

DE Ros, Henry William Fitzgerald, *see* FITZGERALD-DE Ros, Henry William.

DESART, 2d E. of, *see* CUFFE, John Otway.

DES BOUVERIE, Jacob, *see* BOUVERIE, Jacob.

DESPENCER, *see* LE DESPENCER.

DE TABLY, 1st Bn, *see* LEICESTER, John Fleming.

1304. DEVAYNES, William (ca 1730–1809), M.P. Barnstable 1774–80, 1784–96, 1802–6, Winchelsea 1796–1802 (*Genealogist*, N.S., *21*, 202; Manning and Bray's *Surrey*, *3*, 299).

1305. DEVERELL, Robert (ca 1760–1841), M.P. Saltash 1802–6 (*Alumni Oxon.;* DNB).

1306. DEVEREUX, Price (1694–1748), 10th Vct Hereford, M.P. Montgomeryshire 1719–40 (*Alumni Oxon.;* GEC).

1307. DE VIRY, François Joseph Marie Henri (1766–1820), Comte de Viry, M.P. Huntingdon borough 1790–96 (Namier's *England*, p. 93; *Times,* 12 Oct. and 1 Nov. 1928).

DEVON, 11th E. of, *see* COURTENAY, William.

DEVONSHIRE, D. of, *see* CAVENDISH, William.

1308. DEWER, John, M.P. Cricklade 1775–80.

D'EYNCOURT, Charles Tennyson, *see* TENNYSON-D'EYNCOURT, Charles.

1309. DICK, Hugh (ca 1780–1830), M.P. Maldon 1827–30 (*Alumni Dublin.;* Burke's *Irish LG; Gent. Mag., 2,* 189).

1310. DICK, Quintin (ca 1777–1858), M.P. West Looe 1803–6, Cashel 1807–9, Orford 1826–30, Maldon 1830–47, Aylesbury 1848–52 (Burke's *Irish LG;* Boase; *Gent. Mag., 1,* 559; *Linc. Inn Reg.*).

1311. DICKER, Samuel (d. 1760), M.P. Plymouth 1754–60 (Musgrave's *Obituary*).

1312. DICKINS, Francis (ca 1750–1833), M.P. Cambridge borough 1788–90, Northamptonshire 1790–1806 (*Alumni Cantab.; Old Westminsters*).

1313. DICKINSON, Marsh (ca 1703–65), M.P. Brackley 1754–65 (*Old Westminsters*).

1314. DICKINSON, William (ca 1745–1806), M.P. Great Marlow 1768–74, Rye 1777–90, Somerset 1796–1806 (Bates Harbin; Burke's *LG; Gent. Mag., 1,* 487; Namier; Phelps, *Somerset, 2,* 481).

1315. DICKINSON, William (1771–1837), M.P. Ilchester 1796–1802, Lostwithiel 1802–6, Somerset 1806–31 (Bates Harbin; Burke's *LG; Old Westminsters; 1832 List*).

1316. DICKSON, James (d. 1771), M.P. Linlithgow burghs 1768–71 (Foster's *Scots M.P.'s;* Musgrave's *Obituary*).

1317. DICKSON, John (d. 1767), M.P. Peebles-shire 1747–67 (Burke's *LG;* Foster's *Scots M.P.'s;* Grant's *Faculty of Advocates*).

1318. DICKSON, William (1748–1815), M.P. Linlithgow burghs 1802–6 (Burke's *LG;* Foster's *Scots M.P.'s*).

1319. DIGBY, Edward (d. 1746), M.P. Warwickshire 1726–46 (GEC).

1320. DIGBY, Edward (1730–57), 6th Bn Digby, M.P. Malmesbury 1751–54, Wells 1754–57 (GEC; *Old Westminsters*).

1321. DIGBY, Henry (1731–93), 1st E. Digby, M.P. Ludgershall 1755–61, Wells 1761–65 (GEC; *Old Westminsters*).

1322. DIGBY, Robert (1732–1815), M.P. Wells 1757–61 (Burke's *Peerage;* Collins' *Peerage;* Charnock's *Biog. Naval., 6,* 119).

1323. DILLON-LEE, Charles (1745–1813), 12th Vct Dillon, M.P. Westbury 1770–74 (GEC).

1324. DILLON-LEE, Henry Augustus (1777–1832), 13th Vct Dillon, M.P. Harwich 1799–1802, Mayo 1802–13 (GEC).

1325. DIMSDALE, Nathaniel (1748–1811), M.P. Hertford borough 1790–1802 (*Eton Coll. Reg.*).

1326. DIMSDALE, Thomas (1712–1800), M.P. Hertford borough 1780–90 (DNB).

DINEVOR, Bn, *see* RICE, George Talbot; *also* RICE-TREVOR, George Rice; *also* TALBOT, William.

DINORBEN, 1st Bn, *see* HUGHES, William Lewis.

1327. DISBROWE, Edward (ca 1754–1818), M.P. Windsor 1806–18 (*Alumni Oxon.; Gent. Mag., 2,* 642).

1328. DISBROWE, Edward Cromwell (ca 1790–1851), M.P. Windsor 1823–26 (*Alumni Oxon.;* Boase).

1329. DIVETT, Thomas (d. 1828), M.P. Gatton 1820–26, Lymington 1827–28 (*Gent. Mag., 2,* 474).

1330. DIXON, Joseph (ca 1800–44), M.P. Glasgow burghs 1831–32 (Addison's *Glasgow Matric. Albums;* Foster's *Scots M.P.'s*).

1331. DOCMINIQUE, Charles (ca 1689–1745), M.P. Gatton 1735–45 (*Alumni Oxon.;* Manning and Bray's *Surrey, 2,* 237, 248).

1332. DOCMINIQUE, Paul (ca 1644–1735), M.P. Gatton 1705–35 (Manning and Bray's *Surrey, 2,* 234, 237, 248).

1333. DODD, John (1717–82), M.P. Reading 1741–41, 1755–82 (*Alumni Cantab.; Eton Coll. Reg.;* Nichols' *Lit. Illust., 8,* 575).

1334. DODINGTON, George (ca 1681–1757), M.P. Weymouth and Melcombe Regis 1734–41, 1747–54 (Burke's *LG; Linc. Inn Reg.;* Phelps' *Somerset, 1,* 319).

DODINGTON, George Bubb, *see* BUBB-DODINGTON, George.

1335. DODSON, John (1780–1858), M.P. Rye 1819–23 (DNB; *Merchant Taylor School Reg.;* Williamson's *Middle Temple Bench Book*).

1336. DOHERTY, John (ca 1783–1850), M.P. New Ross 1824–26, Kilkenny City 1826–30, Newport 1830–30 (*Alumni Dublin.;* DNB).

1337. DOLBEN, William (1727–1814), 3d Bt, M.P. Oxford Univ. 1768–68, 1780–1806, Northamptonshire 1768–74 (DNB; GEC; *Old Westminsters*).

DOMVILE, Compton Pocklington, *see* POCKLINGTON-DOMVILE, Compton.

1338. DON, Alexander (ca 1779–1826), 6th Bt, M.P. Roxburghshire 1814–26 (GEC; *Eton Coll. Reg.*).

DONEGAL, M. of, *see* CHICHESTER, Arthur and George Hamilton.

DONERAILE, 3d Vct, *see* ST. LEGER, Arthur Mohun.

DONOUGHMORE, E. of, *see* HELY-HUTCHINSON, John.

DORCHESTER, E. of, *see* DAMER, George and Joseph.

1339. DORIEN-MAGENS, Magens (ca 1762–1849), M.P. Carmarthen borough 1796–96, Ludgershall 1804–12 (*Gent. Mag., 2,* 109; Williams' *Wales M.P.'s; 1812 List*).

DORSET, D. of, *see* SACKVILLE, Charles and John Frederick.

1340. DOTTIN, Abel Rous (ca 1769–1852), M.P. Gatton 1818–20, Southampton borough 1826–31, 1835–41 (*Alumni Oxon.;* Burke's *LG* [ed. 1849]; *1832 List*).

1341. DOUGLAS, Archibald (ca 1707–78), M.P. Dumfries burghs 1754–61, Dumfries-shire 1761–74 (P. L. W. Adams, *Douglas Family,* pp. 360–67; Burke's *LG;* Foster's *Scots M.P.'s*).

1342. DOUGLAS, Archibald James Edward (1748–1827), 1st Bn Douglas, M.P. Forfarshire 1782–90 (DNB; GEC).

1343. DOUGLAS, Charles (1726–56), M.P. Dumfries-shire 1747–54 (Foster's *Scots M.P.'s; Old Westminsters; Scots Peerage*).

1344. DOUGLAS, Charles (1775–1848), 3d Bn Douglas, M.P. Lanarkshire 1830–32 (GEC; *Eton Coll. Reg.*).

1345. DOUGLAS, Frederick Sylvester North (1791–1819), M.P. Banbury 1812–19 (DNB; GEC sub Glenbervie; *Old Westminsters*).

1346. DOUGLAS, George (ca 1754–1821), 2d Bt, M.P. Roxburghshire 1784–1806 (GEC; Foster's *Scots M.P.'s*).

1347. DOUGLAS, James (d. 1751), M.P. St. Mawes 1741–47, Malmesbury 1747–51 (Musgrave's *Obituary*).

1348. DOUGLAS, James (ca 1703–87), 1st Bt, M.P. Orkney and Shetland 1754–68 (DNB; GEC).

1349. DOUGLAS, John (ca 1708–78), 3d Bt, M.P. Dumfries-shire 1741–47 (GEC; Foster's *Scots M.P.'s; Scots Peerage*).

1350. DOUGLAS, John (? b. ca 1774), M.P. Orford 1818–21, Minehead 1822–26 (*Alumni Oxon.*).

1351. DOUGLAS, John St. Leger (ca 1732–83), M.P. Hindon 1768–74, Weobley 1774–83 (*Alumni Cantab.; Old Westminsters;* Oliver's *Antigua, 1,* 214–15).

1352. DOUGLAS, Robert (d. 1745), M.P. Orkney and Shetland 1730–45 (Foster's *Scots M.P.'s;* Burke's *Peerage* and *Scots Peerage* sub Morton).

1353. DOUGLAS, Sylvester (1743–1823), 1st Bn Glenbervie, M.P. Fowey 1795–96, Midhurst 1796–1800, Plympton Erle 1801–2, Hastings 1802–6 (DNB; GEC).

1354. DOUGLAS, William (d. 1748), M.P. Roxburghshire 1715–22, 1727–34, 1742–47, Dumfries burghs 1722–27 (Burke's *LG;* Foster's *Scots M.P.'s*).

1355. DOUGLAS, William (ca 1730–83), 4th Bt, M.P. Dumfries burghs 1768–80 (Addison's *Glasgow Matric. Albums;* GEC).

1356. DOUGLAS, William (d. 1821), M.P. Plympton Erle 1812–16 (Grant's *Faculty of Advocates*).

1357. DOUGLAS, William Robert Keith (ca 1783–1859), M.P. Dumfries burghs 1812–32 (Foster's *Scots M.P.'s; Scots Peerage; 1832 List*).

DOURO, M. of, *see* WELLESLEY, Arthur Richard.

DOVER, 1st Bn, *see* YORKE, Philip; *also* ELLIS, George James Wellbore Agar.

1358. DOVETON, Gabriel (d. 1824), M.P. Lancaster borough 1812–24 (Bean; *Gent. Mag., 2*, 283; Pink).

1359. DOWDESWELL, John Edmund (1772–1851), M.P. Tewkesbury 1812–32 (*Old Westminsters;* Williams' *Gloucester M.P.'s*).

1360. DOWDESWELL, William (ca 1721–75), M.P. Tewkesbury 1747–54, Worcestershire 1761–75 (DNB; *Old Westminsters;* Williams' *Worcester M.P.'s*).

1361. DOWDESWELL, William (1760–1828), M.P. Tewkesbury 1792–97 (DNB; *Old Westminsters;* Williams' *Gloucester M.P.'s*).

DOWNE, Vct, *see* DAWNAY, Henry Pleydell and John Pleydell.

DOWNES, 2d Bn, *see* DE BURGH, Ulysses.

1362. DOWNIE, Robert (ca 1771–1841), M.P. Stirling burghs 1820–30 (Foster's *Scots M.P.'s; Gent. Mag., 2*, 547).

1363. DOWNING, George (ca 1685–1749), 3d Bt, M.P. Dunwich 1710–15, 1722–49 (DNB; GEC).

1364. DOWNING, Jacob Garrard (ca 1700–64), 4th Bt, M.P. Dunwich 1741–47, 1749–61, 1763–64 (*Alumni Cantab.;* GEC).

DOWNSHIRE, M. of, *see* HILL, Arthur and Wills.

1365. DOYLE, John (1756–1834), 1st Bt, M.P. Newport (Hants) 1806–7 (*Alumni Dublin.;* DNB; Foster's *Baronetage*).

1366. DOYLE, John Milley (ca 1781–1856), M.P. Carlow 1831–32 (DNB).

1367. D'OYLY, Christopher (1716–95), M.P. Wareham 1774–80, Seaford 1780–84 (*Alumni Oxon.;* Brayley's *Surrey, 2*, 96; Kirby's *Winchester Scholars*, p. 236).

1368. D'OYLY, John (1754–1818), 6th Bt, M.P. Ipswich 1790–96 (GEC).

1369. DRAKE, Francis Henry (1694–1740), 4th Bt, M.P. Tavistock 1715–34, Berealston 1734–40 (GEC).

1370. DRAKE, Francis Henry (1723–94), 5th Bt, M.P. Berealston 1747–70, 1774–80 (*Alumni Cantab.;* GEC; *Eton Coll. Reg.*).

1371. DRAKE, Francis William (1724–87), M.P. Berealston 1771–74 (GEC; Charnock's *Biog. Naval., 6*, 61).

DRAKE, Thomas Tyrwhitt, *see* TYRWHITT-DRAKE, Thomas.

1372. DRAKE, William (1723–96), M.P. Agmondesham 1746–96 (Lipscomb's *Bucks, 3*, 170; *Old Westminsters*).

1373. DRAKE, William (1748–95), M.P. Agmondesham 1768–95 (Burke's *LG; Old Westminsters*).

1374. DRAKE-GARRARD, Charles (ca 1755–1817), M.P. Agmondesham 1796–1805 (Burke's *LG;* Cussàns' *Herts, 3,* pt. 1, 338; *Old Westminsters*).

1375. DRAX, Edward (ca 1726–89), M.P. Wareham 1755–61 (*Alumni Oxon.; Burke's LG; Eton Coll. Reg.*).

1376. DRAX, Henry (ca 1694–1755), M.P. Wareham 1718–22, 1734–48, 1751–55, Lyme Regis 1727–34 (*Alumni Cantab.; Eton Coll. Reg.*).

DRAX, Richard Grosvenor Erle, *see* ERLE-DRAX, Richard Grosvenor.

1377. DRAX, Thomas Erle (ca 1722–89), M.P. Corfe Castle 1744–47, Wareham 1747–48, 1761–68 (*Alumni Oxon.;* Burke's *LG*).

DROGHEDA, M. of, *see* MOORE, Charles.

1378. DRUMMOND, Adam (1713–86), M.P. Lymington 1761–68, St. Ives 1768–78, Aberdeen burghs 1779–84, Shaftesbury 1784–86 (Burke's *LG;* Grant's *Faculty of Advocates*).

1379. DRUMMOND, George Harley (1783–1853), M.P. Kincardineshire 1812–20 (Addison's *Glasgow Matric. Albums; Harrow Reg.; Scots Peerage* sub Strathallan).

1380. DRUMMOND, Henry (1762–94), M.P. Castle Rising 1790–94 (*Scots Peerage* sub Strathallan).

1381. DRUMMOND, Henry (d. 1795), M.P. Wendover 1774–80, Midhurst 1780–90 (*Scots Peerage* sub Strathallan).

1382. DRUMMOND, Henry (1786–1860), M.P. Plympton Erle 1810–12, West Surrey 1847–60 (DNB; *Harrow Reg.; Scotts Peerage* sub Strathallan).

DRUMMOND, Henry Home, *see* HOME-DRUMMOND, Henry.

1383. DRUMMOND, James Andrew John Lawrence Charles (1767–1851), 6th Vct Strathallan, M.P. Perthshire 1812–24 (GEC).

1384. DRUMMOND, John (d. 1742), M.P. Perth burghs 1727–42 (Foster's *Scots M.P.'s*).

1385. DRUMMOND, John (1723–74), M.P. Thetford 1768–74 (*Old Westminsters; Scots Peerage* sub Strathallan).

1386. DRUMMOND, John (ca 1754–1836), M.P. Shaftesbury 1786–90 (Burke's *LG*).

1387. DRUMMOND, William (ca 1770–1828), M.P. St. Mawes 1795–96, Lostwithiel 1796–1802 (DNB).

1388. DRUMMOND-BURRELL, Peter Robert (1782–1865), 2d Bn Gwydir and 2d Bn Willoughby, M.P. Boston 1812–20 (*Alumni Cantab.;* GEC).

1389. DRURY, Thomas (1712–59), 1st Bt, M.P. Maldon 1741–47 (GEC).

1390. DU CANE, Peter (1778–1841), M.P. Steyning 1826–30 (*Alumni Cantab.*).

DUCIE, Bn, *see* MORETON, Matthew Ducie; also REYNOLDS-MORETON, Francis.

DUCIE, 2d E. of, *see* REYNOLDS-MORETON, Henry George Francis.

1391. DUCKETT, George (1725–1822), 1st Bt, M.P. Weymouth and Melcombe Regis 1786–88, Colchester 1788–89, 1790–96 (DNB; GEC; *Duchetiana*, p. 70).

1392. DUCKETT, George (1777–1856), 2d Bt, M.P. Lymington 1807–12, Plympton Erle 1812–12 (GEC).

1393. DUCKETT, Thomas (ca 1713–66), M.P. Calne 1754–57, 1761–66 (*Duchetiana*, p. 47; *Wilts Archaeol. and Nat. Hist. Mag., 44* [1928], 106).

1394. DUCKETT, William (d. 1749), M.P. Calne 1727–41 (*Duchetiana*, pp. 46, 59; *Notes and Queries*, 12th Ser., *2*, 192).

1395. DUCKWORTH, John Thomas (1748–1817), 1st Bt, M.P. New Romney 1812–17 (DNB; *Eton Coll. Reg.*).

DUDLEY AND WARD, Vct and E., *see* WARD, John, John William, and William.

1396. DUFF, Alexander (ca 1778–1851), M.P. Elgin burghs 1826–31 (Boase; *Old Westminsters;* Tayler's *Book of the Duffs, 1,* 182, 193).

1397. DUFF, Arthur (ca 1743–1805), M.P. Elginshire 1774–79 (Foster's *Scots M.P.'s;* Tayler's *Morayshire M.P.'s*).

1398. DUFF, James (1729–1809), 2d E. of Fife, M.P. Banffshire 1754–84, Elginshire 1784–90 (DNB; GEC).

1399. DUFF, James (ca 1755–1839), M.P. Banffshire 1784–89 (DNB; Foster's *Scots M.P.'s;* Tayler's *Memoirs of the Duffs,* pp. 506, 514).

1400. DUFF, James (1776–1857), 4th E. of Fife, M.P. Banffshire 1818–27 (DNB; GEC; *Old Westminsters*).

1401. DUFF-GORDON, William (1772–1823), 2d Bt, M.P. Worcester City 1807–18 (*Scots Peerage* sub Aberdeen; Williams' *Worcester M.P.'s*).

DUFFERIN, 2d Bn, *see* BLACKWOOD, James.

1402. DUGDALE, Dugdale Stratford (ca 1773–1836), M.P. Warwickshire 1802–31 (*Alumni Oxon.;* Burke's *LG*).

1403. DUGDALE, William Stratford (1800–71), M.P. Shaftesbury 1830–31, Bramber 1831–32, North Warwickshire 1832–47 (Burke's *LG; Old Westminsters*).

1404. DUIGENAN, Patrick (ca 1735–1816), M.P. Armagh borough 1801–16 (DNB).

1405. DUKE, John (ca 1714–75), M.P. Honiton 1747–54, 1761–68 (*Devon and Cornwall Notes and Queries, 14,* 360; *Misc. Geneal. et Herald.,* 4th Ser., *3*).

1406. DUMMER, Thomas (ca 1740–81), M.P. Newport (Hants) 1765–68, Yarmouth (Hants) 1769–74, Downton 1774–75, Wendover 1775–80, Lymington 1780–81 (*Old Westminsters*).

1407. DUMMER, Thomas Lee (ca 1713–65), M.P. Southhampton borough 1737–41, Newport (Hants) 1747–65 (*Old Westminsters*).

DUNALLEY, 2d Bn, *see* SADLEIR-PRITTIE, Henry.

DUNCANNON, 1st Bn, *see* PONSONBY, John William.

DUNCANNON, 1st Vct, *see* VANE, William.

1408. DUNCOMBE, Anthony (ca 1695–1763), 1st Bn Feversham, M.P. Salisbury 1721–34, Downton 1734–47 (GEC; *Old Westminsters*).

1409. DUNCOMBE, Arthur (1806–89), M.P. East Retford 1830–51, Yorkshire (East Riding) 1851–68 (Boase; Burke's *Peerage* sub Feversham).

1410. DUNCOMBE, Charles (1764–1841), 1st Bn Feversham, M.P. Shaftesbury 1790–96, Aldborough 1796–1806, Heytesbury 1812–18, Newport (Hants) 1818–26 (GEC; *Harrow Reg.*).

1411. DUNCOMBE, Henry (ca 1728–1818), M.P. Yorkshire 1780–96 (Gooder; *Old Westminsters*).

1412. DUNCOMBE, Thomas (d. 1746), M.P. Ripon 1734–41 (Burke's *Peerage* sub Feversham; Musgrave's *Obituary*).

1413. DUNCOMBE, Thomas (ca 1724–79), M.P. Downton 1751–54, 1768–75, 1779–79, Morpeth 1754–68 (*Old Westminsters*).

1414. DUNCOMBE, Thomas Slingsby (ca 1797–1861), M.P. Hertford borough 1826–32, Finsbury 1834–61 (DNB; *Harrow Reg.*).

1415. DUNCOMBE, William (1798–1867), 2d Bn Feversham, M.P. Great Grimsby 1820–26, Yorkshire 1826–31, Yorkshire (North Riding) 1832–41 (GEC; Gooder).

DUNDAS, Charles, *see* DUNDAS, John Charles.

1416. DUNDAS, Charles (1751–1832), 1st Bn Amesbury, M.P. Richmond 1775–80, 1784–86, Orkney and Shetland 1781–84, Berkshire 1794–1832 (*Alumni Cantab.;* DNB; GEC).

1417. DUNDAS, Charles Lawrence (1771–1810), M.P. Malton 1798–1805, Richmond 1806–10 (*Alumni Cantab.; Harrow Reg.*).

1418. DUNDAS, George (1690–1762), M.P. Linlithgowshire 1722–27, 1741–43 (Grant's *Faculty of Advocates;* McLeod's *Royal Letters,* p. xl).

1419. DUNDAS, George Heneage Lawrence (1778–1834), M.P. Richmond 1802–6, 1812–12, Orkney and Shetland 1818–20, 1826–30 (Burke's *Peerage* sub Zetland; Foster's *Scots M.P.'s*).

1420. DUNDAS, Henry (1742–1811), 1st Vct Melville, M.P. Edinburghshire 1774–82, 1783–90, Newton (Hants) 1782–82, Edinburgh City 1790–1802 (DNB; GEC).

1421. DUNDAS, Henry (1801–76), 3d Vct Melville, M.P. Rochester 1826–30, Winchelsea 1830–31 (DNB; GEC; *Harrow Reg.*).

1422. DUNDAS, James (1721–80), M.P. Linlithgowshire 1770–74 (McLeod's *Royal Letters,* p. xl).

1423. DUNDAS, John Charles (1808–66), M.P. Richmond 1830–34, 1841–47, 1865–66, York City 1835–41 (*Alumni Cantab.*).

1424. DUNDAS, Lawrence (ca 1710–81), 1st Bt, M.P. Linlithgow burghs

1747–48, Newcastle-under-Lyme 1762–68, Edinburgh City 1768–80, 1781–81 (GEC; Wedgwood).

1425. DUNDAS, Lawrence (1766–1839), 1st E. of Zetland, M.P. Richmond 1790–1802, 1808–11, York City 1802–7, 1811–20 (*Alumni Cantab.;* GEC; *Harrow Reg.*).

1426. DUNDAS, Philip (d. 1807), M.P. Gatton 1803–5 (*Gent. Mag., 2,* 1075; Omond's *Arniston Memoirs,* p. 350).

1427. DUNDAS, Robert (1685–1753), M.P. Edinburghshire 1722–37 (DNB).

1428. DUNDAS, Robert (1713–87), M.P. Edinburghshire 1754–60 (DNB).

1429. DUNDAS, Robert (1758–1819), M.P. Edinburghshire 1790–1801 (DNB).

DUNDAS, Robert Adam, *see* CHRISTOPHER-NISBET-HAMILTON, Robert Adam.

1430. DUNDAS, Robert Lawrence (1780–1844), M.P. Malton 1807–12, East Retford 1826–27, Richmond 1828–34, 1839–41 (Burke's *Peerage* sub Zetland; *Harrow Reg.*).

DUNDAS, Robert Saunders, *see* SAUNDERS-DUNDAS, Robert.

1431. DUNDAS, Thomas (d. 1786), M.P. Orkney and Shetland 1768–71 (Burke's *Peerage* sub Zetland; Berry's *County Geneal.: Berkshire,* p. 32; Foster's *Scots M.P.'s*).

1432. DUNDAS, Thomas (1741–1820), 1st Bn Dundas, M.P. Richmond 1763–68, Stirlingshire 1768–94 (GEC; *Eton Coll. Reg.*).

1433. DUNDAS, Thomas (1750–94), M.P. Orkney and Shetland 1771–80, 1784–90 (DNB).

1434. DUNDAS, Thomas (1795–1873), 2d E. of Zetland, M.P. Richmond 1818–30, 1835–39, York City 1830–32, 1833–34 (*Alumni Cantab.;* GEC; *Harrow Reg.*).

1435. DUNDAS, William (ca 1762–1845), M.P. Anstruther Easter burghs 1794–96, Tain burghs 1796–1802, Sutherlandshire 1802–8, Elgin burghs 1810–12, Edinburgh City 1812–31 (*Alumni Oxon.;* DNB).

DUNFERMLINE, 1st Bn, *see* ABERCROMBY, James.

DUNGANNON, Vct, *see* HILL-TREVOR, Arthur; *also* PONSONBY, William.

DUNGARVAN, Vct, *see* BOYLE, Hamilton.

DUNLO, Vct, *see* TRENCH, Richard Le Poer.

1436. DUNLOP, James (d. 1832), M.P. Kirkcudbright Stewarty 1812–26 (DNB).

DUNMORE, 5th E. of, *see* MURRAY, George.

1437. DUNNING, John (1731–83), 1st Bn Ashburton, M.P. Calne 1768–82 (DNB; GEC).

DUNRAVEN, 2d E. of, *see* WYNDHAM-QUIN, Windham Henry.

DUNSANDLE, 1st Bn, *see* DALY, James.

1438. DUNTZE, John (ca 1735–95), 1st Bt, M.P. Tiverton 1768–95 (GEC).

DUPPLIN, Vct, *see* HAY, Thomas.

1439. DUPRE, James (1778–1870), M.P. Gatton 1800–2, Aylesbury 1802–6, Chichester 1807–12 (*Alumni Oxon.;* Boase; Burke's *LG*).

1440. DURAND, John (ca 1719–88), M.P. Aylesbury 1768–74, Plympton Erle 1775–80, Seaford 1780–84 (*Notes and Queries,* 12th Ser., *3,* 72).

1441. DURAND, John Hodsdon (ca 1761–1830), M.P. Maidstone 1802–6 (Brightling's *Carshalton,* p. 96; *1806 List*).

1442. DURANT, George (ca 1733–80), M.P. Evesham 1768–74 (Shrop. Archaeol. Soc. *Trans.,* 1st Ser., *2,* 258; Williams' *Worcester M.P.'s*).

DURHAM, 1st E. *see* LAMBTON, John George.

1443. DURRANT, Thomas (ca 1734–90), 1st Bt, M.P. St. Ives 1768–74 (*Alumni Cantab.;* GEC).

DURSLEY, Vct, *see* BERKELEY, William Fitzhardinge.

1444. DUTTON, James (1744–1820), 1st Bn Sherborne, M.P. Gloucestershire 1781–84 (GEC; *Eton Coll. Reg.*).

1445. DYKE-ACLAND, John (ca 1747–78), M.P. Callington 1774–78 (DNB; GEC; *Eton Coll. Reg.*).

1446. DYKE-ACLAND, Thomas (ca 1723–85), 3d Bt, M.P. Devon 1746–47, Somerset 1767–68 (GEC; Bates Harbin).

1447. DYKE-ACLAND, Thomas (1787–1871), 6th Bt, M.P. Devon 1812–18, 1820–31, North Devon 1837–57 (DNB; GEC; *Harrow Reg.*).

DYSART, E. *see* TOLLEMACHE, Lionel William John and Wilbraham.

1448. DYSON, Jeremiah (ca 1722–76), M.P. Yarmouth (Hants) 1762–68, Weymouth and Melcombe Regis 1768–74, Horsham 1774–76 (DNB).

1449. EAMES, John (ca 1716–95), M.P. Yarmouth (Hants) 1765–68, Newport (Hants) 1768–73 (*Alumni Oxon.*).

1450. EARDLEY, Culling (1805–63), 3d Bt, M.P. Pontefract 1830–31 (*Alumni Oxon.;* DNB).

1451. EARDLEY, Sampson (1745–1824), 1st Bn Eardley, M.P. Cambridgeshire 1770–80, Midhurst 1780–84, Coventry 1784–96, Wallingford 1796–1802 (GEC; *Eton Coll. Reg.*).

1452. EARDLEY-WILMOT, John (1749–1815), M.P. Tiverton 1776–84, Coventry 1784–96 (DNB; Foster's *Baronetage; Old Westminsters*).

1453. EARLE, Giles (ca 1678–1758), M.P. Chippenham 1715–22, Malmesbury 1722–47 (DNB).

1454. EARLE, William Rawlinson (ca 1702–74), M.P. Malmesbury 1727–47, Cricklade 1747–61, 1774–74, Newport (Hants) 1762–68 (DNB sub Giles Earle).

1455. EAST, Edward Hyde (1764–1847), 1st Bt, M.P. Great Bedwin 1792–96, Winchester 1823–31 (*Alumni Oxon.;* DNB; *Harrow Reg.*).

1456. EAST, James Buller (1789–1878), 2d Bt, M.P. Winchester 1831–32, 1835–64 (DNB; *Harrow Reg.*).

1457. EASTHOPE, John (1784–1865), 1st Bt, M.P. St. Albans 1826–30, Banbury 1831–32, Leicester borough 1837–47 (DNB; Williams' *Oxford M.P.'s*).

EASTNOR, Vct, *see* COCKS, John Somers.

EBRINGTON, Vct, *see* FORTESCUE, Hugh.

EBURY, 1st Bn, *see* GROSVENOR, Robert.

EDDISBURY, 1st Bn, *see* STANLEY, Edward John.

1458. EDEN, George (1784–1849), 1st E. of Auckland, M.P. Woodstock 1810–12, 1813–14 (DNB; GEC).

1459. EDEN, John (1740–1812), 4th Bt, M.P. Durham 1774–90 (*Alumni Cantab.;* GEC; *Eton Coll. Reg.*).

EDEN, Robert Henley, *see* HENLEY, Robert Henley.

1460. EDEN, William (1744–1814), 1st Bn Auckland, M.P. Woodstock 1774–84, Heytesbury 1784–93 (DNB; GEC; *Eton Coll. Reg.*).

1461. EDEN, William Frederick (1782–1810), M.P. Woodstock 1806–10 (GEC; Williams' *Oxford M.P.'s*).

1462. EDGCUMBE, Ernest Augustus (1797–1861), 3d E. of Mount Edgcumbe, M.P. Fowey 1819–26, Lostwithiel 1830–32, Plympton Erle 1830–30 (GEC; *Harrow Reg.*).

1463. EDGCUMBE, George (1721–95), 1st E. of Mount Edgcumbe, M.P. Fowey 1746–61 (DNB; GEC).

1464. EDGCUMBE, George (1800–82), M.P. Plympton Erle 1826–26 (*Alumni Oxon.; Harrow Reg.*).

1465. EDGCUMBE, Richard (1680–1758), 1st Bn Edgcumbe, M.P. Cornwall 1701–1, St. Germans 1701–2, Plympton Erle 1702–34, 1741–42, Lostwithiel 1734–41 (DNB; GEC; *Alumni Cantab.*).

1466. EDGCUMBE, Richard (1716–61), 2d Bn Edgcumbe, M.P. Plympton Erle 1742–47, Lostwithiel 1747–54, Penryn 1754–58 (DNB; GEC; *Eton Coll. Reg.*).

1467. EDGCUMBE, Richard (1764–1839), 2d E. of Mount Edgcumbe, M.P. Fowey 1786–95 (DNB; GEC).

1468. EDGCUMBE, William Richard (1794–1818), M.P. Lostwithiel 1816–18, Fowey 1819–19 [*sic*] (GEC; *Harrow Reg.*).

1469. EDMONSTONE, Archibald (1717–1807), 1st Bt, M.P. Dumbartonshire 1761–80, 1790–96, Ayr burghs 1780–90 (GEC; Addison's *Glasgow Matric. Albums*).

1470. EDMONSTONE, Charles (1764–1821), 2d Bt, M.P. Dumbartonshire 1806–7, Stirlingshire 1812–21 (GEC; *Eton Coll. Reg.*).

1471. EDWARDES, Edward Henry (1798–1829), M.P. Bletchingley 1820–26 (*Alumni Oxon.;* GEC sub Kensington; *Eton Lists;* cf. *Alumni Cantab.*).

EDWARDES, Gerard Noel, *see* NOEL, Gerard Noel.

1472. EDWARDES, William (ca 1711–1801), 1st Bn Kensington, M.P. Haverfordwest 1747–84, 1786–1801 (GEC).

1473. EDWARDES, William (1777–1852), 2d Bn Kensington, M.P. Haverfordwest 1802–18 (GEC).

1474. EDWARDS, Bryan (1743–1800), M.P. Grampound 1796–1800 (DNB; Oliver's *Antigua, 1,* 235).

1475. EDWARDS, Samuel (ca 1668–1738), M.P. Wenlock 1722–38 (Musgrave's *Obituary;* Shrop. Archaeol. Soc. *Trans.,* 3d Ser., *2,* 339).

1476. EDWARDS, Thomas (ca 1673–1743), M.P. Bristol 1713–14, Wells 1719–35 (*Alumni Oxon;* Williamson's *Middle Temple Bench Book*).

1477. EDWARDS-FREEMAN, Thomas (ca 1727–1808), M.P. Steyning 1768–80 (*Alumni Oxon.*).

1478. EDWARDS-FREEMAN, Thomas (ca 1754–88), M.P. Steyning 1785–88 (*Alumni Oxon.;* Musgrave's *Obituary*).

1479. EDWARDS-VAUGHAN, John (d. 1833), M.P. Glamorgan 1818–20, Wells 1830–32 (Williams' *Wales M.P.'s*).

1480. EDWIN, Charles (ca 1699–1756), M.P. Westminster 1741–47, Glamorgan 1747–56 (*Herald and Genealogist, 6,* 58; Williams' *Wales M.P.'s*).

1481. EDWIN, Charles (d. 1801), M.P. Glamorgan 1780–89 (*Herald and Genealogist, 6,* 58; *Misc. Geneal. et Herald.,* 1st Ser., *2,* 136).

EFFINGHAM, 4th E. of, *see* HOWARD, Richard.

1482. EGERTON, Francis (1800–57), 1st E. of Ellesmere, M.P. Bletchingley 1822–26, Sutherlandshire 1826–31, South Lancashire 1835–46 (DNB; GEC).

EGERTON, John, *see* GREY-EGERTON, John.

1483. EGERTON, John William (1753–1823), 7th E. of Bridgewater, M.P. Morpeth 1777–80, Brackley 1780–1803 (GEC; *Eton Coll. Reg.*).

EGERTON, Philip de Malpas Grey, *see* GREY-EGERTON, Philip de Malpas.

1484. EGERTON, Samuel (1711–80), M.P. Cheshire 1754–80 (Foster's *Lancashire Pedigrees;* Omerod's *Chester, 1,* 448).

1485. EGERTON, Thomas (1749–1814), 1st E. de Wilton, M.P. Lancashire 1772–84 (GEC).

1486. EGERTON, Thomas Grey (ca 1721–56), 6th Bt, M.P. Newton 1747–54 (*Alumni Oxon.;* GEC).

1487. EGERTON, Wilbraham (1781–1856), M.P. Cheshire 1812–31 (*Alumni Oxon.;* Boase; *Eton Lists*).

1488. EGERTON, William (d. 1783), M.P. Brackley 1768–80 (Collins' *Peerage* sub Bridgewater; Foster's *Lancashire Pedigrees*).

EGERTON, William Tatton, *see* TATTON-EGERTON, William.

1489. EGERTON, William Tatton (1806–83), 1st Bn Egerton, M.P. Lymington 1830–31, North Cheshire 1832–58 (GEC).

EGLETON, Charles, *see* KENT, Charles.

EGLINTOUN, E. of, *see* MONTGOMERIE, Archibald and Hugh.

EGMONT, E. of, *see* PERCEVAL, Henry Frederick John James, John, and John James.

EGREMONT, 2d E. of, *see* WYNDHAM, Charles.

ELDON, E. of, *see* SCOTT, John.

1490. ELFORD, Jonathan (ca 1777–1823), M.P. Westbury 1820–20 (*Alumni Oxon.*).

1491. ELFORD, William (1749–1837), 1st Bt, M.P. Plymouth 1796–1806, Rye 1807–8 (DNB; GEC).

ELIBANK, 7th Bn, *see* MURRAY, Alexander.

ELIOT, Edward, *see* CRAGGS-ELIOT, Edward.

1492. ELIOT, Edward Granville (1798–1877), 3d E. of St. Germans, M.P. Liskeard 1824–32, East Cornwall, 1837–45 (DNB; GEC; *Old Wesminsters*).

1493. ELIOT, Edward James (1758–97), M.P. St. Germans 1780–84, Liskeard 1784–97 (*Alumni Cantab.;* GEC).

1494. ELIOT, John (1761–1823), 1st E. of St. Germans, M.P. Liskeard 1784–1804 (*Alumni Cantab.;* GEC).

1495. ELIOT, Richard (1694–1748), M.P. St. Germans 1733–34, 1747–48, Liskeard 1734–47 (*Alumni Oxon.;* Boase and Courtney, *Biblio. Cornub.; Misc. Geneal. et Herald.,* 7th Ser., *2,* 46).

1496. ELIOT, William (1767–1845), 2d E. of St. Germans, M.P. St. Germans 1791–1802, Liskeard 1802–23 (*Alumni Cantab.;* GEC).

1497. ELIOTT-LOCKHART, William (1764–1832), M.P. Selkirkshire 1806–30 (Burke's *LG;* Foster's *Scots M.P.'s*).

ELLENBOROUGH, 1st Bn, *see* LAW, Edward.

ELLESMERE, E. of, *see* EGERTON, Francis.

1498. ELLICE, Edward (ca 1783–1863), M.P. Coventry 1818–26, 1830–63 (DNB; Burke's *LG;* Dod's *Parl. Companion* [1834], p. 110).

1499. ELLICE, William (ca 1781–1822), M.P. Great Grimsby 1807–12 (Addison's *Glasgow Matric. Albums;* Burke's *LG*).

1500. ELLIOT, Gilbert (1722–77), 3d Bt, M.P. Selkirkshire 1753–65, Roxburghshire 1765–77 (DNB; GEC).

1501. ELLIOT, Gilbert (1751–1814), 1st E. of Minto, M.P. Morpeth 1776–77, Roxburghshire 1777–84, Berwick 1786–90, Helston 1790–95 (DNB; GEC).

1502. ELLIOT, John (1732–1808), M.P. Cockermouth 1767–68 (DNB; G. F. S. Elliot's *Border Elliots,* p. 442).

1503. ELLIOT, William (d. 1764), M.P. Calne 1741–54 (Dalton, *George the First's Army, 2,* 198; *Notes and Queries,* 12th Ser., *2,* 192).

1504. ELLIOT, William (d. 1818), M.P. Portarlington 1801–2, Peterborough 1802–18 (*Alumni Oxon.*).

1505. ELLIOT-MURRAY-KYNYNMOUND, Gilbert (1782–1859), 2d E. of Minto, M.P. Ashburton 1806–7, Roxburghshire 1812–14 (DNB; GEC).

1506. ELLIS, Augustus Frederick (ca 1800–41), M.P. Seaford 1826–27, 1827–31 (Burke's *Peerage* sub Howard de Walden).
1507. ELLIS, Charles Rose (1771–1845), 1st Bn Seaford, M.P. Heytesbury 1793–96, Seaford 1796–1806, 1812–26, East Grinstead 1807–12 (DNB; GEC).
1508. ELLIS, George (1754–1815), M.P. Seaford 1796–1802 (DNB; *Eton Coll. Reg.*).
1509. ELLIS, George James Wellbore Agar (1797–1833), 1st Bn Dover, M.P. Heytesbury 1818–20, Seaford 1820–26, Ludgershall 1826–30, Okehampton 1830–31 (DNB; GEC).
1510. ELLIS, Henry (ca 1777–1855), M.P. Boston 1820–21 (DNB).
1511. ELLIS, Henry Welbore (1761–1836), 2d Vct Clifden, M.P. Heytesbury 1793–1802 (GEC; *Old Westminsters*).
1512. ELLIS, John Thomas (1756–1836), M.P. Lostwithiel 1784–90 (Burke's *LG; Linc. Inn Reg.*).
1513. ELLIS, Thomas (ca 1774–1832), M.P. Dublin City 1820–26 (*Alumni Dublin.;* Burke's *Irish LG; Gent. Mag., 1,* 189).
1514. ELLIS, Welbore (1713–1802), 1st Bn Mendip, M.P. Cricklade 1741–47, Weymouth and Melcombe Regis 1747–61, 1774–90, Aylesbury 1761–68, Petersfield 1768–74, 1791–94 (DNB; GEC; *Old Westminsters*).
1515. ELLIS, Wynne (1790–1875), M.P. Leicester borough 1831–34, 1839–47 (DNB).
1516. ELLISON, Cuthbert (1698–1785), M.P. Shaftesbury 1747–54 (Burke's *LG;* Surtees' *Durham, 2,* 79).
1517. ELLISON, Cuthbert (1783–1860), M.P. Newcastle-upon-Tyne 1812–30 (Burke's *LG; Alumni Cantab.; Harrow Reg.*).
1518. ELLISON, Richard (1754–1827), M.P. Lincoln City 1796–1812, Wootton Bassett 1813–20 (Hunter's *Familiae Min. Gent.; 1798 List*).
ELMLEY, Vct, *see* LYGON, William Beauchamp.
1519. ELPHINSTONE, George Keith (1746–1823), 1st Vct Keith, M.P. Dumbartonshire 1781–90, Stirlingshire 1796–1801 (DNB; GEC).
ELPHINSTONE, James Drummond Buller, *see* BULLER-ELPHINSTONE, James Drummond.
1520. ELPHINSTONE-FLEEMING, Charles (1774–1840), M.P. Stirlingshire 1802–12, 1832–34 (Foster's *Scots M.P.'s; Scots Peerage*).
1521. ELTON, Abraham (1679–1742), 2d Bt, M.P. Taunton 1724–27, Bristol 1727–42 (GEC; Williams' *Gloucester M.P.'s*).
ELWALL, Ralph, *see* ETWALL, Ralph.
1522. ELWES, John (1714–89), M.P. Berks 1772–84 (DNB; *Old Westminsters*).
1523. ELWILL, John (d. 1778), 4th Bt, M.P. Guildford 1747–68 (GEC; *Eton Coll. Reg.*).
EMERSON, Wharton, *see* AMCOTTS, Wharton.

ENCOMBE, Vct, *see* SCOTT, John.

ENNISHOWEN, 1st Bn, *see* CHICHESTER, George Hamilton.

ENNISKILLEN, E. of, *see* COLE, John Willoughby and William Willoughby.

ENNISMORE, Vct, *see* HARE, Richard.

1524. ERLE-DRAX-GROSVENOR, Richard (1762–1819), M.P. East Looe 1786–88, Clitheroe 1794–96, Chester City 1802–7, New Romney 1818–19 (Burke's *LG; Old Westminsters*).

1525. ERLE-DRAX-GROSVENOR, Richard Edward (1797–1828), M.P. New Romney 1819–26 (Burke's *LG;* Hutchins' *Dorset, 3,* 503; *Old Westminsters*).

1526. ERSKINE, Charles (ca 1680–1763), M.P. Dumfries-shire 1722–41, Tain burghs 1741–42 (DNB).

1527. ERSKINE, Charles (1716–49), M.P. Ayr burghs 1747–49 (*Alumni Cantab.*).

1528. ERSKINE, David Montagu (ca 1777–1855), 2d Bn Erskine, M.P. Portsmouth 1806–6 (*Alumni Cantab.;* DNB; GEC).

1529. ERSKINE, Henry (d. 1765), 5th Bt, M.P. Ayr burghs 1749–54, Anstruther Easter burghs 1754–65 (DNB; GEC).

1530. ERSKINE, Henry (1746–1817), M.P. Haddington burghs 1806–6, Dumfries burghs 1806–7 (DNB).

1531. ERSKINE, James (ca 1679–1754), M.P. Aberdeen burghs 1715–15, Clackmannanshire 1734–41, Stirling burghs 1741–47 (DNB).

ERSKINE, James and James Alexander St. Clair, *see* ST. CLAIR-ERSKINE, James and James Alexander.

1532. ERSKINE, Thomas (ca 1706–66), M.P. Stirling burghs 1728–34, Stirlingshire 1747–47, Clackmannanshire 1747–54 (*Old Westminsters; Scots Peerage* sub Mar).

1533. ERSKINE, Thomas (1750–1823), 1st Bn Erskine, M.P. Portsmouth 1783–84, 1790–1806 (*Alumni Cantab.;* DNB; GEC).

1534. ERSKINE, William (1770–1813), 2d Bt, M.P. Fifeshire 1796–1806 (DNB; GEC; Foster's *Scots M.P.'s*).

1535. ERSKINE-WEMYSS, James (1789–1854), M.P. Fifeshire 1820–31, 1832–47 (Boase; Foster's *Scots M.P.'s*).

ESLINGTON, 1st Bn, *see* LIDDELL, Henry Thomas.

ESSEX, 5th E. of, *see* CONINGSBY, George Capel.

1536. ESTCOURT, Thomas (1748–1818), M.P. Cricklade 1790–1806 (*Alumni Oxon.;* Burke's *LG*).

1537. ESTCOURT, Thomas Grimston Bucknall (1775–1853), M.P. Devizes 1805–26, Oxford Univ. 1826–47 (*Alumni Oxon.; Harrow Reg.;* Williams' *Oxford M.P.'s*).

ESTCOURT, Thomas Henry Sutton, *see* SOTHERON-ESTCOURT, Thomas Henry Sutton.

1538. ESTWICK, Samuel (ca 1736–95), M.P. Westbury 1779–95 (*Eton Coll. Reg.*).

1539. ESTWICK, Samuel (1770–97), M.P. Westbury 1795–96 (*Eton Coll. Reg.*).

1540. ETWALL, Ralph (ca 1804–82), M.P. Andover 1831–47 (*Alumni Oxon.;* Boase).

EUSTON, E. of, *see* FITZROY, Augustus Henry, Charles, and Henry.

1541. EVANS, George (d. 1759), 2d Bn Carbery, M.P. Westbury 1734–47 (GEC).

1542. EVANS, George (1766–1804), 4th Bn Carbery, M.P. Rutland 1802–4 (*Alumni Cantab.;* GEC; *Eton Coll. Reg.*).

1543. EVANS, George De Lacy (1787–1870), M.P. Rye 1830–30, 1831–32, Westminster 1833–41, 1846–65 (DNB; Boase).

1544. EVANS, Henry (d. 1842), M.P. Wexford town 1819–20, 1826–29 (*Gent. Mag., 1* [1843], 322).

1545. EVANS, Richard, M.P. Queenborough 1729–54 (*Army Lists*).

1546. EVANS, William (1788–1856), M.P. East Retford 1818–26, Leicester borough 1830–34, North Derbyshire 1837–53 (Burke's *LG; 1832 List;* Boase).

1547. EVANS, William Bertram (ca 1801–50), M.P. Leominster 1831–32 (*Alumni Cantab.; Harrow Reg.;* Williams' *Hereford M.P.'s*).

EVELYN, George Augustus William Shuckburgh, *see* SHUCKBURGH-EVELYN, George William Augustus.

1548. EVELYN, John (1706–67), 2d Bt, M.P. Helston 1727–41, 1747–67, Penryn 1741–47 (GEC; *Eton Coll. Reg.*).

1549. EVELYN, Lyndon (ca 1759–1839), M.P. Wigtown burghs 1809–12, Dundalk 1813–18, St. Ives 1820–26 (*Alumni Dublin.;* Foster's *Scots M.P.'s*).

1550. EVELYN, William (1686–1766), M.P. Hythe 1728–66 (Manning and Bray's *Surrey, 2,* 329; *Misc. Geneal. et Herald.,* 2d Ser., *5*).

1551. EVELYN, William (1723–83), M.P. Helston 1767–74 (Brayley's *Surrey, 1,* 319; *Misc. Geneal. et Herald.,* 2d Ser., *5; Old Westminsters*).

1552. EVELYN, William (ca 1734–1813), M.P. Hythe 1768–1802 (*Old Westminsters*).

1553. EVERETT, Joseph Hague (ca 1777–1853), M.P. Ludgershall 1810–11, 1812–12 (*Alumni Cantab.; 1812 List*).

1554. EVERETT, Thomas (ca 1739–1810), M.P. Ludgershall 1796–1810 (*Admissions to St. John, Cambridge,* sub Joseph Hague Everett; *Wiltshire Notes and Queries, 6,* 572).

1555. EVERSFIELD, Charles (ca 1684–1749), M.P. Horsham 1705–10, 1713–15, 1721–41, Sussex 1710–13, Steyning 1741–47 (Albery's *Horsham;* Burke's *LG*).

EVERSLEY, 1st Vct, *see* SHAW-LEFEVRE, Charles.

1556. EWART, William (1798–1869), M.P. Bletchingley 1828–30, Liverpool 1830–37, Wigan 1839–41, Dumfries burghs 1841–68 (*Alumni Oxon.;* DNB; Pink).

1557. EWER, Charles (d. 1742), M.P. Shaftesbury 1741–42 (Beaven's *Aldermen of London*).

1558. EWER, Thomas (d. 1790), M.P. Dorchester 1789–90 (Musgrave's *Obituary; Parl. Hist., 24,* 781; *Royal Kalendar* [1790], p. 31).

1559. EWER, William (d. 1789), M.P. Dorchester 1765–89 (*Notes and Queries, 179,* 116).

1560. EWING, James (1775–1853), M.P. Wareham 1830–31, Glasgow City 1832–34 (Addison's *Glasgow Matric. Albums;* Boase).

EXETER, E. of, *see* CECIL, Brownlow and Henry.

EXMOUTH, Vct, *see* PELLEW, Edward and Pownoll Bastard.

1561. EYLES, Francis (d. 1750), M.P. Devizes 1727–42 (Musgrave's *Obituary;* MS, *ex inform.* the Reverend E. S. Dabbs).

1562. EYLES, Joseph (ca 1690–1740), M.P. Devizes 1722–27, 1734–40, Southwark 1727–34 (GEC; Beaven's *Aldermen of London; Notes and Queries, 179,* 81).

1563. EYRE, Anthony (1727–88), M.P. Boroughbridge 1774–84 (*Alumni Oxon.;* Burke's *LG*).

1564. EYRE, Anthony Hardolph (1757–1836), M.P. Notts 1803–12 (Burke's *LG; Harrow Reg.*).

1565. EYRE, Francis (ca 1723–97), M.P. Morpeth 1774–75, Great Grimsby 1780–84 (Bean; *Gent. Mag., 1,* 353).

1566. EYRE, Samuel (ca 1730–95), M.P. Salisbury 1765–68 (Burke's *LG; Gent. Mag.,* p. 358).

1567. FAGG, Robert (1704–40), 4th Bt, M.P. Steyning 1734–40 (GEC).

1568. FAIRFAX, Robert (ca 1707–93), 7th Bn Fairfax, M.P. Maidstone 1740–41, 1747–54, Kent 1754–68 (GEC; *Scots Peerage*).

FAIRFORD, Vct, *see* HILL, Arthur.

FAIRLIE, William Cuninghame, *see* CUNINGHAME-FAIRLIE, William.

1569. FALCONAR, John (1674–1764), M.P. Kincardineshire 1734–41 (Foster's *Scots M.P.'s;* Grant's *Faculty of Advocates*).

1570. FALKINER, Frederick John (ca 1768–1815), 1st Bt, M.P. Dublin Co. 1801–7, Carlow borough 1812–18 (*Alumni Dublin.;* Burke's *Ext. Baronetcies*).

1571. FALL, James (d. 1743), M.P. Haddington burghs 1734–41 (Foster's *Scots M.P.'s*).

FALMOUTH, 1st E. of, *see* BOSCAWEN, Edward.

1572. FANE, Charles (ca 1708–66), 2d Vct Fane, M.P. Tavistock 1734–47, Reading 1754–61 (GEC; Devonshire Assoc. *Trans., 43,* 398).

1573. FANE, Francis (ca 1698–1757), M.P. Taunton 1727–41, Petersfield 1741–47, Ilchester 1747–54, Lyme Regis 1754–57 (*Alumni Cantab.;* GEC).

1574. FANE, Francis (1752–1813), M.P. Lyme Regis 1777–80, Dorchester 1790–1807 (*Alumni Cantab.;* Barron's *Northampton Families,* p. 107).

1575. FANE, Henry (1703–77), M.P. Lyme Regis 1757–77 (Barron's *Northampton Families*, p. 106).

1576. FANE, Henry (1739–1802), M.P. Lyme Regis 1772–1802 (Barron's *Northampton Families*, p. 117).

1577. FANE, Henry (1778–1840), M.P. Lyme Regis 1802–18, Sandwich 1829–30, Hastings 1830–31 (DNB; *Eton Lists*).

1578. FANE, Henry Sutton (1804–57), M.P. Lyme Regis 1826–32 (Boase; *Harrow Reg.*).

1579. FANE, John (1728–74), 9th E. of Westmorland, M.P. Lyme Regis 1762–71 (DNB; GEC; *Old Westminsters*).

1580. FANE, John (1751–1824), M.P. Oxfordshire 1796–1824 (Barron's *Northampton Families*, p. 107; Williams' *Oxford M.P.'s*).

1581. FANE, John (1775–1850), M.P. Oxfordshire 1824–31 (*Alumni Cantab.*).

1582. FANE, John (1784–1859), 11th E. of Westmorland, M.P. Lyme Regis 1806–16 (*Alumni Cantab.;* DNB; GEC).

1583. FANE, John Thomas (1790–1833), M.P. Lyme Regis 1816–32 (Barron's *Northampton Families*, p. 108; *Gent. Mag.*, 1, 466).

1584. FANE, Thomas (1700–71), 8th E. of Westmorland, M.P. Lyme Regis 1753–62 (Barron's *Northampton Families*, p. 107; GEC).

1585. FANE, Thomas (1760–1807), M.P. Lyme Regis 1784–1806 (*Old Westminsters*).

1586. FANE, Vere (1785–1863), M.P. Lyme Regis 1818–26 (Barron's *Northampton Families*, p. 119; *Eton Lists*).

1587. FANSHAWE, Robert (1740–1823), M.P. Plymouth 1784–89 (Burke's *LG;* Howard and Crisp's *Visitation of Eng. and Wales, 15,* 17).

1588. FANSHAWE, Simon (1716–77), M.P. Old Sarum 1751–54, Grampound 1754–68 (Burke's *LG; Misc. Geneal. et Herald.*, 1st Ser., *2,* 14).

1589. FARDELL, John (1784–1854), M.P. Lincoln City 1830–31 (Burke's *LG* [ed. 1849]; Boase).

1590. FARMER, Samuel (ca 1748–1839), M.P. Huntingdon borough 1809–18 (Burke's *LG; Gent. Mag., 1,* 669; *Royal Kalendar* [1816], p. 62).

1591. FARMER, William Meeke (ca 1777–1836), M.P. Huntingdon borough 1807–9 (*Alumni Cantab.; Harrow Reg.*).

1592. FARNABY-RADCLIFFE, Charles (ca 1740–98), 3d Bt, M.P. East Grinstead 1765–68, Kent 1769–74, Hythe 1774–98 (GEC; *Eton Coll. Reg.*).

FARNBOROUGH, 1st Bn, *see* LONG, Charles.

FARNHAM, Bn and Vct, *see* MAXWELL, Henry and Robert; *also,* MAXWELL-BARRY, John.

1593. FARQUHAR, James (1764–1833), M.P. Aberdeen burghs 1802–6, 1807–18, Portarlington 1824–30 (Foster's *Scots M.P.'s*).

FARQUHAR, Robert Townsend Townsend, *see* TOWNSEND-FARQUHAR, Robert Townsend.

1594. FARQUHARSON, Archibald (1793–1841), M.P. Elgin burghs 1820–26 (Burke's *LG;* Jervise's *Epitaphs, 2,* 44).

1595. FARRAND, Robert (d. 1855), M.P. Hedon 1818–26, 1830–32, Stafford borough 1837–41 (Wedgwood).

1596. FARRER, Thomas (1744–97), M.P. Wareham 1780–90 (Burke's *LG;* . Foster's *Yorkshire Pedigrees;* Holzman's *Nabobs in Eng.*).

1597. FARRINGTON, Thomas (d. 1758), M.P. Whitchurch 1727–27, St. Michael 1727–34, Ludgershall 1747–54 (Hasted's *Kent, 2,* 16; *London Chronicle,* 28–31 Jan. 1758).

FAUCONBERG, 2d E., *see* BELAYSE, Henry.

1598. FAWCETT, Henry (d. 1816), M.P. Grampound 1806–7, Carlisle 1812–16 (*Gent. Mag., 1,* 281).

1599. FAWKES, Walter Ramsden (1769–1825), M.P. Yorkshire 1806–7 (DNB; Gooder; *Old Westminsters*).

1600. FAZAKERLEY, John Nicholas (ca 1788–1852), M.P. Lincoln City 1812–18, 1826–30, Great Grimsby 1818–20, Tavistock 1820–20, Peterborough 1830–41 (*Alumni Oxon.;* Burke's *LG* [ed. 1849]; Pink).

1601. FAZAKERLEY, Nicholas (ca 1685–1767), M.P. Preston 1732–67 (*Alumni Cantab.;* DNB; *Eton Coll. Reg.*).

1602. FEILDE, Paul (1711–83), M.P. Hertford borough 1770–80 (Burke's *LG* [ed. 1849]; Clutterbuck's *Herts, 3,* 244; *Old Westminsters*).

1603. FEILDING, William Robert (1760–99), M.P. Berealston 1780–90, Newport 1790–96 (GEC sub Denbigh; *Harrow Reg.*).

1604. FELLOWES, Coulson (1696–1769), M.P. Hunts 1741–61 (*Alumni Oxon.;* Burke's *Peerage;* Hutchins' *Dorset, 2,* 565; Nichols' *Lit. Anec., 1,* 589).

1605. FELLOWES, Henry Arthur Wallop (1799–1847), M.P. Andover 1831–34 (*Alumni Cantab.;* GEC sub Portsmouth).

1606. FELLOWES, Newton (1772–1854), 4th E. of Portsmouth, M.P. Andover 1802–20, North Devon 1832–37 (GEC; *Eton Coll Reg.*).

1607. FELLOWES, Robert (ca 1742–1829), M.P. Norwich 1802–7 (*Alumni Cantab.;* Burke's *LG*).

1608. FELLOWES, William (ca 1727–1804), M.P. Ludlow 1768–74, Andover 1784–96 (*Alumni Cantab.*).

1609. FELLOWES, William Henry (1769–1837), M.P. Huntingdon borough 1796–1807, Hunts 1807–30 (*Alumni Cantab.*).

1610. FENTON-CAWTHORNE, John (1753–1831), M.P. Lincoln City 1783–96, Lancaster City 1806–7, 1812–18, 1820–31 (Bean; *Notes and Queries,* 12th Ser., *2,* 266, 417; Pink).

1611. FENWICK, John (1699–1747), M.P. Northumberland 1741–47 (*Alumni Cantab.*).

1612. FENWICK, Nicholas (ca 1693–1752), M.P. Newcastle-upon-Tyne 1727–47 (*New Hist. of Northumberland, 7, 174*).

1613. FENWICK, Robert (1688–1750), M.P. Lancaster borough 1734–47 (*Alumni Cantab.; Chetham Soc., N.S., 104, 57–58*).

1614. FENWICK, Thomas (1733–94), M.P. Westmorland 1768–74 (*Alumni Cantab.; Eton Coll. Reg.*).

1615. FERGUSON, James (1735–1820), M.P. Banffshire 1789–90, Aberdeenshire 1790–1820 (Grant's *Faculty of Advocates*).

1616. FERGUSON, Robert (ca 1768–1840), M.P. Fifeshire 1806–7, Dysart burghs 1831–34, 1837–40, Haddingtonshire 1835–37 (Addison's *Glasgow Matric. Albums;* Grant's *Faculty of Advocates*).

1617. FERGUSON, Robert Alexander (ca 1795–1860), 2d Bt, M.P. Londonderry City 1830–60 (*Alumni Cantab.;* Boase).

1618. FERGUSON, Ronald Craufurd (1773–1841), M.P. Dysart burghs 1806–30, Nottingham borough 1830–41 (DNB).

1619. FERGUSSON, Adam (1733–1813), 3d Bt, M.P. Ayrshire 1774–80, 1781–84, 1790–96, Edinburgh City 1784–90 (GEC; Grant's *Faculty of Advocates*).

1620. FERGUSSON, James (ca 1688–1759), 2d Bt, M.P. Sutherlandshire 1734–35 (DNB; GEC).

1621. FERGUSSON, Robert Cutlar (ca 1768–1838), M.P. Kirkcudbright Stewarty 1826–38 (DNB).

FERMANAGH, Vct, *see* VERNEY, Ralph.

FERRAND, Vct, *see* FOSTER-SKEFFINGTON, Thomas Henry.

1622. FERRAND, Walker (1780–1835), M.P. Tralee 1831–32 (Burke's *LG*).

1623. FETHERSTON, George Ralph (1784–1853), 3d Bt, M.P. Longford 1819–30 (*Alumni Cantab.;* GEC).

1624. FETHERSTON, Thomas (ca 1759–1819), 2d Bt, M.P. Longford 1801–19 (*Alumni Dublin.;* GEC).

1625. FETHERSTONEHAUGH, Henry (1754–1846), 2d Bt, M.P. Portsmouth 1782–96 (GEC; *Eton Coll. Reg.*).

1626. FETHERSTONEHAUGH, Matthew (ca 1715–74), 1st Bt, M.P. Morpeth 1755–61, Portsmouth 1761–74 (GEC).

FEVERSHAM, Bn, *see* DUNCOMBE, Anthony, Charles, and William.

FIFE, E. of, *see* DUFF, James.

1627. FILMER, John (1716–97), 4th Bt, M.P. Steyning 1767–74 (GEC).

FINCASTLE, Vct, *see* MURRAY, George.

1628. FINCH, Charles (1752–1819), M.P. Castle Rising 1775–77, Maidstone 1777–80 (*Old Westminsters*).

FINCH, Charles Wynne, *see* GRIFFITH-WYNNE, Charles Wynne.

1629. FINCH, Edward (1756–1843), M.P. Cambridge borough 1789–1819 (*Alumni Cantab.;* DNB; *Old Westminsters*).

1630. FINCH, George (1794–1870), M.P. Lymington 1820–21, Stamford

1832–37, Rutland 1846–47 (*Alumni Cantab.;* Burke's *LG;* Finch's *Burley-on-the-Hill,* p. 339; *Harrow Reg.*).

1631. FINCH, Heneage (1715–77), 3d E. of Aylesford, M.P. Leicestershire 1739–41, Maidstone 1741–47, 1754–57 (GEC; *Old Westminsters*).

1632. FINCH, Heneage (1751–1812), 4th E. of Aylesford, M.P. Castle Rising 1772–74, Maidstone 1774–77 (GEC; *Old Westminsters*).

1633. FINCH, Heneage (1786–1859), 5th E. of Aylesford, M.P. Weobley 1807–12 (GEC; *Old Westminsters*).

1634. FINCH, Henry (ca 1695–1761), M.P. Malton 1724–61 (*Alumni Cantab.; Eton Coll. Reg.*).

1635. FINCH, John (ca 1692–1739), M.P. Maidstone 1722–39 (*Old Westminsters*).

1636. FINCH, John (ca 1693–1763), M.P. Higham Ferrers 1724–41, Rutland 1741–47 (*Eton Coll. Reg.; Old Westminsters*).

1637. FINCH, Savile (ca 1736–88), M.P. Maidstone 1757–61, Malton 1761–80 (Burke's *Peerage* sub Aylesford; Hunter's *Deanery of Doncaster, 2,* 41).

1638. FINCH, William (ca 1691–1766), M.P. Cockermouth 1727–54, Bewdley 1755–61 (*Alumni Oxon.;* Williams' *Worcester M.P.'s*).

1639. FINCH, William Clement (1753–94), M.P. Surrey 1790–94 (*Old Westminsters*).

1640. FINCH-HATTON, Edward (ca 1697–1771), M.P. Cambridge Univ. 1727–68 (*Alumni Cantab.;* DNB).

1641. FINCH-HATTON, George (1747–1823), M.P. Rochester 1772–84 (*Alumni Cantab.; Old Westminsters*).

FINGALL, 9th E. of, *see* PLUNKETT, Arthur James.

1642. FINLAY, Kirkman (ca 1773–1842), M.P. Glasgow burghs 1812–18, Malmesbury 1818–20 (DNB).

1643. FIREBRACE, Cordell (1712–59), 3d Bt, M.P. Suffolk 1735–59 (GEC).

1644. FISH, John (ca 1758–1835), M.P. Wexford town 1813–14 (*Gent. Mag., 1,* 558).

1645. FISHER, Brice (d. 1767), M.P. Malmesbury 1754–61, Boroughbridge 1761–67 (*Eng. Hist. Rev., 42* [1927], 514–32).

FISHERWICK, 1st Bn, *see* CHICHESTER, Arthur.

FITZGERALD, 2d Bn, *see* VESEY-FITZGERALD, William.

1646. FITZGERALD, Augustine (ca 1765–1834), 1st Bt, M.P. Clare 1808–18, Ennis 1832–32 (*Alumni Dublin.;* Burke's *Peerage; Gent. Mag., 1* [1835], 220).

1647. FITZGERALD, Charles James (1756–1810), 1st Bn Lecale, M.P. Arundel 1807–7 (GEC).

1648. FITZGERALD, Henry (1761–1829), M.P. Kildare 1807–13 (Burke's *Peerage* sub Leinster).

1649. FITZGERALD, James (ca 1742–1835), M.P. Ennis 1802–8, 1812–12 (DNB; GEC).

1650. FITZGERALD, John (1775–1852), M.P. Seaford 1826–32 (*Notes and Queries*, 8th Ser., *4*, 463).

1651. FITZGERALD, Maurice (1774–1849), M.P. Kerry 1801–31 (DNB; *Harrow Reg.*).

1652. FITZGERALD, Robert Stephen (1765–1833), M.P. Kildare 1802–7 (*Alumni Dublin.;* Burke's *Peerage* sub Leinster).

FITZGERALD, Robert Uniacke, *see* UNIACKE-FITZGERALD, Robert.

1653. FITZGERALD, William Charles O'Brien (1793–1864), M.P. Kildare 1813–31 (*Alumni Oxon.;* Burke's *Peerage* sub Leinster).

FITZGERALD, William Vesey, *see* VESEY-FITZGERALD, William.

1654. FITZGERALD-DE ROS, Henry William (1793–1839), 22d Bn De Ros, M.P. West Looe 1816–18 (GEC).

1655. FITZGIBBON, Richard Hobart (1793–1864), 3d E. of Clare, M.P. Limerick Co. 1818–41 (GEC; *Harrow Reg.*).

FITZHARDINGE, Bn and E., *see* BERKELEY, Maurice Frederick Fitzhardinge and William Fitzhardinge.

1656. FITZHERBERT, Thomas, M.P. Arundel 1780–90 (*Parl. Hist., 23,* 635).

1657. FITZHERBERT, William (ca 1712–72), M.P. Bramber 1761–62, Derby borough 1762–72 (Burke's *Peerage; Derby School Reg.;* Hunter's *Familiae Min. Gent., 1,* 252).

1658. FITZHUGH, William (ca 1759–1842), M.P. Tiverton 1803–19 (Devonshire Assoc. *Trans., 67,* 340; *Gent. Mag., 1,* 449).

FITZMAURICE, Vct, *see* PETTY, John and William.

1659. FITZMAURICE, John Hamilton (1778–1820), M.P. Heytesbury 1802–6, Denbigh borough 1812–18 (GEC sub Orkney; *Eton Coll. Reg.*).

FITZMAURICE, John, *see* PETTY, John.

1660. FITZMAURICE, Thomas (1742–93), M.P. Calne 1762–74, Wycombe 1774–80 (*Eton. Coll. Reg.*).

1661. FITZPATRICK, John (ca 1719–58), 1st E. of Upper Ossory, M.P. Bedfordshire 1753–58 (GEC).

1662. FITZPATRICK, John (1745–1818), 2d E. of Upper Ossory, M.P. Bedfordshire 1767–94 (GEC; Ball and Venn's *Admissions to Trinity College; Old Westminsters*).

1663. FITZPATRICK, Richard (1748–1813), M.P. Okehampton 1770–74, Tavistock 1774–1807, 1812–13, Bedfordshire 1807–12 (Ball and Venn's *Admissions to Trinity College;* DNB).

1664. FITZROY, Augustus (1716–41), M.P. Thetford 1739–41 (*Eton Coll. Reg.*).

1665. FITZROY, Augustus Henry (1735–1811), 3d D. of Grafton, M.P. Bury 1756–57 (*Alumni Cantab.;* DNB; GEC).

FITZROY, Charles, *see* FITZROY-SCUDAMORE, Charles.

1666. FITZROY, Charles (1737–97), 1st Bn Southampton, M.P. Orford 1759–61, Bury 1761–74, Thetford 1774–80 (DNB; GEC).

1667. FITZROY, Charles (1764–1829), M.P. Bury 1787–96, 1802–18 (*Alumni Cantab.;* DNB; *Harrow Reg.*).

1668. FITZROY, Charles (1791–1865), M.P. Thetford 1818–30, Bury 1832–47 (Boase; *Harrow Reg.*).

1669. FITZROY, Charles Augustus (1796–1858), M.P. Bury 1831–32 (DNB; *Harrow Reg.*).

1670. FITZROY, George (1715–47), M.P. Coventry 1737–47 (GEC; *Eton Coll. Reg.*).

1671. FITZROY, George Ferdinand (1761–1810), 2d Bn Southampton, M.P. Bury 1784–87 (GEC; *Eton Coll. Reg.*).

1672. FITZROY, George Henry (1760–1844), 4th D. of Grafton, M.P. Thetford 1782–84, Cambridge Univ. 1784–1811 (DNB; GEC).

1673. FITZROY, Henry (1790–1863), 5th D. of Grafton, M.P. Bury 1818–20, 1826–31, Thetford 1834–42 (*Alumni Cantab.;* GEC; *Harrow Reg.*).

1674. FITZROY, Henry (1807–59), M.P. Great Grimsby 1831–32, Lewes 1837–41, 1842–59 (*Alumni Oxon.;* DNB).

1675. FITZROY, James Henry (1804–34), M.P. Thetford 1830–34 (*Alumni Cantab.;* Harrow Reg.*).

1676. FITZROY, John Edward (1785–1856), M.P. Thetford 1812–18, Bury 1820–26 (*Alumni Cantab.;* Boase; *Harrow Reg.*).

1677. FITZROY, William (1782–1857), M.P. Thetford 1806–12 (Burke's *Peerage* sub Grafton).

1678. FITZROY-SCUDAMORE, Charles (ca 1713–82), M.P. Thetford 1733–54, 1774–82, Hereford City 1754–68, Heytesbury 1768–74 (*Old Westminsters;* Williams' *Hereford M.P.'s*).

FITZWILLIAM, Charles William Wentworth, *see* WENTWORTH-FITZWILLIAM, Charles William.

1679. FITZWILLIAM, George (ca 1756–86), M.P. Richmond 1781–84 (*Alumni Cantab.;* Eton Coll. Reg.*).

1680. FITZWILLIAM, John (1714–89), M.P. Windsor 1754–68 (*Notes and Queries,* 12th Ser., *2,* 192; *Old Westminsters*).

1681. FITZWILLIAM, Richard (1745–1816), 7th Vct Fitzwilliam, M.P. Wilton 1790–1806 (*Alumni Cantab.;* DNB; GEC).

1682. FITZWILLIAM, William (1720–56), 1st E. Fitzwilliam, M.P. Peterborough 1741–42 (GEC; *Eton Coll. Reg.*).

1683. FITZWYGRAM, Robert (1773–1843), 2d Bt, M.P. Fowey 1806–18, Lostwithiel 1818–26, Wexford town 1829–30 (*Alumni Oxon.;* Foster's *Baronetage; Notes and Queries, 179,* 148).

FLEEMING, Charles Elphinstone, *see* ELPHINSTONE-FLEEMING, Charles.

FLEETWOOD, George Harry William Hartopp, *see* HARTOPP-FLEETWOOD, George Harry William.

FLEMING, *see* FLEEMING, LE FLEMING, and WILLIS-FLEMING.

1684. FLEMING, John (d. 1827), M.P. Gatton 1818–20, Saltash 1820–26 (*Cornwallis Corr., 3,* 527 n.).

1685. FLEMING, William (d. 1756), 3d Bt, M.P. Cumberland 1756–56 (GEC).

1686. FLETCHER, Andrew (ca 1722–79), M.P. Haddington burghs 1747–61, Haddingtonshire 1761–68 (Addison's *Glasgow Matric. Albums; Alumni Oxon.*).

1687. FLETCHER, Henry (ca 1727–1807), 1st Bt, M.P. Cumberland 1768–1806 (DNB; GEC).

FLETCHER, John Fenton, *see* BOUGHEY-FLETCHER, John Fenton.

1688. FLETCHER, Robert (d. 1776), M.P. Cricklade 1768–74 (Buckland's *Dict. Ind. Biog.;* Hodson's *Bengal Army List;* Holzman's *Nabobs in Eng.*).

1689. FLETCHER-VANE, Frederick (1760–1832), 2d Bt, M.P. Winchelsea 1792–94, 1806–7, Carlisle 1796–1802 (GEC).

1690. FLOOD, Frederick (ca 1741–1824), 1st Bt, M.P. Wexford Co. 1812–18 (*Alumni Dublin.;* DNB; GEC).

1691. FLOOD, Henry (ca 1732–91), M.P. Winchelsea 1783–84, Seaford 1786–90 (*Alumni Dublin.;* DNB).

1692. FLOYER, John (b. 1681), M.P. Tamworth 1741–42 (Namier; Wedgwood).

1693. FLUDYER, George (1761–1837), M.P. Chippenham 1783–1802, Appleby 1818–19 (Burke's *Peerage; Old Westminsters*).

1694. FLUDYER, Samuel (ca 1705–68), 1st Bt, M.P. Chippenham 1754–68 (DNB; GEC; *Old Westminsters*).

1695. FLUDYER, Samuel Brudenell (1759–1833), 2d Bt, M.P. Aldborough 1781–84 (GEC; *Old Westminsters*).

1696. FLUDYER, Thomas (1711–69), M.P. Great Bedwin 1767–68, Chippenham 1768–69 (Burke's *Peerage;* GEC; Hasted's *Blackheath,* p. 223; Namier).

1697. FOLEY, Andrew (ca. 1749–1818), M.P. Droitwich 1774–1818 (*Alumni Oxon.;* Burke's *Peerage;* Williams' *Worcester M.P.'s*).

1698. FOLEY, Edward (d. 1747), M.P. Droitwich 1732–41 (Burke's *Peerage;* Musgrave's *Obituary; Linc. Inn Reg.*).

1699. FOLEY, Edward (1747–1803), M.P. Droitwich 1768–74, Worcestershire 1774–1803 (Burke's *LG; Old Westminsters;* Williams' *Worcester M.P.'s*).

1700. FOLEY, Edward Thomas (1791–1846), M.P. Ludgershall 1826–32, Herefordshire 1832–41 (*Alumni Oxon.;* Burke's *Peerage*).

FOLEY, John Hodgetts, *see* HODGETTS-FOLEY, John.

1701. FOLEY, Thomas (ca 1670–1737), M.P. Weobley 1691–1700, Hereford City 1701–22, Stafford borough 1722–27, 1734–37 (GEC; Wedgwood; Williams' *Hereford M.P.'s*).

1702. FOLEY, Thomas (ca 1695–1749), M.P. Hereford City 1734–41, Herefordshire 1742–47 (*Alumni Cantab.;* GEC).

1703. FOLEY, Thomas (1716–77), 1st Bn Foley, M.P. Droitwich 1741–47, 1754–68, Herefordshire 1768–76 (*Alumni Cantab.;* GEC; *Old Westminsters*).

1704. FOLEY, Thomas (1742–93), 2d Bn Foley, M.P. Herefordshire 1767–74, Droitwich 1774–77 (GEC; *Old Westminsters*).

1705. FOLEY, Thomas (1778–1822), M.P. Droitwich 1805–7, 1819–22, Herefordshire 1807–18 (*Old Westminsters;* Williams' *Worcester M.P.'s*).

1706. FOLEY, Thomas Henry (1808–69), 4th Bn Foley, M.P. Worcestershire 1830–32, West Worcestershire 1832–33 (GEC).

1707. FOLJAMBE, Francis Ferrand (1750–1814), M.P. Yorkshire 1784–84, Higham Ferrers 1801–7 (*Alumni Cantab.;* Gooder).

1708. FOLKES, Martin Browne (1749–1821), 1st Bt, M.P. Lynn 1790–1821 (*Alumni Cantab.;* GEC; *Eton Coll. Reg.*).

1709. FOLKES, William John Henry Browne (1786–1860), 2d Bt, M.P. Norfolk 1830–32, West Norfolk 1832–37 (*Alumni Cantab.;* Boase; GEC).

FOLKESTONE, Vct, *see* BOUVERIE, Jacob and William; *also* PLEYDELL-BOUVERIE, Jacob and William.

FONBLANQUE, John, *see* DE GRENIER-FONBLANQUE, John.

1710. FONNEREAU, Martin (1741–1817), M.P. Aldeburgh 1779–84 (Cussans' *Herts, 3*, pt. 2, 179; Huguenot Soc. *Proceedings, 15*, 247; *Notes and Queries, 179*, 118).

1711. FONNEREAU, Philip (1739–97), M.P. Aldeburgh 1761–68 (Cussans' *Herts, 3*, pt. 2, 179; *Gent. Mag., 1*, 350; *Linc. Inn Reg.*).

1712. FONNEREAU, Thomas (1699–1779), M.P. Sudbury 1741–68, Aldeburgh 1773–79 (Agnew's *Protestant Exiles, 2*, 250; Burke's *LG;* Cussans' *Herts, 3*, pt. 2, 178).

1713. FONNEREAU, Zachary Philip (1706–78), M.P. Aldeburgh 1747–74 (Agnew's *Protestant Exiles, 2, 250;* Cussans' *Herts, 3*, pt. 2, 178; *Misc. Geneal. et Herald.*, 2d Ser., *5;* Prinsep's *Madras Civilians*, p. xii).

1714. FORBES, Arthur (ca 1709–73), 4th Bt, M.P. Aberdeenshire 1731–47 (GEC; Foster's *Scots M.P.'s*).

1715. FORBES, Charles (1773–1849), 1st Bt, M.P. Beverley 1812–18, Malmesbury 1818–32 (DNB; Foster's *Baronetage*).

1716. FORBES, Duncan (1685–1747), M.P. Ayr burghs 1721–22, Inverness burghs 1722–37 (DNB).

1717. FORBES, George (1685–1765), 3d E. of Granard, M.P. Queenborough 1723–27, Ayr burghs 1741–47 (DNB; GEC).

1718. FORBES, George John (1785–1836), M.P. Longford 1806–32, 1833–36 (GEC).

1719. FORBES, John (1801–40), M.P. Malmesbury 1826–32 (*Alumni Oxon.;* Burke's *Peerage*).

1720. FORD, Francis (1758–1801), 1st Bt, M.P. Newcastle-under-Lyme 1793–96 (*Alumni Cantab.;* GEC).

1721. FORD, Richard (ca 1759–1806), M.P. East Grinstead 1789–90, Appleby 1790–91 (*Old Westminsters*).

1722. FORDE, Mathew (ca 1785–1837), M.P. Down 1821–26 (*Alumni Dublin.;* Burke's *Irish LG*).

1723. FORDYCE, John (ca 1738–1809), M.P. New Romney 1796–1802, Berwick 1802–3 (Burke's *LG* sub Hay; *Gent. Mag., 1,* 685; Bean).

FORESTER, Bn, *see* WELD-FORESTER, George Cecil and John George.

1724. FORESTER, Brooke (1717–71), M.P. Wenlock 1739–68 (Shrop. Archaeol. Soc. *Trans.,* 2d Ser., *3,* 172 and 3d Ser., *2,* 340).

1725. FORESTER, Cecil (ca 1721–74), M.P. Wenlock 1761–68 (*Old Westminsters;* Shrop. Archaeol. Soc. *Trans.,* 2d Ser., *3,* 174 and 3d Ser., *2,* 343).

FORESTER, Cecil Weld, *see* WELD-FORESTER, Cecil.

1726. FORESTER, Francis (1774–1861), M.P. Wenlock 1820–26 (Shrop. Archaeol. Soc. *Trans.,* 2d Ser., *3,* 176 and 3d Ser., *2,* 350).

1727. FORESTER, George (1735–1811), M.P. Wenlock 1758–61, 1768–84, 1785–90 (*Alumni Cantab.;* Shrop. Archaeol. Soc. *Trans.,* 2d Ser., *3,* 173 and 3d Ser., *2,* 342; *Shrop. Notes and Queries,* N.S., *3,* 70).

FORESTER, George Cecil Weld and John George Weld, *see* WELD-FORESTER, George Cecil and John George.

1728. FORESTER, William (ca 1690–1758), M.P. Wenlock 1715–22, 1734–41, 1754–58 (Shrop. Archaeol. Soc. *Trans.,* 2d Ser., *3,* 171 and 3d Ser., *2,* 338).

FORRESTER, Bn, *see* GRIMSTON, James Walter.

1729. FORRESTER, Alexander (ca 1711–87), M.P. Dunwich 1758–61, Okehampton 1761–68, Newcastle-under-Lyme 1768–74 (Esdaile's *Temple Church Monuments,* p. 90).

1730. FORTESCUE, George Mathew (1791–1877), M.P. Hindon 1826–31 (Burke's *Peerage;* Boase; *Eton Lists*).

1731. FORTESCUE, Hugh (1753–1841), 1st E. Fortescue, M.P. Beaumaris 1784–85 (GEC; *Eton Coll. Reg.*).

1732. FORTESCUE, Hugh (1783–1861), 2d E. Fortescue, M.P. Barnstable 1804–7, St. Mawes 1807–9, Buckingham borough 1812–17, Devon 1818–20, 1830–32, Tavistock 1820–30, North Devon 1832–39 (GEC).

FORTESCUE, John Inglett, *see* INGLETT-FORTESCUE, John.

1733. FORTESCUE, Theophilus (ca 1707–46), M.P. Barnstable 1727–41, Devon 1741–46 (GEC sub Clinton; Devonshire Assoc. *Trans., 49,* 374).

1734. FORTESCUE, William (1687–1749), M.P. Newport (Hants) 1727–36 (*Alumni Oxon.;* DNB).

1735. FORTESCUE, William Charles (1764–1829), 2d Vct Clermont, M.P. Louth 1801–6 (GEC).

FORTROSE, Vct, *see* MACKENZIE, Kenneth.

1736. FOSTER, Augustus John (1780–1848), 1st Bt, M.P. Cockermouth 1812–16 (DNB).

1737. FOSTER, Frederick Thomas Hervey (b. 1777), M.P. Bury 1812–18 (*Alumni Dublin.; Alumni Oxon.;* Burke's *Peerage*).

1738. FOSTER, James (ca 1787–1853), M.P. Bridgnorth 1831–32 (Burke's *LG; Times,* 14 Apr. 1853).

1739. FOSTER, John (1740–1828), 1st Bn Oriel, M.P. Louth 1801–21 (DNB; GEC).

1740. FOSTER, John Leslie (ca 1781–1842), M.P. Dublin Univ. 1807–12, Yarmouth (Hants) 1816–18, Armagh borough 1818–20, Louth 1824–30 (*Alumni Cantab.; Alumni Dublin.;* DNB).

1741. FOSTER, Thomas, M.P. Bossiney 1742–47.

1742. FOSTER, Thomas (ca 1720–65), M.P. Dorchester 1761–65 (Burke's *LG;* Musgrave's *Obituary*).

1743. FOSTER-BARHAM, John (1800–38), M.P. Stockbridge 1820–26, 1831–32, Kendal 1834–37 (Bean; Burke's *LG; Eton Lists*).

1744. FOSTER-BARHAM, Joseph (1759–1832), M.P. Stockbridge 1793–99, 1802–6, 1807–22, Okehampton 1806–7 (Burke's *LG; Gray's Inn Reg.; Gent. Mag., 2,* 573).

FOSTER-PIGOTT, George Edward Graham, *see* GRAHAM-FOSTER-PIGOTT, George Edward.

1745. FOSTER-SKEFFINGTON, Thomas Henry (ca 1772–1843), 2d Bn Oriel, M.P. Drogheda 1807–12, Louth 1821–24 (*Alumni Cantab.;* GEC; *Eton Coll. Reg.*).

1746. FOULKES, Evan (d. 1825), M.P. Tralee 1807–8, Stamford 1808–18 (*Royal Kalendar* [1816], p. 73; MS, *ex inform.* John Bean King).

1747. FOUNTAYNE-WILSON, Richard (1783–1847), M.P. Yorkshire 1826–30 (Burke's *LG; Eton Lists;* Gooder).

1748. FOWNES-LUTTRELL, Francis (1756–1823), M.P. Minehead 1780–83 (Burke's *LG; Eton Coll. Reg.*).

1749. FOWNES-LUTTRELL, Henry (ca 1724–80), M.P. Minehead 1768–74 (*Alumni Oxon.;* Burke's *LG;* Maxwell-Lyte's *Dunster, 1,* 259).

1750. FOWNES-LUTTRELL, Henry (1790–1867), M.P. Minehead 1816–22 (*Alumni Oxon.;* Burke's *LG; Eton Lists*).

1751. FOWNES-LUTTRELL, John (1752–1816), M.P. Minehead 1774–1806, 1307–16 (Burke's *LG; Eton Coll. Reg.;* Maxwell-Lyte's *Dunster, 1,* 262).

1752. FOWNES-LUTTRELL, John (1787–1857), M.P. Minehead 1812–32 (*Alumni Oxon.;* Burke's *LG*).

1753. FOWNES-LUTTRELL, Thomas (1763–1811), M.P. Minehead 1795–96
(Maxwell-Lyte's *Dunster, 1,* 260, 263).

1754. Fox, Charles James (1749–1806), M.P. Midhurst 1768–74, Malmesbury 1774–80, Westminster 1780–1806 (DNB).

1755. Fox, Charles Richard (1796–1873), M.P. Calne 1831–32, Tavistock 1832–34, Stroud 1835–35, Tower Hamlets 1841–47 (DNB;
Boase; *Eton Lists*).

Fox, George Lane, *see* LANE-FOX, George.

1756. Fox, Henry (1705–74), 1st Bn Holland, M.P. Hindon 1735–41,
Windsor 1741–61, Dunwich 1761–63 (DNB; GEC).

1757. Fox, Henry Edward (1802–59), 4th Bn Holland, M.P. Horsham
1826–27 (GEC).

Fox, Sackville Walter Lane, *see* LANE-FOX, Sackville Walter.

1758. Fox, Stephen (1745–74), 2d Bn Holland, M.P. Salisbury 1768–74
(GEC; *Eton Coll. Reg.; Gent. Mag.,* p. 334).

1759. Fox-LANE, George (ca 1697–1773), 1st Bn Bingley, M.P. Hindon
1734–41, York City 1742–61 (GEC).

1760. Fox-LANE, James (ca 1756–1821), M.P. Horsham 1796–1802
(*Alumni Cantab.*).

1761. Fox-LANE, Robert (1732–68), M.P. York City 1761–68 (GEC sub
Bingley).

1762. Fox-STRANGEWAYS, Henry Thomas (1747–1802), 2d E. of Ilchester,
M.P. Midhurst 1768–74 (GEC; *Eton Coll. Reg.*).

1763. Fox-STRANGEWAYS, Stephen (1704–76), 1st E. of Ilchester, M.P.
Shaftesbury 1726–34, 1735–41 (*Eton Coll. Reg.;* GEC).

1764. FRANCIS, Philip (1740–1818), M.P. Yarmouth (Hants) 1784–90,
Bletchingley 1790–96, Appleby 1802–7 (DNB).

FRANCO, Ralph, *see* LOPES, Ralph.

FRANK, Frank, *see* SOTHERON, Frank.

1765. FRANKLAND, Frederick Meinhardt (ca 1694–1768), M.P. Thirsk
1734–49 (*Alumni Cantab.; Genealogist,* N.S., *19,* 197; *Notes and
Queries, 179,* 96).

1766. FRANKLAND, Thomas (ca 1683–1747), 3d Bt, M.P. Harwich
1708–13, Thirsk 1715–47 (*Alumni Cantab.;* GEC).

1767. FRANKLAND, Thomas (ca 1718–84), 5th Bt, M.P. Thirsk 1747–80,
1784–84 (DNB; GEC).

1768. FRANKLAND, Thomas (1750–1831), 6th Bt, M.P. Thirsk 1774–80,
1796–1801 (GEC; *Eton Coll. Reg.*).

1769. FRANKLAND, William (ca 1722–1805), M.P. Thirsk 1768–74 (*Genealogist,* N.S., *19,* 197; Holzman's *Nabobs in Eng.*).

1770. FRANKLAND, William (ca 1762–1816), M.P. Thirsk 1801–6, 1807–15,
Queenborough 1806–7 (*Alumni Oxon.;* Burke's *Peerage*).

1771. FRANKLAND-RUSSELL, Robert (1784–1849), 7th Bt, M.P. Thirsk
1815–34 (GEC; *Yorkshire Archaeol. Jour., 6,* 394; cf. Lipscomb's
Bucks, 2, 198).

FRASER, Alexander Mackenzie, *see* MACKENZIE-FRASER, Alexander.

1772. FRASER, Archibald Campbell (1736–1815), M.P. Inverness-shire 1782–84 (Addison's *Glasgow Matric. Albums;* DNB; *Scots Peerage* sub Lovat).

FRASER, Charles Mackenzie, *see* MACKENZIE-FRASER, Charles.

1773. FRASER, James, M.P. Gatton 1787–90.

1774. FRASER, John Simon Frederick (ca 1765–1803), M.P. Inverness-shire 1796–1802 (DNB; *Scots Peerage* sub Lovat).

1775. FRASER, Simon (1726–82), M.P. Inverness-shire 1761–82 (Addison's *Glasgow Matric. Albums;* DNB; *Scots Peerage* sub Lovat).

1776. FREDERICK, Charles (1709–85), M.P. Shoreham 1741–54, Queenborough 1754–84 (*Old Westminsters*).

1777. FREDERICK, John (1708–83), 4th Bt, M.P. Shoreham 1740–41, West Looe 1743–61 (GEC; *Old Westminsters*).

1778. FREDERICK, John (1750–1825), 5th Bt, M.P. Newport 1774–80, Christchurch 1781–90, Surrey 1794–1807 (GEC; *Old Westminsters*).

1779. FREDERICK, Thomas (1707–40), M.P. Shoreham 1734–40 (GEC; *Old Westminsters*).

FREEMAN, Inigo, *see* THOMAS, Inigo.

1780. FREEMAN, Sambrooke (ca 1721–82), M.P. Pontefract 1754–61, Bridport 1768–74 (*Alumni Oxon.;* Oliver's *Antigua, 1,* 270).

FREEMAN, Thomas Edwards, *see* EDWARDS-FREEMAN, Thomas.

1781. FREEMAN-HEATHCOTE, Thomas (1769–1825), 4th Bt, M.P. Bletchingley 1807–8, Hampshire 1808–20 (GEC).

1782. FREEMAN-MITFORD, John (1748–1830), 1st Bn Redesdale, M.P. Berealston 1788–99, East Looe 1799–1802 (DNB; GEC).

1783. FREMANTLE, Thomas Francis (1765–1819), M.P. Sandwich 1806–7, Saltash 1807–8 (DNB).

1784. FREMANTLE, Thomas Francis (1798–1890), 1st Bn Cottesloe, M.P. Buckingham borough 1827–46 (DNB; GEC).

1785. FREMANTLE, William Henry (1766–1850), M.P. Enniskillen 1806–6, Harwich 1806–7, Saltash 1807–8, Tain burghs 1808–12, Buckingham borough 1812–27 (DNB).

1786. FRENCH, Arthur (ca 1764–1820), M.P. Roscommon 1801–20 (GEC sub De Freyne; *Cornwallis Corr., 3,* 50).

1787. FRENCH, Arthur (ca 1787–1856), 1st Bn De Freyne, M.P. Roscommon 1821–32 (*Alumni Dublin.; Alumni Oxon.;* GEC).

1788. FRENCH, Jeffery (d. 1754), M.P. Milborne Port 1741–47, Tavistock 1754–54 (Devonshire Assoc. *Trans., 43,* 398).

1789. FRERE, John (1740–1807), M.P. Norwich 1799–1802 (DNB; *Alumni Cantab.*).

1790. FRERE, John Hookham (1769–1846), M.P. West Looe 1796–1802 (*Alumni Cantab.;* DNB; *Eton Coll. Reg.*).

1791. FRESHFIELD, James William (1775–1864), M.P. Penryn 1830–32,

1835–41, 1852–57, Boston 1851–52 (*Alumni Cantab.;* Howard and Crisp's *Visitation of Eng. and Wales, 16,* 168).

1792 FREWEN-TURNER, John (1755–1829), M.P. Athlone 1807–12 (*Alumni Oxon.;* Burke's *LG; Rugby Reg.*).

1793. FULLARTON, William (ca 1754–1808), M.P. Plympton Erle 1779–80, Haddington burghs 1787–90, Horsham 1793–96, Ayrshire 1796–1803 (DNB).

1794. FULLER, John (1706–55), M.P. Boroughbridge 1754–55 (*Alumni Cantab.;* Burke's *LG* [ed. 1849]; *Old Westminsters*).

1795. FULLER, John, M.P. Tregony 1754–61.

1796. FULLER, John (ca 1757–1834), M.P. Southampton borough 1780–84, Sussex 1801–12 (*Eton Coll. Reg.; Gent. Mag., 1,* 106).

1797. FULLER, Richard (ca 1713–82), M.P. Steyning 1764–68, Stockbridge 1768–74 (*Misc. Geneal. et Herald.,* 5th Ser., *1,* 82; Musgrave's *Obituary*).

1798. FULLER, Rose (d. 1777), M.P. New Romney 1756–61, Maidstone 1761–68, Rye 1768–77 (*Alumni Cantab.*).

1799. FULLER-MAITLAND, Ebenezer (1780–1858), M.P. Lostwithiel 1807–12, Wallingford 1812–20, Chippenham 1826–30 (*Misc. Geneal. et Herald.,* 1st Ser., *2,* 210).

1800. FURNESE, Henry (d. 1756), M.P. Dover 1720–34, Morpeth 1738–41, New Romney 1741–56 (*Notes and Queries,* 12th Ser., *10,* 297).

FURNIVAL, 1st Bn, *see* TALBOT, Richard Wogan.

1801. FYDELL, Richard (ca 1710–80), M.P. Boston 1734–41 (*Alumni Cantab.;* Thompson's *Boston,* p. 195).

1802. FYDELL, Thomas (1740–1812), M.P. Boston 1790–1803, 1806–12 (Burke's *LG* [ed. 1849]; Thompson's *Boston,* p. 195).

1803. FYDELL, Thomas (1773–1814), M.P. Boston 1803–6 (Burke's *LG* [ed. 1849]; *Gent. Mag., 1,* 703).

1804. FYLER, Thomas Bilcliffe (1788–1838), M.P. Coventry 1826–31 (*Alumni Oxon.;* Burke's *LG;* Hutchins' *Dorset, 1,* 418; Whitley's *Coventry M.P.'s; 1832 List*).

1805. FYNES-CLINTON, Clinton James (1792–1833), M.P. Aldborough 1826–32 (*Alumni Oxon.; Old Westminsters*).

1806. FYNES-CLINTON, Henry (1781–1852), M.P. Aldborough 1806–26 (DNB; *Old Westminsters*).

1807. GAGE, Henry (1761–1808), 3d Vct Gage, M.P. Warwick borough 1790–91 (GEC; *Old Westminsters*).

1808. GAGE, Thomas (ca 1695–1754), 1st Vct Gage, M.P. Tewkesbury 1721–54 (GEC; MS, *ex inform.* the Reverend F. B. R. Browne).

1809. GAGE, William (ca 1695–1744), 7th Bt, M.P. Seaford 1722–44 (GEC).

1810. GAGE, William Hall (1718–91), 2d Vct Gage, M.P. Seaford 1744–47, 1754–80 (GEC; *Old Westminsters*).

GAINSBOROUGH, 1st E., *see* NOEL, Charles Noel.

1811. GALE-BRADDYLL, Thomas Richmond (1776–1862), M.P. Bodmin 1818–20 (Burke's *LG* [ed. 1849]; *Eton Lists; Misc. Geneal. et Herald.*, N.S., *1; Royal Kalendar* [1820], p. 49).

1812. GALE-BRADDYLL, Wilson (1756–1818), M.P. Lancaster borough 1780–84, Horsham 1790–91, Carlisle 1791–96 (*Alumni Oxon.;* Bean; Burke's *LG*).

GALLOWAY, E. of, *see* STEWART, George, John, and Randolph.

1813. GALLY-KNIGHT, Henry (1786–1846), M.P. Aldborough 1814–15, Malton 1831–32, North Notts 1835–46 (*Alumni Cantab.;* DNB).

1814. GALLY-KNIGHT, John (ca 1741–1804), M.P. Aldborough 1784–96 (*Alumni Cantab.; Eton Coll. Reg.*).

GALWAY, Vct, *see* MONCKTON, John; *also* MONCKTON-ARUNDELL, Henry William, Robert, and William.

1815. GAMON, Richard (1748–1818), 1st Bt, M.P. Winchester 1784–1812 (GEC).

1816. GARDEN, Alexander (ca 1719–85), M.P. Aberdeenshire 1768–85 (Burke's *LG; Scottish Notes and Queries, 6,* 153).

GARDINER, John Whalley, *see* WHALLEY-SMYTHE-GARDINER, John.

1817. GARDNER, Alan (1742–1809), 1st Bn Gardner, M.P. Plymouth 1790–96, Westminster 1796–1806 (DNB; GEC).

GARFORTH, John Baynes, *see* BAYNES-GARFORTH, John.

1818. GARLAND, George (d. 1825), M.P. Poole 1801–7 (*Notes and Queries,* 12th Ser., *2,* 368; Sydenham's *Poole,* p. 287; Boase).

GARLIES, Vct, *see* STEWART, George, John, and Randolph.

1819. GARRARD, Benet (ca 1704–67), 6th Bt, M.P. Agmondesham 1761–67 (GEC).

GARRARD, Charles Drake, *see* DRAKE-GARRARD, Charles.

1820. GARROW, William (1760–1840), M.P. Gatton 1805–6, Callington 1806–7, Eye 1812–17 (DNB; Williams' *Great Sessions in Wales*).

1821. GARTH, Charles (ca 1734–84), M.P. Devizes 1765–80 (*Alumni Oxon.*).

1822. GARTH, John (ca 1701–64), M.P. Devizes 1740–64 (*Bedfordshire Notes and Queries, 3,* 370; Surtees' *Durham, 4,* 29; Waylen's *Devizes,* p. 312).

1823. GARTH-TURNOUR, Edward (ca 1734–88), 1st E. Winterton, M.P. Bramber 1761–69 (GEC).

1824. GARTHSHORE, William (1764–1806), M.P. Launceston 1795–96, Weymouth and Melcombe Regis 1796–1806 (DNB; *Old Westminsters*).

GARVAGH, 1st Bn, *see* CANNING, George.

1825. GASCOIGNE, Thomas (1745–1810), 8th Bt, M.P. Thirsk 1780–84, Malton 1784–84, Arundel 1795–96 (GEC; *Genealogist,* N.S., *25,* 188).

1826. GASCOYNE, Bamber (1725–91), M.P. Maldon 1761–63, Midhurst 1765–68, Weobley 1770–74, Truro 1774–84, Bossiney 1784–86

(*Alumni Felsted.;* DNB; *Westminster Abbey Reg.,* p. 55; Williams' *Hereford M.P.'s*).

1827. GASCOYNE, Bamber (ca 1758–1824), M.P. Liverpool 1780–96 (*Alumni Oxon.*).

1828. GASCOYNE, Isaac (ca 1770–1841), M.P. Liverpool 1796–1831 (*Alumni Felsted.;* DNB).

1829. GASCOYNE-CECIL, James Brownlow William (1791–1868), 2d M. of Salisbury, M.P. Weymouth and Melcombe Regis 1813–17, Hertford borough 1817–23 (GEC).

1830. GASHRY, Francis (ca 1701–62), M.P. Aldeburgh 1741–41, East Looe 1741–62 (*Lloyd's Evening Post,* 19–21 May 1762; Namier).

1831. GASKELL, Benjamin (1781–1856), M.P. Maldon 1806–7, 1812–26 (*Alumni Cantab.;* Boase; Burke's *LG*).

1832. GAUSSEN, Samuel Robert (1759–1812), M.P. Warwick borough 1796–1802 (Burke's *LG;* Cussans' *Herts, 3,* pt. 1, 286; *Royal Kalendar* [1802], p. 64).

1833. GEARY, William (1756–1825), 2d Bt, M.P. Kent 1796–1806, 1812–18 (GEC).

1834. GEERS-COTTERELL, John (1757–1845), 1st Bt, M.P. Herefordshire 1802–3, 1806–31 (Burke's *Peerage;* Williams' *Hereford M.P.'s*).

1835. GEERS-WINFORD, Thomas (ca 1697–1753), M.P. Hereford City 1727–34, 1741–47, Worcester City 1747–48 (Williams' *Hereford M.P.'s*).

1836. GELL, Philip (1775–1842), M.P. Malmesbury 1807–12, Penryn 1812–18 (*Alumni Oxon.;* Hunter's *Familiae Min. Gent.*).

GERMAIN, George, *see* SACKVILLE-GERMAIN, George.

GERVIS, George William Tapps, *see* TAPPS-GERVIS, George William.

1837. GIBBON, Edward (1707–70), M.P. Petersfield 1734–41, Southampton borough 1741–47 (*Alumni Cantab.;* Old Westminsters*).

1838. GIBBON, Edward (1737–94), M.P. Liskeard 1774–80, Lymington 1781–83 (DNB; *Old Westminsters*).

GIBBON, Philips, *see* GYBBON, Philips.

1839. GIBBONS, John (ca 1717–76), 2d Bt, M.P. Stockbridge 1754–61, Wallingford 1761–68 (GEC).

1840. GIBBS, Vicary (1751–1820), M.P. Totnes 1804–6, Great Bedwin 1807–7, Cambridge Univ. 1807–12 (*Alumni Cantab.;* DNB; *Eton Coll. Reg.*).

1841. GIBSON, Thomas (d. 1744), M.P. Marlborough 1722–34, Yarmouth (Hants) 1736–44 (Musgrave's *Obituary*).

GIDDY, Davies, *see* GILBERT, Davies.

GIDEON, Sampson, *see* EARDLEY, Sampson.

1842. GIFFORD, Robert (1779–1826), 1st Bn Gifford, M.P. Eye 1817–24 (DNB; GEC).

1843. GILBERT, Davies (1767–1839), M.P. Helston 1804–6, Bodmin 1806–32 (DNB).

1844. GILBERT, Thomas (ca 1720–98), M.P. Newcastle-under-Lyme 1763–68, Lichfield 1768–95 (DNB).

1845. GILDART, Richard (d. 1771), M.P. Liverpool 1734–54 (Bean; Pink; Prinsep's *Madras Civilians,* p. xiii).

1846. GILES, Daniel (ca 1761–1831), M.P. East Grinstead 1802–7, St. Albans 1809–12 (*Alumni Oxon.;* Cussans' *Herts, 1,* 172; *Gent. Mag., 1* [1832], 82).

1847. GILLON, William Downe (1801–46), M.P. Lanark burghs 1831–32, Falkirk burghs 1832–41 (*Alumni Cantab.;* Burke's *LG;* Dod's *Parl. Companion* [1834], p. 117; Foster's *Scots M.P.'s*).

1848. GILMOUR, Alexander (ca 1736–92), 3d Bt, M.P. Edinburghshire 1761–74 (*Alumni Cantab.;* GEC).

1849. GILMOUR, Charles (d. 1750), 2d Bt, M.P. Edinburghshire 1737–50 (GEC).

1850. GIPPS, George (ca 1728–1800), M.P. Canterbury 1780–96, 1797–1800 (*Admissions to St. John, Cambridge;* Berry's *County Geneal.: Kent,* p. 462).

1851. GIPPS, George (b. ca 1784), M.P. Ripon 1807–26 (*Alumni Cantab.*).

1852. GISBORNE, John (ca 1717–79), M.P. Derby borough 1775–76 (Burke's *LG* [ed. 1879]; Glover's *Derbyshire, 2,* 476).

1853. GISBORNE, Thomas (ca 1790–1852), M.P. Stafford borough 1830–32, North Derbyshire 1832–37, Carlow borough 1839–41, Nottingham borough 1843–47 (*Alumni Cantab.;* DNB).

1854. GLADSTONE, John (1764–1851), 1st Bt, M.P. Lancaster borough 1818–20, Woodstock 1820–26, Berwick-on-Tweed 1826–27 (DNB).

1855. GLADSTONE, Thomas (1804–89), 2d Bt, M.P. Queenborough 1830–31, Portarlington 1832–34, Leicester borough 1835–37, Ipswich 1842–42 (*Alumni Oxon.;* Burke's *Peerage*).

GLANVILLE, 2d E., *see* CARTERET, Robert.

1856. GLANVILLE, Francis (1762–1846), M.P Malmesbury 1794–96, Plymouth 1797–1802 (*Alumni Cantab.;* Burke's *LG*).

GLANVILLE, William, *see* EVELYN, William.

1857. GLASSFORD, Henry (ca 1765–1819), M.P. Dumbartonshire 1806–6, 1807–10 (Addison's *Glasgow Matric. Albums;* Foster's *Scots M.P.'s*)

GLASTONBURY, 1st Bn, *see* GRENVILLE, James.

1858. GLEADOWE-NEWCOMEN, Thomas (1776–1825), 2d Vct Newcomen, M.P. Longford 1802–6 (GEC; *Eton Coll. Reg.*).

1859. GLEADOWE-NEWCOMEN, William (ca 1730–1807), 1st Bt, M.P. Longford 1801–2 (GEC).

GLENBERVIE, 1st Bn, *see* DOUGLAS, Sylvester.

GLENELG, 1st Bn, *see* GRANT, Charles.

GLENGALL, 2d E. of, *see* BUTLER, Richard.

GLENLYON, 1st Bn, *see* MURRAY, James.

GLENORCHY, Vct, *see* CAMPBELL, John.

GLERAWLEY, Vct, *see* ANNESLEY, William Richard.

1860. GLOVER, Richard (ca 1712–85), M.P. Weymouth and Melcombe Regis 1761–68 (DNB).

1861. GLOVER, Richard, M.P. Penryn 1790–96 (DNB).

1862. GLYN, Richard (ca 1712–73), 1st Bt, M.P. London 1758–68, Coventry 1768–73 (GEC; Beaven's *Aldermen of London;* Manning and Bray's *Surrey, 1,* 466).

1863. GLYN, Richard Carr (1755–1838), 1st Bt, M.P. St. Ives 1796–1802 (DNB; GEC; *Old Westminsters*).

1864. GLYNN, John (1722–79), M.P. Middlesex 1768–79 (DNB; Maclean's *Trigg Minor, 2,* 70).

1865. GLYNN-CAMPBELL, Alexander (1796–1836), M.P. Fowey 1819–20 (*Alumni Oxon.;* Berry's *County Geneal.: Hampshire; Eton Lists;* Wade's *Black Book*).

1866. GLYNNE, Henry (1810–72), M.P. Flint borough 1831–32 (*Alumni Oxon.;* Williams' *Wales M.P.'s*).

1867. GLYNNE, John (1712–77), 6th Bt, M.P. Flintshire 1741–47, Flint borough 1753–77 (GEC; *Genealogical Mag., 7,* 69).

1868. GLYNNE, Stephen Richard (1807–74), 9th Bt, M.P. Flint borough 1832–37, Flintshire 1837–41, 1842–47 (*Alumni Cantab.;* DNB; *Genealogical Mag., 7,* 71).

1869. GODDARD, Ambrose (ca 1727–1815), M.P. Wilts 1772–1806 (Burke's *LG; Gent. Mag., 1,* 572 and *2,* 275; Kirby's *Winchester Scholars,* p. 245).

1870. GODDARD, John (1682–1736), M.P. Tregony 1727–36 (Clutterbuck's *Herts, 2,* 327; Musgrave's *Obituary*).

1871. GODDARD, Thomas (1722–70), M.P. Wilts 1767–70 (Burke's *LG* [ed. 1849]; *Notes and Queries,* 12th Ser., *2,* 313).

1872. GODDARD, Thomas (ca 1778–1814), M.P. Cricklade 1806–12 (*Alumni Oxon.;* Burke's *LG; Gent. Mag., 1,* 199).

GODERICH, 1st Vct, *see* ROBINSON, Frederick John.

1873. GODFREY, Thomas (ca 1751–1810), M.P. Hythe 1802–10 (Burke's *LG; Gent. Mag., 1,* 294; *1806 List*).

1874. GODOLPHIN, Francis (1706–85), 2d Bn Godolphin, M.P. Helston 1741–66 (GEC; *Eton Coll. Reg.*).

1875. GODSCHALL, Robert (ca 1692–1742), M.P. London 1741–42 (Beaven's *Aldermen of London; Herald and Genealogist, 5,* 488).

1876. GODSON, Richard (1797–1849), M.P. St. Albans 1831–32, Kidderminster 1832–34, 1837–49 (*Alumni Cantab.;* Williams' *Worcester M.P.'s*).

1877. GOLDING, Edward (1746–1818), M.P. Fowey 1799–1802, Plympton Erle 1802–6, Downton 1813–18 (*Gent. Mag., 2,* 187; Holzman's *Nabobs in Eng.;* Kirby's *Winchester Scholars,* p. 254).

1878. GOLDSWORTHY, Philip (ca 1737–1801), M.P. Wilton 1785–88, 1794–1801 (*Alumni Cantab.; Old Westminsters*).

1879. GOOCH, Thomas Sherlock (1767–1851), 5th Bt, M.P. Suffolk 1806–30 (GEC; *Old Westminsters*).

1880. GOODRICKE, Henry (1741–84), M.P. Lymington 1778–80 (C. A. Goodricke, *Goodricke Family,* p. 38).

1881. GOODRICKE, John (1708–89), 5th Bt, M.P. Pontefract 1774–80, Ripon 1787–89 (GEC).

1882. GORDON, Adam (ca 1726–1801), M.P. Aberdeenshire 1754–68, Kincardineshire 1774–88 (DNB; *Eton Coll. Reg.; Scots Peerage*).

GORDON, Alexander Penrose Cumming, *see* CUMMING-GORDON, Alexander Penrose.

1883. GORDON, Charles (1792–1863), 10th M. of Huntly, M.P. East Grinstead 1818–30, Hunts 1830–31 (*Alumni Cantab.;* GEC).

1884. GORDON, Cosmo (ca 1736–1800), M.P. Nairnshire 1774–77 (Bulloch's *Gordons of Cluny,* p. 9; Grant's *Faculty of Advocates*).

1885. GORDON, George (1751–93), M.P. Ludgershall 1774–80 (DNB; *Eton Coll. Reg.*).

1886. GORDON, George (1770–1836), 5th D. of Gordon, M.P. Eye 1806–7 (*Alumni Cantab.;* DNB; GEC; *Eton Coll. Reg.*).

1887. GORDON, James (ca 1758–1822), M.P. Stockbridge 1785–90, Truro 1790–96, Clitheroe 1808–12 (*Alumni Cantab.*).

1888. GORDON, James Adam (1791–1854), M.P. Tregony 1830–31, 1832–32 (*Alumni Cantab.; Harrow Reg.; 1812 List*).

1889. GORDON, James Edward (1789–1864), M.P. Dundalk 1831–32 (Bulloch's *House of Gordon, 3,* 179).

1890. GORDON, James Willoughby (1772–1851), 1st Bt, M.P. Launceston 1829–31 (DNB; Boase).

1891. GORDON, John (d. 1783), 2d Bt, M.P. Cromartyshire 1742–47, 1754–61 (GEC).

1892. GORDON, John (ca 1750–1840), 7th Vct Kenmure, M.P. Kirkcudbright Stewarty 1781–82 (GEC).

1893. GORDON, John (ca 1773–1858), M.P. Weymouth and Melcombe Regis 1826–32 (*Alumni Cantab.;* Boase; *1832 List*).

1894. GORDON, John (1794–1843), M.P. Athlone 1818–20 (*Alumni Cantab.; Rugby Reg.*).

1895. GORDON, Robert (ca 1787–1864), M.P. Wareham 1812–18, Cricklade 1818–37, Windsor 1837–41 (*Alumni Oxon.;* Burke's *LG; Royal Kalendar* [1816], p. 75).

1896. GORDON, William (d. 1742), 1st Bt, M.P. Sutherlandshire 1708–13, 1714–27, Cromartyshire 1741–42 (GEC).

1897. GORDON, William (d. 1776), M.P. Rochester 1768–71 (Musgrave's *Obituary;* Smith's *Rochester in Parl.*).

1898. GORDON, William (ca 1726–98), M.P. Portsmouth 1777–83 (Addison's *Glasgow Matric. Albums; Scottish Notes and Queries*, 3d Ser., *9*, 188).

1899. GORDON, William (ca 1736–1816), M.P. Woodstock 1767–74, Heytesbury 1774–80 (Addison's *Glasgow Matric. Albums; Scots Peerage* sub Aberdeen).

1900. GORDON, William (1774–1823), M.P. Elginshire 1779–84, Inverness-shire 1784–90, Horsham 1792–96 (*Harrow Reg.; Scots Peerage;* Tayler's *Morayshire M.P.'s*).

1901. GORDON, William (1784–1858), M.P. Aberdeenshire 1820–54 (*Harrow Reg.; Scots Peerage*).

GORDON, William Duff, see DUFF-GORDON, William.

1902. GORDON-CUMMING, William Gordon (1787–1854), 2d Bt, M.P. Elgin burghs 1831–32 (Burke's *Peerage;* Foster's *Scots M.P.'s*).

1903. GORDON-HALYBURTON, Douglas (1777–1841), M.P. Forfarshire 1832–41 (*Scots Peerage*).

1904. GORDON-LENNOX, Arthur (1806–64), M.P. Chichester 1831–46, Great Yarmouth 1847–48 (Burke's *Peerage* sub Richmond; Boase).

1905. GORDON-LENNOX, Charles (1791–1860), 5th D. of Richmond, M.P. Chichester 1812–19 (DNB; GEC; *Old Westminsters*).

1906. GORDON-LENNOX, John George (1793–1873), M.P. Chichester 1819–31, Sussex 1831–32, West Sussex 1832–41 (*Old Westminsters*).

1907. GORE, Arthur Saunders (1761–1837), 3d E. of Arran, M.P. Donegal 1801–6 (GEC).

1908. GORE, Charles (ca 1711–68), M.P. Cricklade 1739–41, Herts 1741–61, Tiverton 1762–68 (Clutterbuck's *Herts, 1,* 502; Devonshire Assoc. *Trans., 67,* 333; *Notes and Queries, 170,* 171).

1909. GORE, John (ca 1689–1763), M.P. Great Grimsby 1747–61 (Clutterbuck's *Herts, 1,* 502; Musgrave's *Obituary*).

1910. GORE, John (d. 1773), M.P. Cricklade 1747–54 (Clutterbuck's *Herts, 1,* 502; *Notes and Queries,* 12th Ser., *2,* 432).

1911. GORE, Thomas (ca 1694–1777), M.P. Cricklade 1722–27, 1754–68, Agmondesham 1735–46, Portsmouth 1746–47, Bedford borough 1747–54 (Clutterbuck's *Herts, 1,* 502; *Lloyd's Evening Post,* 17–19 Mar. 1777).

1912. GORE, William (ca 1675–1739), M.P. Colchester 1711–13, St. Albans 1722–27, Cricklade 1734–39 (*Alumni Cantab.;* Clutterbuck's *Herts, 1,* 502; *Notes and Queries, 179,* 61).

GORE, William Ormsby, see ORMSBY-GORE, William.

1913. GORE-LANGTON, William (1760–1847), M.P. Somerset 1795–1806, 1812–20, 1831–32, Tregony 1808–12, East Somerset 1832–47 (Burke's *Peerage* sub Temple; Bates Harbin).

1914. GORGES, Hamilton (ca 1739–1802), M.P. Meath 1801–2 (R. Gorges, *Story of a Family,* pp. 251–55, 279).

1915. GORGES, Richard (ca 1730–80), M.P. Leominster 1754–61 (R. Gorges, *Story of a Family*, p. 205; Williams' *Hereford M.P.'s*).

1916. GORING, Charles (ca 1744–1829), M.P. Shoreham 1774–80 (*Alumni Oxon.;* Burke's *Peerage*).

1917. GORING, Harry (1739–1824), 6th Bt, M.P. Shoreham 1790–96 (GEC).

GORT, Vct, *see* VEREKER, Charles and John Prendegast.

GOSFORD, E. of, *see* ACHESON, Archibald.

1918. GOSSET, William (ca 1782–1848), M.P. Truro 1820–26 (Burke's *LG; Gent. Mag., 1,* 547).

1919. GOUGH, Frederick (1790–1868), 4th Bn Calthorpe, M.P. Hindon 1818–26, Bramber 1826–31 (GEC; *Harrow Reg.*).

1920. GOUGH, Harry (1681–1751), M.P. Bramber 1734–51 (Burke's *LG* [ed. 1849]; Collins' *Peerage* sub Calthorpe; Musgrave's *Obituary*).

1921. GOUGH, Henry (1708–74), 1st Bt, M.P. Totnes 1732–34, Bramber 1734–41 (GEC; Collins' *Peerage* sub Calthorpe).

1922. GOUGH-CALTHORPE, Arthur (1796–1836), M.P. Bramber 1825–26, Hindon 1826–30 (*Alumni Oxon.;* Burke's *Peerage* sub Calthorpe; *Harrow Reg.*).

1923. GOUGH-CALTHORPE, Henry (1749–98), 1st Bn Calthorpe, M.P. Bramber 1774–96 (GEC; *Eton Coll. Reg.*).

1924. GOULBURN, Henry (1784–1856), M.P. Horsham 1808–12, St. Germans 1812–18, West Looe 1818–26, Armagh borough 1826–31, Cambridge Univ. 1831–56 (*Alumni Cantab.;* DNB).

GOULD, Charles, *see* MORGAN, Charles.

GOWER, *see* LEVESON-GOWER *and* SUTHERLAND-LEVESON-GOWER.

1925. GOWLAND, Ralph (d. ca 1780), M.P. Durham City 1761–62, Cockermouth 1775–80 (Bean; Ferguson; Namier).

GOWRAN, Bn, *see* FITZPATRICK, John.

1926. GRADY, Henry Deane (b. ca 1765), M.P. Limerick City 1801–2 (*Alumni Dublin.;* O'Flanaghan's *Irish Bar*, p. 198).

1927. GRAEME, David (d. 1797), M.P. Perthshire 1764–73 (Foster's *Scots M.P.'s*).

GRAFTON, D. of, *see* FITZROY, Augustus Henry, George Henry, and Henry.

1928. GRAHAM, George (1715–47), M.P. Stirlingshire 1741–47 (Foster's *Scots M.P.'s; Scots Peerage* sub Montrose).

1929. GRAHAM, George (ca 1728–1801), M.P. Kinross-shire 1780–84, 1790–96 (*Misc. Geneal. et Herald.*, 4th Ser., *3*).

1930. GRAHAM, James (1753–1825), 1st Bt, M.P. Cockermouth 1802–5, 1806–12, Wigtown burghs 1805–6, Carlisle 1812–25 (*Alumni Cantab.;* Foster's *Baronetage*).

1931. GRAHAM, James (1755–1836), 3d D. of Montrose, M.P. Richmond 1780–84, Great Bedwin 1784–90 (*Alumni Cantab.;* DNB; GEC).

1932. GRAHAM, James (1761–1824), 1st Bt, M.P. Ripon 1798–1807 (GEC).

1933. GRAHAM, James (1799–1874), 4th D. of Montrose, M.P. Cambridge borough 1825–32 (*Alumni Cantab.;* DNB; GEC).

1934. GRAHAM, James Robert George (1792–1861), 2d Bt, M.P. Hull 1818–20, St. Ives 1820–21, Carlisle 1826–29, 1852–61, Cumberland 1829–32, East Cumberland 1832–37, Pembroke borough 1838–41, Dorchester 1841–47, Ripon 1847–52 (DNB; GEC; *Old Westminsters*).

1935. GRAHAM, Montagu William (1807–78), M.P. Dumbartonshire 1830–32, Grantham 1852–57, Herefordshire 1858–65 (*Eton Lists; Scots Peerage* sub Montrose).

GRAHAM, Robert, *see* CUNNINGHAM-GRAHAM, Robert.

1936. GRAHAM, Sandford (1788–1852), 2d Bt, M.P. Aldeburgh 1812–12, Ludgershall 1812–15, 1818–26, 1830–32 (*Alumni Cantab.;* Foster's *Baronetage*).

1937. GRAHAM, Thomas (1748–1843), 1st Bn Lynedoch, M.P. Perthshire 1794–1807 (DNB; GEC).

1938. GRAHAM, Thomas (1752–1819), M.P. Kinross-shire 1811–12, 1818–19 (*Ann. Biog. and Obit.* [1820], p. 461; Graeme's *Or and Sable,* p. 598; *Misc. Geneal. et Herald.,* 4th Ser., *3*).

1939. GRAHAM-FOSTER-PIGOTT, George Edward (1771–1831), M.P. Kinross-shire 1819–20, 1826–30 (Burke's *LG* sub Pigott; Foster's *Scots M.P.'s; Gent. Mag., 2,* 474; *Misc. Geneal. et Herald.,* 4th Ser., *3*).

GRANARD, 3d E. of, *see* FORBES, George.

GRANBY, M. of, *see* MANNERS, Charles and John.

GRANDISON, Vct and E., *see* VILLIERS, George Bussey *and* MASON-VILLIERS, George.

1940. GRANT, Alexander (d. 1772), 5th Bt, M.P. Inverness burghs 1761–68 (GEC).

1941. GRANT, Alexander Cray (1782–1854), 8th Bt, M.P. Tregony 1812–18, Lostwithiel 1818–26, Aldborough 1826–30, Westbury 1830–31, Cambridge borough 1840–43 (*Alumni Cantab.;* DNB; GEC).

1942. GRANT, Charles (1746–1823), M.P. Inverness-shire 1802–18 (DNB).

1943. GRANT, Charles (1778–1866), 1st Bn Glenelg, M.P. Inverness burghs 1811–14, 1814–18, Inverness-shire 1818–35 (*Alumni Cantab.;* DNB; GEC).

GRANT, David MacDowall, *see* MACDOWALL-GRANT, David.

1944. GRANT, Francis (1717–81), M.P. Elginshire 1768–74 (*Scots Peerage;* Tayler's *Morayshire M.P.'s*).

GRANT, Francis William, *see* OGILVY-GRANT, Francis William.

GRANT, George Macpherson, *see* MACPHERSON-GRANT, George.

1945. GRANT, James (1679–1747), 6th Bt, M.P. Inverness-shire 1722–41, Elgin burghs 1741–47 (GEC; *Scots Peerage*).

1946. GRANT, James (ca 1720–1806), M.P. Tain burghs 1773–80, Sutherlandshire 1787–1802 (DNB; Fraser's *Chiefs of Grant, 1,* 511).

1947. GRANT, James (1738–1811), 7th Bt, M.P. Elginshire 1761–68, Banffshire 1790–95 (*Alumni Cantab.;* DNB; GEC; *Old Westminsters;* Tayler's *Morayshire M.P.'s*).

1948. GRANT, John, M.P. Fowey 1784–86 (Philips' *East India Company,* pp. 309, 343; *Royal Kalendar* [1785], p. 32; *Victoria Hist. Berkshire, 3,* 174).

1949. GRANT, John Colquhoun (ca 1764–1835), M.P. Queenborough 1831–32 (DNB).

1950. GRANT, John Peter (1774–1848), M.P. Great Grimsby 1812–18, Tavistock 1819–26 (DNB; Fraser's *Chiefs of Grant, 1,* 510).

GRANT, Lewis Alexander, *see* OGILVIE-GRANT, Lewis Alexander.

1951. GRANT, Ludovic (1707–73), 7th Bt, M.P. Elginshire 1741–61 (GEC; *Scots Peerage;* Tayler's *Morayshire M.P.'s*).

1952. GRANT, Robert (ca 1779–1838), M.P. Elgin burghs 1818–20, Inverness burghs 1826–30, Norwich 1830–32, Finsbury 1832–34 (*Alumni Cantab.;* DNB).

1953. GRANT, William (1701–64), M.P. Elgin burghs 1747–54 (DNB; Grant's *Faculty of Advocates*).

1954. GRANT, William (1752–1832), M.P. Shaftesbury 1790–93, Windsor 1794–96, Banffshire 1796–1812 (DNB).

1955. GRANT-SUTTIE, James (1759–1836), 4th Bt, M.P. Haddingtonshire 1816–26 (Addison's *Glasgow Matric. Albums;* GEC).

GRANTHAM, Bn, *see* ROBINSON, Thomas.

GRANTLEY, Bn, *see* NORTON, Fletcher and William.

GRANVILLE, 1st E., *see* LEVESON-GOWER, Granville.

1956. GRATTAN, Henry (1746–1820), M.P. Malton 1805–6, Dublin City 1806–20 (DNB).

1957. GRATTAN, Henry (ca 1789–1859), M.P. Dublin City 1826–30, Meath 1831–52 (*Alumni Dublin.;* DNB).

1958. GRATTAN, James (1787–1854), M.P. Wicklow 1821–41 (*Alumni Dublin.;* Boase; DNB).

1959. GRAVES, Thomas (1725–1802), 1st Bn Graves, M.P. East Looe 1775–75 (DNB; GEC).

1960. GRAVES, Thomas North (1775–1830), 2d Bn Graves, M.P. Okehampton 1812–18, Windsor 1819–20, Milborne Port 1820–27 (GEC; *Eton Coll. Reg.*).

1961. GRAVES, William (ca 1724–1801), M.P. West Looe 1768–74, East Looe 1775–83, 1784–86, 1796–98 (Burke's *Peerage; Alumni Oxon.*).

1962. GRAY, Charles (ca 1695–1782), M.P. Colchester 1742–55, 1761–80

(*Essex Review, 6,* 187; *Gray's Inn Reg.;* Musgrave's *Obituary*).

1963. GRAY, George (ca 1710–73), 3d Bt, M.P. Winchelsea 1759–60 (GEC).

1964. GREATHEAD-BERTIE-PERCY, Charles (1794–1870), M.P. Newport 1826–29 (*Alumni Oxon.;* Burke's *Peerage* sub Northumberland; *Eton Lists*).

1965. GREATHEED, Samuel (ca 1711–65), M.P. Coventry 1747–61 (*Alumni Cantab.;* Whitley's *Coventry M.P.'s*).

1966. GREENE, James, M.P. Arundel 1796–1802 (Baines' *Lancaster, 3,* 218).

1967. GREENE, Thomas (1794–1872), M.P. Lancaster borough 1824–52, 1853–57 (*Alumni Oxon.;* Burke's *LG;* Boase).

1968. GREENE, William (1748–1829), M.P. Dungarvan 1802–6 (Burke's *Irish LG;* Hodson's *Bengal Army List*).

1969. GREENHILL-RUSSELL, Robert (ca 1763–1836), 1st Bt, M.P. Thirsk 1806–32 (GEC; *Old Westminsters*).

GREENLY, Isaac, *see* COFFIN, Isaac.

GREENOUGH, George Bellas, *see* BELLAS-GREENOUGH, George.

1970. GREGAN-CRAUFURD, Charles (1761–1821), M.P. East Retford 1806–12 (DNB; *Harrow Reg.*).

1971. GREGG, Francis (d. 1795), M.P. Morpeth 1789–95 (Bean; Musgrave's *Obituary*).

1972. GREGOR, Francis (ca 1760–1815), M.P. Cornwall 1790–1806 (Boase and Courtney, *Biblio. Cornub.;* Alumni Cantab.).

1973. GREGORY, George (1670–1746), M.P. Nottingham borough 1701–1, 1702–5, 1715–27, Boroughbridge 1727–46 (*Alumni Cantab.*).

GREGORY, Glynne Earle Welby, *see* WELBY-GREGORY, Glynne Earle.

1974. GREGORY, Mark (d. 1793), M.P. Newtown 1784–90 (Musgrave's *Obituary*).

1975. GREGORY, Robert (ca 1729–1810), M.P. Maidstone 1768–74, Rochester 1774–84 (*Alumni Oxon.;* Burke's *Irish LG;* Smith's *Rochester in Parl.*).

1976. GREGSON, John (ca 1806–79), M.P. Saltash 1830–31 (*Alumni Oxon.;* Courtney's *Cornwall M.P.'s*).

GREISLEY, Roger, *see* GRESLEY, Roger.

1977. GRENFELL, Pascoe (1761–1838), M.P. Great Marlow 1802–20, Penryn 1820–26 (DNB).

1978. GRENVILLE, George (1712–70), M.P. Buckingham borough 1741–70 (DNB).

GRENVILLE, George Nugent, *see* NUGENT-GRENVILLE, George.

GRENVILLE, George Nugent Temple, *see* NUGENT-TEMPLE-GRENVILLE, George.

1979. GRENVILLE, Henry (1717–84), M.P. Bishop's Castle 1759–61, Thirsk 1761–65, Buckingham borough 1768–74 (*Eton Coll. Reg.*).

1980. GRENVILLE, James (1715–83), M.P. Old Sarum 1742–47, Bridport

1747–54, Buckingham borough 1754–68, Horsham 1768–70 (GEC; *Eton Coll. Reg.*).

1981. GRENVILLE, James (1742–1825), 1st Bn Glastonbury, M.P. Thirsk 1765–68, Buckingham borough 1770–90, Bucks 1790–97 (GEC; *Eton Coll. Reg.*).

1982. GRENVILLE, Richard (1742–1823), M.P. Buckingham borough 1774–80 (*Eton Coll. Reg.*).

GRENVILLE, Richard Plantagenet Temple Nugent Brydges Chandos, *see* TEMPLE-NUGENT-BRYDGES-CHANDOS-GRENVILLE, Richard Plantagenet.

GRENVILLE, Richard Temple Nugent Brydges Chandos, *see* TEMPLE-NUGENT-BRYDGES-CHANDOS-GRENVILLE, Richard.

1983. GRENVILLE, Thomas (1719–47), M.P. Bridport 1746–47 (DNB).

1984. GRENVILLE, Thomas (1755–1846), M.P. Bucks 1779–84, 1813–18, Aldeburgh 1790–96, Buckingham borough 1796–1810 (DNB; *Eton Coll. Reg.*).

1985. GRENVILLE, William Wyndham (1759–1834), 1st Bn Grenville, M.P. Buckingham borough 1782–84, Bucks 1784–90 (DNB; GEC; *Eton Coll. Reg.*).

1986. GRENVILLE-TEMPLE, Richard (1711–79), 2d E. Temple, M.P. Buckingham borough 1734–41, 1747–52, Bucks 1741–47 (DNB; GEC; *Eton Coll. Reg.*).

1987. GRESLEY, Roger (1799–1837), 8th Bt, M.P. Durham City 1830–31, New Romney 1831–31, South Derbyshire 1835–37 (DNB; GEC).

1988. GRESLEY, Thomas (ca 1723–53), 5th Bt, M.P. Lichfield 1753–53 (GEC).

1989. GREVILLE, Charles (1762–1832), M.P. Petersfield 1795–96 (*Old Westminsters*).

1990. GREVILLE, Charles Francis (1749–1809), M.P. Warwick borough 1774–90 (Burke's *Peerage* sub Warwick; *Harrow Reg.*; *Gent. Mag., 1,* 482).

1991. GREVILLE, Charles John (1780–1836), M.P. Warwick borough 1816–31, 1832–36 (Burke's *Peerage* sub Warwick; *Gent. Mag., 1* [1837], 203).

1992. GREVILLE, Fulk (ca 1717–ca 1806), M.P. Monmouth borough 1747–54 (*Alumni Oxon.;* Walpole-Montagu *Corr.* [Yale ed.] *1,* 354 n.).

1993. GREVILLE, George (1746–1816), 2d E. of Warwick, M.P. Warwick borough 1768–73 (GEC; *Eton Coll. Reg.*).

1994. GREVILLE, Henry Richard (1779–1853), 3d E. of Warwick, M.P. Warwick borough 1802–16 (GEC; *Eton Lists*).

1995. GREVILLE, Robert Fulk (1751–1824), M.P. Warwick borough 1774–80, Windsor 1796–1806 (Burke's *Peerage* sub Warwick; *Harrow Reg.*).

1996. GREY, Booth (1740–1802), M.P. Leicester borough 1768–84 (*Alumni Cantab.*).

1997. GREY, Booth (1783–1850), M.P. Petersfield 1807–12 (*Alumni Oxon.;* Burke's *Peerage* and Collins' *Peerage* sub Stamford; *Eton Lists*).

1998. GREY, Charles (1764–1845), 2d E. Grey, M.P. Northumberland 1786–1807, Appleby 1807–7, Tavistock 1807–7 (*Alumni Cantab.;* DNB; GEC; *Eton Coll. Reg.*).

1999. GREY, Charles (1804–70), M.P. Wycombe 1832–37 (DNB).

2000. GREY, George Harry (1737–1819), 5th E. of Stamford, M.P. Staffordshire 1761–68 (*Alumni Cantab.;* GEC).

2001. GREY, George Harry (1765–1845), 6th E. of Stamford, M.P. Aldeburgh 1790–96, St. Germans 1796–1802 (*Alumni Cantab.;* GEC).

2002. GREY, Harry (1715–68), 4th E. of Stamford, M.P. Leicestershire 1738–39 (GEC; *Old Westminsters; Rugby Reg.*).

2003. GREY, Henry (d. 1740), M.P. Reading 1734–40 (Musgrave's *Obituary*).

2004. GREY, Henry (1722–1808), 2d Bt, M.P. Northumberland 1754–68 (GEC).

2005. GREY, Henry George (1802–94), 3d E. Grey, M.P. Winchelsea 1826–30, Higham Ferrers 1830–31, Northumberland 1831–32, North Northumberland 1832–41, Sunderland 1841–45 (GEC; DNB; *Alumni Cantab.*).

2006. GREY, John (ca 1724–77), M.P. Bridgnorth 1754–68, Tregony 1768–74 (*Alumni Cantab.; Old Westminsters*).

GREY, DE WILTON, Bn and Vct, *see* EGERTON, Thomas.

2007. GREY-EGERTON, John (1766–1825), 8th Bt, M.P. Chester City 1807–18 (GEC; Omerod's *Chester, 1,* 301 and *2,* 222).

2008. GREY-EGERTON, Philip de Malpas (1806–81), 10th Bt, M.P. Chester City 1830–31, South Cheshire 1835–68, West Cheshire 1868–81 (DNB; GEC).

2009. GRIEVE, William, M.P. Linlithgow burghs 1790–96.

2010. GRIFFIN, John Griffin (1719–97), 4th Bn Howard de Walden and 1st Bn Braybrooke, M.P. Andover 1749–84 (DNB; GEC).

2011. GRIFFIN, Richard (1750–1825), 2d Bn Braybrooke, M.P. Grampound 1774–80, Buckingham borough 1780–82, Reading 1782–97 (DNB; GEC; *Eton Coll. Reg.*).

2012. GRIFFIN, Richard (1783–1858), 3d Bn Braybrooke, M.P. Thirsk 1805–6, Saltash 1807–7, Buckingham borough 1807–12, Berks 1812–25 (DNB; GEC).

2013. GRIFFIN, Thomas (ca 1693–1771), M.P. Arundel 1754–61 (DNB; Musgrave's *Obituary*).

2014. GRIFFINHOOFE, Benjamin Cooke (1772–ca 1840), M.P. Yarmouth (Hants) 1808–8 (*Alumni Carthusiani; Admissions to St. John, Cambridge, 3,* 490).

2015. GRIFFITH, Christopher (ca 1721–76), M.P. Berks 1774–76 (*Alumni Oxon.;* Burke's *LG;* Musgrave's *Obituary*).

2016. GRIFFITH, John (ca 1687–1739), M.P. Carnarvonshire 1715–39 (*Alumni Oxon.;* Williams' *Wales M.P.'s*).

2017. GRIFFITH, John Wynne (1763–1834), M.P. Denbigh borough 1818–26 (Burke's *LG;* Williams' *Wales M.P.'s*).

2018. GRIFFITH-WYNNE, Charles Wynne (1780–1865), M.P. Carnarvonshire 1830–32 (*Alumni Oxon.; Old Westminsters;* Williams' *Wales M.P.'s*).

2019. GRIGBY, Joshua (ca 1731–98), M.P. Suffolk 1784–90 (*Alumni Cantab.; Parish Reg. Horringer, Suffolk,* p. 315).

2020. GRIMSTON, James (1711–73), 2d Vct Grimston, M.P. St. Albans 1754–61 (GEC).

2021. GRIMSTON, James Bucknal (1747–1808), 3d Vct Grimston, M.P. St. Albans 1783–84, Herts 1784–90 (*Alumni Cantab.;* GEC; *Eton Coll. Reg.*).

2022. GRIMSTON, James Walter (1775–1845), 1st E. of Verulam, M.P. St. Albans 1802–8 (GEC; *Harrow Reg.*).

2023. GRIMSTON, James Walter (1809–95), 2d E. of Verulam, M.P. St. Albans 1830–31, Newport 1831–32, Herts 1832–45 (GEC; *Harrow Reg.*).

GRIMSTON, William Bucknall, *see* BUCKNALL-GRIMSTON, William.

GRINSTEAD, 1st Bn, *see* COLE, John Willoughby.

2024. GROSETT, John Rock (ca 1784–1866), M.P. Chippenham 1820–26 (*Gent. Mag., 2,* 698).

2025. GROSVENOR, Richard (1731–1802), 1st E. Grosvenor, M.P. Chester City 1754–61 (DNB; GEC).

2026. GROSVENOR, Richard (1795–1869), 2d M. of Westminster, M.P. Chester City 1818–30, Cheshire 1830–32, South Cheshire 1832–34 (GEC; *Old Westminsters*).

GROSVENOR, Richard (Edward) Erle Drax, *see* ERLE-DRAX-GROSVENOR, Richard (Edward).

2027. GROSVENOR, Robert (1695–1755), 6th Bt, M.P. Chester City 1733–55 (*Alumni Oxon.;* GEC; *Etoniana, 58,* 127).

2028. GROSVENOR, Robert (1767–1845), 1st M. of Westminster, M.P. East Looe 1788–90, Chester City 1790–1802 (*Alumni Cantab.;* DNB; GEC; *Harrow Reg.; Old Westminsters*).

2029. GROSVENOR, Robert (1801–93), 1st Bn Ebury, M.P. Shaftesbury 1822–26, Chester City 1826–31, 1831–47, Middlesex 1847–57 (DNB; GEC; *Old Westminsters*).

2030. GROSVENOR, Thomas (1734–95), M.P. Chester City 1755–95 (*Old Westminsters;* Omerod's *Chester, 2,* 843).

2031. GROSVENOR, Thomas (1764–1851), M.P. Chester City 1795–1826, Stockbridge 1826–30 (DNB; *Old Westminsters*).

2032. GROVE, Grey James (1682–1742), M.P. Bewdley 1715–22, Bridgnorth 1734–41 (Shrop. Archaeol. Soc. *Trans.,* 4th Ser., 5, 67).

2033. GROVE, William (1702–67), M.P. Coventry 1741–61 (Burke's *Colonial Gentry;* Whitley's *Coventry M.P.'s*).

2034. GROVE, William Chafin (ca 1731–93), M.P. Shaftesbury 1768–74, Weymouth and Melcombe Regis 1774–81 (Burke's *LG; Alumni Cantab.;* Hutchins' *Dorset, 3, 568*).

GUERNSEY, Bn, *see* FINCH, Heneage.

2035. GUEST, Josiah John (1785–1852), 1st Bt, M.P. Honiton 1826–31, Merthyr Tydvil 1832–52 (DNB).

2036. GUIDOTT, William (ca 1672–1745), M.P. Andover 1708–27, 1730–41 (*Alumni Oxon.; Linc. Inn Reg.;* Musgrave's *Obituary*).

GUILDFORD, E. of, *see* NORTH, Frederick and George Augustus.

GUILLAMORE, 2d Vct, *see* O'GRADY, Standish.

2037. GUISE, Berkeley William (1775–1834), 2d Bt, M.P. Gloucestershire 1811–32, East Gloucestershire 1832–34 (*Alumni Oxon.;* GEC; *Eton Lists*).

2038. GUISE, William (1737–83), 5th Bt, M.P. Gloucestershire 1770–83 (GEC; Williams' *Gloucester M.P.'s*).

2039. GULSTON, Joseph (ca 1694–1766), M.P. Tregony 1737–41, Poole 1741–65 (DNB; Nichols' *Lit. Illust., 5,* 1–60; Nicholas' *County Families of Wales, 1,* 288).

2040. GULSTON, Joseph (ca 1745–86), M.P. Poole 1765–68, 1780–84 (DNB; *Eton Coll. Reg.*).

2041. GUMLEY, Samuel (d. 1763), M.P. Hedon 1746–47 (Bean; *Notes and Queries,* 12th Ser., *2,* 313).

2042. GUNDRY, Nathaniel (ca 1701–54), M.P. Dorchester 1741–50 (DNB).

2043. GUNNING, George William (1763–1823), 2d Bt, M.P. Wigan 1800–2, Hastings 1802–6, East Grinstead 1812–18 (*Alumni Cantab.;* GEC).

2044. GUNNING, Robert Henry (1795–1862), 3d Bt, M.P. Northampton borough 1830–31 (*Alumni Cantab.;* GEC; *Harrow Reg.*).

2045. GURNEY, Hudson (1775–1864), M.P. Shaftesbury 1812–13, Newtown 1816–32 (DNB).

2046. GURNEY, Richard Hanbury (ca 1784–1854), M.P. Norwich 1818–26, 1830–32 (Burke's *LG; Gent. Mag., 1,* 320).

GWILLYM, Robert Vernon Atherton, *see* ATHERTON-GWILLYM, Robert Vernon.

GWYDIR, Bn, *see* BURRELL, Peter; *also,* DRUMMOND-BURRELL, Peter Robert.

2047. GWYN, Francis (ca 1698–1777), M.P. Wells 1741–54 (*Alumni Oxon.;* Hutchins' *Dorset, 4,* 528; Musgrave's *Obituary*).

2048. GWYNNE, Howel (b. ca 1701), M.P. Radnorshire 1755–61, Old Sarum 1761–68 (*Alumni Oxon.;* Burke's *LG*).

2049. GYBBON, Philips (1678–1762), M.P. Rye 1707–62 (*Gent. Mag., 2* [1788], 699 n., 834).

2050. GYE, Frederick (ca 1781–1869), M.P. Chippenham 1826–30 (DNB).

HADDINGTON, 9th E. of, see HAMILTON, Thomas.

2051. HADDOCK, Nicholas (ca 1686–1746), M.P. Rochester 1734–46 (DNB).

2052. HADDOCK, Nicholas (ca 1723–81), M.P. Rochester 1754–61 (Musgrave's *Obituary;* Smith's *Rochester in Parl.*).

2053. HALDANE, George (ca 1722–59), M.P. Stirling burghs 1747–58 (J. A. L. Haldane, *Haldanes of Gleneagles,* pp. 159–76).

2054. HALDANE, Robert (1705–67), M.P. Stirling burghs 1758–61 (J. A. L. Haldane, *Haldanes of Gleneagles,* pp. 293–96).

2055. HALDIMAND, William (1784–1862), M.P. Ipswich 1820–27 (DNB).

2056. HALE, Paggen (ca 1715–55), M.P. Herts 1747–55 (Clutterbuck's *Herts, 3,* 133, 136; *Gray's Inn Pension Book, 2,* 232).

2057. HALE-RIGBY, Francis (d. 1827), M.P. St. Michael 1779–84 (Burke's *LG* [ed. 1849]; *Gent. Mag., 2,* 282).

2058. HALES, Philip (d. 1824), 5th Bt, M.P. Downton 1775–80, Marlborough 1784–90 (GEC).

2059. HALES, Thomas (ca 1662–1748), 2d Bt, M.P. Kent 1701–5, Canterbury 1715–34, 1735–41, 1746–47 (GEC).

2060. HALES, Thomas (ca 1694–1762), 3d Bt, M.P. Minehead 1722–27, Camelford 1727–34, Grampound 1734–41, Hythe 1744–61, East Grinstead 1761–62 (GEC).

2061. HALES, Thomas Pym (ca 1726–73), 4th Bt, M.P. Downton 1762–68, Dover 1770–73 (GEC).

2062. HALHED, Nathaniel Brassey (1751–1830), M.P. Lymington 1791–96 (DNB).

HALIFAX, 1st Vct, see WOOD, Charles.

2063. HALKETT, Peter (ca 1695–1755), 2d Bt, M.P. Stirling burghs 1734–41 (GEC).

2064. HALL, Benjamin (1778–1817), M.P. Totnes 1806–12, Westbury 1812–14, Glamorgan 1814–17 (*Old Westminsters;* Williams' *Wales M.P.'s*).

2065. HALL, Benjamin (1802–67), 1st Bn Llanover, M.P. Monmouth borough 1831–31, 1832–37, Marylebone 1837–59 (DNB; GEC; *Old Westminsters*).

2066. HALL, James (1761–1832), 4th Bt, M.P. St. Michael 1807–12 (*Alumni Cantab.;* DNB; GEC).

HALL, John, see WHARTON, John.

2067. HALL, Thomas, M.P. Berwick-on-Tweed 1802–3 (Bean, p. 1195).

HALL, William, see GAGE, William Hall.

2068. HALLIDAY, John (ca 1710–54), M.P. Taunton 1754–54 (Burke's *LG* [ed. 1849]).

2069. HALLIDAY, John (ca 1737–1805), M.P. Taunton 1775–84 (Burke's *LG* [ed. 1849]; *Gent. Mag., 1,* 489).

2070. HALLIFAX, Thomas (ca 1721–89), M.P. Coventry 1780–81, Aylesbury 1784–89 (DNB).

2071. HALSE, James (ca 1769–1838), M.P. St. Ives 1826–30, 1831–38 (*Gent. Mag., 2*, 214).

2072. HALSEY, Joseph Thompson (1774–1818), M.P. St. Albans 1807–18 (*Alumni Cantab.; Burke's LG; Harrow Reg.*).

2073. HALSEY, Thomas (1731–88), M.P. Herts 1768–84 (Burke's *LG*).

HALYBURTON, Douglas Gordon, *see* GORDON-HALYBURTON, Douglas.

2074. HALYBURTON, James, M.P. Orkney and Shetland 1747–54.

2075. HAMILTON, Alexander (ca 1684–1763), M.P. Linlithgowshire 1727–41 (G. Hamilton, *House of Hamilton,* p. 505).

2076. HAMILTON, Alexander (1767–1852), 10th D. of Hamilton, M.P. Lancaster borough 1802–6 (DNB; GEC).

2077. HAMILTON, Archibald (1673–1754), M.P. Lanarkshire 1708–10, 1718–34, Queenborough 1735–41, Dartmouth 1742–47 (*Scots Peerage*).

2078. HAMILTON, Archibald (1740–1819), 9th D. of Hamilton, M.P. Lancashire 1768–72 (GEC; *Eton Coll. Reg.; Scots Peerage*).

2079. HAMILTON, Archibald (1769–1827), M.P. Lanarkshire 1802–27 (DNB; *Eton Coll. Reg.; Harow Reg.; Scots Peerage*).

HAMILTON, Arthur Cole, *see* COLE-HAMILTON, Arthur.

2080. HAMILTON, Basil (1696–1742), M.P. Kirkcudbright Stewarty 1741–42 (GEC and *Scots Peerage* sub Selkirk).

2081. HAMILTON, Charles (1704–86), M.P. Truro 1741–47 (*Old Westminsters; Scots Peerage* sub Abercorn).

2082. HAMILTON, Charles (1767–1849), 2d Bt, M.P. St. Germans 1790–90, Dungannon 1801–2, 1803–6, Honiton 1807–12 (DNB; GEC).

2083. HAMILTON, Claude (1787–1808), M.P. Dungannon 1807–8 (*Alumni Cantab.; Scots Peerage* sub Abercorn).

2084. HAMILTON, George (ca 1698–1775), M.P. Wells 1734–35, 1747–54 (*Scots Peerage* sub Abercorn).

2085. HAMILTON, Gustavus (ca 1710–46), 2d Vct Boyne, M.P. Newport (Hants) 1736–41 (GEC; *Old Westminsters*).

2086. HAMILTON, Hans (d. 1822), M.P. Dublin Co. 1801–22 (*Gent. Mag., 2*, 647; G. Hamilton, *House of Hamilton,* p. 973).

HAMILTON, Hew Dalrymple, *see* DALRYMPLE-HAMILTON, Hew.

2087. HAMILTON, James (ca 1682–1750), 2d Bt, M.P. Lanarkshire 1710–15, 1735–50 (GEC; G. Hamilton, *House of Hamilton,* p. 113).

2088. HAMILTON, James (ca 1691–1758), 1st E. of Clanbrassil, M.P. Wendover 1727–41, Tavistock 1742–47, Morpeth 1747–54 (GEC; Devonshire Assoc. *Trans., 43*, 399).

2089. HAMILTON, James (1730–98), 2d E. of Clanbrassil, M.P. Helston 1768–74 (GEC).

2090. HAMILTON, James (1786–1814), M.P. Dungannon 1807–7, Liskeard 1807–12 (GEC and *Scots Peerage* sub Abercorn).

2091. HAMILTON, John (1715–96), M.P. Wigtown burghs 1754–61, 1762–68, Wigtownshire 1761–62 (Grant's *Faculty of Advocates; Scots Peerage* sub Stair).

2092. HAMILTON, John (1751–1804), M.P. Haddingtonshire 1786–95 (Foster's *Scots M.P.'s*).

HAMILTON, John Dalrymple, *see* DALRYMPLE-HAMILTON, John.

2093. HAMILTON, John James (1756–1818), 1st M. of Abercorn, M.P. East Looe 1783–84, St. Germans 1784–89 (*Alumni Cantab.;* GEC; *Harrow Reg.*).

HAMILTON, Robert Adam Christopher Nisbet, *see* CHRISTOPHER-NISBET-HAMILTON, Robert Adam.

2094. HAMILTON, Thomas (1780–1858), 9th E. of Haddington, M.P. St. Germans 1802–6, Cockermouth 1807–7, Callington 1807–12, St. Michael 1814–18, Rochester 1818–26, Yarmouth (Hants) 1826–27 (DNB; GEC).

2095. HAMILTON, William (ca 1706–34), M.P. Lanarkshire 1734–34 (*Scots Peerage*).

2096. HAMILTON, William (1730–1803), M.P. Midhurst 1761–64 (DNB; *Old Westminsters*).

2097. HAMILTON, William Gerard (1729–96), M.P. Petersfield 1754–61, Pontefract 1761–68, Old Sarum 1768–74, Wareham 1774–80, Wilton 1780–90, Haslemere 1790–96 (DNB; *Harrow Reg.*).

2098. HAMILTON-DALRYMPLE, Hew (1746–1800), 3d Bt, M.P. Haddingtonshire 1780–86 (GEC; *Scots Peerage* sub Stair).

2099. HAMILTON-DALRYMPLE, John (1780–1835), 5th Bt, M.P. Haddington burghs 1805–6 (GEC; *Scots Peerage* sub Stair).

2100. HAMILTON-NISBET, William (ca 1749–1822), M.P. Haddingtonshire 1777–80, East Grinstead 1790–96, Newport (Hants) 1796–1800 (*Eton Coll. Reg.;* G. Hamilton, *House of Hamilton,* p. 677; *Gent. Mag., 2,* 189).

2101. HAMLYN, James (d. 1811), 1st Bt, M.P. Carmarthenshire 1793–1802 (GEC).

2102. HAMLYN-WILLIAMS, James (1765–1829), 2d Bt, M.P. Carmarthenshire 1802–6 (*Alumni Cantab.;* GEC; *Old Westminsters*).

2103. HAMLYN-WILLIAMS, James (ca 1791–1861), 3d Bt, M.P. Carmarthenshire 1831–32, 1835–37 (GEC; Williams' *Wales M.P.'s*).

2104. HAMMERSLEY, Hugh (ca 1767–1828), M.P. Helston 1812–18 (*Alumni Oxon.;* Burke's *LG; Eton Coll. Reg.*).

2105. HAMMETT, Benjamin (ca 1736–1800), M.P. Taunton 1782–1800 (Beaven's *Aldermen of London; Gent. Mag., 2,* 798; Kite and Palmer's *Taunton,* pp. 29, 93).

HAMMETT, James, *see* HAMLYN, James.

2106. HAMMETT, John (d. 1811), M.P. Taunton 1800–11 (*Gent. Mag.*, *2* [1800], 799, and *1* [1811], 497; *Royal Kalendar* [1802], p. 63).

2107. HAMMOND, James (1710–42), M.P. Truro 1741–42 (DNB; *Old Westminsters*).

2108. HAMMOND, William (ca 1721–63), M.P. Southwark 1754–61 (*Alumni Oxon.*; Musgrave's *Obituary*).

2109. HAMOND, Andrew Snape (1738–1828), 1st Bt, M.P. Ipswich 1796–1806 (DNB; GEC).

2110. HAMPDEN, George Robert (1789–1849), 5th E. of Buckinghamshire, M.P. St. Michael 1812–13 (GEC; *Old Westminsters*).

2111. HAMPDEN, John (ca 1696–1754), M.P. Wendover 1734–54 (GEC sub Buckinghamshire; Lipscomb's *Bucks*, *2*, 269, 286).

2112. HAMPDEN, Thomas (1746–1824), 2d Vct Hampden, M.P. Lewes 1768–74 (GEC).

2113. HANBURY, Capel (1707–65), M.P. Leominster 1741–47, Monmouthshire 1747–65 (*Alumni Oxon.*; Burke's *LG;* Williams' *Wales M.P.'s*).

2114. HANBURY, John (ca 1664–1734), M.P. Gloucester City 1701–8, Monmouthshire 1721–34 (DNB; Burke's *LG;* Williams' *Wales M.P.'s*).

2115. HANBURY, John (1744–84), M.P. Monmouthshire 1766–84 (Burke's *LG; Eton Coll. Reg.;* Williams' *Wales M.P.'s*).

HANBURY, William, *see* BATEMAN-HANBURY, William.

2116. HANBURY-TRACY, Charles (1778–1858), 1st Bn Sudeley, M.P. Tewkesbury 1807–12, 1832–37 (GEC).

2117. HANBURY-TRACY, Thomas Charles (1801–63), 2d Bn Sudeley, M.P. Wallingford 1831–32 (GEC).

2118. HANBURY-WILLIAMS, Charles (1708–59), M.P. Monmouthshire 1735–47, Leominster 1754–59 (DNB; *Eton Coll. Reg.*).

2119. HANDASYDE, Roger (ca 1685–1763), M.P. Huntingdon borough 1722–41, Scarborough 1747–54 (*Notes and Queries*, 12th Ser., *2*, 394, and *3*, 112; *Old Westminsters*).

2120. HANDCOCK, Richard (1791–1869), 3d Bn Castlemaine, M.P. Athlone 1826–32 (GEC).

2121. HANDCOCK, William (1761–1839), 1st Vct Castlemaine, M.P. Athlone 1801–3 (GEC).

2122. HANDLEY, Henry (ca 1797–1846), M.P. Heytesbury 1820–26, Lincolnshire (parts of Kesteven and Holland) 1832–41 (*Alumni Oxon.*; Burke's *LG* [ed. 1855]; *Eton Lists; Gent. Mag.*, *2*, 205; Parish's *List of Carthusians*).

2123. HANDLEY, William Farnworth (1780–1851), M.P. Newark 1831–34 (Burke's *LG* [ed. 1849]; *Gent. Mag.*, *1* [1852], 193).

2124. HANGER, Gabriel (1697–1773), 1st Bn Coleraine, M.P. Maidstone 1753–61, Bridgwater 1763–68 (GEC).

2125. HANGER, William (1744–1814), 3d Bn Coleraine, M.P. East Retford 1775–78, Aldborough 1778–80, St. Michael 1780–84 (GEC).

2126. HANKEY, Joseph Chaplin (ca 1754–1803), M.P. Wareham 1799–1802 (Burke's LG; Gent. Mag., 1, 480; Royal Kalendar [1802], p. 64).

2127. HANKEY, Richard (d. 1817), M.P. Plympton Erle 1799–1802 (Gent. Mag., 1, 375; Gray's Inn Reg.; Royal Kalendar [1802], p. 58).

2128. HANMER, Henry (1789–1868), M.P. Westbury 1831–31, Aylesbury 1832–37 (Alumni Cantab.; Rugby Reg.).

2129. HANMER, Thomas (1702–37), M.P. Castle Rising 1734–37 (Alumni Cantab.; Old Westminsters).

2130. HANMER, Walden (1717–83), 1st Bt, M.P. Sudbury 1768–74, 1775–80 (GEC).

2131. HANNAY, Samuel (d. 1790), 3d Bt, M.P. Camelford 1784–90 (GEC).

HANNING, John Lee, see LEE, John Lee.

2132. HARBORD, Edward (1781–1835), 3d Bn Suffield, M.P. Great Yarmouth 1806–12, Shaftesbury 1820–21 (DNB; GEC).

2133. HARBORD, Harbord (1734–1810), 1st Bn Suffield, M.P. Norwich 1756–86 (Alumni Cantab.; GEC).

2134. HARBORD, William (ca 1697–1770), 1st Bt, M.P. Berealston 1734–34, 1741–54, Dunwich 1738–41 (Burke's Peerage sub Suffield; GEC).

2135. HARBORD, William Assheton (1766–1821), 2d Bn Suffield, M.P. Ludgershall 1790–96, Plympton Erle 1807–10 (GEC).

HARBOROUGH, 5th E. of, see SHERARD, Philip.

2136. HARCOURT, George Granville (1785–1861), M.P. Lichfield 1806–31, Oxfordshire 1831–61 (Burke's LG; Boase; Old Westminsters).

2137. HARCOURT, George Simon (1736–1809), 2d E. Harcourt, M.P. St. Albans 1761–68 (GEC; Old Westminsters).

2138. HARCOURT, George William Richard (1775–1812), M.P. Westbury 1796–1800 (Burke's LG; Lipscomb's Bucks, 4, 592).

2139. HARCOURT, John, M.P. Ilchester 1785–86, 1790–96, Leominster 1812–18, 1819–20.

2140. HARCOURT, John Simon (1772–1810), M.P. Westbury 1800–2 (Burke's LG).

2141. HARCOURT, Richard (ca 1714–77), M.P. Sussex 1768–74 (Burke's LG; Old Westminsters).

2142. HARCOURT, William (1743–1830), 3d E. Harcourt, M.P. Oxford City 1768–74 (DNB; GEC).

2143. HARCOURT-VERNON, Granville (1792–1879), M.P. Aldborough 1815–20, East Retford 1831–47 (Boase; Old Westminsters).

2144. HARDINGE, George (1743–1816), M.P. Old Sarum 1784–1802 (Alumni Cantab.; DNB; Eton Coll. Reg.).

2145. HARDINGE, Henry (1785–1856), 1st Vct Hardinge, M.P. Durham City 1820–30, St. Germans 1830–30, Newport 1830–32, Launceston 1832–44 (DNB; GEC).

2146. HARDINGE, Nicholas (1699–1758), M.P. Eye 1748–58 (*Alumni Cantab.;* DNB; *Eton Coll. Reg.*).

2147. HARDMAN, Edward (b. cà 1767), M.P. Drogheda 1801–6 (*Alumni Dublin.*).

2148. HARDMAN, John (ca 1698–1755), M.P. Liverpool 1754–55 (Burke's *LG* [ed. 1849], sub Crompton; Fishwick's *Rochdale,* p. 521; Pink).

2149. HARDRES, William (1686–1736), 4th Bt, M.P. Kent 1711–13, Dover 1713–15, Canterbury 1727–35 (GEC).

HARDWICKE, E. of, *see* YORKE, Charles Philip and Philip.

2150. HARDY, Charles (ca 1680–1744), M.P. Portsmouth 1743–44 (DNB).

2151. HARDY, Charles (ca 1713–80), M.P. Rochester 1764–68, Plymouth 1771–80 (DNB; Musgrave's *Obituary*).

2152. HARE, James (1747–1804), M.P. Stockbridge 1772–74, Knaresborough 1781–1804 (*Alumni Cantab.;* DNB; *Eton Coll. Reg.*).

2153. HARE, Richard (1773–1827), M.P. Cork Co. 1812–27 (GEC sub Listowel; *Eton Coll. Reg.*).

2154. HARE, William (1801–56), 2d E. of Listowel, M.P. Kerry 1826–30, St. Albans 1841–46 (*Alumni Cantab.;* GEC).

HAREWOOD, E. of, *see* LASCELLES, Edward and Henry.

HARINGTON, Arthur, *see* CHAMPERNOWNE, Arthur.

2155. HARLEY, Edward (ca 1699–1755), 3d E. of Oxford, M.P. Herefordshire 1727–41 (GEC; *Old Westminsters*).

2156. HARLEY, Edward (1726–90), 4th E. of Oxford, M.P. Herefordshire 1747–55 (GEC; *Old Westminsters*).

2157. HARLEY, Robert (ca 1707–74), M.P. Leominster 1734–41, 1742–47, Droitwich 1754–74 (Collins' *Peerage* sub Oxford; *Old Westminsters;* Williams' *Worcester M.P.'s*).

2158. HARLEY, Thomas (1730–1804), M.P. London 1761–74, Herefordshire 1776–1802 (DNB; GEC sub Oxford; *Old Westminsters*).

2159. HARPUR, Henry (ca 1709–48), 5th Bt, M.P. Worcester City 1744–47, Tamworth 1747–48 (GEC; Williams' *Worcester M.P.'s*; Wedgwood).

2160. HARPUR, Henry (ca 1739–89), 6th Bt, M.P. Derbyshire 1761–68 (GEC; *Old Westminsters*).

HARRINGTON, E. of, *see* STANHOPE, Charles and William.

2161. HARRIS, George (ca 1787–1836), M.P. Great Grimsby 1830–31 (*Gent. Mag., 1* [1837], 432; *1832 List*).

2162. HARRIS, James (1709–80), M.P. Christchurch 1761–80 (*Alumni Oxon.;* DNB).

2163. HARRIS, James (1746–1820), 1st E. of Malmesbury, M.P. Christchurch 1770–74, 1780–88 (DNB; GEC).

2164. HARRIS, James Edward (1778–1841), 2d E. of Malmesbury, M.P. Helston 1802–4, Horsham 1804–6, Heytesbury 1807–12, Wilton 1816–20 (*Alumni Oxon.;* GEC).

2165. HARRIS, John (ca 1690–1767), M.P. Helston 1727–41, Ashburton 1741–67 (Courtney's *Cornwall M.P.'s,* pp. 49–50; Vivian's *Visitation of Devon,* p. 450).

2166. HARRIS, John (1703–68), M.P. Barnstable 1741–47, 1754–61 (Devonshire Assoc. *Trans., 73,* 185; *Devon and Cornwall Notes and Queries, 7,* 212).

2167. HARRIS, John Rawlinson (ca 1780–1830), M.P. Southwark 1830–30 (*Gent. Mag., 2,* 283).

2168. HARRISON, George (1680–1759), M.P. Hertford borough 1727–34, 1741–59 (*Alumni Carthusiani;* Clutterbuck's *Herts, 2,* 158, 186).

2169. HARRISON, John (ca 1738–1811), M.P. Great Grimsby 1780–96, Thetford 1796–1806 (*Alumni Cantab.; Eton Coll. Reg.*).

2170. HARRISON-BATLEY, Charles (ca 1786–1835), M.P. Beverley 1826–30 (*Alumni Cantab.*).

HARROWBY, Bn and E. of, *see* RYDER, Dudley and Nathaniel.

2171. HART, George Vaughan (ca 1752–1832), M.P. Donegal 1812–31 (*Alumni Dublin.;* DNB).

2172. HART, William Nevill (1741–1804), M.P. Stafford borough 1770–74 (*Notes and Queries,* 10th Ser., *6,* 473 and *10,* 263; Wedgwood).

HARTINGTON, M. of, *see* CAVENDISH, William.

HARTLAND, 2d Bn, *see* MAHON, Thomas.

2173. HARTLEY, David (ca 1732–1813), M.P. Hull 1774–80, 1782–84 (*Alumni Oxon.;* DNB).

2174. HARTLEY, Winchcombe Henry (ca 1740–94), M.P. Berks 1776–84, 1790–94 (*Alumni Oxon.;* Humphrey's *Bucklebury,* pp. 176, 326; Musgrave's *Obituary*).

HARTOPP, Edmund Cradock, *see* CRADOCK-HARTOPP, Edmund.

2175. HARTOPP-FLEETWOOD, George Harry William (1785–1824), M.P. Dundalk 1820–24 (*Alumni Oxon.;* Burke's *Peerage;* Fletcher's *Leicester Pedigrees*).

2176. HARTY, Robert Way (1779–1832), 1st Bt, M.P. Dublin City 1831–31 (Burke's *Peerage;* Foster's *Baronetage*).

HARVEY, Charles, *see* SAVILL-ONLEY, Charles.

2177. HARVEY, Daniel Whittle (ca 1786–1863), M.P. Colchester 1818–20, 1826–34, Southwark 1835–40 (DNB).

2178. HARVEY, Edward (1718–78), M.P. Gatton 1761–68, Harwich 1768–78 (Cussans' *Herts, 1,* 191; *Old Westminsters*).

2179. HARVEY, Eliab (1716–69), M.P. Dunwich 1761–68 (*Alumni Cantab.; Old Westminsters*).

2180. HARVEY, Eliab (1758–1830), M.P. Maldon 1780–84, Essex 1802–12, 1820–30 (DNB; *Harrow Reg.; Old Westminsters*).

2181. HARVEY, Michael (1694–1748), M.P. Milborne Port 1717–17, 1722–41, 1742–47 (Manning and Bray's *Surrey, 1,* 402; *Misc. Geneal. et Herald.,* 2d Ser., *3*).

2182. HARVEY, William (1714–63), M.P. Essex 1747–63 (*Alumni Oxon.; Misc. Geneal. et Herald.,* 2d Ser., *3*).

2183. HARVEY, William (1754–79), M.P. Essex 1775–79 (*Alumni Cantab.;* Cussans' *Herts, 1,* 191).

2184. HARVEY-THURSBY, John (ca 1710–64), M.P. Wootton Bassett 1741–47, Stamford 1754–61 (Baker's *Northampton, 1,* 11, 17; Burke's *LG* [ed. 1849]; Musgrave's *Obituary*).

HARWICH, 1st Bn, *see* HILL, Wills.

HASTINGS, Charles Abney, *see* ABNEY-HASTINGS, Charles.

HATHERTON, 1st Bn, *see* LITTELTON, John.

HATTON, Edward Finch, *see* FINCH-HATTON, Edward.

2185. HATTON, George (b. ca 1761), M.P. Lisburn 1801–2 (*Alumni Dublin.;* Burke's *Irish LG*).

HATTON, George Finch, *see* FINCH-HATTON, George.

2186. HAWKE, Edward (1710–81), 1st Bn Hawke, M.P. Portsmouth 1747–76 (DNB; GEC).

2187. HAWKE, Martin Bladen (1744–1805), 2d Bn Hawke, M.P. Saltash 1768–74 (DNB; GEC; *Eton Coll. Reg.*).

HAWKESBURY, Bn, *see* JENKINSON, Charles and Robert Bankes.

2188. HAWKINS, Christopher (1758–1829), 1st Bt, M.P. St. Michael 1784–99, Grampound 1800–7, Penryn 1818–20, St. Ives 1821–28 (GEC; *Etoniana, 94,* 695).

2189. HAWKINS, John Heywood (1802–77), M.P. St. Michael 1830–31, Tavistock 1831–32, Newport 1832–41 (*Alumni Cantab.*).

2190. HAWKINS, Philip (ca 1701–38), M.P. Grampound 1727–38 (*Alumni Cantab.*).

2191. HAWKINS, Thomas (ca 1728–70), M.P. Grampound 1747–54 (GEC).

HAWKSWORTH, Walter Ramsden, *see* FAWKES, Walter Ramsden.

2192. HAWTHORNE, Charles Stewart, M.P. Downpatrick 1802–6, 1812–15.

2193. HAY, Adam (d. 1775), M.P. Peebles-shire 1767–68, 1775–75 (Buchan's *Peebleshire, 2,* 364; Foster's *Scots M.P.'s*).

2194. HAY, Adam (1795–1867), 7th Bt, M.P. Linlithgow burghs 1826–30 (GEC).

2195. HAY, Charles (ca 1700–60), M.P. Haddingtonshire 1741–47 (DNB; *Scots Peerage* sub Tweeddale).

2196. HAY, George (1715–78), M.P. Stockbridge 1754–56, Calne 1757–61, Sandwich 1761–68, Newcastle-under-Lyme 1768–78 (DNB).

2197. HAY, John (1788–1838), 6th Bt, M.P. Peebles-shire 1831–37 (GEC).

2198. HAY, John (1793–1851), M.P. Haddingtonshire 1826–31, Windsor 1847–50 (DNB; *Scots Peerage* sub Tweeddale).

2199. HAY, Thomas (1710–87), 9th E. of Kinnoull, M.P. Scarborough 1736–36, Cambridge borough 1741–58 (DNB; GEC; *Old Westminsters*).

2200. HAY, Thomas (ca 1733–86), M.P. Lewes 1768–80 (Berry's *County Geneal.: Sussex,* p. 118; Nichols' *Lit. Anec., 6,* 356).

2201. HAY, William (1695–1755), M.P. Seaford 1734–55 (*Alumni Oxon.;* DNB).

2202. HAYES, Edmund Samuel (1806–60), 3d Bt, M.P. Donegal 1831–60 (GEC).

2203. HAYES, James (1715–1800), M.P. Downton 1753–57, 1761–68, 1771–74 (*Alumni Cantab.; Eton Coll. Reg.;* Williams' *Great Sessions in Wales*).

HAYES, William Parnell, *see* PARNELL-HAYES, William.

2204. HAYLEY, George (d. 1781), M.P. London 1774–81 (Beaven's *Aldermen of London; Lloyd's Evening Post,* 29–31 Aug. 1781).

2205. HAYNES, Samuel (d. 1811), M.P. Brackley 1789–1802 (*Gent. Mag., 1,* 682).

2206. HAYWARD, Thomas (ca 1702–81), M.P. Ludgershall 1741–47, 1754–61 (DNB).

HEADFORT, 2d M. of, *see* TAYLOUR, Thomas.

HEADLEY, Bn, *see* ALLANSON-WINN, George, *and* WINN-ALLANSON, Charles.

HEATH, John, *see* DUKE, John.

2207. HEATH, Richard (ca 1706–52), M.P. Bossiney 1747–52 (*Alumni Oxon.; Old Westminsters*).

2208. HEATHCOTE, George (1700–68), M.P. Hindon 1727–34, Southwark 1734–41, London 1741–47 (*Alumni Cantab.;* Beaven's *Aldermen of London;* E. D. Heathcote, *Account of . . . Heathcote,* pp. 69–72).

2209. HEATHCOTE, Gilbert (ca 1724–85), 3d Bt, M.P. Shaftesbury 1761–68 (*Alumni Cantab.;* GEC).

2210. HEATHCOTE, Gilbert (1773–1851), 4th Bt, M.P. Lincolnshire 1796–1807, Rutland 1812–41 (GEC; E. D. Heathcote, *Account of . . . Heathcote,* p. 91).

2211. HEATHCOTE, Gilbert John (1795–1867), 1st Bn Aveland, M.P. Boston 1820–30, 1831–32, Lincolnshire (parts of Kesteven and Holland) 1832–41, Rutland 1841–56 (*Alumni Cantab.;* GEC; *Old Westminsters*).

2212. HEATHCOTE, John (ca 1689–1759), 2d Bt, M.P. Grantham 1715–22, Bodmin 1733–41 (GEC; *Notes and Queries, 179,* 82).

2213. HEATHCOTE, John (ca 1727–95), M.P. Rutland 1790–95 (*Alumni Cantab.;* Burke's *LG;* E. D. Heathcote, *Account of . . . Heathcote,* pp. 95–96).

2214. HEATHCOTE, John (1767–1838), M.P. Gatton 1796–98, Ripon 1798–
1806 (Burke's *LG;* E. D. Heathcote, *Account of . . . Heathcote,*
pp. 95–96).

2215. HEATHCOTE, Richard Edensor (1780–1850), M.P. Coventry 1826–
30, Stoke 1835–36 (E. D. Heathcote, *Account of . . . Heathcote,* pp. 95–96; *Old Westminsters*).

2216. HEATHCOTE, Samuel (1699–1775), M.P. Berealston 1740–47 (E. D.
Heathcote, *Account of . . . Heathcote,* p. 107; *Linc. Inn Reg.*).
HEATHCOTE, Thomas Freeman, *see* FREEMAN-HEATHCOTE, Thomas.

2217. HEATHCOTE, William (1693–1751), 1st Bt, M.P. Buckingham borough 1722–27, Southampton borough 1729–41 (GEC).

2218. HEATHCOTE, William (1746–1819), 3d Bt, M.P. Hampshire 1790–
1806 (GEC).

2219. HEATHCOTE, William (1801–81), 5th Bt, M.P. Hampshire 1826–31,
North Hampshire 1837–49, Oxford Univ. 1854–68 (GEC).

2220. HEBER, Richard (1774–1833), M.P. Oxford Univ. 1821–26 (DNB;
Genealogist, N.S., *21,* 262; *Notes and Queries,* 7th Ser., *9,* 310).

2221. HEDGES, John (1688–1737), M.P. St. Michael 1722–27, Bossiney
1727–34, Fowey 1734–37 (*Alumni Cantab.; Misc. Geneal. et
Herald.,* 5th Ser., *2*).

2222. HEDWORTH, John (1683–1747), M.P. Durham Co. 1713–47 (*Alumni
Oxon.;* Surtees' *Durham, 2,* 151).

2223. HELY-HUTCHINSON, Christopher (1767–1826), M.P. Cork City
1802–12, 1818–26 (*Alumni Dublin.;* DNB).

2224. HELY-HUTCHINSON, John (1757–1832), 2d E. of Donoughmore,
M.P. Cork City 1801–1 (DNB; GEC; *Eton Coll. Reg.*).

2225. HELY-HUTCHINSON, John (ca 1787–1851), 3d E. of Donoughmore,
M.P. Tipperary 1826–30, 1831–32 (DNB; GEC; *Alumni Dublin.*).

2226. HELY-HUTCHINSON, John (ca 1795–1842), M.P. Cork City 1826–30
(Burke's *Peerage* sub Donoughmore).

2227. HENDERSON, Anthony (ca 1763–1810), M.P. Brackley 1803–10
(*Alumni Oxon.; Gent. Mag., 1,* 597; *1806 List*).

2228. HENDERSON, John (1752–1817), 5th Bt, M.P. Fifeshire 1780–80,
Dysart burghs 1780–84, Seaford 1785–86, Stirling burghs 1806–7
(GEC; Grant's *Faculty of Advocates*).

2229. HENEAGE, George Fieschi (1800–68), M.P. Great Grimsby 1826–
30, Lincoln City 1831–34, 1852–62 (*Alumni Cantab.;* Boase).
HENEAGE, John Walker, *see* WALKER-HENEAGE, John.

2230. HENLEY, Henry Holt (d. 1748), M.P. Lyme Regis 1722–27, 1728–
48 (Musgrave's *Obituary*).

2231. HENLEY, Robert (ca 1682–1758), M.P. Lyme Regis 1748–54
(*Alumni Oxon.;* Hutchins' *Dorset, 3,* 744).

2232. HENLEY, Robert (ca 1708–72), 1st E. of Northington, M.P. Bath
1747–57 (DNB; GEC; *Old Westminsters*).

2233. HENLEY, Robert (1747–86), 2d E. of Northington, M.P. Hampshire 1768–72 (DNB; GEC; *Old Westminsters*).

2234. HENLEY, Robert Henley (1789–1841), 2d Bn Henley, M.P. Fowey 1826–30 (DNB; GEC).

2235. HENLEY-ONGLEY, Robert (ca 1724–85), 1st Bn Ongley, M.P. Bedford borough 1754–61, Bedfordshire 1761–80, 1784–85 (GEC).

2236. HENNIKER, John (1724–1803), 1st Bn Henniker, M.P. Sudbury 1761–68, Dover 1774–84 (GEC).

2237. HENNIKER-MAJOR, John (1752–1821), 2d Bn Henniker, M.P. New Romney 1785–90, Steyning 1794–1802, Rutland 1805–12, Stamford 1812–18 (GEC).

2238. HEPBURN, Robert Rickart (ca 1720–1804), M.P. Kincardineshire 1768–74 (Foster's *Scots M.P.'s*).

2239. HEPBURNE-SCOTT, Francis (1800–67), 7th Bn Polwarth, M.P. Roxburghshire 1826–32 (GEC; *Scots Peerage*).

2240. HEPBURNE-SCOTT, Hugh (1758–1841), 6th Bn Polwarth, M.P. Berwickshire 1780–84 (GEC).

2241. HERBERT, Charles (1743–1816), M.P. Wilton 1775–80, 1806–16 (*Eton Coll. Reg.; Gent. Mag., 2,* 286).

2242. HERBERT, Edward (ca 1701–70), M.P. Ludlow 1754–70 (*Alumni Oxon.;* Burke's *Irish LG*).

2243. HERBERT, Edward (1785–1848), 2d E. of Powis, M.P. Ludlow 1806–39 (*Alumni Cantab.;* DNB; GEC).

2244. HERBERT, Edward Charles Hugh (1802–52), M.P. Callington 1831–32 (*Alumni Oxon.;* Burke's *Peerage* sub Carnarvon; *Eton Lists*).

2245. HERBERT, Francis, M.P. Montgomery borough 1748–54 (Williams' *Wales M.P.'s*).

2246. HERBERT, George Augustus (1759–1827), 11th E. of Pembroke, M.P. Wilton 1780–84, 1788–94 (DNB; GEC; *Harrow Reg.*).

2247. HERBERT, Henry (d. 1748), M.P. Montgomery borough 1747–48 (Williams' *Wales M.P.'s*).

2248. HERBERT, Henry (1741–1811), 1st E. of Carnarvon, M.P. Wilton 1768–80 (*Alumni Cantab.;* GEC; *Eton Coll. Reg.*).

2249. HERBERT, Henry Arthur (ca 1703–72), 1st E. of Powis, M.P. Bletchingley 1724–27, Ludlow 1727–43 (GEC).

2250. HERBERT, Henry Arthur (ca 1756–1821), M.P. East Grinstead 1782–86, Kerry 1806–12, Tralee 1812–13 (*Alumni Cantab.;* Burke's *Irish LG; Harrow Reg.;* Namier).

2251. HERBERT, Henry George (1772–1833), 2d E. of Carnarvon, M.P. Cricklade 1794–1811 (GEC; *Eton Coll. Reg.*).

2252. HERBERT, Henry John George (1800–49), 3d E. of Carnarvon, M.R. Wootton Bassett 1831–32 (DNB; GEC).

2253. HERBERT, James (d. 1740), M.P. Oxford City 1739–40 (Lipscomb's *Bucks, 1,* 298; Williams' *Oxford M.P.'s*).

2254. HERBERT, Nicholas (ca 1706–75), M.P. Newport 1740–54, Wilton

1757–75 (*Alumni Oxon.; Eton Coll. Reg.; Gent. Mag., 1* [1829], 207).

2255. HERBERT, Philip (ca 1717–49), M.P. Oxford City 1740–49 (Williams' *Oxford M.P.'s*).

2256. HERBERT, Richard (ca 1705–54), M.P. Ludlow 1727–41, 1743–54 (*Alumni Cantab., supp.;* Shrop. Archaeol. Soc. *Trans.*, 2d Ser., *7*, 41).

2257. HERBERT, Robert Sawyer (ca 1693–1769), M.P. Wilton 1722–68 (*Alumni Oxon.;* Burke's *Peerage* sub Pembroke).

2258. HERBERT, Thomas (ca 1695–1739), M.P. Newport 1726–39 (Burke's *Peerage* sub Pembroke; *Notes and Queries*, 12th Ser., *3*, 11, 234).

2259. HERBERT, Thomas (ca 1727–79), M.P. Ludlow 1770–74 (*Alumni Cantab., supp.;* Burke's *Irish LG*).

2260. HERBERT, William (ca 1696–1757), M.P. Wilton 1734–57 (Burke's *Peerage* sub Carnarvon.; *Notes and Queries*, 12th Ser., *2*, 230).

2261. HERBERT, William (1778–1847), M.P. Hampshire 1806–7, Cricklade 1811–12 (DNB; *Eton Coll. Reg.*).

HEREFORD, 10th Vct, *see* DEVEREUX, Price.

2262. HERNE, Francis (d. 1776), M.P. Bedford borough 1754–68, Camelford 1774–76 (Musgrave's *Obituary*).

2263. HERON, Patrick (d. 1761), M.P. Kirkcudbright Stewarty 1727–41 (Foster's *Scots M.P.'s*).

2264. HERON, Patrick (ca 1732–1803), M.P. Kirkcudbright Stewarty 1795–1803 (Addison's *Glasgow Matric. Albums;* Foster's *Scots M.P.'s*).

2265. HERON, Peter (1770–1848), M.P. Newton 1806–14 (Bean; Burke's *LG* [ed. 1849]; Pink).

2266. HERON, Robert (1765–1854), 2d Bt, M.P. Great Grimsby 1812–18, Peterborough 1819–47 (*Alumni Cantab.;* DNB; GEC).

2267. HERON-MAXWELL, John Shaw Stewart (1772–1830), 4th Bt, M.P. Dumfries burghs 1807–12 (GEC).

2268. HERRIES, John Charles (1778–1855), M.P. Harwich 1823–41, Stamford 1847–53 (DNB).

2269. HERRIES, Robert (ca 1730–1815), M.P. Dumfries burghs 1780–84 (Foster's *Scots M.P.'s; Misc. Geneal. et Herald.*, 4th Ser., *4*).

HERTFORD, M. of, *see* SEYMOUR-CONWAY, Francis Charles and Richard; *also* INGRAM-SEYMOUR-CONWAY, Francis.

2270. HERVEY, Augustus John (1724–79), 3d E. of Bristol, M.P. Bury 1757–63, 1768–75, Saltash 1763–68 (DNB; GEC; *Old Westminsters*).

2271. HERVEY, Felton (1712–73), M.P. Bury 1747–61 (GEC sub Bristol; *Eton Coll. Reg.*).

2272. HERVEY, Frederick William (1769–1859), 1st M. of Bristol, M.P. Bury 1796–1803 (*Alumni Cantab.;* GEC).

2273. HERVEY, Frederick William (1800–64), 2d M. of Bristol, M.P. Bury 1826–59 (*Alumni Cantab.;* GEC).

2274. HERVEY, John (1696–1764), M.P. Reigate 1739–41, Wallingford 1754–64 (*Notes and Queries,* 9th Ser., *4,* 51; Williams' *Great Sessions in Wales*).

2275. HERVEY, Thomas (1699–1775), M.P. Bury 1733–47 (DNB; *Old Westminsters*).

2276. HERVEY, William (1732–1815), M.P. Bury 1763–68 (*Alumni Cantab.; Old Westminsters*).

2277. HEWETT, John (ca 1722–87), M.P. Notts 1747–74 (*Alumni Cantab.;* Maddison's *Lincs Pedigrees*).

2278. HEWITT, James (ca 1709–89), 1st Vct Lifford, M.P. Coventry 1761–66 (DNB; GEC).

HEWITT, William Hughes, *see* HUGHES-HUGHES, William.

2279. HEY, William (ca 1734–97), M.P. Sandwich 1774–76 (*Gent. Mag., 1,* 261).

2280. HEYGATE, William (1782–1844), 1st Bt, M.P. Sudbury 1818–26 (Burke's *Peerage;* Foster's *Baronetage*).

2281. HEYWOOD, Benjamin (1793–1865), 1st Bt, M.P. Lancashire 1831–32 (Addison's *Glasgow Matric. Albums;* Burke's *Peerage;* DNB).

2282. HEYWOOD, James Modyford (ca 1730–98), M.P. Fowey 1768–74 (*Alumni Cantab.; Eton Coll. Reg.; Gent. Mag., 1,* 356).

2283. HIBBERT, George (1757–1837), M.P. Seaford 1806–12 (DNB; Cussans' *Herts, 3* pt. 2, 179; Hunter's *Familiae Min. Gent.*).

2284. HICKS-BEACH, Michael (1760–1830), M.P. Cirencester 1794–1818 (*Alumni Oxon.;* Burke's *LG;* Williams' *Worcester M.P.'s*).

HICKS-BEACH, William, *see* BEACH, William.

2285. HILDYARD, Robert (1716–81), 3d Bt, M.P. Great Bedwin 1754–61 (*Alumni Cantab.;* GEC; *Eton Coll. Reg.*).

2286. HILL, Andrew (d. 1755), M.P. Bishop's Castle 1741–47 (Musgrave's *Obituary;* Shrop. Archaeol. Soc. *Trans.,* 2d Ser., *10*).

2287. HILL, Arthur (1753–1801), 2d M. of Downshire, M.P. Lostwithiel 1774–80, Malmesbury 1780–84 (GEC; *Eton Coll. Reg.*).

2288. HILL, Arthur Moyses William (1793–1860), 2d Bn Sandys, M.P. Down 1817–36 (GEC; *Eton Lists*).

2289. HILL, George Augusta (1801–79), M.P. Carrickfergus 1830–32 (Burke's *Peerage* sub Downshire; Boase).

2290. HILL, George Fitzgerald (1763–1839), 2d Bt, M.P. Londonderry Co. 1801–2, Londonderry City 1802–30 (*Alumni Dublin.;* GEC).

2291. HILL, John (ca 1700–53), M.P. Higham Ferrers 1747–53 (*Alumni Oxon.;* Musgrave's *Obituary*).

2292. HILL, John (1740–1824), 3d Bt, M.P. Shrewsbury 1784–96, 1805–6 (GEC; *Shrewsbury School Reg.*).

2293. HILL, Noel (1745–89), 1st Bn Berwick, M.P. Shrewsbury 1768–74, Salop 1774–84 (*Alumni Cantab.;* GEC).

2294. HILL, Richard (1732–1808), 2d Bt, M.P. Shropshire 1780–1806 (DNB; GEC; *Old Westminsters; Shrewsbury School Reg.*).

2295. HILL, Rowland (1705–83), 1st Bt, M.P. Lichfield 1734–41 (Burke's *Peerage;* GEC; Wedgwood).

2296. HILL, Rowland (1772–1842), 1st Vct Hill, M.P. Shrewsbury 1812–14 (DNB; GEC).

2297. HILL, Rowland (1800–75), 2d Vct Hill, M.P. Salop 1821–32, North Salop 1832–42 (GEC; *Harrow Reg.*).

2298. HILL, Thomas (ca 1693–1782), M.P. Shrewsbury 1749–68 (GEC sub Berwick; Musgrave's *Obituary;* Namier).

2299. HILL, Thomas (1721–76), M.P. Leominster 1774–76 (Burke's *LG;* Musgrave's *Obituary;* Namier).

HILL, William, *see* NOEL-HILL, William.

2300. HILL, Wills (1718–93), 1st M. of Downshire, M.P. Warwick borough 1741–56 (DNB; GEC).

2301. HILL-TREVOR, Arthur (1798–1862), 3d Vct Dungannon, M.P. New Romney 1830–31, Durham City 1831–32, 1835–41, 1843–43 (DNB; GEC; *Harrow Reg.*).

2302. HILLIARD, Edward (d. 1815), M.P. Horsham 1802–6 (*Gent. Mag., 1* [1816], 88; *1806 List; Linc. Inn Reg.;* cf. *Alumni Oxon.*).

HILLSBOROUGH, Vct and E. of, *see* HILL, Arthur and Wills.

HINCHINBROKE, Vct, *see* MONTAGU, George John and John.

HINDE, John Hodgson, *see* HODGSON-HINDE, John.

2303. HINXMAN, Joseph (ca 1702–40), M.P. Christchurch 1727–40 (*Alumni Oxon.;* Kirby's *Winchester Scholars,* p. 225).

2304. HIPPISLEY, John Coxe (1747–1825), 1st Bt, M.P. Sudbury 1790–96, 1802–18 (DNB; GEC; *Genealogists Mag., 6,* 506).

2305. HOARE, Henry (1705–85), M.P. Salisbury 1734–41 (Hoare's *Modern Wiltshire, 5,* 14; Burke's *Peerage;* Lipscomb's *Bucks, 4,* 390).

2306. HOARE-HUME, William (1772–1815), M.P. Wicklow 1801–15 (Burke's *Irish LG*).

2307. HOBART, George (1731–1804), 3d E. of Buckinghamshire, M.P. St. Ives 1754–61, Berealston 1761–80 (DNB; GEC; *Old Westminsters*).

HOBART, George Robert, *see* HAMPDEN, George Robert.

2308. HOBART, Henry (1738–99), M.P. Norwich 1786–99 (*Old Westminsters*).

2309. HOBART, John (1723–93), 2d E. of Buckinghamshire, M.P. Norwich 1747–56 (*Alumni Cantab.;* DNB; GEC; *Old Westminsters*).

2310. HOBART, Robert (1760–1816), 4th E. of Buckinghamshire, M.P. Bramber 1788–90, Lincoln City 1790–96 (DNB; GEC; *Old Westminsters*).

2311. HOBHOUSE, Benjamin (1757–1831), 1st Bt, M.P. Bletchingley 1797–1802, Grampound 1802–6, Hindon 1806–18 (DNB).

2312. HOBHOUSE, John Cam (1786–1869), 1st Bn Broughton, M.P. West-

minster 1820–33, Nottingham borough 1834–47, Harwich 1848–
51 (DNB; GEC; *Old Westminsters*).

2313. HOBLYN, Robert (1710–56), M.P. Bristol 1742–54 (DNB; Burke's
Family Records; Eton Coll. Reg.; Williams' *Gloucester M.P.'s*).

2314. HOBY, Thomas (ca 1714–44), 4th Bt, M.P. Great Marlow 1732–44
(GEC).

2315. HODGES, Thomas Law (1776–1857), M.P. Kent 1830–32, West Kent
1832–41, 1847–52 (*Alumni Cantab.;* Boase; *Harrow Reg.*).

2316. HODGETTS-FOLEY, John Hodgetts (1797–1861), M.P. Droitwich
1822–34, East Worcestershire 1847–61 (Burke's *LG;* Williams'
Worcester M.P.'s).

HODGKINSON, Robert Banks, *see* BANKS-HODGKINSON, Robert.

2317. HODGSON, Frederick (ca 1795–1854), M.P. Barnstable 1824–30,
1831–32, 1837–47 (Boase; *Notes and Queries,* 7th Ser., *6,* 417).

2318. HODGSON-HINDE, John (1806–69), M.P. Newcastle-upon-Tyne
1830–34, 1836–47 (*Alumni Cantab.;* Boase; Burke's *LG*).

2319. HODSON, James Alexander (b. ca 1787), M.P. Wigan 1820–31
(*Alumni Cantab.;* Bean; Pink).

2320. HODSON, John (ca 1758–1828), M.P. Wigan 1802–20 (Pink).

2321. HOGHTON, Henry (ca 1678–1768), 5th Bt, M.P. Preston 1710–13,
1715–22, 1727–41, East Looe 1722–27 (GEC; Foster's *Lancashire Pedigrees;* Pink).

2322. HOGHTON, Henry (1728–95), 6th Bt, M.P. Preston 1768–95 (GEC).

2323. HOGHTON, Henry Philip (1768–1835), 7th Bt, M.P. Preston 1795–
1802 (*Alumni Cantab.;* GEC).

2324. HOLBECH, William (ca 1748–1812), M.P. Banbury 1794–96 (*Eton
Coll. Reg.*).

2325. HOLBURNE, Francis (ca 1704–71), M.P. Stirling burghs 1761–68,
Plymouth 1768–71 (DNB).

2326. HOLDEN, Samuel (ca 1670–1740), M.P. East Looe 1735–40 (*Notes
and Queries,* 12th Ser., *12,* 31; *159,* 443; *160,* 33; *179,* 81).

2327. HOLDSWORTH, Arthur (ca 1757–87), M.P. Dartmouth 1780–87
(*Alumni Cantab.; Eton Coll. Reg.*).

2328. HOLDSWORTH, Arthur Howe (ca 1780–1860), M.P. Dartmouth
1802–20, 1829–32 (Burke's *LG;* Boase; *Devon and Cornwall
Notes and Queries, 10,* 235; *Eton Lists; 1832 List*).

2329. HOLFORD, George Peter (1767–1839), M.P. Bossiney 1803–6, Lostwithiel 1807–12, Dungannon 1812–18, Hastings 1818–20, Queenborough 1820–26 (*Alumni Cantab.; Harrow Reg.*).

HOLLAND, Bn, *see* Fox, Henry, Henry Edward, and Stephen.

2330. HOLLAND, Henry (b. ca 1774), M.P. Okehampton 1802–6 (*Alumni
Cantab.; Harrow Reg.*).

2331. HOLLAND, Nathaniel (1735–1811), 1st Bt, M.P. East Grinstead
1790–1802, 1807–11, Great Bedwin 1802–6 (DNB; GEC; *Merchant Taylor School Reg.*).

2332. HOLLAND, Rogers (d. 1761), M.P. Chippenham 1727–37 (Williams'
        Great Sessions in Wales).

HOLLIS, Thomas Brand, *see* BRAND-HOLLIS, Thomas.

2333. HOLME-SUMNER, George (1760–1838), M.P. Ilchester 1787–90,
        Guildford 1790–96, 1806–7, 1830–31, Surrey 1807–26 (*Harrow
        Reg.; Gent. Mag., 2*, 326).

2334. HOLMES, Charles (1711–61), M.P. Newport (Hants) 1758–61
        (DNB).

2335. HOLMES, Henry (ca 1703–62), M.P. Newtown (Hants) 1741–47,
        Yarmouth (Hants) 1747–62 (Burke's *Ext. Peerage, 2* [ed. 1866],
        282; Musgrave's *Obituary;* Namier).

HOLMES, Leonard Thomas Worsley and Richard Fleming Worsley,
        see WORSLEY-HOLMES, Leonard Thomas and Richard Fleming.

2336. HOLMES, Thomas (1699–1764), 1st Bn Holmes, M.P. Newtown
        (Hants) 1727–29, 1734–41, Yarmouth (Hants) 1747–64 (GEC).

2337. HOLMES, William (ca 1778–1851), M.P. Grampound 1808–12,
        Tregony 1812–18, Totnes 1818–20, Bishop's Castle 1820–30,
        Haslemere 1830–32, Berwick-on-Tweed 1837–41 (*Alumni Dub-
        lin.;* DNB; *1832 List*).

HOLMESDALE, Vct, *see* AMHERST, William Pitt.

HOLROYD, John Baker, *see* BAKER-HOLROYD, John.

2338. HOLT, Rowland (ca 1723–86), M.P. Suffolk 1759–68, 1771–80
        (*Alumni Oxon.;* Burke's *LG* sub Wilson; Howard's *Visitation of
        Suffolk, 2*, 54).

2339. HOLTE, Charles (ca 1722–82), 6th Bt, M.P. Warwickshire 1774–80
        (GEC).

2340. HOLTE, Lister (ca 1721–70), 5th Bt, M.P. Lichfield 1741–47 (GEC;
        Wedgwood).

2341. HOME, Patrick (1728–1808), M.P. Berwickshire 1784–96 (Burke's
        LG; Foster's *Scots M.P.'s;* Grant's *Faculty of Advocates*).

2342. HOME-DRUMMOND, Henry (1783–1867), M.P. Stirlingshire
        1821–31, Perthshire 1840–52 (*Alumni Oxon.;* Burke's *LG* sub
        Moray).

2343. HOMFRAY, Samuel (ca 1756–1822), M.P. Stafford borough 1818–20
        (Hunter's *Familiae Min. Gent.; Gent. Mag., 1*, 572; Wedgwood).

2344. HONYMAN, Richard Bemptde Johnstone (1787–1842), 2d Bt, M.P.
        Orkney and Shetland 1812–18 (Burke's *Peerage; Eton Lists;*
        Foster's *Scots M.P.'s*).

2345. HONYMAN, Robert (ca 1781–1808), M.P. Orkney and Shetland
        1806–7 (Burke's *Peerage;* Foster's *Scots M.P.'s*).

2346. HONYMAN, Robert (ca 1765–1848), M.P. Orkney and Shetland
        1796–1806 (Burke's *Peerage;* Foster's *Scots M.P.'s; Gent. Mag.,
        2*, 423; O'Byrne's *Naval Biog. Dict.*).

2347. HONYWOOD, Filmer (ca 1745–1809), M.P. Steyning 1774–80, Kent

1780–96, 1802–6 (*Alumni Oxon.;* Burke's *Peerage;* Chancellor's *Essex Monuments,* p. 140; *Gent. Mag., 1,* 588).

2348. HONYWOOD, Fraser (d. 1764), M.P. Steyning 1759–64 (Burke's *Peerage;* Musgrave's *Obituary; Topographer and Genealogist, 2,* 191).

2349. HONYWOOD, John (ca 1757–1806), 4th Bt, M.P. Steyning 1784–85, 1788–90, Canterbury 1790–96, 1797–1802, Honiton 1802–6 (GEC).

2350. HONYWOOD, Philip (ca 1710–85), M.P. Appleby 1754–56, 1756–84 (Chancellor's *Essex Monuments,* p. 119; *Notes and Queries,* 12th Ser., *2,* 353).

2351. HONYWOOD, William (ca 1760–1818), M.P. Kent 1806–12 (Chancellor's *Essex Monuments,* p. 140; *Gent. Mag., 1,* 379; *Notes and Queries,* 12th Ser., *4,* 264).

2352. HONYWOOD, William Philip (ca 1790–1831), M.P. Kent 1818–30 (Chancellor's *Essex Monuments,* p. 140; *Rugby Reg.*).

2353. HOOD, Alexander (1726–1814), 1st Vct Bridport, M.P. Bridgwater 1784–90, Buckingham borough 1790–96 (DNB; GEC).

2354. HOOD, Samuel (1724–1816), 1st Vct Hood, M.P. Westminster 1785–88, 1790–96, Reigate 1789–90 (DNB; GEC).

2355. HOOD, Samuel (1762–1814), 1st Bt, M.P. Westminster 1806–7, Bridport 1807–12 (DNB).

2356. HOOD, Samuel (1788–1868), 2d Bn Bridport, M.P. Heytesbury 1812–18 (*Alumni Cantab.;* GEC).

2357. HOOPER, Edward (ca 1702–95), M.P. Christchurch 1734–48 (*Alumni Oxon.*).

2358. HOPE, Alexander (1769–1837), M.P. Dumfries burghs 1796–1800, Linlithgowshire 1800–34 (DNB; *Scots Peerage* sub Hopetoun).

2359. HOPE, Charles (1763–1851), M.P. Dumfries burghs 1802–2, Edinburgh City 1803–4 (DNB; *Scots Peerage* sub Hopetoun).

2360. HOPE, Charles (1768–1828), M.P. Dysart burghs 1790–96, Haddingtonshire 1800–16 (*Scots Peerage* sub Hopetoun).

2361. HOPE, George Johnstone (1767–1818), M.P. East Grinstead 1815–18 (*Scots Peerage* sub Hopetoun).

2362. HOPE, Henry Thomas (1807–62), M.P. East Looe 1829–32, Gloucester City 1833–41, 1847–52 (*Alumni Cantab.*).

2363. HOPE, John (1739–85), M.P. Linlithgowshire 1768–70 (DNB; *Scots Peerage* sub Hopetoun).

2364. HOPE, John (1765–1823), 4th E. of Hopetoun, M.P. Linlithgowshire 1790–1800 (DNB; GEC).

HOPE, John Bruce, *see* BRUCE-HOPE, John.

2365. HOPE, John Thomas (1807–35), M.P. Gatton 1830–31, Okehampton 1831–32 (*Alumni Oxon.;* Bean; Burke's *LG;* Pink).

HOPE, William Johnstone, *see* JOHNSTONE-HOPE, William.

2366. HOPE-JOHNSTONE, John James (1796–1876), M.P. Dumfries-shire 1830–47, 1857–65 (Boase; *Scots Peerage* sub Hopetoun).

2367. HOPE-VERE, Charles (1710–91), M.P. Linlithgowshire 1743–68 (*Scots Peerage* sub Hopetoun).

2368. HOPE-VERE, James Joseph (1785–1843), M.P. Ilchester 1830–31, Newport (Hants) 1831–32 (*Alumni Cantab.; Scots Peerage* sub Hopetoun).

HOPETOUN, 4th E. of, *see* HOPE, John.

2369. HOPKINS, Benjamin (ca 1734–79), M.P. Great Bedwin 1771–74 (Burke's *LG* [ed. 1849]; Beaven's *Aldermen of London; Notes and Queries, 179,* 116).

HOPKINS, Benjamin Bond, *see* BOND-HOPKINS, Benjamin.

HOPKINS, John Probyn, *see* PROBYN-HOPKINS, John.

2370. HOPKINS, Richard (ca 1728–99), M.P. Dartmouth 1766–80, 1784–90, Thetford 1780–84, Queenborough 1790–96, Harwich 1796–99 (*Alumni Cantab.*).

2371. HOPTON, Edward Cope (1707–54), M.P. Hereford City 1741–47 (Burke's *LG;* Williams' *Hereford M.P.'s*).

2372. HORNBY, Edmund (1773–1857), M.P. Preston 1812–26 (*Alumni Cantab.;* Burke's *LG*).

2373. HORNE, William (ca 1774–1860), M.P. Helston 1812–18, Bletchingley 1831–31, Newtown (Hants) 1831–32, Marylebone 1832–34 (DNB).

2374. HORNE-TOOKE, John (1736–1812), M.P. Old Sarum 1801–2 (DNB; *Eton Coll. Reg.; Old Westminsters*).

2375. HORNER, Francis (1778–1817), M.P. St. Ives 1806–7, Wendover 1807–12, St. Mawes 1813–17 (DNB).

HORNER, Thomas Strangeways, *see* STRANGEWAYS-HORNER, Thomas.

2376. HORROCKS, John (1768–1804), M.P. Preston 1802–4 (DNB).

2377. HORROCKS, Samuel (1766–1842), M.P. Preston 1804–26 (Bean; Burke's *LG; Gent Mag., 2,* 430; Pink).

HORSEY, Spencer Horsey, *see* DE HORSEY, Spencer Horsey.

2378. HORT, Josiah William (1791–1876), 2d Bt, M.P. Kildare 1831–32 (*Alumni Cantab.;* GEC; *Old Westminsters*).

HORTON, Robert John Wilmot, *see* WILMOT-HORTON, Robert John.

2379. HOSKINS, Kedgwin (1775–1852), M.P. Herefordshire 1831–47 (Boase; *Williams' Hereford M.P.'s*).

2380. HOTHAM, Beaumont (1737–1814), 2d Bn Hotham, M.P. Wigan 1768–75 (DNB; GEC; *Old Westminsters*).

2381. HOTHAM, Beaumont (1794–1870), 3d Bn Hotham, M.P. Leominster 1820–31, 1831–41, Yorkshire (East Riding) 1841–68 (DNB; GEC; *Old Westminsters*).

2382. HOTHAM, Charles (1693–1738), 5th Bt, M.P. Beverley 1723–27, 1729–38 (GEC; Stirling's *Hothams*).

2383. HOTHAM, Charles (1729–94), 8th Bt, M.P. St. Ives 1761–68 (GEC; *Old Westminsters;* Stirling's *Hothams*).

2384. HOTHAM, Richard (ca 1723–99), M.P. Southwark 1780–84 (Dalloway's *Western Division of Sussex, 1,* pt. 2, 46; *Notes and Queries,* 11th Ser., *3,* 267).

2385. HOUBLON, Jacob (1710–70), M.P. Colchester 1735–41, Herts 1741–47, 1761–68 (*Alumni Cantab.*).

HOUBLON, John Archer, *see* ARCHER-HOUBLON, John.

2386. HOULDSWORTH, Thomas (1771–1852), M.P. Pontefract 1818–30, Newton 1830–32, North Nottinghamshire 1832–52 (Bean; Burke's *LG;* Pink).

2387. HOUSTOUN, Alexander (ca 1769–1822), M.P. Glasgow burghs 1802–3, 1809–12, 1818–20 (Addison's *Glasgow Matric. Albums;* Burke's *LG;* Foster's *Scots M.P.'s*).

HOWARD DE WALDEN, 4th Bn, *see* GRIFFIN, John Griffin.

2388. HOWARD, Charles (d. 1765), M.P. Carlisle 1727–61 (DNB).

2389. HOWARD, Charles (1719–41), M.P. Yorkshire 1741–41 (Gooder).

2390. HOWARD, Charles (1746–1815), 11th D. of Norfolk, M.P. Carlisle 1780–86 (DNB; GEC).

2391. HOWARD, Fulke Greville (1773–1846), M.P. Castle Rising 1808–32 (*Old Westminsters*).

2392. HOWARD, George (1718–96), M.P. Lostwithiel 1761–66, Stamford 1768–96 (DNB; *Old Westminsters*).

2393. HOWARD, George (1773–1848), 6th E. of Carlisle, M.P. Morpeth 1795–1806, Cumberland 1806–20 (DNB; GEC; *Eton Coll. Reg.*).

2394. HOWARD, George William Frederick (1802–64), 7th E. of Carlisle, M.P. Morpeth 1826–30, Yorkshire 1830–32, Yorkshire (West Riding) 1832–41, 1846–48 (DNB; GEC; Gooder).

2395. HOWARD, Henry (ca 1694–1758), 4th E. of Carlisle, M.P. Morpeth 1715–38 (DNB; GEC; *Eton Coll. Reg.*).

2396. HOWARD, Henry (1802–75), M.P. Steyning 1824–26, Shoreham 1826–32 (Burke's *Peerage* sub Norfolk; Boase; *Harrow Reg.*).

2397. HOWARD, Henry Charles (1791–1856), 13th D. of Norfolk, M.P. Horsham 1829–32, West Sussex 1832–41 (DNB; GEC).

2398. HOWARD, Henry Thomas (1766–1824), M.P. Arundel 1790–95, 1818–20, Gloucester City 1795–1818, Steyning 1820–24 (Burke's *Peerage* sub Norfolk; *Gent. Mag., 2,* 81).

2399. HOWARD, Philip Henry (1801–83), M.P. Carlisle 1830–47, 1848–52 (Boase; Burke's *Peerage* sub Norfolk).

2400. HOWARD, Ralph (ca 1801–73), 1st Bt, M.P. Wicklow 1829–47, 1848–52 (Boase; *Eton Lists;* Williams' *Worcester M.P.'s*).

2401. HOWARD, Richard (1748–1816), 4th E. of Effingham, M.P. Steyning 1784–90 (GEC; *Eton Coll. Reg.*).

2402. HOWARD, Thomas (1721–83), 14th E. of Suffolk, M.P. Castle Rising

1747–68, Malmesbury 1768–74, St. Michael 1774–79 (GEC; *Eton Coll. Reg.*).

2403. HOWARD, Thomas (1776–1851), 16th E. of Suffolk, M.P. Arundel 1802–6 (GEC; *Eton Coll. Reg.*).

2404. HOWARD, William (1714–56), M.P. Castle Rising 1737–47 (GEC; *Eton Coll. Reg.*).

2405. HOWARD, William (1781–1843), M.P. Morpeth 1806–26, 1830–32, Sutherland 1837–40 (*Alumni Oxon.; Bean; Burke's Peerage* sub Carlisle).

HOWARD-MOLYNEUX-HOWARD, Henry Thomas, *see* HOWARD, Henry Thomas.

2406. HOWARD-VYSE, Richard William (1784–1853), M.P. Beverley 1807–12, Honiton 1812–18 (DNB).

2407. HOWARTH, Henry (ca 1746–83), M.P. Abingdon 1782–83 (*Old Westminsters; Williams' Worcester M.P.'s*).

2408. HOWARTH, Humphrey (ca 1685–1755), M.P. Radnorshire 1722–55 (*Musgrave's Obituary; Williams' Wales M.P.'s*).

2409. HOWARTH, Humphrey (ca 1751–1827), M.P. Evesham 1806–7, 1808–20 (*Williams' Worcester M.P.'s*).

HOWDEN, 2d Bn, *see* CARADOC, John Hobart.

2410. HOWE, George Augustus (ca 1724–58), 3d Vct Howe, M.P. Nottingham borough 1747–58 (DNB; GEC; *Eton Coll. Reg.*).

2411. HOWE, John (d. 1742), 1st Bn Chedworth, M.P. Gloucester borough 1727–27, Wilts 1729–41 (GEC).

2412. HOWE, Richard (1726–99), 1st E. Howe, M.P. Dartmouth 1757–82 (DNB; GEC; *Eton Coll. Reg.; Old Westminsters*).

2413. HOWE, Stephens (d. 1796), M.P. Great Yarmouth 1795–96 (*Army Lists*).

2414. HOWE, Thomas (ca 1730–71), M.P. Northampton borough 1768–71 (Collins' *Peerage;* Clutterbuck's *Herts, 1,* 480).

2415. HOWE, William (1729–1814), 5th Vct Howe, M.P. Nottingham borough 1758–80 (DNB; GEC; *Eton Coll. Reg.*).

2416. HOWELL, David (ca 1751–1804), M.P. St. Michael 1784–96 (*Chetham Soc.,* N.S., *85,* 46).

HOWICK, Vct, *see* GREY, Henry George.

HOY, James Barlow, *see* BARLOW-HOY, James.

2417. HUCKS, Robert (1699–1745), M.P. Abingdon 1722–41 (*Alumni Cantab.;* Cussans' *Herts, 3,* pt. 1, 246, 252).

2418. HUCKS, William (d. 1740), M.P. Abingdon 1709–10, Wallingford 1715–40 (Cussans' *Herts, 3,* pt. 1, 246, 252; *Notes and Queries,* 12th Ser., *2,* 93).

2419. HUDLESTON, John (ca 1749–1835), M.P. Bridgwater 1804–6 (Burke's *LG; Genealogists Mag., 6,* 162).

2420. HUDSON, Giles (d. 1783), M.P. Chippenham 1780–83 (Musgrave's *Obituary*).

2421. Hudson, Harrington (1772–1826), M.P. Helston 1818–26 (*Alumni Cantab.; Old Westminsters*).

2422. Hudson, Thomas (ca 1772–1852), M.P. Evesham 1831–34 (Burke's *LG;* May's *Evesham,* p. 299; Williams' *Worcester M.P.'s*).

2423. Hughan, Thomas (d. 1811), M.P. East Retford 1806–7, Dundalk 1808–11 (*Gent. Mag., 2,* 491).

2424. Hughes, James (d. 1845), M.P. Grantham 1820–20, 1831–32 (MS, *ex inform.* John Bean King).

2425. Hughes, William Lewis (1767–1852), 1st Bn Dinorben, M.P. Wallingford 1802–31 (*Alumni Felsted.;* GEC).

2426. Hughes-Hughes, William (ca 1792–1874), M.P. Oxford City 1830–32, 1833–37 (Boase; Williams' *Oxford M.P.'s*).

2427. Hulkes, James (ca 1770–1821), M.P. Rochester 1802–6 (*Gent. Mag., 1,* 188; Smith's *Rochester in Parl.*).

2428. Hulse, Charles (1771–1854), 4th Bt, M.P. West Looe 1816–26, 1827–32 (GEC; *Eton Coll. Reg.*).

2429. Humberston, Thomas (d. 1755), M.P. Brackley 1754–55 (Musgrave's *Obituary*).

2430. Hume, Abraham (ca 1703–72), 1st Bt, M.P. Steyning 1747–54, Tregony 1761–68 (GEC; Clutterbuck's *Herts, 2,* 238).

2431. Hume, Abraham (1749–1838), 2d Bt, M.P. Petersfield 1774–80, Hastings 1807–18 (*Alumni Cantab.;* DNB; *Eton Coll. Reg.*).

2432. Hume, Alexander (ca 1693–1765), M.P. Southwark 1743–54, 1761–65, Steyning 1754–61 (Clutterbuck's *Herts, 2,* 238; Cussans' *Herts, 2,* pt. 2, 250).

Hume, Gustavus Rochfort, *see* Rochfort-Hume, Gustavus.

2433. Hume, Joseph (1777–1855), M.P. Weymouth and Melcombe Regis 1812–12, Aberdeen burghs 1818–30, 1842–55, Middlesex 1830–37, Kilkenny Co. 1837–41 (DNB).

Hume, William Hoare, *see* Hoare-Hume, William.

2434. Hume-Campbell, Hugh (1708–94), 3d E. of Marchmont, M.P. Berwick-on-Tweed 1734–40 (DNB; GEC).

2435. Humfrey, Paul (ca 1687–1751), M.P. Gatton 1745–51 (Manning and Bray's *Surrey, 2,* 237, 248).

Hungerford, John Peach, *see* Peach-Hungerford, John.

2436. Hungerford, Walter (d. 1754), M.P. Calne 1734–47 (Musgrave's *Obituary*).

2437. Hunt, George (ca 1721–98), M.P. Bodmin 1753–84 (*Alumni Oxon.;* Burke's *LG*).

2438. Hunt, Henry (1773–1835), M.P. Preston 1830–32 (DNB).

2439. Hunt, Joseph, M.P. Queenborough 1807–10.

2440. Hunt, Thomas (ca 1723–89), M.P. Bodmin 1784–89 (*Alumni Oxon.;* Burke's *LG*).

2441. Hunter, John (ca 1724–1802), M.P. Leominster 1784–97 (Cussans' *Herts, 3,* pt. 1, 288, 297; Williams' *Hereford M.P.'s*).

2442. HUNTER, Thomas Orby (d. 1769), M.P. Winchelsea 1741–59, 1760–69 (*Genealogist,* 1st Ser., *3,* 273; Musgrave's *Obituary*).

2443. HUNTER, William, M.P. Ilchester 1802–3.

2444. HUNTER-BLAIR, James (1741–87), 1st Bt, M.P. Edinburgh City 1781–84 (DNB; GEC).

2445. HUNTER-BLAIR, James (d. 1822), M.P. Wigtownshire 1816–22 (GEC; Foster's *Scots M.P.'s*).

HUNTINGFIELD, Bn, *see* VANNECK, Joshua.

HUNTLEY, 10th M. of, *see* GORDON, Charles.

2446. HURST, Robert (ca 1750–1843), M.P. Shaftesbury 1802–6, Steyning 1806–12, Horsham 1812–29 (Albery's *Horsham; Gent. Mag., 2,* 96).

2447. HUSKE, John (1724–73), M.P. Maldon 1763–73 (*Notes and Queries,* 12th Ser., *8,* 335).

2448. HUSKISSON, William (1770–1830), M.P. Morpeth 1796–1802, Liskeard 1804–7, Harwich 1807–12, Chichester 1812–23, Liverpool 1823–30 (DNB).

2449. HUSSEY, Richard (ca 1715–70), M.P. St. Michael 1755–61, St. Mawes 1761–68, East Looe 1768–70 (DNB).

2450. HUSSEY, Thomas (ca 1746–1824), M.P. Aylesbury 1809–14 (*Gent. Mag., 1,* 574).

2451. HUSSEY, William (1724–1813), M.P. St. Germans 1765–68, Hindon 1768–74, Salisbury 1774–1813 (*Gent. Mag., 1,* 188; Hoare's *Modern Wiltshire, 5,* 107; *1812 List*).

2452. HUSSEY-BICKERTON, Richard (1759–1832), 2d Bt, M.P. Poole 1808–12 (DNB; GEC).

2453. HUSSEY-DELAVAL, John (1728–1808), 1st Bn Delaval, M.P. Berwick-on-Tweed 1754–61, 1765–74, 1780–86 (*Alumni Cantab.;* GEC; *Old Westminsters*).

2454. HUSSEY-MONTAGU, Edward (ca 1721–1802), 1st E. Beaulieu, M.P. Tiverton 1758–62 (GEC).

2455. HUSSEY-MONTAGU, John (1747–87), M.P. Windsor 1772–87 (GEC sub Beaulieu; *Eton Coll. Reg.*).

2456. HUTCHINGS-MEDLYCOTT, Thomas (d. 1795), M.P. Milborne Port 1763–70, 1780–81 (Burke's *Peerage;* Musgrave's *Obituary*).

HUTCHINSON, *see* HELY-HUTCHINSON.

2457. HUXLEY, George (ca 1687–1744), M.P. Newport (Hants) 1726–41 (*Alumni Cantab.*).

HYDE, Bn, *see* VILLIERS, Thomas.

2458. HYDE, Henry (1710–53), Bn Hyde, M.P. Oxford Univ. 1732–51 (DNB; GEC).

2459. HYDE, John (ca 1775–1832), M.P. Youghal 1820–26 (*Alumni Dublin.;* Burke's *Irish LG*).

HYDE, Thomas Villiers, *see* VILLIERS, Thomas.

HYLTON, 1st Bn, *see* JOLLIFFE, William George Hylton.

2460. HYLTON, John (1699–1746), M.P. Carlisle 1727–41, 1742–46 (GEC sub Musgrave; Surtees' *Durham, 2,* 27).

2461. IDLE, Christopher (ca 1771–1819), M.P. Weymouth and Melcombe Regis 1813–18 (*Gent. Mag., 1,* 285).

ILCHESTER, E. of, *see* FOX-STRANGEWAYS, Henry Thomas and Stephen.

2462. IMPEY, Elijah (1732–1809), M.P. New Romney 1790–96 (*Alumni Cantab.;* DNB; *Old Westminsters*).

INCHIQUIN, Bn and E. of, *see* O'BRIEN, Lucius, Murrough, and William.

INGESTRE, Vct, *see* CHETWYND-TALBOT, Henry John.

2463. INGILBY, John (ca 1758–1815), 1st Bt, M.P. East Retford 1790–96 (*Alumni Cantab.;* GEC; *Eton Coll. Reg.*).

INGILBY, William Amcotts, *see* AMCOTTS-INGILBY, William.

2464. INGLETT-FORTESCUE, John (1758–1840), M.P. Callington 1801–3 (*Alumni Oxon.;* Burke's LG [ed. 1849]).

2465. INGLIS, Hugh (ca 1744–1820), 1st Bt, M.P. Ashburton 1802–6 (DNB sub Robert Harry Inglis; *Gent. Mag., 2,* 277).

2466. INGLIS, Robert Harry (1786–1855), 2d Bt, M.P. Dundalk 1824–26, Ripon 1828–29, Oxford Univ. 1829–54 (DNB).

2467. INGRAM, Charles (1696–1748), M.P. Horsham 1737–48 (GEC; *Scots Peerage*).

2468. INGRAM, Charles (1727–78), 9th Vct Irvine, M.P. Horsham 1747–63 (GEC; *Old Westminsters; Scots Peerage*).

2469. INGRAM, Henry (1691–1761), 7th Vct Irvine, M.P. Horsham 1722–36 (GEC; *Scots Peerage*).

2470. INGRAM-SEYMOUR-CONWAY, Francis (1743–1822), 2d M. of Hertford, M.P. Lostwithiel 1766–68, Orford 1768–94 (DNB; GEC; *Eton Coll. Reg.*).

2471. INNES, Hugh (ca 1764–1831), 1st Bt, M.P. Ross-shire 1809–12, Tain burghs 1812–30, Sutherlandshire 1831–31 (Addison's *Glasgow Matric. Albums;* Foster's *Scots M.P.'s*).

2472. INNES, John (d. 1838), M.P. Grampound 1818–26 (*Gent. Mag., 1* [1839], 105; *Notes and Queries, 159,* 153).

2473. INNES, William (ca 1720–95), M.P. Ilchester 1774–75 (*Court and City Register* [1776], p. 38; Musgrave's *Obituary*).

2474. INWEN, Thomas (d. 1743), M.P. Southwark 1730–43 (*Gent. Mag.,* p. 218; Namier).

2475. IRBY, William (1707–75), 1st Bn Boston, M.P. Launceston 1735–47, Bodmin 1747–61 (GEC; *Old Westminsters*).

2476. IRELAND-BLACKBURNE, John (1783–1874), M.P. Newton 1807–18, Warrington 1835–47 (*Alumni Oxon.;* Boase; Burke's *LG;* Pink).

IRNHAM, 1st Bn, *see* LUTTRELL, Simon.

2477. IRONMONGER, Richard (ca 1772–1826), M.P. Stafford borough 1826–26 (Wedgwood).

IRVINE, Vct, *see* INGRAM, Charles and Henry.

2478. IRVINE, Alexander (d. 1789), M.P. East Looe 1786–89 (*Gent. Mag.,* p. 1214).

IRVINE, Alexander Ramsay, *see* RAMSAY-IRVINE, Alexander.

2479. IRVING, John (ca 1767–1845), M.P. Bramber 1806–32, Antrim 1837–45 (Bean; *Gent. Mag., 1* [1846], 93; *1832 List*).

2480. IRWIN, John (ca 1728–88), M.P. East Grinstead 1762–83 (DNB).

2481. ISHAM, Edmund (1690–1772), 6th Bt, M.P. Northamptonshire 1737–72 (Barron's *Northampton Families,* p. 161; GEC).

2482. ISHAM, Justinian (1687–1737), 5th Bt, M.P. Northamptonshire 1730–37 (GEC).

2483. ISHERWOOD, Henry (d. 1797), M.P. Windsor 1796–97 (*Gent. Mag., 1* [1797], 350, and *1* [1798], 536).

2484. IVORY-TALBOT, John (d. 1772), M.P. Ludgershall 1715–22, Wilts 1727–41 (Burke's *LG; Notes and Queries,* 7th Ser., *10,* 214).

JACKSON, George, *see* DUCKETT, George.

2485. JACKSON, George (ca 1761–1805), M.P. Mayo 1801–2 (*Alumni Dublin.;* Burke's *Irish LG*).

2486. JACKSON, John (1763–1820), 1st Bt, M.P. Dover 1806–20 (Burke's *Peerage;* Foster's *Baronetage; Etoniana, 94,* 695).

2487. JACKSON, Josias, M.P. Southampton borough 1807–12.

2488. JACKSON, Richard (ca 1722–87), M.P. Weymouth and Melcombe Regis 1762–68, New Romney 1768–84 (*Alumni Cantab.;* DNB).

2489. JACOB, William (ca 1762–1851), M.P. Westbury 1806–7, Rye 1808–12 (DNB).

2490. JAFFRAY, John, M.P. East Retford 1802–6 (*1806 List*).

2491. JAMES, William (ca 1721–83), 1st Bt, M.P. West Looe 1774–83 (DNB; GEC).

2492. JAMES, William (1791–1861), M.P. Carlisle 1820–26, 1831–34, East Cumberland 1836–47 (*Alumni Cantab.;* Burke's *LG*).

2493. JAMES-KECK, Anthony (ca 1741–82), M.P. Leicester borough 1765–68, Newton 1768–80 (*Alumni Cantab.; Eng. Hist. Rev., 42* [1927], 413; *Eton Coll. Reg.;* Nichols' *Leicester, 2,* pt. 2, 861).

2494. JANSSEN, Stephen Theodore (d. 1777), 4th Bt, M.P. London 1747–54 (GEC; Nichols' *Lit. Anec., 3,* 408).

2495. JEAFFRESON, Christopher (1699–1749), M.P. Cambridge borough 1744–47, 1748–49 (Burke's *LG* [ed. 1849]; Oliver's *Antigua, 2,* 106).

2496. JEFFERY, John (ca 1751–1822), M.P. Poole 1796–1809 (*Gent. Mag., 1,* 574).

2497. JEFFERYS, Nathaniel, M.P. Coventry 1796–1803 (*Notes and Queries,* 6th Ser., *1,* 465; Whitley's *Coventry M.P.'s*).

2498. JEFFREY, Francis (1773–1850), M.P. Perth burghs 1831–31, 1831–32, Malton 1831–31, Edinburgh City 1832–34 (DNB).

2499. JEFFREYS, John (ca 1706–66), M.P. Brecon Co. 1734–47, Dartmouth 1747–66 (Devonshire Assoc. *Trans.*, *43*, 368; Williams' *Wales M.P.'s*).

2500. JEKYLL, Joseph (ca 1663–1738), M.P. Eye 1697–1713, Lymington 1713–22, Reigate 1722–38 (DNB).

2501. JEKYLL, Joseph (1754–1837), M.P. Calne 1787–1816 (DNB; Martin's *Masters of the Bench, Inner Temple; Old Westminsters*).

2502. JENISON, Ralph (1696–1758), M.P. Northumberland 1724–41, Newport (Hants) 1749–58 (*Alumni Cantab.; New Hist. of Northumberland, 13*, 248).

2503. JENKINS, Richard (1785–1853), M.P. Shrewsbury 1830–32, 1837–41 (*Bengal Past and Present, 24* [1922], 127; DNB).

2504. JENKINSON, Charles (1729–1808), 1st E. of Liverpool, M.P. Cockermouth 1761–66, Appleby 1767–72, Harwich 1772–74, Hastings 1774–80, Saltash 1780–86 (*Alumni Carthusiani;* DNB; GEC).

2505. JENKINSON, Charles (1779–1855), 10th Bt, M.P. Dover 1806–18 (GEC).

2506. JENKINSON, Charles Cecil Cope (1784–1851), 3d E. of Liverpool, M.P. Sandwich 1807–12, Bridgnorth 1812–18, East Grinstead 1818–28 (DNB; GEC).

2507. JENKINSON, John (1734–1805), M.P. Corfe Castle 1768–80 (*Alumni Carthusiani;* GEC).

2508. JENKINSON, Robert Bankes (1770–1828), 2d E. of Liverpool, M.P. Rye 1790–1803 (DNB; GEC).

2509. JENNINGS, George (ca 1721–90), M.P. Whitchurch 1757–68, St. Germans 1768–74, Thetford 1784–90 (*Alumni Cantab.; Old Westminsters*).

2510. JENNINGS-CLERKE, Philip (ca 1722–88), 1st Bt, M.P. Totnes 1768–88 (GEC; *Old Westminsters*).

2511. JENYNS, Soame (1704–87), M.P. Cambridgeshire 1741–54, Dunwich 1754–58, Cambridge borough 1758–80 (*Alumni Cantab.;* DNB).

2512. JEPHSON, Denham (ca 1748–1813), M.P. Mallow 1802–12 (*Alumni Oxon.;* Burke's *Peerage; Linc. Inn Reg.*).

2513. JEPHSON-NORREYS, Charles Denham Orlando (ca 1799–1888), 1st Bt, M.P. Mallow 1826–32, 1833–59 (*Alumni Oxon.;* Boase; Burke's *Peerage*).

JERMYN, E., *see* HERVEY, Frederick William.

JERNINGHAM, Henry Valentine Stafford, *see* STAFFORD-JERNINGHAM, Henry Valentine.

JERSEY, E. of, *see* VILLIERS, George Bussey; *also* CHILD-VILLIERS, George Augustus Frederick.

2514. JERVIS, John (1735–1823), 1st E. St. Vincent, M.P. Launceston 1783–84, Great Yarmouth 1784–90, Wycombe 1790–94 (DNB; GEC).

2515. JERVIS, Thomas (ca 1768–1838), M.P. Great Yarmouth 1802–6

(Burke's *Peerage,* sub St. Vincent; Esdaile's *Temple Church Monuments,* p. 156; Williamson's *Middle Temple Bench Book*).

JERVOISE, George Purefoy, *see* PUREFOY-JERVOISE, George.

JERVOISE, Jervoise Clarke and Thomas Clarke, *see* CLARKE-JERVOISE, Jervoise and Thomas.

2516. JESSOP, William (1665–1734), M.P. Aldborough 1702–13, 1715–34 (*Genealogist,* N.S., *17, 55; The Reliquary,* N.S., *4,* 213; Williams' *Great Sessions in Wales*).

2517. JEWKES, John (ca 1683–1743), M.P. Bridport 1730–34, Aldborough 1735–43 (*Alumni Cantab.; Eton Coll. Reg.*).

2518. JOCELYN, John (ca 1769–1828), M.P. Louth 1807–9, 1820–26 (Burke's *Peerage* sub Roden).

2519. JOCELYN, Robert (1788–1870), 3d E. of Roden, M.P. Louth 1806–7, 1810–20 (DNB; GEC; *Harrow Reg.*).

2520. JODRELL, Henry (ca 1750–1814), M.P. Great Yarmouth 1796–1802, Bramber 1802–12 (Burke's *Peerage; Eton Coll. Reg.*).

2521. JODRELL, Paul (1713–51), M.P. Old Sarum 1751–51 (*Alumni Oxon.;* Foster's *Baronetage*).

2522. JODRELL, Richard Paul (1745–1831), M.P. Seaford 1790–92, 1794–96 (DNB; *Eton Coll. Reg.*).

2523. JOHNES, Thomas (d. 1780), M.P. Radnorshire 1777–80 (Burke's *LG;* Williams' *Wales M.P.'s*).

2524. JOHNES, Thomas (1748–1816), M.P. Cardigan borough 1775–80, Radnorshire 1780–96, Cardiganshire 1796–1816 (DNB; *Eton Coll. Reg.*).

2525. JOHNSON, Richard (d. 1807), M.P. Milborne Port 1791–94 (*Annual Register,* p. 588; *Gent. Mag., 2,* 890; Philips' *East India Co.,* pp. 312, 343).

2526. JOHNSON, William Augustus (1777–1863), M.P. Boston 1821–26, Oldham 1837–47 (Bean; Boase; *Misc. Geneal. et Herald.,* N.S., *2;* Pink).

2527. JOHNSTON, Andrew (ca 1798–1862), M.P. Anstruther Easter burghs 1831–37 (Foster's *Scots M.P.'s;* Grant's *Faculty of Advocates*).

2528. JOHNSTON, James (1802–41), M.P. Stirling burghs 1830–32 (*Alumni Oxon.;* Foster's *Scots M.P.'s*).

2529. JOHNSTON, Peter (1749–1837), M.P. Kirkcudbright Stewarty 1780–81, 1782–86 (*Alumni Cantab.; Eton Coll. Reg.*).

2530. JOHNSTON, William (1760–1844), 7th Bt, M.P. Windsor 1797–1802 (GEC; *Harrow Reg.*).

JOHNSTONE, Andrew Cochrane, *see* COCHRANE-JOHNSTONE, Andrew.

2531. JOHNSTONE, George (ca 1730–87), M.P. Cockermouth 1768–74, Appleby 1774–80, Lostwithiel 1780–84, Ilchester 1786–87 (DNB).

2532. JOHNSTONE, George (ca 1767–1813), M.P. Aldeburgh 1800–2, Hedon 1802–13 (Bean; *Westminster Abbey Reg.*).

2533. JOHNSTONE, James (1697–1772), 3d Bt, M.P. Dumfries burghs 1743–54 (GEC; Grant's *Faculty of Advocates*).

2534. JOHNSTONE, James (1726–94), 4th Bt, M.P. Dumfries burghs 1784–90, Weymouth and Melcombe Regis 1791–94 (GEC).

2535. JOHNSTONE, John (1721–42), M.P. Dumfries burghs 1741–42 (Addison's *Glasgow Matric. Albums; Scots Peerage* sub Annandale).

2536. JOHNSTONE, John (1734–95), M.P. Dysart burghs 1774–80 (Burke's *Peerage;* Foster's *Scots M.P.'s*).

JOHNSTONE, John James Hope, *see* HOPE-JOHNSTONE, John James.

2537. JOHNSTONE, John Lowther (ca 1783–1811), 6th Bt, M.P. Weymouth and Melcombe Regis 1810–11 (Burke's *Peerage;* GEC).

JOHNSTONE, John Vanden Bempde, *see* VANDEN-BEMPDE-JOHNSTONE, John.

2538. JOHNSTONE, Richard (1732–1807), 1st Bt, M.P. Weymouth and Melcombe Regis 1790–96 (GEC).

2539. JOHNSTONE-HOPE, William (1766–1831), M.P. Dumfries burghs 1800–2, Dumfries-shire 1804–30 (DNB).

2540. JOHNSTONE-PULTENEY, William (1729–1805), 5th Bt, M.P. Cromartyshire 1768–74, Shrewsbury 1775–1805 (GEC; Foster's *Scots M.P.'s*).

2541. JOLLIFFE, Gilbert East (ca 1802–33), M.P. Petersfield 1830–31 (Burke's *Peerage* sub Hylton; *Gent. Mag., 1* [1834], 118).

2542. JOLLIFFE, Hylton (1773–1843), M.P. Petersfield 1796–97, 1802–30, 1831–32, 1833–34 (Burke's *Peerage* sub Hylton; *Old Westminsters*).

2543. JOLLIFFE, John (ca 1697–1771), M.P. Petersfield 1741–54, 1761–68 (*Old Westminsters*).

2544. JOLLIFFE, Thomas Samuel (ca 1746–1824), M.P. Petersfield 1780–87 (Burke's *LG* [ed. 1849]).

2545. JOLLIFFE, William (ca 1666–1750), M.P. Petersfield 1734–41 (Morant's *Essex, 2,* 453; Musgrave's *Obituary; Notes and Queries, 179,* 80).

2546. JOLLIFFE, William (ca 1745–1802), M.P. Petersfield 1768–1802 (*Alumni Oxon.;* Burke's *Peerage* sub Hylton; Manning and Bray's *Surrey, 2,* 263).

2547. JOLLIFFE, William George Hylton (1800–76), M.P. Petersfield 1830–32, 1837–38, 1841–66 (DNB; GEC).

2548. JONES, Gilbert (d. 1830), M.P. Aldeburgh 1806–12 (Bean; *Gent. Mag., 2,* 285).

2549. JONES, Henry (ca 1714–92), M.P. Devizes 1780–84 (Cunnington's *Annals of Devizes, 2,* 260; Musgrave's *Obituary*).

2550. JONES, Hugh Valence (1722–1800), M.P. Dover 1756–59 (Yorke's *Hardwicke, 1,* 36–37).

2551. JONES, John (1777–1842), M.P. Pembroke borough 1815–18, Carmarthen borough 1821–32, Carmarthenshire 1837–42 (*Alumni

Oxon.; Burke's *LG* [ed. 1849]; *Gent. Mag., 2,* 653; Williams' *Wales M.P.'s*).

2552. JONES, Robert (d. 1774), M.P. Huntingdon borough 1754–74 (Musgrave's *Obituary; British Topographer* [1790], pp. 50–51; *Wilts Archaeol. and Nat. Hist. Mag., 44* [1928], 106–7).

2553. JONES, Theobald (ca 1790–1868), M.P. Londonderry Co. 1830–57 (Boase; Burke's *Irish LG*).

2554. JONES, Theophilus (ca 1729–1811), M.P. Leitrim 1801–2 (Burke's *Irish LG; Jour. of Assoc. for Preserv. Mem. of Dead, Irel., 9,* 472).

2555. JONES, Thomas (1765–1811), 1st Bt, M.P. Weymouth and Melcombe Regis 1790–91, Denbigh borough 1797–1802, Athlone 1803–6, Shrewsbury 1807–11 (Burke's *Peerage* sub Wilson-Tyrwhitt; Foster's *Baronetage;* Williams' *Wales M.P.'s*).

JONES, Thomas John Tyrwhitt, *see* TYRWHITT-JONES, Thomas John.

2556. JONES, Walter (1754–1839), M.P. Coleraine 1801–6, 1807–9 (Burke's *Irish LG*).

2557. JONES-PARRY, Love Parry (1781–1853), M.P. Horsham 1806–8, Carnarvon borough 1835–37 (*Old Westminsters;* Williams' *Wales M.P.'s*).

2558. JONES-SKELTON, Arnoldus (ca 1750–93), M.P. Eye 1780–82 (Burke's *LG* [ed. 1849]; *Eton Coll. Reg.*).

JULL, Thomas, *see* GODFREY, Thomas.

2559. KAVANAGH, Thomas (1767–1837), M.P. Carlow Co. 1826–31, 1835–37 (*Alumni Dublin.; Annual Register,* p. 169; Burke's *Irish LG; Linc. Inn Reg.*).

KAYE, John Lister, *see* LISTER-KAYE, John.

2560. KEANE, John (ca 1757–1829), 1st Bt, M.P. Youghal 1801–6, 1807–18 (*Alumni Dublin.; Alumni Oxon.;* Burke's *Peerage*).

2561. KEARSLEY, John Hodson (ca 1784–1842), M.P. Wigan 1831–32, 1835–37 (Bean; *Gent. Mag., 2,* 548).

2562. KEATING, Maurice Bagenal St. Leger (d. 1835), M.P. Kildare 1801–2 (DNB).

KECK, Anthony, *see* TRACY-KECK, Anthony.

KECK, Anthony James, *see* JAMES-KECK, Anthony.

KECK, George Anthony Legh, *see* LEGH-KECK, George Anthony.

2563. KEENE, Benjamin (ca 1697–1757), M.P. Maldon 1740–41, West Looe 1741–47 (*Alumni Cantab.;* DNB).

2564. KEENE, Benjamin (ca 1752–1837), M.P. Cambridge borough 1776–84 (*Eton Coll. Reg.*).

2565. KEENE, Whitshed (ca 1732–1822), M.P. Wareham 1768–74, Ludgershall 1774–74, Montgomery borough 1774–1818 (*Alumni Dublin.;* Williams' *Wales M.P.'s*).

KEITH, 1st Vct, *see* ELPHINSTONE, George Keith.

2566. KEITH, Robert Murray (1730–95), M.P. Peebles-shire 1775–80 (DNB).

2567. KEKEWICH, Samuel Trehawke (1796–1873), M.P. Exeter 1826–30, South Devon 1858–73 (*Alumni Oxon.;* Burke's *LG;* Boase).

2568. KEMEYS-TYNTE, Charles (1710–85), 5th Bt, M.P. Monmouth borough 1745–47, Somerset 1747–74 (GEC; Williams' *Wales M.P.'s*).

2569. KEMEYS-TYNTE, Charles Kemeys (1779–1860), M.P. Bridgwater 1820–37 (*Admissions to St. John, Cambridge; Eton Coll. Reg.*).

2570. KEMMIS, Thomas Arthur (1806–58), M.P. East Looe 1830–32 (*Alumni Oxon.;* Burke's *Irish LG*).

2571. KEMP, Robert (1667–1734), 3d Bt, M.P. Dunwich 1701–5, 1708–9, 1713–15, Suffolk 1732–34 (*Alumni Cantab.;* GEC).

2572. KEMP, Thomas (ca 1746–1811), M.P. Lewes 1780–1802, 1806–11 (*Admissions to St. John, Cambridge;* Burke's *LG* [ed. 1849]; *Gent. Mag., 1,* 600 and *2,* 87).

2573. KEMP, Thomas Read (ca 1781–1844), M.P. Lewes 1811–16, 1826–37, Arundel 1823–26 (*Admissions to St. John, Cambridge;* DNB; Dod's *Parl. Companion* [1834], p. 132).

KENLIS, 1st Bn, *see* TAYLOUR, Thomas.

KENMURE, 10th Vct, *see* GORDON, John.

2574. KENNEDY, Archibald (1794–1832), M.P. Evesham 1830–31 (GEC and *Scots Peerage* sub Ailsa).

2575. KENNEDY, David (ca 1727–92), 10th E. of Cassilis, M.P. Ayrshire 1768–74 (Addison's *Glasgow Matric. Albums;* GEC and *Scots Peerage* sub Ailsa).

2576 KENNEDY, Thomas Francis (1788–1879), M.P. Ayr burghs 1818–34 (Addison's *Glasgow Matric. Albums;* DNB; *Harrow Reg.*).

2577. KENRICK, John (ca 1735–99), M.P. Bletchingley 1780–90 (Christie's *Bletchingley, 1,* 312; *Genealogist,* N.S., *24,* 97–98; *Harrow Reg.;* Manning and Bray's *Surrey, 2,* 306).

2578. KENRICK, William (1774–1829), M.P. Bletchingley 1806–14 (Christie's *Bletchingley, 1,* 312; Howard and Crisp's *Visitation of Eng. and Wales, 13,* 61).

KENSINGTON, 2d Bn, *see* EDWARDES, William.

2579. KENT, Charles (ca 1744–1811), 1st Bt, M.P. Thetford 1784–90 (GEC).

2580. KENT, Samuel (ca 1683–1759), M.P. Ipswich 1734–59 (*Notes and Queries,* 12th Ser., *5,* 107; *Genealogist,* 1st Ser., *1;* Musgrave's *Obituary*).

2581. KENYON, Lloyd (1732–1802), 1st Bn Kenyon, M.P. Hindon 1780–84, Tregony 1784–88 (DNB; GEC).

2582. KENYON, Lloyd (1805–69), 3d Bn Kenyon, M.P. St. Michael 1830–32 (GEC; *Harrow Reg.*).

83. KEPPEL, Augustus (1725–86), 1st Vct Keppel, M.P. Chichester

1755-61, Windsor 1761-80, Surrey 1780-82 (DNB; GEC; *Old Westminsters*).

2584. KEPPEL, Augustus Frederick (1794-1851), 5th E. of Albemarle, M.P. Arundel 1820-26 (GEC).

2585. KEPPEL, George (1724-72), 3d E. of Albemarle, M.P. Chichester 1746-54 (DNB; GEC; *Old Westminsters*).

2586. KEPPEL, William (1727-82), M.P. Chichester 1767-82 (*Old Westminsters*).

2587. KER, David (ca 1772-1844), M.P. Athlone 1820-26, Downpatrick 1835-41 (*Eton Coll. Reg.*).

2588. KER, Richard Gervas (ca 1757-1822), M.P. Newport (Hants) 1802-6 (*Alumni Oxon.; Misc. Geneal. et Herald.*, 5th Ser., 7).

2589. KERR, James (d. 1768), M.P. Edinburgh City 1747-54 (Burke's *LG;* Foster's *Scots M.P.'s*).

2590. KERR, John William Robert (1794-1841), 7th M. of Lothian, M.P. Huntingdon borough 1820-24 (GEC; *Scots Peerage*).

2591. KERR, William Henry (ca 1710-75), 4th M. of Lothian, M.P. Richmond 1747-63 (DNB; GEC; *Scots Peerage*).

2592. KERRISON, Edward (1776-1853), 1st Bt, M.P. Shaftesbury 1813-18, Northampton borough 1818-20, Eye 1824-52 (DNB; Boase; Dod's *Parl. Companion* [1834], p. 133; Foster's *Baronetage*).

2593. KEYT, William (1688-1741), 3d Bt, M.P. Warwick borough 1722-35 (GEC).

2594. KIBBLEWHITE, James (ca 1770-1845), M.P. Wootton Bassett 1812-13 (*Gent. Mag., 2*, 658; *1812 List*).

2595. KIELY, John, M.P. Clonmel 1819-20.

KILDERBEE, Spencer Horsey, *see* DE HORSEY, Spencer Horsey.

KILLEEN, Bn, *see* PLUNKETT, Arthur James.

KILMOREY, E. of, *see* NEEDHAM, Francis Jack.

2596. KINASTON, William (ca 1682-1749), M.P. Shrewsbury 1734-49 (*Alumni Cantab.;* Shrop. Archaeol. Soc. *Trans.*, 3d Ser., *1*, 221 and 4th Ser., *6*, 73; *Shrop. Notes and Queries,* 1st Ser., *1*, 64).

2597. KING, Edward (ca 1775-1807), M.P. Roscommon 1802-6 (*Eton Coll. Reg.; Harrow Reg.*).

2598. KING, Edward (1795-1837), M.P. Cork Co. 1818-26 (DNB; GEC).

2599. KING, Edward Bolton (ca 1801-78), M.P. Warwick borough 1831-37, South Warwickshire 1857-59 (*Alumni Oxon.;* Burke's *LG;* Boase).

2600. KING, Henry (ca 1776-1839), M.P. Sligo Co. 1822-31 (*Eton Coll. Reg.; Harrow Reg.; Royal Kalendar* [1824], p. 74).

2601. KING, John (1706-40), 2d Bn King, M.P. Launceston 1727-34 (*Alumni Cantab.;* GEC).

2602. KING, John (1759-1830), M.P. Enniskillen 1806-6 (*Alumni Oxon.; Cornwallis Corr., 3,* 156 n.; *Line. Inn Reg.*).

KING, John Dashwood, see DASHWOOD-KING, John.

2603. KING, Richard (1730–1806), 1st Bt, M.P. Rochester 1794–1802 (DNB; GEC).

2604. KING, Robert Edward (1804–69), 6th E. of Kingston, M.P. Roscommon 1826–30 (GEC).

2605. KING, Robert Henry (1796–1867), 4th E. of Kingston, M.P. Cork Co. 1826–32 (GEC).

KINGSBOROUGH, Vct, see KING, Edward.

KINGSDOWN, 1st Bn, see PEMBERTON-LEIGH, Thomas.

2606. KINGSMILL, Robert Brice (ca 1730–1805), 1st Bt, M.P. Yarmouth (Hants) 1779–80, Tregony 1784–90 (DNB; GEC).

KINGSTON, E. of, see KING, Robert Edward and Robert Henry.

2607. KINGSTON, John, M.P. Lymington 1802–14 (*Admissions to St. John, Cambridge;* Cass' *East Barnet,* pp. 82, 87; *1812 List*).

2608. KINNAIRD, Charles (1780–1826), 8th Bn Kinnaird, M.P. Leominster 1802–5 (Ball and Venn's *Admissions to Trinity College;* DNB; GEC; *Eton Lists; Scots Peerage*).

2609. KINNAIRD, Douglas James William (1788–1830), M.P. Bishop's Castle 1819–20 (DNB; *Scots Peerage*).

2610. KINNERSLEY, William Shepherd (ca 1780–1823), M.P. Newcastle-under-Lyme 1818–23 (Wedgwood).

KINNOULL, 9th E. of, see HAY, Thomas.

2611. KIRKMAN, John (d. 1780), M.P. London 1780–80 (Beaven's *Aldermen of London*).

2612. KIRKPATRICK, William (ca 1705–78), M.P. Dumfries burghs 1735–38 (Burke's *Peerage;* Foster's *Scots M.P.'s;* Grant's *Faculty of Advocates*).

KIRKWALL, Vct, see FITZMAURICE, John Hamilton.

2613. KNAPP, George (1754–1809), M.P. Abingdon 1807–9 (*Gent. Mag., 2,* 1085; *Notes and Queries,* 11th Ser., *2,* 35).

2614. KNATCHBULL, Edward (ca 1760–1819), 8th Bt, M.P. Kent 1790–1802, 1806–19 (GEC).

2615. KNATCHBULL, Edward (1781–1849), 9th Bt, M.P. Kent 1819–31, East Kent 1832–45 (DNB; GEC).

2616. KNATCHBULL-WYNDHAM, Wyndham (1737–63), 6th Bt, M.P. Kent 1760–63 (GEC).

KNIGHT, Bulstrode Peachey, see PEACHEY-KNIGHT, Bulstrode.

2617. KNIGHT, Henry (1728–62), M.P. Great Grimsby 1761–62 (GEC sub Catherlough).

KNIGHT, Henry Gally and John Gally, see GALLY-KNIGHT, Henry and John.

2618. KNIGHT, Richard Payne (1750–1824), M.P. Leominster 1780–84, Ludlow 1784–1806 (DNB).

2619. KNIGHT, Robert (1702–72), 1st E. of Catherlough, M.P. Great

Grimsby 1734–47, 1762–68, Castle Rising 1747–54, Milborne Port 1770–72 (GEC).

2620. KNIGHT, Robert (1768–1855), M.P. Wootton Bassett 1806–7, 1811–12, Rye 1823–26, Wallingford 1826–32 (Burke's *LG* [ed. 1849]; *Gent. Mag., 1,* 313; Shrop. Archaeol. Soc. *Trans.,* 2d Ser., *10;* Venn MS).

2621. KNIGHT, Thomas (ca 1702–81), M.P. Canterbury 1734–41 (*Alumni Oxon.;* Burke's *LG*).

2622. KNIGHT, Thomas (1735–94), M.P. New Romney 1761–68, Kent 1774–80 (*Eton Coll. Reg.*).

2623. KNIGHT-BRUCE, James Lewis (1791–1866), M.P. Bishop's Castle 1831–32 (DNB; Boase).

2624. KNIGHTLEY, Lucy (1742–91), M.P. Northampton borough 1763–68, Northamptonshire 1773–84 (*Eton Coll. Reg.; Rugby Reg.*).

2625. KNIGHTLEY, Valentine (1718–54), M.P. Northamptonshire 1748–54 (Barron's *Northampton Families,* p. 194; *Eton Coll. Reg.*).

2626. KNOLLYS, Francis (ca 1722–72), 1st Bt, M.P. Reading 1761–68 (GEC).

2627. KNOLLYS, William (ca 1695–1740), M.P. Banbury 1733–40 (GEC sub Banbury; Williams' *Oxford M.P.'s*).

2628. KNOWLES, Charles (ca 1704–77), 1st Bt, M.P. Gatton 1749–52 (DNB; GEC).

2629. KNOX, George (ca 1765–1827), M.P. Dublin Univ. 1801–7 (*Alumni Oxon.;* Burke's *Peerage* sub Ranfurly; *Cornwallis Corr., 3,* 31 n.).

2630. KNOX, John (ca 1757–1800), M.P. Dungannon 1801–1 [*sic*] (Burke's *Peerage* sub Ranfurly).

2631. KNOX, John Henry (1788–1872), M.P. Newry 1826–32 (Boase; Burke's *Peerage* sub Ranfurly; *Harrow Reg.*).

2632. KNOX, John James (1790–1856), M.P. Dungannon 1830–37 (Burke's *Peerage* sub Ranfurly; Venn MS).

2633. KNOX, Thomas (1754–1840), 1st E. of Ranfurly, M.P. Tyrone 1806–12 (GEC).

2634. KNOX, Thomas (1786–1858), 2d E. of Ranfurly, M.P. Tyrone 1812–18, Dungannon 1818–30, 1837–38 (GEC; *Harrow Reg.*).

2635. KNUBLEY, Edward (d. 1815), M.P. Carlisle 1786–87, 1790–91 (Bean; Ferguson; *Gent. Mag., 1,* 474).

2636. KYNASTON, Corbet (1690–1740), M.P. Shrewsbury 1714–23, Salop 1734–40 (*Calendar Inner Temple Records, 4,* 69; Shrop. Archaeol. Soc. *Trans.,* 2d Ser., *6,* 217).

2637. KYNASTON, Edward (1709–72), M.P. Bishop's Castle 1734–41, Montgomeryshire 1747–72 (*Alumni Cantab.; Eton Coll. Reg.*).

KYNASTON, William, *see* KINASTON, William.

2638. KYNASTON-POWELL, John (1753–1822), 1st Bt, M.P. Salop 1784–1822 (*Alumni Oxon.; Admissions to St. John, Cambridge,* sub Edward Kynaston-Powell).

2639. LABOUCHERE, Henry (1798–1869), 1st Bn Taunton, M.P. St. Michael 1826–30, Taunton 1830–59 (DNB; GEC; *Linc. Inn Reg.*).

2640. LACON, Edmund Knowles (1780–1839), 2d Bt, M.P. Great Yarmouth 1812–18 (Burke's *Peerage; Eton Lists; Linc. Inn Reg.;* Palmer's *Perlustration of Great Yarmouth, 1,* 263).

2641. LADBROKE, Robert (ca 1713–73), M.P. London 1754–73 (Beaven's *Aldermen of London;* Musgrave's *Obituary*).

2642. LADBROKE, Robert (ca 1740–1814), M.P. Warwick borough 1780–90, Okehampton 1791–96, Winchelsea 1802–6, Malmesbury 1806–7 (*Gent. Mag., 2,* 91; *Royal Kalendar* [1803], p. 65; Wright's *Okehampton,* p. 142).

2643. LADE, John (d. 1759), 1st Bt, M.P. Camelford 1754–59 (GEC).

2644. LAING, Malcolm (ca 1762–1818), M.P. Orkney and Shetland 1807–12 (DNB).

2645. LAKE, Gerrard (1744–1808), 1st Vct Lake, M.P. Aylesbury 1790–1802 (DNB; GEC; *Eton Coll. Reg.*).

2646. LAMB, George (1784–1834), M.P. Westminster 1819–20, Dungarvan 1822–34 (DNB).

2647. LAMB, James (1752–1824), 1st Bt, M.P. Helston 1787–90 (DNB; GEC).

2648. LAMB, Matthew (ca 1705–68), 1st Bt, M.P. Stockbridge 1741–47, Peterborough 1747–68 (DNB; GEC).

2649. LAMB, Peniston (1745–1828), 1st Vct Melbourne, M.P. Ludgershall 1768–84, Malmesbury 1784–90, Newport (Hants) 1790–93 (GEC; *Eton Coll. Reg.*).

2650. LAMB, Peniston (1770–1805), M.P. Newport (Hants) 1793–96, Herts 1802–5 (GEC; *Eton Coll. Reg.*).

2651. LAMB, Thomas Davis (1775–1818), M.P. Rye 1802–6 (*Old Westminsters*).

2652. LAMB, Thomas Phillipps (d. 1819), M.P. Rye 1812–16, 1819–19 (*Gent. Mag., 2,* 89; *1812 List*).

2653. LAMB, William (1779–1848), 2d Vct Melbourne, M.P. Leominster 1806–6, Haddington burghs 1806–7, Portarlington 1807–12; Peterborough 1816–19, Herts 1819–26, Newport (Hants) 1827–27, Bletchingley 1827–28 (DNB; GEC).

2654. LAMBERT, Daniel (1685–1750), M.P. London 1741–47 (Beaven's *Aldermen of London;* Burke's *LG;* Manning and Bray's *Surrey, 2,* 589, 593).

2655. LAMBERT, Henry (1786–1861), M.P. Wexford Co. 1831–34 (Burke's *Irish LG*).

2656. LAMBERT, James Staunton (1789–1867), M.P. Galway Co. 1827–32 (*Alumni Dublin.;* Burke's *Irish LG*).

2657. LAMBTON, Henry (1697–1761), M.P. Durham City 1734–61 (*Alumni Oxon.;* Surtees' *Durham, 2,* 175).

2658. LAMBTON, John (1710–94), M.P. Durham City 1762–68 (DNB; Namier).

2659. LAMBTON, John George (1792–1840), 1st E. of Durham, M.P. Durham Co. 1813–28 (DNB; GEC).

2660. LAMBTON, Ralph John (ca 1768–1844), M.P. Durham City 1798–1813 (*Eton Coll. Reg.*).

2661. LAMBTON, William Henry (1764–97), M.P. Durham City 1787–97 (*Eton Coll. Reg.*).

LANDAFF, 2d E. of, *see* MATHEW, Francis James.

LANE, *see* FOX-LANE.

2662. LANE-FOX, George (1793–1848), M.P. Beverley 1820–26, 1837–40 (*Alumni Oxon.; Old Westminsters*).

2663. LANE-FOX, Sackville Walter (1797–1874), M.P. Helston 1831–34, Ipswich 1842–47, Beverley 1840–41, 1847–52 (Burke's *LG; Eton Lists*).

2664. LANGHAM, James (1736–95), 7th Bt, M.P. Northamptonshire 1784–90 (GEC).

2665. LANGHAM, James (1776–1833), 10th Bt, M.P. St. Germans 1802–6 (GEC; *Eton Coll. Reg.*).

2666. LANGLOIS, Benjamin (ca 1727–1802), M.P. St. Germans 1768–80 (*Alumni Oxon.;* Agnew's *Protestant Exiles, 3,* 238; *Herald and Genealogist, 6,* 127).

2667. LANGMEAD, Philip (ca 1739–1816), M.P. Plymouth 1802–6 (*Gent. Mag., 2,* 283; *1806 List*).

2668. LANGSTON, James Haughton (ca 1797–1863), M.P. Woodstock 1820–26, Oxford City 1826–34, 1841–63 (*Alumni Oxon.;* Boase; Williams' *Oxford M.P.'s*).

2669. LANGSTON, John (d. 1812), M.P. Sudbury 1784–90, Bridgwater 1790–96, 1806–7, Minehead 1796–1802, Portarlington 1806–6 (*Eton Coll. Reg.*).

LANGTON, William Gore, *see* GORE-LANGTON, William.

LANDSDOWNE, M. of, *see* PETTY, John Henry and William; *also* PETTY-FITZMAURICE, Henry.

2670. LAROCHE, James (1734–ca 1804), 1st Bt, M.P. Bodmin 1768–80 (Agnew's *Protestant Exiles, 2,* 298; GEC; *Eton Coll. Reg.*).

2671. LAROCHE, John (ca 1700–52), M.P. Bodmin 1727–52 (Agnew's *Protestant Exiles, 2,* 298; *Alumni Cantab.;* GEC).

2672. LASCELLES, Daniel (1714–84), M.P. Northallerton 1752–80 (Burke's *Peerage* sub Harewood).

2673. LASCELLES, Edward (1740–1820), 1st E. of Harewood, M.P. Northallerton 1761–74, 1790–96 (GEC).

2674. LASCELLES, Edward (1764–1814), M.P. Northallerton 1796–1814 (GEC sub Harewood; *Harrow Reg.*).

2675. LASCELLES, Edwin (1713–95), 1st Bn Harewood, M.P. Scarborough

1744–54, Northallerton 1754–61, 1780–90, Yorkshire 1761–80 (*Alumni Cantab.;* GEC; Gooder).

2676. LASCELLES, Henry (1690–1753), M.P. Northallerton 1745–52 (GEC sub Harewood).

2677. LASCELLES, Henry (1767–1841), 2d E. of Harewood, M.P. Yorkshire 1796–1806, 1812–18, Westbury 1807–12, Northallerton 1818–20 (DNB; GEC; Gooder; *Harrow Reg.*).

2678. LASCELLES, Henry (1797–1857), 3d E. of Harewood, M.P. Northallerton 1826–31 (GEC).

2679. LASCELLES, William Saunders Sebright (1798–1851), M.P. Northallerton 1820–26, 1831–32, East Looe 1826–30, Wakefield 1837–41, 1842–47, Knaresborough 1847–51 (Burke's *Peerage* sub Harewood; Boase).

2680. LATOUCHE, David (ca 1769–1816), M.P. Carlow Co. 1802–16 (*Alumni Dublin.;* Burke's *Irish LG; Gent. Mag., 1,* 377; *Manchester School Reg.;* Namier).

2681. LATOUCHE, John (ca 1732–1810), M.P. Kildare 1801–2 (Burke's *Irish LG; Gent. Mag., 1,* 289; Huguenot Soc. *Proceedings, 10,* 237).

2682. LATOUCHE, John (ca 1775–1820), M.P. Dublin City 1802–6, Leitrim 1807–20 (*Alumni Dublin.; Eton Coll. Reg.; 1812 List*).

2683. LATOUCHE, Peter (ca 1777–1830), M.P. Leitrim 1802–6 (*Alumni Dublin.;* Burke's *Irish LG; Harrow Reg.*).

2684. LATOUCHE, Robert (ca 1783–1849), M.P. Carlow Co. 1816–18 (Burke's *Irish LG; Eton Lists; Gent. Mag., 1* [1850], 222).

2685. LATOUCHE, Robert (ca 1773–1844), M.P. Kildare 1802–30 (*Alumni Dublin.;* Burke's *Irish LG; Eton Coll. Reg.; Harrow Reg.*).

LAUDERDALE, E. of, *see* MAITLAND, Anthony and James.

2686. LAURENCE, French (1757–1809), M.P. Peterborough 1796–1809 (DNB).

2687. LAURIE, Robert (d. 1779), 4th Bt, M.P. Kirkcudbright Stewarty 1738–41 (GEC).

2688. LAURIE, Robert (d. 1804), 5th Bt, M.P. Dumfries-shire 1774–1804 (GEC).

LAVINGTON, 1st Bn, *see* PAYNE, Ralph.

2689. LAW, Edward (1750–1818), 1st Bn Ellenborough, M.P. Newtown (Hants) 1801–2 (DNB; GEC).

2690. LAW, Edward (1790–1871), 1st E. of Ellenborough, M.P. St. Michael 1813–18 (DNB; GEC).

2691. LAW, Evan (1747–1829), M.P. Westbury 1790–95, Newtown (Hants) 1802–2 (Burke's *Peerage* sub Ellenborough; Holzman's *Nabobs in England*).

2692. LAWLEY, Francis (ca 1782–1851), 7th Bt, M.P. Warwickshire 1820–32 (GEC; *Rugby Reg.*).

2693. LAWLEY, Robert (1736–93), 5th Bt, M.P. Warwickshire 1780–93 (GEC; *Old Westminsters*).

2694. LAWLEY, Robert (ca 1768–1834), 1st Bn Wenlock, M.P. Newcastle-under-Lyme 1802–6 (GEC).

2695. LAWLEY-THOMPSON, Paul Beilby (1784–1852), 1st Bn Wenlock, M.P. Wenlock 1826–32, Yorkshire (East Riding) 1832–37 (GEC; *Harrow Reg.; Rugby Reg.*).

2696. LAWRENCE, William (ca 1723–98), M.P. Ripon 1761–68, 1775–80, 1781–98 (*Admissions to St. John, Cambridge;* Bean; Park).

2697. LAWSON, Marmaduke (ca 1794–1823), M.P. Boroughbridge 1818–23 (Burke's *LG; Gent. Mag., 1,* 571; *Shrewsbury School Reg.*).

2698. LAWSON, Wilfrid (ca 1697–1737), 3d Bt, M.P. Boroughbridge 1718–22, Cockermouth 1722–37 (GEC).

2699. LAWSON, Wilfrid (d. 1762), 8th Bt, M.P. Cumberland 1761–62 (GEC).

2700. LAWTON, John (ca 1700–40), M.P. Newcastle-under-Lyme 1734–40 (Burke's *LG;* Wedgwood).

2701. LEACH, John (1760–1834), M.P. Seaford 1806–16 (DNB).

2702. LEADER, Nicholas Philpot (ca 1773–1836), M.P. Kilkenny City 1830–32 (*Alumni Dublin.;* Burke's *Irish LG;* Burtchaell's *Kilkenny M.P.'s*).

2703. LEADER, William, M.P. Camelford 1812–18, Winchelsea 1823–26.

2704. LEAKE, William. M.P. St. Michael 1818–20, 1826–30, Malmesbury 1820–26.

2705. LEATHES, Carteret (ca 1698–1787), M.P. Sudbury 1727–34, 1741–47, Harwich 1734–41 (*Alumni Oxon.;* Burke's *LG*).

LECALE, 1st Bn, *see* FITZGERALD, Charles James.

2706. LECHMERE, Edmund (1710–1805), M.P. Worcestershire 1734–47 (*Alumni Cantab.;* Burke's *Peerage;* Williams' *Worcester M.P.'s*).

2707. LECHMERE, Edmund (ca 1748–98), M.P. Worcester City 1790–96 (*Alumni Oxon.;* Williams' *Worcester M.P.'s*).

2708. LECHMERE-CHARLTON, Nicholas (ca 1733–1807), M.P. Worcester City 1774–74 (*Alumni Cantab.;* Burke's *Peerage;* Williams' *Worcester M.P.'s*).

LE DESPENCER, 14th Bn, *see* DASHWOOD, Francis.

LEE, Charles Dillon, *see* DILLON-LEE, Charles.

2709. LEE, Edward (b. ca 1761), M.P. Dungarvan 1801–2, Waterford Co. 1802–6 (*Alumni Dublin.*).

2710. LEE, George (ca 1700–58), M.P. Brackley 1733–42, Devizes 1742–47, Liskeard 1747–54, Launceston 1754–58 (*Alumni Cantab.; Alumni Oxon.;* DNB).

2711. LEE, George Henry (1718–72), 3d E. of Lichfield, M.P. Oxfordshire 1740–43 (DNB; GEC; *Old Westminsters*).

LEE, Henry Augustus Dillon, *see* DILLON-LEE, Henry Augustus.

2712. LEE, John (1695–1761), M.P. Malmesbury 1747–54, Newport 1754–61 (Clutterbuck's *Herts, 2,* 453; Lipscomb's *Bucks, 2,* 308; *Notes and Queries,* 12th Ser., *3,* 11, 234).

2713. LEE, John (1733–93), M.P. Clitheroe 1782–90, Higham Ferrers 1790–93 (DNB).

2714. LEE, John Lee (1802–74), M.P Wells 1830–37 (*Old Westminsters*).

2715. LEE, Robert (1706–76), 4th E. of Lichfield, M.P. Oxford City 1754–68 (GEC).

2716. LEE, Thomas (1687–1749), 3d Bt, M.P. Wycombe 1710–22, Bucks 1722–27, 1729–41 (GEC).

2717. LEE, William (ca 1727–78), M.P. Appleby 1754–56 (*Alumni Cantab.; Alumni Oxon.;* GEC; Clutterbuck's *Herts, 2,* 453).

2718. LEE-ANTONIE, William (1764–1815), M.P. Great Marlow 1790–96, Bedford borough 1802–12 (*Old Westminsters*).

LEEDS, 7th D. of, *see* D'ARCY-OSBORNE, Francis Godolphin.

2719. LEEDS, Edward (1728–1803), M.P. Reigate 1784–87 (DNB).

2720. LE FEBURE [LEFEVRE?], Charles, M.P. Wareham 1784–86 (*Notes and Queries,* 12th Ser., *2,* 457).

LEFEVRE, Charles Shaw, *see* SHAW-LEFEVRE, Charles.

2721. LE FLEMING, Michael (1748–1806), 4th Bt, M.P. Westmorland 1774–1806 (GEC; *Eton Coll. Reg.*).

2722. LEFROY, Anthony (1800–90), M.P. Longford 1830–32, 1833–37, 1842–47, Dublin Univ. 1858–70 (*Alumni Dublin.;* Burke's *Irish LG; Linc. Inn Reg.; 1832 List*).

2723. LEFROY, Thomas Langlois (1776–1869), M.P. Dublin Univ. 1830–41 (DNB).

2724. LEGGE, Arthur Charles (1800–90), M.P. Banbury 1826–30 (Boase; Burke's *Peerage* sub Dartmouth; Williams' *Oxford M.P.'s*).

2725. LEGGE, Edward (ca 1710–47), M.P. Portsmouth 1747–47 (DNB).

2726. LEGGE, George (1755–1810), 3d E. of Dartmouth, M.P. Plymouth 1778–80, Staffordshire 1780–84 (DNB; GEC; *Harrow Reg.*).

2727. LEGGE, Heneage (1788–1844), M.P. Banbury 1819–26 (*Alumni Oxon.;* Burke's *Peerage* sub Dartmouth; *Eton Lists;* Williams' *Oxford M.P.'s*).

LEGGE, Henry Bilson, *see* BILSON-LEGGE, Henry.

2728. LEGGE, William (1784–1853), 4th E. of Dartmouth, M.P. Milborne Port 1810–10 (GEC).

2729. LEGH, Peter (1706–92), M.P. Newton 1743–74 (*Alumni Cantab.; Alumni Oxon.; Old Westminsters*).

2730. LEGH, Peter (1723–1804), M.P. Ilchester 1765–74 (Burke's *LG;* Omerod's *Chester, 1,* 500).

2731. LEGH, Thomas (ca 1793–1857), M.P. Newton 1814–32 (*Alumni Oxon.;* Bean; Burke's *Peerage* sub Newton; Foster's *Lancashire Pedigrees;* Pink).

2732. LEGH, Thomas Peter (ca 1755–97), M.P. Newton 1780–97 (*Alumni*

Oxon.; Bean; Burke's *LG* [ed. 1849]; Foster's *Lancashire Pedigrees;* Pink).

2733. LEGH-KECK, George Anthony (1774–1860), M.P. Leicestershire 1797–1818, 1820–31 (*Eton Coll. Reg.*).

2734. LE HEUP, Isaac (ca 1686–1747), M.P. Bodmin 1722–27, Grampound 1732–34, Callington 1734–41 (*Alumni Cantab.; Misc. Geneal. et Herald.,* 4th Ser., *2*).

LEICESTER, 1st E. of, *see* COKE, Thomas William.

2735. LEICESTER, John Fleming (1762–1827), 1st Bn de Tabley, M.P. Yarmouth (Hants) 1791–96, Heytesbury 1796–1802, Stockbridge 1807–7 (DNB; GEC).

2736. LEICESTER, Peter (1732–70), 4th Bt, M.P. Preston 1767–68 (*Alumni Oxon.;* GEC).

2737. LEIGH, Charles (d. 1836), M.P. New Ross 1806–7, 1812–18 (*Army Lists;* Burke's *Irish LG; Gent. Mag., 2,* 221).

2738. LEIGH, Francis (ca 1755–1839), M.P. Wexford town 1801–1, New Ross 1821–24 (*Alumni Dublin.;* Burke's *Irish LG*).

2739. LEIGH, James Henry (1765–1823), M.P. Marlborough 1802–6, Great Bedwin 1806–18, Winchester 1818–23 (*Alumni Oxon.;* Burke's *Peerage; Harrow Reg.*).

2740. LEIGH, Richard (ca 1728–72), M.P. East Looe 1770–72 (*Alumni Oxon.;* Musgrave's *Obituary*).

2741. LEIGH, Robert (ca 1729–ca 1803), M.P. New Ross 1801–2 (*Alumni Dublin.;* Burke's *Irish LG*).

2742. LEIGH, Robert Holt (ca 1763–1843), 1st Bt, M.P. Wigan 1802–20 (*Alumni Oxon.;* Bean).

LEIGH, Thomas Charles, *see* HANBURY-TRACY, Thomas Charles.

LEIGH, Thomas Pemberton, *see* PEMBERTON-LEIGH, Thomas.

2743. LEIGHTON, Charlton (ca 1747–84), 4th Bt, M.P. Shrewsbury 1774–75, 1780–84 (*Admissions to St. John, Cambridge;* GEC).

2744. LEIGHTON, Daniel (1694–1765), M.P. Hereford City 1747–54 (GEC; *Notes and Queries,* 12th Ser., *2,* 354; Williams' *Hereford M.P.'s*).

2745. LEITH, Alexander Charles George (ca 1741–81), 1st Bt, M.P. Tregony 1774–80 (GEC; Lawrence-Archer, *Monument. Insc. Brit. West Indies,* p. 81).

LEITRIM, 2d E. of, *see* CLEMENTS, Nathaniel.

2746. LELAND, John (d. 1808), M.P. Stamford 1796–1808 (*Gent. Mag., 1,* 89).

2747. LE MESURIER, Paul (1755–1805), M.P. Southwark 1784–96 (DNB).

2748. LEMON, Charles (1784–1868), 2d Bt, M.P. Penryn 1807–12, 1830–31, Cornwall 1831–32, West Cornwall 1832–41, 1842–57 (Boase; GEC; *Harrow Reg.;* Venn MS).

2749. LEMON, John (1754–1814), M.P. West Looe 1784–84, Saltash 1787–

90, Truro 1796–1814 (Boase and Courtney, *Biblio. Cornub.;* GEC; *Harrow Reg.*).

2750. LEMON, William (1748–1824), 1st Bt, M.P. Penryn 1770–74, Cornwall 1774–1824 (*Alumni Oxon.;* GEC; Olivey's *Mylor,* pp. 120, 198).

LENNARD, Thomas Barrett, *see* BARRETT-LENNARD, Thomas.

LENNOX, Arthur, *see* GORDON-LENNOX, Arthur.

2751. LENNOX, Charles (1764–1819), 4th D. of Richmond, M.P. Sussex 1790–1806 (DNB; GEC).

LENNOX, Charles, *see* GORDON-LENNOX, Charles.

2752. LENNOX, George Henry (1737–1805), M.P. Chichester 1761–67, Sussex 1767–90 (DNB; *Old Westminsters*).

LENNOX, John George, *see* GORDON-LENNOX, John George.

2753. LENNOX, William Pitt (1799–1881), M.P. Lynn 1831–34 (DNB; *Old Westminsters*).

2754. LESLIE, Charles Powell (ca 1767–1831), M.P. Monaghan 1801–26, New Ross 1830–31 (*Alumni Oxon.;* Burke's *Peerage*).

2755. LESLIE, Thomas (ca 1701–72), M.P. Dysart burghs 1734–41, Perth burghs 1743–61 (*Scots Peerage* sub Rothes).

2756. LESTER, Benjamin (ca 1724–1802), M.P. Poole 1790–96 (Hutchins' *Dorset, 1,* 48; Sydenham's *Poole,* p. 319)..

2757. LESTER, Benjamin Lester (ca 1780–1838), M.P. Poole 1809–34 (*Gent. Mag., 2,* 343; *Notes and Queries,* 12th Ser., *2,* 369).

2758. LETHBRIDGE, John (ca 1746–1815), 1st Bt, M.P. Minehead 1806–7 (Burke's *Peerage; Gent. Mag., 1* [1816], 87).

LETHBRIDGE, Thomas Buckler, *see* BUCKLER-LETHBRIDGE, Thomas.

2759. LETHIEULLIER, Benjamin (d. 1797), M.P. Andover 1768–97 (*Gent. Mag., 2* 1076).

2760. LEVESON-GOWER, Baptist (ca 1704–82), M.P. Newcastle-under-Lyme 1727–61 (*Alumni Cantab.; Old Westminsters*).

2761. LEVESON-GOWER, Edward (1776–1853), M.P. Truro 1802–7, St. Michael 1807–7 (Burke's *Peerage* sub Sutherland).

LEVESON-GOWER, Francis, *see* EGERTON, Francis.

2762. LEVESON-GOWER, George Granville (1758–1833), 1st D. of Sutherland, M.P. Newcastle-under-Lyme 1779–84, Staffordshire 1787–99 (DNB; GEC).

LEVESON-GOWER, George Granville, *see* SUTHERLAND-LEVESON-GOWER, George Granville.

2763. LEVESON-GOWER, Granville (1721–1803), 1st M. of Stafford, M.P. Bishop's Castle 1744–47, Westminster 1747–54, Lichfield 1754–54 (DNB; GEC).

2764. LEVESON-GOWER, Granville (1773–1846), 1st E. Granville, M.P. Lichfield 1795–99, Staffordshire 1799–1815 (DNB; GEC).

2765. LEVESON-GOWER, John (1740–92), M.P. Appleby 1784–90, Newcastle-under-Lyme 1790–92 (DNB).

2766. LEVESON-GOWER, John (1774–1816), M.P. Truro 1796–1802 (Burke's *Peerage* sub Sutherland; *Harrow Reg.*).

2767. LEVESON-GOWER, Richard (1726–53), M.P. Lichfield 1747–53 (*Alumni Oxon.;* Burke's *Peerage* sub Sutherland; Wedgwood).

2768. LEVESON-GOWER, William (ca 1696–1756), M.P. Staffordshire 1720–56 (Burke's *Peerage* sub Sutherland; Wedgwood).

2769. LEVETT, John (1721–99), M.P. Lichfield 1761–62 (Burke's *LG; Old Westminsters;* Wedgwood).

2770. LEVINZ, William (ca 1713–65), M.P. Notts 1732–47 (*Alumni Cantab.; Eton Coll. Reg.; Westminster Abbey Reg.*).

2771. LEWES, Watkin (ca 1737–1821), M.P. London 1781–96 (Beaven's *Aldermen of London; Shrewsbury School Reg.;* Williams' *Worcester M.P.'s*).

2772. LEWIS, Edward, M.P. New Radnor 1761–90 (Williams' *Wales M.P.'s*).

2773. LEWIS, John (1738–97), M.P. New Radnor 1768–69, 1774–75, 1780–81 (Burke's *Peerage; Linc. Inn Reg.;* Williams' *Wales M.P.'s*).

2774. LEWIS, Matthew Gregory (1775–1818), M.P. Hindon 1796–1802 (DNB; *Old Westminsters*).

2775. LEWIS, Thomas (ca 1679–1736), M.P. Whitchurch 1708–8, Winchester 1710–15, Southampton borough 1715–27, Salisbury 1727–34, Portsmouth 1734–36 (GEC sub Plymouth; MS, *ex inform.* C. Twynam).

2776. LEWIS, Thomas (1690–1777), M.P. New Radnor 1715–61 (*Alumni Oxon.;* Burke's *Peerage;* Williams' *Wales M.P.'s*).

2777. LEWIS, Thomas Frankland (1780–1855), 1st Bt, M.P. Beaumaris 1812–26, Ennis 1826–28, Radnorshire 1828–34, New Radnor 1847–55 (DNB).

2778. LEWIS, Wyndham (1780–1838), M.P. Cardiff 1820–26, Aldeburgh 1827–29, Maidstone 1835–38 (*Gent. Mag., 1,* 658; Williams' *Wales M.P.'s*).

LEWISHAM, Vct, *see* LEGGE, George and William.

LEYCESTER, Edward, *see* PENRHYN, Edward.

2779. LEYCESTER, Hugh (1748–1836), M.P. Milborne Port 1802–12 (*Eton Coll. Reg.*).

2780. LEYCESTER, Ralph (1764–1835), M.P. Shaftesbury 1821–30 (Burke's *LG; Eton Coll. Reg.*).

LICHFIELD, E. of, *see* ANSON, Thomas William; *also* LEE, George Henry and Robert.

2781. LIDDELL, George (1678–1740), M.P. Berwick-on-Tweed 1727–40 (Surtees' *Durham, 2,* 213).

2782. LIDDELL, Henry (1708–84), 1st Bn Ravensworth, M.P. Morpeth 1734–47 (*Alumni Cantab.;* GEC).

2783. LIDDELL, Henry Thomas (1797–1878), 1st E. of Ravensworth, M.P. Northumberland 1826–30, North Durham 1837–47, Liverpool 1853–55 (DNB; GEC).

2784. LIDDELL, Richard (ca 1695–1746), M.P. Bossiney 1742–46 (*Alumni Oxon.; Calendar Inner Temple Records, 4,* 514; Musgrave's *Obituary*).

2785. LIDDELL, Thomas Henry (1775–1855), 1st Bn Ravensworth, M.P. Durham Co. 1806–7 (GEC; *Eton Coll. Reg.*).

LIFFORD, 1st Vct, *see* HEWITT, James.

2786. LIGONIER, John Louis (1680–1770), 1st E. Ligonier, M.P. Bath 1748–63 (DNB; GEC).

LILFORD, 1st Bn, *see* POWYS, Thomas.

LIMERICK, 1st Vct, *see* HAMILTON, James.

LINCOLN, E. of, *see* PELHAM-CLINTON, Henry Fiennes and Thomas.

2787. LIND, George (d. 1763), M.P. Edinburgh City 1761–62 (Foster's *Scots M.P.'s*).

2788. LINDSAY, Hugh (1763–1844), M.P. Perth burghs 1820–30 (Foster's *Scots M.P.'s;* Scots *Peerage* sub Balcarres).

2789. LINDSAY, James (1783–1869), 7th E. of Balcarres, M.P. Wigan 1820–25 (GEC).

2790. LINDSAY, James (1793–1855), M.P. Wigan 1825–31, Fifeshire 1831–32 (Bean; Foster's *Scots M.P.'s*).

2791. LINDSAY, John (ca 1737–88), M.P. Aberdeen burghs 1767–68 (DNB).

2792. LINDSAY, Patrick (1686–1753), M.P. Edinburgh City 1734–41 (DNB).

LINDSEY, 9th E. of, *see* BERTIE, Albemarle.

2793. LINWOOD, Nicholas (d. 1773), M.P. Stockbridge 1761–68, Aldeburgh 1768–73 (*Eng. Hist. Rev., 42* [1927], 519; Musgrave's *Obituary*).

2794. LIPPINCOTT, Henry (1737–80), 1st Bt, M.P. Bristol 1780–80 (GEC).

LISBURNE, 1st E. of, *see* VAUGHAN, Wilmot.

LISGAR, 1st Bn, *see* YOUNG, John.

2795. LISLE, Edward (1692–1753), M.P. Marlborough 1727–34, Hampshire 1734–41 (*Alumni Oxon.;* Berry's *County Geneal.: Hampshire*).

2796. LISLE, Warren, M.P. Weymouth and Melcombe Regis 1780–80.

LISMORE, 1st Vct, *see* O'CALLAGHAN, Cornelius.

2797. LISTER, Nathaniel (1725–93), M.P. Clitheroe 1761–73 (*Old Westminsters*).

2798. LISTER, Thomas (1688–1745), M.P. Clitheroe 1713–45 (*Alumni Oxon.;* Burke's *Peerage* sub Ribblesdale; *Genealogist,* N.S., *17,* 255).

2799. LISTER, Thomas (1723–61), M.P. Clitheroe 1745–61 (*Alumni Cantab.; Old Westminsters*).

2800. LISTER, Thomas (1752–1826), 1st Bn Ribblesdale, M.P. Clitheroe 1773–90 (GEC; *Old Westminsters*).

2801. LISTER-KAYE, John (1697–1752), 4th Bt, M.P. York City 1734–41 (GEC; *Genealogist*, N.S., *10, 172*).

LISTOWEL, 2d E. of, *see* HARE, William.

2802. LITTLETON, Edward (ca 1727–1812), 4th Bt, M.P. Staffordshire 1784–1812 (*Alumni Cantab.;* GEC; Wedgwood).

2803. LITTLETON, Edward John (1791–1863), 1st Bn Hatherton, M.P. Staffordshire 1812–32, South Staffordshire 1832–35 (DNB; GEC).

LIVERPOOL, E. of, *see* JENKINSON, Charles, Charles Cecil Cope, and Robert Bankes.

2804. LIVINGSTONE, Adam (d. 1795), M.P. Argyllshire 1772–80 (Musgrave's *Obituary*).

LLANDAFF, 2d E. of, *see* MATHEW, Francis John.

LLANOVER, 1st Bn, *see* HALL, Benjamin.

2805. LLOYD, Edward Pryce (1768–1854), 1st Bn Mostyn, M.P. Flint borough 1806–7, 1812–31, Beaumaris 1807–12 (GEC; *Old Westminsters*).

2806. LLOYD, Francis (ca 1748–99), M.P. Montgomeryshire 1795–99 (*Alumni Oxon.;* Williams' *Wales M.P.'s*).

2807. LLOYD, Hardress (ca 1782–1860), M.P. Kings 1807–18 (*Alumni Dublin.;* Burke's *LG* [ed. 1849]; Burtchaell's *Kilkenny M.P.'s,* p. 168).

2808. LLOYD, Herbert (ca 1719–69), 1st Bt, M.P. Cardigan borough 1761–68 (GEC).

2809. LLOYD, James Martin (1762–1844), 1st Bt, M.P. Steyning 1790–91, 1791–92, 1796–1806, 1806–18, Shoreham 1818–26 (*Alumni Oxon.; Gent. Mag., 2,* 646).

2810. LLOYD, John (ca 1718–55), M.P. Cardiganshire 1747–55 (*Alumni Oxon.;* Williams' *Wales M.P.'s*).

2811. LLOYD, John (ca 1749–1815), M.P. Flintshire 1797–99 (*Alumni Oxon.;* Williams' *Wales M.P.'s;* Williamson's *Middle Temple Bench Book*).

2812. LLOYD, Maurice, M.P. Gatton 1782–87.

2813. LLOYD, Philip (d. 1735), M.P. Saltash 1723–27, Aylesbury 1727–30, Christchurch 1732–34, Lostwithiel 1734–35 (Musgrave's *Obituary*).

2814. LLOYD, Richard (ca 1697–1757), M.P. Cardigan borough 1730–41 (*Alumni Oxon.;* Williams' *Wales M.P.'s*).

2815. LLOYD, Richard (ca 1697–1761), M.P. St. Michael 1745–47, Maldon 1747–54, Totnes 1754–59 (*Alumni Cantab.*).

2816. LLOYD, Richard Savage (ca 1730–1810), M.P. Totnes 1759–68
(*Alumni Cantab.; Eton Coll. Reg.; Gent. Mag., 1,* 498).

LLOYD, Samuel Jones, *see* LOYD, Samuel Jones.

2817. LLOYD, Thomas (ca 1771–1829), M.P. Limerick Co. 1826–29
(Burke's *Irish LG; Alumni Dublin.;* cf. *Alumni Oxon.*).

2818. LLOYD, Walter (d. 1747), M.P. Cardiganshire 1734–41 (Williams'
Wales M.P.'s).

2819. LLOYD-MOSTYN, Edward Mostyn (1795–1884), 2d Bn Mostyn, M.P.
Flintshire 1831–37, 1841–42, 1847–54, Lichfield 1846–47 (GEC;
Old Westminsters).

2820. LOCH, James (1780–1855), M.P. St. Germans 1827–30, Tain burghs
1830–52 (DNB; *1832 List*).

2821. LOCH, John (1781–1868), M.P. Hythe 1830–32 (Boase; Burke's
Peerage; Wilks' *Barons of the Cinque Ports,* p. 120).

2822. LOCK, William (ca 1680–1761), M.P. Great Grimsby 1741–61
(*Court and City Register* [1760], p. 36; *Lloyd's Evening Post,*
21–23 Oct. 1761; *Notes and Queries, 165,* 333).

LOCKHART, Alexander Macdonald, *see* MACDONALD-LOCKHART,
Alexander.

LOCKHART, John Ingram, *see* WASTIE, John.

2823. LOCKHART, Thomas (ca 1739–75), M.P. Elgin burghs 1771–74
(Fisher's *Masham,* p. 384 n.; Foster's *Scots M.P.'s; Linc. Inn
Reg.;* Venn MS).

LOCKHART, William Eliott, *see* ELIOTT-LOCKHART, William.

2824. LOCKHART-ROSS, Charles (ca 1763–1814), 7th Bt, M.P. Tain burghs
1786–96, Ross-shire 1796–1806, Linlithgow burghs 1806–7
(GEC).

2825. LOCKHART-ROSS, John (1721–90), 6th Bt, M.P. Linlithgow burghs
1761–68, Lanarkshire 1768–74 (DNB; GEC).

2826. LOCKWOOD, Richard (ca 1672–1756), M.P. Hindon 1713–15, London 1722–27, Worcester City 1734–41 (Burke's *LG; Old Westminsters*).

2827. LOCKYER, Charles (d. 1752), M.P. Ilchester 1727–47 (Musgrave's
Obituary).

2828. LOCKYER, Joseph Tolson (d. 1765), M.P. Ilchester 1756–65 (*Court
and City Register* [1763], p. 33; *Linc. Inn Reg.;* Musgrave's
Obituary).

2829. LOCKYER, Thomas (ca 1696–1785), M.P. Ilchester 1747–61 (*Gent.
Mag.,* p. 574).

2830. LOFT, John Henry (ca 1769–1849), M.P. Great Grimsby 1802–3,
1807–12 (*Army Lists;* MS, *ex inform.* John Bean King; *Royal
Kalendar* [1809], p. 59).

2831. LOFTUS, John (1770–1845), 2d M. of Ely, M.P. Wexford Co.
1801–6 (GEC).

2832. LOFTUS, William (ca 1752–1831), M.P. Great Yarmouth 1796–1802, 1812–18, Tamworth 1802–12 (Burke's *Peerage* sub Ely; *Gent. Mag., 2,* 467; Wedgwood).

2833. LOMBE, Edward (ca 1800–52), M.P. Arundel 1826–30 (Carthew's *Launditch, 3,* 401; *Gent. Mag., 2,* 105).

LONDONDERRY, E. of, *see* PITT, Ridgeway and Thomas.

LONDONDERRY, M. of, *see* STEWART, Frederick William Robert and Robert; *also* STEWART-VANE, Charles William.

2834. LONG, Charles (ca 1760–1838), 1st Bn Farnborough, M.P. Rye 1789–96, Midhurst 1796–1802, Wendover 1802–6, Haslemere 1806–26 (DNB; GEC).

LONG, James Tylney, *see* TYLNEY-LONG, James.

2835. LONG, Richard (ca 1692–1760), M.P. Chippenham 1734–41 (Burke's *LG*).

2836. LONG, Richard Godolphin (1761–1835), M.P. Wilts 1806–18 (Burke's *LG; Gent. Mag., 2,* 324; *Misc. Geneal. et Herald.,* N.S., *3*).

2837. LONG, Robert (ca 1705–67), 6th Bt, M.P. Wootton Bassett 1734–41, Wilts 1741–67 (GEC; *Misc. Geneal. et Herald.,* N.S., *3; Old Westminsters*).

2838. LONG, Samuel (d. 1807), M.P. Ilchester 1790–96 (*Gent. Mag., 2,* 990; Burke's *LG*).

2839. LONG-NORTH, Dudley (1749–1829), M.P. St. Germans 1780–84, Great Grimsby 1784–93, 1793–96, Banbury 1796–1806, 1808–12, Richmond 1812–18, Haddington burghs 1818–20, Newtown (Hants) 1820–21 (Burke's *LG; DNB*).

LONG-WELLESLEY, William Pole Tylney, *see* POLE-TYLNEY-LONG-WELLESLEY, William.

2840. LONGFIELD, John (1741–1815), M.P. Mallow 1801–2 (Burke's *Irish LG; Jour. of Assoc. for Preserv. Mem. of Dead, Irel., 10,* 266).

2841. LONGFIELD, Montifort (1746–1819), M.P. Cork City 1801–18 (Burke's *Irish LG*).

2842. LONGMAN, George, M.P. Maidstone 1806–12, 1818–20 (*Royal Kalendar* [1808], p. 65).

2843. LONGUEVILLE, Charles (ca 1678–1750), M.P. Downton 1715–22, Great Bedwin 1722–27, East Looe 1727–41 (*Alumni Cantab.*).

LONSDALE, E. of, *see* LOWTHER, James and William.

2844. LOPES, Manasseh Masseh (1755–1831), 1st Bt, M.P. New Romney 1802–6, Evesham 1807–8, Barnstable 1812–20, Westbury 1820–29 (DNB).

2845. LOPES, Ralph (1788–1854), 2d Bt, M.P. Westbury 1814–19, 1831–37, 1841–47, South Devon 1849–54 (*Alumni Oxon.;* Boase; Burke's *Peerage;* Dod's *Parl. Companion* [1834], p. 138).

2846. LORAINE-SMITH, Charles (1751–1835), M.P. Leicester borough 1784–90 (Burke's *Peerage; Eton Coll. Reg.*).

LORD, John, *see* OWEN, John.

LORNE, M. of, *see* CAMPBELL, George and John.

LORTON, 2d Vct, *see* KING, Robert Edward.

LOTHIAN, M. of, *see* KERR, John William Robert and William.

2847. LOTT, Henry Baines (1781–1833), M.P. Honiton 1826–30, 1831–32 (Devonshire Assoc. *Trans., 66,* 268; Farquharson's *Honiton,* pp. 14, 49; *Gent. Mag., 1,* 572).

LOUGHBOROUGH, Bn, *see* WEDDERBURN, Alexander; *also* ST. CLAIR-ERSKINE, James Alexander.

LOVAINE, Bn, *see* PERCY, Hugh and Algernon George.

2848. LOVEDEN, Edward Loveden (ca 1751–1822), M.P. Abingdon 1783–96, Shaftesbury 1802–12 (*Alumni Oxon.;* Burke's *Peerage* sub Pryse).

LOVEDEN, Pryse, *see* PRYSE, Pryse.

LOVEL, Bn, *see* PERCEVAL, John, John James, and Henry Frederick John James.

2849. LOVETT, Verney (ca 1705–71), M.P. Wendover 1761–65 (*Alumni Dublin.;* Burke's *LG; Rugby Reg.*).

LOWDHAM, Lewis Allsopp, *see* ALLSOPP-LOWDHAM, Lewis.

2850. LOWNDES, Charles (ca 1700–84), M.P. Bramber 1768–69 (Burke's *LG;* Lipscomb's *Bucks, 3,* 544; Musgrave's *Obituary*).

2851. LOWNDES, Richard (ca 1707–75), M.P. Bucks 1741–74 (*Alumni Oxon.;* Burke's *LG; Etoniana, 99, 776*).

LOWNDES, William Selby, *see* SELBY-LOWNDES, William.

2852. LOWRY-CORRY, Armar (1801–45), 3d E. of Belmore, M.P. Fermanagh 1823–31 (GEC).

2853. LOWRY-CORRY, Henry Thomas (1803–73), M.P. Tyrone 1825–73 (DNB).

2854. LOWRY-CORRY, Somerset (1774–1841), 2d E. of Belmore, M.P. Tyrone 1801–2 (GEC).

2855. LOWTHER, Anthony (d. 1741), M.P. Cockermouth 1721–22, Westmorland 1722–41 (Collins' *Peerage* sub Lonsdale; Ferguson; Musgrave's *Obituary*).

2856. LOWTHER, Henry Cecil (1790–1867), M.P. Westmorland 1812–67 (*Old Westminsters*).

2857. LOWTHER, James (ca 1673–1755), 4th Bt, M.P. Carlisle 1694–1702, Cumberland 1708–22, 1727–55, Appleby 1723–27 (GEC).

2858. LOWTHER, James (1753–1837), M.P. Westmorland 1775–1812, Appleby 1812–18 (*Cumberland and Westmorland Antiq. and Archaeol. Soc., N.S., 43,* 127).

2859. LOWTHER, James (1736–1802), 1st E. of Lonsdale, M.P. Cumberland 1757–61, 1762–68, 1774–84, Westmorland 1761–62, Cockermouth 1769–74 (DNB; GEC).

2860. LOWTHER, John (1759–1844), 1st Bt, M.P. Cockermouth 1780–86, Carlisle 1786–86, Haslemere 1786–90, Cumberland 1796–1831 (*Old Westminsters*).

2861. LOWTHER, John Henry (1793–1868), 2d Bt, M.P. Cockermouth 1816–26, 1831–32, Wigtown burghs 1826–31, York City 1835–47 (*Old Westminsters*).

2862. LOWTHER, Robert (1741–77), M.P. Westmorland 1759–61, 1763–63 (Ferguson; Foster's *Lancashire Pedigrees;* Namier; Walker's *Peterhouse Admissions,* p. 306).

2863. LOWTHER, Thomas (1699–1745), 2d Bt, M.P. Lancaster borough 1722–45 (GEC; *Cumberland and Westmorland Antiq. and Archaeol. Soc.,* N.S., *44,* 115).

2864. LOWTHER, William (1694–1763), 2d Bt, M.P. Pontefract 1729–41 (*Alumni Cantab.;* GEC; *Cumberland and Westmorland Antiq. and Archaeol. Soc.,* N.S., *42,* 85).

2865. LOWTHER, William (ca 1727–56), 3d Bt, M.P. Cumberland 1755–56 (*Alumni Cantab.;* GEC).

2866. LOWTHER, William (1757–1844), 1st E. of Lonsdale, M.P. Carlisle 1780–84, Cumberland 1784–90, Rutland 1796–1802 (DNB; GEC; *Old Westminsters*).

2867. LOWTHER, William (1787–1872), 2d E. of Lonsdale, M.P. Cockermouth 1808–13, Westmorland 1813–31, 1832–41, Dunwich 1832–32 (DNB; GEC; *Harrow Reg.*).

2868. LOYD, Samuel Jones (1796–1883), 1st Bn Overstone, M.P. Hythe 1819–26 (DNB; GEC).

2869. LUBBOCK, John (1744–1816), 1st Bt, M.P. Bossiney 1796–1802, Leominster 1802–12 (Burke's *Peerage;* Williams' *Hereford M.P.'s*).

2870. LUBBOCK, John William (1774–1840), 2d Bt, M.P. Leominster 1812–20 (Williams' *Hereford M.P.'s*).

LUCAN, E. of, *see* BINGHAM, Charles, George Charles, and Richard.

2871. LUCAS, Thomas (d. 1784), M.P. Grampound 1780–84 (Musgrave's *Obituary; Royal Kalendar* [1782], p. 32).

2872. LUCY, George (1798–1845), M.P. Fowey 1818–19, 1820–30 (*Alumni Oxon.;* Burke's *LG; Gent. Mag., 2,* 534; *Harrow Reg.*).

2873. LUDLOW, Peter (1730–1803), 1st E. Ludlow, M.P. Hunts 1768–96 (GEC).

2874. LUMLEY, James (ca 1706–66), M.P. Chichester 1729–34, Arundel 1741–47 (*Alumni Cantab.; Eton Coll. Reg.*).

2875. LUMLEY, John (d. 1739), M.P. Arundel 1728–39 (Collins' *Peerage* sub Scarborough; Musgrave's *Obituary*).

2876. LUMLEY-SAUNDERSON, George Augusta (1753–1807), 5th E. of Scarborough, M.P. Lincoln City 1774–80 (GEC; *Eton Coll. Reg.*).

2877. LUMLEY-SAUNDERSON, Richard (1757–1832), 6th E. of Scarborough, M.P. Lincoln City 1784–90 (GEC).

2878. LUMLEY-SAUNDERSON, Thomas (ca 1690–1752), 3d E. of Scarborough, M.P. Arundel 1722–27, Lincolnshire 1727–40 (GEC; *Eton Coll. Reg.*).

2879. LUMLEY-SAVILE, John (1788–1856), 8th E. of Scarborough, M.P. Notts 1826–32, North Nottinghamshire 1832–35 (GEC; *Eton Lists*).

LURGAN, 1st Bn, *see* BROWNLOW, Charles.

2880. LUSHINGTON, James Law (ca 1779–1859), M.P. Petersfield 1825–26, Hastings 1826–27, Carlisle 1827–31 (DNB; *Harrow Reg.*).

2881. LUSHINGTON, Stephen (1744–1807), 1st Bt, M.P. Hedon 1783–84, Helston 1790–96, St. Michael 1796–1802, Penryn 1802–6, Plympton Erle 1806–7 (GEC).

2882. LUSHINGTON, Stephen (1782–1873), M.P. Great Yarmouth 1806–8, Ilchester 1820–26, 1831–32, Tregony 1826–30, Winchelsea 1831–31, Tower Hamlets 1832–41 (DNB; *Eton Coll. Reg.*).

2883. LUSHINGTON, Stephen Rumbold (1776–1868), M.P. Rye 1807–12, Canterbury 1812–30, 1835–37 (DNB; *Rugby Reg.*).

2884. LUSHINGTON, William (1747–1823), M.P. London 1795–1802 (Beaven's *Aldermen of London;* Foster's *Baronetage*).

2885. LUTHER, John (ca 1739–86), M.P. Essex 1763–84 (Ball and Venn's *Admissions to Trinity College; Essex Review, 26* [1917], 178; Huguenot Soc. *Proceedings, 9,* 122; *Notes and Queries,* 11th Ser., *7, 513*).

2886. LUTTRELL, Alexander (1705–37), M.P. Minehead 1727–37 (*Alumni Oxon.;* Burke's *LG;* Musgrave's *Obituary*).

LUTTRELL, Francis Fownes and Henry Fownes, *see* FOWNES-LUTTRELL, Francis and Henry.

2887. LUTTRELL, Henry Lawes (1743–1821), 2d E. of Carhampton, M.P. Bossiney 1768–69, 1774–84, Middlesex 1769–74, Plympton Erle 1790–94, Ludgershall 1817–21 (DNB; GEC; *Old Westminsters*).

2888. LUTTRELL, James (ca 1751–88), M.P. Stockbridge 1775–84, Dover 1784–88 (DNB).

LUTTRELL, John Fownes, *see* FOWNES-LUTTRELL, John.

2889. LUTTRELL, Simon (ca 1713–87), 1st E. of Carhampton, M.P. St. Michael 1755–61, Wigan 1761–68, Weobley 1768–74, Stockbridge 1774–80 (GEC).

2890. LUTTRELL, Temple Simon (ca 1739–1803), M.P. Milborne Port 1775–80 (DNB; *Old Westminsters*).

LUTTRELL, Thomas Fownes, *see* FOWNES-LUTTRELL, Thomas.

2891. LUTTRELL-OLMIUS, John (ca 1745–1829), 3d E. of Carhampton, M.P. Stockbridge 1774–75, 1780–85 (DNB; GEC).

2892. LUTWYCHE, Thomas (1674–1734), M.P. Appleby 1710–22, Callington 1722–27, Agmondesham 1728–34 (DNB; *Old Westminsters*).

LUXBOROUGH, 1st Bn, *see* KNIGHT, Robert.

2893. LUXMORE, John (1756–88), M.P. Okehampton 1784–85 (Burke's *LG*).

2894. LYGON, Edward Pyndar (ca 1786–1860), M.P. Callington 1818–20 (Boase; *Old Westminsters*).

2895. LYGON, Henry Beauchamp (1784–1863), 4th E. Beauchamp, M.P. Worcestershire 1816–31, West Worcestershire 1832–53 (GEC).

2896. LYGON, William (1747–1816), 1st E. Beauchamp, M.P. Worcestershire 1775–1806 (DNB; GEC).

2897. LYGON, William Beauchamp (ca 1782–1823), 2d E. Beauchamp, M.P. Worcestershire 1806–16 (GEC; *Old Westminsters*).

LYMINGTON, Vct, *see* WALLOP, John.

2898. LYNCH, William (ca 1731–85), M.P. Weobley 1762–68, 1774–80, Canterbury 1768–74 (*Alumni Cantab.*).

LYNDHURST, 1st Bn, *see* COPLEY, John Singleton.

2899. LYNE-STEPHENS, Stephens (ca 1801–60), M.P. Barnstable 1830–31 (Boase).

LYNEDOCH, 1st Bn, *see* GRAHAM, Thomas.

2900. LYON, David (ca 1794–1872), M.P. Berealston 1831–32 (Boase; Burke's LG; *Harrow Reg.*).

2901. LYON, Thomas (1704–53), 8th E. of Strathmore, M.P. Forfarshire 1734–35 (*Scots Peerage*).

2902. LYON, Thomas (ca 1741–96), M.P. Aberdeen burghs 1768–79 (*Scots Peerage;* Venn MS).

2903. LYON, William (ca 1807–92), M.P. Seaford 1831–32 (Boase; Burke's *LG; Harrow Reg.*).

2904. LYSTER, Richard (ca 1691–1766), M.P. Shrewsbury 1722–23, 1727–34, Salop 1740–66 (Burke's *LG* [ed. 1849]; Shrop. Archaeol. Soc. *Trans.*, 4th Ser., *6*, 74).

2905. LYSTER, Richard (ca 1772–1819), M.P. Shrewsbury 1814–19 (Burke's *LG* [ed. 1849]; *Gent. Mag., 1,* 584).

2906. LYTTELTON, George (1709–73), 1st Bn Lyttelton, M.P. Okehampton 1735–56 (DNB; GEC; *Eton Coll. Reg.*).

2907. LYTTELTON, George Fulke (1763–1828), 2d Bn Lyttelton, M.P. Bewdley 1790–96 (GEC; *Harrow Reg.*).

2908. LYTTELTON, Richard (d. 1770), M.P. Brackley 1747–54, Poole 1754–61 (Burke's *Peerage; Notes and Queries*, 12th Ser., *6*, 42).

2909. LYTTELTON, Thomas (ca 1686–1751), 4th Bt, M.P. Worcestershire 1721–34, Camelford 1734–41 (GEC).

2910. LYTTELTON, Thomas (1744–79), 2d Bn Lytteleton, M.P. Bewdley 1768–69 (DNB; GEC; *Eton Coll. Reg.*).

2911. LYTTELTON, William Henry (1724–1808), 1st Bn Lyttelton, M.P. Bewdley 1748–55, 1774–90 (DNB; GEC; *Eton Coll. Reg.*).

2912. LYTTELTON, William Henry (1782–1837), 3d Bn Lyttelton, M.P. Worcestershire 1806–20 (DNB; GEC; *Rugby Reg.*).

LYTTON, 1st Bn, *see* BULWER-LYTTON, Edward George Earle.

LYTTON, John Robinson, *see* ROBINSON-LYTTON, John.

LYVEDEN, 1st Bn, *see* VERNON, Robert Vernon.

2913. MABBOT, William (ca 1694–1764), M.P. Hindon 1756–61 (Leaning's *Tadworth Court,* pp. 48–59; Musgrave's *Obituary;* Prinsep's *Madras Civilians,* p. xiv).

2914. MABERLY, John (ca 1780–1845), M.P. Rye 1816–18, Abingdon 1818–32 (*Bon Accord* 24 May 1930, copy in Aberdeen Pub. Lib.).

2915. MABERLY, William Leader (1798–1885), M.P. Westbury 1819–20, Northampton borough 1820–30, Shaftesbury 1831–32, Chatham 1832–34 (*Alumni Oxon.;* DNB).

2916. MACARTNEY, George (1737–1806), 1st E., Macartney, M.P. Cockermouth 1768–69, Ayr burghs 1774–76, Berealston 1780–81 (DNB; GEC).

2917. MACAULAY, Colin (ca 1760–1836), M.P. Saltash 1826–30 (*Army Lists; Gent. Mag., 1,* 443).

2918. MACAULAY, Thomas Babington (1800–59), 1st Bn Macaulay, M.P. Calne 1830–32, Leeds 1832–34, Edinburgh City 1839–47, 1852–56 (DNB; GEC).

2919. MACBRIDE, John (d. 1800), M.P. Plympton Erle 1784–90 (DNB).

MACCLESFIELD, E. of, *see* PARKER, George and Thomas.

2920. MACCORMICK, William (1742–1816), M.P. Truro 1784–87 (*Army Lists; Journal of the Royal Institution of Cornwall, 19,* 237; *Parish Reg. St. Mary, Truro,* p. 534).

2921. MACDONALD, Alexander (1773–1824), 2d Bn Macdonald, M.P. Saltash 1796–1802 (GEC).

2922. MACDONALD, Archibald (1747–1826), 1st Bt, M.P. Hindon 1777–80, Newcastle-under-Lyme 1780–93 (GEC; *Old Westminsters*).

2923. MACDONALD, James (1784–1832), 2d Bt, M.P. Tain burghs 1805–6, Newcastle-under-Lyme 1806–12, Sutherland 1812–16, Calne 1816–31, Hampshire 1831–32 (*Old Westminsters*).

2924. MACDONALD, Reginald George (1788–1873), M.P. Plympton Erle 1812–24 (Burke's *LG; Eton Lists*).

2925. MACDONALD-LOCKHART, Alexander (ca 1776–1816), 1st Bt, M.P. Berwick-on-Tweed 1807–12 (Burke's *Peerage; Gent. Mag., 2,* 185).

2926. MACDONNELL, Charles (ca 1761–1803), M.P. Yarmouth (Hants) 1803–3 (*Admissions to St. John, Cambridge;* Burke's *Irish LG*).

2927. McDOWALL, Andrew (ca 1759–1834), M.P. Wigtownshire 1784–96, 1802–5 (Burke's *LG;* Foster's *Scots M.P.'s*).

2928. MACDOWALL, William (ca 1700–84), M.P. Renfrewshire 1768–74 (Addison's *Glasgow Matric. Albums;* Burke's *LG*).

2929. MacDowall, William (ca 1746–1810), M.P. Renfrewshire 1783–86, 1802–10, Ayrshire 1789–90, Glasgow burghs 1790–1802 (Addison's *Glasgow Matric. Albums;* Grant's *Faculty of Advocates*).

2930. MacDowall-Grant, David (d. 1840), M.P. Banffshire 1795–96 (Burke's *LG;* Foster's *Scots M.P.'s*).

MacDuff, Vct, *see* Duff, James.

2931. Mackay, Alexander (ca 1717–89), M.P. Sutherlandshire 1761–68, Tain burghs 1768–73 (Leslie's *Landguard Fort,* p. 108; *Scots Peerage* sub Reay).

2932. Mackay, George (ca 1715–82), M.P. Sutherlandshire 1747–61 (Burke's *Peerage* sub Reay; Grant's *Faculty of Advocates*).

Mackenzie, Charles Stuart Wortley, *see* Stuart-Wortley-Mackenzie, Charles.

2933. Mackenzie, Francis Humberston (1754–1815), 1st Bn Seaforth and Mackenzie, M.P. Ross-shire 1784–90, 1794–96 (DNB; GEC).

Mackenzie, James Alexander Stewart, *see* Stewart-Mackenzie, James Alexander.

Mackenzie, James Archibald Stuart Wortley, *see* Stuart-Wortley-Mackenzie, James Archibald.

Mackenzie, James Stuart, *see* Stuart-Mackenzie, James.

2934. Mackenzie, James Wemyss (1770–1843), 5th Bt, M.P. Ross-shire 1822–31 (GEC).

2935. Mackenzie, John (ca 1727–89), M.P. Ross-shire 1780–84 (DNB; GEC).

2936. Mackenzie, John Randoll (ca 1763–1809), M.P. Tain burghs 1806–8, Sutherlandshire 1808–9 (Burke's *Peerage; Gent. Mag., 2,* 780; Venn MS).

Mackenzie, John Stuart Wortley, *see* Stuart-Wortley-Mackenzie, John.

2937. Mackenzie, Kenneth (ca 1718–61), M.P. Inverness burghs 1741–47, Ross-shire 1747–61 (GEC and *Scots Peerage* sub Seaforth).

2938. Mackenzie, Kenneth (1744–81), 1st E. of Seaforth, M.P. Caithness-shire 1768–74 (GEC).

2939. Mackenzie, Thomas (ca 1789–1822), M.P. Ross-shire 1818–22 (Foster's *Scots M.P.'s; Gent. Mag., 2,* 379; MS, *ex inform.* the Reverend H. J. Matthew).

2940. Mackenzie, William Frederick (ca 1791–1814), M.P. Ross-shire 1812–14 (GEC sub Seaforth; *Harrow Reg.*).

2941. Mackenzie-Fraser, Alexander (ca 1756–1809), M.P. Cromarty-shire 1802–6, Ross-shire 1806–9 (DNB).

2942. Mackenzie-Fraser, Charles (1792–1871), M.P. Ross-shire 1814–18 (Burke's *LG;* Foster's *Scots M.P.'s*).

Mackie, John Ross, *see* Ross-Mackye, John.

2943. Mackillop, James, M.P. Tregony 1830–32 (*1832 List*).

2944. MACKINNON, Charles (d. 1833), M.P. Ipswich 1827–31 (*Gent. Mag., 1* [1834], 656).

2945. MACKINNON, William Alexander (ca 1784–1870), M.P. Dunwich 1819–20, Lymington 1831–32, 1835–52, Rye 1853–65 (DNB; *Admissions to St. John, Cambridge*).

2946. MACKINTOSH, James (1765–1832), M.P. Nairnshire 1813–18, Knaresborough 1818–32 (DNB).

2947. MACKRETH, Robert (ca 1726–1819), M.P. Castle Rising 1774–84, Ashburton 1784–1802 (DNB).

2948. MACKWORTH, Herbert (1687–1765), M.P. Cardiff 1739–65 (*Alumni Oxon.; Old Westminsters*).

2949. MACKWORTH, Herbert (1737–91), 1st Bt, M.P. Cardiff 1766–90 (GEC; *Old Westminsters*).

2950. MACKWORTH-PRAED, Humphry (1719–1803), M.P. St. Ives 1761–68, Cornwall 1772–74 (*Alumni Cantab.;* Foster's *Baronetage*).

2951. MACKWORTH-PRAED, William (1694–1752), M.P. St. Ives 1734–41 (Boase and Courtney, *Biblio. Cornub.;* Foster's *Baronetage;* Lipscomb's *Bucks, 4,* 378).

2952. MACKWORTH-PRAED, William (1749–1833), M.P. St. Ives 1774–75, 1780–1806, Banbury 1806–8 (Boase and Courtney, *Biblio. Cornub.; Eton Coll. Reg.*).

2953. MACKWORTH-PRAED, Winthrop (1802–39), M.P. St. Germans 1830–32, Great Yarmouth 1835–37, Aylesbury 1837–39 (DNB).

2954. McLEAN-CLEPHANE, William Douglas (d. 1803), M.P. Kinross-shire 1802–3 (Foster's *Scots M.P.'s*).

2955. MACLEANE, Lauchlin (ca 1728–78), M.P. Arundel 1768–71 (*Alumni Dublin.;* Holzman's *Nabobs in Eng.*).

MACLEOD, Bn, *see* MACKENZIE, John.

2956. MACLEOD, Alexander, M.P. Honiton 1780–81.

2957. MACLEOD, John Norman (1788–1835), M.P. Sudbury 1828–30 (*Alumni Oxon.;* Burke's *LG*).

2958. MACLEOD, Norman (ca 1706–72), M.P. Inverness-shire 1741–54 (Burke's *LG;* A. Mackenzie, *Hist. of the Macleods,* p. 122).

2959. MACLEOD, Norman (1754–1801), M.P. Inverness-shire 1790–96 (*Alumni Oxon.;* Burke's *LG*).

2960. MACLEOD, Robert Bruce Aeneas (1764–1844), M.P. Cromartyshire 1807–12 (Addison's *Glasgow Matric. Albums;* Burke's *LG; Eton Coll. Reg.;* Grant's *Faculty of Advocates*).

2961. MACLEOD, Roderick (ca 1786–1853), M.P. Cromartyshire 1818–20, Sutherland 1831–37, Inverness burghs 1837–40 (*Eton Lists;* Foster's *Scots M.P.'s;* Grant's *Faculty of Advocates*).

2962. McCLINTOCK, John (1770–1855), M.P. Athlone 1820–20, Louth 1830–31 (*Alumni Dublin.;* Burke's *Irish LG*).

2963. McMahon, John (ca 1754–1817), 1st Bt, M.P. Aldeburgh 1802–12 (*Ann. Biog. and Obit.* [1817], p. 312; Burke's *Peerage*).

2964. MacNaghton, Edmund Alexander (1762–1832), M.P. Antrim 1801–12, 1826–30, Orford 1812–20 (Foster's *Baronetage; Gent. Mag., 1,* 563).

2965. Macnamara, John, M.P. Leicester borough 1784–90 (*Notes and Queries, 170,* 393).

2966. McNamara, William Nugent (ca 1775–1856), M.P. Clare 1830–52 (Burke's *Irish LG;* Boase).

2967. Maconochie-Welwood, Alexander (1777–1861), M.P. Yarmouth (Hants) 1817–18, Anstruther Easter burghs 1818–19 (DNB).

2968. Macpherson, James (1736–96), M.P. Camelford 1780–96 (DNB).

2969. Macpherson, John (ca 1745–1821), 1st Bt, M.P. Cricklade 1779–82, Horsham 1796–1802 (DNB; GEC).

2970. Macpherson-Grant, George (1781–1846), 1st Bt, M.P. Sutherlandshire 1809–12, 1816–26 (Burke's *Peerage;* Foster's *Scots M.P.'s*).

2971. Macqueen, Thomas Potter (1792–1854), M.P. East Looe 1816–26, Bedfordshire 1826–30 (Cathrall's *Oswestry,* p. 147; *Gent. Mag., 1,* 558; Venn's *Biog. Hist. Gonville and Caius, 2,* 155; Williams' *Great Sessions in Wales*).

2972. Madan, Martin (ca 1701–56), M.P. Wootton Bassett 1747–54 (*Alumni Cantab.; Notes and Queries,* 12th Ser., *2,* 231).

2973. Maddock, John Finchett, M.P. Chester City 1832–32.

2974. Madocks, John (ca 1723–94), M.P. Westbury 1786–90 (DNB sub W. A. Madocks; Lloyd's *Powys Fadog, 5,* 328; *Shrewsbury School Reg.*).

2975. Madocks, William Alexander (1773–1828), M.P. Boston 1802–20, Chippenham 1820–26 (*Alumni Oxon.;* DNB; *Notes and Queries, 193,* 15).

2976. Magenis, Richard (ca 1763–1831), M.P. Enniskillen 1812–28 (Burke's *Irish LG*).

Magens, Dorien Magens, *see* Dorien-Magens, Magens.

Mahon, Vct, *see* Stanhope, Charles and Philip Henry.

2977. Mahon, Charles James Patrick O'Gorman (1800–91), M.P. Clare 1830–31, 1879–85, Ennis 1847–52, Carlow 1887–91 (DNB).

2978. Mahon, Ross (1763–1835), 1st Bt, M.P. Ennis 1820–20 (*Alumni Dublin.;* Foster's *Baronetage*).

2979. Mahon, Stephen (1768–1828), M.P. Roscommon 1806–26 (Burke's *Irish LG*).

2980. Mahon, Thomas (1766–1835), 2d Bn Hartland, M.P. Roscommon 1801–2 (*Admissions to St. John, Cambridge;* GEC).

2981. Mainwaring, George Boulton (b. ca 1773), M.P. Middlesex 1804–5, 1806–6 (*Admissions to St. John, Cambridge*).

2982. MAINWARING, William (1735–1821), M.P. Middlesex 1784–1802 (*Admissions to St. John, Cambridge; Merchant Taylor School Reg.*).

2983. MAISTER, Henry (1699–1744), M.P. Hull 1734–41 (Burke's *LG* [ed. 1849]; Gunnell's *Hull Celebrities*, p. 356; Poulson's *Holderness, 2,* 445).

2984. MAITLAND, Anthony (1785–1863), 10th E. of Lauderdale, M.P. Haddington burghs 1813–18, Berwickshire 1826–32 (DNB; GEC).

2985. MAITLAND, Charles (d. 1751), M.P. Aberdeen burghs 1748–51 (Burke's *Peerage* sub Arbuthnot; Foster's *Scots M.P.'s*).

MAITLAND, Ebenezer Fuller, *see* FULLER-MAITLAND, Ebenezer.

2986. MAITLAND, James (1759–1839), 8th E. of Lauderdale, M.P. Newport 1780–84, Malmesbury 1784–89 (DNB; GEC).

2987. MAITLAND, James (1784–1860), 9th E. of Lauderdale, M.P. Camelford 1806–7, Richmond 1818–20, Appleby 1826–32 (GEC).

2988. MAITLAND, John (ca 1732–79), M.P. Haddington burghs 1774–79 (*Scots Peerage* sub Lauderdale).

2989. MAITLAND, John (ca 1754–1831), M.P. Chippenham 1803–7,·1808–12, 1817–18 (Burke's *LG; Misc. Geneal. et Herald.,* 1st Ser., *2,* 210).

MAITLAND, John Bushby, *see* BUSHBY-MAITLAND, John.

2990. MAITLAND, Thomas (1759–1824), M.P. Haddington burghs 1790–96, 1802–5, 1812–13 (DNB).

2991. MAJOR, John (1698–1781), 1st Bt, M.P. Scarborough 1761–68 (GEC).

MAJOR, John, *see* HENNIKER-MAJOR, John.

2992. MALCOLM, John (1769–1833), M.P. Launceston 1831–32 (DNB).

2993. MALCOLM, Neill (ca 1798–1857), M.P. Boston 1826–31 (*Alumni Oxon.;* Burke's *LG;* Boase; *Harrow Reg.; 1832 List*).

MALMESBURY, E. of, *see* HARRIS, James and James Edward.

MALPAS, Vct, *see* CHOLMONDELEY, George.

MANCHESTER, D. of, *see* MONTAGU, George and Robert.

MANDEVILLE, Vct, *see* MONTAGU, George.

2994. MANGLES, James (ca 1762–1838), M.P. Guildford 1831–37 (*Annual Register,* p. 236; Dod's *Parl. Companion* [1834], p. 140; *Gent. Mag., 1* [1839], 96).

2995. MANN, Horatio (1744–1814), 2d Bt, M.P. Maidstone 1774–84, Sandwich 1790–1807 (GEC; Walker's *Peterhouse Admissions,* p. 320).

2996. MANN, James (1778–1852), 5th E. Cornwallis, M.P. Eye 1799–1806, 1807–7 (GEC; *Alumni Cantab.; Eton Coll. Reg.*).

2997. MANNERS, Charles (1754–87), 4th D. of Rutland, M.P. Cambridge Univ. 1774–79 (DNB; GEC; *Eton Coll. Reg.*).

2998. MANNERS, Charles Henry Somerset (1780–1855), M.P. Cambridge-
      shire 1802–30, North Leicestershire 1835–52 (Burke's *Peerage*
      sub Rutland; Boase).
2999. MANNERS, George (d. 1772), M.P. Scarborough 1768–72 (*Eton
      Coll. Reg.*).
3000. MANNERS, John (1721–70), M.P. Grantham 1741–54, Cambridge-
      shire 1754–70 (*Alumni Cantab.;* DNB; GEC; *Eton Coll. Reg.*).
3001. MANNERS, John (1730–92), M.P. Newark 1754–74 (GEC; Nichols'
      Leicester, 2, pt. 1, 100; *Old Westminsters*).
3002. MANNERS, Robert (ca 1718–82), M.P. Hull 1747–82 (Burke's
      Peerage sub Rutland; Bean; Musgrave's *Obituary; Notes and
      Queries,* 12th Ser., *2,* 231 and *3,* 304).
3003. MANNERS, Robert (1758–82), M.P. Cambridgeshire 1780–82
      (DNB).
3004. MANNERS, Robert (1758–1823), M.P. Great Bedwin 1784–90, Cam-
      bridgeshire 1791–1820 (Burke's *Peerage* sub Rutland).
3005. MANNERS, Robert William (1781–1835), M.P. Scarborough 1802–6,
      Leicestershire 1806–31, North Leicestershire 1832–35 (Burke's
      Peerage sub Rutland).
3006. MANNERS, Russell (ca 1774–1840), M.P. Grantham 1806–7 (MS,
      ex inform. John Bean King; Venn MS).
3007. MANNERS, Sherard (ca 1713–42), M.P. Tavistock 1741–42 (Collins'
      Peerage sub Rutland; Fletcher's *Leicester Pedigrees*).
3008. MANNERS, William (1697–1772), M.P. Leicestershire 1719–34,
      Newark 1738–54 (Collins' *Peerage* sub Rutland; Fletcher's
      Leicester Pedigrees).
      MANNERS, William, *see* TALMASH, William.
3009. MANNERS-SUTTON, Charles (1780–1845), 1st Vct Canterbury, M.P.
      Scarborough 1806–32, Cambridge Univ. 1832–35 (DNB; GEC).
3010. MANNERS-SUTTON, George (1723–83), M.P. Grantham 1754–80,
      Newark 1780–83 (*Eton Coll. Reg.*).
3011. MANNERS-SUTTON, George (1751–1804), M.P. Newark 1774–80,
      Grantham 1780–1802, Bramber 1802–4 (*Eton Coll. Reg.*).
3012. MANNERS-SUTTON, John (1752–1826), M.P. Newark 1783–96, Il-
      chester 1804–6 (Burke's *Peerage* sub Canterbury; *Gent. Mag.,
      1,* 463).
3013. MANNERS-SUTTON, Thomas (1756-1842), 1st Bn Manners, M.P.
      Newark 1796–1805 (DNB; GEC).
3014. MANNING, William (1763–1835), M.P. Plympton Erle 1794–96,
      Lymington 1796–1806, 1818–20, 1821–26, Evesham 1806–18,
      Penryn 1826–30 (Oliver's *Antigua, 3,* 439; Williams' *Worcester
      M.P.'s*).
      MANSEL, Richard, *see* PHILLIPS, Richard.
3015. MANSEL, Bussey (ca 1701–50), 4th Bn Mansel, M.P. Cardiff 1727–
      34, Glamorgan 1737–44 (*Alumni Oxon.;* GEC).

3016. MANSEL, William (1739–1804), 9th Bt, M.P. Carmarthenshire 1784–90 (GEC).

3017. MANSEL-TALBOT, Christopher Rice (1803–90), M.P. Glamorgan 1830–85, Mid-Glamorgan 1885–90 (Burke's *LG;* Nicholas' *County Families of Wales, 2,* 641; Williams' *Wales M.P.'s*).

MANSFIELD, E. of, *see* MURRAY, William and William David.

3018. MANSFIELD, James (1734–1821), M.P. Cambridge Univ. 1779–84 (*Alumni Cantab.; DNB; Eton Coll. Reg.*).

3019. MANSFIELD, John (1778–1841), M.P. Leicester borough 1818–26 (*Gent. Mag., 1* [1839], 319; Venn MS).

MARCH, E. of, *see* GORDON-LENNOX, Charles.

3020. MARCH-PHILLIPPS, Charles (1779–1862), M.P. Leicestershire 1818–20, 1831–32, North Leicestershire 1832–37 (Burke's *LG;* Boase; *Eton Lists*).

MARCHMONT, 3d E. of, *see* HUME-CAMPBELL, Hugh.

3021. MARJORIBANKS, John (1763–1833), 1st Bt, M.P. Buteshire 1812–18; Berwickshire 1818–26 (Burke's *Peerage* sub Tweedmouth; Foster's *Baronetage*).

3022. MARJORIBANKS, Stewart (ca 1774–1863), M.P. Hythe 1820–37, 1841–47 (Foster's *Baronetage;* Wilks' *Barons of the Cinque Ports,* p. 123).

3023. MARKHAM, John (1761–1827), M.P. Portsmouth 1801–18, 1820–26 (DNB; *Old Westminsters*).

3024. MARKHAM, Osborn (1769–1827), M.P. Calne 1806–7 (*Old Westminsters*).

MARLBOROUGH, D. of, *see* SPENCER-CHURCHILL, George.

3025. MARRIOTT, James (ca 1731–1803), M.P. Sudbury 1781–84, 1796–1802 (*Alumni Cantab.; DNB; Notes and Queries,* 8th Ser., *8,* 215).

3026. MARRYAT, Joseph (1757–1824), M.P. Horsham 1808–12, Sandwich 1812–24 (Bayley's *Surrey, 3,* 227; *Gent. Mag., 1, 372; Misc. Geneal. et Herald.,* 4th Ser., *3*).

3027. MARRYAT, Joseph (1789–1876), M.P. Sandwich 1826–34 (Boase; Burke's *Colonial Gentry; 1832 List*).

3028. MARSH, Charles (ca 1774–1835), M.P. East Retford 1812–18 (*Admissions to St. John, Cambridge;* DNB).

3029. MARSH, Samuel, M.P. Chippenham 1774–80.

3030. MARSHALL, Henry (1688–1754), M.P. Agmondesham 1734–54 (Beaven's *Aldermen of London;* MS, *ex inform.* the Reverend H. F. E. Harfitt; *Yorkshire Archaeol. Jour., 7,* 95).

3031. MARSHALL, John (1765–1845), M.P. Yorkshire 1826–30 (Gooder).

3032. MARSHALL, William (1796–1872), M.P. Petersfield 1826–30, Leominster 1830–31, Beverley 1831–32, Carlisle 1835–47, East Cumberland 1847–68 (Burke's *LG;* Boase; Williams' *Hereford M.P.'s*).

3033. Marsham, Charles (1744–1811), 1st E. of Romney, M.P. Maidstone 1768–74, Kent 1774–90 (GEC; *Eton Coll. Reg.*).

3034. Marsham, Charles (1777–1845), 2d E. of Romney, M.P. Hythe 1798–1802, 1806–7, Downton 1803–6 (GEC; *Eton Coll. Reg.*).

3035. Martin, Henry (1733–94), 1st Bt, M.P. Southampton borough 1790–94 (GEC).

3036. Martin, Henry (1763–1839), M.P. Kinsale 1806–18 (Burke's *LG; Harrow Reg.*).

Martin, Isaac Martin Rebow, *see* Rebow-Martin, Isaac Martin.

3037. Martin, James (d. 1744), M.P. Cambridge borough 1741–44 (Burke's *LG*).

3038. Martin, James (1738–1810), M.P. Tewkesbury 1776–1807 (Burke's *LG;* Martin, *The Grasshopper,* p. 96; Williams' *Gloucester M.P.'s*).

3039. Martin, John (1692–1767), M.P. Tewkesbury 1741–47 (Burke's *LG;* Williams' *Gloucester M.P.'s*).

3040. Martin, John (1724–94), M.P. Tewkesbury 1754–61 (Burke's *LG;* Williams' *Gloucester M.P.'s*).

3041. Martin, John (1774–1832), M.P. Tewkesbury 1812–32 (Martin, *The Grasshopper,* p. 97; Williams' *Gloucester M.P.'s*).

3042. Martin, Joseph (1726–76), M.P. Gatton 1768–74, Tewkesbury 1774–76 (Beaven's *Aldermen of London;* Burke's *LG;* Williams' *Gloucester M.P.'s*).

3043. Martin, Matthew (d. 1749), M.P. Colchester 1722–27, 1734–42 (*Essex Review, 11,* 158; *Gent. Mag.,* p. 332; Morant's *Essex, 2,* 188–89).

3044. Martin, Richard (1754–1834), M.P. Galway Co. 1801–12, 1818–27 (DNB).

3045. Martin, Samuel (1714–88), M.P. Camelford 1747–68, Hastings 1768–74 (Burke's *Peerage;* Oliver's *Antigua, 2,* 240; Martin's *Masters of the Bench, Inner Temple*).

3046. Martin, Thomas Byam (1773–1854), M.P. Plymouth 1818–32 (DNB).

3047. Marton, Edward (ca 1715–58), M.P. Lancaster borough 1747–58 (*Alumni Cantab.; Chetham Soc.,* N.S., *95,* 65).

3048. Mason-Villiers, George (1751–1800), 2d E. of Grandison, M.P. Ludlow 1774–80 (GEC; *Eton Coll. Reg.*).

3049. Massey, Hugh Dillon (ca 1768–1842), 2d Bt, M.P. Clare 1801–2 (*Alumni Dublin.;* GEC).

3050. Massy-Dawson, James Hewitt (1779–1834), M.P. Clonmel 1820–30, Limerick Co. 1830–30 (*Alumni Oxon.;* Foster's *Peerage*).

3051. Master, Legh (ca 1694–1750), M.P. Newton 1727–47 (*Alumni Cantab.*).

3052. Master, Richard (ca 1746–1800), M.P. Cirencester 1785–92 (Burke's *LG;* Williams' *Gloucester M.P.'s*).

3053. MASTER, Thomas (1690–1769), M.P. Cirencester 1712–47 (*Alumni Oxon.;* Burke's *LG;* Williams' *Gloucester M.P.'s*).

3054. MASTER, Thomas (1717–49), M.P. Cirencester 1747–49 (*Alumni Oxon.;* Burke's *LG; Old Westminsters;* Williams' *Gloucester M.P.'s*).

3055. MASTER, Thomas (ca 1744–1823), M.P. Gloucestershire 1784–96 (Burke's *LG; Old Westminsters;* Williams' *Gloucester M.P.'s*).

3056. MASTERMAN, William (ca 1722–86), M.P. Bodmin 1780–84 (Everett's *Masterman Family,* pp. 15, 27).

3057. MASTERMAN-SYKES, Mark (1771–1823), 3d Bt, M.P. York City 1807–20 (DNB; GEC; *Old Westminsters*).

3058. MASTERTON, James (1715–78), M.P. Stirling burghs 1768–74 (Foster's *Scots M.P.'s; Scots Hist. Soc., 15,* 462).

3059. MATHEW, Francis James (1768–1833), 2d E. of Landaff, M.P. Tipperary 1801–6 (GEC; *Harrow Reg.*).

3060. MATHEW, Montague James (1773–1819), M.P. Tipperary 1806–19 (GEC sub Landaff).

3061. MATHEWS, Thomas (1676–1751), M.P. Glamorgan 1745–47, Carmarthen borough 1747–51 (DNB).

3062. MATHEWS, Thomas William (ca 1711–68), M.P. Glamorgan 1756–61 (*Alumni Oxon.; Notes and Queries,* 12th Ser., *2,* 431; Williams' *Wales M.P.'s*).

3063. MATTHEWS, John (1755–1826), M.P. Herefordshire 1803–6 (DNB; *Eton Coll. Reg.*).

3064. MAUGER, Joshua (d. 1788), M.P. Poole 1768–80 (Huguenot Soc. *Proceedings, 11,* 150; Musgrave's *Obituary*).

3065. MAULE, John (ca 1706–81), M.P. Aberdeen burghs 1739–48 (Grant's *Faculty of Advocates; Scots Peerage* sub Panmure).

3066. MAULE, William (ca 1700–82), 1st E. of Panmure, M.P. Forfarshire 1735–82 (GEC).

3067. MAULE, William (1771–1852), 1st Bn Panmure, M.P. Forfarshire 1796–96, 1805–31 (DNB; GEC).

3068. MAWBEY, Joseph (1730–98), 1st Bt, M.P. Southwark 1761–74, Surrey 1775–90 (DNB; GEC).

3069. MAXWELL, Henry (1799–1868), 7th Bn Farnham, M.P. Cavan 1824–38 (*Alumni Dublin.;* Ball and Venn's *Admissions to Trinity College;* GEC).

3070. MAXWELL, John (ca 1700–54), M.P. Kirkcudbright Stewarty 1742–47 (Foster's *Scots M.P.'s;* Fraser's *Book of Calaverock, 1,* 604).

3071. MAXWELL, John (1791–1865), 8th Bt, M.P. Renfrewshire 1818–30, Lanarkshire 1832–37 (*Old Westminsters*).

MAXWELL, John Shaw Heron, *see* HERON-MAXWELL, John Shaw.

3072. MAXWELL, John Waring, M.P. Downpatrick 1820–30, 1832–34.

3073. MAXWELL, Robert (ca 1721–79), 1st E. Farnham, M.P. Taunton 1754–68 (*Alumni Dublin.;* GEC).

3074. MAXWELL, William (b. ca 1768), M.P. Linlithgow burghs 1807–12 (*Alumni Oxon.; Linc. Inn Reg.*).

3075. MAXWELL, William (1779–1838), 5th Bt, M.P. Wigtownshire 1805–12, 1822–30 (GEC).

3076. MAXWELL-BARRY, John (1767–1838), 5th Bn Farnham, M.P. Cavan 1806–23 (GEC).

3077. MAY, James Edward (ca 1753–1814), 2d Bt, M.P. Belfast 1801–14 (GEC; *Cornwallis Corr., 3,* 139 n.; *1806 List*).

3078. MAY, Stephen (ca 1763–1845), M.P. Belfast 1814–16 (*Alumni Oxon.;* GEC).

MAY, Thomas, *see* KNIGHT, Thomas.

3079. MAYHEW, William (ca 1787–1855), M.P. Colchester 1831–32 (Burke's *LG;* Boase; *Essex Rev., 8,* 239).

3080. MAYNARD, William (1721–72), 4th Bt, M.P. Essex 1759–72 (GEC).

MAYNE, John, *see* COGHILL, John.

3081. MAYNE, Robert (ca 1724–82), M.P. Gatton 1774–82 (Burke's *Ext. Peerage* [ed. 1866], sub Newhaven; Musgrave's *Obituary*).

3082. MAYNE, William (ca 1722–94), 1st Bn Newhaven, M.P. Canterbury 1774–80, Gatton 1780–90 (GEC).

3083. MAYOR, John, M.P. Abingdon 1774–82.

3084. MEADE, John (ca 1775–1849), M.P. Down 1805–17 (Burke's *Peerage* sub Clanwilliam; *Gent. Mag., 2,* 420).

MEATH, 11th E. of, *see* BRABAZON, William.

3085. MEDLEY, George (1720–96), M.P. Seaford 1768–80, East Grinstead 1783–90 (Hills' *East Grinstead,* p. 53; *Misc. Geneal. et Herald.,* 2d Ser., *4*).

3086. MEDLYCOTT, Thomas (1697–1763), M.P. Milborne Port 1734–42, 1747–63 (Burke's *Peerage*).

MEDLYCOTT, Thomas Hutchings, *see* HUTCHINGS-MEDLYCOTT, Thomas.

3087. MEDLYCOTT, William Coles (1767–1835), 1st Bt, M.P. Milborne Port 1790–91 (Burke's *Peerage; Harrow Reg.*).

MEDOWS, Charles, *see* PIERREPONT, Charles.

3088. MEDOWS, Sydney (ca 1699–1792), M.P. Penryn 1722–27, Tavistock 1727–41 (Collins' *Peerage* sub Manvers; Devonshire Assoc. *Trans., 43,* 399; Musgrave's *Obituary*).

3089. MEEKE, William (b. ca 1759), M.P. Penryn 1796–1802 (*Linc. Inn Reg.;* Venn MS).

MEGGOTT, John, *see* ELWES, John.

MELBOURNE, Vct, *see* LAMB, Peniston and William.

MELCOMBE, 1st Bn, *see* BUBB-DODINGTON, George.

3090. MELLISH, Charles (ca 1737–96), M.P. Pontefract 1774–80, Aldborough 1780–84 (Bean; C. Brown, *Newark, 2,* 261; *Genealogist, N.S., 28,* 39; *Gent. Mag.,* p. 1117).

3091. MELLISH, Joseph (ca 1716–90), M.P. Great Grimsby 1761–80 (Hunter's *Familiae Min. Gent.;* Musgrave's *Obituary*).

3092. MELLISH, William (ca 1711–91), M.P. East Retford 1741–51 (*Alumni Cantab.;* Clutterbuck's *Herts, 1,* 502; *Eton Coll. Reg.; Genealogist, N.S., 28,* 38; *Notes and Queries, 168,* 140).

3093. MELLISH, William (ca 1764–1838), M.P. Great Grimsby 1796–1802, 1803–6, Middlesex 1806–20 (*Genealogist, N.S., 28,* 38; *Gent. Mag., 2,* 325; *Notes and Queries, 179,* 133).

MELROSS, 1st Bn, *see* HAMILTON, Thomas.

MELVILLE, Vct, *see* DUNDAS, Henry; *also* SAUNDERS-DUNDAS, Robert.

MENDIP, Bn, *see* ELLIS, Henry Welbore and Welbore.

3094. MEREDITH, William (ca 1725–90), 3d Bt, M.P. Wigan 1754–61, Liverpool 1761–80 (DNB; GEC; *Old Westminsters*).

3095. MEREST, John William Drage (1789–1873), M.P. Ilchester 1818–20 (*Bury Grammar School List*).

3096. METCALFE, Henry (ca 1781–1822), M.P. Drogheda 1820–22 (*Alumni Dublin.; Gent. Mag., 1,* 478).

3097. METCALFE, Lascelles, M.P. Great Bedwin 1741–54 (*Court and City Reg.* [1753], p. 47).

3098. METCALFE, Philip (1733–1818), M.P. Horsham 1784–90, Plympton Erle 1790–96, 1802–6, Malmesbury 1796–1802 (Burke's *LG* [ed. 1849]; Courtney's *Eight Friends of the Great,* p. 14).

3099. METCALFE, Thomas Theophilus (1745–1813), 1st Bt, M.P. Abingdon 1796–1807 (Foster's *Baronetage*).

3100. METGE, John, M.P. Dundalk 1806–7, 1812–13, 1820–20 (Burke's *Irish LG*).

3101. METHAM, George Montgomery (ca 1716–93), M.P. Hull 1757–66 (*Alumni Cantab.;* Musgrave's *Obituary*).

3102. METHUEN, Paul (ca 1672–1757), M.P. Devizes 1708–10, Brackley 1713–14, 1715–47, Westbury 1747–48 (DNB).

3103. METHUEN, Paul (1723–95), M.P. Warwick borough 1762–74, Great Bedwin 1774–81 (GEC).

3104. METHUEN, Paul (1779–1849), 1st Bn Methuen, M.P. Wilts 1812–19, North Wiltshire 1832–37 (GEC; *Eton Coll. Reg.*).

3105. METHUEN, Paul Cobb (1752–1816), M.P. Great Bedwin 1781–84 (*Alumni Oxon.;* GEC; *Gent. Mag., 2,* 465).

MEXBOROUGH, E. of, *see* SAVILE, John and John Charles George.

3106. MEYLER, Richard (ca 1792–1818), M.P. Winchester 1812–18 (*Alumni Oxon.; Eton Lists; Gent. Mag., 1,* 470).

3107. MEYNELL, Henry (1789–1865), M.P. Lisburn 1826–47 (Boase; *Harrow Reg.;* Nichols' *Leicester, 3,* pt. 1, 102).

3108. MEYNELL, Hugo (1735–1808), M.P. Lichfield 1762–68, Lymington 1769–74, Stafford borough 1774–80 (Burke's *LG* [ed. 1849]; *Gent. Mag., 2,* 1134; Wedgwood).

3109. MEYRICK, Owen (ca 1705–70), M.P. Anglesey 1761–70 (*Alumni Cantab.; Old Westminsters*).

3110. MEYSEY-WIGLEY, Edmund (ca 1758–1821), M.P. Worcester City 1789–1802 (*Genealogist,* N.S., *7,* 113; Williams' *Worcester M.P.'s*).

3111. MICHEL, David Robert (ca 1736–1805), M.P. Lyme Regis 1780–84 (*Alumni Oxon.;* Burke's *LG; Gent. Mag.,* pp. 290–91; Namier).

3112. MICHEL, John (ca 1765–1844), M.P. Belfast 1816–18 (Burke's *LG; Gent. Mag., 1,* 554).

3113. MICHELL, John (1710–66), M.P. Boston 1741–54, 1761–66 (*Alumni Cantab.;* Burke's *LG*).

3114. MICHELL, Matthew (d. 1752), M.P. Westbury 1747–52 (DNB).

MIDDLESEX, E. of, *see* SACKVILLE, Charles.

MIDDLETON, 4th Bn, *see* WILLOUGHBY, Thomas.

3115. MIDDLETON, Charles (1726–1813), 1st Bn Barham, M.P. Rochester 1784–90 (DNB; GEC).

MIDDLETON, Charles Miles Lambert, *see* MONCK, Charles Miles Lambert.

3116. MIDDLETON, John (1678–1739), M.P. Aberdeen burghs 1713–39 (Biscoe, *Earls of Middleton,* p. 381; Foster's *Scots M.P.'s*).

3117. MIDDLETON, William (ca 1700–57), 3d Bt, M.P. Northumberland 1722–57 (GEC).

3118. MIDDLETON, William (1738–95), 5th Bt, M.P. Northumberland 1774–95 (GEC).

3119. MIDDLETON-FOWLE, William (1749–1829), 1st Bt, M.P. Ipswich 1784–90, 1803–6, Hastings 1806–7 (Copinger's *Suffolk, 2,* 244; *East Anglian,* N.S., *6,* 180; Venn's *Biog. Hist. Gonville and Caius, 2,* 85).

MIDLETON, Vct, *see* BRODRICK, George.

3120. MILBANK, Mark (1795–1881), M.P. Camelford 1818–19, 1820–32 (*Alumni Oxon.;* Burke's *Peerage; Harrow Reg.*).

3121. MILBANKE, Ralph (ca 1722–98), 5th Bt, M.P. Scarborough 1754–61, Richmond 1761–68 (GEC; *Old Westminsters*).

MILBANKE, Ralph Noel, *see* NOEL, Ralph.

MILDMAY, *see* ST. JOHN-MILDMAY.

3122. MILES, Philip John (1774–1845), M.P. Westbury 1820–26, Corfe Castle 1829–32, Bristol 1835–37 (Burke's *Peerage;* Williams' *Gloucester M.P.'s*).

3123. MILES, William (1797–1878), 1st Bt, M.P. Chippenham 1818–20, New Romney 1830–32, East Somerset 1834–65 (*Alumni Oxon.;* Boase; Foster's *Baronetage*).

MILFORD, 1st Bn, *see* PHILIPPS, Richard Bulkeley Philipps.

3124. MILL, Richard (ca 1690–1760), 5th Bt, M.P. Midhurst 1721–22, 1729–34, Penryn 1734–41, Horsham 1741–47 (GEC).

3125. MILL, Richard (ca 1717–70), 6th Bt, M.P. Hampshire 1765–68 (GEC).

3126. MILLER, Patrick (d. 1845), M.P. Dumfries burghs 1790–96 (Burke's *Peerage; Gent. Mag., 1, 565;* cf. Foster's *Scots M.P.'s* and Addison's *Glasgow Matric. Albums*).

3127. MILLER, Thomas (1717–89), 1st Bt, M.P. Dumfries burghs 1761–66 (DNB; GEC).

3128. MILLER, Thomas (ca 1735–1816), 5th Bt, M.P. Lewes 1774–80, Portsmouth 1806–16 (GEC; Venns MS).

3129. MILLER, William (1755–1846), 2d Bt, M.P. Edinburgh City 1780–81 (DNB; GEC).

3130. Miller, William Henry (ca 1789–1848), M.P. Newcastle-under-Lyme 1830–41 (DNB; Venn MS).

3131. MILLES, Richard (ca 1735–1820), M.P. Canterbury 1761–80 (*Admissions to St. John, Cambridge; Old Westminsters*).

3132. MILLS, Charles (1755–1826), M.P. Warwick borough 1802–26 (Burke's *LG; Gent. Mag., 1, 366;* cf. *Rugby Reg.*).

3133. MILLS, George Galway, M.P. Wallingford 1804–6, St. Michael 1807–8, Winchelsea 1818–20 (*Linc. Inn Reg.;* Oliver's *Antigua, 3, 259*).

3134. MILLS, John (1789–1871), M.P. Rochester 1831–34 (Burke's *LG; Harrow Reg.;* Smith's *Rochester in Parl.*).

3135. MILLS, Robert William (1777–1851), M.P. Bletchingley 1830–31 (*Gent. Mag., 1, 449;* Surtees' *Willington and Crook,* p. 12).

3136. MILLS, William (1750–1820), M.P. St. Ives 1790–96, Coventry 1805–12 (*Alumni Felsted.;* Burke's *LG;* Philips' *East India Co.,* pp. 337, 344; Whitley's *Coventry M.P.'s*).

3137. MILNE, David (1763–1845), M.P. Berwick-on-Tweed 1820–20 (DNB).

3138. MILNE, Patrick, M.P. Elgin burghs 1812–18.

3139. MILNER, William Mordaunt (1754–1811), 3d Bt, M.P. York City 1790–1811 (GEC; *Eton Coll. Reg.*).

3140. MILNES, James (1755–1805), M.P. Bletchingley 1802–5 (Hunter's *Familiae Min. Gent., 1,* 54).

3141. MILNES, Richard Slater (1759–1804), M.P. York City 1784–1802 (Addison's *Glasgow Matric. Albums;* Burke's *Peerage* sub Crewe; Hunter's *Familiae Min. Gent., 1,* 52).

3142. MILNES, Robert Pemberton (1784–1858), M.P. Pontefract 1806–18 (DNB).

MILSINGTOWN, Vct, *see* COLYEAR, Thomas Charles.

MILTON, 1st Bn, *see* DAMER, Joseph; *also* FITZWILLIAM, William.

MILTON, Vct, *see* DAMER, George; *also* FITZWILLIAM, Charles William Wentworth.

3143. MINCHIN, Humphrey (ca 1728–96), M.P. Okehampton 1778–84, 1785–90, Bossiney 1790–96 (*Alumni Dublin.;* Burke's *Irish LG;* Gent. Mag., p. 262).

3144. MINGAY, James (1752–1812), M.P. Thetford 1806–7 (Ball and Venn's *Admissions to Trinity College;* Martin's *Masters of the Bench, Inner Temple*).

MINSTER, 2d Bn, see CONYNGHAM, Francis Nathaniel.

MINTO, E. of, see ELLIOT, Gilbert; *also* ELLIOT-MURRAY-KYNYN-MOUND, Gilbert.

3145. MISSING, Thomas, M.P. Poole 1741–47.

3146. MITCHELL, Andrew (1708–71), M.P. Aberdeenshire 1747–54, Elgin burghs 1755–71 (DNB).

3147. MITCHELL, John (ca 1781–1827), M.P. Hull 1818–26 (*Alumni Oxon.;* Gunnel's *Hull Celebrities,* p. 444; *Old Westminsters*).

3148. MITCHELL, William (d. 1745), M.P. Huntingdonshire 1741–45 (Musgrave's *Obituary*).

3149. MITCHELL, William, M.P. Plympton Erle 1796–99.

MITFORD, John Freeman, see FREEMAN-MITFORD, John.

3150. MITFORD, William (1744–1827), M.P. Newport 1785–90, Berealston 1796–1806, New Romney 1812–18 (DNB).

3151. MOFFAT, William, M.P. Winchelsea 1802–6 (Brayley's *Surrey, 2,* 371; *1806 List*).

3152. MOLESWORTH, John (1705–66), 4th Bt, M.P. Newport 1734–41, Cornwall 1744–61 (GEC).

3153. MOLESWORTH, John (1729–75), 5th Bt, M.P. Cornwall 1765–75 (GEC).

3154. MOLESWORTH, William (1758–98), 6th Bt, M.P. Cornwall 1784–90 (GEC; *Eton Coll. Reg.*).

3155. MOLINEUX, Crisp (1730–92), M.P. Castle Rising 1771–74, Lynn 1774–90 (*Alumni Cantab.; Caribbeana, 3,* 2; Namier).

3156. MOLYNEUX, Charles William (1748–94), 1st E. of Sefton, M.P. Lancashire 1771–74 (GEC).

3157. MOLYNEUX, James More (ca 1723–59), M.P. Haslemere 1754–59 (*Alumni Oxon.;* Musgrave's *Obituary*).

3158. MOLYNEUX, Thomas More (ca 1724–76), M.P. Haslemere 1759–76 (*Alumni Oxon.;* Brayley's *Surrey, 1,* 204; Manning and Bray's *Surrey, 1,* 68).

3159. MOLYNEUX, William Philip (1772–1838), 1st Bn Sefton, M.P. Droitwich 1816–31 (GEC).

MOLYNEUX-HOWARD, Henry Thomas, see HOWARD, Henry Thomas.

3160. MONCK, Charles Miles Lambert (1779–1867), 6th Bt, M.P. Northumberland 1812–20 (GEC; *Rugby Reg.*).

3161. MONCK, John Berkeley (1769–1834), M.P. Reading 1820–30 (*Eton Coll. Reg.*).

3162. MONCKTON, Edward (1744–1832), M.P. Stafford borough 1780–

1812 (Burke's *Peerage* sub Galway; Holzman's *Nabobs in Eng.*).

3163. MONCKTON, John (ca 1695–1751), 1st Vct Galway, M.P. Clitheroe 1727–34, Pontefract 1734–47, 1749–51 (*Alumni Cantab.;* GEC).

3164. MONCKTON, Robert (1726–82), M.P. Pontefract 1751–54, 1774–74, Portsmouth 1778–82 (DNB; *Old Westminsters*).

3165. MONCKTON-ARUNDELL, Henry William (1749–74), 3d Vct Galway, M.P. Pontefract 1772–74 (GEC; *Eton. Coll. Reg.*).

3166. MONCKTON-ARUNDELL, Robert (1752–1810), 4th Vct Galway, M.P. Pontefract 1780–83, 1796–1802, York City 1783–90 (GEC).

3167. MONCKTON-ARUNDELL, William (ca 1725–72), 2d Vct Galway, M.P. Pontefract 1747–48, 1754–72, Thirsk 1749–54 (*Alumni Cantab.;* GEC; *Old Westminsters*).

3168. MONEY, William Taylor (1769–1840), M.P. Wootton Bassett 1816–20, St. Michael 1820–26 (Burke's *LG* [ed. 1849]; *Genealogists Mag., 6,* 295).

3169. MONOUX, Humphrey (ca 1703–57), 4th Bt, M.P. Tavistock 1728–34, Stockbridge 1734–41 (GEC).

MONRO, Hector, *see* MUNRO, Hector.

3170. MONSON, Charles (ca 1696–1764), M.P. Lincoln City 1734–54 (*Alumni Cantab.;* Clutterbuck's *Herts, 2,* 55, 65).

3171. MONSON, George (1730–76), M.P. Lincoln City 1754–68 (DNB; *Old Westminsters*).

MONSON, Lewis, *see* WATSON, Lewis.

3172. MONSON, William (1760–1807), M.P. Lincoln City 1806–7 (DNB; *Eton Coll. Reg.; Harrow Reg.*).

3173. MONTAGU, Charles (d. 1759), M.P. Westminster 1722–27, St. Germans 1734–41, Camelford 1741–47, Northampton borough 1754–59 (DNB sub Frederick Montagu; *Walpole-Montagu Corr.* [Yale ed.]).

3174. MONTAGU, Charles Greville (1741–84), M.P. Hunts 1762–65 (Burke's *Peerage* and Collins' *Peerage* sub Manchester).

MONTAGU, Edward, *see* HUSSEY-MONTAGU, Edward.

3175. MONTAGU, Edward (1692–1775), M.P. Huntingdon borough 1734–68 (*Alumni Cantab.; Eton Coll. Reg.*).

MONTAGU, Edward Wortley, see WORTLEY-MONTAGU, Edward.

3176. MONTAGU, Frederick (1733–1800), M.P. Northampton borough 1759–68, Higham Ferrers 1768–90 (*Alumni Cantab.;* DNB; *Eton Coll. Reg.*).

3177. MONTAGU, Frederick (1774–1827), M.P. Hunts 1796–1806, 1818–20 (Burke's *Peerage* and Collins' *Peerage* sub Manchester; *Harrow Reg.*).

3178. MONTAGU, George (ca 1713–80), M.P. Northampton borough 1744–54 (*Alumni Cantab.; Eton Coll. Reg.; Walpole-Montagu Corr.* [Yale ed.]).

3179. MONTAGU, George (1737–88), 4th D. of Manchester, M.P. Hunts 1761–62 (DNB; GEC).

3180. MONTAGU, George (1799–1855), 6th D. of Manchester, M.P. Hunts 1826–37 (GEC).

3181. MONTAGU, George John (1773–1818), 6th E. of Sandwich, M.P. Hunts 1794–1814 (GEC; *Eton Coll. Reg.*).

MONTAGU, John, *see* HUSSEY-MONTAGU, John.

3182. MONTAGU, John (d. 1734), M.P. Stockbridge 1734–34 (Musgrave's *Obituary;* Collins' *Peerage* sub Sandwich).

3183. MONTAGU, John (ca 1719–95), M.P. Huntingdon borough 1748–54 (Charnock's *Biog. Naval., 5,* 480; DNB).

3184. MONTAGU, John (1735–70), 1st Bn Montagu, M.P. Marlborough 1761–62 (GEC; *Eton Coll. Reg.*).

3185. MONTAGU, John (1743–1814), 5th E. of Sandwich, M.P. Brackley 1765–68, Hunts 1768–92 (GEC; *Eton Coll. Reg.*).

3186. MONTAGU, John George (1767–90), M.P. Huntingdon borough 1790–90 (GEC sub Sandwich; *Eton Coll. Reg.*).

3187. MONTAGU, Matthew (1762–1831), 4th Bn Rokeby, M.P. Bossiney 1786–90, Tregony 1790–96, St. Germans 1806–12 (Ball and Venn's *Admissions to Trinity College;* GEC; *Harrow Reg.*).

3188. MONTAGU, Robert (ca 1710–62), 3d D. of Manchester, M.P. Hunts 1734–39 (GEC).

3189. MONTAGU, William (ca 1720–57), M.P. Hunts 1745–47, Bossiney 1752–54 (DNB).

3190. MONTAGU, William Augustus (1752–76), M.P. Huntingdon borough 1774–76 (Collins' *Peerage* sub Sandwich; *Eton Coll. Reg.*).

3191. MONTAGU, William Augustus (ca 1786–1852), M.P. Huntingdon borough 1818–20 (*Gent. Mag., 1,* 407; O'Byrne's *Naval Biog. Dict.*).

3192. MONTAGU-SCOTT, Charles William Henry (1772–1819), 4th D. of Buccleuch and 6th D. of Queensberry, M.P. Marlborough 1793–96, 1806–7, Ludgershall 1796–1804, St. Michael 1805–6 (GEC; *Eton Coll. Reg.*).

MONTEAGLE, 1st Bn, *see* RICE, Thomas Spring.

3193. MONTEITH, Henry (ca 1764–1848), M.P. Linlithgow burghs 1820–26, 1830–31, Saltash 1826–26 (Addison's *Glasgow Matric. Albums;* Burke's *LG;* Foster's *Scots M.P.'s*).

MONTFORT, Bn, *see* BROMLEY, Henry and Thomas.

3194. MONTGOMERIE, Archibald (1726–96), 11th E. of Eglinton, M.P. Ayrshire 1761–68 (DNB; GEC).

3195. MONTGOMERIE, George (1712–66), M.P. Ipswich 1759–61 (*Alumni Cantab.; Eton Coll. Reg.*).

3196. MONTGOMERIE, Hugh (1739–1819), 12th E. of Eglinton, M.P. Ayrshire 1780–81, 1784–89, 1796–96 (DNB; GEC).

3197. MONTGOMERIE, James (1755–1829), M.P. Ayrshire 1818–29 (Foster's *Scots M.P.'s; Scots Peerage* sub Eglinton).

3198. MONTGOMERY, George (ca 1765–1831), 2d Bt, M.P. Peebles-shire 1831–31 (GEC).

3199. MONTGOMERY, Henry Conyngham (1765–1830), 1st Bt, M.P. St. Michael 1807–7, Donegal 1808–12, Yarmouth (Hants) 1812–16 (Burke's *Peerage;* Foster's *Baronetage*).

3200. MONTGOMERY, James (1766–1839), 2d Bt, M.P. Peebles-shire 1800–31 (Foster's *Baronetage;* Grant's *Faculty of Advocates*).

3201. MONTGOMERY, James William (1721–1803), 1st Bt, M.P. Dumfries burghs 1766–68, Peebles-shire 1768–75 (DNB).

3202. MONTGOMERY, William (ca 1764–1800), M.P. Peebles-shire 1790–1800 (Burke's *Peerage;* Foster's *Scots M.P.'s; Scots Mag.* [1763], p. 301).

MONTROSE, 4th D. of, see GRAHAM, James.

3203. MOORE, Abraham (1766–1822), M.P. Shaftesbury 1820–22 (*Eton Coll. Reg.; Gent. Mag., 2,* 569).

3204. MOORE, Arthur (ca 1765–1846), M.P. Tralee 1801–2 (*Alumni Dublin.;* Ball's *Judges in Ireland, 2,* 339; *Gent. Mag., 1,* 669).

3205. MOORE, Charles (1730–1822), 1st M. of Drogheda, M.P. Horsham 1776–80 (DNB; GEC).

3206. MOORE, Charles (ca 1771–1826), M.P. Woodstock 1799–1802, Heytesbury 1802–6, 1807–12 (*Eton Coll. Reg.;* Williams' *Oxford M.P.'s*).

3207. MOORE, Daniel, M.P. Great Marlow 1754–61 (*Millan's Univ. Reg.* [1760], p. 21).

MOORE, Francis Ferrand, see FOLJAMBE, Francis Ferrand.

3208. MOORE, George (b. ca 1779), M.P. Dublin City 1826–31 (*Alumni Dublin.*).

3209. MOORE, George Peter (b. ca 1779), M.P. Queenborough 1802–6 (Burke's *LG; Old Westminsters*).

3210. MOORE, Henry Seymour (ca 1784–1825), M.P. Orford 1806–12, Lisburn 1812–18 (Burke's *Peerage* sub Drogheda; *Rugby Reg.*).

3211. MOORE, John (1761–1809), M.P. Peebles 1784–90 (DNB).

3212. MOORE, John (b. ca 1738), M.P. Newry 1801–2 (Venn MS).

3213. MOORE, Peter (1753–1828), M.P. Coventry 1803–26 (DNB).

3214. MOORE, William (1699–1746), M.P. Banbury 1740–46 (*Westminster Abbey Reg.,* p. 34; Williams' *Oxford M.P.'s*).

3215. MOORSOM, Robert (1760–1835), M.P. Queenborough 1812–20 (*Ann. Biog. and Obit.* [1836], p. 17; *Gent. Mag., 2,* 321).

3216. MORANT, Edward (1730–91), M.P. Hindon 1761–68, Lymington 1774–80, Yarmouth (Hants) 1780–87 (*Alumni Oxon.;* Burke's *LG;* Lawrence-Archer, *Monument. Insc. Brit. West Indies,* p. 300).

MORAY, 12th E. of, *see* STUART, John.

3217. MORDAUNT, Charles (ca 1698–1778), 6th Bt, M.P. Warwickshire 1734–74 (GEC; *Rugby Reg.*).

3218. MORDAUNT, Charles (1771–1823), 8th Bt, M.P. Warwickshire 1804–20 (GEC; Baker's *Northampton, 2,* 256; *Eton Coll. Reg.*).

3219. MORDAUNT, John (ca 1697–1780), M.P. Pontefract 1730–34, Whitchurch 1735–41, Cockermouth 1741–68 (DNB).

3220. MORDAUNT, John (ca 1709–67), M.P. Notts 1739–47, Winchelsea 1747–54, Christchurch 1754–61 (*Old Westminsters*).

3221. MORDAUNT, John (ca 1735–1806), 7th Bt, M.P. Warwickshire 1793–1802 (GEC).

MORDEN, William, *see* HARBORD, William.

3222. MORE, Robert (1703–80), M.P. Bishop's Castle 1727–41, Shrewsbury 1754–61 (*Alumni Cantab.;* DNB; Shrop. Archaeol. Soc. *Trans., 2, 10*).

MORETON, Francis Reynolds and Henry George Francis, *see* REYNOLDS-MORETON, Francis and Henry George Francis.

3223. MORETON, Matthew Ducie (ca 1700–70), 1st Bn Ducie, M.P. Cricklade 1721–22, Calne 1723–27, Tregony 1734–34, Lostwithiel 1735–35 (GEC; *Harrow Reg.*).

3224. MORETON, William (ca 1696–1763), M.P. Brackley 1755–61 (Burke's *LG* [ed. 1849]; Martin's *Masters of the Bench, Inner Temple;* Omerod's *Chester, 3,* 51).

3225. MORGAN, Charles (1726–1806), 1st Bt, M.P. Brecon borough 1778–87, Breconshire 1787–1806 (DNB; GEC; *Old Westminsters*).

3226. MORGAN, Charles (1736–87), M.P. Brecon borough 1763–69, Breconshire 1769–87 (Burke's *Peerage* sub Tredegar; Williams' *Wales M.P.'s*).

3227. MORGAN, Charles (1760–1846), 2d Bt, M.P. Brecon borough 1787–96, Monmouthshire 1796–1831 (GEC; *Old Westminsters*).

3228. MORGAN, Charles Morgan Robinson (1792–1875), 1st Bn Tredegar, M.P. Brecon borough 1812–18, 1830–32, 1835–47 (GEC; *Harrow Reg.; Old Westminsters*).

3229. MORGAN, George Gould (1794–1845), M.P. Brecon borough 1818–30 (*Old Westminsters*).

3230. MORGAN, John (1710–67), 4th Bt, M.P. Hereford City 1734–41, Herefordshire 1755–67 (GEC; *Old Westminsters*).

3231. MORGAN, John (1732–92), M.P. Brecon borough 1769–71, Monmouthshire 1771–92 (Burke's *Peerage* sub Tredegar; Williams' *Wales M.P.'s*).

3232. MORGAN, Thomas (1702–69), M.P. Brecon borough 1723–34, Monmouthshire 1734–47, Breconshire 1747–69 (Burke's *Peerage* sub Tredegar; Williams' *Wales M.P.'s*).

3233. MORGAN, Thomas (1727–71), M.P. Brecon borough 1754–63, Monmouthshire 1763–71 (Burke's *Peerage* sub Tredegar; Williams' *Wales M.P.'s*).

3234. MORGAN, William (1725–63), M.P. Monmouthshire 1747–63 (*Alumni Oxon.;* Burke's *Peerage* sub Tredegar; Clutterbuck's *Herts, 2,* 191; Williams' *Wales M.P.'s*).

3235. MORICE, Humphry (ca 1723–85), M.P. Launceston 1750–80 (DNB).

3236. MORICE, William (ca 1707–50), 3d Bt, M.P. Newport 1727–34, Launceston 1734–50 (Boase and Courtney's *Biblio. Cornub.;* GEC).

3237. MORISON, John (ca 1758–1835), M.P. Banffshire 1827–32 (Jervise, *Epitaphs, 2,* 180).

3238. MORLAND, William (ca 1739–1815), M.P. Taunton 1796–1806 (*Gent. Mag., 2,* 94).

MORLAND, Scrope Bernard, *see* BERNARD-MORLAND, Scrope.

MORNINGTON, 2d E. of, *see* WELLESLEY, Richard Colley.

MORPETH, Vct, *see* HOWARD, Charles, George, George William Frederick, and Henry.

3239. MORRIS, Edward (ca 1769–1815), M.P. Newport 1803–12 (*Genealogists Mag., 6,* 278; *Old Westminsters*).

3240. MORRIS, John (ca 1734–1814), M.P. Calne 1790–92 (*Gent. Mag., 2,* 507; *Royal Kalendar* [1791], p. 27).

3241. MORRIS, Matthew (1713–1800), 2d Bn Rokeby, M.P. Canterbury 1747–61 (*Alumni Cantab.;* GEC; *Old Westminsters*).

3242. MORRIS, Robert (ca 1758–1816), M.P. Gloucester City 1805–16 (Fowler's *Barnwood,* p. 27; Williams' *Gloucester M.P.'s*).

3243. MORRIS, Staats Long (ca 1731–1800), M.P. Elgin burghs 1774–84 (*Scots Peerage* sub Huntley; *Westminster Abbey Reg.*).

3244. MORRISON, James (ca 1790–1857), M.P. St. Ives 1830–31, Ipswich 1831–34, 1835–37, Inverness burghs 1840–47 (DNB).

3245. MORRITT, John Bacon Sawrey (ca 1771–1843), M.P. Beverley 1799–1802, Northallerton 1814–18, Shaftesbury 1818–20 (*Admissions to St. John, Cambridge;* DNB).

3246. MORSHEAD, John (1747–1813), 1st Bt, M.P. Callington 1780–84, Bodmin 1784–1802 (GEC).

3247. MORTIMER, Hans Winthrop (1734–1807), M.P. Shaftesbury 1775–80, 1781–90 (*Gent. Mag., 1,* 283; *Linc. Inn Reg.; Misc. Geneal. et Herald.,* 3d Ser., *3,* 23).

3248. MORTLOCK, John (ca 1755–1816), M.P. Cambridge borough 1784–88 (*Gent. Mag., 1* [1816], 477 and *2* [1848], 208; Palmer's *Perlustration of Great Yarmouth, 1,* 262 n.).

3249. MORTON, John (ca 1715–80), M.P. Abingdon 1747–70, New Romney 1770–74, Wigan 1775–80 (*Alumni Oxon.;* Martin's *Masters of the Bench, Inner Temple;* Pink; Bean; Williams' *Great Sessions in Wales*).

Morton, Matthew Ducie, *see* Moreton, Matthew Ducie.

3250. Mosley, Oswald (1785–1871), 2d Bt, M.P. Portarlington 1806–7, Winchelsea 1807–12, Midhurst 1817–18, North Staffordshire 1832–37 (*Alumni Oxon.*; GEC).

Mostyn, Bn, *see* Lloyd, Edward Pryce; *also* Lloyd-Mostyn, Edward Mostyn.

Mostyn, Edward Mostyn Lloyd, *see* Lloyd-Mostyn, Edward Mostyn.

3251. Mostyn, John (ca 1710–79), M.P. Malton 1741–68 (DNB; *Old Westminsters*).

3252. Mostyn, Roger (1734–96), 5th Bt, M.P. Flintshire 1758–96 (GEC; *Old Westminsters*).

3253. Mostyn, Savage (ca 1714–57), M.P. Weobley 1747–57 (DNB; *Old Westminsters*).

3254. Mostyn, Thomas (1704–58), 4th Bt, M.P. Flintshire 1734–41, 1747–58 (GEC; Mostyn and Glenn, *Mostyn of Mostyn,* p. 170; *Old Westminsters*).

3255. Mostyn, Thomas (1776–1831), 6th Bt, M.P. Flintshire 1796–97, 1799–1831 (GEC; *Old Westminsters*).

3256. Mostyn-Owen, William (d. 1795), M.P. Montgomeryshire 1774–95 (Williams' *Wales M.P.'s*).

3257. Moulton-Barrett, Samuel Barrett (1787–1837), M.P. Richmond 1820–28 (J. Marks, *Family of the Barrett,* pp. 209, 347, 461).

3258. Mount, William (1787–1869), M.P. Yarmouth (Hants) 1818–19, Newport (Hants) 1831–32 (*Alumni Oxon.*; Burke's *LG*).

Mount Charles, E. of, *see* Conyngham, Francis Nathaniel and Henry Joseph.

Mountedgcumbe, E. of, *see* Edgcumbe, Ernest Augustus, George, and Richard.

Mountnorris, 2d E. of, *see* Annesley, George.

Mountrath, 7th E. of, *see* Coote, Charles Henry.

Mountstuart, Bn, *see* Stuart, John.

3259. Moysey, Abel (1743–1831), M.P. Bath 1774–90 (*Old Westminsters;* Williams' *Great Sessions in Wales*).

Mozley, Oswill, *see* Mosley, Oswald.

3260. Muilman-Trench-Chiswell, Richard (ca 1735–97), M.P. Aldborough 1790–97 (DNB).

Muir, William, *see* Mure, William.

Mulgrave, Bn and E. of, *see* Phipps, Constantine Henry, Constantine John, and Henry.

Mullins, Frederick William, *see* De Moleyns, Frederick William Beaufort.

Muncaster, 1st Bn, *see* Pennington, John.

3261. Mundy, Edward Miller (1750–1822), M.P. Derbyshire 1784–1822 (GEC sub Middleton; *Eton Coll. Reg.*).

3262. MUNDY, Francis (1771–1837), M.P. Derbyshire 1822–31 (*Alumni Oxon.;* Burke's *LG*).

3263. MUNDY, George (ca 1777–1861), M.P. Boroughbridge 1818–20, 1824–30 (Boase; Burke's *LG; Eton Coll. Reg.*).

3264. MUNDY, Wrightson (ca 1715–62), M.P. Leicestershire 1747–54 (*Alumni Cantab.*).

3265. MUNRO, Harry (ca 1720–81), 7th Bt, M.P. Ross-shire 1746–47, Tain burghs 1747–61 (GEC; *Old Westminsters*).

3266. MUNRO, Hector (ca 1726–1805), M.P. Inverness burghs 1768–1802 (DNB).

3267. MUNRO, Robert (ca 1684–1746), 6th Bt, M.P. Tain burghs 1710–41 (DNB; GEC).

3268. MURE, William (ca 1718–76), M.P. Renfrewshire 1742–61 (Addison's *Glasgow Matric. Albums;* DNB).

3269. MURE-CAMPBELL, James (1726–86), 5th E. of Loudoun, M.P. Ayrshire 1754–61 (Addison's *Glasgow Matric. Albums;* GEC).

3270. MURRAY, Alexander (d. 1755), M.P. Peebles-shire 1712–13, 1715–22, 1741–47 (Burke's *LG;* Buchan's *Peebleshire, 2,* 494).

3271. MURRAY, Alexander (1736–95), M.P. Peebles-shire 1780–83 (DNB; Grant's *Faculty of Advocates*).

3272. MURRAY, Alexander (1747–1820), 7th Bn Elibank, M.P. Peebles-shire 1783–84 (GEC).

3273. MURRAY, David (1748–94), M.P. Peebles-shire 1784–90, Radnor borough 1790–94 (*Scots Peerage* sub Elibank; Williams' *Wales M.P.'s*).

3274. MURRAY, George (1741–97), M.P. Perth burghs 1790–96 (*Scots Peerage* sub Atholl).

3275. MURRAY, George (1762–1836), 5th E. of Dunmore, M.P. Liskeard 1800–2 (GEC).

3276. MURRAY, George (1772–1846), M.P. Perthshire 1824–32, 1834–34 (DNB).

3277. MURRAY, James (1734–94), M.P. Perthshire 1773–94 (*Scots Peerage* sub Atholl).

3278. MURRAY, James (ca 1726–99), M.P. Wigtownshire 1762–68, Kirkcudbright Stewarty 1768–74 (Addison's *Glasgow Matric. Albums;* Foster's *Scots M.P.'s*).

3279. MURRAY, James (1782–1837), 1st Bn Glenlyon, M.P. Perthshire 1807–12 (GEC).

3280. MURRAY, James Patrick (ca 1781–1834), M.P. Yarmouth (Hants) 1802–3 (*Scots Peerage* sub Elibank).

3281. MURRAY, John (d. 1753), M.P. Linlithgow burghs 1725–27, Selkirkshire 1727–53 (Burke's *LG;* Craig-Brown's *Selkirkshire, 2,* 346).

3282. MURRAY, John (1711–87), M.P. Perthshire 1734–61 (DNB; *Scots Peerage* sub Atholl).

3283. MURRAY, John (1729–74), 3d D. of Atholl, M.P. Perthshire 1761–64 (DNB; GEC; *Eton Coll. Reg.*).

3284. MURRAY, John (1726–1800), M.P. Linlithgow burghs 1754–61 (Addison's *Glasgow Matric. Albums;* Grant's *Faculty of Advocates*).

3285. MURRAY, John (ca 1768–1827), 8th Bt, M.P. Wootton Bassett 1807–11, Weymouth and Melcombe Regis 1811–18 (DNB; GEC; *Old Westminsters*).

3286. MURRAY, Patrick (1771–1837), 6th Bt, M.P. Edinburgh City 1806–12 (Addison's *Glasgow Matric. Albums;* GEC).

3287. MURRAY, Robert (1689–1738), M.P. Wootton Bassett 1722–27, Great Bedwin 1734–38 (*Scots Peerage* sub Dunmore).

3288. MURRAY, William (1705–93), 1st E. of Mansfield, M.P. Boroughbridge 1742–56 (DNB; GEC).

3289. MURRAY, William David (1806–98), 4th E. of Mansfield, M.P. Aldborough 1830–31, Woodstock 1831–32, Norwich 1832–37, Perthshire 1837–40 (GEC; *Old Westminsters*).

3290. MURRAY-PULTENEY, James (ca 1755–1811), 7th Bt, M.P. Weymouth and Melcombe Regis 1790–1811 (DNB; GEC; *Old Westminsters*).

3291. MUSGRAVE, George (ca 1740–1824), M.P. Carlisle 1768–74 (*Old Westminsters*).

3292. MUSGRAVE, Philip (ca 1712–95), 6th Bt, M.P. Westmorland 1741–47 (GEC; *Eton Coll. Reg.*).

3293. MUSGRAVE, Philip Christopher (1794–1827), 8th Bt, M.P. Petersfield 1820–25, Carlisle 1825–27 (*Alumni Oxon.;* GEC; *Eton Lists*).

3294. MUSGRAVE, Richard (1790–1859), 3d Bt, M.P. Waterford Co. 1831–32, 1835–37 (*Alumni Dublin.;* GEC).

MUSSENDEN, Carteret, *see* LEATHES, Carteret.

3295. MUSSENDEN, Hill (ca 1699–1772), M.P. Harwich 1741–47 (Burke's *LG;* Musgrave's *Obituary*).

3296. MYDDELTON, John (1685–1747), M.P. Denbigh borough 1733–41, Denbighshire 1741–42 (*Misc. Geneal. et Herald.*, 3d Ser., *2;* Williams' *Wales M.P.'s*).

3297. MYDDELTON, Richard (ca 1726–95), M.P. Denbigh borough 1747–88 (*Alumni Oxon.;* Burke's *LG; Misc. Geneal. et Herald.*, 3d Ser., *2;* Williams' *Wales M.P.'s*).

3298. MYDDELTON, Richard (ca 1764–96), M.P. Denbigh borough 1788–96 (*Alumni Oxon.; Eton Coll. Reg.;* Williams' *Wales M.P.'s*).

3299. MYDDELTON-BIDDULPH, Robert (1761–1814), M.P. Herefordshire 1796–1802, Denbigh borough 1806–12 (Burke's *LG;* Williams' *Hereford M.P.'s*).

3300. MYDDELTON-BIDDULPH, Robert (1805–72), M.P. Denbigh borough 1830–32, Denbighshire 1832–34, 1852–68 (*Alumni Oxon.;* Burke's *LG*).

3301. MYERS, Thomas (b. ca 1764), M.P. Harwich 1802–3, Yarmouth (Hants) 1810–12 (Hodson's *Bengal Army Officers, 3,* 366).

3302. MYTTON, John (1796–1834), M.P. Shrewsbury 1819–20 (DNB; *Harrow Reg.; Old Westminsters*).

3303. NAPER, James Lennox William (1791–1868), M.P. Weobley 1813–18 (*Alumni Oxon.;* Burke's *Irish LG;* Williams' *Hereford M.P.'s*).

3304. NAPIER, Gerard (ca 1740–65), 6th Bt, M.P. Bridport 1761–65 (GEC; *Eton Coll. Reg.*).

3305. NARES, George (ca 1716–86), M.P. Oxford City 1768–71 (*Alumni Oxon.;* DNB).

3306. NASMITH, James (ca 1704–79), 2d Bt, M.P. Peebles-shire 1732–34, 1735–41 (GEC).

3307. NASSAU, Richard Savage (1723–80), M.P. Colchester 1747–54, Malden 1774–80 (*Old Westminsters*).

NEALE, Harry Burrard, *see* BURRARD-NEALE, Harry.

3308. NEALE, John (1687–1746), M.P. Wycombe 1722–22, Coventry 1722–34, 1737–41 (*Alumni Oxon.;* Burke's *LG*).

3309. NEALE, Robert (1706–76), M.P. Wootton Bassett 1741–54 (Burke's *LG;* Musgrave's *Obituary*).

3310. NEDHAM, Robert (ca 1704–62), M.P. Old Sarum 1734–41 (*Alumni Oxon.;* Burke's *LG* [ed. 1849]).

3311. NEDHAM, William (ca 1741–1806), M.P. Winchelsea 1774–74, 1775–80, 1784–90, Pontefract 1780–84 (*Eton Coll. Reg.; Jour. Mod. Hist., 18* [1946], 215).

3312. NEEDHAM, Francis (1748–1832), 1st E. of Kilmorey, M.P. Newry 1806–18 (DNB; GEC).

3313. NEEDHAM, Francis Jack (1787–1880), 2d E. of Kilmorey, M.P. Newry 1819–26 (GEC).

3314. NEELD, Joseph (1789–1856), M.P. Gatton 1830–30, Chippenham 1830–56 (Boase; Burke's *Peerage;* Dod's *Parl. Companion* [1834], p. 145; *Harrow Reg.*).

3315. NEPEAN, Evan (ca 1751–1822), 1st Bt, M.P. Queenborough 1796–1802, Bridport 1802–12 (DNB).

3316. NESBITT, Albert (d. 1753), M.P. Huntingdon borough 1741–47, St. Michael 1747–53 (Burke's *LG* [ed. 1875]; *Notes and Queries, 174,* 331).

3317. NESBITT, Arnold (ca 1722–79), M.P. St. Michael 1753–54, Winchelsea 1754–61, 1770–74, Cricklade 1761–68, 1774–79 (Horsfield's *Sussex, 1,* 476; *Notes and Queries, 174,* 331).

3318. NESBITT, John (ca 1746–1817), M.P. Winchelsea 1780–90, Gatton 1790–96, Bodmin 1796–1802 (*Gent. Mag., 1,* 375; *Notes and Queries, 174,* 331).

3319. NEVILL, Henry (1755–1843), 2d E. of Abergavenny, M.P. Monmouthshire 1784–85 (GEC; *Old Westminsters*).

3320. NEVILLE, Richard (ca 1745–1822), M.P. Wexford town 1802–6,

1807–10, 1811–13, 1814–19 (Burke's *Irish LG; Cornwallis Corr.,
3, 46 n.).

NEVILLE, Richard Aldworth, *see* GRIFFIN, Richard.

NEVILLE-ALDWORTH, Richard, *see* ALDWORTH-NEVILLE, Richard.

NEWARK, Vct, *see* PIERREPONT, Charles Evelyn.

3321. NEWBOLT, John Henry (ca 1769–1823), M.P. Bramber 1800–2
(*Alumni Oxon.*).

NEWBOROUGH, Bn, *see* WYNN, Thomas and Thomas John.

NEWCOMEN, Thomas Gleadowe and William Gleadowe, *see* GLEA-
DOWE-NEWCOMEN, Thomas and William.

3322. NEWDIGATE, Roger (1719–1806), 5th Bt, M.P. Middlesex 1742–47,
Oxford Univ. 1750–80 (DNB; GEC; *Old Westminsters*).

NEWHAVEN, 1st Bn, *see* MAYNE, William.

3323. NEWLAND, George (ca 1692–1749), M.P. Gatton 1738–49 (*Lond.
Visit. Pedigrees* (Harl. Soc.), p. 141; *Alumni Oxon.*).

3324. NEWLAND, William (ca 1686–1738), M.P. Gatton 1710–38 (*Alumni
Oxon.*).

3325. NEWMAN, Robert William (1776–1848), 1st Bt, M.P. Bletchingley
1812–18, Exeter 1818–26 (Burke's *Peerage;* Foster's *Baronetage*).

3326. NEWNHAM, George Lewis (ca 1734–1800), M.P. Arundel 1774–80
(*Alumni Cantab.; Eton Coll. Reg.*).

3327. NEWNHAM, Nathaniel (ca 1699–1778), M.P. Aldborough 1743–54,
Bramber 1754–61 (Musgrave's *Obituary;* Sealy, *Newnham Family,* p. 7).

3328. NEWNHAM, Nathaniel (ca 1742–1809), M.P. London 1780–90,
Ludgershall 1793–96 (*Annual Register* [1810], p. 362; Beaven's
Aldermen of London).

3329. NEWNHAM, Thomas (d. 1761), M.P. Queenborough 1741–54 (*London Chronicle* 29 Sept. to 1 Oct. 1761; Musgrave's *Obituary*).

3330. NEWPORT, Simon John (1756–1843), 1st Bt, M.P. Waterford City
1803–32 (DNB; GEC; *Eton Coll. Reg.*).

NEWRY, Vct, *see* NEEDHAM, Francis Jack.

NEWSHAM, James, *see* CRAGGS, James Newsham.

3331. NEWTON, Michael (ca 1695–1743), 4th Bt, M.P. Beverley 1722–27,
Grantham 1727–43 (GEC).

3332. NEWTON, Michael (ca 1727–1803), M.P. Beverley 1761–68 (*Misc.
Geneal. et Herald.,* N.S., *1;* MS, *ex inform.* the Reverend Cyril
Britton).

3333. NEWTON, William (ca 1784–1862), M.P. Ipswich 1818–20 (*Alumni
Oxon.*).

3334. NICHOLAS, Robert (1758–1826), M.P. Cricklade 1785–90 (*Alumni
Oxon.; Wiltshire Notes and Queries, 7,* 238–39).

3335. NICHOLL, John (1759–1838), M.P. Penryn 1802–6, Hastings

1806–7, Great Bedwin 1807–32 (*Alumni Oxon.;* Burke's *LG;* Williams' *Oxford M.P.'s*).

3336. NICHOLLS, John (ca 1746–1832), M.P. Bletchingley 1783–87, Tregony 1796–1802 (*Alumni Oxon.;* Boase and Courtney's *Biblio. Cornub.*).

NISBET, William, *see* HAMILTON-NISBET, William.

NISBET-HAMILTON, Robert Adam, *see* CHRISTOPHER-NISBET-HAMILTON, Robert Adam.

3337. NIGHTINGALL, Miles (1768–1829), M.P. Eye 1820–29 (DNB).

3338. NOEL, Charles Noel (1781–1866), 1st E. of Gainsborough, M.P. Rutland 1808–14 (GEC; Ball and Venn's *Admissions to Trinity College*).

3339. NOEL, Gerard Noel (1759–1838), 2d Bt, M.P. Maidstone 1784–88, Rutland 1788–1808, 1814–38 (GEC; *Eton Coll. Reg.*).

3340. NOEL, James (1712–52), M.P. Rutland 1734–52 (Hill's *Market Harborough,* p. 221; *Old Westminsters*).

3341. NOEL, Ralph (ca 1748–1825), 6th Bt, M.P. Durham Co. 1790–1812 (GEC; *Old Westminsters*).

3342. NOEL, Thomas (ca 1705–88), M.P. Rutland 1728–41, 1753–88 (Hill's *Market Harborough,* p. 221; Musgrave's *Obituary*).

3343. NOEL, Thomas (1745–1815), 2d Vct Wentworth, M.P. Leicestershire 1774–74 (GEC; *Eton Coll. Reg.*).

3344. NOEL, William (1695–1762), M.P. Stamford 1722–47, West Looe 1747–57 (*Alumni Cantab.;* DNB).

3345. NOEL-HILL, William (1773–1842), 3d Bn Berwick, M.P. Shrewsbury 1796–1812, Marlborough 1814–18 (DNB; GEC; *Rugby Reg.*).

3346. NOLAN, Michael (ca 1764–1827), M.P. Barnstable 1820–24 (*Alumni Dublin.;* DNB).

NORFOLK, D. of, *see* HOWARD, Charles and Henry Charles.

3347. NORMAN, Richard (ca 1758–1847), M.P. Bramber 1804–6 (*Gent. Mag., 1,* 331; *Royal Kalendar* [1805], p. 40).

NORMANBY, Vct and M., *see* PHIPPS, Constantine Henry.

NORREYS, Charles Denham Orlando Jephson, *see* JEPHSON-NORREYS, Charles Denham Orlando.

3348. NORRIS, John (ca 1660–1749), M.P. Rye 1708–22, 1734–49, Portsmouth 1722–34 (DNB).

3349. NORRIS, John, M.P. Rye 1762–74 (Haslewood's *Benenden,* p. 186).

NORTH, Dudley, *see* LONG-NORTH, Dudley.

3350. NORTH, Frederick (1732–92), 2d E. of Guilford, M.P. Banbury 1754–90 (DNB; GEC).

3351. NORTH, Frederick (1766–1827), 5th E. of Guilford, M.P. Banbury 1792–94 (DNB; GEC; *Eton Coll. Reg.*).

3352. NORTH, Frederick (1800–69), M.P. Hastings 1831–37, 1854–65,

1868–69 (Boase; Burke's *Peerage* sub Guilford; Carthew's *Launditch, 3,* 303; *Harrow Reg.*).

3353. NORTH, George Augustus (1757–1802), 3d E. of Guilford, M.P. Harwich 1778–84, Wootton Bassett 1784–90, Petersfield 1790–90, Banbury 1790–92 (DNB; GEC; *Eton Coll. Reg.*).

3354. NORTH, John Henry (ca 1788–1831), M.P. Plympton Erle 1824–26, Milborne Port 1827–30, Drogheda 1830–31 (*Alumni Dublin.; Gent. Mag., 2,* 466).

NORTHAMPTON, E. of and M. of, *see* COMPTON, Charles, George, Spencer, and Spencer Joshua Alwyne.

NORTHBROOK, 1st Bn, *see* BARING, Francis Thornhill.

3355. NORTHCOTE, Henry (ca 1710–43), 5th Bt, M.P. Exeter 1735–43 (GEC).

3356. NORTHCOTE, Henry Stafford (1792–1850), M.P. Heytesbury 1826–30 (*Alumni Oxon.;* GEC sub Iddesleigh).

3357. NORTHEY, William (ca 1722–70), M.P. Calne 1747–61, Maidstone 1761–68, Great Bedwin 1768–70 (*Alumni Cantab.; Genealogist,* N.S., *10,* 178).

3358. NORTHEY, William (ca 1753–1826), M.P. Newport 1796–1826 (*Eton Coll. Reg.; Genealogist,* N.S., *10,* 178).

NORTHINGTON, E. of, *see* HENLEY, Robert.

NORTHLAND, 2d E., *see* KNOX, Thomas.

3359. NORTHMORE, William (1690–1735), M.P. Okehampton 1713–22, 1727–35 (Burke's *LG;* Musgrave's *Obituary*).

NORTHUMBERLAND, D. of, *see* PERCY, Algernon George, George, and Hugh.

NORTHWICK, 1st Bn, *see* RUSHOUT, John.

3360. NORTON, Chapple (1746–1818), M.P. Guildford 1784–90, 1796–1806, 1807–12 (DNB).

3361. NORTON, Charles Francis (1807–35), M.P. Guildford 1831–32 (Burke's *Peerage* sub Grantley; *Gent. Mag., 1* [1836], 445).

3362. NORTON, Edward (1750–86), M.P. Haslemere 1780–84, Carlisle 1784–86 (*Alumni Oxon.;* Bean; Burke's and Collins' *Peerage* sub Grantley; Ferguson).

3363. NORTON, Fletcher (1716–89), 1st Bn Grantley, M.P. Appleby 1756–61, Wigan 1761–68, Guildford 1768–82 (*Alumni Cantab.;* DNB; GEC).

3364. NORTON, Fletcher (1744–1820), M.P. Appleby 1773–74, Carlisle 1774–75 (*Eton Coll. Reg.; Harrow Reg.*).

3365. NORTON, George Chapple (1800–75), M.P. Guildford 1826–30 (Burke's *Peerage* sub Grantley; Boase).

3366. NORTON, Thomas (ca 1684–1748), M.P. Bury 1727–47 (*Bury Grammar School List;* Musgrave's *Obituary*).

3367. NORTON, William (1742–1822), 2d Bn Grantley, M.P. Richmond 1768–74, 1775–80, Wigtown burghs 1774–75, Guildford 1782–

84, Surrey 1784–89 (*Admissions to St. John, Cambridge;* GEC; *Harrow Reg.*).

3368. NOWELL, Alexander (ca 1762–1842), M.P. Westmorland 1831–32 (Bean; Burke's *LG;* Ferguson; *Gent. Mag., 1* [1843], 108).

3369. NUGENT, Charles Edmund (ca 1759–1844), M.P. Buckingham borough 1784–90 (DNB).

3370. NUGENT, Edmund (ca 1731–71), M.P. Liskeard 1754–59, St. Mawes 1761–70 (GEC).

3371. NUGENT, George (1757–1849), 1st Bt, M.P. Buckingham borough 1790–1802, 1818–32, Aylesbury 1806–12 (DNB; *Cork Archaeol. Jour.* [1896], p. 40).

NUGENT, Robert Craggs, *see* CRAGGS-NUGENT, Robert.

3372. NUGENT-GRENVILLE, George (1789–1850), 2d Bn Nugent, M.P. Buckingham borough 1810–12, Aylesbury 1812–32, 1847–50 (DNB; GEC; *1832 List*).

3373. NUGENT-TEMPLE-GRENVILLE, George (1753–1813), 1st M. of Buckingham, M.P. Bucks 1774–79 (DNB; GEC; *Eton Coll. Reg.*).

NUNEHAM, Vct, *see* HARCOURT, George Simon.

3374. O'BRIEN, Edward (1773–1837), 4th Bt, M.P. Clare 1802–26 (*Alumni Dublin.;* GEC).

3375. O'BRIEN, Lucius (1800–72), 13th Bn Inchiquin, M.P. Clare 1826–30, 1847–52 (GEC; *Harrow Reg.*).

3376. O'BRIEN, Murrough (ca 1724–1808), 1st M. of Thomond, M.P. Richmond 1784–96, Liskeard 1797–1800 (GEC).

O'BRIEN, Percy Wyndham, *see* WYNDHAM-O'BRIEN, Percy.

3377. O'BRIEN, William (d. 1777), 4th E. of Inchiquin, M.P. Windsor 1722–27, Tamworth 1727–34, Camelford 1741–47, Aylesbury 1747–54 (GEC).

O'BRIEN, William Smith, *see* SMITH-O'BRIEN, William.

3378. O'CALLAGHAN, Cornelius (1775–1857), 1st Vct Lismore, M.P. Lostwithiel 1806–7 (Ball and Venn's *Admissions to Trinity College;* GEC).

3379. O'CALLAGHAN, James (b. ca 1777), M.P. Tregony 1806–12, 1818–26 (*Notes and Queries,* 24 July 1948).

3380. OCKENDEN, William (d. 1761), M.P. Great Marlow 1744–54 (Musgrave's *Obituary*).

3381. O'CONNELL, Daniel (1775–1847), M.P. Clare 1828–29, 1829–30, Waterford Co. 1830–31, Kerry 1831–32, Dublin City 1832–36, 1837–41, Kilkenny City 1836–37, Cork Co. 1841–47 (DNB).

3382. O'CONNELL, Maurice (ca 1801–53), M.P. Clare 1831–32, Tralee 1832–37, 1838–53 (*Alumni Dublin.;* Burke's *Irish LG*).

3383. O'CONNOR, Denis (1794–1847), M.P. Roscommon 1831–47 (*Alumni Dublin.;* Burke's *Irish LG; Gent. Mag., 2,* 434; *Linc. Inn Reg.*).

3384. O'CONNOR, Owen (1763–1831), M.P. Roscommon 1830–31 (Burke's Irish LG; Gent. Mag., 1, 650).

3385. ODELL, William, M.P. Limerick Co. 1801–18 (Burke's Irish LG).

3386. O'FERRALL, Richard More (ca 1797–1880), M.P. Kildare 1830–47, 1859–65, Longford 1851–52 (DNB).

OFFLEY, Foster Cunliffe, see CUNLIFFE-OFFLEY, Foster.

3387. OFFLEY, John (ca 1718–84), M.P. Bedford borough 1747–54, Orford 1754–68, East Retford 1768–74 (Genealogist, N.S., 19, 221; London Chronicle, 3–6 Apr. 1784).

3388. OGILVY, Charles, M.P. West Looe 1774–75.

3389. OGILVY, Donald (1788–1863), M.P. Forfarshire 1831–32 (Scots Peerage sub Airlie).

3390. OGILVY, William (ca 1794–1871), M.P. Perth burghs 1831–31 (Annual Register, p. 148; Scots Peerage sub Airlie).

3391. OGILVY-GRANT, Francis William (1778–1853), 6th E. of Seafield, M.P. Elgin burghs 1802–6, Inverness burghs 1806–7, Elginshire 1807–32, Elgin and Nairnshire 1832–40 (GEC).

3392. OGILVY-GRANT, Lewis Alexander (1767–1840), 5th E. of Seafield, M.P. Elginshire 1790–96 (GEC; Old Westminsters).

3393. OGLANDER, William (1769–1852), 6th Bt, M.P. Bodmin 1807–12 (GEC).

3394. OGLE, Chaloner (ca 1681–1750), M.P. Rochester 1746–50 (DNB).

3395. OGLE, Charles (1775–1858), 2d Bt, M.P. Portarlington 1830–31 (DNB; Eton Coll. Reg.).

3396. OGLE, George (1742–1814), M.P. Dublin City 1801–2 (DNB; Alumni Dublin.).

3397. OGLE, Henry Meade (b. ca 1762), M.P. Drogheda 1806–7, 1812–20 (Alumni Dublin.).

3398. OGLETHORPE, James Edward (1696–1785), M.P. Haslemere 1722–54 (Alumni Oxon.; DNB; Etoniana, 45, 710; Genealogist, N.S., 21, 174).

3399. O'GRADY, Standish (1792–1848), 2d Vct Guillamore, M.P. Limerick Co. 1820–26, 1830–30, 1830–34 (DNB; GEC; Old Westminsters).

3400. O'HARA, Charles (1746–1822), M.P. Sligo Co. 1801–22 (Alumni Oxon.; Burke's Irish LG).

3401. O'HARA, James (ca 1796–1838), M.P. Galway town 1826–31 (Alumni Dublin.; Burke's Irish LG).

3402. OLIVER, Charles Silver (d. 1817), M.P. Limerick Co. 1802–6 (Burke's Irish LG; Eton Coll. Reg.).

3403. OLIVER, Richard (1735–84), M.P. London 1770–80 (DNB).

3404. OLMIUS, Drigue Billiers (1746–87), 2d Bn Waltham, M.P. Weymouth and Melcombe Regis 1768–74, Maldon 1784–87 (GEC).

3405. OLMIUS, John (ca 1711–62), 1st Bn Waltham, M.P. Weymouth and

Melcombe Regis 1737–41, 1761–62, Colchester 1741–42, 1754–61 (GEC).

3406. OMMANNEY, Francis Molineux (ca 1774–1840), M.P. Barnstable 1818–26 (Palmer's *Perlustration of Great Yarmouth, 1,* 328 n.; *Times,* 11 Nov. 1840).

3407. O'NEILL, John Augustus (b. 1799), M.P. Hull 1826–30 (Burke's *LG* [ed. 1849]; Gunnell's *Hull Celebrities,* p. 448).

3408. O'NEILL, John Bruce Richard (1780–1855), 3d Vct O'Neill, M.P. Antrim 1802–41 (DNB; GEC).

ONGLEY, Robert Henley, *see* HENLEY-ONGLEY, Robert.

3409. ONGLEY, Samuel (ca 1697–1747), M.P. Shoreham 1729–34, Bedford borough 1734–47 (*Alumni Oxon.;* GEC).

ONLEY, Charles Savill, *see* SAVILL-ONLEY, Charles.

3410. ONSLOW, Arthur (1691–1768), M.P. Guildford 1720–27, Surrey 1727–61 (DNB).

3411. ONSLOW, Arthur (1759–1833), M.P. Guildford 1812–30 (Woolrych's *Serjeants at Law, 2,* 772).

3412. ONSLOW, Denzil (ca 1698–1765), M.P. Guildford 1740–47 (*Misc. Geneal. et Herald.,* N.S., *3*).

3413. ONSLOW, Edward (1758–1829), M.P. Aldborough 1780–81 (*Old Westminsters;* Venn MS).

3414. ONSLOW, George (1731–92), M.P. Guildford 1760–84 (DNB).

3415. ONSLOW, George (1731–1814), 1st E. of Onslow, M.P. Rye 1754–61, Surrey 1761–74 (*Alumni Cantab.;* GEC; *Old Westminsters*).

3416. ONSLOW, Middleton (d. 1801), M.P. Rye 1774–75 (*Gent. Mag., 2,* 964).

3417. ONSLOW, Richard (ca 1697–1760), M.P. Guildford 1727–60 (*London Chronicle,* 15–18 Mar. 1760; Maclean's *Trigg Minor, 3,* 400).

3418. ONSLOW, Richard (ca 1713–76), 3d Bn Onslow, M.P. Guildford 1734–40 (*Alumni Cantab.;* GEC; *Eton Coll. Reg.*).

3419. ONSLOW, Thomas (1754–1827), 2d E. of Onslow, M.P. Rye 1775–84, Guildford 1784–1806 (DNB; GEC; *Old Westminsters*).

3420. ONSLOW, Thomas Cranley (1778–1861), M.P. Guildford 1806–18 (Burke's *Peerage; Harrow Reg.*).

ORANMORE, 1st Bn, *see* BROWNE, Dominick.

3421. ORCHARD, Paul (1739–1812), M.P. Callington 1784–1806 (*Alumni Oxon.; Gent. Mag., 1,* 393, 494; *Parish Reg. Hartland, Devon,* p. 507).

3422. ORD, John (1710–45), M.P. St. Michael 1741–45 (*Alumni Cantab.; Archaeol. Aeliana,* 4th Ser., *18,* 91).

3423. ORD, John (1729–1814), M.P. Midhurst 1774–80, Hastings 1780–84, Wendover 1784–90 (*Alumni Cantab.;* DNB).

3424. ORD, Robert (ca 1700–78), M.P. St. Michael 1734–41, Morpeth

1741–55 (DNB; Burke's *LG;* Hodgson's *Northumberland, 2,* pt. 3, 433).

3425. ORD, William (d. 1789), M.P. Bossiney 1747–54 (Burke's *LG*).

3426. ORD, William (1781–1855), M.P. Morpeth 1802–32, Newcastle-upon-Tyne 1835–52 (Boase; Ball and Venn's *Admissions to Trinity College;* Burke's *LG; Eton Lists*).

3427. ORDE, John (1751–1824), 1st Bt, M.P. Yarmouth (Hants) 1807–12 (DNB; GEC).

3428. ORDE-POWLETT, Thomas (1746–1807), 1st Bn Bolton, M.P. Aylesbury 1780–84, Harwich 1784–96 (DNB; GEC; *Eton Coll. Reg.; Gent. Mag.,* p. 785; Namier).

3429. ORDE-POWLETT, William (1782–1850), 2d Bn Bolton, M.P. Yarmouth (Hants) 1807–7 (GEC).

ORFORD, E. of, *see* WALPOLE, Horatio and Robert.

ORIEL, Bn, *see* FOSTER, John; *also* FOSTER-SKEFFINGTON, Thomas Henry.

ORMATHWAITE, 1st Bn, *see* BENN-WALSH, John.

3430. ORME, Garton (ca 1700–58), M.P. Arundel 1739–54 (Burke's *LG* [ed. 1849], sub Garton; Elwes' *Western Sussex,* p. 272).

ORMELIE, E. of, *see* CAMPBELL, John.

ORMONDE, M. of, *see* BUTLER, James Wandesford and John.

3431. ORMSBY, Charles Montagu (1767–1818), 1st Bt, M.P. Carlow borough 1801–6 (*Alumni Dublin.;* Burke's *Irish LG* sub Hamilton).

3432. ORMSBY-GORE, William (1779–1860), M.P. Leitrim 1806–7, Carnarvon borough 1830–31, North Salop 1835–57 (*Alumni Oxon.;* Boase; *Eton Lists;* Williams' *Wales M.P.'s*).

ORWELL, 1st Bn, *see* VERNON, Francis.

3433. OSBALDESTON, Fountayne Wentworth (1696–1770), M.P. Scarborough 1766–70 (*Alumni Cantab.*).

3434. OSBALDESTON, George (ca 1754–93), M.P. Scarborough 1784–90 (Burke's *LG* [ed. 1849]; Musgrave's *Obituary;* Venn MS).

3435. OSBALDESTON, George (1787–1866), M.P. East Retford 1812–18 (*Alumni Oxon.;* DNB).

3436. OSBALDESTON, William (1688–1766), M.P. Scarborough 1736–47, 1754–66 (*Alumni Cantab.*).

3437. OSBORN, Danvers (1715–53), 3d Bt, M.P. Bedfordshire 1747–53 (*Alumni Cantab.;* GEC; *Old Westminsters*).

3438. OSBORN, George (1742–1818), 4th Bt, M.P. Bossiney 1769–74, Penryn 1774–80, Horsham 1780–84 (GEC; *Old Westminsters*).

3439. OSBORN, Henry (1694–1771), M.P. Bedfordshire 1758–61 (Burke's *Peerage;* Blaydes' *Genealogica Bedfordiensis,* p. 62).

3440. OSBORN, John (1772–1848), 5th Bt, M.P. Bedfordshire 1794–1807, 1818–20, Cockermouth 1807–8, Queenborough 1812–18, Wigtown burghs 1821–24 (GEC; *Old Westminsters*).

3441. OSBORNE, Francis Godolphin (1751–99), 5th D. of Leeds, M.P. Eye 1774–74, Helston 1774–75 (DNB; GEC).

3442. OSBORNE, Francis Godolphin (1777–1850), 1st Bn Godolphin, M. P. Helston 1799–1802, Lewes 1802–6, Cambridgeshire 1810–31 (GEC).

OSBORNE, Francis Godolphin D'Arcy, see D'ARCY-OSBORNE, Francis Godolphin.

OSSINGTON, 1st Vct, see DENISON, John Evelyn.

3443. OSWALD, James (1715–69), M.P. Dysart burghs 1741–47, 1754–68, Fifeshire 1747–54 (DNB).

3444. OSWALD, James Townsend (ca 1748–1813), M.P. Dysart burghs 1768–74, Fifeshire 1776–79 (*Alumni Oxon.;* Burke's *LG*).

3445. OTWAY-CAVE, Robert (ca 1796–1844), M.P. Leicester borough 1826–30, Tipperary 1832–32, 1835–44 (GEC sub Braye; *Eton Lists; Gent. Mag., 1* [1845], 201).

3446. OUGHTON, Adolphus (ca 1685–1736), 1st Bt, M.P. Coventry 1722–36 (GEC).

3447. OURRY, Paul Henry (1719–83), M.P. Plympton Erle 1763–75 (Burke's *LG* [ed. 1849], sub Treby; Charnock's *Biog. Naval., 6, 265; Misc. Geneal. et Herald.,* 3d Ser., *5*).

OURRY, Paul Treby, see TREBY, Paul Treby.

OVERSTONE, 1st Bn, see LOYD, Samuel Jones.

OXMANTOWN, Bn, see PARSONS, William.

3448. OWEN, Edward Campbell Rich (ca 1771–1849), M.P. Sandwich 1826–29 (DNB).

3449. OWEN, Francis (ca 1746–74), M.P. Helston 1774–74 (*Eton Coll. Reg.*).

OWEN, Hugh, see BARLOW, Hugh.

3450. OWEN, Hugh (ca 1730–86), 5th Bt, M.P. Pembrokeshire 1770–86 (GEC; J. R. Phillips, *Owen of Orielton,* pp. 70–71).

3451. OWEN, Hugh (1782–1809), 6th Bt, M.P. Pembroke borough 1809–9 (GEC).

3452. OWEN, Hugh Owen (1804–91), 2d Bt, M.P. Pembroke borough 1826–38, 1861–68 (*Alumni Oxon.;* Boase; Williams' *Wales M.P.'s*).

3453. OWEN, John (d. 1754), M.P. Anglesey 1741–47, Beaumaris 1753–54 (Musgrave's *Obituary;* Williams' *Wales M.P.'s*).

3454. OWEN, John (ca 1698–1776), M.P. West Looe 1735–41 (*Alumni Oxon.;* Williams' *Wales M.P.'s*).

3455. OWEN, John (ca 1776–1861), 1st Bt, M.P. Pembroke borough 1809–12, 1841–61, Pembrokeshire 1812–41 (Boase; Williams' *Wales M.P.'s*).

3456. OWEN, William (ca 1697–1781), 4th Bt, M.P. Pembroke borough 1722–47, 1761–74, Pembrokeshire 1747–61 (GEC).

OWEN, William, see MOSTYN-OWEN, William.

3457. OXENDEN, George (1694–1775), 5th Bt, M.P. Sandwich 1720–54 (*Alumni Cantab.;* DNB; GEC).

OXFORD, E. of, *see* HARLEY, Edward.

3458. PACKER, Winchcombe Howard (1702–46), M.P. Berks 1731–46 (Burke's *Peerage*).

3459. PAGE, Francis (ca 1727–1803), M.P. Oxford Univ. 1768–1801 (*Alumni Oxon.;* Brookes' *Steeple Aston,* p. 235; Williams' *Oxford M.P.'s*).

3460. PAGE, John (ca 1696–1779), M.P. Great Grimsby 1727–34, Chichester 1741–68 (Dalloway's *Western Division of Sussex, 1,* pt. 2, 54–55; Musgrave's *Obituary*).

3461. PAGE-TURNER, Gregory (1748–1805), 3d Bt, M.P. Thirsk 1784–1805 (GEC; *Eton Coll. Reg.*).

3462. PAGET, Arthur (1771–1840), M.P. Anglesey 1794–1807 (DNB; *Old Westminsters*).

3463. PAGET, Berkeley Thomas (1780–1842), M.P. Anglesey 1807–20, Milborne Port 1820–26 (*Rugby Reg.;* Williams' *Wales M.P.'s*).

3464. PAGET, Charles (1778–1839), M.P. Milborne Port 1804–6, Carnarvon borough 1806–26, 1831–33, 1833–34 (DNB).

3465. PAGET, Edward (1775–1849), M.P. Carnarvon borough 1796–1806, Milborne Port 1810–20 (DNB; *Old Westminsters*).

3466. PAGET, Henry (1797–1869), 2d M. of Anglesey, M.P. Anglesey 1820–32 (GEC; *Old Westminsters*).

3467. PAGET, Henry William (1768–1854), 1st M. of Anglesey, M.P. Carnarvon borough 1790–96, Milborne Port 1796–1804, 1806–10 (DNB; GEC; *Old Westminsters*).

3468. PAGET, Thomas (1778–1862), M.P. Leicestershire 1831–32 (Burke's *LG;* Boase).

3469. PAGET, William (1769–94), M.P. Anglesey 1790–94 (*Old Westminsters*).

3470. PAGET, William (1803–73), M.P. Carnarvon borough 1826–30, Andover 1841–47 (*Old Westminsters*).

3471. PAKENHAM, Hercules Robert (1781–1850), M.P. Westmeath 1808–26 (DNB; Venn's *Biog. Hist. Gonville and Caius, 2,* 135).

3472. PAKINGTON, Herbert Perrott (ca 1701–48), 5th Bt, M.P. Worcestershire 1727–41 (GEC).

3473. PALK, Lawrence (ca 1766–1813), 2d Bt, M.P. Ashburton 1787–96, Devon 1796–1812 (GEC; *Harrow Reg.*).

3474. PALK, Lawrence Vaughan (1793–1860), 3d Bt, M.P. Ashburton 1818–31 (GEC).

3475. PALK, Robert (1717–98), 1st Bt, M.P. Ashburton 1767–68, 1774–87, Wareham 1768–74 (DNB; GEC).

3476. PALK, Walter (ca 1743–1819), M.P. Ashburton 1796–1811 (*Gent. Mag., 1,* 189; *1806 List*).

3477. PALLISER, Hugh (1723–96), 1st Bt, M.P. Scarborough 1774–79, Huntingdon borough 1780–84 (DNB; GEC).

3478. PALLMER, Charles Nicholas (d. 1830), M.P. Ludgershall 1815–17, Surrey 1826–30 (Cobbett's *Rural Rides,* ed. Cole, *3,* 1016; *Linc. Inn Reg.*).

3479. PALMER, Charles (1777–1851), M.P. Bath 1808–26, 1830–37 (DNB).

3480. PALMER, Charles Fyshe (ca 1769–1843), M.P. Reading 1818–26, 1827–34, 1837–41 (*Gent. Mag., 2,* 95; *Notes and Queries, 160,* 401).

3481. PALMER, John (1735–1817), 5th Bt, M.P. Leicestershire 1765–80 (GEC; Barron's *Northampton Families,* p. 248).

3482. PALMER, John (ca 1742–1818), M.P. Bath 1801–8 (DNB).
PALMER, John Acland, *see* ACLAND-PALMER, John.

3483. PALMER, Peregrine (ca 1703–62), M.P. Oxford Univ. 1745–62 (*Alumni Oxon.;* Musgrave's *Obituary*).

3484. PALMER, Robert (1793–1872), M.P. Berks 1825–31, 1832–59 (Boase; Burke's *LG; Eton Lists*).

3485. PALMER, Thomas (ca 1685–1735), M.P. Bridgwater 1715–27, 1731–35 (*Alumni Oxon.;* Collinson's *Somerset, 1,* 258).

3486. PALMER, Thomas (ca 1702–65), 4th Bt, M.P. Leicestershire 1754–65 (*Alumni Cantab.;* GEC).
PALMERSTON, Vct, *see* TEMPLE, Henry and Henry John.
PANMURE, Bn and E., *see* MAULE, William.

3487. PAPILLON, David (ca 1691–1762), M.P. New Romney 1722–34, Dover 1734–41 (Burke's *LG;* Martin's *Masters of the Bench, Inner Temple;* Nichols' *Leicester, 2,* pt. 2, 709).

3488. PARDOE, John (ca 1757–96), M.P. Camelford 1780–84, Plympton Erle 1784–90, West Looe 1790–96 (Burke's *LG;* Ball and Venn's *Admissions to Trinity College;* Oliver's *Antigua, 3,* 447).

3489. PARES, Thomas (1790–1866), M.P. Leicester borough 1818–26 (Burke's *LG;* Boase).

3490. PARKER, Armistead (ca 1699–1777), M.P. Peterborough 1734–41, 1742–47, 1761–68 (Cussans' *Herts, 3,* pt. 2, 178; Musgrave's *Obituary; 1747 List*).

3491. PARKER, George (1755–1842), 4th E. of Macclesfield, M.P. Woodstock 1777–84, Minehead 1790–95 (GEC).

3492. PARKER, George Lane (1724–91), M.P. Yarmouth (Hants) 1769–74, Tregony 1774–80 (DNB).

3493. PARKER, John (ca 1735–88), 1st Bn Boringdon, M.P. Bodmin 1761–62, Devon 1762–84 (GEC).

3494. PARKER, John (ca 1755–97), M.P. Clitheroe 1780–82 (*Eton Coll. Reg.*).

3495. PARKER, Peter (ca 1721–1811), 1st Bt, M.P. Seaford 1784–86, Maldon 1787–90 (DNB; GEC).

3496. PARKER, Peter (ca 1785–1814), 2d Bt, M.P. Wexford town 1810–11 (DNB; GEC).

3497. PARKER, Thomas (1723–95), 3d E. of Macclesfield, M.P. Newcastle-under-Lyme 1747–54, Oxfordshire 1755–61, Rochester 1761–64 (GEC).

3498. PARKYNS, George Augustus Henry Anne (1785–1850), 2d Bn Rancliffe, M.P. Minehead 1806–7, Nottingham borough 1812–20, 1826–30 (GEC; *Harrow Reg.*).

3499. PARKYNS, Thomas Boothby (1755–1800), 1st Bn Rancliffe, M.P. Stockbridge 1784–90, Leicester borough 1790–1800 (GEC).

3500. PARNELL, Henry Brooke (1776–1842), 1st Bn Congleton, M.P. Queens 1802–2, 1806–32, Portarlington 1802–2, Dundee 1832–41 (DNB; GEC).

3501. PARNELL, John (1744–1801), 2d Bt, M.P. Queens 1801–1 (*Alumni Dublin.;* DNB; GEC; *Eton Coll. Reg.; Harrow Reg.*).

3502. PARNELL-HAYES, William (ca 1777–1821), M.P. Wicklow 1817–21 (DNB; Ball and Venn's *Admissions to Trinity College; Eton Lists*).

3503. PARRY, John (ca 1724–97), M.P. Carnarvonshire 1780–90 (*Alumni Cantab.*).

PARRY, Love Parry Jones, *see* JONES-PARRY, Love Parry.

3504. PARSONS, Henry (1687–1739), M.P. Lostwithiel 1724–27, Maldon 1727–39 (*Daily Advertiser,* 31 Dec. 1739; Musgrave's *Obituary; Parish Reg. Christ Church Newgate,* p. 66).

3505. PARSONS, Humphrey (ca 1676–1741), M.P. Harwich 1722–27, London 1727–41 (DNB).

3506. PARSONS, John Clere (b. ca 1760), M.P. Kings 1818–21 (*Alumni Dublin.;* Burke's *Peerage* sub Rosse).

3507. PARSONS, Laurence (1758–1841), 2d E. of Rosse, M.P. Kings 1801–7 (DNB; GEC).

3508. PARSONS, William (1800–67), 3d E. of Rosse, M.P. Kings 1821–34 (DNB; GEC).

3509. PATERSON, John (ca 1705–89), M.P. Ludgershall 1761–68 (Beaven's *Aldermen of London;* Musgrave's *Obituary;* Namier).

3510. PATERSON, John (d. 1782), 3d Bt, M.P. Berwickshire 1779–80 (GEC).

PATERSON, Philip Anstruther, *see* ANSTRUTHER-PATERSON, Philip.

PATTEN, John Wilson and Thomas Wilson, *see* WILSON-PATTEN, John and Thomas.

3511. PATTEN-BOLD, Peter (ca 1764–1819), M.P. Newton 1797–1806, Lancaster borough 1807–12, Malmesbury 1813–18 (*Alumni Oxon.;* Burke's *LG* [ed. 1849]).

3512. PATTERSON, John (1755–1833), M.P. Minehead 1802–6, Norwich 1806–12 (Burke's *LG;* Cozens-Hardy and Kent, *Mayors of Norwich,* p. 140).

PAULET, *see* POWLETT.

PAULET, Charles Ingoldsby Burroughs, *see* BURROUGHS-PAULET, Charles Ingoldsby.

3513. PAULET, George (1722–1800), 12th M. of Winchester, M.P. Winchester 1765–74 (GEC).

3514. PAULL, James (ca 1770–1808), M.P. Newtown 1805–6 (DNB).

3515. PAXTON, William (ca 1744–1824), M.P. Carmarthen borough 1803–6, Carmarthenshire 1806–7 (Burke's *LG* [ed. 1849]; Williams' *Wales M.P.'s*).

3516. PAXTON, William Gill (1789–1850), M.P. Plympton Erle 1821–26 (*Alumni Oxon.;* Burke's *LG* [ed. 1849]; *Harrow Reg.*).

3517. PAYNE, John Willett (ca 1752–1803), M.P. Huntingdon borough 1787–96 (DNB; Oliver's *Antigua, 3,* 9).

3518. PAYNE, Peter (ca 1762–1843), 3d Bt, M.P. Bedfordshire 1831–32 (DNB; GEC; Oliver's *Antigua, 3,* 9).

3519. PAYNE, Ralph (1739–1807), 1st Bn Lavington, M.P. Shaftesbury 1768–71, Camelford 1776–80, Plympton Erle 1780–84, Woodstock 1795–99 (DNB; GEC).

3520. PEACH, Nathaniel William (ca 1786–1835), M.P. Corfe Castle 1828–29, Truro 1829–32 (*Gent. Mag., 2,* 444; *Linc. Inn Reg.; Shrewsbury School Reg.*).

3521. PEACH-HUNGERFORD, John (ca 1719–1809), M.P. Leicestershire 1775–90 (Burke's *LG* [ed. 1849]; *Gent. Mag., 1,* 589).

3522. PEACHEY, Henry (ca 1671–1737), 1st Bt, M.P. Sussex 1701–2, 1708–10, Midhurst 1736–37 (GEC; *Eton Coll. Reg.*).

3523. PEACHEY, James (1683–1771), M.P. Leominster 1747–54 (Clutterbuck's *Herts, 3,* 366).

3524. PEACHEY, James (1723–1808), 1st Bn Selsey, M.P. Seaford 1755–68 (GEC; *Old Westminsters*).

3525. PEACHEY, John (ca 1680–1744), 2d Bt, M.P. Midhurst 1738–44 (GEC).

3526. PEACHEY, John (ca 1720–65), 3d Bt, M.P. Midhurst 1744–61 (GEC; *Old Westminsters*).

3527. PEACHEY, John (1749–1816), 2d Bn Selsey, M.P. St. Germans 1776–80, Shoreham 1780–90 (GEC; *Eton Coll. Reg.*).

3528. PEACHEY, William (ca 1763–1838), M.P. Yarmouth (Hants) 1797–1802, Taunton 1826–30 (*Alumni Oxon.; Gent. Mag., 1* [1839], 96).

3529. PEACHEY-KNIGHT, Bulstrode (ca 1682–1736), M.P. Midhurst 1722–36 (Burke's *LG;* GEC sub Selsey; Dalloway's *Western Division of Sussex, 1,* pt. 2, 167, 169).

3530. PEARCE, Thomas (d. ca 1756), M.P. Weymouth and Melcombe Regis 1722–27, 1727–41 (DNB; cf. *Alumni Cantab.*).

3531. PEARSE, John (ca 1760–1836), M.P. Devizes 1818–32 (*Gent. Mag., 2,* 331; *Notes and Queries, 179,* 133).

PECHELL, *see* BROOKE-PECHELL.

3532. PEDLEY, John, M.P. Hindon 1802–6, Saltash 1808–9 (*Royal Kalendar* [1806], p. 49; *1806 List*).

PEDLEY, Robert, *see* DEVERELL, Robert.

3533. PEEL, Edmund (1791–1850), M.P. Newcastle-under-Lyme 1831–32, 1835–37 (Burke's *Peerage; Harrow Reg.*).

3534. PEEL, Jonathan (1799–1879), M.P. Norwich 1826–30, Huntingdon borough 1831–68 (DNB; *Rugby Reg.*).

3535. PEEL, Lawrence (1799–1884), M.P. Cockermouth 1827–30 (*Alumni Oxon.;* Bean; Boase; Ferguson; Foster's *Lancashire Pedigrees; Rugby Reg.*).

3536. PEEL, Robert (1750–1830), 1st Bt, M.P. Tamworth 1790–1820 (DNB; GEC).

3537. PEEL, Robert (1788–1850), 2d Bt, M.P. Cashel 1809–12, Chippenham 1812–17, Oxford Univ. 1817–29, Westbury 1829–30, Tamworth 1830–50 (DNB; GEC).

3538. PEEL, William Yates (1789–1858), M.P. Bossiney 1817–18, Tamworth 1818–30, 1835–37, 1847–47, Yarmouth (Hants) 1830–31, Cambridge Univ. 1831–32 (DNB).

PEERS, Richard, *see* SYMONS, Richard.

3539. PEIRS, William, M.P. Wells 1716–22, 1729–34, 1735–41.

3540. PEIRSE, Henry (1692–1759), M.P. Northallerton 1713–15, 1722–54 (Burke's *LG* [ed. 1849]; *Genealogist,* N.S., *24,* 117).

3541. PEIRSE, Henry (ca 1754–1824), M.P. Northallerton 1774–1824 (*Eton Coll. Reg.; Genealogist,* N.S., *24,* 117).

3542. PELHAM, Charles (ca 1679–1763), M.P. Great Grimsby 1722–27, Beverley 1727–34, 1738–54 (Burke's *Peerage* and Collins' *Peerage* sub Yarborough).

PELHAM, Charles Anderson, *see* ANDERSON-PELHAM, Charles.

PELHAM, Henry, *see* CRESSETT-PELHAM, Henry.

3543. PELHAM, Henry (ca 1696–1754), M.P. Seaford 1717–22, Sussex 1722–54 (*Alumni Cantab.;* DNB; *Old Westminsters*).

3544. PELHAM, Henry (1759–97), M.P. Lewes 1780–96 (*Old Westminsters*).

3545. PELHAM, James (ca 1683–1761), M.P. Newark 1727–41, Hastings 1741–61 (Collins' *Peerage* sub Chichester; *London Chronicle,* 26–29 Dec. 1761; Musgrave's *Obituary*).

PELHAM, John Cressett, *see* CRESSETT-PELHAM, John.

3546. PELHAM, Thomas (b. ca 1678), M.P. Lewes 1705–41 (*Alumni Oxon.;* GEC; Comber's *Sussex Geneal., Lewes,* p. 212; Namier).

3547. PELHAM, Thomas (ca 1705–37), M.P. Lewes 1727–37 (*Alumni Cantab.;* M. A. Lower, *Pelham Family,* p. 47).

3548. PELHAM, Thomas (ca 1705–43), M.P. Hastings 1728–41, Lewes 1741–43 (Comber's *Sussex Geneal., Lewes,* p. 212; Musgrave's *Obituary;* Namier).

3549. PELHAM, Thomas (1728–1805), 1st E. of Chichester, M.P. Rye
1749–54, Sussex 1754–68 (*Alumni Cantab.;* DNB; GEC; *Old
Westminsters*).

3550. PELHAM, Thomas (1756–1826), 2d E. of Chichester, M.P. Sussex
1780–1801 (DNB; GEC; *Old Westminsters*).

3551. PELHAM-CLINTON, Henry Fiennes (1750–78), M.P. Aldborough
1772–74, Notts 1774–78 (GEC sub Newcastle; *Eton Coll. Reg.*).

3552. PELHAM-CLINTON, John (1755–81), M.P. East Retford 1778–81
(*Alumni Cantab.; Eton Coll. Reg.*).

3553. PELHAM-CLINTON, Thomas (1752–95), 3d D. of Newcastle, M.P.
Westminster 1774–80, East Retford 1781–94 (GEC; *Eton Coll.
Reg.*).

3554. PELLEW, Edward (1757–1833), 1st Vct Exmouth, M.P. Barnstable
1802–4 (DNB; GEC).

3555. PELLEW, Pownoll Bastard (1786–1833), 2d Vct Exmouth, M.P.
Launceston 1812–29 (GEC).

3556. PEMBERTON-LEIGH, Thomas (1793–1867), 1st Bn Kingsdown, M.P.
Rye 1831–32, Ripon 1835–43 (DNB; GEC; *Harrow Reg.*).

PEMBROKE, 11th E. of, *see* HERBERT, George Augustus.

PENDARVES, Edward William Wynne, *see* WYNNE-PENDARVES, Edward William.

3557. PENLEAZE, John Story (ca 1786–1855), M.P. Southampton borough 1831–32, 1833–34 (*Alumni Oxon.;* Boase; Dod's *Parl.
Companion* [1834], p. 152).

3558. PENN, John (1760–1834), M.P. Helston 1802–5 (DNB; *Eton
Coll. Reg.*).

3559. PENN, Richard (ca 1736–1811), M.P. Appleby 1784–90, Haslemere 1790–91, 1802–6, Lancaster borough 1796–1802 (DNB;
Admissions to St. John, Cambridge; Eton Coll. Reg.).

PENNANT, George Hay Dawkins, *see* DAWKINS-PENNANT, George
Hay.

3560. PENNANT, Richard (ca 1737–1808), 1st Bn Penrhyn, M.P. Petersfield 1761–67, Liverpool 1767–80, 1784–90 (DNB; GEC; Ball
and Venn's *Admissions to Trinity College*).

3561. PENNEFATHER, Matthew (ca 1784–1858), M.P. Cashel 1830–31
(Burke's *Irish LG*).

3562. PENNEFATHER, Richard (ca 1756–1831), M.P. Cashel 1818–19
(*Alumni Dublin.;* Burke's *Irish LG; Gent. Mag., 1,* 650).

3563. PENNINGTON, John (ca 1710–68), 3d Bt, M.P. Cumberland 1745–
68 (GEC).

3564. PENNINGTON, John (ca 1737–1813), 1st Bn Muncaster, M.P. Milborne Port 1781–96, Colchester 1796–1802, Westmorland 1806–
13 (DNB; GEC).

3565. PENNINGTON, Joseph (1677–1744), 2d Bt, M.P. Cumberland 1734–
44 (GEC).

3566. PENNYMAN, James (1736–1808), 6th Bt, M.P. Scarborough 1770–74, Beverley 1774–96 (GEC; *Old Westminsters*).

PENRHYN, 1st Bn, *see* PENNANT, Richard.

3567. PENRHYN, Edward (1794–1861), M.P. Shaftesbury 1830–32 (Burke's *LG*).

3568. PENRUDDOCKE, Charles (1743–88), M.P. Wilts 1770–88 (*Alumni Oxon.;* Burke's *LG;* Hoare's *Modern Wiltshire, 4,* 80).

3569. PENRUDDOCKE, John Hungerford (1770–1841), M.P. Wilton 1821–37 (*Alumni Oxon.;* Burke's *LG; Harrow Reg.*).

3570. PENTON, Henry (ca 1706–62), M.P. Tregony 1734–47, Winchester 1747–61 (*Alumni Oxon.;* Musgrave's *Obituary*).

3571. PENTON, Henry (1736–1812), M.P. Winchester 1761–96 (*Gent. Mag., 1,* 93; *Linc. Inn Reg.;* Venn MS).

3572. PEPYS, Charles Christopher (1781–1851), 1st E. of Cottenham, M.P. Higham Ferrers 1831–31, Malton 1831–36 (DNB; GEC; *Harrow Reg.*).

3573. PERCEVAL, Alexander (1787–1858), M.P. Sligo Co. 1831–41 (*Alumni Dublin.;* DNB).

3574. PERCEVAL, Charles George (1756–1840), 1st Bn Arden (U.K.), M.P. Launceston 1780–90, Warwick borough 1790–96, Totnes 1796–1802 (GEC).

3575. PERCEVAL, Henry Frederick John James (1796–1841), 5th E. of Egmont, M.P. East Looe 1826–26 (GEC).

3576. PERCEVAL, John (1711–70), 2d E. of Egmont, M.P. Westminster 1741–47, Weobley 1747–54, Bridgwater 1754–62 (DNB; GEC).

3577. PERCEVAL, John James (1738–1822), 3d E. of Egmont, M.P. Bridgwater 1762–69 (GEC; *Eton Coll. Reg.*).

3578. PERCEVAL, Spencer (1762–1812), M.P. Northampton borough 1796–1812 (DNB).

3579. PERCEVAL, Spencer (1795–1859), M.P. Ennis 1818–20, Newport (Hants) 1827–31, Tiverton 1831–32 (Burke's *Peerage* sub Egmont; Boase).

3580. PERCY, Algernon (1750–1830), 1st E. of Beverley, M.P. Northumberland 1774–86 (GEC; *Eton Coll. Reg.*).

3581. PERCY, Algernon George (1810–99), 6th D. of Northumberland, M.P. Berealston 1831–32, North Northumberland 1852–65 (GEC).

PERCY, Charles, *see* GREATHEAD-BERTIE-PERCY, Charles.

3582. PERCY, George (1778–1867), 5th D. of Northumberland, M.P. Berealston 1799–1830 (GEC; *Eton Coll. Reg.*).

3583. PERCY, Henry (1785–1825), M.P. Berealston 1820–25 (DNB).

3584. PERCY, Hugh (1715–86), 1st D. of Northumberland, M.P. Middlesex 1740–50 (Burke's *Peerage;* GEC).

3585. PERCY, Hugh (1742–1817), 2d D. of Northumberland, M.P. Westminster 1763–76 (DNB; GEC; *Eton Coll. Reg.*).

3586. PERCY, Hugh (1785–1847), 3d D. of Northumberland, M.P. Buckingham borough 1806–6, Westminster 1806–6, Launceston 1806–7, Northumberland 1807–12 (*Admissions to St. John, Cambridge;* DNB; GEC).

3587. PERCY, Josceline (1784–1856), M.P. Berealston 1806–20 (DNB).

3588. PERCY, William Henry (1788–1855), M.P. Stamford 1818–26 (DNB).

3589. PERIAM, John (b. ca 1702), M.P. Minehead 1742–47 (*Alumni Oxon.*).

3590. PERRIN, Louis (1782–1864), M.P. Dublin City 1831–31, Monaghan 1832–34, Cashel 1835–35 (DNB).

3591. PERRING, John (1765–1831), 1st Bt, M.P. New Romney 1806–7, Hythe 1810–20 (Foster's *Baronetage;* Wilks' *Barons of the Cinque Ports,* p. 119).

3592. PERROTT, Henry (1689–1740), M.P. Oxfordshire 1721–40 (*Alumni Oxon.; Westminster Abbey Reg.,* p. 44; Williams' *Oxford M.P.'s*).

3593. PERRY, Micajah (d. 1753), M.P. London 1727–41 (Beaven's *Aldermen of London;* Oliver's *Antigua, 3,* 20).

PETERS, Edmund, *see* TURTON, Edmund.

PETERS, Henry, *see* BURTON-PETERS, Henry.

3594. PETERS, Henry (ca 1763–1827), M.P. Oxford City 1796–1802 (Williams' *Oxford M.P.'s; Admissions to St. John, Cambridge*).

PETERSHAM, Vct, *see* STANHOPE, Charles and William.

3595. PETIT, Louis Hayes (1774–1849), M.P. Ripon 1827–32 (Agnew's *Protestant Exiles, 2,* 256; *Gent. Mag., 1* [1850], 90).

3596. PETRE, Edward Robert (ca 1795–1848), M.P. Ilchester 1831–32, York City 1832–34 (Burke's *Peerage*).

3597. PETRIE, John (ca 1742–1826), M.P. Gatton 1796–1800 (*Notes and Queries,* 10th Ser., *6,* 401).

3598. PETRIE, William (ca 1748–1816), M.P. East Retford 1796–1802 (*Notes and Queries,* 10th Ser., *6,* 401).

3599. PETTY, John (ca 1706–61), 1st E. of Shelburne, M.P. Wycombe 1754–60 (GEC; *Old Westminsters*).

3600. PETTY, John Henry (1765–1809), 2d M. of Lansdowne, M.P. Wycombe 1786–1802 (GEC).

3601. PETTY, William (1737–1805), 1st M. of Lansdowne, M.P. Wycombe 1760–61 (DNB; GEC).

3602. PETTY-FITZMAURICE, Henry (1780–1863), 3d M. of Lansdowne, M.P. Calne 1802–6, Cambridge Univ. 1806–7, Camelford 1807–9 (DNB; GEC; *Old Westminsters*).

3603. PEYTON, Henry (1736–89), 1st Bt, M.P. Cambridgeshire 1782–89 (GEC; Howard's *Visitation of Suffolk, 2,* 131).

3604. PEYTON, Henry (1779–1854), 2d Bt, M.P. Cambridgeshire 1802–2 (GEC; *Harrow Reg.*).

3605. PHELIPS, Edward (1725–97), M.P. Somerset 1774–80 (Burke's *LG; Old Westminsters*).

3606. PHELIPS, Edward (1753–92), M.P. Somerset 1784–92 (Burke's *LG; Old Westminsters*).

3607. PHILIPPS, Erasmus (ca 1700–43), 5th Bt, M.P. Haverfordwest 1726–43 (DNB; GEC).

3608. PHILIPPS, Griffith (d. 1781), M.P. Carmarthen borough 1751–61, 1768–74 (Burke's *LG;* Williams' *Wales M.P.'s*).

3609. PHILIPPS, John (ca 1701–64), 6th Bt, M.P. Carmarthen borough 1741–47, Petersfield 1754–61, Pembrokeshire 1761–64 (GEC; Williams' *Wales M.P.'s*).

3610. PHILIPPS, John George (ca 1761–1816), M.P. Carmarthen borough 1784–96, 1796–1803 (*Alumni Oxon.;* Burke's *LG;* Williams' *Wales M.P.'s*).

3611. PHILIPPS, Richard (ca 1744–1823), 1st Bn Milford, M.P. Pembrokeshire 1765–70, 1786–1812, Plympton Erle 1774–79, Haverfordwest 1784–86 (GEC).

3612. PHILIPPS, Richard Bulkeley Philipps Grant (1801–57), 1st Bn Milford, M.P. Haverfordwest 1826–34, 1837–47 (GEC).

3613. PHILIPS, George (ca 1743–84), M.P. Carmarthen borough 1780–84 (Ball and Venn's *Admissions to Trinity College; Old Westminsters;* Williams' *Wales M.P.'s*).

3614. PHILIPS, George (1766–1847), 1st Bt, M.P. Ilchester 1812–18, Steyning 1818–20, Wootton Bassett 1820–30, South Warwickshire 1832–34 (Foster's *Baronetage; 1821 List*).

3615. PHILIPS, George Richard (1789–1874), 2d Bt, M.P. Horsham 1818–20, Steyning 1820–32, Kidderminster 1835–37, Poole 1837–52 (Burke's *LG;* Williams' *Worcester M.P.'s*).

3616. PHILIPSON, John (d. 1756), M.P. Shoreham 1734–41, Harwich 1741–56 (Musgrave's *Obituary*).

3617. PHILLIMORE, Joseph (1775–1855), M.P. St. Mawes 1817–26, Yarmouth (Hants) 1826–30 (DNB; *Old Westminsters*).

3618. PHILLIPPS, Ambrose (ca 1707–37), M.P. Leicestershire 1734–37 (*Alumni Oxon.;* Burke's *LG* [ed. 1849]; Musgrave's *Obituary*).
PHILLIPPS, Charles March, *see* MARCH-PHILLIPPS, Charles.

3619. PHILLIPPS, Jonathan (ca 1724–98), M.P. Camelford 1784–84 (Maclean's *Trigg Minor, 1,* 652).

3620. PHILLIPPS, Robert (1749–1822), M.P. Hereford borough 1784–85 (Burke's *LG* [ed. 1849]; Williams' *Hereford M.P.'s*).

3621. PHILLIPS, Charles (d. 1774), M.P. Camelford 1768–74 (Musgrave's *Obituary*).

3622. PHILLIPS, Richard (ca 1768–1844), M.P. Stafford borough 1806–12 (Burke's *Peerage* sub Mansel; Clarke's *Mon. Insc. St. Mary's, Wimbledon,* p. 5; Foster's *Baronetage;* Wedgwood).

3623. PHILLIPS, William (d. 1781), M.P. Boroughbridge 1775–80 (*Army*

Lists; Bean; Musgrave's *Obituary; Royal Kalendar* [1780], p. 25).

PHILLIPSON, Richard Burton, *see* BURTON-PHILLIPSON, Richard.

3624. PHILLPOTTS, John (ca 1775–1849), M.P. Gloucester City 1830–31, 1832–34, 1837–47 (Burke's *LG* [ed. 1849]; Williams' *Gloucester M.P.'s*).

3625. PHIPPS, Charles (1753–86), M.P. Scarborough 1779–84, Minehead 1784–86 (Bean; Collins' *Peerage* sub Mulgrave; Musgrave's *Obituary*).

3626. PHIPPS, Constantine Henry (1797–1863), 1st M. of Normanby, M.P. Scarborough 1818–20, Higham Ferrers 1822–26, Malton 1826–30 (DNB; GEC).

3627. PHIPPS, Constantine John (1744–92), 1st Bn Mulgrave (U.K.), M.P. Lincoln City 1768–74, Huntingdon borough 1776–84, Newark 1784–90 (DNB; GEC; *Eton Coll. Reg.*).

3628. PHIPPS, Edmund (1760–1837), M.P. Scarborough 1794–1818, 1820–32, Queenborough 1818–20 (*Admissions to St. John, Cambridge; Eton Coll. Reg.*).

3629. PHIPPS, Henry (1755–1831), 1st E. of Mulgrave, M.P. Totnes 1784–90, Scarborough 1790–94 (DNB; GEC; *Eton Coll. Reg.*).

3630. PHIPPS, James Farrill (ca 1745–86), M.P. Peterborough 1780–86 (*Alumni Oxon.; Notes and Queries, 175,* 301).

3631. PICKERING, Edward (ca 1716–49), 4th Bt, M.P. St. Michael 1745–47 (GEC).

3632. PICTON, Thomas (1758–1815), M.P. Pembroke borough 1813–15 (DNB).

3633. PIERREPONT, Charles (1737–1816), 1st E. Manvers, M.P. Notts 1778–96 (GEC).

3634. PIERREPONT, Charles Evelyn (1805–50), M.P. East Retford 1830–34 (*Alumni Oxon.;* GEC sub Manvers).

3635. PIERREPONT, Charles Herbert (1778–1860), 2d E. Manvers, M.P. Notts 1801–16 (GEC).

3636. PIERREPONT, Evelyn Henry Frederick (1775–1801), M.P. Bossiney 1796–96, Notts 1796–1801 (*Alumni Oxon.;* GEC sub Manvers).

3637. PIGOT, George (1719–77), 1st Bn Pigot, M.P. Wallingford 1765–68, Bridgnorth 1768–77 (DNB; GEC).

3638. PIGOT, Hugh (1722–92), M.P. Penryn 1768–74, Bridgnorth 1778–84 (DNB; *Notes and Queries,* 8th Ser., *9,* 406; Shrop. Archaeol. Soc. *Trans.,* 4th Ser., *5,* 69).

3639. PIGOT, Robert (1720–96), 2d Bt, M.P. Wallingford 1768–71 (DNB; GEC).

3640. PIGOTT, Arthur Leary (1749–1819), M.P. Steyning 1806–6, Arundel 1806–12, 1818–19, Horsham 1812–18 (*Alumni Oxon.;* DNB; Williamson's *Middle Temple Bench Book*).

PIGOTT, George Edward Graham Foster, *see* GRAHAM-FOSTER-PIGOTT, George Edward.

3641. PIGOTT, George Grenville Wandesford (1796-1865), M.P. St. Mawes 1830-32 (Burke's *LG; Rugby Reg.*).

3642. PIGOTT, Robert (d. 1746), M.P. Hunts 1713-22, 1730-41 (Musgrave's *Obituary*).

3643. PILKINGTON, Lionel (1707-78), 5th Bt, M.P. Horsham 1748-68 (GEC; *Old Westminsters*).

3644. PILSWORTH, Charles (d. 1749), M.P. Aylesbury 1741-47 (Musgrave's *Obituary*).

3645. PINNEY, John Frederick (ca 1718-62), M.P. Bridport 1747-61 (Burke's *LG*).

3646. PITT, George (1721-1803), 1st Bn Rivers, M.P. Shaftesbury 1742-47, Dorset 1747-74 (DNB; GEC).

3647. PITT, George (1751-1828), 2nd Bn Rivers, M.P. Dorset 1774-90 (GEC).

3648. PITT, George Morton (ca 1693-1756). M.P. Old Sarum 1722-24, Pontefract 1741-54 (Collins' *Peerage* sub Rivers; Musgrave's *Obituary; Notes and Queries*, 12th Ser., *4*, 99, 198, 284).

3649. PITT, John (ca 1706-87), M.P. Wareham 1734-47, 1748-51, 1761-68, Dorchester 1751-61 (*Alumni Oxon.;* Collins' *Peerage* sub Rivers; Hutchins' *Dorset, 1*, 517 and *2*, 564).

3650. PITT, John (1725-1805), M.P. Gloucester City 1789-1805 (*Alumni Carthusiani;* Williams' *Gloucester M.P.'s*).

3651. PITT, Joseph (ca 1759-1842), M.P. Cricklade 1812-31 (*Gent. Mag., 1*, 340; *1812 List*).

3652. PITT, Ridgeway (ca 1722-65), 3d E. of Londonderry, M.P. Camelford 1747-54 (*Alumni Cantab.;* GEC; *Old Westminsters*).

3653. PITT, Thomas (ca 1705-61), M.P. Okehampton 1727-54, Old Sarum 1754-55, 1761-61 (Boase and Courtney's *Biblio. Cornub.; Eton Coll. Reg.;* Ruville's *Chatham, 1*, 69).

3654. PITT, Thomas (1737-93), 1st Bn Camelford, M.P. Old Sarum 1761-68, 1774-84, Okehampton 1768-74 (DNB; GEC).

3655. PITT, William (1708-78), 1st E. of Chatham, M.P. Old Sarum 1735-47, Seaford 1747-54, Aldborough 1754-56, Okehampton 1756-57, Bath 1757-66 (DNB; GEC; *Eton Coll. Reg.*).

3656. PITT, William (1759-1806), M.P. Appleby 1781-84, Cambridge Univ. 1784-1806 (DNB).

3657. PITT, William Augustus (ca 1728-1809), M.P. Wareham 1754-61 (DNB; Hutchins' *Dorset, 4*, 92; *Notes and Queries*, 8th Ser., *9*, 406).

3658. PITT, William Morton (1754-1836), M.P. Poole 1780-90, Dorset 1790-1826 (*Alumni Oxon.;* Collins' *Peerage* sub Rivers; Hutchins' *Dorset, 2*, 564; *Linc. Inn Reg.;* Sydenham's *Poole*, p. 285).

3659. PLANTA, Joseph (1787–1847), M.P. Hastings 1827–31, 1837–44 (DNB).

3660. PLEYDELL, Edmund Morton (ca 1695–1754), M.P. Dorchester 1722–23, Dorset 1727–47 (*Alumni Oxon.;* Burke's *LG;* Hutchins' *Dorset, 1,* 198; Musgrave's *Obituary*).

3661. PLEYDELL-BOUVERIE, Jacob (1750–1828), 2d E. of Radnor, M.P. Salisbury 1771–76 (GEC).

3662. PLEYDELL-BOUVERIE, William (1779–1869), 3d E. of Radnor, M.P. Downton 1801–2, Salisbury 1802–28 (DNB; GEC).

3663. PLUMER, Richard (ca 1685–1750), M.P. Lichfield 1722–34, St. Mawes 1734–41, Aldeburgh 1741–47, Weymouth and Melcombe Regis 1747–50 (Berry's *County Geneal.: Herts;* Wedgwood).

3664. PLUMER, Thomas (1753–1824), M.P. Downton 1807–13 (DNB; *Eton Coll. Reg.*).

3665. PLUMER, William (ca 1687–1767), M.P. Yarmouth (Hants) 1721–22, Herts 1734–41, 1755–61 (*Alumni Cantab.;* Berry's *County Geneal.: Herts*).

3666. PLUMER, William (1736–1822), M.P. Lewes 1763–68, Herts 1768–1807, Higham Ferrers 1812–22 (Berry's *County Geneal.: Herts;* Cussans' *Herts, 1,* 141; *Gent. Mag., 1,* 376).

3667. PLUMER-WARD, Robert (1765–1846), M.P. Cockermouth 1802–6, Haslemere 1807–23 (*Alumni Oxon.;* DNB).

3668. PLUMMER, John, M.P. Hindon 1820–26 (*1821 List;* query *Gent. Mag., 2* [1839], 545).

3669. PLUMMER, Thomas William, M.P. Ilchester 1802–3, Yarmouth (Hants) 1806–7 (*1812 List*).

3670. PLUMMER, Walter (ca 1683–1746), M.P. Aldeburgh 1719–27, Appleby 1730–41 (*Alumni Cantab.; Eton Coll. Reg.*).

3671. PLUMPTRE, John (1679–1751), M.P. Nottingham borough 1706–13, 1715–27, 1734–47, Bishop's Castle 1727–34, St. Ives 1747–51 (Berry's *County Geneal.: Kent,* p. 90; Burke's *LG;* Shrop. Archaeol. Soc. *Trans.,* 2d Ser., *10,* 58).

3672. PLUMPTRE, John (1711–91), M.P. Penryn 1758–61, Nottingham borough 1761–74 (Berry's *County Geneal.: Kent,* p. 90; Burke's *LG;* Musgrave's *Obituary*).

3673. PLUNKET, William Conyngham (1765–1854), 1st Bn Plunket, M.P. Midhurst 1807–7, Dublin Univ. 1812–27 (*Alumni Dublin.;* DNB; GEC).

3674. PLUNKETT, Arthur James (1791–1869), 9th E. of Fingall, M.P. Meath 1830–32 (GEC).

3675. POCHIN, Charles William (1777–1817), M.P. Enniskillen 1807–12 (Burke's *LG;* Fletcher's *Leicester Pedigrees;* Nichols' *Leicester, 3,* pt. 1, 52).

3676. POCHIN, William (1731–98), M.P. Leicestershire 1780–98 (*Alumni Cantab.;* Burke's *LG;* Fletcher's *Leicester Pedigrees*).

3677. POCKLINGTON-DOMVILE, Compton (d. 1857), 1st Bt, M.P. Bossiney 1818–26, Okehampton 1826–30, Plympton Erle 1830–32 (Burke's *Peerage;* Boase).

3678. POCOCK, George (1706–92), M.P. Plymouth 1760–68 (DNB).

3679. POCOCK, George (1765–1840), 1st Bt, M.P. Bridgwater 1796–1806, 1807–20 (*Eton Coll. Reg.*).

8680. POLE, Charles (1695–1779), M.P. Liverpool 1756–61 (Bean; Burke's *LG*).

3681. POLE, Charles Morice (1757–1830), 1st Bt, M.P. Newark 1802–6, Plymouth 1806–18 (DNB).

POLE, John William, *see* DE LA POLE, John William.

3682. POLE, Peter (1770–1850), 2d Bt, M.P. Yarmouth (Hants) 1819–26 (GEC).

POLE, William Wellesley, *see* WELLESLEY-POLE, William.

3683. POLE-CAREW, Reginald (1753–1835), M.P. Penryn 1782–84, Reigate 1787–90, Lostwithiel 1790–96, 1812–16, Fowey 1796–99, 1802–12 (*Alumni Oxon.;* Burke's *LG*).

3684. POLE-TYLNEY-LONG-WELLESLEY, William (1788–1857), 4th E. of Mornington, M.P. St. Ives 1812–18, 1830–31, Wilts 1818–20, Essex 1831–32 (DNB; GEC).

3685. POLHILL, David (ca 1674–1754), M.P. Kent 1710–10, Bramber 1723–27, Rochester 1727–41, 1743–54 (Berry's *County Geneal.: Sussex,* p. 268; *Notes and Queries,* 10th Ser., *11,* 314; Smith's *Rochester in Parl.; Topographer and Genealogist, 1,* 186).

3686. POLHILL, Frederick (ca 1798–1848), M.P. Bedford borough 1830–32, 1835–47 (Burke's *LG; Gent. Mag., 2,* 545).

3687. POLHILL, Nathaniel (1723–82), M.P. Southwark 1774–82 (Burke's *LG;* Musgrave's *Obituary; Topographer and Genealogist, 1,* 191).

3688. POLLEN, George Augustus (ca 1775–1807), M.P. Leominster 1796–1802 (Burke's *LG* [ed. 1849]; *Gent. Mag., 1* [1808], 461; Venn MS; Williams' *Hereford M.P.'s*).

3689. POLLEN, John (ca 1702–75), M.P. Andover 1734–54 (*Alumni Oxon.;* GEC; Williams' *Great Sessions in Wales*).

3690. POLLEN, John Walter (1784–1863), 2d Bt, M.P. Andover 1820–31, 1835–41 (*Alumni Oxon.;* GEC).

POLLINGTON, Bn and Vct, *see* SAVILE, John.

3691. POLLOCK, Jonathan Frederick (1783–1870), 1st Bt, M.P. Huntingdon borough 1831–44 (DNB; *St. Paul's School Reg.*).

POLWARTH, Bn, *see* HEPBURNE-SCOTT, Henry Francis and Hugh; *also* HUME-CAMPBELL, Hugh.

3692. PONSONBY, Frederick (1758–1844), 3d E. of Bessborough, M.P. Knaresborough 1780–93 (GEC).

3693. PONSONBY, Frederick (d. 1849), M.P. Galway town 1811–13 (Burke's *Peerage* sub Bessborough; Burtchaell's *Kilkenny M.P.'s,* p. 176; J. Ponsonby, *Ponsonby Family,* p. 95).

3694. Ponsonby, Frederick Cavendish (1783–1837), M.P. Kilkenny Co. 1806–26, Higham Ferrers 1826–30 (DNB; Howard and Crisp's *Visitation of Eng. and Wales, 12,* 109).

3695. Ponsonby, George (1755–1817), M.P. Wicklow 1801–6, 1816–17, Cork Co. 1806–7, Tavistock 1808–12, Peterborough 1812–16 (DNB).

3696. Ponsonby, George (ca 1773–1863), M.P. Kilkenny Co. 1806–6, Cork Co. 1807–12, Youghal 1826–32 (*Alumni Dublin.;* Burtchaell's *Kilkenny M.P.'s;* Foster's *Peerage* sub Bessborough).

3697. Ponsonby, John (ca 1772–1855), 1st Vct Ponsonby, M.P. Galway town 1801–2 (DNB; GEC).

3698. Ponsonby, John George Brabazon (1809–80), 5th E. of Bessborough, M.P. Bletchingley 1831–31, Higham Ferrers 1831–32, Derby borough 1835–37, 1841–47 (GEC).

3699. Ponsonby, John William (1781–1847), 4th E. of Bessborough, M.P. Knaresborough 1805–6, Higham Ferrers 1810–12, Malton 1812–26, Kilkenny Co. 1826–32, Nottingham borough 1832–34 (DNB; GEC; *Harrow Reg.*).

3700. Ponsonby, William (ca 1704–93), 2d E. of Bessborough, M.P. Derby borough 1742–54, Saltash 1754–56, Harwich 1756–58 (DNB; GEC).

3701. Ponsonby, William (ca 1772–1815), M.P. Londonderry Co. 1812–15 (DNB; Ball and Venn's *Admissions to Trinity College; Cork Archaeol. Jour.* [1896], p. 178).

3702. Ponsonby, William Brabazon (1744–1806), 1st Bn Ponsonby, M. P. Kilkenny Co. 1801–6 (DNB; GEC; Venn MS).

3703. Ponsonby, William Francis Spencer (1787–1855), 1st Bn De Mauley, M.P. Poole 1826–31, Knaresborough 1832–32, Dorset 1832–37 (GEC; *Harrow Reg.*).

3704. Poole, Francis (ca 1683–1763), 2d Bt, M.P. Lewes 1743–63 (GEC).

3705. Poore, Edward (1705–88), M.P. Salisbury 1747–54, Downton 1756–61 (Burke's *Peerage;* Williams' *Great Sessions in Wales*).

3706. Popham, Alexander (ca 1729–1810), M.P. Taunton 1768–74, 1775–80, 1784–96 (DNB).

3707. Popham, Edward (ca 1712–72), M.P. Great Bedwin 1738–41, Wilts 1741–72 (*Alumni Oxon.;* Burke's *LG;* Musgrave's *Obituary*).

3708. Popham, Home Riggs (1760–1820), M.P. Yarmouth (Hants) 1804–6, Shaftesbury 1806–7, Ipswich 1807–12 (DNB; *Old Westminsters*).

3709. Popham, William (1740–1821), M.P. Milborne Port 1787–90 (Hodson's *Bengal Army Officers, 3,* 556).

3710. Porcher, Henry (ca 1795–1857), M.P. Clitheroe 1822–26 (Burke's *LG* [ed. 1849]; *Gent. Mag., 1* [1858], 113; *Notes and Queries, 179,* 150; Pink; Venn MS).

3711. PORCHER, Josias Dupré (ca 1761–1820), M.P. Bodmin 1802–6, Dundalk 1807–7, Bletchingley 1806–7, Old Sarum 1807–18 (Agnew's *Protestant Exiles, 2,* 256; Prinsep's *Madras Civilians,* p. 115; *Times,* 4 May 1820).

PORCHESTER, Bn, see HERBERT, Henry, Henry George, and Henry John George.

3712. PORTER, George (ca 1761–1828), M.P. Stockbridge 1793–1820 (Baker's *Northampton, 2,* 244; *1812 List*).

3713. PORTER, John (d. 1756), M.P. Evesham 1754–56 (Beaven's *Aldermen of London;* Williams' *Worcester M.P.'s*).

PORTLAND, D. of, see CAVENDISH-BENTINCK, William Henry; also CAVENDISH-SCOTT-BENTINCK, William Henry and William John.

3714. PORTMAN, Edward Berkeley (1771–1823), M.P. Boroughbridge 1802–6, Dorset 1806–23 (*Admissions to St. John, Cambridge*).

3715. PORTMAN, Edward Berkeley (1799–1888), 1st Vct Portman, M.P. Dorset 1823–32, Marylebone 1832–33 (DNB; GEC).

3716. PORTMAN, Henry Berkeley (ca 1768–1803), M.P. Wells 1790–96 (Hutchins' *Dorset, 1,* 256; *Old Westminsters*).

PORTMAN, Henry William, see BERKELEY-PORTMAN, Henry William.

PORTMORE, 4th E. of, see COLYEAR, Thomas Charles.

PORTSMOUTH, 4th E. of, see FELLOWES, Newton.

3717. POSTLETHWAITE, Thomas, M.P. Haslemere 1784–86.

3718. POTTENGER, Richard (ca 1690–1739), M.P. Reading 1727–39 (*Alumni Oxon.;* Williams' *Great Sessions in Wales*).

3719. POTTER, Christopher (d. 1817), M.P. Colchester 1781–82, 1784–84 (*Ann. Biog. and Obit.* [1817], p. 352; *Essex Review, 8,* 231–32; *Gent. Mag., 2,* 569).

3720. POTTER, Thomas (ca 1718–59), M.P. St. Germans 1747–54, Aylesbury 1754–57, Okehampton 1757–59 (DNB).

3721. POTTER, Thomas (ca 1740–1801), M.P. Lostwithiel 1776–80 (Williams' *Great Sessions in Wales*).

3722. POULETT, Anne (1711–85), M.P. Bridgwater 1769–85 (*Alumni Oxon.;* Burke's *Peerage;* Collins' *Peerage;* Musgrave's *Obituary*).

3723. POULETT, Peregrine (1708–52), M.P. Bossiney 1737–41, Bridgwater 1747–52 (Burke's *Peerage;* Collins' *Peerage*).

3724. POULETT, Vere (1710–88), 3d E. Poulett, M.P. Bridgwater 1741–47 (GEC).

3725. POULETT, Vere (1761–1812), M.P. Bridgwater 1790–96, 1806–7 (Burke's *Peerage;* Collins' *Peerage; Harrow Reg.*).

3726. POULETT-THOMSON, Charles Edward (1799–1841), 1st Bn Sydenham, M.P. Dover 1826–32, Manchester 1832–39 (DNB; GEC).

3727. POWELL, Alexander (1782–1847), M.P. Downton 1826–30 (*Alumni Oxon.;* Burke's *LG*).

3728. POWELL, Christopher (ca 1690–1742), 4th Bt, M.P. Kent 1735–41 (GEC).

3729. POWELL, Harcourt (d. 1782), M.P. Newtown 1754–75 (*Linc. Inn Reg.;* Lipscomb's *Bucks, 4,* 591; Musgrave's *Obituary*).

POWELL, John Kynaston, *see* KYNASTON-POWELL, John.

3730. POWELL, Mansell (ca 1693–1775), M.P. Weobley 1747–47 (*Lloyd's Evening Post,* 9–12 June 1775; Robinson's *Hereford,* p. 215; Williams' *Hereford M.P.'s*).

3731. POWELL, Thomas (d. 1752), M.P. Cardigan borough 1725–27, Cardiganshire 1741–47 (Williams' *Wales M.P.'s*).

3732. POWELL, William Edward (1788–1854), M.P. Cardiganshire 1816–54 (Burke's *LG; Old Westminsters;* Williams' *Wales M.P.'s*).

3733. POWER, Richard (d. 1814), M.P. Waterford Co. 1801–2, 1806–14.

3734. POWER, Richard (b. ca 1776), M.P. Waterford Co. 1814–30 (*Alumni Dublin.*).

3735. POWER, Robert (ca 1793–1842), M.P. Waterford Co. 1831–32 (*Alumni Dublin.; Gent. Mag., 1* [1843], 104).

POWERSCOURT, 2d Vct, *see* WINGFIELD, Edward.

POWIS, E. of, *see* CLIVE, Edward; *also* HERBERT, Edward and Henry Arthur.

3736. POWLETT, Charles (ca 1718–65), 5th D. of Bolton, M.P. Lymington 1741–55, Hampshire 1755–59 (*Alumni Cantab.;* GEC).

3737. POWLETT, Charles Armand (d. 1751), M.P. Newtown 1729–34, Christchurch 1740–51 (Collins' *Peerage* sub Winchester; Musgrave's *Obituary; Notes and Queries,* 12th Ser., *2,* 191).

3738. POWLETT, Charles Frederick (1785–1823), 2d Bn Bayning, M.P. Truro 1808–10 (GEC).

POWLETT, Charles Ingoldsby, *see* BURROUGHS-PAULET, Charles Ingoldsby.

POWLETT, George, *see* PAULET, George.

3739. POWLETT, Harry (1691–1759), 4th D. of Bolton, M.P. St. Ives 1715–22, Hampshire 1722–54 (GEC).

3740. POWLETT, Harry (1720–94), 6th D. of Bolton, M.P. Christchurch 1751–54, Lymington 1755–61, Winchester 1761–65 (DNB; GEC).

3741. POWLETT, Nassau (ca 1699–1741), M.P. Hampshire 1720–27, Lymington 1727–34, 1741–41 (Burke's *Peerage* and Collins' *Peerage* sub Winchester; Musgrave's *Obituary*).

3742. POWLETT, William (ca 1693–1757), M.P. Lymington 1729–34, Winchester 1741–47, Whitchurch 1754–57 (*Alumni Oxon.;* Collins' *Peerage* sub Winchester).

POWLETT, William John Frederick Vane, *see* VANE, William John Frederick.

3743. POWLETT, William Powlett (ca 1759–1821), M.P. Totnes 1790–96 (*Gent. Mag., 1,* 285).

POWLETT-WRIGHTE-DE-BEAUVOIR, Richard Benyon, *see* DE BEAU-
VOIR, Richard Benyon.

3744. POWNALL, John (ca 1725–95), M.P. St. Germans 1775–76 (*Gent.
Mag.*, p. 621; *Genealogists Mag., 6,* 280; Nichols' *Lit. Anec., 8,*
66).

3745. POWNALL, Thomas (ca 1722–1805), M.P. Tregony 1767–74, Minehead 1774–80 (*Alumni Cantab.;* DNB).

3746. POWNEY, Penyston (ca 1699–1757), M.P. Berks 1739–57 (*Eton
Coll. Reg.*).

3747. POWNEY, Penyston Portlock (ca 1744–94), M.P. Windsor 1780–94
(*Alumni Oxon.*).

3748. POWYS, Richard (ca 1707–43), M.P. Orford 1734–41 (*Alumni
Cantab.; Old Westminsters*).

3749. POWYS, Thomas (1743–1800), 1st Bn Lilford, M.P. Northamptonshire 1774–97 (GEC; *Eton Coll. Reg.*).

3750. POYNTZ, William Stephen (ca 1770–1840), M.P. St. Albans 1800–7,
Callington 1810–18, Chichester 1823–30, Ashburton 1831–34,
Midhurst 1835–37 (Dalloway's *Western Division of Sussex, 1,*
pt. 2, 286; *Eton Coll. Reg.; Gent. Mag., 1,* 653).

PRAED, *see* MACKWORTH-PRAED.

3751. PRATT, Charles (1714–94), 1st E. Camden, M.P. Downton 1757–
62 (*Alumni Cantab.;* DNB; GEC; *Eton Coll. Reg.*).

3752. PRATT, George Charles (1799–1866), 2d M. Camden, M.P. Ludgershall 1821–26, Bath 1826–30, Dunwich 1831–32 (GEC).

3753. PRATT, John (d. 1770), M.P. Sandwich 1741–47 (Burke's *Peerage*
sub Camden; Musgrave's *Obituary*).

3754. PRATT, John Jeffries (1759–1840), 1st M. Camden, M.P. Bath
1780–94 (DNB; GEC).

3755. PRATT, Robert (ca 1728–75), M.P. Horsham 1763–74 (Burke's
Peerage sub Camden; *Alumni Oxon.*).

3756. PRENDERGAST, Guy Lenox (ca 1779–1845), M.P. Lymington 1826–
27 (*Gent. Mag., 1,* 448).

3757. PRENDERGAST, Michael George, M.P. Saltash 1809–18, Galway
town 1820–26, Gatton 1826–30, Westbury 1830–31 (*1832 List*).

3758. PRESCOTT, George (ca 1712–90), M.P. Stockbridge 1761–68, Milborne Port 1772–74 (Burke's *Peerage;* Cussans' *Herts, 2,* pt. 2,
210, 238; Musgrave's *Obituary*).

3759. PRESTON, Charles (ca 1735–1800), 5th Bt, M.P. Dysart burghs
1784–90 (GEC).

3760. PRESTON, Richard (ca 1768–1850), M.P. Ashburton 1812–18
(DNB).

3761. PRESTON, Robert (1740–1834), 6th Bt, M.P. Dover 1784–90, Cirencester 1792–1806 (GEC; Williams' *Gloucester M.P.'s*).

3762. PRICE, Charles (1748–1818), 1st Bt, M.P. London 1802–12
(Beaven's *Aldermen of London;* Burke's *Peerage*).

3763. PRICE, Chase (ca 1731–77), M.P. Leominster 1759–67, Radnor 1768–77 (*Old Westminsters;* Williams' *Hereford M.P.'s* and *Wales M.P.'s*).

3764. PRICE, Richard (b. ca 1708), M.P. Sudbury 1734–41 (*Alumni Oxon.*).

3765. PRICE, Richard (ca 1774–1861), M.P. New Radnor 1799–1847 (*Alumni Oxon.;* Burke's *Peerage;* Williams' *Wales M.P.'s*).

3766. PRICE, Richard Thelwall (1720–94), M.P. Beaumaris 1754–68 (Lloyd's *Powis Fadog, 6,* 423, 476; Williams' *Wales M.P.'s*).

3767. PRICE, Robert (1786–1857), 2d Bt, M.P. Herefordshire 1818–41, 1845–57 (*Alumni Oxon.;* Boase; *Eton Lists*).

3768. PRICE, Samuel Grove (1793–1839), M.P. Sandwich 1830–31, 1835–37 (*Eton Lists; Gent. Mag., 2,* 200).

3769. PRIMROSE, Archibald John (1783–1868), 4th E. of Rosebery, M.P. Helston 1805–6, Cashel 1806–7 (DNB; GEC; *Scots Peerage*).

3770. PRIMROSE, Francis Ward (1785–1860), M.P. Stirling burghs 1819–20 (Foster's *Scots M.P.'s; Scots Peerage* sub Rosebery).

3771. PRINGLE, Alexander (1791–1857), M.P. Selkirkshire 1830–32, 1835–46 (Ball and Venn's *Admissions to Trinity College;* Burke's *LG;* Foster's *Scots M.P.'s; 1832 List*).

3772. PRINGLE, James (1726–1809), 4th Bt, M.P. Berwickshire 1761–79 (GEC; Foster's *Scots M.P.'s*).

3773. PRINGLE, John (d. 1792), M.P. Selkirkshire 1765–86 (Burke's *LG* [ed. 1849]; Foster's *Scots M.P.'s;* A. Pringle, *Records of the Pringles,* p. 175).

3774. PRINGLE, John (ca 1796–1831), M.P. Linlithgow burghs 1819–20 (*Alumni Oxon.;* Burke's *LG* [ed. 1849]; Foster's *Scots M.P.'s*).

3775. PRINGLE, Mark (1754–1812), M.P. Selkirkshire 1786–1802 (Burke's *LG* [ed. 1849]; Foster's *Scots M.P.'s;* Grant's *Faculty of Advocates*).

3776. PRINGLE, William Henry (ca 1772–1840), M.P. St. Germans 1812–18, Liskeard 1818–32 (*Alumni Dublin.; Gent. Mag., 1* [1841], 317).

3777. PRINSEP, John (ca 1746–1831), M.P. Queenborough 1802–6 (Beaven's *Aldermen of London; Gent. Mag., 2,* 569; *1806 List*).

3778. PRITTIE, Francis Aldborough (1779–1853), M.P. Carlow borough 1801–1, Tipperary 1806–18, 1819–31 (*Alumni Dublin.;* Burke's *Peerage* sub Dunalley; *Cork Archaeol. Jour.* [1896], p. 179).

3779. PRITTIE, Henry Sadleir (1775–1854), 2d Bn Dunalley, M.P. Carlow borough 1801–1, Okehampton 1819–24 (*Alumni Dublin.;* GEC).

3780. PROBY, Granville Leveson (ca 1782–1868), 3d E. of Carysfort, M.P. Wicklow 1816–29 (DNB; GEC; *Rugby Reg.*).

3781. PROBY, John (ca 1698–1762), M.P. Hunts 1722–27, Stamford 1734–

47 (*Alumni Cantab.;* GEC sub Carysfort; *East Anglian,* N.S., *10,* 42).

3782. PROBY, John (1720–72), 1st Bn Carysfort, M.P. Stamford 1747–54, Hunts 1754–68 (*Alumni Cantab.;* DNB; GEC; *Old Westminsters*).

3783. PROBY, John (ca 1780–1855), 2d E. of Carysfort, M.P. Buckingham borough 1805–6, Hunts 1806–7, 1814–18 (GEC; *Rugby Reg.*).

3784. PROBY, John Joshua (1751–1828), 1st E. of Carysfort, M.P. East Looe 1790–90, Stamford 1790–1801 (DNB; GEC; *Old Westminsters*).

3785. PROBY, William Allen (1779–1804), M.P. Buckingham borough 1802–4 (GEC sub Carysfort; DNB; *Rugby Reg.*).

3786. PROBYN-HOPKINS, John (1702–73), M.P. Wootton Bassett 1754–61 (Burke's *LG*).

3787. PROCTOR, George (1704–51), M.P. Downton 1746–51 (*Alumni Cantab.; Eton Coll. Reg.*).

PROCTOR, William Beauchamp, *see* BEAUCHAMP-PROCTOR, William.

3788. PROTHEROE, Edward (1774–1856), M.P. Bristol 1812–20 (Boase; Williams' *Gloucester M.P.'s*).

PROTHEROE, Edward Davis, *see* DAVIS-PROTHEROE, Edward.

3789. PROWSE, Thomas (ca 1708–67), M.P. Somerset 1740–67 (Bates Harbin; *Misc. Geneal. et Herald.,* N.S., *3*).

3790. PRYSE, John Pughe (ca 1739–74), M.P. Cardigan borough 1761–68, Merioneth 1768–74 (*Old Westminsters;* Williams' *Wales M.P.'s*).

3791. PRYSE, Pryse (1774–1849), M.P. Cardigan borough 1818–41, 1842–49 (*Eton Coll. Reg.;* Williams' *Wales M.P.'s*).

3792. PRYSE, Thomas (ca 1716–45), M.P. Cardigan borough 1741–45 (*Old Westminsters;* Williams' *Wales M.P.'s*).

3793. PULTENEY, Daniel (1749–1811), M.P. Bramber 1784–88 (*Eton Coll. Reg.*).

3794. PULTENEY, Harry (ca 1686–1767), M.P. Hedon 1722–34, 1739–41, Hull 1744–47 (*Lloyd's Evening Post,* 26–28 Oct. 1767; *Old Westminsters*).

PULTENEY, James Murray, *see* MURRAY-PULTENEY, James.

3795. PULTENEY, William (1684–1764), 1st E. of Bath, M.P. Hedon 1705–34, Middlesex 1734–42 (DNB; GEC; *Old Westminsters*).

3796. PULTENEY, William (1731–63), M.P. Old Sarum 1754–61, Westminster 1761–63 (GEC sub Bath; *Old Westminsters*).

PULTENEY, William Johnstone, *see* JOHNSTONE-PULTENEY, William.

3797. PUREFOY-JERVOISE, George (1770–1847), M.P. Salisbury 1813–18, Hampshire 1820–26 (Burke's *LG; Old Westminsters*).

3798. PURLING, John (ca 1730–1800), M.P. Shoreham 1770–70, East

Looe 1772–74, Weymouth and Melcombe Regis 1774–90 (*Gent. Mag., 2*, 903; Namier; Prinsep's *Madras Civilians*, p. xvi).

3799. PURVIS, George (1680–1741), M.P. Aldeburgh 1732–41 (Burke's *LG* [ed. 1849]; Charnock's *Biog. Naval., 4*, 14; Musgrave's *Obituary; Topographer and Genealogist, 1*, 477).

3800. PUSEY, Philip (1799–1855), M.P. Rye 1830–30, Chippenham 1830–31, Cashel 1831–32, Berks 1835–52 (DNB).

3801. PYBUS, Charles Small (1766–1810), M.P. Dover 1790–1802 (*Admissions to St. John, Cambridge; Harrow Reg.*).

3802. PYE, Henry (ca 1709–66), M.P. Berks 1746–66 (*Alumni Oxon.;* Burke's *LG*).

3803. PYE, Henry James (1745–1813), M.P. Berks 1784–90 (DNB).

3804. PYE, Thomas (ca 1713–85), M.P. Rochester 1771–74 (DNB).

3805. PYM, Francis (ca 1757–1833), M.P. Bedfordshire 1806–18, 1820–26 (Ball and Venn's *Admissions to Trinity College;* Burke's *LG; Gent. Mag., 1* [1834], 116).

3806. PYTCHES, John (ca 1774–1829), M.P. Sudbury 1802–7 (Burke's *LG; Gent. Mag., 1*, 569).

3807. PYTTS, Edmund (ca 1695–1753), M.P. Worcestershire 1741–53 (Burke's *LG* sub Childe; Williams' *Worcester M.P.'s*).

3808. PYTTS, Edmund (1729–81), M.P. Worcestershire 1753–61 (Burke's *Peerage* sub Baldwyn; *Genealogist*, 1st Ser., *1; Linc. Inn Reg.;* Williams' *Worcester M.P.'s*).

QUARENDON, Vct, *see* LEE, George Henry.

QUEENSBERRY, 6th D. of, *see* MONTAGU-SCOTT, Charles William Henry.

QUIN, Windham Henry Wyndham, *see* WYNDHAM-QUIN, Windham Henry.

RADCLIFFE, Charles, *see* FARNABY-RADCLIFFE, Charles.

3809. RADCLIFFE, John (1739–83), M.P. St. Albans 1768–83 (*Eton Coll. Reg.;* Burke's *LG;* Dalloway's *Western Division of Sussex, 1*, pt. 2, 219).

RADNOR, E. of, *see* BOUVERIE and PLEYDELL-BOUVERIE.

3810. RAE, William (1769–1842), 3d Bt, M.P. Anstruther Easter burghs 1819–26, Harwich 1827–30, Buteshire 1830–31, 1833–42, Portarlington 1831–32 (Addison's *Glasgow Matric. Albums;* DNB).

RAGLAN, 1st Bn, *see* SOMERSET, Fitzroy James Henry.

3811. RAINE, Jonathan (1763–1831), M.P. St. Ives 1802–6, Wareham 1806–7, Launceston 1812–12, Newport 1812–31 (*Eton Coll. Reg.*).

3812. RAINIER, Peter (ca 1741–1808), M.P. Sandwich 1807–8 (DNB).

3813. RAINIER, John Spratt (d. 1822), M.P. Sandwich 1808–12 (*Gent. Mag., 2*, 573).

3814. RAINSFORD, Charles (1728–1809), M.P. Maldon 1773–74, Berealston 1787–88, Newport 1790–96 (DNB).

3815. RAM, Abel (ca 1756-1830), M.P. Wexford Co. 1801-6, 1807-12 (Burke's *Irish LG; Linc. Inn Reg.*).

3816. RAMSAY, Alexander (1785-1852), 2d Bt, M.P. Kincardineshire 1820-26 (Burke's *Peerage;* Foster's *Scots M.P.'s*).

3817. RAMSAY, John (1775-1842), M.P. Aberdeen burghs 1806-7 (Foster's *Scots M.P.'s; Scots Peerage* sub Dalhousie).

RAMSAY, Robert Balfour, *see* BALFOUR-RAMSAY, Robert.

3818. RAMSAY, William Ramsay (1809-50), M.P. Stirlingshire 1831-32, Edinburghshire 1841-45 (*Alumni Oxon.;* Burke's *Peerage* sub Torphichen; Foster's *Scots M.P.'s*).

3819. RAMSAY-IRVINE, Alexander (d. 1806), 6th Bt, M.P. Kincardineshire 1765-68 (GEC; Foster's *Scots M.P.'s*).

3820. RAMSBOTTOM, John (d. 1845), M.P. Windsor 1810-45 (*Eton Lists; Gent. Mag., 2,* 647).

3821. RAMSBOTTOM, Richard (ca 1750-1813), M.P. Windsor 1806-10 (*Gent. Mag., 1,* 291).

3822. RAMSDEN, John (1699-1769), 3d Bt, M.P. Appleby 1727-54 (*Alumni Cantab.;* GEC).

3823. RAMSDEN, John (1755-1839), 4th Bt, M.P. Grampound 1780-84 (GEC).

3824. RAMSDEN, John Charles (1788-1836), M.P. Malton 1812-31, 1833-36, Yorkshire 1831-32 (Gooder; *Harrow Reg.*).

RANCLIFFE, Bn, *see* PARKYNS, George Augustus Henry Anne, and Thomas Boothby.

RANFURLY, E., *see* KNOX, Thomas.

3825. RASHLEIGH, Jonathan (1690-1764), M.P. Fowey 1727-64 (Boase and Courtney, *Biblio. Cornub.;* Burke's *LG*).

3826. RASHLEIGH, Philip (1729-1811), M.P. Fowey 1765-1802 (DNB; Boase and Courtney, *Biblio. Cornub.*).

3827. RASHLEIGH, William (1777-1855), M.P. Fowey 1812-18 (Boase; Burke's *LG*).

RAVENSWORTH, Bn, *see* LIDDELL, Henry and Thomas Henry.

3828. RAWDON, George (1761-1800), M.P. Lincoln City 1796-1800 (*Gent. Mag., 1,* 393; Lodge and Archdall's *Irish Peerage, 3,* 109).

3829. RAWDON, John (1757-1808), M.P. Appleby 1791-96, Launceston 1796-1802 (Bean; Ferguson; *Gent. Mag., 1,* 468).

3830. RAWLINSON, Abram (ca 1738-1803), M.P. Lancaster borough 1780-90 (Bean; Burke's *LG* sub Ford; Foster's *Lancashire Pedigrees;* Pink).

3831. RAWLINSON, Henry (1743-86), M.P. Liverpool 1780-84 (Foster's *Lancashire Pedigrees;* Pink).

3832. RAWLINSON, Walter (ca 1735-1805), M.P. Queenborough 1774-84, Huntingdon borough 1784-90 (Ball and Venn's *Admissions*

to *Trinity College;* Beaven's *Aldermen of London;* Copinger's
Suffolk, 1, 370; Foster's *Lancashire Pedigrees*).

RAWLINSON, William, *see* EARLE, William Rawlinson.

3833. RAYMOND, John (ca 1712–82), M.P. Weymouth and Melcombe
Regis 1741–47 (Hunter's *Familiae Min. Gent.; Misc. Geneal.
et Herald.,* 1st Ser., *3,* 211; *Notes and Queries, 157,* 30).

3834. READE, Thomas (ca 1683–1752), 4th Bt, M.P. Cricklade 1713–47
(GEC).

3835. REBOW, Isaac Lemyng (d. 1735), M.P. Colchester 1734–35
(Burke's *LG; Calendar Inner Temple Records, 4,* 167; Musgrave's *Obituary*).

3836. REBOW-MARTIN, Isaac Martin (1731–81), M.P. Colchester
1755–81 (*Alumni Cantab.; Essex Review, 8,* 227; *Eton Coll.
Reg.*).

REDESDALE, 1st Bn, *see* FREEMAN-MITFORD, John.

3837. REID, John Rae (1791–1867), 2d Bt, M.P. Dover 1830–31, 1832–
47 (Boase; Burke's *Peerage;* Dod's *Parl. Companion* [1834],
p. 156; *Eton Lists*).

RENDLESHAM, 1st Bn, *see* THELLUSSON, Peter Isaac.

REPINGTON, *see* A'COURT-REPINGTON.

3838. REVELL, Thomas (d. 1752), M.P. Dover 1734–52 (Jones' *Annals
of Dover,* p. 389; Musgrave's *Obituary*).

3839. REYNOLDS, Francis (d. 1773), M.P. Lancaster borough 1745–73
(GEC sub Ducie; Bean; Pink).

3840. REYNOLDS-MORETON, Francis (1739–1808), 3d Bn Ducie, M.P.
Lancaster borough 1784–85 (GEC).

3841. REYNOLDS-MORETON, Henry George Francis (1802–53), 2d E. of
Ducie, M.P. Gloucestershire 1831–32, East Gloucestershire
1832–34 (DNB; GEC).

RIBBLESDALE, 1st Bn, *see* LISTER, Thomas.

3842. RICARDO, David (1772–1823), M.P. Portarlington 1819–23
(DNB).

3843. RICE, George (ca 1724–79), M.P. Carmarthenshire 1754–79 (DNB;
GEC sub Dinevor).

3844. RICE, George Talbot (1765–1852), 3d Bn Dinevor, M.P. Carmarthenshire 1790–93 (GEC; *Old Westminsters*).

3845. RICE, Thomas Spring (1790–1866), 1st Bn Monteagle, M.P.
Limerick City 1820–32, Cambridge borough 1832–39 (DNB;
GEC).

3846. RICE-TREVOR, George Rice (1795–1869), 4th Bn Dinevor, M.P.
Carmarthenshire 1820–31, 1832–52 (GEC; *Old Westminsters*).

RICH, Richard Slater, *see* MILNES, Richard Slater.

3847. RICH, Robert (1685–1768), 4th Bt, M.P. Dunwich 1715–22,
Berealston 1724–27, St. Ives 1727–41 (DNB; GEC).

3848. RICH, Thomas (ca 1733–1803), 5th Bt, M.P. Great Marlow 1784–90 (GEC).

3849. RICHARDS, Bisse (ca 1716–55), M.P. Hindon 1747–55 (*Alumni Oxon.;* Musgrave's *Obituary*).

3850. RICHARDS, George (d. 1746), M.P. Bridport 1741–46 (Hutchins' *Dorset, 2,* 184; Musgrave's *Obituary*).

3851. RICHARDS, Richard (1752–1823), M.P. Helston 1796–99, 1807–7 (DNB).

3852. RICHARDSON, Joseph (ca 1755–1803), M.P. Newport 1796–1803 (DNB; *Notes and Queries,* 12th Ser., *2,* 211).

3853. RICHARDSON, William (b. ca 1749), M.P. Armagh Co. 1807–20 (*Alumni Oxon.;* Burke's *Irish LG*).

RICHMOND, 5th D. of, *see* GORDON-LENNOX, Charles.

3854. RICKARDS, Robert (1769–1836), M.P. Wootton Bassett 1813–16 (Boase and Courtney, *Biblio. Cornub.*).

RICKART, Robert Hepburn, *see* HEPBURN, Robert Rickart.

3855. RICKETTS, Charles Milner (1776–1867), M.P. Dartmouth 1820–22 (*Old Westminsters*).

3856. RICKFORD, William (1768–1854), M.P. Aylesbury 1818–41 (Boase; Burke's *LG* [ed. 1849]; Lipscomb's *Bucks, 1,* 474 and *2,* 27).

RIDDELL, John Buchanan, *see* BUCHANAN-RIDDELL, John.

3857. RIDER, Thomas (1765–1847), M.P. Kent 1831–32, West Kent 1832–34 (*Alumni Oxon.; Alumni Carthusiani*).

3858. RIDLEY, Matthew (1711–78), M.P. Newcastle-upon-Tyne 1747–74 (*Alumni Cantab.; Archaeol. Aeliana,* 4th Ser., *18,* 12; GEC; *Old Westminsters*).

3859. RIDLEY, Matthew White (1745–1813), 2d Bt, M.P. Morpeth 1768–74, Newcastle-upon-Tyne 1774–1812 (GEC; *Old Westminsters;* Welford's *Men of Mark*).

3860. RIDLEY, Matthew White (1778–1836), 3d Bt, M.P. Newcastle-upon-Tyne 1812–36 (GEC; *Old Westminsters;* Phillips' *Hist. of Banks,* p. 193).

3861. RIDLEY-COLBORNE, Nicholas William (1779–1854), 1st Bn Colborne, M.P. Bletchingley 1805–6, Malmesbury 1806–7, Appleby 1807–12, Thetford 1818–26, Horsham 1827–32, Wells 1834–37 (GEC; *Old Westminsters*).

RIGBY, Francis Hale, *see* HALE-RIGBY, Francis.

3862. RIGBY, Richard (ca 1722–88), M.P. Castle Rising 1745–47, Sudbury 1747–54, Tavistock 1754–88 (*Alumni Cantab.;* DNB).

3863. RIGGS-MILLER, John (ca 1744–98), 1st Bt, M.P. Newport 1784–90 (GEC; Collinson's *Somerset, 1,* 105; *Eton Coll. Reg.*).

RIPON, 1st E. of, *see* ROBINSON, Frederick John.

RIVERS, Bn, *see* PITT, George.

3864. RIVETT, Thomas (ca 1713–63), M.P. Derby borough 1748–54 (Burke's *Peerage* sub Carnac; Glover's *Derbyshire, 2,* 467).

3865. ROBARTS, Abraham (ca 1745–1816), M.P. Worcester City 1796–
1816 (Williams' *Worcester M.P.'s; 1806 List*).

3866. ROBARTS, Abraham Wildey (ca 1780–1858), M.P. Maidstone 1818–
37 (Boase; Burke's *LG;* Dod's *Parl. Companion* [1834], p. 157;
Williams' *Worcester M.P.'s*).

3867. ROBARTS, George James (ca 1782–1829), M.P. Wallingford 1820–
26 (*Gent. Mag., 2,* 379).

3868. ROBARTS, William Tierney (d. 1820), M.P. St. Albans 1818–20
(*Gent. Mag., 2,* 573; *Notes and Queries, 179,* 148; Williams'
Worcester M.P.'s).

3869. ROBERTS, John (ca 1712–72), M.P. Harwich 1761–72 (DNB;
Eng. Hist. Rev., 42 [1927], 408; *Old Westminsters*).

3870. ROBERTS, John (d. 1782), M.P. Taunton 1780–82 (Musgrave's
Obituary).

ROBERTS, Wenman, *see* COKE, Wenman.

3871. ROBERTS, Wilson Aylesbury (1760–1853), M.P. Bewdley 1818–32
(Boase; Burke's *LG;* Wade's *Black Book;* Williams' *Worcester
M.P.'s*).

3872. ROBERTSON, Alexander (d. 1856), M.P. Grampound 1818–26 (Bean,
p. 155; *Gent. Mag., 1* [1857], 251; *Royal Kalendar* [1825], p.
55).

3873. ROBINS, John (ca 1714–54), M.P. Stafford borough 1747–54
(Wedgwood).

3874. ROBINSON, Charles (ca 1733–1807), M.P. Canterbury 1780–90
(*Gent. Mag., 1,* 386; Jones' *Annals of Dover,* p. 348).

3875. ROBINSON, Christopher (ca 1766–1833), M.P. Callington 1818–20
(DNB).

3876. ROBINSON, Frederick (1746–92), M.P. Ripon 1780–87 (Ball and
Venn's *Admissions to Trinity College;* Bean; Collins' *Peerage*
sub Grantham; *Linc. Inn Reg.;* Musgrave's *Obituary*).

3877. ROBINSON, Frederick John (1782–1859), 1st E. of Ripon, M.P.
Carlow borough 1806–7, Ripon 1807–27 (DNB; GEC).

3878. ROBINSON, George (1730–1815), 5th Bt, M.P. Northampton borough 1774–80 (*Alumni Cantab.;* GEC).

3879. ROBINSON, George (1764–1833), 6th Bt, M.P. Northampton borough 1820–32 (Ball and Venn's *Admissions to Trinity College;*
Barron's *Northampton Families,* p. 277; GEC).

3880. ROBINSON, George Abercrombie (ca 1759–1832), 1st Bt, M.P.
Honiton 1812–18 (Burke's *Peerage; Gent. Mag., 1,* 270).

3881. ROBINSON, George Richard (ca 1781–1850), M.P. Worcester City
1826–37, Poole 1847–50 (Williams' *Worcester M.P.'s*).

3882. ROBINSON, John (1727–1802), M.P. Westmorland 1764–74, Harwich 1774–1802 (DNB).

3883. ROBINSON, John (ca 1757–1819), M.P. Bishop's Castle 1802–19
(Copinger's *Suffolk, 5,* 229; *Gent. Mag., 1,* 654).

3884. ROBINSON, Luke, M.P. Hedon 1741-42, 1747-54 (Bean; *Linc. Inn Reg.; Notes and Queries*, 11th Ser., *11*, 197).

ROBINSON, Matthew, *see* MONTAGU, Matthew; *also* MORRIS, Matthew.

3885. ROBINSON, Morris (1757-1829), 3d Bn Rokeby, M.P. Boroughbridge 1790-96 (GEC).

3886. ROBINSON, Nicholas (d. 1753), M.P. Wootton Bassett 1734-41 (Charnock's *Biog. Naval.*, *4*, 302; *Genealogist*, N.S., *26*, 228; Musgrave's *Obituary; Parl. Hist.*, *9*, 629).

3887. ROBINSON, Thomas (1695-1770), 1st Bn Grantham, M.P. Thirsk 1727-34, Christchurch 1748-61 (*Alumni Cantab.*; DNB; GEC; *Old Westminsters*).

3888. ROBINSON, Thomas (1738-86), 2d Bn Grantham, M.P. Christchurch 1761-70 (DNB; GEC; *Old Westminsters*).

3889. ROBINSON-LYTTON, John (ca 1725-62), M.P. Bishop's Castle 1747-54 (*Alumni Oxon.*; GEC sub Lytton).

ROBSON, Richard Bateman, *see* BATEMAN-ROBSON, Richard.

3890. ROCHFORT, Gustavus (ca 1782-1848), M.P. Westmeath 1826-32 (Burke's *Irish LG; Gent. Mag.*, *1*, 548; *Herald and Genealogist*, *2*, 240; *United Service Jour.*, *1*, 478).

3891. ROCHFORT-HUME, Gustavus (d. 1824), M.P. Westmeath 1801-24 (Burke's *Irish LG; Gent. Mag.*, *1*, 382).

ROCKINGHAM, 3d E. of, *see* WATSON, Thomas.

ROCKSAVAGE, E. of, *see* CHOLMONDELEY, George Horatio.

RODEN, E. of, *see* JOCELYN, Robert.

3892. RODNEY, George (1753-1802), 2d Bn Rodney, M.P. Northampton borough 1780-84 (GEC).

3893. RODNEY, George Brydges (1718-92), 1st Bn Rodney, M.P. Saltash 1751-54, Okehampton 1759-61, Penryn 1761-68, Northampton borough 1768-74, Westminster 1780-82 (DNB; GEC).

3894. RODNEY, John (1765-1847), M.P. Launceston 1790-96 (Burke's *Peerage; Royal Kalendar* [1791], p. 36).

3895. ROGERS, Augustus (d. 1794), M.P. Queenborough 1793-94 (Musgrave's *Obituary*).

3896. ROGERS, Edward (ca 1782-1852), M.P. Bishop's Castle 1820-32 (*Shrop. Archaeol. Soc. Trans.*, 2d Ser., *10*).

3897. ROGERS, Frederick Leman (1746-97), 5th Bt, M.P. Plymouth 1780-84, 1790-97 (GEC).

3898. ROGERS, John (1708-73), 3d Bt, M.P. Plymouth 1739-40 (GEC).

3899. ROGERS, John (1750-1832), M.P. West Looe 1775-80, Penryn 1780-82, Helston 1784-86 (*Alumni Oxon.*; Burke's *LG*).

3900. ROGERS, John Leman (1780-1847), 6th Bt, M.P. Callington 1812-13 (GEC).

3901. ROGERS, Thomas (1735-93), M.P. Coventry 1780-81 (DNB sub

Samuel Rogers; *Misc. Geneal. et Herald.*, N.S., *3;* Musgrave's *Obituary;* Whitley's *Coventry M.P.'s*).

ROKEBY, Bn, *see* MONTAGU, Matthew; *also* MORRIS, Matthew; *also* ROBINSON, Matthew.

3902. ROLLE, Dennis (ca 1726–97), M.P. Barnstable 1761–74 (*Alumni Oxon.;* DNB sub John Rolle; Collins' *Peerage*).

3903. ROLLE, Henry (1708–50), 1st Bn Rolle, M.P. Devon 1730–41, Barnstable 1741–48 (GEC).

3904. ROLLE, John (1756–1842), 1st Bn Rolle, M.P. Devon 1780–96 (DNB; GEC; Venn MS).

3905. ROLLE-WALTER, John (ca 1714–79), M.P. Exeter 1754–76, Devon 1776–79 (*Alumni Oxon.;* Burke's *Ext. Peerage;* Musgrave's *Obituary*).

ROLT, *see* BAYNTUN-ROLT.

3906. ROMILLY, Samuel (1757–1818), M.P. Queenborough 1806–7, Horsham 1807–8, Wareham 1808–12, Arundel 1812–18, Westminster 1818–18 (DNB).

ROMNEY, E. of, *see* MARSHAM, Charles.

3907. ROOKE, James (ca 1738–1805), M.P. Monmouthshire 1785–1805 (Bristol and Glouc. Archaeol. Soc. *Trans.*, *24*, 149; Williams' *Wales M.P.'s*).

3908. ROOPER, John Bonfoy (1778–1855), M.P. Hunts 1831–37 (Burke's *LG; Rugby Reg.*).

3909. ROSCOE, William (1753–1831), M.P. Liverpool 1806–7 (DNB).

3910. ROSE, George (1744–1818), M.P. Launceston 1784–88, Lymington 1788–90, Christchurch 1790–1818 (DNB; *Old Westminsters*).

3911. ROSE, George Henry (1771–1855), M.P. Southampton borough 1794–1818, Christchurch 1818–32, 1837–44 (*Admissions to St. John, Cambridge;* DNB; *1832 List*).

3912. ROSE, George Pitt (1797–1851), M.P. Christchurch 1826–32 (*Admissions to St. John, Cambridge;* Foster's *Peerage* sub Strathnairn).

3913. ROSE, Hugh (ca 1684–1755), M.P. Nairnshire 1708–10, Ross-shire 1734–41 (Burke's *LG;* Foster's *Scots M.P.'s;* Innes' *Rose of Kilravock,* p. 405).

3914. ROSE, Hugh (ca 1780–1827), M.P. Nairnshire 1812–13 (Burke's *LG;* Foster's *Scots M.P.'s;* Innes' *Rose of Kilravock,* p. 503).

3915. ROSE, William Stewart (ca 1775–1843), M.P. Christchurch 1796–1800 (*Admissions to St. John, Cambridge;* DNB).

ROSEBERY, 4th E. of, *see* PRIMROSE, Archibald John.

3916. ROSEWARNE, Henry (ca 1732–83), M.P. Truro 1780–83 (*Alumni Cantab.*).

3917. Ross, Charles (1721–45), M.P. Ross-shire 1741–45 (Addison's *Glasgow Matric. Albums; Scots Peerage*).

3918. Ross, Charles (ca 1729–97), M.P. Tain burghs 1780–84 (Reid's *Earls of Ross*, pp. 16, 74; *Scots Mag.*, p. 214).

3919. Ross, Charles (ca 1800–60), M.P. Orford 1822–26, St. Germans 1826–32, Northampton borough 1832–37 (*Alumni Oxon.;* Boase; Dod's *Parl. Companion* [1834], p. 159).

Ross, Charles Lockhart, *see* Lockhart-Ross, Charles.

3920. Ross, George (ca 1705–86), M.P. Cromartyshire 1780–84, Tain burghs 1786–86 (Coleridge's *Life of Thomas Coutts, 1,* 132; Foster's *Scots M.P.'s;* Musgrave's *Obituary;* Namier).

3921. Ross, Horatio (1801–86), M.P. Aberdeen burghs 1831–34 (DNB; Dod's *Parl. Companion* [1834], p. 159).

Ross, John Lockhart, *see* Lockhart-Ross, John.

3922. Ross, Patrick (ca 1740–1804), M.P. Horsham 1802–4 (DNB).

3923. Ross-Mackie, John (1707–97), M.P. Linlithgow burghs 1742–47, Kirkcudbright Stewarty 1747–68 (Foster's *Scots M.P.'s;* Grant's *Faculty of Advocates*).

Rosse, E. of, *see* Parsons, Laurence and William.

Rosslyn, E. of, *see* St. Clair-Erskine, James and James Alexander; *also* Wedderburn, Alexander.

Rossmore, Bn, *see* Cuninghame, Robert; *also* Westenra, Henry Robert and Warren William.

3924. Round, John (1783–1860), M.P. Ipswich 1812–18, Maldon 1837–47 (*Alumni Oxon.;* Boase; Burke's *LG* [ed. 1849]; *1812 List*).

3925. Rous, George (ca 1744–1802), M.P. Shaftesbury 1776–80 (*Eton Coll. Reg.*).

3926. Rous, John (ca 1727–71), 5th Bt, M.P. Suffolk 1768–71 (*Alumni Cantab.;* GEC).

3927. Rous, John (1750–1827), 1st E. of Stradbroke, M.P. Suffolk 1780–96 (GEC; *Old Westminsters*).

3928. Rous, Thomas Bates (d. 1799), M.P. Worcester City 1773–74, 1774–84 (Williams' *Worcester M.P.'s*).

3929. Rouse-Boughton, Charles William (1747–1821), 9th Bt, M.P. Evesham 1780–90, Bramber 1796–99 (GEC; Holzman's *Nabobs in Eng.;* Williams' *Worcester M.P.'s*).

3930. Rouse-Boughton, William Edward (1788–1856), 10th Bt, M.P. Evesham 1818–19, 1820–26 (GEC; Williams' *Worcester M.P.'s*).

3931. Rowley, Clotworthy (ca 1731–1805), M.P. Downpatrick 1801–1 (*Alumni Cantab.*).

3932. Rowley, Josias (ca 1765–1842), 1st Bt, M.P. Kinsale 1821–26 (DNB).

3933. Rowley, Samuel Campbell (1774–1846), M.P. Downpatrick 1801–2, Kinsale 1802–6 (Burke's *Peerage; Cork Archaeol. Jour.* [1896], p. 226).

3934. ROWLEY, William (ca 1690–1768), M.P. Taunton 1750–54, Portsmouth 1754–61 (DNB).

3935. ROWLEY, William (ca 1764–1812), M.P. Kinsale 1801–2 (*Alumni Dublin.;* Burke's *Peerage; Cork Archaeol. Jour.* [1896], p. 226).

3936. ROWLEY, William (1761–1832), 2d Bt, M.P. Suffolk 1812–30 (GEC; *Harrow Reg.*).

3937. ROWNEY, Thomas (ca 1693–1759), M.P. Oxford City 1722–59 (*Alumni Oxon.; Eton Coll. Reg.;* Williams' *Oxford M.P.'s*).

ROYSTON, Vct, *see* YORKE, Philip.

3938. RUDGE, Edward (1703–63), M.P. Aylesbury 1728–34, Evesham 1741–54, 1756–61 (Burke's *LG* [ed. 1849]; Williams' *Worcester M.P.'s*).

3939. RUMBOLD, Charles Edmund (1788–1857), M.P. Great Yarmouth 1818–34, 1837–47, 1848–57 (*Alumni Oxon.;* Boase; Burke's *Peerage*).

3940. RUMBOLD, Thomas (1736–91), 1st Bt, M.P. Shoreham 1770–74, Shaftesbury 1774–75, 1780–81, Yarmouth (Hants) 1781–84, Weymouth and Melcombe Regis 1784–90 (DNB; GEC).

3941. RUMBOLD, William Richard (1760–86), M.P. Weymouth and Melcombe Regis 1781–84 (Burke's *Peerage; Harrow Reg.*).

3942. RUSH, John, M.P. Wallingford 1741–47 (MS, *ex inform.* John Bean King).

3943. RUSHOUT, John (ca 1684–1775), 4th Bt, M.P. Malmesbury 1713–22, Evesham 1722–68 (DNB; GEC).

3944. RUSHOUT, John (1738–1800), 1st Bn Northwick, M.P. Evesham 1761–96 (GEC; *Eton Coll. Reg.; Harrow Reg.*).

3945. RUSHWORTH, Edward (1755–1817), M.P. Yarmouth (Hants) 1780–81, 1790–91, 1796–97, Newport (Hants) 1784–90 (*Alumni Oxon.; Misc. Geneal. et Herald.*, 4th Ser., *4*).

3946. RUSSELL, Charles (1786–1856), M.P. Reading 1830–37, 1841–47 (Boase; Dod's *Parl. Companion* [1834], p. 160).

3947. RUSSELL, Francis (1739–67), M.P. Bedfordshire 1761–67 (GEC sub Bedford; *Old Westminsters*).

3948. RUSSELL, Francis (1788–1861), 7th D. of Bedford, M.P. Peterborough 1809–12, Bedfordshire 1812–32 (GEC; *Old Westminsters*).

3949. RUSSELL, Francis (1793–1832), M.P. Tavistock 1831–32 (*Old Westminsters*).

3950. RUSSELL, George William (1790–1846), M.P. Bedford borough 1812–30 (DNB; *Old Westminsters*).

RUSSELL, Jesse Watts, *see* WATTS-RUSSELL, Jesse.

3951. RUSSELL, John (1766–1839), 6th D. of Bedford, M.P. Tavistock 1788–90, 1790–1802 (DNB; GEC; *Old Westminsters*).

3952. Russell, John (1792–1878), 1st E. Russell, M.P. Tavistock 1813–
17, 1818–20, 1830–31, Hunts 1820–26, Bandon 1826–30, Devon
1831–32, South Devon 1832–35, Stroud 1835–41, London 1841–
61 (DNB; GEC).

3953. Russell, John (1796–1835), M.P. Kinsale 1826–32 (*Old Westminsters*).

3954. Russell, Matthew (1765–1822), M.P. Saltash 1802–7, 1808–22
(*Alumni Oxon.;* Burke's *LG* [ed. 1849]; *Gent Mag., 1,* 472;
Bean; Surtees' *Castle of Brancepeth,* p. 38).

Russell, Robert Frankland, *see* Frankland-Russell, Robert.

Russell, Robert Greenhill, *see* Greenhill-Russell, Robert.

3955. Russell, William (1767–1840), M.P. Surrey 1789–1807, Tavistock
1807–19, 1826–30 (*Old Westminsters*).

3956. Russell, William (1798–1850), M.P. Saltash 1822–26, Bletchingley 1826–27, Durham Co. 1828–32 (*Eton Lists;* Surtees' *Castle
of Brancepeth,* p. 38; Venn MS).

3957. Russell, William (1809–72), 8th D. of Bedford, M.P. Tavistock
1830–31, 1832–41 (GEC; Devonshire Assoc. *Trans., 43,* 401).

3958. Rutherford, John (1712–58), M.P. Roxburghshire 1734–42
(Burke's *LG;* Foster's *Scots M.P.'s;* Grant's *Faculty of Advocates*).

3959. Rutherford, John (ca 1748–1834), M.P. Selkirkshire 1802–6,
Roxburghshire 1806–12 (Burke's *LG;* Foster's *Scots M.P.'s;*
Grant's *Faculty of Advocates*).

3960. Ruthven, Edward Southwell (ca 1772–1836), M.P. Downpatrick
1806–7, 1830–32, Dublin City 1832–36 (DNB).

Rutland, 4th D. of, *see* Manners, Charles.

3961. Ryder, Dudley (1691–1756), M.P. St. Germans 1733–34, Tiverton 1734–54 (DNB; GEC sub Harrowby).

3962. Ryder, Dudley (1762–1847), 1st E. of Harrowby, M.P. Tiverton
1784–1803 (DNB; GEC; *Harrow Reg.*).

3963. Ryder, Dudley (1798–1882), 2d E. of Harrowby, M.P. Tiverton
1819–31, Liverpool 1831–47 (DNB; GEC).

3964. Ryder, Granville Dudley (1799–1879), M.P. Tiverton 1830–32,
Herts 1841–47 (Burke's *Peerage* sub Harrowby; Boase).

3965. Ryder, Nathaniel (1735–1803), 1st Bn Harrowby, M.P. Tiverton
1756–76 (DNB; GEC).

3966. Ryder, Richard (1766–1832), M.P. Tiverton 1795–1830 (*Admissions to St. John, Cambridge;* DNB; *Harrow Reg.;* Williams'
Great Sessions in Wales).

3967. Ryder, Thomas (ca 1731–1812), M.P. Tiverton 1755–56 (*Alumni
Cantab.; Notes and Queries, 170,* 40).

3968. Sabine, John, M.P. Bossiney 1741–42.

3969. Sackville, Charles (1711–69), 2d D. of Dorset, M.P. East Grinstead 1734–42, 1761–65, Sussex 1742–47, Old Sarum 1747–54 (DNB; GEC; *Old Westminsters*).

3970. SACKVILLE, John Frederick (1745–99), 3d D. of Dorset, M.P. Kent 1768–69 (DNB; GEC; *Old Westminsters*).

3971. SACKVILLE, John Philip (1713–65), M.P. Tamworth 1734–47 (*Old Westminsters*).

3972. SACKVILLE-GERMAIN, George (1716–85), 1st Vct Sackville, M.P. Dover 1741–61, Hythe 1761–68, East Grinstead 1768–82 (DNB; GEC; *Old Westminsters*).

3973. SADLER, Michael Thomas (1780–1835), M.P. Newark 1829–31, Aldborough 1831–32 (DNB).

ST. ALBANS, D. of, see BEAUCLERK, Aubrey.

3974. ST. AUBYN, John (1696–1744), 3d Bt, M.P. Cornwall 1722–44 (DNB; GEC).

3975. ST. AUBYN, John (1726–72), 4th Bt, M.P. Launceston 1747–54, 1758–59, Cornwall 1761–72 (GEC).

3976. ST. AUBYN, John (1758–1839), 5th Bt, M.P. Truro 1784–84, Penryn 1784–90, Helston 1807–12 (DNB; GEC; *Old Westminsters*).

3977. ST. CLAIR-ERSKINE, James (1762–1837), 2d E. of Rosslyn, M.P. Castle Rising 1782–84, Morpeth 1784–96, Dysart burghs 1796–1805 (DNB; GEC; *Eton Coll. Reg.*).

3978. ST. CLAIR-ERSKINE, James Alexander (1802–66), 3d E. of Rosslyn, M.P. Dysart burghs 1830–31, Great Grimsby 1831–32 (GEC).

ST. GERMANS, E. of, see ELIOT, Edward Granville and John.

3979. ST. JOHN, Ambrose (ca 1760–1822), M.P. Callington 1803–6 (*Alumni Oxon.; Gent. Mag., 2*, 646).

3980. ST. JOHN, Frederick (1765–1844), M.P. Oxford City 1818–20 (Burke's *Peerage* sub Bolingbroke; *Harrow Reg.;* Williams' *Oxford M.P.'s*).

3981. ST. JOHN, George Richard (1761–1824), 3d Vct Bolingbroke, M.P. Cricklade 1782–84 (GEC; *Harrow Reg.*).

3982. ST. JOHN, Henry (ca 1738–1818), M.P. Wootton Bassett 1761–84, 1802–2 (*Eton Coll. Reg.*).

3983. ST. JOHN, Henry Paulet (ca 1737–84), 2d Bt, M.P. Hampshire 1772–80 (GEC).

3984. ST. JOHN, John (ca 1746–93), M.P. Newport (Hants) 1773–74, 1780–84, Eye 1774–80 (DNB; *Eton Coll. Reg.*).

3985. ST. JOHN, Paulet (1704–80), 1st Bt, M.P. Winchester 1734–41, 1751–54, Hampshire 1741–47 (GEC).

3986. ST. JOHN, St. Andrew (1759–1817), 14th Bn St. John, M.P. Bedfordshire 1780–1805 (GEC; Venn MS).

3987. ST. JOHN-MILDMAY, Henry Carew (1787–1848), 4th Bt, M.P. Winchester 1807–18 (GEC).

3988. St. John-Mildmay, Henry Paulet (1764–1808), 3d Bt, M.P. Westbury 1796–1802, Winchester 1802–7, Hampshire 1807–8 (*Admissions to St. John, Cambridge;* GEC).

3989. St. John-Mildmay, Paulet (1791–1845), M.P. Winchester 1818–34, 1837–41 (Burke's *Peerage*).

3990. St. Leger, Anthony (1731–86), M.P. Great Grimsby 1768–74 (*Alumni Cantab.; Eton Coll. Reg.*).

3991. St. Leger, Arthur Mohun (1718–50), 3d Vct Doneraile, M.P. Winchelsea 1741–47, Old Sarum 1747–50 (GEC; *Old Westminsters*).

3992. St. Leger, John Hayes (1756–1800), M.P. Okehampton 1791–96 (*Eton Coll. Reg.*).

    St. Leonards, 1st Bn, *see* Sugden, Edward Burtenshaw.

    St. Maur, 1st E., *see* Seymour, Edward Adolphus.

3993. St. Paul, Henry Heneage (1777–1820), M.P. Berwick-on-Tweed 1812–20, 1820–20 (G. G. Butler's *Colonel St. Paul, 1,* clxx; *Eton Lists; Gent. Mag., 2,* 469).

3994. St. Paul, Horace David Cholwell (1775–1840), 1st Bt, M.P. Bridport 1812–20, 1820–32 (*Eton Coll. Reg.*).

    St. Vincent, 1st E. of, *see* Jervis, John.

    Salisbury, M. of, *see* Cecil, James; *also* Gascoyne-Cecil, James Brownlow William.

3995. Salt, Samuel (d. 1792), M.P. Liskeard 1768–84, Aldeburgh 1784–90 (DNB).

    Saltersford, Bn, *see* Stopford, James, James George, and James Thomas.

3996. Salusbury, Robert (1756–1817), 1st Bt, M.P. Monmouthshire 1792–96, Brecon borough 1796–1812 (GEC; Venn MS).

    Salusbury, Thomas, *see* Brereton-Salusbury, Thomas.

3997. Salusbury-Brereton, Owen (ca 1716–98), M.P. Ilchester 1775–80 (*Alumni Cantab.;* DNB; *Old Westminsters*).

    Sambrooke, Jeremy Vanacker, *see* Vanacker-Sambrooke, Jeremy.

3998. Sanderson, James (1741–98), 1st Bt, M.P. Malmesbury 1792–96, Hastings 1796–98 (GEC).

3999. Sanderson, Richard (ca 1783–1857), M.P. Colchester 1829–30, 1832–47 (*Essex Review, 8,* 238; *Gent. Mag., 2,* 687).

    Sandon, Vct, *see* Ryder, Dudley.

    Sandwich, E. of, *see* Montagu, George John and John.

    Sandys, 2d Bn, *see* Hill, Arthur Moyses William.

4000. Sandys, Edwin (1726–97), 2d Bn Sandys, M.P. Droitwich 1747–54, Bossiney 1754–61, Westminster 1762–70 (GEC; *Eton Coll. Reg.*).

4001. Sandys, Samuel (1695–1770), 1st Bn Sandys, M.P. Worcester City 1718–43 (DNB; GEC).

4002. Sanford, Edward Ayshford (1794–1871), M.P. Somerset 1830–

32, West Somerset 1832–41 (*Alumni Oxon.;* Boase; Burke's *LG; Eton Lists;* Bates Harbin).

4003. SARGENT, John (ca 1715–91), M.P. Midhurst 1754–61, West Looe 1765–68 (*Gent. Mag., 1* [1833], 636; *Genealogist,* N.S., *33,* 189; *Notes and Queries,* 8th Ser., *8,* 369).

4004. SARGENT, John (ca 1750–1831), M.P. Seaford 1790–93, Queenborough 1794–1802, Bodmin 1802–6 (DNB sub John Sargent, 1780–1833; *Eton Coll. Reg.; Genealogist,* N.S., *33,* 191).

4005. SATTERTHWAITE, James Clarke, M.P. Cockermouth 1784–90, Carlisle 1790–91, Haslemere 1791–1802 (*Admissions to St. John, Cambridge,* sub James Satterthwaite; Bean; Ferguson).

4006. SAUNDERS, Charles (ca 1713–75), M.P. Plymouth 1750–54, Hedon 1754–75 (DNB).

4007. SAUNDERS, George (ca 1671–1734), M.P. Queenborough 1728–34 (DNB).

4008. SAUNDERS-DUNDAS, Robert (1771–1851), 2d Vct Melville, M.P. Hastings 1794–96, Rye 1796–1801, Edinburghshire 1801–11 (*Alumni Cantab.;* DNB; GEC).

4009. SAUNDERSON, Alexander (1783–1857), M.P. Cavan 1826–31 (Boase; Burke's *Irish LG; 1832 List*).

4010. SAUNDERSON, Francis (1754–1827), M.P. Cavan 1801–6 (*Eton Coll. Reg.; Gray's Inn Reg.*).

SAUNDERSON, George Augustus Lumley, Richard Lumley, and Thomas Lumley, *see* LUMLEY-SAUNDERSON, George Augustus, Richard, and Thomas.

4011. SAVAGE, Francis (ca 1769–1823), M.P. Down 1801–12 (Burke's *Family Records*).

4012. SAVILE, Albany (ca 1784–1831), M.P. Okehampton 1807–20 (*Alumni Oxon.;* Burke's *LG*).

4013. SAVILE, Christopher (ca 1739–1819), M.P. Hedon 1780–83, 1796–1806, Okehampton 1818–19 (Burke's *LG; Gent. Mag., 1,* 488).

4014. SAVILE, George (1726–84), 8th Bt, M.P. Yorkshire 1759–83 (*Alumni Cantab.;* DNB; GEC; Gooder).

4015. SAVILE, John (1719–78), 1st E. of Mexborough, M.P. Hedon 1747–54, Shoreham 1761–68 (GEC).

4016. SAVILE, John (1761–1830), 2d E. of Mexborough, M.P. Lincoln City 1808–12 (GEC; *Old Westminsters*).

4017. SAVILE, John (1783–1860), 3d E. of Mexborough, M.P. Pontefract 1807–12, 1812–26, 1831–32 (GEC).

4018. SAVILE, John Charles George (1810–99), 4th E. of Mexborough, M.P. Gatton 1831–32, Pontefract 1835–37, 1841–47 (GEC).

SAVILE, John Lumley, *see* LUMLEY-SAVILE, John.

SAVILE, Richard Lumley, *see* LUMLEY-SAUNDERSON, Richard.

4019. SAVILL, Samuel (ca 1700–63), M.P. Colchester 1742–47 (*Essex Review, 6,* 186; Musgrave's *Obituary*).

4020. SAVILL-ONLEY, Charles (1756–1843), M.P. Norwich 1812–18, Carlow borough 1818–26 (Burke's *LG;* Foster's *Baronetage; Gent. Mag., 2,* 546; Venn's *Biog. Hist. Gonville and Caius, 2,* 92).

4021. SAWBRIDGE, John (ca 1732–95), M.P. Hythe 1768–74, London 1774–95 (DNB).

4022. SAWBRIDGE, Samuel Elias (ca 1769–1850), M.P. Canterbury 1796–97, 1807–7 (*Eton Coll. Reg.; Harrow Reg.*).

4023. SAWYER, John (ca 1762–1845), M.P. Leominster 1790–91 (Burke's *LG* [ed. 1849]; *Eton Coll. Reg.;* Williams' *Hereford M.P.'s*).

4024. SAXON, Nathaniel, M.P. Ilchester 1806–7 (query, *Gent. Mag., 1* [1844], 664).

4025. SAXTON, Charles (1773–1838), 2d Bt, M.P. Cashel 1812–18 (*Eton Coll. Reg.*).

SCARBOROUGH, E. of, *see* LUMLEY-SAUNDERSON, George Augustus and Thomas; *also* LUMLEY-SAVILE, Richard.

4026. SCARLETT, James (1769–1844), 1st Bn Abinger, M.P. Peterborough 1819–30, Malton 1830–31, Cockermouth 1831–32, Norwich 1832–34 (DNB; GEC).

SCARSDALE, Bn, *see* CURZON, Nathaniel.

4027. SCAWEN, James (d. 1801), M.P. St. Michael 1761–74, Surrey 1774–80 (*Gent. Mag., 1,* 281; Vivian's *Visitation of Cornwall,* p. 423).

4028. SCAWEN, Thomas (d. 1774), M.P. Surrey 1727–41 (Berry's *County Geneal.: Surrey,* p. 43; Boase and Courtney's *Biblio. Cornub.*).

4029. SCHONSWAR, George (1775–1859), M.P. Hull 1830–32 (Bean; Boase; Burke's *LG* [ed. 1849]).

SCOTT, Charles William Henry Montagu, *see* MONTAGU-SCOTT, Charles William Henry.

4030. SCOTT, Claude (1742–1830), 1st Bt, M.P. Malmesbury 1802–6, Dungannon 1809–12 (Burke's *Peerage; Gent. Mag., 1,* 467).

4031. SCOTT, David (d. 1766), M.P. Fifeshire 1741–47, Aberdeen burghs 1751–66 (Foster's *Scots M.P.'s;* Grant's *Faculty of Advocates*).

4032. SCOTT, David (ca 1746–1805), M.P. Forfarshire 1790–96, Perth burghs 1796–1805 (Foster's *Scots M.P.'s;* Jervise, *Epitaphs, 2,* 394–95).

4033. SCOTT, David (1782–1851), 2d Bt, M.P. Yarmouth (Hants) 1806–6 (Burke's *Peerage;* Venn MS).

4034. SCOTT, Edward Dolman (1793–1851), 2d Bt, M.P. Lichfield 1831–37 (Boase; GEC).

4035. SCOTT, Francis (1721–50), M.P. Boroughbridge 1746–50 (*Alumni Cantab.; Eton Coll. Reg.*).

SCOTT, Henry Francis Hepburne and Hugh Hepburne, *see* HEPBURNE-SCOTT, Henry Francis and Hugh.

4036. SCOTT, James (d. 1835), M.P. Bridport 1820–26 (*Royal Kalendar* [1821], p. 51; *Victoria Hist. Hampshire, 4,* 424).

4037. SCOTT, John (ca 1725–75), M.P. Caithness-shire 1754–61, Tain burghs 1761–68, Fifeshire 1768–75 (Foster's *Scots M.P.'s; Scots Peerage;* Wood's *East Neuk of Fife,* p. 389).

4038. Scott, John (1751–1838), 1st E. of Eldon, M.P. Weobley 1783–96, Boroughbridge 1796–99 (DNB; GEC).

4039. Scott, John (1774–1805), M.P. Boroughbridge 1799–1805 (*Alumni Oxon.;* GEC sub Eldon).

4040. Scott, John (1805–54), 2d E. of Eldon, M.P. Truro 1829–32 (GEC).

4041. Scott, Joseph (1752–1828), 1st Bt, M.P. Worcester City 1802–6 (*Alumni Oxon.;* Burke's *Peerage;* Williams' *Worcester M.P.'s*).

4042. Scott, Robert, M.P. Wootton Bassett 1774–80 (*Court and City Reg.* [1775], p. 45).

4043. Scott, Samuel (1772–1849), 2d Bt, M.P. Malmesbury 1802–6, Camelford 1812–18, Whitchurch 1818–32 (Burke's *Peerage; 1806 List*).

4044. Scott, Thomas (1783–1838), 2d E. of Clonmell, M.P. New Romney 1807–12 (Ball and Venn's *Admissions to Trinity College;* GEC).

4045. Scott, Thomas (ca 1723–1816), M.P. Bridport 1780–90 (MS, *ex inform.* Maj. J. R. Bush).

4046. Scott, Walter (1724–93), M.P. Roxburghshire 1747–65 (Burke's *Peerage* sub Polwarth; Foster's *Scots M.P.'s*).

4047. Scott, William (1745–1836), 1st Bn Stowell, M.P. Downton 1790–1801, Oxford Univ. 1801–21 (DNB; GEC).

4048. Scott, William (ca 1794–1835), M.P. Gatton 1826–30 (*Alumni Oxon.;* GEC sub Eldon).

4049. Scott, William (1803–71), 6th Bt, M.P. Carlisle 1829–30, Roxburghshire 1859–70 (GEC).

4050. Scott, William Henry John (1795–1832), M.P. Heytesbury 1818–20, Hastings 1820–26, Newport (Hants) 1826–30 (*Alumni Oxon.;* Burke's *Peerage* sub Eldon).

4051. Scott-Waring, John (1747–1819), M.P. West Looe 1784–90 (DNB).

4052. Scourfield, William Henry (ca 1776–1843), M.P. Haverfordwest 1818–26, 1835–37 (*Alumni Oxon.;* Burke's *Peerage;* Williams' *Wales M.P.'s*).

4053. Scrope, John (ca 1662–1752), M.P. Ripon 1722–27, Bristol 1727–34, Lyme Regis 1734–52 (DNB).

4054. Scrope, Thomas (1723–92), M.P. Lincoln City 1768–74 (*Alumni Oxon.;* Foster's *Yorkshire Pedigrees;* Maddison's *Lincs. Pedigrees*).

Scudamore, Charles Fitzroy, *see* Fitzroy-Scudamore, Charles.

4055. Scudamore, John (1727–96), M.P. Hereford City 1764–96 (Burke's *LG;* Robinson's *Hereford,* p. 157; *Linc. Inn Reg.;* Williams' *Hereford M.P.'s*).

4056. SCUDAMORE, John (1757–1805), M.P. Hereford City 1796–1805 (*Eton Coll. Reg.*).

4057. SCUDAMORE, Richard Philip (1752–1831), M.P. Hereford City 1805–18, 1819–26 (Burke's *LG;* Williams' *Hereford M.P.'s*).

SEAFIELD, E. of, *see* OGILVIE-GRANT, Francis William and Lewis Alexander.

SEAFORD, 1st Bn, *see* ELLIS, Charles Rose.

SEAFORTH, 1st E., *see* MACKENZIE, Kenneth.

4058. SEBRIGHT, John Saunders (1725–94), 6th Bt, M.P. Bath 1763–74, 1775–80 (GEC; *Old Westminsters*).

4059. SEBRIGHT, John Saunders (1767–1846), 7th Bt, M.P. Herts 1807–34 (GEC; DNB; *Old Westminsters*).

4060. SEBRIGHT, Thomas Saunders (1692–1736), 4th Bt, M.P. Herts 1715–36 (GEC).

4061. SEDLEY, Charles (ca 1722–78), 2d Bt, M.P. Nottingham borough 1747–54, 1774–78 (GEC; *Old Westminsters*).

SEFTON, E. of, *see* MOLYNEUX, Charles William and William Philip.

SEGRAVE, 1st Bn, *see* BERKELEY, William Fitzhardinge.

4062. SELBY-LOWNDES, William (ca 1768–1840), M.P. Bucks 1810–20 (Burke's *LG; Gent. Mag., 2,* 542; Lipscomb's *Bucks, 3,* 544).

SELSEY, Bn, *see* PEACHEY, James and John.

4063. SELWYN, Charles (ca 1689–1749), M.P. St. Michael 1722–27, Gloucester City 1728–34, Ludgershall 1741–47 (Williams' *Gloucester M.P.'s*).

4064. SELWYN, George Augustus (1719–91), M.P. Ludgershall 1747–54, 1780–91, Gloucester City 1754–80 (DNB; *Eton Coll. Reg.*).

4065. SELWYN, John (1688–1751), M.P. Whitchurch 1727–34, Gloucester City 1734–51 (Fenwick and Metcalfe's *Visitation of Gloucester,* p. 162; Williams' *Gloucester M.P.'s*).

4066. SELWYN, John (ca 1709–51), M.P. Whitchurch 1734–51 (*Alumni Cantab.*).

4067. SELWYN, William (1732–1817), M.P. Whitchurch 1783–90 (*Alumni Cantab.; Old Westminsters*).

4068. SENHOUSE, Humphrey (ca 1731–1814), M.P. Cockermouth 1786–90, Cumberland 1790–96 (*Alumni Cantab.;* Burke's *LG*).

4069. SERGISON, Thomas (1701–66), M.P. Lewes 1747–66 (Burke's *LG;* Musgrave's *Obituary;* Sussex Archaeol. Soc. *Trans., 25,* 84).

SEVERN, John Cheesment, *see* CHEESMENT-SEVERN, John.

4070. SEWELL, Robert (ca 1751–1828), M.P. Grampound 1796–1802 (M. C. Owen, *Sewells of the Isle of Wight,* p. 167; *Royal Kalendar* [1802], p. 49).

4071. SEWELL, Thomas (ca 1712–84), M.P. Harwich 1758–61, Winchelsea 1761–68 (DNB; Rolls Chapel Reg. [G.D. 21/3 (1), f. 64], in *Deputy Keeper's Report, 57, 44, ex inform.* C. S. Drew).

4072. SEYMOUR, Edward (1695–1757), 8th D. of Somerset, M.P. Salisbury 1741–47 (GEC).

4073. SEYMOUR, Edward Adolphus (1804–85), 12th D. of Somerset, M.P. Okehampton 1830–31, Totnes 1834–55 (DNB; GEC).

4074. SEYMOUR, Francis (1697–1761), M.P. Great Bedwin 1732–34, Marlborough 1734–41 (Burke's *Peerage* and Collins' *Peerage* sub Somerset; *Collectanea Topographica et Genealogica, 5,* 39).

4075. SEYMOUR, George (1763–1848), M.P. Orford 1784–90, Totnes 1796–1801 (*Eton Coll. Reg.; Harrow Reg.*).

4076. SEYMOUR, Henry (ca 1729–1807), M.P. Totnes 1763–68, Huntingdon Borough 1768–74, Evesham 1774–80 (DNB; *Notes and Queries,* 11th Ser., *5,* 515; *Old Westminsters*).

4077. SEYMOUR, Henry (1746–1830), M.P. Coventry 1766–74, Midhurst 1774–80, Downton 1780–84 (*Eton Coll. Reg.*).

4078. SEYMOUR, Henry (1776–1849), M.P. Taunton 1826–30 (Collins' *Peerage* sub Somerset; *Gent. Mag., 1* [1850], 212).

4079. SEYMOUR, Horace Beauchamp (1791–1851), M.P. Lisburn 1819–26, 1847–51, Bodmin 1826–32, Midhurst 1841–45, Antrim 1845–47 (Boase; *Harrow Reg.*).

4080. SEYMOUR, Hugh (1759–1801), M.P. Newport (Hants) 1784–86, Tregony 1788–90, Wendover 1790–96, Portsmouth 1796–1801 (DNB).

4081. SEYMOUR, Hugh Henry John (1790–1821), M.P. Antrim 1818–21 (Burke's *Peerage* sub Hertford; *Harrow Reg.*).

4082. SEYMOUR, Robert (1748–1831), M.P. Orford 1771–84, 1794–1807, Wootton Bassett 1784–90, Carmarthenshire 1807–20 (*Eton Coll. Reg.*).

4083. SEYMOUR, William (1759–1837), M.P. Coventry 1783–84, Downton 1785–90, Orford 1790–96 (Burke's *Peerage* sub Hertford; *Gent. Mag., 1,* 333; *Harrow Reg.*).

SEYMOUR-CONWAY, Francis, *see* INGRAM-SEYMOUR-CONWAY, Francis.

4084. SEYMOUR-CONWAY, Francis Charles (1777–1842), 3d M. of Hertford, M.P. Orford 1797–1802, Lisburn 1802–12, Antrim 1812–18, Camelford 1820–22 (DNB; GEC).

4085. SEYMOUR-CONWAY, Richard (1800–70), 4th M. of Hertford, M.P. Antrim 1822–26 (GEC).

4086. SHADWELL, Lancelot (1779–1850), M.P. Ripon 1826–27 (*Admissions to St. John, Cambridge;* DNB).

SHAFTESBURY, E. of, *see* ASHLEY-COOPER, Anthony; *also* COOPER, Cropley Ashley.

SHAFTO, George, *see* DELAVAL, George.

4087. SHAFTO, Jennison (d. 1771), M.P. Leominster 1761–68, Castle Rising 1768–71 (*New Hist. of Northumberland, 13,* 224; Williams' *Hereford M.P.'s*).

4088. SHAFTO, John (ca 1694–1742), M.P. Durham City 1730–42 (*Alumni Oxon.;* Burke's *LG*).

4089. SHAFTO, Robert (ca 1732–97), M.P. Durham Co. 1760–68, Downton 1779–90 (*Eton Coll. Reg.; Old Westminsters*).

4090. SHAFTO, Robert Eden Duncombe (1776–1848), M.P. Durham City 1804–6 (Burke's *LG*).

4091. SHAKESPEARE, Arthur (ca 1748–1818), M.P. Richmond 1798–1808, Portarlington 1812–16 (Stopes, *Shakespeare's Family*, p. 154).

SHANNON, E. of, *see* BOYLE, Henry and Richard.

4092. SHARP, Richard (ca 1759–1835), M.P. Castle Rising 1806–12, Portarlington 1816–19, Ilchester 1826–27 (DNB).

4093. SHARPE, Fane William (ca 1728–71), M.P. Callington 1756–71 (*Old Westminsters*).

4094. SHARPE, John (ca 1700–56), M.P. Callington 1754–56 (Cass' *East Barnet*, p. 112; Clutterbuck's *Herts, 1*, 155; Oliver's *Antigua, 3*, 323).

4095. SHAW, Benjamin, M.P. Westbury 1812–18 (Bean; *Royal Kalendar* [1816], p. 76).

4096. SHAW, Frederick (1799–1876), 3d Bt, M.P. Dublin City 1830–31, 1831–32, Dublin Univ. 1832–48 (DNB).

4097. SHAW, James (ca 1764–1843), 1st Bt, M.P. London 1806–18 (DNB).

4098. SHAW, Robert (1774–1849), 1st Bt, M.P. Dublin City 1804–26 (*Alumni Dublin.;* Burke's *Peerage; 1812 List*).

4099. SHAW-LEFEVRE, Charles (ca 1758–1823), M.P. Newtown (Hants) 1796–1802, Reading 1802–20 (Ball and Venn's *Admissions to Trinity College;* Burke's *Peerage; 1812 List*).

4100. SHAW-LEFEVRE, Charles (1794–1888), 1st Vct Eversley, M.P. Downton 1830–31, Hampshire 1831–32, North Hampshire 1832–57 (DNB; GEC).

4101. SHAW-STEWART, John (ca 1740–1812), 4th Bt, M.P. Renfrewshire 1780–83, 1786–96 (GEC).

4102. SHAW-STEWART, Michael (ca 1788–1836), 6th Bt, M.P. Lanarkshire 1827–30, Renfrewshire 1830–36 (GEC; *Dod's Parl. Companion* [1834], p. 167).

4103. SHAWE, William Cunliffe (1745–1821), M.P. Preston 1792–96 (Addison's *Glasgow Matric. Albums;* Burke's *LG;* Fishwick's *Preston*, p. 341).

SHEFFIELD, 1st E. of, *see* HOLROYD, John Baker.

4104. SHEIL, Richard Lalor (1791–1851), M.P. Milborne Port 1831–31, Louth 1831–32, Tipperary 1832–41, Dungarvan 1841–51 (DNB).

SHELBURNE, E. of, *see* PETTY, John and William.

4105. SHELDON, Ralph (d. 1822), M.P. Wilton 1804–22 (*Alumni Oxon.;* Burke's *LG* [ed. 1849]).

4106. SHELLEY, Henry (1767–1811), M.P. Lewes 1802–11 (*Old Westminsters*).

4107. SHELLEY, John (1692–1771), 4th Bt, M.P. Arundel 1727–41, Lewes 1743–47 (GEC).

4108. SHELLEY, John (ca 1730–83), 5th Bt, M.P. East Retford 1751–68, Newark 1768–74, Shoreham 1774–80 (*Alumni Cantab.;* GEC; *Old Westminsters*).

4109. SHELLEY, John (1772–1852), 6th Bt, M.P. Helston 1806–6, Lewes 1816–31 (GEC; *Eton Coll. Reg.*).

4110. SHELLEY, John Villiers (1808–67), 7th Bt, M.P. Gatton 1830–31, Great Grimsby 1831–31, Westminster 1852–65 (GEC).

4111. SHELLEY, Timothy (1753–1844), 2d Bt, M.P. Horsham 1790–92, Shoreham 1802–18 (*Eton Coll. Reg.*).

4112. SHEPHEARD, Samuel (d. 1748), M.P. Malmesbury 1701–1, Cambridge borough 1708–22, 1747–48, Cambridgeshire 1724–47 (GEC sub Irvine; Musgrave's *Obituary; Notes and Queries,* 8th Ser., *10,* 404).

4113. SHEPHERD, Henry John (ca 1784–1855), M.P. Shaftesbury 1818–20 (Ball and Venn's *Admissions to Trinity College; Eton Lists; Gent. Mag., 2,* 108; *Linc. Inn Reg.*).

4114. SHEPHERD, Samuel (1760–1840), M.P. Dorchester 1814–19 (DNB).

4115. SHERARD, Philip (1767–1807), 5th E. of Harborough, M.P. Rutland 1795–96 (GEC; *Harrow Reg.*).

SHERBORNE, 1st Bn, *see* DUTTON, James.

4116. SHERIDAN, Richard Brinsley (1751–1816), M.P. Stafford borough 1780–1806, Westminster 1806–7, Ilchester 1807–12 (DNB).

4117. SHIFFNER, George (1762–1842), 1st Bt, M.P. Lewes 1812–26 (Burke's *Peerage*).

4118. SHIFFNER, Henry (1721–95), M.P. Minehead 1761–68 (Burke's *Peerage; Gent. Mag., 1* [1842], 552; Namier).

SHIPBROOKE, 1st E. of, *see* VERNON, Francis.

4119. SHIPLEY, William (ca 1778–1820), M.P. St. Mawes 1807–7, 1812–13, Flint borough 1807–12 (DNB sub William Davies Shipley; *Gent. Mag., 2,* 572).

4120. SHIPPEN, William (1673–1743), M.P. Bramber 1707–9, 1710–13, Saltash 1713–15, Newton 1715–43 (*Alumni Cantab.;* DNB).

4121. SHIRLEY, Evelyn John (1788–1856), M.P. Monaghan 1826–31, South Warwickshire 1836–49 (Burke's *LG; Rugby Reg.;* Venn MS).

4122. SHIRLEY, Sewallis (ca 1709–65), M.P. Brackley 1742–54, Callington 1754–61 (Baker's *Northampton, 1,* 733; GEC sub Clinton).

SHREWSBURY, 18th E. of, *see* CHETWYND-TALBOT, Henry John.

4123. SHUCKBURGH-EVELYN, George Augustus William (1751–1804), 6th Bt, M.P. Warwickshire 1780–1804 (DNB; GEC; *Misc. Geneal. et Herald.,* 2d Ser., *4*).

4124. SHULDHAM, Molineux (ca 1717–98), 1st Bn Shuldham, M.P. Fowey 1774–84 (DNB; GEC).

4125. SHUM, George (ca 1752–1805), M.P. Honiton 1796–1805 (Farquharson's *Honiton*, p. 48; *Gent. Mag., 1,* 290).

SHUTE, William Wildman Barrington, *see* BARRINGTON-SHUTE, William Wildman.

4126. SHUTTLEWORTH, James (1714–73), M.P. Preston 1741–54, Lancashire 1761–68 (Bean; Foster's *Lancashire Pedigrees; Old Westminsters;* Pink).

4127. SHUTTLEWORTH, Richard (1683–1749), M.P. Lancashire 1705–49 (Bean; Burke's *LG* [ed. 1849]; Foster's *Lancashire Pedigrees;* Pink).

SIBTHORP, Charles De Laet Waldo, *see* WALDO-SIBTHORP, Charles De Laet.

4128. SIBTHORP, Coningsby (ca 1706–79), M.P. Lincoln City 1734–41, 1747–54, 1761–68 (*Alumni Oxon.;* Burke's *LG;* Maddison's *Lincs. Pedigrees; Old Westminsters*).

4129. SIBTHORP, Coningsby Waldo (ca 1781–1822), M.P. Lincoln City 1814–22 (Burke's *LG; Old Westminsters*).

SIBTHORP, Humphrey, *see* WALDO-SIBTHORP, Humphrey.

4130. SIDNEY, Philip Charles (1800–51), 1st Bn de L'Isle and Dudley, M.P. Eye 1829–31 (*Alumni Oxon.;* GEC).

4131. SIMCOE, John Graves (1752–1806), M.P. St. Mawes 1790–92 (DNB; *Eton Coll. Reg.*).

4132. SIMEON, John (1756–1824), 1st Bt, M.P. Reading 1797–1802, 1806–18 (DNB; *Eton Coll. Reg.*).

4133. SIMMONS, James (1741–1807), M.P. Canterbury 1806–7 (*Annual Register,* p. 557; *Gent. Mag., 1,* 94, 177).

4134. SIMPSON, Edward (ca 1701–64), M.P. Dover 1759–64 (*Alumni Cantab.*).

4135. SIMPSON, John (1763–1850), M.P. Wenlock 1784–85, 1794–1820 (Burke's *Peerage* sub Bradford).

4136. SIMPSON, John, M.P. St. Michael 1799–1802.

4137. SIMSON, George, M.P. Maidstone 1806–18 (*Victoria Hist. Berks, 3,* 135; *1812 List*).

4138. SINCLAIR, George (1790–1868), 2d Bt, M.P. Caithness-shire 1811–12, 1818–20, 1831–41 (DNB; GEC; *Harrow Reg.*).

4139. SINCLAIR, James (ca 1688–1762), M.P. Dysart burghs 1722–34, 1747–54, Sutherlandshire 1736–47, Fifeshire 1754–62 (DNB; *Scots Peerage*).

4140. SINCLAIR, James (1797–1856), M.P. Caithness-shire 1826–30 (*Scots Peerage*).

4141. SINCLAIR, John (1754–1835), 1st Bt, M.P. Caithness-shire 1780–84, 1790–96, 1802–6, 1807–11, Lostwithiel 1784–90, Petersfield 1797–1802 (DNB; GEC).

4142. SINGLETON, Mark (ca 1762–1840), M.P. Eye 1796–99, 1807–20 (*Alumni Oxon.;* Burke's *Irish LG; Harrow Reg.; Linc. Inn Reg.*).

4143. Sitwell, Francis (ca 1777–1813), M.P. Berwick-on-Tweed 1803–6 (Bean; Burke's *Peerage; Gent. Mag., 1,* 291).

4144. Sitwell, Sitwell (1769–1811), 1st Bt, M.P. West Looe 1796–1802 (*Alumni Oxon.;* Burke's *Peerage; Gent. Mag., 2,* 91; Hunter's *Hallamshire,* p. 373).

Skeffington, Thomas Henry Foster, *see* Foster-Skeffington, Thomas Henry.

Skelmersdale, 1st Bn, *see* Bootle-Wilbraham, Edward.

Skelton, Arnoldus Jones, *see* Jones-Skelton, Arnoldus.

4145. Skene, George (1749–1825), M.P. Aberdeenshire 1786–90, Elgin burghs 1806–7 (Foster's *Scots M.P.'s;* Grant's *Faculty of Advocates*).

4146. Skene, Robert (d. 1787), M.P. Fifeshire 1779–80, 1780–87 (Burke's *LG;* Foster's *Scots M.P.'s*).

4147. Skinner, Matthew (1689–1749), M.P. Oxford City 1734–38 (DNB; *Old Westminsters*).

4148. Skipwith, George (1771–1852), 8th Bt, M.P. Warwickshire 1831–32, South Warwickshire 1832–34 (GEC; *Eton Coll. Reg.*).

4149. Skipwith, Thomas George (ca 1736–90), 4th Bt, M.P. Warwickshire 1769–80, Steyning 1780–84 (Ball and Venn's *Admissions to Trinity College;* GEC; *Rugby Reg.*).

4150. Skrine, William (ca 1722–83), M.P. Callington 1771–80 (*Alumni Oxon.;* Musgrave's *Obituary*).

4151. Skynner, John (ca 1724–1805), M.P. Woodstock 1771–77 (DNB; *Old Westminsters*).

4152. Slaney, Robert Aglionby (1791–1862), M.P. Shrewsbury 1826–34, 1837–41, 1847–52, 1857–62 (DNB; Burke's *LG;* Hughes, *Sheriffs of Shrop.,* p. 47).

4153. Slingsby, Henry (ca 1693–1763), 5th Bt, M.P. Knaresborough 1714–15, 1722–63 (GEC).

4154. Sloane-Stanley, Hans (1739–1827), M.P. Newport (Hants) 1768–80, Southampton borough 1780–84, Christchurch 1788–96, Lostwithiel 1796–1806 (Ball and Venn's *Admissions to Trinity College;* Burke's *LG; Jour. Mod. Hist., 18* [1946], 215).

4155. Sloane-Stanley, William (ca 1781–1860), M.P. Orford 1807–12. Stockbridge 1830–31 (Burke's *LG; Eton Lists; Gent. Mag., 1,* 533).

4156. Sloper, William (ca 1669–1743), M.P. Great Bedwin 1715–22, 1729–41, Camelford 1722–27, Whitchurch 1742–43 (*Alumni Oxon.;* Musgrave's *Obituary*).

4157. Sloper, William (ca 1708–89), M.P. Great Bedwin 1747–56 (*Alumni Cantab.; Gent. Mag.,* p. 865).

4158. Sloper, William Charles, M.P. St. Albans 1780–90 (*Royal Kalendar* [1786], p. 23).

4159. Smelt, Leonard (ca 1683–1740), M.P. Thirsk 1709–10, Northallerton 1713–40 (*Alumni Cantab.*).

4160. SMELT, William (1690–1755), M.P. Northallerton 1740–45 (Ingle-
dew's *Northallerton,* p. 138; Walker's *Yorkshire Pedigrees*).

4161. SMITH, Abel (1717–88), M.P. Aldborough 1774–78, St. Ives 1780–
84, St. Germans 1784–88 (Burke's *LG*).

4162. SMITH, Abel (1748–79), M.P. Nottingham borough 1778–79
(Burke's *LG*).

4163. SMITH, Abel (1788–1859), M.P. Malmesbury 1810–12, Wendover
1812–18, 1830–32, Midhurst 1820–30, Herts 1835–47 (Burke's
LG; Boase; *Harrow Reg.*).

4164. SMITH, Charles (1756–1814), M.P. Saltash 1796–1802, Westbury
1802–6 (Howard and Crisp's *Visitation of Eng. and Wales, 2,*
129; Venn MS).

SMITH, Charles Loraine, *see* LORAINE-SMITH, Charles.

4165. SMITH, Christopher (d. 1835), M.P. St. Albans 1812–18, 1820–30
(Beaven's *Aldermen of London; Gent. Mag., 1,* 666 and *2,* 669;
1812 List).

SMITH, Culling Eardley, *see* EARDLEY, Culling.

4166. SMITH, Edward (ca 1705–62), M.P. Leicestershire 1734–62
(*Alumni Cantab.;* Nichols' *Leicester, 2,* pt. 1, 182; *Rugby Reg.*).

4167. SMITH, George (1765–1836), M.P. Lostwithiel 1791–96, Midhurst
1800–6, 1830–31, Wendover 1806–30 (Burke's *Peerage* sub Carrington; Venn MS).

4168. SMITH, George Robert (1793–1869), M.P. Midhurst 1831–32,
Wycombe 1838–41 (Boase; Burke's *LG; Eton Lists*).

4169. SMITH, Henry, M.P. Calne 1807–12.

SMITH, Jarrit, *see* SMYTH, Jarrit.

4170. SMITH, John (ca 1727–75), M.P. Bath 1766–75 (*Notes and Queries,*
11th Ser., *11,* 161; MS, *ex inform.* the Reverend D. A. Yerbury).

4171. SMITH, John, M.P. New Romney 1784–84 (*Parl. Hist., 21,* 789).

4172. SMITH, John (1767–1842), M.P. Wendover 1802–6, Nottingham
borough 1806–18, Midhurst 1818–30, Chichester 1830–31, Bucks
1831–34 (Burke's *LG;* Dod's *Parl. Companion* [1834], p. 164).

4173. SMITH, John (1767–1827), M.P. East Looe 1799–99 (*Eton Coll.
Reg.*).

4174. SMITH, John Abel (1802–71), M.P. Midhurst 1830–31, Chichester
1831–59, 1863–68 (Burke's *LG;* DNB; Dod's *Parl. Companion*
[1834], p. 164; *Eton Lists*).

4175. SMITH, John Mansell (b. ca 1759), M.P. Wendover 1780–84 (*Admissions to St. John, Cambridge*).

4176. SMITH, John Spencer (1769–1845), M.P. Dover 1802–6 (*Alumni
Oxon.;* Fetis, *Biog. Univ. des Musiciens,* 8, 54; Jones' *Annals of
Dover,* p. 393).

4177. SMITH, Joshua (ca 1733–1819), M.P. Devizes 1788–1818 (Oliver's
Antigua, 2, 12).

4178. SMITH, Martin Tucker (1803–80), M.P. Midhurst 1831–32, Wycombe 1847–65 (Boase; Burke's *LG; Eton Lists*).

4179. SMITH, Nathaniel (ca 1721–94), M.P. Pontefract 1783–83, Rochester 1784–90, 1792–94 (*Alumni Oxon.;* C. Reade, *Smith Family;* Bean).

4180. SMITH, Richard (d. 1803), M.P. Hindon 1774–76, 1776–77, Wendover 1780–84, Wareham 1790–96 (*Admissions to St. John, Cambridge,* sub John M. Smith; Holzman's *Nabobs in Eng.*).

4181. SMITH, Robert (1752–1838), 1st Bn Carrington, M.P. Nottingham borough 1779–97 (DNB; GEC).

SMITH, Robert John, *see* CARRINGTON, Robert John.

4182. SMITH, Robert Percy (1770–1845), M.P. Grantham 1812–18, Lincoln City 1820–26 (DNB; *Eton Coll. Reg.*).

SMITH, Robert Vernon, *see* VERNON, Robert Vernon.

4183. SMITH, Samuel (1754–1834), M.P. St. Germans 1788–90, Leicester borough 1790–1818, Midhurst 1818–20, Wendover 1820–32 (Burke's *LG; Gent. Mag., 2,* 317).

4184. SMITH, Samuel (1755–93), M.P. Ilchester 1780–84, Worcester City 1784–90, Ludgershall 1791–93 (C. Reade, *Smith Family;* Williams' *Worcester M.P.'s*).

4185. SMITH, Thomas (b. ca 1780), M.P. West Looe 1802–3 (Venn MS).

SMITH, Thomas Assheton, *see* ASSHETON-SMITH, Thomas.

4186. SMITH, William (1756–1835), M.P. Sudbury 1784–90, 1796–1802, Camelford 1791–96, Norwich 1802–30 (DNB).

4187. SMITH, William Sidney (1764–1840), M.P. Rochester 1802–6 (DNB).

4188. SMITH-O'BRIEN, William (1803–64), M.P. Ennis 1828–31, Limerick Co. 1835–49 (DNB; Boase; *Harrow Reg.*).

4189. SMITH-STANLEY, Edward (1752–1834), 12th E. of Derby, M.P. Lancashire 1774–76 (GEC; *Eton Coll. Reg.*).

4190. SMITH-STANLEY, Edward (1775–1851), 13th E. of Derby, M.P. Preston 1796–1812, Lancashire 1812–32 (DNB; GEC; *Eton Coll. Reg.*).

4191. SMITH-STANLEY, Edward George Geoffrey (1799–1869), 14th E. of Derby, M.P. Stockbridge 1822–26, Preston 1826–30, Windsor 1831–32, North Lancashire 1832–44 (DNB; GEC).

4192. SMITH-STANLEY, James (1717–71), M.P. Lancashire 1741–71 (GEC; *Old Westminsters*).

SMITHSON, Hugh, *see* PERCY, Hugh.

SMOLLETT, Alexander Telfer, *see* TELFER-SMOLLETT, Alexander.

4193. SMYTH, George Henry (1784–1852), 6th Bt, M.P. Colchester 1826–29, 1835–50 (GEC).

4194. SMYTH, Jarrit (ca 1692–1783), 1st Bt, M.P. Bristol 1756–68 (GEC; Williams' *Gloucester M.P.'s*).

4195. SMYTH, John (1748–1811), M.P. Pontefract 1783–1807 (*Old Westminsters;* C. Reade, *Smith Family*).

4196. SMYTH, John Henry (1780–1822), M.P. Cambridge Univ. 1812–22 (Burke's *LG* [ed. 1849]; *Eton Lists;* C. Reade, *Smith Family*).

4197. SMYTH, Robert (1744–1802), 5th Bt, M.P. Cardigan borough 1774–
75, Colchester 1780–90 (GEC; *Old Westminsters;* Williams'
Wales M.P.'s).

4198. SMYTH, Robert (b. 1777), M.P. Westmeath 1824–26 (*Alumni Dublin.;* Burke's *Irish LG*).

4199. SMYTH, William (ca 1745–1827), M.P. Westmeath 1801–8 (Burke's
Irish LG; Gent. Mag., 2, 93; C. Reade, *Smith Family*).

4200. SMYTHE, Sidney Stafford (ca 1705–78), M.P. East Grinstead
1747–50 (*Alumni Cantab.;* DNB).

4201. SMYTHE, William Meade (1786–1866), M.P. Drogheda 1822–26
(Burke's *Irish LG;* Boase; Venn MS).

SMYTHE-GARDINER, John Whalley, *see* WHALLEY-SMYTHE-GARDINER, John.

4202. SNEYD, Nathaniel (ca 1767–1833), M.P. Cavan 1801–26 (Belmore's *Fermanagh M.P.'s; Gent. Mag., 2,* 183; MS, *ex inform.*
the Reverend E. H. L. Crosby).

4203. SNEYD, Walter (1752–1829), M.P. Castle Rising 1784–90 (*Alumni
Oxon.;* Burke's *LG*).

SOMERS, Bn and E., *see* COCKS, Charles and John Somers.

SOMERSET, D. of, *see* SEYMOUR, Edward and Edward Adolphus.

4204. SOMERSET, Arthur John Henry (1780–1816), M.P. Monmouthshire
1805–16 (Burke's *Peerage* sub Beaufort; Williams' *Wales
M.P.'s*).

4205. SOMERSET, Charles Henry (1767–1831), M.P. Scarborough 1796–
1802, Monmouth borough 1802–13 (*Old Westminsters;* Williams'
Wales M.P.'s).

4206. SOMERSET, Charles Noel (1709–56), 4th D. of Beaufort, M.P. Monmouthshire 1731–34, Monmouth borough 1734–45 (GEC; *Old
Westminsters*).

4207. SOMERSET, Fitzroy James Henry (1788–1855), 1st Bn Raglan,
M.P. Truro 1818–20, 1826–29 (DNB; GEC; *Old Westminsters*).

4208. SOMERSET, Granville Charles Henry (1792–1848), M.P. Monmouthshire 1816–48 (DNB).

4209. SOMERSET, Henry (1792–1853), 7th D. of Beaufort, M.P. Monmouth borough 1813–31, 1831–32, West Gloucestershire 1835–35
(DNB; GEC; *Old Westminsters*).

4210. SOMERSET, Henry Charles (1766–1835), 6th D. of Beaufort, M.P.
Monmouth borough 1788–90, Bristol 1790–96, Gloucestershire
1796–1803 (GEC; *Old Westminsters*).

4211. SOMERSET, Robert Edward Henry (1776–1842), M.P. Monmouth
borough 1799–1802, Gloucestershire 1803–31, Cirencester 1834–
37 (DNB; *Old Westminsters*).

4212. SOMERVILLE, Marcus (ca 1775–1831), 4th Bt, M.P. Meath 1801–31
(*Alumni Dublin.;* GEC).

SONDES, Bn, *see* WATSON, Lewis and Lewis Thomas.

4213. SOTHERON, Frank (1765–1839), M.P. Notts 1814–31 (*Misc. Geneal. et Herald.*, N.S., *1*, 141).

4214. SOTHERON, William (ca 1755–1806), M.P. Pontefract 1784–96 (Bean; *Misc. Geneal. et Herald.*, N.S., *1*, 140).

4215. SOTHERON-ESTCOURT, Thomas Henry Sutton (1801–76), M.P. Marlborough 1829–32, Devizes 1835–44, North Wilts 1844–65. (DNB).

4216. SOUTHEY, Robert (1774–1843), M.P. Downton 1826–26 (DNB).

4217. SOUTHWELL, Edward (1705–55), M.P. Bristol 1739–54 (GEC sub Clifford; *Old Westminsters*).

4218. SOUTHWELL, Edward (1738–77), 20th Bn de Clifford, M.P. Bridgwater 1761–63, Gloucestershire 1763–76 (GEC; *Old Westminsters*).

4219. SPALDING, John (ca 1763–1815), M.P. Wigtown burghs 1796–1803 (Burke's *LG;* Foster's *Scots M.P.'s*).

4220. SPARROW, Robert (1741–1822), M.P. Bedford borough 1774–75 (Copinger's *Suffolk, 7,* 226).

SPEED, Henry, *see* DE VIRY, François Joseph Marie Henry.

4221. SPEIRS, Archibald (1758–1832), M.P. Renfrewshire 1810–18 (Burke's *LG;* Foster's *Scots M.P.'s*).

4222. SPEKE, George (d. 1753), M.P. Milborne Port 1722–27, Taunton 1727–34, Wells 1735–47 (Musgrave's *Obituary*).

4223. SPENCE, George (ca 1787–1850), M.P. Reading 1826–27, Ripon 1829–32 (DNB).

4224. SPENCER, Brent (ca 1760–1828), M.P. Sligo borough 1815–18 (DNB).

4225. SPENCER, Charles (1740–1820), M.P. Oxfordshire 1761–90, 1796–1801 (DNB; *Eton Coll. Reg.*).

4226. SPENCER, Francis Almeric (1779–1845), 1st Bn Churchill, M.P. Oxfordshire 1801–15 (GEC).

4227. SPENCER, Frederick (1798–1857), 4th E. Spencer, M.P. Worcestershire 1831–32, Midhurst 1832–34, 1837–41 (GEC).

4228. SPENCER, George John (1758–1834), 2d E. Spencer, M.P. Northampton borough 1780–82, Surrey 1782–83 (DNB; GEC).

4228. SPENCER, George John (1758–1834), 2d E. Spencer, M.P. Northampton borough 1780–82, Surrey 1782–83 (DNB; GEC).

4229. SPENCER, Henry John (1770–95), M.P. Woodstock 1790–95 (DNB; *Eton Coll. Reg.*).

4230. SPENCER, John (1708–46), M.P. Woodstock 1732–46 (GEC; *Eton Coll. Reg.*).

4231. SPENCER, John (1734–83), 1st E. Spencer, M.P. Warwick borough 1756–61 (GEC).

4232. SPENCER, John (1767–1831), M.P. Wilton 1801–4 (*Alumni Oxon.;* Burke's *Peerage* sub Marlborough; *Harrow Reg.*).

4233. SPENCER, John Charles (1782–1845), 3d E. Spencer, M.P. Okehampton 1804–6, Northamptonshire 1806–32, South Northamptonshire 1832–34 (DNB; GEC).

4234. SPENCER, Joshua (ca 1758–1829), M.P. Sligo borough 1813–15 (*Alumni Dublin.; Cornwallis Corr., 3, 32*).

4235. SPENCER, Robert (1747–1831), M.P. Woodstock 1768–71, 1818–20, Oxford City 1771–90, Wareham 1790–99, Tavistock 1802–7, 1817–18 (Collins' *Peerage* and Burke's *Peerage* sub Marlborough; Williams' *Oxford M.P.'s; Harrow Reg.*).

4236. SPENCER-CHURCHILL, Charles (1794–1840), M.P. St. Albans 1818–20, Woodstock 1830–32, 1835–37 (Burke's *Peerage* sub Marlborough; *Eton Lists*).

4237. SPENCER-CHURCHILL, George (1766–1840), 5th D. of Marlborough, M.P. Oxfordshire 1790–96, Tregony 1802–4 (DNB; GEC).

4238. SPENCER-CHURCHILL, George (1793–1857), 6th D. of Marlborough, M.P. Chippenham 1818–20, Woodstock 1826–34, 1838–40 (GEC).

4239. SPENCER-STANHOPE, Walter (1749–1821), M.P. Carlisle 1775–80, 1802–12, Haslemere 1780–84, Hull 1784–90, Cockermouth 1800–2 (*Alumni Oxon.;* Burke's *LG;* Hunter's *Deanery of Doncaster, 2,* 232).

4240. SPICER, William (ca 1735–88), M.P. Exeter 1767–68 (Devonshire Assoc. *Trans., 62,* 215; Musgrave's *Obituary*).

4241. SPOONER, Richard (1783–1864), M.P. Boroughbridge 1820–24, Birmingham 1844–47, North Warwickshire 1847–64 (Bean; Boase; Burke's *LG; Rugby Reg.*).

4242. SPOTTISWOODE, Andrew (ca 1787–1866), M.P. Saltash 1826–30, Colchester 1830–31 (Boase; Burke's *LG*).

SPRING-RICE, Thomas, *see* RICE, Thomas Spring.

4243. SPURRIER, Christopher (ca 1784–1876), M.P. Bridport 1820–20 (*Alumni Oxon.*).

STACKHOUSE, Edward William, *see* WYNNE-PENDARVES, Edward William.

STAFFORD, M. of, *see* LEVESON-GOWER, George Granville and Granville.

4244. STAFFORD-JERNINGHAM, Henry Valentine (1802–84), 2d Bn Stafford, M.P. Pontefract 1830–34 (GEC).

STAMFORD, E. of, *see* GREY, George Harry and Harry.

4245. STANDERT, Frederick (d. 1785), M.P. Bletchingley 1769–80 (Musgrave's *Obituary; Royal Kalendar* [1770], p. 25).

4246. STANDISH, Frank (ca 1746–1812), 3d Bt, M.P. Preston 1768–68 (GEC; *Old Westminsters*).

4247. STANHOPE, Charles (ca 1673–1760), M.P. Milborne Port 1717–22, Aldborough 1722–34, Harwich 1734–41 (DNB; GEC sub Harrington).

4248. STANHOPE, Charles (1708–36), M.P. Derby borough 1730–36 (Collins' *Peerage* and Burke's *Peerage* sub Chesterfield; Musgrave's *Obituary*).

4249. STANHOPE, Charles (1753–1829), 3d E. of Harrington, M.P. Thetford 1774–74, Westminster 1776–79 (DNB; GEC; *Eton Coll. Reg.*).

4250. STANHOPE, Charles (1753–1816), 3d E. Stanhope, M.P. Wycombe 1780–86 (DNB; GEC; *Eton Coll. Reg.*).

4251. STANHOPE, Henry Fitzroy (1754–1828), M.P. Bramber 1782–84 (*Eton Coll. Reg.*).

4252. STANHOPE, James Hamilton (1788–1825), M.P. Buckingham borough 1817–18, Fowey 1818–19, Dartmouth 1822–25 (Collins' *Peerage* and Burke's *Peerage* sub Stanhope; *Gent. Mag., 1,* 465).

4253. STANHOPE, John (1705–48), M.P. Nottingham borough 1727–34, Derby borough 1736–48 (Collins' *Peerage* and Burke's *Peerage* sub Chesterfield).

4254. STANHOPE, Lovell (1720–83), M.P. Winchester 1774–83 (Collins' *Peerage* and Burke's *Peerage* sub Chesterfield; Glover's *Derbyshire, 2,* 164; *Linc. Inn Reg.*).

4255. STANHOPE, Philip (1732–68), M.P. Liskeard 1754–61, St. Germans 1761–64 (DNB; Chesterfield's *Letters,* ed. Dobree, *1,* 66).

4256. STANHOPE, Philip Henry (1781–1855), 4th E. Stanhope, M.P. Wendover 1806–7, Hull 1807–12, Midhurst 1812–16 (GEC).

4257. STANHOPE, Philip Henry (1805–75), 5th E. Stanhope, M.P. Wootton Bassett 1830–32, Hertford borough 1832–52 (DNB; GEC).

4258. STANHOPE, Robert Henry (1802–39), M.P. Dover 1831–32 (Burke's *Peerage* sub Harrington).

STANHOPE, Walter Spencer, *see* SPENCER-STANHOPE, Walter.

4259. STANHOPE, William (1702–72), M.P. Lostwithiel 1727–27, Bucks 1727–41, 1747–68 (Collins' *Peerage* and Burke's *Peerage* sub Chesterfield; Musgrave's *Obituary*).

4260. STANHOPE, William (1719–79), 2d E. of Harrington, M.P. Aylesbury 1741–47, Bury 1747–56 (DNB; GEC; *Eton Coll. Reg.*).

4261. STANIFORTH, John (d. 1830), M.P. Hull 1802–18 (*Annual Register,* p. 259; *Notes and Queries, 179,* 148).

4262. STANLEY, Edward (1689–1776), 11th E. of Derby, M.P. Lancashire 1727–36 (*Alumni Cantab.;* GEC).

STANLEY, Edward George Geoffrey Smith, see SMITH-STANLEY, Edward George Geoffrey.

4263. STANLEY, Edward John (1802–69), 2d Bn Stanley and 1st Bn Eddisbury, M.P. Hindon 1831–32, North Cheshire 1832–41, 1847–48 (DNB; GEC; *Eton Lists*).

STANLEY, Edward Smith, see SMITH-STANLEY, Edward.

4264. STANLEY, Hans (ca 1720–80), M.P. St. Albans 1743–47, Southampton borough 1754–80 (DNB).

STANLEY, Hans Sloane, *see* SLOANE-STANLEY, Hans.

STANLEY, James Smith, *see* SMITH-STANLEY, James.

4265. STANLEY, John (ca 1740–99), M.P. Hastings 1784–96 (*Notes and Queries*, 11th Ser., *11*, 235).

4266. STANLEY, John Thomas (1766–1850), 1st Bn Stanley, M.P. Wootton Bassett 1790–96 (GEC).

4267. STANLEY, Thomas (1749–1818), M.P. Lancashire 1780–1812 (Burke's *LG*).

4268. STANLEY, Thomas Smith (ca 1753–79), M.P. Lancashire 1776–79 (*Eton Coll. Reg.*).

STANLEY, William Sloane, *see* SLOANE-STANLEY, William.

4269. STANTON, Robert, M.P. Penryn 1824–26.

4270. STANWIX, John (ca 1690–1766), M.P. Carlisle 1741–42, 1746–61; Appleby 1761–66 (DNB).

4271. STAPLES, John (b. 1736), M.P. Antrim 1801–2 (*Alumni Dublin.;* Burke's *Peerage*).

4272. STAPLETON, Thomas (1727–81), 5th Bt, M.P. Oxford City 1759–68 (GEC).

4273. STAPLETON, William (ca 1698–1740), 4th Bt, M.P. Oxfordshire 1727–40 (GEC).

4274. STAPYLTON, Miles (ca 1708–52), 4th Bt, M.P. Yorkshire 1734–50 (GEC; Gooder; *Old Westminsters*).

4275. STARKIE, Edmund (d. 1773), M.P. Preston 1754–68 (Dobson's *Preston M.P.'s;* Foster's *Lancashire Pedigrees;* Martin's *Masters of the Bench, Inner Temple*).

4276. STARKIE, Le Gendre Nicholas (1799–1868), M.P. Pontefract 1826–30 (*Alumni Oxon.;* Howard and Crisp's *Visitation of Eng. and Wales, 6,* 152).

4277. STAUNTON, George Thomas (1781–1859), 2d Bt, M.P. St. Michael 1818–26, Heytesbury 1830–32, South Hampshire 1832–34,. Portsmouth 1838–52 (DNB; GEC).

4278. STAUNTON, Thomas (d. 1784), M.P. Ipswich 1757–84 (*Gent. Mag.*, p. 798).

4279. STEELE, Robert (1757–1817), M.P. Weobley 1802–7 (*Old Westminsters*).

4280. STEELE, Thomas (1753–1823), M.P. Chichester 1780–1807 (*Old Westminsters*).

4281. STEELE, William (d. 1748), M.P. Hindon 1741–47 (*London Evening Post*, 5–7 July 1748).

4282. STEIN, John (b. 1769), M.P. Bletchingley 1796–1802 (Manning and Bray's *Surrey, 3,* 589; MS Pedigree at Society of Genealogists, London).

4283. STEPHEN, James (1758–1832), M.P. Tralee 1808–12, East Grinstead 1812–15 (DNB).

4284. STEPHENS, Philip (1723–1809), 1st Bt, M.P. Liskeard 1759–68, Sandwich 1768–1806 (DNB; GEC).

4285. STEPHENS, Samuel (ca 1728–94), M.P. St. Ives 1751–54 (*Alumni Cantab.*).

4286. STEPHENS, Samuel (ca 1768–1834), M.P. St. Ives 1806–12, 1818–20 (*Admissions to St. John, Cambridge;* Burke's *LG* [ed. 1849]).

STEPHENS, Stephen Lyne, *see* LYNE-STEPHENS, Stephen.

4287. STEPHENSON, Edward, M.P. Sudbury 1734–41.

4288. STEPHENSON, Henry Frederick (1790–1858), M.P. Westbury 1831–32 (Boase; *Sedbergh School Reg.*).

4289. STEPHENSON, John (ca 1710–94), M.P. St. Michael 1754–55, 1761–80, Tregony 1780–84, 1790–94, Plympton Erle 1784–90 (*Gent. Mag.*, p. 388; Namier, *England*, p. 295).

4290. STEPHENSON, Rowland (ca 1728–1807), M.P. Carlisle 1786–90 (*Gent. Mag., 2*, 1179; *Notes and Queries*, 12th Ser., *11*, 88).

4291. STEPHENSON, Rowland (b. ca 1778), M.P. Leominster 1827–30 (*Eton Lists; Notes and Queries*, 12th Ser., *10*, 491 and *11*, 88).

4292. STEPNEY, John (1743–1811), 8th Bt, M.P. Monmouth borough 1767–88 (GEC).

4293. STERT, Arthur (d. 1755), M.P. Plymouth 1727–54 (Musgrave's *Obituary*).

4294. STEUART, James (d. 1757), M.P. Weymouth and Melcombe Regis 1741–47 (Charnock's *Biog. Naval., 4*, 18; Musgrave's *Obituary; 1747 List*).

4295. STEUART, Robert (ca 1807–43), M.P. Haddington burghs 1831–31, 1832–41 (*Alumni Oxon.;* Foster's *Scots M.P.'s*).

4296. STEUART-DENHAM, James (1744–1839), 8th Bt, M.P. Lanarkshire 1784–1802 (DNB; GEC).

4297. STEVENS, Richard, M.P. Callington 1761–68.

4298. STEWARD, Gabriel (1731–92), ·M.P. Weymouth and Melcombe Regis 1778–86, 1788–90 (Burke's *LG* [ed. 1849]; Hutchins' *Dorset, 2*, 481; Musgrave's *Obituary;* Namier).

4299. STEWARD, Gabriel Tucker (b. ca 1768), M.P. Weymouth and Melcombe Regis 1794–1810 (Burke's *LG* [ed. 1849]; *Harrow Reg.;* Irish House of Commons *Jour.* [1781], app., p. cccxlvi; *Royal Kalendar* [1802], p. 65).

4300. STEWARD, Richard Augustus Tucker (1773–1842), M.P. Weymouth and Melcombe Regis 1806–12 (Burke's *LG* [ed. 1849]; *Harrow Reg.*).

STEWART, 1st Bn, *see* VANE, Charles William.

4301. STEWART, Alexander (d. 1794), M.P. Kirkcudbright Stewarty 1786–94 (Foster's *Scots M.P.'s*).

4302. STEWART, Alexander (1746–1831), M.P. Londonderry Co. 1814–18 (Burke's *Irish LG*).

4303. STEWART, Alexander Robert (1795–1850), M.P. Londonderry Co. 1818–30 (Burke's *Irish LG*).
4304. STEWART, Archibald (d. 1780), M.P. Edinburgh City 1741–47 (Foster's *Scots M.P.'s*).
4305. STEWART, Charles (ca 1681–1741), M.P. Portsmouth 1737–41 (Charnock's *Biog. Naval., 3,* 304; Musgrave's *Obituary*).
4306. STEWART, Charles (ca 1802–91), M.P. Penryn 1831–32 (Boase).
     STEWART, Charles William, *see* VANE, Charles William.
4307. STEWART, Edward (1808–75), M.P. Wigtown burghs 1831–34 (*Alumni Oxon.;* Boase; *Eton Lists; Scots Peerage* sub Galloway).
4308. STEWART, Edward Richard (1782–1851), M.P. Wigtown burghs 1806–9 (*Scots Peerage* sub Galloway).
4309. STEWART, Frederick William Robert (1805–72), 4th M. of Londonderry, M.P. Down 1826–52 (GEC).
4310. STEWART, George (1768–1834), 8th E. of Galloway, M.P. Saltash 1790–95, Cockermouth 1805–6, Haslemere 1806–6 (GEC; *Old Westminsters*).
4311. STEWART, Hugh (1792–1854), 2d Bt, M.P. Tyrone 1830–34 (*Alumni Dublin.;* Burke's *Peerage;* Boase).
4312. STEWART, James (d. 1768), M.P. Wigtown burghs 1734–41, 1747–54, Wigtownshire 1741–47, 1754–61 (*Scots Peerage* sub Galloway).
4313. STEWART, James (d. 1762), M.P. Buteshire 1761–62 (Foster's *Scots M.P.'s; Scots Notes and Queries,* 3d Ser., *9,* 16).
4314. STEWART, James (b. ca 1741), M.P. Tyrone 1801–12 (Burke's *Irish LG*).
4315. STEWART, James (ca 1760–1827), 7th Bt, M.P. Donegal 1802–18 (GEC).
4316. STEWART, James Henry Keith (1783–1836), M.P. Wigtown burghs 1812–21 (Ball and Venn's *Admissions to Trinity College; Scots Peerage* sub Galloway).
4317. STEWART, John (ca 1708–96), M.P. Anstruther Easter burghs 1741–47 (*Scots Peerage* sub Moray).
4318. STEWART, John (1736–1806), 7th E. of Galloway, M.P. Morpeth 1761–68, Ludgershall 1768–73 (Addison's *Glasgow Matric. Albums;* GEC).
4319. STEWART, John, M.P. Wigtownshire 1747–54 (Foster's *Scots M.P.'s*).
4320. STEWART, John, M.P. Arundel 1771–74.
4321. STEWART, John (ca 1757–1825), 1st Bt, M.P. Tyrone 1802–6, 1812–25 (*Alumni Dublin.;* Burke's *Peerage*).
4322. STEWART, John (ca 1784–1873), M.P. Bevereley 1826–30 (Boase).
4323. STEWART, John (ca 1789–1860), M.P. Camelford 1819–20, Lymington 1832–47 (*Alumni Dublin.*).
     STEWART, John Shaw, *see* SHAW-STEWART, John.

4324. STEWART, Keith (ca 1739–95), M.P. Wigtown burghs 1762–62, Wigtownshire 1768–84 (Charnock's *Biog. Naval., 6,* 471; *Scots Peerage* sub Galloway).

STEWART, Michael Shaw, *see* SHAW-STEWART, Michael.

4325. STEWART, Montgomery Granville John (1780–1860), M.P. Kirkcudbright Stewarty 1803–12 (*Scots Peerage* sub Galloway).

4326. STEWART, Patrick Maxwell (ca 1791–1846), M.P. Lancaster borough 1831–37, Renfrewshire 1841–46 (Burke's *Peerage;* Bean; Foster's *Scots M.P.'s;* Pink).

4327. STEWART, Randolph (1800–73), 9th E. of Galloway, M.P. Cockermouth 1826–31 (GEC; *Harrow Reg.*).

4328. STEWART, Robert (1769–1822), 2d M. of Londonderry, M.P. Tregony 1794–96, Orford 1796–97, 1821–22, Down 1801–5, 1812–21, Boroughbridge 1806–6, Plympton Erle 1806–12 (DNB; GEC).

4329. STEWART, William (1686–1768), M.P. Inverness burghs 1713–22, Ayr burghs 1722–34, Elgin burghs 1734–41 (Grant's *Faculty of Advocates*).

4330. STEWART, William, M.P. Wigtown burghs 1741–47 (*Scots Peerage* sub Galloway).

4331. STEWART, William (ca 1734–97), M.P. Wigtown burghs 1770–74, Kirkcudbright Stewarty 1774–80 (Addison's *Glasgow Matric. Albums;* Foster's *Scots M.P.'s*).

4332. STEWART, William (1774–1827), M.P. Saltash 1795–96, Wigtownshire 1796–1802, 1812–16, Wigtown burghs 1803–5 (DNB; *Scots Peerage* sub Galloway).

4333. STEWART, William (ca 1780–1850), M.P. Tyrone 1818–30 (*Alumni Oxon.;* Burke's *Irish LG*).

4334. STEWART-MACKENZIE, James Alexander (1784–1843), M.P. Rossshire 1831–37 (Ball and Venn's *Admissions to Trinity College; Scots Peerage* sub Galloway).

4335. STIRLING, Walter (1758–1832), 1st Bt, M.P. Gatton 1799–1802, St. Ives 1807–20 (GEC).

4336. STONE, Andrew (1703–73), M.P. Hastings 1741–61 (DNB; *Old Westminsters*).

4337. STOPFORD, Edward (1766–1837), M.P. Marlborough 1810–18 (*Eton Coll. Reg.*).

4338. STOPFORD, James (1731–1810), 2d E. of Courtown, M.P. Great Bedwin 1774–74, Marlborough 1780–93 (*Alumni Dublin.;* GEC).

4339. STOPFORD, James George (1765–1835), 3d E. of Courtown, M.P. Great Bedwin 1790–96, 1806–7, Linlithgow burghs 1796–1802, Dumfries burghs 1803–6, Marlborough 1807–10 (GEC; *Eton Coll. Reg.*).

4340. STOPFORD, James Thomas (1794–1858), 4th E. of Courtown, M.P. Wexford Co. 1820–30 (GEC).

4341. STOPFORD, Robert (1768–1847), M.P. Ipswich 1806–7 (DNB; *Eton Coll. Reg.*).

4342. STORER, Anthony Morris (1746–99), M.P. Carlisle 1774–80, Morpeth 1780–84 (DNB; *Eton Coll. Reg.*).

STORMONT, Vct, *see* MURRAY, William David.

STOWELL, 1st Bn, *see* SCOTT, William.

4343. STRACHEY, Henry (1736–1810), 1st Bt, M.P. Pontefract 1768–74, Bishop's Castle 1774–78, 1780–1802, Saltash 1778–80, East Grinstead 1802–7 (DNB; Holzman's *Nabobs in Eng.; Old Westminsters*).

STRADBROKE, 1st E. of, *see* ROUS, John.

STRAFFORD, E. of, *see* BYNG, George Stevens and John.

4344. STRAHAN, Andrew (ca 1749–1831), M.P. Newport (Hants) 1796–1802, Wareham 1802–7, Carlow borough 1807–12, Aldeburgh 1812–18, New Romney 1818–20 (DNB sub William Strahan; *Gent. Mag., 2, 274*).

4345. STRAHAN, William (1715–85), M.P. Malmesbury 1774–80, Wootton Bassett 1780–84 (DNB).

4346. STRANGE, James Charles Stuart (1753–1840), M.P. East Grinstead 1796–1802, Okehampton 1802–4 (Buckland, *Dict. Ind. Biog.,* addenda, p. 470).

4347. STRANGE, John (ca 1696–1754), M.P. West Looe 1737–41, Totnes 1742–54 (DNB; Cussans' *Herts, 3,* pt. 2, 90; *St. Paul's School Reg.*).

STRANGWAYS, *see* FOX-STRANGWAYS.

4348. STRANGWAYS-HORNER, Thomas (ca 1688–1741), M.P. Somerset 1713–15, 1727–41, Wells 1715–16, 1716–17 (Burke's *LG;* Hutchins' *Dorset, 2,* 667; *Harrow Reg.;* Bates Harbin).

STRATFORD, 1st Vct, *see* CANNING, Stratford.

4349. STRATFORD, Edward Augustus (ca 1734–1801), 2d E. of Aldborough, M.P. Taunton 1774–75 (DNB; GEC).

STRATHALLAN, 6th Vct, *see* DRUMMOND, James Andrew John Lawrence Charles.

STRATHMORE, 8th E. of, *see* LYON, Thomas.

4350. STRATTON, George (ca 1734–1800), M.P. Callington 1778–79, 1779–84 (Holzman's *Nabobs in Eng.*).

4351. STRATTON, Richard (ca 1705–58), M.P. Shoreham 1754–58 (Clutterbuck's *Herts, 1,* 301; *Notes and Queries, 179,* 98).

STRICKLAND, George, *see* CHOLMLEY, George.

4352. STRICKLAND, William (ca 1686–1735), 4th Bt, M.P. Malton 1708–15, Carlisle 1715–22, Scarborough 1722–35 (GEC).

4353. STRICKLAND, William (1714–88), M.P. Beverley 1741–47 (Burke's *Peerage;* Foster's *Yorkshire Pedigrees;* Musgrave's *Obituary*).

4354. STRODE, William (ca 1719–55), M.P. Reading 1740–47, 1754–55 (*Alumni Oxon.;* Musgrave's *Obituary*).

4355. STRODE, William (ca 1738–1809), M.P. Yarmouth (Hants) 1768–69 (*Alumni Oxon.;* Burke's *Peerage* sub Salisbury; Clutterbuck's *Herts, 2,* 417; *Court and City Reg.* [1769], p. 42; Cussans' *Herts, 2,* pt. 2, 270 and *3,* pt. 2, 16).

4356. STRUTT, Edward (1801–80), 1st Bn Belper, M.P. Derby borough 1830–48, Arundel 1851–52, Nottingham borough 1852–56 (DNB; GEC).

4357. STRUTT, John (ca 1727–1816), M.P. Maldon 1774–90 (*Alumni Felsted.;* GEC and Burke's *Peerage* sub Rayleigh; *Gent. Mag., 1,* 373).

4358. STRUTT, Joseph Holden (1758–1845), M.P. Maldon 1790–1826, Okehampton 1826–30 (*Alumni Felsted.; Alumni Oxon.;* Burke's *Peerage* and GEC sub Rayleigh).

4359. STUART, Andrew (d. 1801), M.P. Lanarkshire 1774–84, Weymouth and Melcombe Regis 1790–1801 (DNB).

4360. STUART, Charles (1753–1801), M.P. Bossiney 1776–90, Ayr burghs 1790–94, Poole 1796–1801 (DNB; *Scots Peerage*).

4361. STUART, Dudley Coutts (1803–54), M.P. Arundel 1830–37, Marylebone 1847–54 (DNB; *Scots Peerage*).

4362. STUART, Evelyn James (1773–1842), M.P. Cardiff 1794–1802, 1814–18 (*Eton Coll. Reg.; Scots Peerage*).

4363. STUART, Frederick (1751–1802), M.P. Ayr burghs 1776–80, Buteshire 1796–1802 (*Notes and Queries, 171,* 119; *Scots Peerage*).

STUART, Henry Villiers, see VILLIERS-STUART, Henry.

4364. STUART, James (d. 1743), M.P. Ayr burghs 1734–41 (Foster's *Scots M.P.'s*).

4365. STUART, James (d. 1833), M.P. Huntingdon borough 1824–31 (*Gent. Mag., 1,* 466).

4366. STUART, John (1744–1814), 1st M. of Bute, M.P. Bossiney 1766–76 (GEC; *Harrow Reg.*).

4367. STUART, John (1767–94), M.P. Cardiff 1790–94 (*Eton Coll. Reg.*).

4368. STUART, John (1768–91), M.P. Great Bedwin 1790–91 (*Eton Coll. Reg.;* Venn MS).

4369. STUART, John (d. 1810), 3d Bt, M.P. Kincardineshire 1797–1806 (GEC; Grant's *Faculty of Advocates*).

4370. STUART, John (1797–1867), 12th E. of Moray, M.P. Newport (Hants) 1825–26 (GEC).

4371. STUART, Patrick (ca 1684–1760), M.P. Lanarkshire 1750–54 (Foster's *Scots M.P.'s;* Musgrave's *Obituary*).

STUART, Patrick James Herbert Crichton, see CRICHTON-STUART, Patrick James Herbert.

4372. STUART, Simeon (ca 1721–79), 3d Bt, M.P. Hampshire 1761–79 (GEC; *Old Westminsters*).

4373. STUART, William (1778–1814), M.P. Cardiff 1802–14 (*Eton Coll. Reg.*).

4374. STUART, William (1798–1874), M.P. Armagh borough 1820–26, Bedfordshire 1830–31, 1832–34 (Boase).

4375. STUART-MACKENZIE, James (ca 1718–1800), M.P. Argyllshire 1742–47, Buteshire 1747–54, Ayr burghs 1754–61, Ross-shire 1761–80 (GEC sub Bute; *Eton Coll. Reg.;* Foster's *Scots M.P.'s*).

4376. STUART-WORTLEY, James Archibald (1776–1845), 1st Bn Wharn-cliffe, M.P. Bossiney 1802–18, Yorkshire 1818–26 (GEC; Gooder; *Scots Peerage*).

4377. STUART-WORTLEY, John (1773–97), M.P. Bossiney 1796–97 (*Scots Peerage*).

4378. STUART-WORTLEY-MACKENZIE, Charles (1802–44), M.P. Bossiney 1830–31 (Burke's *Peerage* sub Wharncliffe; *Harrow Reg.*).

4379. STUART-WORTLEY-MACKENZIE, James Archibald (1747–1818), M.P. Ayr burghs 1768–74, Buteshire 1774–80, 1784–90, 1806–7, Plympton Erle 1780–84, Bossiney 1790–96, 1797–1802 (*Scots Peerage*).

4380. STUART-WORTLEY-MACKENZIE, John (1801–55), 2d Bn Wharn-cliffe, M.P. Bossiney 1823–30, 1831–32, Perth burghs 1830–31, Yorkshire 1841–45 (DNB; GEC; *Harrow Reg.*).

STUART DE DECIES, 1st Bn, *see* VILLIERS-STUART, Henry.

4381. STURGES-BOURNE, William (1769–1845), M.P. Hastings 1798–1802, Christchurch 1802–12, 1818–26, Bandon 1815–18, Ashburton 1826–30, Milborne Port 1830–31 (DNB).

4382. STURT, Charles (1763–1812), M.P. Bridport 1784–1802 (Burke's *Peerage* sub Alington; *Gent. Mag., 1,* 596).

4383. STURT, Henry Charles (1795–1866), M.P. Bridport 1817–20, Dor-chester 1830–30, Dorset 1835–46 (Boase; *Harrow Reg.;* Burke's *Peerage* sub Alington).

4384. STURT, Humphrey (ca 1724–86), M.P. Dorset 1754–84 (*Alumni Oxon.;* Burke's *Peerage* sub Alington).

4385. SUCKLING, Maurice (1725–78), M.P. Portsmouth 1776–78 (DNB).

SUDELEY, Bn, *see* HANBURY-TRACY, Charles and Thomas Charles.

SUDLEY, Vct, *see* GORE, Arthur Saunders.

SUFFIELD, Bn, *see* HARBORD, Edward, Harbord, and William Asshe-ton.

SUFFOLK, 16th E. of, *see* HOWARD, Thomas.

4386. SUGDEN, Edward Burtenshaw (1781–1875), 1st Bn St. Leonards, M.P. Weymouth and Melcombe Regis 1828–31, St. Mawes 1831–32, Ripon 1837–41 (DNB; GEC).

4387. SULIVAN, Lawrence (d. 1786), M.P. Taunton 1762–68, Ashburton 1768–74 (Musgrave's *Obituary*).

4388. SULLIVAN, Henry (1785–1814), 2d Bt, M.P. Lincoln City 1812–14 (Burke's *Peerage*).

4389. SULLIVAN, John (1749–1839), M.P. Old Sarum 1790–96, Aldbor-

ough 1802–6, Ashburton 1811–18 (Burke's *Peerage; Gent. Mag.,*
1 [1840], 428; Lipscomb's *Bucks, 4,* 519).

4390. SULLIVAN, Richard Joseph (1752–1806), 1st Bt, M.P. New Romney
1787–96, Seaford 1802–6 (DNB).

SUMNER, George Holme, *see* HOLME-SUMNER, George.

SUNDON, 1st Bn, *see* CLAYTON, William.

SUNDRIDGE, 1st Bn, *see* CAMPBELL, John.

SURREY, E. of, *see* HOWARD, Charles and Henry Charles.

SUTHERLAND, D. of, *see* LEVESON-GOWER, George Granville; *also*
SUTHERLAND-LEVESON-GOWER, George Granville.

4391. SUTHERLAND-LEVESON-GOWER, George Granville (1786–1861), 2d
D. of Sutherland, M.P. St. Mawes 1808–12, Newcastle-under-
Lyme 1812–15, Staffordshire 1815–20 (GEC).

4392. SUTTIE, George (1715–83), 3d Bt, M.P. Haddingtonshire 1768–77
(GEC).

SUTTIE, James Grant, *see* GRANT-SUTTIE, James.

SUTTON, Charles Manners and George Manners, *see* MANNERS-
SUTTON, Charles and George.

4393. SUTTON, James (ca 1733–1801), M.P. Devizes 1765–80 (Waylen's
Devizes, p. 307).

SUTTON, John, *see* MANNERS-SUTTON, John.

4394. SUTTON, Richard (ca 1674–1737), M.P. Newark 1708–10, 1712–37
(Burke's *Peerage*).

4395. SUTTON, Richard (1733–1802), 1st Bt, M.P. St. Albans 1768–80,
Sandwich 1780–84, Boroughbridge 1784–96 (*Alumni Cantab.;*
GEC; *Old Westminsters*).

4396. SUTTON, Robert (ca 1671–1746), M.P. Notts 1722–32, Great
Grimsby 1734–41 (*Alumni Oxon.;* GEC sub Sunderland).

4397. SUTTON, Robert (1722–62), M.P. Notts 1747–62 (Collins' *Peerage*
and Burke's *Peerage* sub Rutland).

4398. SUTTON, Thomas (ca 1755–1813), 1st Bt, M.P. Surrey 1812–13
(*Alumni Oxon.*).

SUTTON, Thomas Manners, *see* MANNERS-SUTTON, Thomas.

4399. SWANN, Henry (d. 1824), M.P. Yarmouth (Hants) 1803–4, Penryn
1806–24 (*Gent. Mag., 2,* 185; *1812 List*).

4400. SWINBURNE, John Edward (1762–1860), 6th Bt, M.P. Launceston
1788–90 (GEC).

4401. SWYMMER, Anthony Langley (d. 1760), M.P. Southampton borough 1747–60 (Musgrave's *Obituary*).

SYDENHAM, 1st Bn, *see* POULETT-THOMSON, Charles Edward.

4402. SYDENHAM, Humphrey (ca 1695–1757), M.P. Exeter 1741–54
(*Alumni Cantab.;* Collinson's *Somerset, 3,* 524).

SYDNEY, Vct and E., *see* TOWNSHEND, John Robert, John Thomas,
and Thomas.

4403. SYKES, Christopher (1749–1801), 2d Bt, M.P. Beverley 1784–90 (GEC; Phillips' *Hist. of Banks,* p. 402).

4404. SYKES, Daniel (1766–1832), M.P. Hull 1820–30, Beverley 1830–31 (Foster's *Yorkshire Pedigrees; Gent. Mag., 1,* 178; Hunter's *Familiae Min. Gent.;* Taylor's *Biog. Leodiensis,* p. 337; *1832 List*).

4405. SYKES, Francis (1732–1804), 1st Bt, M.P. Shaftesbury 1771–75, 1780–84, Wallingford 1784–1804 (Burke's *Peerage;* GEC).

4406. SYKES, Francis William (ca 1767–1804), 2d Bt, M.P. Wallingford 1794–96 (GEC; *Eton Coll. Reg.*).

SYKES, Mark Masterman, *see* MASTERMAN-SYKES, Mark.

4407. SYMES, Michael (ca 1753–1809), M.P. Carlow borough 1806–6, Heytesbury 1807–7 (*Alumni Dublin.;* DNB).

4408. SYMMONS, John (1701–64), M.P. Cardigan borough 1746–61 (*West Wales Hist. Records,* Vol. *14, ex inform.* E. H. Stuart Jones; Williams' *Wales M.P.'s*).

4409. SYMONDS, Thomas Powell (ca 1762–1819), M.P. Hereford City 1800–19 (*Alumni Oxon.;* Burke's *LG;* Williams' *Hereford M.P.'s*).

4410. SYMONS, John (ca 1709–63), M.P. Hereford City 1754–63 (*Alumni Oxon.;* Burke's *LG;* Williams' *Hereford M.P.'s*).

4411. SYMONS, Richard (ca 1744–96), 1st Bt, M.P. Hereford City 1768–84 (GEC).

4412. TAFFE, Theobald (b. ca 1705), M.P. Arundel 1747–54 (Walpole-Montagu *Corr.* [Yale ed.]).

4413. TAIT, William (d. 1800), M.P. Stirling burghs 1797–1800 (Foster's *Scots M.P.'s;* Grant's *Faculty of Advocates; Gent. Mag., 1,* 89).

4414. TALBOT, Charles (1751–1812), 2d Bt, M.P. Weobley 1800–2, Rye 1803–6, Bletchingley 1812–12 (GEC).

TALBOT, Christopher Rice Mansel, *see* MANSEL-TALBOT, Christopher Rice.

TALBOT, George, *see* RICE, George.

TALBOT, Henry John Chetwynd, *see* CHETWYND-TALBOT, Henry John.

4415. TALBOT, John (ca 1712–56), M.P. Brecon borough 1734–54, Ilchester 1754–56 (Burke's *Peerage* sub Shrewsbury; Williams' *Wales M.P.'s* and *Great Sessions in Wales*).

4416. TALBOT, John (ca 1718–78), M.P. Marlborough 1747–54 (Burke's *LG; Old Westminsters*).

TALBOT, John Chetwynd, *see* CHETWYND-TALBOT, John.

TALBOT, John Ivory, *see* IVORY-TALBOT, John.

4417. TALBOT, Richard Wogan (ca 1766–1849), 2d Bn Talbot, M.P. Dublin Co. 1807–30 (GEC).

4418. TALBOT, Roger (1713–77), M.P. Thirsk 1754–61 (*Alumni Cantab.; Eton Coll. Reg.*).

4419. TALBOT, William (1710–82), 1st E. Talbot, M.P. Glamorgan 1734–37 (GEC; *Eton Coll. Reg.*).

4420. TALBOTT, William (ca 1776–1851), M.P. Kilkenny City 1801–1 (*Alumni Oxon.;* Burtchaell's *Kilkenny M.P.'s; Gent. Mag., 2,* 101).

TALMASH, *see* TOLLEMACHE.

4421. TALMASH, William (ca 1766–1833), 1st Bt, M.P. Ilchester 1803–4, 1806–7 (GEC sub Dysart; *Scots Peerage*).

TANKERVILLE, E. of, *see* BENNETT, Charles and Charles Augustus.

4422. TAPPS-GERVIS, George William (1795–1842), 2d Bt, M.P. New Romney 1826–30, Christchurch 1832–37 (GEC).

4423. TARLETON, Banastre (1754–1833), 1st Bt, M.P. Liverpool 1790–1806, 1807–12 (DNB).

4424. TARLETON, John (1755–1820), M.P. Seaford 1792–96 (Burke's *LG;* Hunter's *Familiae Min. Gent., 1,* 133; Omerod's *Chester, 2,* 677).

4425. TATTON, William (1774–99), M.P. Beverley 1796–99 (Burke's *LG; Alumni Oxon.;* Foster's *Lancashire Pedigrees;* Omerod's *Chester, 1,* 446).

4426. TATTON-EGERTON, William (1749–1806), M.P. Hindon 1784–90, Newcastle-under-Lyme 1792–1802, Cheshire 1802–6 (Burke's *LG;* Foster's *Lancashire Pedigrees;* Omerod's *Chester, 1,* 446).

TAUNTON, 1st Bn, *see* LABOUCHERE, Henry.

TAVISTOCK, M. of, *see* RUSSELL, Francis.

4427. TAYLOR, Charles (ca 1692–1766), M.P. Totnes 1747–54 (*Alumni Oxon.;* Musgrave's *Obituary*).

4428. TAYLOR, Charles William (1770–1857), 1st Bt, M.P. Wells 1796–1830 (*Alumni Oxon.;* Boase).

4429. TAYLOR, Clement (d. 1804), M.P. Maidstone 1780–96 (Berry's *County Geneal.: Kent,* p. 193; *Gent. Mag.,* p. 977; Namier).

4430. TAYLOR, Edward (1774–1843), M.P. Canterbury 1807–12 (*Alumni Oxon.;* Burke's *LG*).

TAYLOR, George Watson, *see* WATSON-TAYLOR, George.

4431. TAYLOR, Herbert (1775–1839), M.P. Windsor 1820–23 (DNB).

4432. TAYLOR, John (ca 1761–1820), M.P. Lymington 1814–18, Yarmouth (Hants) 1818–19 (*Annual Register,* p. 570; *Gent. Mag., 1,* 93).

4433. TAYLOR, John Bladen (1764–1820), M.P. Hythe 1818–19 (*Annual Register,* p. 579; *Notes and Queries,* 12th Ser., *2,* 456).

4434. TAYLOR, Joseph (ca 1693–1746), M.P. Ashburton 1739–41 (*Alumni Oxon.;* Devonshire Assoc. *Trans., 32,* 240).

4435. TAYLOR, Michael Angelo (ca 1757–1834), M.P. Poole 1784–90, 1791–96, 1812–18, Heytesbury 1790–91, Aldborough 1796–1800, Durham City 1800–2, 1818–31, Rye 1806–7, Ilchester 1807–12, Sudbury 1832–34 (DNB; *Old Westminsters*).

4436. TAYLOR, Peter (1714–77), M.P. Wells 1765–66, Portsmouth 1774–77 (*Gent. Mag., 2* [1800], 731).

4437. TAYLOR, Robert Paris (ca 1736–92), M.P. Berwick-on-Tweed 1768–74 (Bean; Musgrave's *Obituary*).

4438. TAYLOR, William (ca. 1697–1741), M.P. Evesham 1734–41 (*Alumni Oxon.;* Williams' *Worcester M.P.'s*).

4439. TAYLOR, William (ca 1754–1825), M.P. Leominster 1797–1802, Barnstable 1806–12 (Williams' *Hereford M.P.'s*).

4440. TAYLOUR, Thomas (1787–1870), 2d M. of Headfort, M.P. Meath 1812–29 (GEC).

4441. TEED, John, M.P. Grampound 1808–8, 1812–18.

4442. TELFER-SMOLLETT, Alexander (d. 1799), M.P. Dumbartonshire 1797–99 (Burke's *LG;* Foster's *Scots M.P.'s*).

TEMPEST, Henry Vane, *see* VANE-TEMPEST, Henry.

4443. TEMPEST, John (1710–76), M.P. Durham City 1742–68 (*Alumni Cantab.; Six North Country Diaries* [Surtees Soc.], 174 n.).

4444. TEMPEST, John (ca 1742–94), M.P. Durham City 1768–94 (*Old Westminsters*).

TEMPLE, E., *see* GRENVILLE-TEMPLE, NUGENT-TEMPLE-GRENVILLE, and TEMPLE-NUGENT-BRYDGES-CHANDOS-GRENVILLE.

4445. TEMPLE, Henry (ca 1673–1757), 1st Vct Palmerston, M.P. East Grinstead 1727–34, Bossiney 1734–41, Weobley 1741–47 (*Alumni Cantab.;* DNB; GEC; *Eton Coll. Reg.*).

4446. TEMPLE, Henry (1739–1802), 2d Vct Palmerston, M.P. East Looe 1762–68, Southampton borough 1768–74, Hastings 1774–84, Boroughbridge 1784–90, Newport (Hants) 1790–96, Winchester 1796–1802 (DNB; GEC).

4447. TEMPLE, Henry John (1784–1865), 3d Vct Palmerston, M.P. Newport (Hants) 1807–11, Cambridge Univ. 1811–31, Bletchingley 1831–32, South Hampshire 1832–34, Tiverton 1835–65 (DNB; GEC).

4448. TEMPLE, Richard (ca 1726–49), M.P. Downton 1747–49 (*Alumni Cantab.*).

4449. TEMPLE-NUGENT-BRYDGES-CHANDOS-GRENVILLE, Richard (1776–1839), 1st D. of Buckingham and Chandos, M.P. Bucks 1797–1813 (DNB; GEC).

4450. TEMPLE-NUGENT-BRYDGES-CHANDOS-GRENVILLE, Richard Plantagenet (1797–1861), 2d D. of Buckingham and Chandos, M.P. Bucks 1818–39 (DNB; GEC).

TEMPLEMORE, 1st Bn, *see* CHICHESTER, Arthur.

4451. TEMPLER, George (ca 1755–1819), M.P. Honiton 1790–96 (*Old Westminsters*).

TEMPLETOWN, 1st Vct, *see* UPTON, John Henry.

4452. TENNANT, Charles (1796–1873), M.P. St. Albans 1830–31 (Boase; *Harrow Reg.; 1832 List*).

4453. TENNYSON, George (1750–1835), M.P. Bletchingley 1818–19 (Burke's *Peerage; Genealogist*, N.S., *23*, 82).

4454. TENNYSON-D'EYNCOURT, Charles (1784–1861), M.P. Great Grimsby 1818–26, Bletchingley 1826–31, Stamford 1831–32, Lambeth 1832–52 (*Admissions to St. John, Cambridge;* DNB).

THANET, 11th E. of, *see* TUFTON, Henry.

4455. THELLUSSON, Charles (1770–1815), M.P. Evesham 1796–1806 (Agnew's *Protestant Exiles, 3,* 246; Burke's *Peerage* sub Rendlesham; *Harrow Reg.*).

4456. THELLUSSON, George Woodford (1764–1811), M.P. Southwark 1796–96, Tregony 1804–6, Barnstable 1807–11 (Agnew's *Protestant Exiles, 3,* 246; Burke's *Peerage* sub Rendlesham; *Harrow Reg.;* Hunter's *Deanery of Doncaster, 1,* 318; *Western Antiquary, 6,* 31).

4457. THELLUSSON, Peter Isaac (1761–1808), 1st Bn Rendlesham, M.P. Midhurst 1795–96, Malmesbury 1796–1802, Castle Rising 1802–6, Bossiney 1807–8 (GEC; *Harrow Reg.*).

4458. THICKNESSE, Ralph (ca 1768–1842), M.P. Wigan 1831–34 (Burke's *LG; Gent. Mag.,* 1 [.1843], 657; MS, *ex inform.* W. A. Cowen).

4459. THISTLETHWAYTE, Alexander (ca 1718–71), M.P. Hampshire 1751–61 (Burke's *LG;* Hutchins' *Dorset, 2,* 294).

THISTLETHWAYTE, Francis, *see* WHITHEAD, Francis.

4460. THISTLETHWAYTE, Robert (1755–1802), M.P. Hampshire 1780–90 (*Alumni Oxon.;* Burke's *LG;* Hutchins' *Dorset, 2,* 294).

4461. THISTLETHWAYTE, Thomas (1779–1850), M.P. Hampshire 1806–7 (*Alumni Oxon.;* Burke's *LG;* Hutchins' *Dorset, 2,* 294).

4462. THOMAS, Edmond (1712–67), 3d Bt, M.P. Chippenham 1741–54, Glamorgan 1761–67 (GEC; *Old Westminsters*).

4463. THOMAS, George (ca 1740–1815), 3d Bt, M.P. Arundel 1790–97 (GEC; *Eton Coll. Reg.;* Oliver's *Antigua, 3,* 132; Venn MS).

THOMAS, George White, *see* WHITE-THOMAS, George.

4464. THOMAS, Inigo (ca 1766–1847), M.P. Weobley 1796–1800 (*Alumni Oxon.;* Oliver's *Antigua, 1,* 260; Williams' *Hereford M.P.'s*).

THOMLINSON, John, *see* TOMLINSON, John.

THOMOND, 1st M. of, *see* O'BRIEN, Murrough.

4465. THOMPSON, Beilby (1742–99), M.P. Hedon 1768–80, 1790–96, Thirsk 1780–84 (Hunter's *Familiae Min. Gent.;* Peile's *Biog. Reg. of Christ's College*).

4466. THOMPSON, Charles (ca 1740–99), 1st Bt, M.P. Monmouth borough 1796–99 (DNB; GEC).

THOMPSON, Charles Hotham, *see* HOTHAM, Charles.

THOMPSON, Charles Poulett, *see* POULETT-THOMSON, Charles Edward.

4467. THOMPSON, Edward (1697–1742), M.P. York City 1722–42

(*Alumni Oxon.;* Foster's *Yorkshire Pedigrees;* Hunter's *Familiae Min. Gent.*).

THOMPSON, George, *see* FINCH, George.

4468. THOMPSON, George Lowther (1786–1841), M.P. Haslemere 1823–30, Yarmouth (Hants) 1830–31 (Burke's *LG* [ed. 1853]; *Harrow Reg.*).

THOMPSON, Paul Beilby, *see* LAWLEY-THOMPSON, Paul Beilby.

4469. THOMPSON, Peter (1698–1770), M.P. St. Albans 1747–54 (Nichols' *Lit. Anec., 5,* 511; Sydenham's *Poole,* p. 317).

4470. THOMPSON, Thomas (ca 1768–1818), M.P. Evesham 1790–1802 (Williams' *Worcester M.P.'s;* Venn MS).

4471. THOMPSON, Thomas (1754–1828), M.P. Midhurst 1807–18 (*Genealogist,* N.S., *13,* 43).

4472. THOMPSON, Thomas Boulden (1766–1828), 1st Bt, M.P. Rochester 1807–16 (DNB; Foster's *Yorkshire Pedigrees*).

4473. THOMPSON, William (ca 1680–1744), M.P. Scarborough 1701–22, 1730–44 (*Alumni Oxon.;* Foster's *Yorkshire Pedigrees*).

4474. THOMPSON, William (ca 1792–1854), M.P. Callington 1820–26, London 1826–32, Sunderland 1833–41, Westmorland 1841–54 (*Herald and Genealogist, 5,* 491; *Notes and Queries, 179,* 168).

THOMSON, Charles Edward Poulett, *see* POULETT-THOMSON, Charles Edward.

THORNE, Patrick, *see* HOME, Patrick.

THORNHAGH, John, *see* HEWITT, John.

4475. THORNTON, Henry (1760–1815), M.P. Southwark 1782–1815 (DNB).

4476. THORNTON, Robert (1759–1826), M.P. Bridgwater 1785–90, Colchester 1790–1817 (Burke's *LG;* Philips' *East India Co.,* p. 337).

4477. THORNTON, Samuel (1754–1838), M.P. Hull 1784–1806, Surrey 1807–12, 1813–18 (Burke's *LG;* DNB; Hunter's *Familiae Min. Gent.*).

THORNTON, William, *see* ASTELL, William.

4478. THORNTON, William (ca 1713–69), M.P. York City 1747–54, 1758–61 (*Alumni Cantab.*).

4479. THORNTON, William (1763–1841), M.P. Woodstock 1812–13, 1814–18 (Baker's *Northampton, 1,* 115; Barron's *Northampton Families,* p. 307; Burke's *LG; Notes and Queries,* 5th Ser., *1,* 355).

4480. THOROLD, John (1734–1815), 9th Bt, M.P. Lincolnshire 1779–96 (*Alumni Oxon.;* GEC).

4481. THOROTON, Thomas (ca 1753–1814), M.P. Grantham 1802–12 (*Gent. Mag., 1,* 203).

4482. THOROTON, Thomas (ca 1723–94), M.P. Boroughbridge 1757–61, Newark 1761–68, Bramber 1769–82 (*Alumni Cantab.;* DNB; *Old Westminsters*).

4483. THORP, John Thomas (d. 1835), M.P. London 1818–20 (Beaven's *Aldermen of London; Gent. Mag., 1* [1836], 210).

4484. THRALE, Henry (ca 1729–81), M.P. Southwark 1765–80 (DNB sub Piozzi; Clifford's *Piozzi*, p. 34; Manning and Bray's *Surrey, 3, 391*).

4485. THRALE, Ralph (ca 1698–1758), M.P. Southwark 1741–47 (Clifford's *Piozzi*, p. 34; Manning and Bray's *Surrey, 3, 392*).

4486. THROCKMORTON, Robert George (1800–62), 8th Bt, M.P. Berks 1831–34 (GEC).

4487. THURLOW, Edward (1731–1806), 1st Bn Thurlow, M.P. Tamworth 1765–78 (*Alumni Cantab.;* DNB; GEC; Wedgwood).

THURSBY, John Harvey, *see* HARVEY-THURSBY, John.

4488. THYNNE, Edward (1807–84), M.P. Weobley 1831–32, Frome 1859–65 (*Alumni Oxon.;* Burke's *Peerage* sub Bath; Williams' *Hereford M.P.'s*).

4489. THYNNE, George (1770–1838), 2d Bn Carteret, M.P. Weobley 1790–1812 (*Admissions to St. John, Cambridge;* GEC).

THYNNE, Henry Frederick, *see* CARTERET, Henry Frederick.

4490. THYNNE, Henry Frederick (1797–1837), 3d M. of Bath, M.P. Weobley 1824–26, 1828–32 (GEC).

4491. THYNNE, John (1772–1849), 3d Bn Carteret, M.P. Weobley 1796–96, Bath 1796–1805, 1805–32 (*Admissions to St. John, Cambridge;* GEC).

4492. THYNNE, Thomas (1765–1837), 2d M. of Bath, M.P. Weobley 1786–90, Bath 1790–96 (*Admissions to St. John, Cambridge;* GEC).

4493. THYNNE, Thomas (1796–1837), M.P. Weobley 1818–20 (GEC sub Bath).

4494. THYNNE, William (1803–90), M.P. Weobley 1826–31 (Burke's *Peerage* sub Bath; Boase; Williams' *Hereford M.P.'s*).

4495. TIERNEY, George (1761–1830), M.P. Colchester 1789–90, Southwark 1796–1806, Athlone 1806–7, Bandon 1807–12, Appleby 1812–18, Knaresborough 1818–30 (DNB; *Eton Coll. Reg.*).

4496. TIGHE, William (ca 1766–1816), M.P. Wicklow 1806–16 (Burtchaell's *Kilkenny M.P.'s;* Burke's *Irish LG; Eton Coll. Reg.*).

4497. TINDAL, Nicolas Conyngham (1776–1846), M.P. Wigtown burghs 1824–26, Harwich 1826–27, Cambridge Univ. 1827–29 (DNB).

TITCHFIELD, M. of, *see* CAVENDISH-BENTINCK and CAVENDISH-SCOTT-BENTINCK.

4498. TOLLEMACHE, Felix Thomas (ca 1796–1843), M.P. Ilchester 1827–30 (Burke's *Peerage* sub Dysart; *Harrow Reg.*).

4499. TOLLEMACHE, Frederick James (1804–88), M.P. Grantham 1826–30, 1837–52, 1857–65, 1868–74 (Boase; Burke's *Peerage* sub Dysart; *Harrow Reg.*).

4500. TOLLEMACHE, Lionel William John (1794–1878), 8th E. of Dysart, M.P. Ilchester 1827–30 (GEC; Harrow Reg.).

4501. TOLLEMACHE, Wilbraham (1739–1821), 6th E. of Dysart, M.P. Northampton borough 1771–80, Liskeard 1780–84 (GEC).

TOLLEMACHE, William, see TALMASH, William.

4502. TOMES, John (ca 1761–1844), M.P. Warwick borough 1826–32 (*Gent. Mag., 2,* 94).

4503. TOMLINE, William Edward (1787–1836), M.P. Christchurch 1812–18, Truro 1818–20, 1826–29, Minehead 1830–31 (Burke's *LG*).

4504. TOMLINSON, John (ca 1731–67), M.P. Steyning 1761–67 (*Alumni Cantab.*).

TOMPSON, Charles, see THOMPSON, Charles.

4505. TONSON, Richard (d. 1772), M.P. Wallingford 1747–54, Windsor 1768–72 (DNB).

TOOKE, John Horne, see HORNE-TOOKE, John.

4506. TOPPING, James (1756–1821), M.P. Bodmin 1806–6, Thirsk 1806–7 (Omerod's *Chester, 3,* 244).

4507. TORRENS, Robert (ca 1780–1864), M.P. Ipswich 1826–27, Ashburton 1831–32, Bolton 1832–34 (DNB).

4508. TOTTENHAM, Charles (1743–1823), M.P. New Ross 1802–5 (*Alumni Dublin.;* Burke's *Irish LG*).

4509. TOTTENHAM, Charles (1807–86), M.P. New Ross 1831–31, 1856–63 (Burke's *Irish LG;* Venn MS).

4510. TOTTENHAM, Ponsonby (ca 1746–1818), M.P. Wexford town 1801–2, New Ross 1805–6 (Burke's *Irish LG*).

4511. TOUCHET, Samuel (d. 1773), M.P. Shaftesbury 1761–68 (Musgrave's *Obituary*).

4512. TOWER, Alexander (d. 1813), M.P. Berwick-on-Tweed 1806–7 (*Archaeol. Aeliana,* 4th Ser., *24*).

4513. TOWER, Christopher (ca 1692–1771), M.P. Lancaster borough 1727–34, Aylesbury 1734–41, Bossiney 1741–42 (*Alumni Oxon.;* Burke's *LG;* Lipscomb's *Bucks, 4,* 530; *Notes and Queries, 179,* 96; Pink).

4514. TOWER, Thomas (ca 1699–1778), M.P. Wareham 1729–34, Wallingford 1734–41 (*Alumni Oxon.;* Burke's *LG*).

4515. TOWNLEY, Richard Greaves (1786–1855), M.P. Cambridgeshire 1831–41, 1847–52 (Burke's *LG;* Boase; *Eton Lists;* Foster's *Lancashire Pedigrees; Linc. Inn Reg.*).

4516. TOWNSEND, Chauncy (1707–70), M.P. Westbury 1748–68, Wigtown burghs 1768–70 (Foster's *Scots M.P.'s; Misc. Geneal. et Herald.,* N.S., *3* and *4; Parish Reg. St. Christopher le Stocks, London,* p. 37).

4517. TOWNSEND, Isaac (ca 1685–1765), M.P. Portsmouth 1744–54, Rochester 1757–65 (DNB; Smith's *Rochester in Parl.*).

4518. TOWNSEND, James (1737–87), M.P. West Looe 1767–74, Calne

1782–87 (*Alumni Oxon.;* Beaven's *Aldermen of London; Notes and Queries,* 11th Ser., *5*, 2).

4519. TOWNSEND, Joseph, M.P. Wallingford 1740–41, 1747–54, Westbury 1741–47 (*Admissions to St. John, Cambridge* sub Gore Townsend; Burke's *LG* [ed. 1849]).

4520. TOWNSEND-FARQUHAR, Robert Townsend (1776–1830), 1st Bt, M.P. Newton 1825–26, Hythe 1826–30 (DNB; *Old Westminsters*).

4521. TOWNSHEND, Charles (1725–67), M.P. Great Yarmouth 1747–56, Harwich 1761–67, Saltash 1756–61 (*Alumni Cantab.;* DNB).

4522. TOWNSHEND, Charles (1728–1810), 1st Bn Bayning, M.P. Great Yarmouth 1756–84, 1790–96 (*Alumni Cantab.;* DNB; GEC; *Eton Coll. Reg.*).

TOWNSHEND, Charles Frederick, *see* POWLETT, Charles Frederick.

4523. TOWNSHEND, Charles Patrick Thomas (1768–96), M.P. Great Yarmouth 1796–96 (Burke's *Peerage*).

4524. TOWNSHEND, Charles Vere Ferrers (1785–1853), M.P. Tamworth 1812–18, 1820–34 (Burke's *Peerage; Harrow Reg.*).

TOWNSHEND, Chauncy, *see* TOWNSEND, Chauncy.

4525. TOWNSHEND, George (1724–1807), 1st M. Townshend, M.P. Norfolk 1747–64 (*Alumni Cantab.;* DNB; GEC; *Eton Coll. Reg.*).

4526. TOWNSHEND, Henry (ca 1736–62), M.P. Eye 1758–60, 1761–62 (Collins' *Peerage* sub Sydney; Musgrave's *Obituary;* Venn MS).

4527. TOWNSHEND, Horatio George Powys (1780–1843), M.P. Whitchurch 1816–26, 1831–32 (*Eton Coll. Reg.*).

TOWNSHEND, James, *see* TOWNSEND, James.

4528. TOWNSHEND, James Nugent Boyle Bernardo (1785–1842), M.P. Helston 1818–32, 1835–37 (Burke's *Peerage;* Clutterbuck's *Herts, 2,* 187; *Eton Lists; Harrow Reg.*).

4529. TOWNSHEND, John (1757–1833), M.P. Cambridge Univ. 1780–84, Westminster 1788–90, Knaresborough 1793–1818 (*Eton Coll. Reg.; Admissions to St. John, Cambridge*).

4530. TOWNSHEND, John Robert (1805–90), 1st E. Sydney, M.P. Whitchurch 1826–31 (GEC).

4531. TOWNSHEND, John Thomas (1764–1831), 2d Vct Sydney, M.P. Newport (Hants) 1786–89, Whitchurch 1790–1800 (GEC; *Eton Coll. Reg.*).

4532. TOWNSHEND, Roger (1708–60), M.P. Great Yarmouth 1738–47, Eye 1747–48 (DNB; GEC; *Eton Coll. Reg.*).

4533. TOWNSHEND, Thomas (1701–80), M.P. Winchelsea 1722–27, Cambridge Univ. 1727–74 (*Alumni Cantab.;* DNB; *Eton Coll. Reg.*).

4534. TOWNSHEND, Thomas (1733–1800), 1st Vct Sydney, M.P. Whitchurch 1754–83 (*Alumni Cantab.;* DNB; GEC; *Eton Coll. Reg.*).

4535. TOWNSHEND, William (ca 1702–38), M.P. Great Yarmouth 1723–38 (DNB).

4536. TOWNSHEND, William Augustus (1776–1816), M.P. Whitchurch 1800–16 (*Eton Coll. Reg.*).

4537. TOWNSON, John (ca 1725–97), M.P. Milborne Port 1780–87 (*Gent. Mag., 1,* 261; Intro. to R. Churton, *The Works of the Reverend Thomas Townshend;* Namier).

TRACY, Charles Hanbury, *see* HANBURY-TRACY, Charles.

4538. TRACY, Robert (ca 1706–67), M.P. Tewkesbury 1734–41, Worcester City 1748–54 (*Alumni Oxon.;* Musgrave's *Obituary;* Williams' *Gloucester M.P.'s*).

4539. TRACY, Thomas (d. 1770), M.P. Gloucestershire 1763–70 (Williams' *Gloucester M.P.'s*).

TRACY, Thomas Charles Hanbury, *see* HANBURY-TRACY, Thomas Charles.

4540. TRACY-KECK, Anthony (d. 1767), M.P. Woodstock 1753–67 (*Eng. Hist. Rev., 42* [1927], 412).

4541. TRAIL, Henry (ca 1755–1835), M.P. Weymouth and Melcombe Regis 1812–13 (*Gent. Mag., 1,* 331; *Notes and Queries,* 12th Ser., *2,* 297).

4542. TRAIL, James (1750–1808), M.P. Orford 1802–6 (Addison's *Glasgow Matric. Albums*).

4543. TRAILL, George (ca 1789–1871), M.P. Orkney and Shetland 1830–34, Caithness-shire 1841–69 (Boase; Burke's *LG;* Foster's *Scots M.P.'s; Old Westminsters*).

4544. TRANT, William Henry (ca 1782–1859), M.P. Okehampton 1824–26, 1831–31, Dover 1828–30 (Burke's *Irish LG; Eton Coll. Reg.*).

4545. TREBY, George (ca 1684–1742), M.P. Plympton Erle 1708–22, Dartmouth 1722–42 (*Alumni Oxon.;* Burke's *LG* [ed. 1849]).

4546. TREBY, George (ca 1726–61), M.P. Plympton Erle 1747–61 (*Alumni Oxon.;* Burke's *LG* [ed. 1849]).

4547. TREBY, George Hele (d. 1763), M.P. Plympton Erle 1761–63 (Burke's *LG* [ed. 1849]).

4548. TREBY, Paul Treby (1758–1832), M.P. Plympton Erle 1784–84 (Burke's *LG* [ed. 1849]; *Eton Coll. Reg.*).

4549. TRECOTHICK, Barlow (ca 1719–75), M.P. London 1768–74 (Beaven's *Aldermen of London; Notes and Queries,* 11th Ser., *3,* 330).

TREDEGAR, 1st Bn, *see* MORGAN, Charles Morgan Robinson.

4550. TREFUSIS, Charles Rodolph (1791–1866), 19th Bn Clinton, M.P. Callington 1813–18 (GEC).

4551. TREFUSIS, Robert (1708–42), M.P. Truro 1734–41 (*Alumni Cantab.;* GEC sub Clinton; Boase and Courtney's *Biblio. Cornub.*).

4552. TREFUSIS, Thomas (1687–1754), M.P. Grampound 1739–41 (Boase and Courtney's *Biblio. Cornub.;* Vivian's *Visitation of Cornwall,* p. 568).

4553. TREISE, Christopher (1728–80), M.P. Bodmin 1762–68 (*Alumni Oxon.;* Maclean's *Trigg Minor, 1,* 83).

4554. TRELAWNY, Charles (ca 1706–64), M.P. Liskeard 1740–54 (*Old Westminsters*).

4555. TRELAWNY, Edward (1699–1754), M.P. West Looe 1724–32, East Looe 1734–35 (DNB; Boase and Courtney's *Biblio. Cornub.;* Old *Westminsters*).

4556. TRELAWNY, William (ca 1723–72), 6th Bt, M.P. West Looe 1757–67 (DNB; GEC; Boase and Courtney's *Biblio. Cornub.;* Old *Westminsters*).

4557. TRELAWNY-BRERETON, Charles (ca 1757–1820), M.P. St. Michael 1808–9, 1814–14 (Boase and Courtney's *Biblio. Cornub.;* Burke's *LG; Old Westminsters*).

4558. TREMAYNE, John Hearle (1780–1851), M.P. Cornwall 1806–26 (*Alumni Oxon.;* Burke's *LG; Eton Lists*).

4559. TRENCH, Frederick (1755–1840), 1st Bn Ashtown, M.P. Portarlington 1801–1 (*Alumni Dublin.;* GEC).

4560. TRENCH, Frederick William (ca 1775–1859), M.P. St. Michael 1806–7, Dundalk 1812–12, Cambridge borough 1819–32, Scarborough 1835–47 (*Alumni Dublin.;* DNB).

4561. TRENCH, Richard Le Poer (1767–1837), 2d E. of Clancarty, M.P. Galway Co. 1801–5, Rye 1807–7 (DNB; GEC).

4562. TRENCHARD, George (ca 1684–1758), M.P. Poole 1713–41, 1747–54 (*Alumni Cantab.;* Burke's *LG;* Sydenham's *Poole,* p. 284).

TRENTHAM, Vct, *see* LEVESON-GOWER, Granville.

4563. TREVANION, John (d. 1810), M.P. Dover 1774–84, 1789–1806 (Boase and Courtney's *Biblio. Cornub.;* Jones' *Annals of Dover,* p. 391).

TREVANION, John Trevanion Purnell Bettesworth, *see* BETTESWORTH-TREVANION, John Trevanion Purnell.

4564. TREVANION, William (1728–67), M.P. Tregony 1747–67 (Boase and Courtney's *Biblio. Cornub.; Etoη Coll. Reg.*).

4565. TREVELYAN, John (1735–1828), 4th Bt, M.P. Newcastle-upon-Tyne 1777–80, Somerset 1780–96 (*Alumni Oxon.;* GEC).

TREVOR, Arthur Hill, *see* HILL-TREVOR, Arthur.

TREVOR, George Rice, *see* RICE-TREVOR, George.

4566. TREVOR, John (ca 1717–43), M.P. Lewes 1738–43 (*Eton Coll. Reg.*).

4567. TREVOR, John (1695–1764), 3d Bn Trevor, M.P. Woodstock 1746–53 (*Alumni Cantab.;* GEC).

TREVOR, Thomas, *see* HAMPDEN, Thomas.

4568. TRIST, Browse (ca 1698–1777), M.P. Totnes 1754–63 (*Alumni Oxon.;* Burke's *LG;* Devonshire Assoc. *Trans., 32,* 466).

4569. Trotman, Fiennes (ca 1752–1823), M.P. Northampton borough 1784–90 (*Gloucestershire Notes and Queries, 5* [1891–93], 337).

Trotter, Edward Southwell, *see* Ruthven, Edward Southwell.

4570. Troubridge, Edward Thomas (ca 1787–1852), 2d Bt, M.P. Sandwich 1831–47 (DNB; GEC).

4571. Troubridge, Thomas (ca 1758–1807), 1st Bt, M.P. Great Yarmouth 1802–6 (DNB; GEC).

Truro, 1st Bn, *see* Wilde, Thomas.

4572. Tucker, Edward (d. 1739), M.P. Weymouth and Melcombe Regis 1727–37 (Musgrave's *Obituary*).

4573. Tucker, John (ca 1713–79), M.P. Weymouth and Melcombe Regis 1735–47, 1754–78 (*Alumni Oxon.;* Musgrave's *Obituary*).

4574. Tuckfield, John (ca 1719–67), M.P. Exeter 1747–67 (Devonshire Assoc. *Trans., 62,* 214).

4575. Tuckfield, Roger (ca 1685–1739), M.P. Ashburton 1708–11, 1713–39 (*Alumni Oxon.;* Devonshire Assoc. *Trans., 62,* 214).

4576. Tudor, George (1792–1857), M.P. Barnstable 1830–31 (*Misc. Geneal. et Herald.,* 3d Ser., *1,* 22).

4577. Tudway, Charles (1713–70), M.P. Wells 1754–61 (Oliver's *Antigua, 3,* 148).

4578. Tudway, Clement (1734–1815), M.P. Wells 1761–1815 (*Alumni Oxon.;* Burke's *LG;* Oliver's *Antigua, 3,* 148).

4579. Tudway, John Payne (1775–1835), M.P. Wells 1815–30 (*Alumni Oxon.;* Burke's *LG;* Oliver's *Antigua, 3,* 148).

4580. Tufnell, George Foster (ca 1723–98), M.P. Beverley 1761–68, 1774–80 (Burke's *LG; Gent. Mag., 2,* 635).

4581. Tufnell, John Jolliffe (ca 1720–94), M.P. Beverley 1754–61 (*Alumni Cantab.;* Burke's *LG; Essex Review, 34,* 34).

4582. Tufnell, Samuel (ca 1682–1758), M.P. Colchester 1727–34, Great Marlow 1741–47 (Burke's *LG; Essex Review, 34,* 34; Williamson's *Middle Temple Bench Book*).

4583. Tufnell, William (ca 1769–1809), M.P. Colchester 1806–7 (Burke's *LG; Essex Review, 8,* 235; Venn MS).

4584. Tufton, Henry (1775–1849), 11th E. of Thanet, M.P. Rochester 1796–1802, Appleby 1826–32 (GEC; *Old Westminsters*).

4585. Tufton, John (1773–99), M.P. Appleby 1796–99 (GEC sub Thanet; *Old Westminsters*).

4586. Tuite, Hugh Morgan (ca 1795–1868), M.P. Westmeath 1826–30, 1841–47 (*Alumni Oxon.;* Burke's *Peerage;* Boase).

4587. Tulk, Charles Augustus (1786–1849), M.P. Sudbury 1820–26, Poole 1835–37 (DNB; *Old Westminsters*).

Tullamore, Bn, *see* Bury, Charles William.

4588. Tunno, Edward Rose (ca 1795–1863), M.P. Bossiney 1826–32 (Ball and Venn's *Admissions to Trinity College;* Boase; *Harrow Reg.; Linc. Inn Reg.*).

4589. TURBERVILL, Richard (ca 1707–71), M.P. Glamorgan 1767–68 (Burke's *LG;* Williams' *Wales M.P.'s*).

4590. TURNER, Barnard (ca 1736–84), M.P. Southwark 1784–84 (Beaven's *Aldermen of London;* Clutterbuck's *Herts, 3,* 592; *Gent. Mag.,* p. 477).

4591. TURNER, Charles (1666–1738), 1st Bt, M.P. Lynn 1695–1738 (*Alumni Cantab.;* GEC; Carthew's *Launditch, 3,* 129).

4592. TURNER, Charles (ca 1726–83), 1st Bt, M.P. York City 1768–83 (*Alumni Cantab.;* GEC).

4593. TURNER, Charles (1773–1810), 2d Bt, M.P. Hull 1796–1802 (GEC).

4594. TURNER, Cholmley (1685–1757), M.P. Northallerton 1715–22, Yorkshire 1727–41, 1742–47 (Gooder).

4595. TURNER, Edward (1719–66), 2d Bt, M.P. Great Bedwin 1741–47, Oxfordshire 1755–61, Penryn 1761–66 (GEC; *Eton Coll. Reg.*).

TURNER, Gregory Page, *see* PAGE-TURNER, Gregory.

4596. TURNER, John (1712–80), 3d Bt, M.P. Lynn 1739–74 (GEC; *Alumni Cantab.*).

TURNER, John Frewen, *see* FREWEN-TURNER, John.

4597. TURNER, William Horsemonden (d. 1753), M.P. Maidstone 1734–41, 1747–53 (Musgrave's *Obituary; Notes and Queries,* 12th Ser., *2,* 297).

4598. TURNOR, Edmund (ca 1755–1829), M.P. Midhurst 1802–6 (DNB; *Linc. Inn Reg.*).

TURNOUR, Edward, *see* GARTH-TURNOUR, Edward.

4599. TURTON, Edmund (1796–1857), M.P. Hedon 1818–20 (*Alumni Oxon.;* Burke's *LG*).

4600. TURTON, Thomas (1764–1844), 1st Bt, M.P. Southwark 1806–12 (GEC; *St. Paul's School Reg.*).

4601. TWISDEN, Roger (ca 1705–72), 5th Bt, M.P. Kent 1741–54 (*Alumni Oxon.;* GEC).

4602. TWISS, Horace (ca 1787–1849), M.P. Wootton Bassett 1820–30, Newport (Hants) 1830–31, Bridport 1835–37 (DNB).

TYLNEY, John Child, *see* CHILD-TYLNEY, John.

4603. TYLNEY-LONG, James (ca 1736–94), 7th Bt, M.P. Marlborough 1762–80, Devizes 1780–88, Wilts 1788–94 (GEC; *Old Westminsters*).

TYLNEY-LONG-WELLESLEY, *see* POLE-TYLNEY-LONG-WELLESLEY.

TYNTE, *see* KEMEYS-TYNTE.

TYRCONNEL, E. of, *see* CARPENTER, George.

TYRCONNEL, 1st Vct, *see* BROWNLOW, John.

4604. TYRELL, Charles (ca 1776–1872), M.P. Suffolk 1830–32, West Suffolk 1832–34 (*Misc. Geneal. et Herald.,* 4th Ser., *1;* Boase).

4605. TYRREL, James (ca 1674–1742), M.P. Boroughbridge 1722–42 (Bean; Lipscomb's *Buck's, 1,* 363; Musgrave's *Obituary*).

4606. TYRRELL, John Tyssen (1795–1877), 2d Bt, M.P. Essex 1830–31, North Essex 1832–57 (*Alumni Felsted.;* Ball and Venn's *Admissions to Trinity College;* Chancellor's *Essex Monuments,* p. 172).

4607. TYRWHITT, John de la Fountain (1708–60), 6th Bt. M.P. Lincoln City 1741–47 (GEC; *Eton Coll. Reg.*).

TYRWHITT, Thomas, *see* JONES, Thomas.

4608. TYRWHITT, Thomas (ca 1763–1833), M.P. Okehampton 1796–1802, Portarlington 1802–6, Plymouth 1806–12 (*Eton Coll. Reg.*).

4609. TYRWHITT-DRAKE, Thomas (1749–1810), M.P. Agmondesham 1795–1810 (Burke's *LG;* Clutterbuck's *Herts, 1,* 515; *Old Westminsters*).

4610. TYRWHITT-DRAKE, Thomas (1783–1852), M.P. Agmondesham 1805–32 (*Old Wesminsters*).

4611. TYRWHITT-DRAKE, William (1785–1848), M.P. Agmondesham 1810–32 (*Old Westminsters*).

4612. TYRWHITT-JONES, Thomas John (1793–1839), 2d Bt, M.P. Bridgnorth 1818–20 (*Alumni Oxon.;* Burke's *Peerage; Eton Lists;* Shrop. Archaeol. Soc. *Trans.,* 4th Ser., *5,* 71).

4613. UNIACKE-FITZGERALD, Robert (ca 1751–1814), M.P. Cork Co. 1801–6 (Burke's *Peerage; Cork Archaeol. Jour.* [1895], p. 327).

UPPER OSSORY, E. of, *see* FITZPATRICK, John.

4614. UPTON, Arthur Percy (1777–1855), M.P. Bury 1818–26 (*Old Westminsters*).

UPTON, Fulke Greville, *see* HOWARD, Fulke Greville.

4615. UPTON, John (b. ca 1715), M.P. Westmorland 1761–68 (*Alumni Cantab.; Eton Coll. Reg.; Misc. Geneal. et Herald.,* 2d Ser., *4,* 75).

4616. UPTON, John Henry (1771–1846), 2d Bn Templetown, M.P. Bury 1803–12 (GEC; *Eton Coll. Reg.*).

4617. URE, Masterton (ca 1776–1863), M.P. Weymouth and Melcombe Regis 1813–32 (Addison's *Glasgow Matric. Albums;* Burke's *LG* [ed. 1849]; Boase; *1832 List*).

4618. URQUHART, Duncan (d. 1742), M.P. Inverness burghs 1737–41 (Foster's *Scots M.P.'s;* H. Tayler, *Urquhart Family,* p. 235).

UXBRIDGE, E. of, *see* PAGET, Henry.

VALENTIA, Vct, *see* ANNESLEY, George.

VALLETORT, Vct, *see* EDGCUMBE, Ernest Augustus and William Richard.

4619. VAN, Charles (d. 1778), M.P. Brecon borough 1772–78 (Williams' *Wales M.P.'s*).

4620. VANACKER-SAMBROOKE, Jeremy (ca 1703–40), 4th Bt, M.P. Bedford borough 1731–40 (*Alumni Cantab.;* GEC).

4621. VANBRUGH, Charles (1680–1740), M.P. Plymouth 1740–40 (Charnock's *Biog. Naval., 4,* 20; Musgrave's *Obituary; Notes and Queries,* 2d Ser., *1,* 116; *Parish Reg. Holy Trinity, Chester,* p. 134).

4622. VANDELEUR, John Ormsby (ca 1765–1828), M.P. Ennis 1801–2 (Burke's *Irish LG; Cornwallis Corr., 3,* 108 n.; *Linc. Inn Reg.*).

4623. VANDEN-BEMPDE-JOHNSTONE, John (1799–1869), 2d Bt, M.P. Yorkshire 1830–32, Scarborough 1832–37, 1841–69 (GEC; Gooder; *Rugby Reg.*).

4624. VANDERHEYDEN, David (d. 1828), M.P. East Looe 1807–16 (*Gent. Mag., 2,* 190).

4625. VANE, Charles William (1778–1854), 1st E. Vane, M.P. Londonderry Co. 1801–14 (DNB; GEC; *Eton Coll. Reg.*).

4626. VANE, Frederick (1732–1801), M.P. Durham Co. 1761–74 (*Alumni Cantab.; Old Westminsters*).

VANE, Frederick Fletcher, *see* FLETCHER-VANE, Frederick.

VANE, Frederick William Robert, *see* STEWART, Frederick William Robert.

4627. VANE, Henry (ca 1705–58), 1st E. of Darlington, M.P. Launceston 1726–27, St. Mawes 1727–41, Ripon 1741–47, Durham Co. 1747–53 (GEC).

4628. VANE, Henry (ca 1726–92), 2d E. of Darlington, M.P. Downton 1749–53, Durham Co. 1753–58 (*Alumni Cantab.;* GEC; *Old Westminsters*).

4629. VANE, Henry (1788–1864), 2d D. of Cleveland, M.P. Durham Co. 1812–15, Winchelsea 1816–18, Tregony 1818–26, Totnes 1826–30, Saltash 1830–31, South Salop 1832–42 (GEC).

4630. VANE, Raby (1736–69), M.P. Durham Co. 1758–61, Carlisle 1761–68 (Burke's *Peerage* sub Barnard; Bean; Ferguson).

4631. VANE, William (ca 1680–1734), 1st Vct Duncannon, M.P. Durham Co. 1708–10, Steyning 1727–34, Kent 1734–34 (GEC).

4632. VANE, William Harry (1766–1842), 1st D. of Cleveland, M.P. Totnes 1788–90, Winchelsea 1790–92 (DNB; GEC).

4633. VANE, William John Frederick (1792–1864), 3d D. of Cleveland, M.P. Winchelsea 1812–15, Durham Co. 1815–31, St. Ives 1846–52, Ludlow 1852–57 (GEC).

4634. VANE-TEMPEST, Henry (1771–1813), 2d Bt, M.P. Durham City 1794–1800, Durham Co. 1807–13 (GEC).

4635. VAN HOMRIGH, Peter (b. ca 1768), M.P. Drogheda 1826–30 (*Alumni Dublin.*).

4636. VANNECK, Gerard William (1743–91), 2d Bt, M.P. Dunwich 1768–90 (GEC; *Eton Coll. Reg.; Parish Reg. Putney, Suffolk,* p. 269).

4637. VANNECK, Joshua Henry (1745–1816), 1st Bn Huntingfield, M.P. Dunwich 1790–1816 (GEC; *Eton Coll. Reg.*).

4638. VANNECK, Joshua (1778–1844), 2d Bn Huntingfield, M.P. Dunwich 1816–19 (GEC; *Eton Lists;* Venn MS).

VAN NOTTEN, Peter, *see* POLE, Peter.

4639. VANSITTART, Arthur (1726–1804), M.P. Berks 1757–74 (*Eton Coll. Reg.*).

4640. Vansittart, Arthur (1775–1829), M.P. Windsor 1804–6 (Burke's *LG; Eton Lists*).

4641. Vansittart, George (1745–1825), M.P. Berks 1784–1812 (Burke's *LG;* Holzman's *Nabobs in Eng.*).

4642. Vansittart, Henry (1732–70), M.P. Reading 1768–70 (DNB; GEC; Holzman's *Nabobs in Eng.*).

4643. Vansittart, Nicholas (1766–1851), 1st Bn Bexley, M.P. Hastings 1796–1802, Old Sarum 1802–12, East Grinstead 1812–12, Harwich 1812–23 (DNB; GEC).

Vassal, Godfrey, *see* Webster, Godfrey.

4644. Vaughan, Benjamin (1751–1835), M.P. Calne 1792–96 (DNB; Venn MS).

4645. Vaughan, Evan Lloyd (ca 1710–91), M.P. Merioneth 1774–91 (*Alumni Cantab.; Eton Coll. Reg.*).

4646. Vaughan, John (ca 1693–1765), M.P. Carmarthenshire 1745–54 (Williams' *Wales M.P.'s*).

4647. Vaughan, John (ca 1748–95), M.P. Berwick-on-Tweed 1774–95 (DNB).

4648. Vaughan, John (ca 1752–1804), M.P. Carmarthenshire 1779–84 (Williams' *Wales M.P.'s*).

4649. Vaughan, John (1769–1831), 3d E. of Lisburne, M.P. Cardigan borough 1796–1818 (GEC; *Harrow Reg.*).

Vaughan,.John Edwards, *see* Edwards–Vaughan, John.

4650. Vaughan, Robert Williams (ca 1768–1843), 2d Bt, M.P. Merioneth 1792–1836 (GEC).

4651. Vaughan, William (ca 1707–75), M.P. Merioneth 1734–68 (*Alumni Cantab.;* Williams' *Wales M.P.'s*).

4652. Vaughan, Wilmot (ca 1730–1800), 1st E. of Lisburne, M.P. Cardiganshire 1755–61, 1768–96, Berwick-on-Tweed 1765–68 (GEC; *Eton Coll. Reg.*).

4653. Veitch, James (1712–93), M.P. Dumfries-shire 1755–61 (DNB).

4654. Venables, William (ca 1786–1840), M.P. London 1831–32 (Beaven's *Aldermen of London; Gent. Mag., 2, 435*).

4655. Venables-Vernon, George (1708–80), 1st Bn Vernon, M.P. Lichfield 1731–47, Derby borough 1754–62 (GEC).

4656. Venables-Vernon, George (1735–1813), 2d Bn Vernon, M.P. Weobley 1757–61, Bramber 1762–68, Glamorgan 1768–80 (GEC; *Old Westminsters*).

Venables-Vernon, George Granville, *see* Harcourt, George Granville.

Venables-Vernon, George John, *see* Warren, George John.

Vere, Bn, *see* Beauclerk, Aubrey and Vere.

4657. Vere, James (d. 1759), M.P. Lanarkshire 1754–59 (Foster's *Scots M.P.'s*).

Vere, James Joseph Hope, *see* Hope-Vere, James Joseph.

4658. VERE, Thomas (ca 1681–1766), M.P. Norwich 1735–47 (Cozens-Hardy and Kent, *Mayors of Norwich,* p. 120; Rye's *Norfolk Families,* p. 967).

4659. VEREKER, Charles (ca 1768–1842), 2d Vct Gort, M.P. Limerick City 1802–17 (GEC).

4660. VEREKER, John Prendergast (1790–1865), 3d Vct Gort, M.P. Limerick City 1817–20 (GEC; *Harrow Reg.*).

4661. VERNEY, John (1699–1741), M.P. Downton 1722–34, 1741–41 (DNB).

4662. VERNEY, Ralph (1683–1752), 1st E. Verney, M.P. Agmondesham 1717–27, Wendover 1741–52 (*Alumni Oxon.;* GEC).

4663. VERNEY, Ralph (ca 1712–91), 2d E. Verney, M.P. Wendover 1753–61, Carmarthen borough 1761–68, Bucks 1768–84, 1790–91 (*Alumni Cantab.;* DNB; GEC).

VERNON, 5th Bn, *see* WARREN, George John.

4664. VERNON, Charles (ca 1684–1762), M.P. Wycombe 1731–41, Ripon 1747–61 (Manning and Bray's *Surrey, 2,* 160; Shaw's *Knights, 2,* 281).

4665. VERNON, Charles (ca 1719–1810), M.P. Tamworth 1768–74 (*Notes and Queries,* 12th Ser., *2,* 251 and *3,* 305; Wedgwood).

4666. VERNON, Edward (1684–1757), M.P. Penryn 1722–34, Portsmouth 1741–41, Ipswich 1741–57 (DNB; *Old Westminsters*).

4667. VERNON, Francis (ca 1716–83), 1st E. of Shipbrooke, M.P. Ipswich 1761–68 (*Alumni Cantab.;* GEC; *Old Westminsters*).

VERNON, George Granville Venables, *see* HARCOURT, George Granville.

VERNON, George John, *see* WARREN, George John.

VERNON, George Venables, *see* VENABLES-VERNON, George.

VERNON, Granville Harcourt, *see* HARCOURT-VERNON, Granville.

4668. VERNON, Henry (1718–65), M.P. Lichfield 1754–54, 1755–61, Newcastle-under-Lyme 1761–62 (*Alumni Cantab.;* Old Westminsters).

4669. VERNON, Richard (1726–1800), M.P. Tavistock 1754–61, Bedford borough 1761–74, Okehampton 1774–84, Newcastle-under-Lyme 1784–90 (DNB).

4670. VERNON, Robert Vernon (1800–73), 1st Bn Lyveden, M.P. Tralee 1829–31, Northampton borough 1831–59 (DNB; GEC).

4671. VERNON, Thomas (1724–71), M.P. Worcester City 1746–61 (Burke's *Peerage;* Williams' *Worcester M.P.'s*).

VERULAM, Bn and E. of, *see* GRIMSTON, James Bucknal and James Walter.

4672. VESEY-FITZGERALD, William (ca 1783–1843), 2d Bn Fitzgerald, M.P. Ennis 1808–12, 1813–18, 1831–32, Clare Co. 1818–28, Newport 1829–30, Lostwithiel 1830–30 (DNB; GEC).

VILLIERS, George, *see* MASON-VILLIERS, George.

4673. VILLIERS, George (1759–1827), M.P. Warwick borough 1792–1802 (*Eton Coll. Reg.*).

VILLIERS, George Augustus Frederick, *see* CHILD-VILLIERS, George Augustus Frederick.

4674. VILLIERS, George Bussey (1735–1805), 4th E. of Jersey, M.P. Tamworth 1756–65, Aldborough 1765–68, Dover 1768–69 (GEC).

4675. VILLIERS, John Charles (1757–1838), 3d E. of Clarendon, M.P. Old Sarum 1784–90, Dartmouth 1790–1802, Tain burghs 1802–5, Queenborough 1807–12, 1820–24 (DNB; GEC; *Eton Coll. Reg.*).

4676. VILLIERS, Thomas (ca 1709–86), 1st E. of Clarendon, M.P. Tamworth 1747–56 (*Alumni Cantab.;* DNB; GEC; *Eton Coll. Reg.*).

4677. VILLIERS, Thomas (1753–1824), 2d E. of Clarendon, M.P. Christchurch 1774–79, 1779–80, Helston 1781–86 (*Admissions to St. John, Cambridge;* GEC; *Eton Coll. Reg.*).

4678. VILLIERS, Thomas Hyde (1801–32), M.P. Hedon 1826–30, Wootton Bassett 1830–31, Bletchingley 1831–32 (DNB).

4679. VILLIERS-MEYNELL, Frederick (ca 1801–ca 1871), M.P. Saltash 1831–32, Canterbury 1835–35, Sudbury 1841–47 (Ball and Venn's *Admissions to Trinity College; Eton Lists; Linc. Inn Reg.; Notes and Queries,* 12th Ser., *3,* 366).

4680. VILLIERS-STUART, Henry (1803–74), 1st Bn Stuart de Decies, M.P. Waterford Co. 1826–30, Banbury 1830–31 (GEC).

4681. VINCENT, Francis (ca 1718–75), 7th Bt, M.P. Surrey 1761–75 (GEC; MS, *ex inform.* the Reverend J. J. Cowan).

4682. VINCENT, Francis (1803–80), 10th Bt, M.P. St. Albans 1831–34 (GEC; *Eton Lists*).

VIRY, *see* DE VIRY.

4683. VIVIAN, Richard Hussey (1775–1842), 1st Bn Vivian, M.P. Truro 1820–26, 1832–34, Windsor 1826–31, East Cornwall 1837–41 (DNB; GEC; *Harrow Reg.*).

4684. VYNER, Robert (ca 1685–1777), M.P. Lincolnshire 1724–61 (Burke's *LG*).

4685. VYNER, Robert (1717–99), M.P. Okehampton 1754–61, Lincoln City 1774–84, Thirsk 1785–96 (*Alumni Cantab.;* Burke's *LG*).

4686. VYNER, Robert (1762–1810), M.P. Lincolnshire 1794–1802 (*Admissions to St. John, Cambridge;* Burke's *LG; Harrow Reg.*).

4687. VYSE, Richard (1746–1825), M.P. Beverley 1806–7 (DNB; Burke's *LG*).

VYSE, Richard William Howard, *see* HOWARD-VYSE, Richard William.

VYVYAN, Richard Hussey, *see* VIVIAN, Richard Hussey.

4688. VYVYAN, Richard Rawlinson (1800–79), 8th Bt, M.P. Cornwall 1825–31, Okehampton 1831–32, Bristol 1832–37, Helston 1841–57 (DNB; GEC).

4689. WADE, George (ca 1673–1748), M.P. Hindon 1715–22, Bath 1722–48 (DNB).

4690. WAGER, Charles (ca 1666–1743), M.P. Portsmouth 1710–11, 1715–34, West Looe 1713–15, 1741–43, Westminster 1734–41 (DNB).

4691. WAITHMAN, Robert (ca 1764–1833), M.P. London 1818–20, 1826–33 (DNB).

4692. WAKE, William (ca 1742–85), 8th Bt, M.P. Bedford borough 1774–84 (GEC; *Eton Coll. Reg.*).

4693. WALCOT, Charles (1738–99), M.P. Weymouth and Melcombe Regis 1763–68 (*Alumni Oxon.; Burke's LG*).

4694. WALDEGRAVE, George (1751–89), 4th E. Waldegrave, M.P. Newcastle-under-Lyme 1774–80 (GEC; *Eton Coll. Reg.*).

4695. WALDEGRAVE, John (1718–84), 3d E. Waldegrave, M.P. Orford 1747–54, Newcastle-under-Lyme 1754–63 (DNB; GEC).

4696. WALDEGRAVE, William (1788–1859), 8th E. Waldegrave, M.P. Bedford borough 1815–18 (GEC).

4697. WALDO-SIBTHORP, Charles De Laet (1783–1855), M.P. Lincoln City 1826–32, 1835–55 (DNB).

4698. WALDO-SIBTHORP, Humphrey (1744–1815), M.P. Boston 1777–84, Lincoln City 1800–6 (Burke's *LG; Harrow Reg.; Old Westminsters*).

WALHOUSE, Edward John, see LITTELTON, Edward John.

4699. WALKER, Charles Arthur (ca 1790–1873), M.P. Wexford Town 1831–41 (*Alumni Dublin.;* Burke's *Irish LG;* Boase; *Linc. Inn Reg.*).

4700. WALKER, Joshua (b. 1786), M.P. Aldeburgh 1818–29 (Burke's *LG* [ed. 1849]; Foster's *Yorkshire Pedigrees; 1821 List*).

4701. WALKER, Samuel (1779–1851), M.P. Aldeburgh 1818–20 (Foster's *Yorkshire Pedigrees*).

4702. WALKER, Thomas (d. 1748), M.P. West Looe 1733–34, Plympton Erle 1735–41, Helston 1741–47 (Musgrave's *Obituary*).

4703. WALKER-CORNEWALL, Frederick (1752–83), M.P. Leominster 1776–80, Ludlow 1780–83 (*Eton Coll. Reg.*).

4704. WALKER-HENEAGE, John (d. 1806), M.P. Cricklade 1785–94 (Burke's *LG*).

WALL, Charles Baring, see BARING-WALL, Charles.

4705. WALLACE, James (1729–83), M.P. Horsham 1770–83 (GEC; Williamson's *Middle Temple Bench Book*).

4706. WALLACE, Thomas (ca 1768–1844), 1st Bn Wallace, M.P. Grampound 1790–96, Penryn 1796–1802, Hindon 1802–6, Shaftesbury 1807–12, Weymouth and Melcombe Regis 1812–13, 1818–28, Cockermouth 1813–18 (DNB; GEC; *Eton Coll. Reg.*).

4707. WALLACE, Thomas (b. ca 1766), M.P. Yarmouth (Hants) 1827–30, Drogheda 1831–32, Carlow Co. 1832–34 (*Alumni Dublin.*).

4708. WALLER, Edmund (d. 1771), M.P. Great Marlow 1722–41, Wycombe 1741–54 (Burke's *LG;* Lipscomb's *Bucks, 3,* 182).

4709. WALLER, Edmund (ca 1726–88), M.P. Wycombe 1747–61 (*Alumni Oxon.;* Burke's *LG*).

4710. WALLER, Harry, M.P. Wycombe 1726–47 (Lipscomb's *Bucks, 3,* 182).

4711. WALLER, John (d. 1757), M.P. Wycombe 1754–57 (Lipscomb's *Bucks, 3,* 182; Burke's *LG*).

4712. WALLER, John (ca 1762–1836), M.P. Limerick Co. 1801–2 (*Alumni Dublin.;* Burke's *Irish LG; Harrow Reg.*).

4713. WALLER, Robert (b. ca 1733), M.P. Wycombe 1761–90 (*Alumni Oxon.;* Burke's *LG*).

WALLINGFORD, Vct, *see* KNOLLYS, William.

WALLIS, Lewis Bayly, *see* BAYLY-WALLIS, Lewis.

4714. WALLOP, Bluett (1726–49), M.P. Newport (Hants) 1747–49 (Collins' *Peerage* sub Portsmouth).

4715. WALLOP, Charles (1722–71), M.P. Whitchurch 1747–54 (*Alumni Cantab.;* Collins' *Peerage* sub Portsmouth).

4716. WALLOP, Coulson (1774–1807), M.P. Andover 1796–1802 (Collins' *Peerage* sub Portsmouth; *Eton Coll. Reg.*).

4717. WALLOP, Henry (ca 1743–94), M.P. Whitchurch 1768–74 (Burke's *Peerage* and Collins' *Peerage* sub Postsmouth).

4718. WALLOP, John (1718–49), M.P. Andover 1741–49 (*Alumni Oxon.;* Burke's *Peerage* sub Portsmouth; GEC).

WALLOP, Newton, *see* FELLOWES, Newton.

4719. WALPOLE, Edward (ca 1706–84), M.P. Lostwithiel 1730–34, Great Yarmouth 1734–68 (*Alumni Cantab.;* Burke's *Peerage* and Collins' *Peerage* sub Orford; *Eton Coll. Reg.*).

4720. WALPOLE, George (1758–1835), M.P. Derby borough 1797–1806, Dungarvan 1807–20 (DNB; *Eton Coll. Reg.*).

4721. WALPOLE, Horatio (1678–1757), 1st Bn Walpole, M.P. Castle Rising 1702–15, Berealston 1715–17, East Looe 1718–22, Great Yarmouth 1722–34, Norwich 1734–56 (DNB; GEC).

4722. WALPOLE, Horatio (1717–97), 4th E. of Orford, M.P. Callington 1741–54, Castle Rising 1754–57, Lynn 1757–68 (DNB; GEC).

4723. WALPOLE, Horatio (1723–1809), 1st E. of Orford, M.P. Lynn 1747–57 (GEC).

4724. WALPOLE, Horatio (1752–1822), 2d E. of Orford, M.P. Wigan 1780–84, Lynn 1784–1809 (GEC; *Eton Coll. Reg.*).

4725. WALPOLE, Horatio (1783–1858), 3d E. of Orford, M.P. Lynn 1809–22 (GEC).

4726. WALPOLE, John (1787–1859), M.P. Lynn 1822–31 (Burke's *Peerage* sub Orford).

4727. WALPOLE, Richard (ca 1729–98), M.P. Great Yarmouth 1768–84 (Burke's *LG* [ed. 1849]; Burke's *Peerage* and Collins' *Peerage* sub Orford).

4728. WALPOLE, Robert (1676–1745), 1st E. of Orford, M.P. Castle Rising 1701–2, Lynn 1702–12, 1713–42 (DNB; GEC).

4729. WALPOLE, Thomas (1727–1803), M.P. Sudbury 1754–61, Ashburton 1761–68, Lynn 1768–84 (Burke's *Peerage* sub Orford; *Eton Coll. Reg.; Parl. Hist., 15,* 312, 1078).

4730. WALROND, Bethel (1801–76), M.P. Sudbury 1826–31, Saltash 1831–32 (Burke's *LG;* Boase; Oliver's *Antigua, 3,* 180; *1832 List*).

4731. WALSH, Benjamin, M.P. Wootton Bassett 1808–12 (*Gent. Mag., 1* [1812], 82–83, 286).

4732. WALSH, John (ca 1725–95), M.P. Worcester City 1761–80 (DNB; Holzman's *Nabobs in Eng.;* Williams' *Worcester M.P.'s*).

4733. WALSH, John (1798–1881), 1st Bn Ormathwaite, M.P. Sudbury 1830–34, 1838–40, Radnorshire 1840–68 (DNB; GEC).

WALSH, John Benn, see BENN-WALSH, John.

WALSINGHAM, Bn, see DE GREY, Thomas and William.

WALSINGHAM, Robert Boyle, see BOYLE-WALSINGHAM, Robert.

4734. WALTER, Edward (1727–80), M.P. Milborne Port 1754–74 (*Herald and Genealogist, 8,* 3; *Misc. Geneal. et Herald.,* N.S., *2,* 8; Namier).

WALTER, John Rolle, see ROLLE-WALTER, John.

4735. WALTER, Peter (ca 1717–53), M.P. Shaftesbury 1741–47 (*Herald and Genealogist, 8,* 3).

WALTHAM, Bn, see OLMIUS, Drigue Billers and John.

4736. WALWYN, James (1744–1800), M.P. Hereford City 1785–1800 (Williams' *Hereford M.P.'s; Alumni Oxon.;* Robinson's *Hereford,* p. 203).

4737. WARBURTON, Henry (ca 1784–1858), M.P. Bridport 1826–41, Kendal 1843–47 (DNB).

4738. WARBURTON, Philip Henry (ca 1700–60), M.P. Chester City 1742–54 (Grazebrook's *Heraldry of Worcestershire,* p. 470 n.; *Linc. Inn Reg.;* Musgrave's *Obituary;* Omerod's *Chester, 2,* 175).

4739. WARD, John (1725–88), 2d Vct Dudley and Ward, M.P. Marlborough 1754–61, Worcestershire 1761–74 (*Alumni Oxon.;* GEC).

4740. WARD, John (1779–1855), M.P. Leominster 1830–31 (Burke's *LG;* Boase; Williams' *Hereford M.P.'s*).

4741. WARD, John William (1781–1833), 1st E. Dudley, M.P. Downton 1802–3, Worcestershire 1803–6, Petersfield 1806–7, Wareham 1807–12, Ilchester 1812–18, Bossiney 1819–23 (DNB; GEC).

4742. WARD, Robert (1754–1831), M.P. Down 1812–12 (*Alumni Dublin.;* Burke's *Peerage* sub Bangor; *Gent. Mag., 1,* 464; *Harrow Reg.*).

WARD, Robert Plumer, see PLUMER-WARD, Robert.

4743. WARD, William (1750–1823), 3d Vct Dudley, M.P. Worcester City 1780–88 (GEC; *Eton Coll. Reg.*).

4744. WARD, William (1787–1849), M.P. London 1826–31 (DNB; Burke's *LG;* Venn MS).

WARDEN, Thomas, see SERGISON, Thomas.

4745. WARDLE, Gwyllm Lloyd (ca 1762–1833), M.P. Okehampton 1807–12 (DNB; *Harrow Reg.*).

4746. WARDOUR, William (1686–1746), M.P. Calne 1727–34, Fowey 1737–46 (*Alumni Oxon.; Westminster Abbey Reg.*).

4747. WARING, Walter (ca 1727–80), M.P. Bishop's Castle 1755–59, Coventry 1773–80 (*Alumni Cantab.; Shrewsbury School Reg.;* Shrop. Archaeol. Soc. *Trans.*, 2d Ser., *10;* Whitley's *Coventry M.P.'s*).

4748. WARRE, John Ashley (1787–1860), M.P. Lostwithiel 1812–18, Taunton 1820–26, Hastings 1831–34, Ripon 1857–60 (*Alumni Oxon.;* Burke's *LG;* Dod's *Parl. Companion* [1834], p. 176; *Harrow Reg.*).

4749. WARREN, Borlase (1677–1747), M.P. Nottingham borough 1713–15, 1727–47 (*Genealogist*, N.S., *2*, 288; *Misc. Geneal. et Herald.*, 1st Ser., *3*, 51; *Notts and Derby Notes and Queries*, *1*, 42).

4750. WARREN, Charles (1764–1829), M.P. Dorchester 1819–26 (*Old Westminsters;* Williams' *Great Sessions in Wales*).

4751. WARREN, George (ca 1734–1801), M.P. Lancaster borough 1758–80, 1786–96, Beaumaris 1780–84 (Bean; Omerod's *Chester, 3*, 687; Pink; Williams' *Wales M.P.'s*).

4752. WARREN, George John (1803–66), 5th Bn Vernon, M.P. Derbyshire 1831–32, South Derbyshire 1832–34 (DNB; GEC).

4753. WARREN, John Borlase (1753–1832), 1st Bt, M.P. Great Marlow 1774–84, Nottingham borough 1797–1806, Buckingham borough 1807–7 (DNB; GEC).

4754. WARREN, Peter (ca 1703–52), M.P. Westminster 1747–52 (DNB).

4755. WARREN-BULKELEY, Thomas James (1752–1822), 7th Vct Cashel, M.P. Anglesey 1774–84 (GEC; *Old Westminsters*).

4756. WARRENDER, George (1782–1849), 4th Bt, M.P. Haddington burghs 1807–12, Truro 1812–18, Sandwich 1818–26, Westbury 1826–30, Honiton 1830–32 (*Alumni Oxon.;* GEC; *1832 List*).

4757. WARRENDER, Patrick (1731–99), 3d Bt, M.P. Haddington burghs 1768–74 (GEC; Foster's *Scots M.P.'s*).

WARRINGTON, 1st E. of, *see* GREY, George Harry.

WARRICK, E. of, *see* GREVILLE, George and Henry Richard.

4758. WASON, Peter Rigby (ca 1798–1875), M.P. Ipswich 1831–35, 1835–37, 1841–42 (Boase).

4759. WASTIE, John (1765–1835), M.P. Oxford City 1807–18, 1820–30 (*Eton Coll. Reg.*).

WATERPARK, 3d Bn, *see* CAVENDISH, Henry Manners.

4760. WATHERSTON, Dalhousie, M.P. Boston 1784–90 (Holzman's *Nabobs in Eng.*).

4761. WATSON, Brook (1735–1807), 1st Bt, M.P. London 1784–93 (DNB).

4762. WATSON, George (1768–1824), M.P. Canterbury 1800–6 (Debrett's *Peerage* [1834], sub Sondes; *Royal Kalendar* [1802], p. 44).

4763. WATSON, James (ca 1748–96), M.P. Bridport 1790–95 (*Alumni Oxon.*).

4764. WATSON, Lewis (1728–95), 1st Bn Sondes, M.P. Boroughbridge 1750–54, Kent 1754–60 (GEC; *Old Westminsters*).

4765. WATSON, Lewis Thomas (1754–1806), 2d Bn Sondes, M.P. Hedon 1776–80 (GEC; *Eton Coll. Reg.*).

4766. WATSON, Richard (1800–52), M.P. Canterbury 1830–34, Peterborough 1852–52 (GEC sub Sondes; *Eton Lists; Gent. Mag., 2,* 307).

4767. WATSON, Thomas (1715–46), 3d E. of Rockingham, M.P. Canterbury 1741–45 (GEC; *Eton Coll. Reg.*).

4768. WATSON, Thomas (ca 1701–66), M.P. Berwick-on-Tweed 1740–65 (*Archaeol. Aeliana,* 4th Ser., *24;* Bean; Musgrave's *Obituary*).

4769. WATSON-TAYLOR, George (ca 1770–1841), M.P. Newport (Hants) 1816–18, Seaford 1818–20, East Looe 1820–26, Devizes 1826–32 (*Alumni Oxon.;* Burke's *LG; Times,* 12 June 1841; *1832 List*).

4770. WATTS, Thomas (d. 1742), M.P. St. Michael 1734–41, Tregony 1741–42 (Musgrave's *Obituary; Notes and Queries,* 12th Ser., *2,* 190).

4771. WATTS-RUSSELL, Jesse (1786–1875), M.P. Gatton 1820–26 (*Alumni Oxon.;* Boase).

4772. WAUCHOPE, Henry (d. 1768), M.P. Buteshire 1762–68 (*Whitehall Evening Post* and *London Chronicle,* 27–29 Sept. 1768).

4773. WAY, Benjamin (1740–1808), M.P. Bridport 1765–68 (*Eton Coll. Reg.*).

4774. WEAVER, Arthur (d. 1759), M.P. Bridgnorth 1747–54 (Shrop. Archaeol. Soc. *Trans.,* 4th Ser., *5,* 67).

4775. WEBB, Edward (d. 1839), M.P. Gloucester City 1816–32 (Williams' *Gloucester M.P.'s*).

4776. WEBB, John (ca 1730–95), M.P. Gloucester City 1780–95 (Rudge's *Gloucester,* p. 346; Williams' *Gloucester M.P.'s*).

4777. WEBB, John Richmond (d. 1766), M.P. Bossiney 1761–66 (*Misc. Geneal. et Herald.,* 5th Ser., *7,* Williams' *Great Sessions in Wales*).

4778. WEBB, Nathaniel (1725–86), M.P. Taunton 1768–75, Ilchester 1775–80 (*Eton Coll. Reg.;* Oliver's *Antigua, 3,* 214, 217).

4779. WEBB, Philip Carteret (ca 1700–70), M.P. Haslemere 1754–68 (DNB; Burke's *Family Records*).

4780. WEBB, Robert (d. 1765), M.P. Taunton 1747–54 (*Court and City Reg.* [1753], p. 39; Musgrave's *Obituary;* Oliver's *Antigua, 3,* 214).

4781. WEBBER, Daniel Webb (ca 1757–1847), M.P. Armagh borough 1816–18 (*Alumni Oxon.; Alumni Dublin.;* Burke's *Irish LG*).

4782. WEBSTER, Godfrey (ca 1719–1800), 4th Bt, M.P. Seaford 1786–90, Wareham 1796–1800 (GEC).

4783. WEBSTER, Godfrey Vassal (1789–1836), 5th Bt, M.P. Sussex 1812–20 (GEC; *Harrow Reg.;* Venn MS).

4784. WEBSTER, Whistler (ca 1690–1779), 2d Bt, M.P. East Grinstead 1741–61 (GEC).

4785. WEDDELL, William (1736–92), M.P. Hull 1766–74, Malton 1775–92 (*Admissions to St. John, Cambridge;* Bean; Hunter's *Familiae Min. Gent.;* Park, p. 139).

4786. WEDDERBURN, Alexander (1733–1805), 1st E. of Rosslyn, M.P. Ayr burghs 1761–68, Richmond 1768–69, Bishop's Castle 1770–74, 1778–80, Okehampton 1774–78 (Addison's *Glasgow Matric. Albums;* DNB; GEC).

4787. WEDDERBURN, David (1775–1858), 7th Bt, M.P. Perth burghs 1805–18 (GEC).

WEIR, Charles Hope, *see* HOPE-WEIR, Charles.

WELBY, Glynne Earle, *see* WELBY-GREGORY, Glynne Earle.

4788. WELBY, William Earle (ca 1734–1815), 1st Bt, M.P. Grantham 1802–6 (*Eton Coll. Reg.;* Foster's *Baronetage*).

4789. WELBY, William Earle (1769–1852), 2d Bt, M.P. Grantham 1807–20 (Foster's *Baronetage; Gent. Mag., 1* [1853], 91).

4790. WELBY-GREGORY, Glynne Earle (1806–75), 3d Bt, M.P. Grantham 1830–57 (*Alumni Oxon.;* Burke's *Peerage;* Boase; *Rugby Reg.*).

4791. WELD-FORESTER, Cecil (1767–1828), 1st Bn Forester, M.P. Wenlock 1790–1820 (GEC; *Old Westminsters*).

4792. WELD-FORESTER, George Cecil (1807–86), 3d Bn Forester, M.P. Wenlock 1828–74 (GEC; *Old Westminsters*).

4793. WELD-FORESTER, John George (1801–74), 2d Bn Forester, M.P. Wenlock 1826–28 (GEC; *Old Westminsters*).

4794. WELLESLEY, Arthur (1769–1852), 1st D. of Wellington, M.P. Rye 1806–6, St. Michael 1807–7, Newport 1807–9 (DNB; GEC).

4795. WELLESLEY, Arthur Richard (1807–84), 2d D. of Wellington, M.P. Aldeburgh 1829–32, Norwich 1837–52 (GEC; *Alumni Oxon.*).

4796. WELLESLEY, Henry (1773–1847), 1st Bn Cowley, M.P. Eye 1807–9 (DNB; GEC; *Eton Coll. Reg.*).

4797. WELLESLEY, Richard (ca 1787–1831), M.P. Queenborough 1810–12, East Grinstead 1812–12, Yarmouth (Hants) 1812–17, Ennis 1820–26 (*Alumni Oxon.;* GEC sub Mornington).

4798. WELLESLEY, Richard Colley (1760–1842), 1st M. of Wellesley, M.P. Berealston 1784–86, Saltash 1786–87, Windsor 1787–96, Old Sarum 1796–97 (DNB; GEC; *Eton Coll. Reg.; Harrow Reg.*).

WELLESLEY-POLE, William, *see* POLE-TYLNEY-LONG-WELLESLEY, William.

4799. WELLESLEY-POLE, William (1763–1845), 3d E. of Mornington, M.P. East Looe 1790–95, Queens 1801–21 (DNB; GEC; *Eton Coll. Reg.*).

WELLINGTON, D. of, *see* WELLESLEY, Arthur and Arthur Richard.

4800. WELLS, John (ca 1761–1848), M.P. Maidstone 1820–30 (*Gent. Mag.,* 1 [1849], 103; *1821 List*).

WELWOOD, Alexander Maconochie, *see* MACONOCHIE-WELWOOD, Alexander.

WEMYSS, Francis Charteris, *see* CHARTERIS-WEMYSS, Francis.

4801. WEMYSS, James (1726–86), M.P. Fifeshire 1763–68, Sutherlandshire 1768–84 (*Scots Peerage*).

WEMYSS, James Erskine, *see* ERSKINE-WEMYSS, James.

4802. WEMYSS, William (1760–1822), M.P. Sutherlandshire 1784–87, Fifeshire 1787–96, 1807–20 (*Scots Peerage*).

WENLOCK, Bn, *see* LAWLEY, Robert; *also* LAWLEY-THOMPSON, Paul Beilby.

4803. WENMAN, Philip (1719–60), 3d Vct Wenman, M.P. Oxford City 1749–54, Oxfordshire 1754–55 (GEC).

4804. WENMAN, Philip (1742–1800), 4th Vct Wenman, M.P. Oxfordshire 1768–96 (GEC).

4805. WENMAN, Thomas Francis (1745–96), M.P. Westbury 1774–80 (DNB).

WENTWORTH, 2d Vct, *see* NOEL, Thomas.

4806. WENTWORTH, Godfrey (1704–89), M.P. York City 1741–47 (Burke's *LG; Genealogist,* N.S., *20,* 260).

4807. WENTWORTH, Paul (d. 1793), M.P. Saltash 1780–80 (*Dict. Am. Biog.*).

4808. WENTWORTH, Thomas (ca 1694–1747), M.P. Whitchurch 1743–47 (*Alumni Oxon.;* Musgrave's *Obituary; Parl. Hist., 12,* 205).

4809. WENTWORTH, William (1686–1763), 4th Bt, M.P. Malton 1731–41 (GEC).

4810. WENTWORTH-ARMYTAGE, Godfrey (1773–1834), M.P. Tregony 1806–8 (Burke's *LG;* Ball and Venn's *Admissions to Trinity College*).

4811. WENTWORTH-FITZWILLIAM, Charles William (1786–1857), 3d E. Fitzwilliam, M.P. Malton 1806–7, Yorkshire 1807–30, Peterborough 1830–30, Northamptonshire 1831–33 (DNB; GEC; Gooder).

4812. WEST, Frederick (ca 1767–1852), M.P. Denbigh borough 1802–6 (Burke's *LG;* Williams' *Wales M.P.'s;* Boase).

4813. WEST, Frederick Richard (ca 1799–1862), M.P. Denbigh borough 1827–30, 1847–57, East Grinstead 1830–32 (*Alumni Oxon.;* Burke's *LG;* Williams' *Wales M.P.'s*).

4814. WEST, James (ca 1704–72), M.P. St. Albans 1741–68, Boroughbridge 1768–72 (DNB).

4815. WEST, James (1742–95), M.P. Boroughbridge 1767–68 (Burke's *LG; Harrow Reg.*).

4816. WEST, Temple (ca 1713–57), M.P. Buckingham borough 1753–54 (DNB).

WESTCOTE, 1st Bn, *see* LYTTELTON, William Henry.

4817. WESTENRA, Henry Robert (1792–1860), 3d Bn Rossmore, M.P. Monoghan 1818–30, 1831–32, 1834–34, 1835–42 (GEC; *Old Westminsters*).

4818. WESTENRA, Warner William (1765–1842), 2d Bn Rossmore, M.P. Monaghan 1801–1 (*Alumni Dublin.;* GEC).

4819. WESTERN, Charles Callis (1767–1844), 1st Bn Western, M.P. Maldon 1790–1806, 1807–12, Essex 1812–32 (*Alumni Felsted.;* DNB; GEC; *Eton Coll. Reg.*).

4820. WESTFALING, Herbert (ca 1700–73), M.P. Thetford 1754–61 (*Alumni Oxon.;* Williams' *Hereford M.P.'s*).

WESTMINSTER, 2d M. of, *see* GROSVENOR, Richard.

WESTMORLAND, E. of, *see* FANE, John and Thomas.

4821. WETHERELL, Charles (1770–1846), M.P. Rye 1812–13, Shaftesbury 1813–18, Oxford City 1820–26, Hastings 1826–26, Plympton Erle 1826–30, Boroughbridge 1830–32 (*Alumni Oxon.;* DNB; Burke's *LG; St. Paul's School Reg.*).

4822. WEYLAND, John (1774–1854), M.P. Hindon 1830–32 (DNB; Burke's *LG; 1832 List*).

4823. WEYLAND, Richard (1780–1864), M.P. Oxfordshire 1831–37 (*Admissions to St. John, Cambridge;* Burke's *LG;* Williams' *Oxford M.P.'s*).

WEYMOUTH, Vct, *see* THYNNE, Thomas.

4824. WHALLEY-SMYTHE-GARDINER, John (1743–97), 1st Bt, M.P. Westbury 1780–84 (GEC).

WHARNCLIFFE, Bn, *see* STUART-WORTLEY-MACKENZIE, James Archibald and John.

4825. WHARTON, John (1765–1843), M.P. Beverley 1790–1826 (Burke's *LG;* Surtees' *Durham, 2,* 292).

4826. WHARTON, Richard (ca 1774–1828), M.P. Durham City 1802–4, 1806–20 (Burke's *LG; Gent. Mag., 2,* 468).

WHATELY, Joseph Thompson, *see* HALSEY, Joseph Thompson.

4827. WHATELY, Thomas (d. 1772), M.P. Ludgershall 1761–68, Castle Rising 1768–72 (DNB).

4828. WHICHCOTE, Thomas (ca 1700–76), M.P. Lincolnshire 1740–74 (Musgrave's *Obituary;* Maddison's *Lincs. Pedigrees*).

4829. WHITBREAD, Samuel (1726–96), M.P. Bedford borough 1768–74, 1775–90, Steyning 1792–96 (Burke's *LG;* Lipscomb's *Bucks, 2,* 117).

4830. WHITBREAD, Samuel (ca 1764–1815), M.P. Bedford borough 1790–1815 (DNB; *Eton Coll. Reg.*).

4831. WHITBREAD, Samuel Charles (1796–1879), M.P. Middlesex 1820–30 (*Eton Lists;* Boase; Lipscomb's *Bucks, 2,* 117).

4832. WHITBREAD, William Henry (1795–1867), M.P. Bedford borough 1818–34 (Boase; Burke's *LG; Eton Lists*).

4833. WHITE, Henry (ca 1791–1873), 1st Bn Annaly, M.P. Dublin Co.

1823–32, Longford 1837–47, 1857–61 (*Alumni Dublin.;* GEC; Venn MS).

4834. WHITE, John (ca 1700–69), M.P. East Retford 1733–68 (Burke's *Peerage*).

4835. WHITE, Luke (ca 1783–1824), M.P. Leitrim 1818–24 (*Alumni Dublin.;* Burke's *Peerage* sub Annaly; *Gent. Mag., 1,* 642).

4836. WHITE, Matthew, M.P. Hythe 1802–6, 1812–18 (*Notes and Queries,* 12th Ser., *2,* 456; *1812 List*).

4837. WHITE, Samuel (ca 1784–1854), M.P. Leitrim 1824–47 (Burke's *Peerage* sub Annaly; Boase).

4838. WHITE-THOMAS, George (ca 1750–1821), M.P. Chichester 1784–1812 (*Eton Coll. Reg.;* Oliver's *Antigua, 3,* 224–27).

4839. WHITHEAD, Francis (ca 1719–51), M.P. Hampshire 1747–51 (*Alumni Oxon.;* Burke's *LG*).

4840. WHITMORE, John (ca 1750–1826), M.P. Bridgnorth 1795–1806 (Burke's *LG; Gent. Mag., 2,* 379; Shrop. Archaeol. Soc. *Trans.,* 4th Ser., *5,* 70).

4841. WHITMORE, Thomas (1711–73), M.P. Bridgnorth 1734–54 (*Eton Coll. Reg.;* Shrop. Archaeol. Soc. *Trans.,* 4th Ser., *5,* 67).

4842. WHITMORE, Thomas (ca 1743–95), M.P. Bridgnorth 1771–95 (Shrop. Archaeol. Soc. *Trans.,* 4th Ser., *5,* 69).

4843. WHITMORE, Thomas (1782–1846), M.P. Bridgnorth 1806–31 (*Alumni Oxon.;* Shrop. Archaeol. Soc. *Trans.,* 4th Ser., *5,* 70).

4844. WHITMORE, William (1714–71), M.P. Bridgnorth 1741–47, 1754–71 (Shrop. Archaeol. Soc. *Trans.,* 4th Ser., *5,* 67).

WHITMORE, William Wolryche, *see* WOLRYCHE-WHITMORE, William.

4845. WHITSHED, James (b. ca 1718), M.P. St. Ives 1754–61, Cirencester 1761–83 (*Alumni Dublin.;* Williams' *Gloucester M.P.'s*).

4846. WHITTINGTON, Isaac (d. 1773), M.P. Agmondesham 1754–61 (Musgrave's *Obituary*).

4847. WHITTLE, Francis, M.P. Westbury 1809–10.

WHITWELL, John Griffin, *see* GRIFFIN-GRIFFIN, John.

4848. WHITWORTH, Charles (ca 1714–78), M.P. Minehead 1747–61, 1768–74, Bletchingley 1761–68, East Looe 1774–74, Saltash 1775–78 (DNB; *Old Westminsters*).

4849. WHITWORTH, Francis (d. 1742), M.P. Minehead 1723–42 (*Old Westminsters*).

4850. WHITWORTH, Richard (1734–1811), M.P. Stafford borough 1768–80 (*Eton Coll. Reg.; Etoniana, 51,* 32).

WICKENS, George, *see* OSBALDESTON, George.

4851. WICKHAM, William (1761–1840), M.P. Heytesbury 1802–2, Cashel 1802–6, Callington 1806–7 (*Alumni Oxon.;* DNB; *Genealogist,* N.S., *11,* 220; *Harrow Reg.*).

4852. WIGGENS, Thomas (d. 1785), M.P. Okehampton 1784–85 (*Linc. Inn Reg.;* Musgrave's *Obituary; Scots Peerage* sub Kinnaird).

WIGLEY, Edmund Meysey, *see* MEYSEY-WIGLEY, Edmund.

4853. WIGLEY, James (ca 1701–65), M.P. Leicester borough 1737–65 (*Alumni Oxon.;* Nichols' *Leicester, 2,* pt. 2, 786; *Rugby Reg.*).

4854. WIGRAM, Robert (1744–1830), 1st Bt, M.P. Fowey 1802–6, Wexford town 1806–7 (Cussans' *Herts, 1,* pt. 2, 173; Foster's *Baronetage; Gent. Mag., 2,* 563).

WIGRAM, Robert, *see* FITZWYGRAM, Robert.

4855. WIGRAM, William (1780–1858), M.P. New Ross 1807–12, 1826–30, 1831–32, Wexford town 1820–26, 1830–31 (Foster's *Baronetage*).

4856. WILBERFORCE, William (1759–1833), M.P. Hull 1780–84, Yorkshire 1784–1812, Bramber 1812–25 (DNB).

WILBRAHAM, Edward, *see* BOOTLE-WILBRAHAM, Edward.

4857. WILBRAHAM, George (1741–1813), M.P. Bodmin 1789–90 (Ball and Venn's *Admissions to Trinity College;* Burke's *LG;* Foster's *Lancashire Pedigrees*).

4858. WILBRAHAM, George (1779–1852), M.P. Stockbridge 1826–31, Cheshire 1831–32, South Cheshire 1832–41 (Burke's *LG;* Foster's *Lancashire Pedigrees; Rugby Reg.;* Venn MS).

4859. WILBRAHAM, Randle (ca 1695–1770), M.P. Newcastle-under-Lyme 1740–47, Appleby 1747–54, Newton 1754–68 (*Alumni Oxon.;* Foster's *Lancashire Pedigrees*).

4860. WILBRAHAM, Roger (ca 1743–1829), M.P. St. Michael 1784–84, Helston 1786–90, Bodmin 1790–96 (Ball and Venn's *Admissions to Trinity College;* Burke's *LG;* Cobbett's *Twickenham,* p. 77; Omerod's *Chester, 2,* 138).

4861. WILBRAHAM-BOOTLE, Richard (ca 1725–96), M.P. Chester City 1761–90 (*Alumni Oxon.;* Foster's *Lancashire Pedigrees*).

4862. WILDE, Thomas (1782–1855), 1st Bn Truro, M.P. Newark 1831–32, 1835–41, Worcester City 1841–46 (DNB; GEC).

4863. WILDER, Francis John (ca 1775–1824), M.P. Horsham 1807–7, Arundel 1807–18 (*Eton Coll. Reg.; Gent. Mag., 1,* 372).

4864. WILDMAN, James (ca 1749–1816), M.P. Hindon 1796–1802 (*Gent. Mag., 1,* 375).

4865. WILDMAN, James Beckford (ca 1789–1867), M.P. Colchester 1818–26 (*Alumni Oxon.;* Boase).

4866. WILDMAN, Thomas (ca 1740–95), M.P. Hindon 1795–95 (Burke's *LG* [ed. 1849]; Cobbett's *Twickenham,* pp. 74, 77, 99; *Notes and Queries, 171,* 105).

WILDMAN, William, *see* BARRINGTON-SHUTE, William Wildman.

4867. WILKES, John (1727–97), M.P. Aylesbury 1757–64, Middlesex 1768–69, 1774–90 (DNB).

4868. WILKINS, Walter (1741–1828), M.P. Radnorshire 1796–1828 (Williams' *Wales M.P.'s*).

4869. WILKINSON, Andrew (ca 1698–1784), M.P. Aldborough 1735–65 (Turner's *Aldborough and Boroughbridge,* p. 124).

4870. WILKINSON, Andrew (ca 1728–85), M.P. Aldborough 1768–72 (Turner's *Aldborough and Boroughbridge,* p. 126).
4871. WILKINSON, Charles (d. 1782), M.P. Aldborough 1774–77 (Burke's *Ext. Peerage* sub Darcy).
4872. WILKINSON, Jacob (ca 1717–91), M.P. Berwick-on-Tweed 1774–80, Honiton 1781–84 (*Archaeol. Aeliana,* 4th Ser., *24;* Philips' *East India Co.,* pp. 337, 347).
4873. WILKINSON, Pinckney (ca 1694–1784), M.P. Old Sarum 1774–84 (Musgrave's *Obituary*).
4874. WILKS, John (ca 1765–1854), M.P. Boston 1830–37 (DNB).
4875. WILKS, John (d. 1846), M.P. Sudbury 1826–28 (DNB).
4876. WILLES, Edward (1723–87), M.P. Old Sarum 1747–47, Aylesbury 1747–54, Leominster 1767–68 (*Alumni Oxon.;* Baker's *Northampton, 1,* 695).
4877. WILLES, John (1685–1761), M.P. Launceston 1722–26, Weymouth and Melcombe Regis 1726–27, West Looe 1727–37 (DNB).
4878. WILLES, John (ca 1722–84), M.P. Banbury 1746–54, Aylesbury 1754–61 (*Alumni Oxon.;* Burke's *LG*).
4879. WILLETT, John Willett (ca 1744–1815), M.P. New Romney 1796–1806 (Hutchins' *Dorset, 3,* 311).
WILLIAMS, Charles Hanbury, *see* HANBURY-WILLIAMS, Charles.
4880. WILLIAMS, Hugh (ca 1718–94), 8th Bt, M.P. Beaumaris 1768–80, 1785–94 (GEC).
WILLIAMS, James Hamlyn, *see* HAMLYN-WILLIAMS, James.
4881. WILLIAMS, John, M.P. Saltash 1772–72.
4882. WILLIAMS, John, M.P. Windsor 1802–4 (Burke's *LG*).
4883. WILLIAMS, John (1777–1846), M.P. Lincoln City 1822–26, Ilchester 1826–27, Winchelsea 1830–32 (DNB).
4884. WILLIAMS, Kyffin (d. 1753), M.P. Flint borough 1747–53 (Williams' *Wales M.P.'s*).
4885. WILLIAMS, Nicholas (ca 1672–1745), 1st Bt, M.P. Carmarthenshire 1724–45 (*Alumni Cantab.; Eton Coll. Reg.*).
4886. WILLIAMS, Owen (1764–1832), M.P. Great Marlow 1796–1832 (*Old Westminsters*).
4887. WILLIAMS, Richard (d. 1759), M.P. Flint borough 1741–47 (Shrop. Archaeol. Soc. *Trans.,* 1st Ser., *7,* 72; Williams' *Wales M.P.'s*).
4888. WILLIAMS, Robert (ca 1695–1763), M.P. Montgomeryshire 1740–41, 1742–47 (*Alumni Oxon.;* Williams' *Wales M.P.'s*).
4889. WILLIAMS, Robert (1735–1814), M.P. Dorchester 1807–12 (*Alumni Oxon.;* Cussans' *Herts, 3,* pt. 2, 155; Hutchins' *Dorset, 2,* 525).
4890. WILLIAMS, Robert (1764–1830), 9th Bt, M.P. Carnarvonshire 1790–1826, Beaumaris 1826–30 (GEC; *Harrow Reg.; Old Westminsters*).
4891. WILLIAMS, Robert (1767–1847), M.P. Wootton Bassett 1802–7, Grampound 1808–8, Kilkenny City 1809–12, Dorchester 1812–34

(Beaven's *Aldermen of London;* Burke's *LG;* Burtchaell's *Kilkenny M.P.'s*).

4892. WILLIAMS, Thomas (d. 1802), M.P. Great Marlow 1790–1802 (Burke's *LG*).

4893. WILLIAMS, Thomas Peers (1795–1875), M.P. Great Marlow 1820–68 (*Old Westminsters*).

4894. WILLIAMS, Watkin (1742–1808), M.P. Montgomeryshire 1772–74, Flint borough 1777–1806 (*Alumni Oxon.;* Burke's *LG*).

4895. WILLIAMS, William (1774–1839), M.P. Weymouth and Melcombe Regis 1818–26 (Burke's *LG; Gent. Mag., 1,* 661; *1821 List*).

WILLIAMS, William Addams, *see* ADDAMS-WILLIAMS, William.

4896. WILLIAMS, William Peere (ca 1730–61), 2d Bt, M.P. Shoreham 1758–61 (GEC; *Etoniana, 45,* 711).

4897. WILLIAMS-BULKELEY, Richard Bulkeley (1801–75), 10th Bt, M.P. Beaumaris 1831–32, Anglesey 1832–37, 1847–68, Flint borough 1841–47 (GEC; *Old Westminsters*).

4898. WILLIAMS-WYNN, Charles Watkin (1775–1850), M.P. Old Sarum 1797–99, Montgomeryshire 1799–1850 (DNB; *Old Westminsters*).

4899. WILLIAMS-WYNN, Henry Watkin (1783–1856), M.P. Midhurst 1807–7 (DNB).

4900. WILLIAMS-WYNN, Watkin (1692–1749), 3d Bt, M.P. Denbighshire 1716–41, 1742–49 (DNB; GEC).

4901. WILLIAMS-WYNN, Watkin (1748–89), 4th Bt, M.P. Salop 1772–74, Denbighshire 1774–89 (GEC; *Old Westminsters*).

4902. WILLIAMS-WYNN, Watkin (1772–1840), 5th Bt, M.P. Beaumaris 1794–96, Denbighshire 1796–1840 (GEC; *Old Westminsters*).

4903. WILLIAMSON, Hedworth (1797–1861), 7th Bt, M.P. Durham Co. 1831–32, Durham Co. (Northern Division) 1832–37, Sunderland 1847–52 (GEC).

4904. WILLIMOTT, Robert (d. 1746), M.P. London 1734–41 (Beaven's *Aldermen of London*).

4905. WILLIS-FLEMING, John (ca 1743–1802), M.P. Southampton borough 1774–80, 1784–90 (*Eton Coll. Reg.*).

4906. WILLIS-FLEMING, John (ca 1782–1844), M.P. Hampshire 1820–31, South Hampshire 1835–42 (*Alumni Oxon.;* Burke's *LG*).

WILLOUGHBY, 2d Bn, *see* DRUMMOND-BURRELL, Peter Robert.

4907. WILLOUGHBY, Henry (1780–1849), M.P. Newark 1805–31 (GEC sub Middleton; *Gent. Mag., 1* [1850], 541; *Rugby Reg.*).

4908. WILLOUGHBY, Henry Pollard (1796–1865), 3d Bt, M.P. Yarmouth (Hants) 1831–32, Newcastle-under-Lyme 1832–34, Evesham 1847–65 (*Alumni Oxon.;* GEC).

4909. WILLOUGHBY, Thomas (1728–81), 4th Bn Middleton, M.P. Notts 1762–74 (GEC).

4910. WILLS, Charles (1666–1741), M.P. Totnes 1718–41 (DNB; *Eton Coll. Reg.*).

4911. WILLY, William (1703–65), M.P. Devizes 1747–65 (Musgrave's *Obituary;* Namier; Prinsep's *Madras Civilians,* p. xviii).

4912. WILMER, William (ca 1693–1744), M.P. Northampton borough 1715–27, 1734–44 (*Alumni Oxon.;* Foster and Green, *Wilmer Family,* pp. 70–72).

WILMOT, John Eardley, *see* EARDLEY-WILMOT, John.

4913. WILMOT-HORTON, Robert John (1784–1841), 3d Bt, M.P. Newcastle-under-Lyme 1818–30 (DNB; GEC).

4914. WILSON, Daniel (ca 1680–1754), M.P. Westmorland 1708–22, 1727–47 (Burke's *LG* [ed. 1849]; Bean; Ferguson; Musgrave's *Obituary*).

4915. WILSON, Edward (ca 1719–64), M.P. Westmorland 1747–54 (Bellasis' *Westmorland Church Notes, 1,* 121; Bean; Burke's *LG* [ed. 1849]; Ferguson).

4916. WILSON, Giffin (ca 1766–1848), M.P. Great Yarmouth 1808–12 (Williams' *Great Sessions in Wales*).

WILSON, Henry Wright, *see* WRIGHT-WILSON, Henry.

4917. WILSON, James (ca 1777–1830), M.P. York City 1826–30 (Bean; *Eton Lists; Notes and Queries,* 12th Ser., *2,* 178; Venn MS).

4918. WILSON, Richard (ca 1744–ca 1809), M.P. Barnstable 1796–1802 (Devonshire Assoc. *Trans., 74,* 169).

4919. WILSON, Richard (1759–1834), M.P. Ipswich 1806–7 (Devonshire Assoc. *Trans., 74,* 169; *Notes and Queries,* 12th Ser., *2,* 75, 213; Venn MS).

WILSON, Richard Fountayne; *see* FONTAYNE-WILSON, Richard.

4920. WILSON, Robert Thomas (1777–1849), M.P. Southwark 1818–31 (DNB).

WILSON, Thomas, *see* FENWICK, Thomas; *also* WILSON-PATTEN, Thomas.

4921. WILSON, Thomas (ca 1767–1852), M.P. London 1818–26 (*Gent. Mag., 2,* 637).

4922. WILSON, Thomas Spencer (1726–98), 6th Bt, M.P. Sussex 1774–80 (*Alumni Carthusiani;* GEC).

4923. WILSON, William (ca 1736–96), M.P. Ilchester 1761–68, Camelford 1768–74 (Nichols' *Leicester, 3,* pt. 1, 514; Venn MS).

WILSON, William Wilson Carus, *see* CARUS-WILSON, William Wilson.

4924. WILSON-PATTEN, John (1802–92), 1st Bn Winmarleigh, M.P. Lancashire 1830–31, North Lancashire 1832–74 (DNB; GEC).

4925. WILSON-PATTEN, Thomas (1770–1827), M.P. Stafford borough 1812–18 (GEC sub Winmarleigh; Foster's *Lancashire Pedigrees;* Bean; Wedgwood).

4926. WILSONN, Charles Edward (ca 1752–1829), M.P. Bewdley 1814–18

(Horsfield's *Sussex, 2,* 65; Williams' *Worcester M.P.'s;* MS, *ex inform.* Charles Hemingfield).

WILTON, E. of, *see* EDGERTON, Thomas.

WINCHESTER, M. of, *see* PAULET, POWLETT, and BURROUGHES-PAULET.

4927. WINCHESTER, Henry (ca 1777–1838), M.P. Maidstone 1830–31 (Beaven's *Aldermen of London; Gent. Mag., 1,* 662).

4928. WINDHAM, William (d. 1789), M.P. Aldeburgh 1747–61, Helston 1766–68 (Musgrave's *Obituary;* MS, *ex inform.* Hon. H. A. Wyndham).

4929. WINDHAM, William (1750–1810), M.P. Norwich 1784–1802, St. Mawes 1802–6, New Romney 1806–7, Higham Ferrers 1807–10 (DNB).

4930. WINDHAM-ASHE, Joseph (d. 1746), M.P. Downton 1734–41, 1742–46 (Burke's *LG;* Manning and Bray's *Surrey, 3,* 409; Musgrave's *Obituary;* MS, *ex inform.* Hon. H. A. Wyndham).

4931. WINDSOR, Herbert (1703–58), 2d Vct Windsor, M.P. Cardiff 1734–38 (GEC).

WINFORD, Thomas Geers, *see* GEERS-WINFORD, Thomas.

4932. WINGFIELD, Edward (1729–64), 2d Vct Powerscourt, M.P. Stockbridge 1756–61 (*Alumni Cantab.; Alumni Dublin.;* GEC).

WINMARLEIGH, 1st Bn, *see* WILSON-PATTEN, John.

WINN, George Allanson, *see* ALLANSON-WINN, George.

4933. WINN, Rowland (1739–85), 5th Bt, M.P. Pontefract 1768–68 (GEC).

4934. WINN-ALLANSON, Charles (1784–1840), 2d Bn Headley, M.P. Ripon 1806–7, Malton 1807–8, Ludgershall 1811–12 (GEC).

4935. WINNINGTON, Edward (ca 1728–91), 1st Bt, M.P. Bewdley 1761–68, 1769–74 (GEC; *Eton Coll. Reg.*).

4936. WINNINGTON, Edward (1749–1805), 2d Bt, M.P. Droitwich 1777–1805 (GEC; *Eton Coll. Reg.*).

4937. WINNINGTON, Francis (b. ca 1704), M.P. Droitwich 1747–54 (*Old Westminsters*).

4938. WINNINGTON, Thomas (1696–1746), M.P. Droitwich 1726–41, Worcester City 1741–46 (DNB; *Old Westminsters*).

4939. WINNINGTON, Thomas Edward (ca 1780–1839), 3d Bt, M.P. Droitwich 1807–16, 1831–32, Worcestershire 1820–30, Bewdley 1832–37 (*Alumni Oxon.;* GEC).

WINTERTON, 1st E, *see* GARTH-TURNOUR, Edward Garth.

4940. WISE, Ayshford (1786–1847), M.P. Totnes 1812–18 (*Alumni Oxon.;* Burke's *LG*).

WISHART, John Belches, *see* STUART, John.

4941. WODEHOUSE, Armine (ca 1714–77), 5th Bt, M.P. Norfolk 1737–68 (GEC).

4942. WODEHOUSE, Edmund (1784–1855), M.P. Norfolk 1817–30, East

Norfolk 1835–55 (*Alumni Oxon.;* Burke's *Peerage* sub Kimberley; *Harrow Reg.*).

4943. WODEHOUSE, John (1741–1834), 1st Bn Wodehouse, M.P. Norfolk 1784–97 (GEC; *Old Westminsters*).

4944. WODEHOUSE, John (1771–1846), 2d Bn Wodehouse, M.P. Great Bedwin 1796–1802, Marlborough 1818–26 (GEC; *Old Westminsters*).

4945. WODEHOUSE, William (d. 1735), M.P. Cirencester 1734–35 (Musgrave's *Obituary;* Williams' *Gloucester M.P.'s*).

4946. WOLLASTON, William (1693–1757), M.P. Ipswich 1733–41 (*Alumni Cantab.*).

4947. WOLLASTON, William (1731–97), M.P. Ipswich 1768–84 (*Alumni Cantab.*).

4948. WOLRYCHE-WHITMORE, William (ca 1787–1858), M.P. Bridgnorth 1820–32, Wolverhampton 1832–34 (Burke's *LG; Shrewsbury School Reg.;* Wedgwood).

4949. WOLSELEY, Charles (ca 1741–1808), M.P. Milborne Port 1775–80 (Charnock's *Biog. Naval., 6,* 452; *Gent. Mag., 1,* 373).

4950. WOMBWELL, George (1734–80), 1st Bt, M.P. Huntingdon borough 1774–80 (GEC).

4951. WOOD, Charles (1800–85), 1st Vct Halifax, M.P. Great Grimsby 1826–31, Wareham 1831–32, Halifax 1832–65, Ripon 1865–66 (DNB; GEC).

4952. WOOD, George (1743–1824), M.P. Haslemere 1796–1806 (DNB).

4953. WOOD, James Athol (ca 1756–1829), M.P. Gatton 1806–7 (DNB).

4954. WOOD, John (ca 1788–1856), M.P. Preston 1826–32 (Addison's *Glasgow Matric. Albums;* Boase; Bean; Pink).

4955. WOOD, Mark (ca 1747–1829), 1st Bt, M.P. Milborne Port 1794–96, Newark 1796–1802, Gatton 1802–18 (DNB).

4956. WOOD, Mark (1794–1837), 2d Bt, M.P. Gatton 1816–18 (DNB sub Mark Wood [1747–1829]; *Gent. Mag., 2,* 422; *Harrow Reg.*).

4957. WOOD, Matthew (1768–1843), 1st Bt, M.P. London 1817–43 (DNB).

4958. WOOD, Robert (ca 1717–71), M.P. Brackley 1761–71 (DNB).

4959. WOOD, Robert, M.P. Minehead 1786–90, East Looe 1790–96 (*Army Lists*).

4960. WOOD, Thomas (1708–99), M.P. Middlesex 1779–80 (*Eton Coll. Reg.*).

4961. WOOD, Thomas (1777–1860), M.P. Brecon Co. 1806–47 (Burke's *LG; Harrow Reg.;* Williams' *Wales M.P.'s*).

4962. WOODLEY, William (ca 1722–93), M.P. Great Bedwin 1761–66, Marlborough 1780–84 (*Alumni Oxon.;* Musgrave's *Obituary*).

4963. WOOLMORE, John (ca 1755–1837), M.P. Westbury 1806–7 (*Gent. Mag., 1* [1838], 106).

WORCESTER, M. of, *see* SOMERSET, Henry and Henry Charles.

4964. WORGE, Richard Alchorne (ca 1707–74), M.P. Stockbridge 1768–72 (Lower's *Worthies of Sussex,* p. 327).

WORLINGHAM, Bn, *see* ACHESON, Archibald.

WORSLEY, Bn, *see* ANDERSON-PELHAM.

4965. WORSLEY, Edward Meux (ca 1747–82), M.P. Yarmouth (Hants) 1774–75, Newtown 1775–82 (*Alumni Oxon.;* Berry's *County Geneal.: Hampshire*).

4966. WORSLEY, James (ca 1672–1756), 5th Bt, M.P. Newtown 1695–1701, 1705–22, 1727–29, 1734–41 (GEC).

4967. WORSLEY, James (ca 1725–87), M.P. Yarmouth (Hants) 1775–80, Newtown 1784–84 (Berry's *County Geneal.: Hampshire,* p. 142).

4968. WORSLEY, Richard (1751–1805), 7th Bt, M.P. Newport (Hants) 1774–84, Newtown 1790–93, 1796–1801 (DNB; GEC).

4969. WORSLEY, Thomas (1711–78), M.P. Orford 1761–68, Callington 1768–74 (*Old Westminsters*).

4970. WORSLEY-HOLMES, Leonard Thomas (1787–1825), 9th Bt, M.P. Newport (Hants) 1809–25 (*Alumni Oxon.;* GEC).

4971. WORSLEY-HOLMES, Richard Fleming (ca 1791–1814), M.P. Newport (Hants) 1812–14 (*Alumni Oxon.;* Berry's *County Geneal.: Hampshire*).

WORTLEY, *see* STUART-WORTLEY and STUART-WORTLEY-MACKENZIE.

4972. WORTLEY-MONTAGU, Edward (1678–1761), M.P. Huntingdon borough 1705–13, 1722–34, Westminster 1715–22, Peterborough 1734–61 (*Alumni Cantab.; Old Westminsters*).

4973. WORTLEY-MONTAGU, Edward (1713–76), M.P. Huntingdonshire 1747–54, Bossiney 1754–68 (DNB; *Old Westminsters*).

4974. WRANGHAM, Digby Cayley (ca 1806–63), M.P. Sudbury 1831–32 (*Alumni Oxon.;* Boase).

4975. WRAXALL, Nathaniel William (1751–1831), 1st Bt, M.P. Hindon 1780–84, Ludgershall 1784–90, Wallingford 1790–94 (DNB).

4976. WRAY, Cecil (1734–1805), 13th Bt, M.P. East Retford 1768–80, Westminster 1782–84 (*Alumni Cantab.;* DNB; GEC; *Old Westminsters*).

4977. WREY, Bourchier (ca 1714–84), 6th Bt, M.P. Barnstable 1748–54 (DNB; GEC).

4978. WRIGHT, John, M.P. Abingdon 1741–47.

WRIGHT, John Atkyns, *see* ATKYNS-WRIGHT, John.

4979. WRIGHT-WILSON, Henry (d. 1832), M.P. St. Albans 1821–26 (Burke's *LG*).

4980. WRIGHTE, George (d. 1766), M.P. Leicester borough 1727–66 (Lipscomb's *Bucks,* 4, 152).

4981. WRIGHTSON, William (1752–1827), M.P. Aylesbury 1784–90 (*Alumni Oxon.;* Burke's *LG; Genealogist,* N.S., *14,* 47).

WRIGHTSON, William Battie, *see* BATTIE-WRIGHTSON, William.

4982. WRIXON-BECHER, William (1780–1850), 1st Bt, M.P. Mallow 1818–26 (Burke's *Peerage;* Foster's *Baronetage*).

4983. WROTTESLEY, Henry (1772–1825), M.P. Brackley 1810–25 (*Old Westminsters*).

4984. WROTTESLEY, John (1744–87), 8th Bt, M.P. Newcastle-under-Lyme 1768–68, Staffordshire 1768–87 (GEC; *Old Westminsters*).

4985. WROTTESLEY, John (1771–1841), 1st Bn Wrottesley, M.P. Lichfield 1799–1806, Staffordshire 1823–32, South Staffordshire 1832–37 (DNB; GEC; *Old Westminsters*).

4986. WROTTESLEY, Richard (1721–69), 7th Bt, M.P. Tavistock 1747–54 (*Alumni Oxon.;* DNB; GEC; *Genealogist,* N.S., *20, 346*).

4987. WYATT, Charles (ca 1759–1819), M.P. Sudbury 1812–18 (*Gent. Mag., 1,* 377; *Notes and Queries, 156,* 461).

WYCOMBE, Bn, *see* PETTY, John, John Henry, and William.

4988. WYLDBORE, Matthew (ca 1716–81), M.P. Peterborough 1768–80 (*Alumni Cantab.* sub Wildbore; *Fenland Notes and Queries, 1, 354*).

WYLDE, Thomas, *see* WILDE, Thomas.

WYNDHAM, Charles, *see* EDWIN, Charles.

4989. WYNDHAM, Charles (1710–63), 2d E. of Egremont, M.P. Bridgwater 1735–41, Appleby 1742–47, Taunton 1747–50 (DNB; GEC; *Old Westminsters*).

4990. WYNDHAM, Charles William (1760–1828), M.P. Midhurst 1790–95, Shoreham 1795–1802, Sussex 1807–12 (*Old Westminsters*).

4991. WYNDHAM, Henry Penruddocke (1736–1819), M.P. Wilts 1795–1812 (DNB; *Eton Coll. Reg.*).

4992. WYNDHAM, Percy Charles (1757–1833), M.P. Chichester 1782–84, Midhurst 1790–96 (*Notes and Queries, 164,* 318; *Old Westminsters*).

4993. WYNDHAM, Thomas (b. ca 1696), M.P. Poole 1732–41 (*Alumni Oxon.*).

4994. WYNDHAM, Thomas (ca 1763–1814), M.P. Glamorgan 1789–1814 (*Eton Coll. Reg.*).

4995. WYNDHAM, Wadham (1773–1843), M.P. Salisbury 1818–33, 1835–43 (Burke's *LG; Eton Lists; Gent. Mag., 2* [1844], 93).

4996. WYNDHAM, William (ca 1687–1740), 3d Bt, M.P. Somerset 1710–40 (DNB; GEC; *Eton Coll. Reg.*).

WYNDHAM, Wyndham Knatchbull, *see* KNATCHBULL-WYNDHAM, Wyndham.

4997. WYNDHAM-O'BRIEN, Percy (ca 1713–74), 1st E. of Thomond, M.P. Taunton 1745–47, Cockermouth 1754–61, Minehead 1747–54, 1761–68, Winchelsea 1768–74 (GEC).

4998. WYNDHAM-QUIN, Windham Henry (1782–1850), 2d E. of Dunraven, M.P. Limerick Co. 1806–20 (GEC).

WYNFORD, Bn, *see* BEST, William Draper and William Samuel.

WYNN, *see* WINN; *also* WILLIAMS-WYNN.

4999. WYNN, Glynn (d. 1793), M.P. Carnarvon borough 1768–90 (Burke's *Peerage* sub Newborough; Williams' *Wales M.P.'s*).

5000. WYNN, Glynn (b. ca 1766), M.P. Westbury 1807–9 (Burke's *Peerage* sub Newborough; *Linc. Inn Reg.*).

5001. WYNN, John (ca 1701–73), 2d Bt, M.P. Carnarvonshire 1740–41, 1754–61, Denbigh borough 1741–47, Carnarvan borough 1761–68 (GEC).

5002. WYNN, Robert Watkin (ca 1757–1806), M.P. Denbighshire 1789–96 (Williams' *Wales M.P.'s*).

5003. WYNN, Thomas (ca 1678–1749), 1st Bt, M.P. Carnarvon borough 1713–49 (GEC).

5004. WYNN, Thomas (ca 1736–1807), 1st Bn Newborough, M.P. Carnarvonshire 1761–74, St. Ives 1775–80, Beaumaris 1796–1807 (GEC).

5005. WYNN, Thomas John (1802–32), 2d Bn Newborough, M.P. Carnarvonshire 1826–30 (GEC).

WYNNE, Charles Wynne Griffith, *see* GRIFFITH-WYNNE, Charles Wynne.

5006. WYNNE, George (1700–56), 1st Bt, M.P. Flint borough 1734–41 (GEC).

5007. WYNNE, John Arthur (1801–65), M.P. Sligo borough 1830–32, 1856–57, 1857–60 (*Alumni Oxon.;* Boase; Burke's *Irish LG*).

5008. WYNNE, Owen (ca 1756–1841), M.P. Sligo borough 1801–6, 1820–30 (Burke's *Irish LG; Gent. Mag., 1* [1842], 329).

5009. WYNNE, Robert, M.P. Carnarvon borough 1754–61 (Williams' *Wales M.P.'s*).

5010. WYNNE, William (d. 1754), M.P. Carnarvon borough 1749–54 (Williams' *Wales M.P.'s*).

5011. WYNNE-PENDARVES, Edward William (1775–1853), M.P. Cornwall 1826–32, West Cornwall 1832–53 (*Alumni Oxon.;* Burke's *LG; Harrow Reg.*).

5012. WYSE, Thomas (1791–1862), M.P. Tipperary 1830–32, Waterford 1835–41, 1842–47 (DNB).

5013. WYVILL, Marmaduke (1791–1872), M.P. York City 1820–30 (Ball and Venn's *Admissions to Trinity College;* Burke's *LG; Eton Lists*).

YARBOROUGH, E. of, *see* ANDERSON-PELHAM.

YARMOUTH, E. of, *see* SEYMOUR-CONWAY, Francis Charles.

YARDE-BULLER, Francis, *see* BULLER-YARDE-BULLER, Francis.

5014. YATES, Thomas, M.P. Chichester 1734–41.

5015. YEO, Edward Rooe (1742–82), M.P. Coventry 1774–80, 1781–82 (*Eton Coll. Reg.;* Vivian's *Visitation of Devonshire,* p. 836).

5016. YONGE, George (ca 1731–1812), 5th Bt, M.P. Honiton 1754–61,

1763–96, Old Sarum 1799–1801 (DNB; GEC; *Eton Coll. Reg.*).

5017. YONGE, William (ca 1693–1755), 4th Bt, M.P. Honiton 1715–54, Tiverton 1754–55 (DNB; GEC).

5018. YORKE, Charles (1722–70), M.P. Reigate 1747–68, Cambridge Univ. 1768–70 (DNB; GEC).

5019. YORKE, Charles Philip (1764–1834), M.P. Cambridgeshire 1790–1810, St. Germans 1810–12, Liskeard 1812–18 (DNB).

5020. YORKE, Charles Philip (1799–1873), 4th E. of Hardwicke, M.P. Reigate 1831–32, Cambridgeshire 1832–34 (DNB; GEC).

5021. YORKE, John (1685–1757), M.P. Richmond 1710–13, 1717–27, 1728–57 (*Alumni Cantab.; Eton Coll. Reg.*).

5022. YORKE, John (1728–1801), M.P. Higham Ferrers 1753–68, Reigate 1768–84 (Burke's *Peerage* sub Hardwicke; *Gent. Mag., 2,* 862; W. M. Palmer, *Monumental Inscriptions,* p. 200).

5023. YORKE, Joseph (1724–92), 1st Bn Dover, M.P. East Grinstead 1750–61, Dover 1761–74, Grampound 1774–80 (DNB; GEC).

5024. YORKE, Joseph (1807–89), M.P. Reigate 1831–32 (Burke's *Peerage* sub Hardwicke; Boase; *Eton Lists*).

5025. YORKE, Joseph Sydney (1768–1831), M.P. Reigate 1790–1806, 1818–31, St. Germans 1806–10, West Looe 1812–12, Sandwich 1812–18 (DNB; *Harrow Reg.*).

5026. YORKE, Philip (1720–90), 2d E. of Hardwicke, M.P. Reigate 1741–47, Cambridgeshire 1747–64 (DNB; GEC).

5027. YORKE, Philip (ca 1743–1804), M.P. Helston 1775–81, Grantham 1792–93 (DNB; *Eton Coll. Reg.*).

5028. YORKE, Philip (1757–1834), 3d E. of Hardwicke, M.P. Cambridgeshire 1780–90 (DNB; GEC; *Harrow Reg.*).

5029. YORKE, Philip (1784–1808), M.P. Reigate 1806–8 (GEC sub Hardwicke; *Admissions to St. John, Cambridge; Harrow Reg.*).

5030. YORKE, Simon (1771–1834), M.P. Grantham 1793–1802 (*Eton Coll. Reg.; Admissions to St. John, Cambridge*).

5031. YORKE, Thomas (1688–1768), M.P. Richmond 1757–61 (Burke's *LG; Genealogist,* N.S., *21,* 26; Whitaker's *Craven,* p. 157).

5032. YOUNG, John (1807–76), 1st Bn Lisgar, M.P. Cavan 1831–55 (DNB; GEC).

5033. YOUNG, William (1749–1815), 2d Bt, M.P. St. Mawes 1784–1806, Buckingham borough 1806–7 (DNB; GEC; *Eton Coll. Reg.;* Oliver's *Antigua, 3,* 282).

5034. YOUNGE, Hitch (d. 1759), M.P. Steyning 1740–59 (Musgrave's *Obituary*).

ZETLAND, E. of, *see* DUNDAS, Lawrence and Thomas.

ZOUCHE, 14th Bn, *see* CURZON, Robert.

Index

Age of M.P.'s, 20–6; ages on first election, 22–3; average ages, 21 ff.; during 1734–1831, 20–1; during 1918–35, 21, 23; in 1950, 21; average age according to nationality, education, and profession, 25–6; entry-age for commercial interests, 26; for landed interests, 26; life span of those born before 1750, 22; born 1750 or later, 22; significance of, in historical perspective, 20; significance of increase in average ages, 21 ff.; stability of average ages and age groupings, 22

Americans. *See* Colonials

Aristocracy: degree of governmental control of, 30–1, 32; family groups, 33; prevalent view of role of, 30

Army officers, 1–2, 4, 16–17, 25, 49–50

Bagehot, Walter, 36, 73

Banker M.P.'s, 57 ff., 61, 62–3; geographical distribution of, 61; interest of, in other commercial enterprises, 61; relation between Bank of England and, 62–3; between East India Company and, 63

Barnes, Donald, 30

Baronets. *See* Aristocracy, Social status and family backgrounds

Beauclerk, Topham, 36

Boswell, James, 34, 36

British ruling class, 1734–1832: adaptability, 75; as trustees of national government, 77; cohesiveness, 74; cosmopolitanism, 74; degree of plutocracy, 76; inertia, 75–6

Busby, Richard, headmaster of Westminster, 38

Butler, Samuel, headmaster of Shrewsbury, 39

Cambridge University, 42 f., 45, 46; St. John's College, 43; King's College, 37; Trinity College, 43, 44; Trinity Hall, 43

Charterhouse, 39

Class system, vertical mobility within, 56

Clergy, 48–9

Colonials, 3, 14–17; M.P.'s with personal knowledge of North America, 16–17; North Americans, 15–17

Commercial interest, 26, 54–73; antagonism to, 55–6; approval of by ruling class, 55; as avenue to aristocracy, 56; characteristics of M.P.'s with commercial connections, 57; interpenetration of aristocracy and businessmen, 57–8; proportion of M.P.'s engaged in commercial activity, 56–7; trades and types of business of commercial M.P.'s, 4, 58–61; varied activities of commercial men, 58. *See also* Bankers, Manufacturers in the House, Nabobs in the House, West Indian group

Continental universities, 45

East India Company, 2–3, 63 ff. *See also* Nabobs in the House

Education, 36–47; as binding force, 36; proportion of M.P.'s receiving upper-class education, 46–7; social importance of, 36. *See also* Public schools, Universities, *and under* names of schools

Emerson, Ralph Waldo, 56

Eton, 37–8, 43; importance of, 37 f.; number of M.P.'s from, 37; as "recruiting ground," 38

Fielding, Henry, 20

Fort William College, Bengal, 45

Gay, John, 55, 58

Ginsberg, Morris, 36

Goldsmith, Oliver, 41

Graham, Henry G., 13

Halévy, Élie, 50

Harrow: number of M.P.'s from, 38–9; rapid growth of, 38

Hinton, Lord, 50

Huguenots, 17–18

Inns of Court, 46

Insurance, M.P.'s connected with, 61–2

Irish: number of seats, 14; percentage of total M.P.'s, 14; types of constituency, 14